The study of ancient science and its relations with Greek philosophy has made a significant and growing contribution to our understanding of ancient thought and civilisation. This collection of articles on Greek science contains fifteen of the most important papers published by G. E. R. Lloyd in this area since 1961, together with three unpublished articles. The topics range over all areas and periods of Greek science, from the earliest Presocratic philosophers to Ptolemy and Galen. In each case the article is preceded by an introduction that assesses scholarly debate on the topic since the original publication. Professor Lloyd also suggests modifications and developments to his own position in the light of those debates and his own further research.

METHODS AND PROBLEMS IN GREEK SCIENCE

METHODS AND PROBLEMS IN GREEK SCIENCE

G. E. R. LLOYD

Professor of Ancient Philosophy and Science, University of Cambridge, and Master of Darwin College

CAMBRIDGE UNIVERSITY PRESS

CAMBRIDGE

NEW YORK PORT CHESTER

MELBOURNE SYDNEY

Published by the Press Syndicate of the University of Cambridge
The Pitt Building, Trumpington Street, Cambridge CB2 1RP
40 West 20th Street, New York, NY 10011, USA
10 Stamford Road, Oakleigh, Melbourne 3166, Australia

First published 1991

Printed in Great Britain by the University Press, Cambridge

British Library cataloguing in publication data

Lloyd, G. E. R. (Geoffrey Ernest Richard)
Methods and problems in Greek science.
1. Greece. Science, ancient period
I. Title
509.38

Library of Congress cataloguing in publication data

Lloyd, G. E. R. (Geoffrey Ernest Richard), 1933–
Methods and problems in Greek science/G. E. R. Lloyd.
p. cm.
ISBN 0 521 37419 7
1. Science–Greece–History. 2. Science–Methodology–History.
I. Title.
Q127.G7L593 1991
509′.38–dc20 90-1539
CIP

ISBN 0 521 37419 7 hardback

UP

CONTENTS

ACKNOWLEDGEMENTS

Chapters 1–15 were published in their original form in the following publications, and we are grateful for permission to reprint them. Chapters 16–18 are as yet unpublished: details of their forthcoming publication are also given below. In this respect we are grateful to the Board of Trustees of the Herbert Spencer Lectures in the University of Oxford for permission to print here the text of G. E. R. Lloyd's 1989 Herbert Spencer Lecture, 'Greek antiquity: the invention of nature' in advance of publication of the complete Lectures.

1 The development of Aristotle's theory of the classification of animals: from *Phronesis* 6 (1961), 59–81.
2 Right and left in Greek philosophy: from *Right and Left*, ed. R. Needham (Chicago, 1973), 167–86; originally published in *Journal of Hellenic Studies* 82 (1962), 56–66.
3 Who is attacked in *On Ancient Medicine*?: from *Phronesis* 8 (1963), 108–26.
4 Experiment in early Greek philosophy and medicine: from *Proceedings of the Cambridge Philological Society* N.S. 10 (1964), 50–72.
5 Popper versus Kirk: a controversy in the interpretation of Greek science: from *British Journal for the Philosophy of Science* 18 (1967), 21–38.
6 The social background of early Greek philosophy and science: from *Literature and Western Civilisation*, I. *The Classical World*, edd. D. Daiches and A. Thorlby (London (Aldus), 1972), ch. 16, 381–95.
7 Greek cosmologies: from *Ancient Cosmologies*, edd. C. Blacker and M. Loewe (London (George Allen and Unwin), 1975), 198–224.
8 Alcmaeon and the early history of dissection: from *Sudhoffs Archiv* 59 (1975), 113–47.
9 The Hippocratic Question: from *The Classical Quarterly* 25 (1975), 171–92.
10 The empirical basis of the physiology of the *Parva Naturalia*: from *Aristotle on Mind and the Senses*, edd. G. E. R. Lloyd and G. E. L. Owen (Cambridge University Press, 1978), 215–39.
11 Saving the appearances: from *Classical Quarterly* 28 (1978), 202–22.
12 The debt of Greek philosophy and science to the ancient Near East: from *Pedilavium* – a Quarterly Bulletin of Hebraic and Hellenistic Studies (Tokyo) – 14 (1982), 1–19.
13 Observational error in later Greek science: from *Science and Speculation*, edd. J. Barnes, J. Brunschwig, M. Burnyeat and M. Schofield (Cambridge University Press, 1982) 128–64.

14 Plato on mathematics and nature, myth and science: from *Humanities – International Christian University Publication* IV-B (Mitaka, Tokyo) – 18 (1983), 11–30.

15 *Science and morality in Greco-roman antiquity*: an inaugural lecture (Cambridge University Press, 1985).

16 Aristotle's zoology and his metaphysics: the status quaestionis. A critical review of some recent theories: as yet (November 1989) unpublished paper to Oléron conference on Aristotle's zoology (proceedings to be edited by P. Pellegrin).

17 Galen on Hellenistics and Hippocrateans: contemporary battles and past authorities: paper for Berlin conference on Galen, August 1989 (proceedings to be edited by J. Kollesch).

18 The invention of nature: Herbert Spencer lecture, Oxford, October 1989.

Note: To give help in following up references, the original pagination of articles is indicated at the top of each page and the original page divisions are marked in the course of the text by a double line (‖).

PREFACE

My studies of some thirty years in Greek science have increasingly brought home to me the importance of the subject, the opportunities it offers, and the difficulties it presents. The study of the science of a given society, of what it or what some of its members claim to know, takes one to the heart of the values of that society and to the interactions of power and knowledge, and the structures in which they are deployed, within it. The study of a society undergoing rapid development such as that of ancient Greece in the classical period allows one further to investigate questions to do with changes in both the content of what was known and in how claims to know were to be justified or legitimated. What stimulated, what permitted, such changes in the very conception of what the inquiry into nature consisted in? How deep-seated were those changes? How far did links with traditional attitudes and positions still persist? Where do new démarches depend primarily on new methods or the perception of new problems, or on new aims and ambitions, and where on institutional factors, or on factors to do with the educational, social or political background?

When I first embarked on the study of Greek science, the emphasis in much current work was still on *their* legacy, *our* inheritance, and it was only with time that I became more fully aware of some deep-seated positivist preconceptions colouring or even determining commonly accepted interpretations. Their science was unproblematic since it could be seen as just the first hesitant steps towards ours. It is also fair to say that – whatever may have been the case in other countries and at other times – in England thirty years ago the study of Greek science was very much a poor relation in comparison with other aspects of the investigation of classical antiquity. Even now the development of the subject has been sporadic and patchy, and great names such as those of Neugebauer in astronomy and Sambursky in physics draw attention, by their very pre-eminence, to their own isolation.

That takes me to some of the difficulties the subject presents – where again it has only been with time that some major points have been borne in on me. I am not referring to the well-known problems that stem from the fragmentary nature of much of our information and the bias of our sources, nor even to the general difficulties of interpreting ancient texts written in dead languages, the products of civilisations whose workings and belief-systems in many cases escape us. The difficulties go further than that and relate to the combination of skills needed to do justice to the challenge of interpretation. The student of the science of Greco-Roman antiquity needs not just the ordinary qualifications and competences of the philosophically aware historian of science – though these are difficult enough to come by: the craft of the historian – a training in historical methodology and in what it is to study the history of scientific ideas and practices in particular – must here be combined with a grasp of issues in contemporary philosophy of science. Over and above these qualifications, the specific challenge of Greco-Roman antiquity calls, ideally, for a critical, comparativist perspective, and that can only be obtained from social anthropology and from the study of other ancient civilisations.

The relevance of social anthropology derives from the rich evidence ethnography yields concerning the cosmologies, world-views, practical and speculative thinking of the vast diversity of contemporary human societies – and the same may be said, *mutatis mutandis*, of the study of ancient civilisations. Although in the past a comparativist perspective has all too often been brought to bear in gross contrasts between 'them' and 'us' – with a view to establishing the superiority of our, broadly Western European, traditions – it is precisely to avoid such narrowmindedness, not to say ethnocentricity, that such a perspective is most useful. It is of course by now abundantly clear that many so-called primitive peoples display impressive knowledge both practical and theoretical, and equally obvious that the same is true of many ancient civilisations besides the Greeks.

But it is not that the skills and learning acquired and valued are always and everywhere the same: nor is there, among ancient or modern societies, any necessary uniformity in the manner in which knowledge is transmitted, in the kinds of scrutiny or modification to which it may be liable, or in the roles of those who claim, or pass as the possessors of, special wisdom. It is not as if there is some common, let alone universal, fund of lore that all societies possess on to which may be grafted, as mere exotica, their own peculiar speculative beliefs and interpretations. While what we *now* know as science has *become* universal, it had diverse, pluralist, origins to which a variety of ancient and modern civilisations, worldwide, have had their contribution to make. That much, at least, one might hope, should be uncontroversial as between relativists and their opponents, even though they will disagree on the question of the status and interpretation of many specific knowledge claims.

Without a comparativist perspective, students of Greek antiquity will easily mistake, indeed can hardly fail to mistake, what may be distinctive, and what may be said to be in no way exceptional, either in the intellectual products of the society they study or in the circumstances and manner of their production. Only with such a perspective can the twin and opposite temptations be avoided, of somehow representing the developments we refer to under the rubric of early Greek science as inevitable, or as seeing them as miraculous. It is the very specificity of those developments in all their great complexity that poses the special challenge of the subject.

This said, it becomes clear that the ideal student of early Greek science would indeed be a paragon, philosopher, historian, anthropologist, a student of ancient civilisations in general as well as of ancient Greece in particular, Egyptologist, Assyriologist, Sinologist, Indologist – the list could be extended indefinitely. Although it is evidently impossible for the same individual to encompass all these specialisations, that does not mean I am any the less unhappily aware of the enormous gaps in my own range and competence.

But however precipitately I may have entered the field, I have attempted forays of a variety of kinds, some more, some less specialised, into topics to do with ancient Greek science. A number of pieces that I have published over the last thirty years have opened up new problems or otherwise stimulated controversy and debate. The object of collecting some of them here is twofold: first simply to assemble within the covers of a single volume a number of papers published in different books and journals of varying degrees of accessibility – together with three as yet unpublished studies. Secondly, and more importantly, to update them with some introductory comments, the aim of which is to take stock of work done subsequently on the problems discussed. It is not my business to attempt to justify and defend my earlier positions. On the contrary these introductions give me the opportunity to record where I have now modified and revised my views, in response either to direct criticism, or to my own further reflections on the problems, or to both. But if in some cases a recantation is in order, in some others I wish now to attempt to strengthen and elaborate positions I initially stated too weakly. On a number of topics I shall accordingly try to develop points that now seem to me to have greater significance than I originally recognised.

The collection contains a heterogeneous mixture of studies dealing with different authors, fields, periods and problems, but they all have to do with aspects of the aims, methods and assumptions of what the Greeks called the inquiry into nature. Ideally the more specialised papers should continue to bear in mind the strategic issues to which they relate and conversely the more general studies should pay close attention to the results of detailed analyses – though once again I am conscious that it is one thing to express an ideal, another to implement it.

That there are strategic issues here to be explored, as well as much more detailed work to be undertaken, is, however, clear. On the side of detailed studies, the present situation and future outlook, in certain areas at least, now appear much more promising than was the case in the 1960s and 1970s. Some indication of this is given by the further references I am able now to include in the addenda to some of these papers. A number of ancient authors who could simply not be studied at all systematically – since no proper collection of the evidence concerning their work existed – have now been made the subject of pioneering scholarly editions and commentaries. Such is the case with von Staden's Herophilus and Vallance's Asclepiades for instance, and the study of the Hellenistic period generally has been transformed by the collection of source material by Long and Sedley as well as by much work by colleagues specialising in Hellenistic philosophy. There is, of course, no orthodoxy, nor even any obvious dominant trends, in recent work done on Greek science across the world. Rather the very fact that such work has recently been very much on the increase is a most hopeful sign for the future. That too will be agreed by those with otherwise quite divergent views on the methods and emphases we should adopt, whether on externalist, sociological, questions or on internalist, intellectual ones, whether, again, on the more purely historical issues, or on those that are illuminated by, and can illuminate, current controversies in the philosophy of science.

As for the more strategic issues I mentioned, the *most* strategic may be stated briefly. If Greek science has occupied a privileged place in relation to Western European society and with respect to later European science, it is all the more important to place that in perspective – in at least two ways. First, to understand our own present – not least the role that science currently occupies in modern industrial societies – it is essential to be aware of the past developments that have led up to it, including even those that go back to the first beginnings of systematic scientific inquiry. Secondly, European developments have to be set in that wider, global perspective I advocated. If, as I remarked, to live fully up to that ideal is by now beyond the capacity of any single scholar, even with the inspiring example of a Joseph Needham to follow, that makes it all the more urgent for collaborative work to be undertaken where the resources of many specialisations can be pooled. The present papers stem mostly from questions that relate in the first instance to one of the constituent specialisations and certainly several of them were initially addressed to my fellow specialists: but they also mark some of the stages whereby I have come to recognise how far the potential of the subject rests on the interdependence of those specialisations.

I

THE DEVELOPMENT OF ARISTOTLE'S THEORY OF THE CLASSIFICATION OF ANIMALS (*PHRONESIS* 1961)

INTRODUCTION

The article I published in *Phronesis* in 1961 on the development of Aristotle's theory of the classification of animals set out to try to establish the relative chronology of various passages in the Corpus in which the groupings of animals and their differentiae are discussed. At the time it was written such developmental studies still enjoyed a certain vogue, although that is now very much a thing of the past. My own efforts were subsequently criticised on two basic grounds: first that I was mistaken in believing that a chronological sequence could be established in this material; secondly and more fundamentally that I was mistaken in holding that Aristotle had a classification of animals or was in any way concerned to try to establish one. I shall limit my remarks here to reviewing what may be said, now, nearly thirty years later, on these two issues.

I

On developmental problems the difficulties of securing even moderately solid results would now be recognised to be a good deal more severe than was originally assumed by those (including myself) who embarked on such studies in the decades following Jaeger's *Aristotle* (p. 8 n. 2). One major difficulty is recognised already in my text (pp. 8, 24): the date of a book cannot be inferred from the date of any particular passage it contains. Individual passages, especially those that deal with topics that are subsidiary to the main argument, may easily be later additions by Aristotle or even interpolations by other hands. In relation to the particular material I discussed concerning animal groupings and differentiae, the further difficulty arises that in passages in the Organon Aristotle uses such examples to illustrate logical points (for example about definition), and given that (as again I noted, p. 9 and p. 11 at n. 17) many of the examples may well have been stock Academic ones, it is hazardous to infer Aristotle's own substantive views on the underlying issues from his comments on the logical features that interest him. Here, then, more should have been conceded to the possibility that Aristotle used some differentiae non-committally.

An even more important point which I did not explicitly mention relates to the motivation for any change or development that is detected in

Aristotle's views on a particular subject. The difficulty here too tended to be underestimated by those (again including myself) who held that it is possible to identify which of two contrasting positions is superior (or rather would have been thought by Aristotle to be) and further supposed that the superior is bound to be later. Where there is no other ground than that supposed superiority on which to base a relative chronology, the dangers of circularity are obvious: a point that was urged against my article by Pellegrin (1982). Reconstructing the sequence of any conjectured change in Aristotle's views depends upon being able to give moderately satisfactory answers to the following questions: (1) why he should have held the supposed 'earlier' view in the first place; (2) why he should have come to be dissatisfied with it; (3) why he came to be more satisfied with his 'later' theory. In other words, there should be *philosophical* reasons, not just biographical ones, to underpin the hypothesis of the change. The underlying – Jaegerian – assumption that still influenced my article unduly was that Aristotle only gradually achieved his independence from Plato and that signs of an apparent readiness to accept or use Platonic positions may be taken as signs of relative immaturity.

Faced with these and many other difficulties, developmental studies have declined if not quite ground to a halt, and there are now fewer widely accepted positions than in 1961. Even on the question of the relation between the main zoological works and the rest of the Corpus, where I wrote (p. 8) that this was fairly clear, recent work belies that statement. The association of the zoological treatises with Aristotle's middle period, the period of his stay in the Troad, Lesbos and Macedon areas, which I believed had been established by the arguments from place-names advanced by Thompson and Lee, has itself been called into question by Solmsen.[1] He protests first that most of the texts cited come in later books of *HA* which are of doubtful authenticity, and further that the information they contain is mostly common knowledge in any event and required no first-hand research by Aristotle in those areas. To that Lee has in turn replied[2] with a restatement of his position and an appeal to the occurrence of at least one important reference to Lesbos in *PA*. Meanwhile even those who go along with the Thompson–Lee hypothesis do not necessarily agree on what follows from their arguments. Those who take it that (most of) *HA* antedates the more theoretical works, *PA*, *MA*, *IA* and *GA*, see Aristotle's theoretical interests in zoology as an important component of the last – second Athenian – period. However, Balme (1987a) recently argued that *HA* is later than those other treatises, partly on the grounds that it summarises information they contain and in some cases does so so elliptically that the account in *HA* can hardly be understood without reference to those other

[1] F. Solmsen, 'The fishes of Lesbos and their alleged significance for the development of Aristotle', *Hermes* 106 (1978), 467–84.

[2] H. D. P. Lee, 'The fishes of Lesbos again', in *Aristotle On Nature and Living Things*, ed. A. Gotthelf (Pittsburgh, 1985), 3–8.

passages. Thus Balme, accepting the Thompson–Lee arguments associating *HA* with the middle period, nevertheless presented a radically different picture of the relations within the zoological works and of their place in the Corpus as a whole.

If developmental studies certainly have not fulfilled the hopes originally placed in them, should that effort now be written off? Jaeger's fundamental insight was that Aristotle's thought was not the static or monolithic entity that it had previously often been taken to be. Stated in those general terms, that is a thesis with which most Aristotelian scholars still agree. However Jaeger believed he could determine not just the order of the treatises but also basic shifts in Aristotle's attitudes, and in neither case have his conclusions stood the test of time. Nor have those who subsequently attempted equally determinate grand syntheses – as for example Düring did in his magnum opus (1966) – been much more successful than Jaeger. The sum total of what may be described as widely agreed views does not amount to much. For instance the *Categories* is still generally taken to be an early work, and the *Topics* similarly held to antedate the *Analytics*. Conversely the central books of the *Metaphysics* (*Zeta*, *Eta*, *Theta*) are generally considered late.[3] But against that, fundamental disagreements remain on many questions to do with both the relative and the absolute chronology of the treatises, and it would be very foolish to believe that even those positions that are now agreed are not subject to revision or modification.

Nevertheless the challenge that Jaeger's work presented remains. As soon as Aristotle's thought is seen as a flexible, tentative and shifting, rather than as a static, whole, the temptation to interpret *away* minor, or even major, discrepancies between one passage and another disappears. That is not to say that those discrepancies generally, or even very often, reflect changes in his substantive positions. What we have learnt since Jaeger, and in part because of the impasse that developmental studies face, is that chronological hypotheses – which are never by themselves a complete answer – are only one of a set of interpretative options that have to be kept open. The apparent discrepancies we encounter between different texts may be a sign of a shift in Aristotle's views or of a certain tentativeness as he tried out different approaches or different lines of argument on a set of related problems: or again they may reflect different audiences or his sense of the appropriateness or inappropriateness of using stock examples, commonplaces and the like – as opposed, that is, to restricting himself, on every occasion, to the most precise statement of his own considered positions.

[3] Whether that is true of everything we find in our present texts of those books is, however, more controversial. Thus the possibility that the first chapter of *Eta* recapitulates a different version of *Zeta* from the one we have has been aired in *Notes on Eta and Theta of Aristotle's Metaphysics recorded by Myles Burnyeat and others*, ed. M. Woods (Oxford, 1984) to 1042a3–24. Where, as in the case with *Physics* VII, chh. 1–3, two different versions are extant, there is no reason *a priori* to rule out the possibility that both stem from Aristotle himself: cf. R. B. B. Wardy, 'A study of *Physics* VII', Ph.D. dissertation, Cambridge.

From that point of view, that of the challenge to interpretation they present, the difficulties raised in this article are still worth pondering. So far as the texts from outside the zoological treatises go, they still present problems of interpretation *whether or not* chronological hypotheses can contribute to their solution. Judged by the yardstick of the opinions expressed in the zoology itself, some of the uses of zoological examples in the Organon, *Metaphysics* and *Politics* must still be considered anomalous[4] – more so than is generally assumed by scholars who specialise in those works. We may allow that Aristotle might choose to stick with stock Academic examples for certain purposes where these were part of the common currency of those who discussed logical issues. But it scarcely makes sense for Aristotle to deploy differentiae he knows to be systematically ambiguous or misleading, nor to write as if the definitions of animals could be secured by a method that he knows to be fundamentally inadequate to the task. That is the high – to my mind still unacceptably high – price that has to be paid if one does not agree to a development of his thought on this topic.

Then within the zoological treatises themselves, the apparent discrepancies between different texts studied in my article take me to the second main subject on which some further comments may be made, namely the prior question of the extent of Aristotle's interest in the classification of animals.

II

In my article a fundamental assumption was that Aristotle was indeed concerned to give a classification of animals, and indeed that his various discussions of animal groupings and differentiae indicated a succession of attempted solutions to that problem. Much work has subsequently been done on this question, and both that fundamental assumption, and my chronological hypotheses, have been challenged and rejected. Apart from Balme, who himself modified his views on this topic after the two classic papers he published in 1961 and 1962, there have been major studies by Pellegrin (1982, 1985, 1987), Kullmann (1974), Preus (1975), Lennox (1980, 1987a, 1987b), to name only the most important contributions. Balme's own revisions to his views indicate the increasing scepticism, generally registered, on the question of Aristotle's interests in zoological classification. In 1961 he attacked the then common view that a detailed Linnaean style taxonomy was to be found anywhere in the zoological treatises, but still expressed the opinion that the *HA* is a preliminary to a classification. In the 1987b revised version of that article the preferred view is that the *HA* is a study of differentiae and itself as such a theoretical treatise, not a descriptive one.

Pellegrin's monograph (1982) took Balme's study of *eidos* and *genos* as one of its starting-points and argued not just that there was no taxonomy in

[4] As striking examples of this may be cited the contrast between *PA* 643a7–24 and *Metaph.* 1038a17f. and that between *PA* 643b28ff. and *Metaph.* 1038a19f., discussed in my article at pp. 18–19.

Aristotle but that the terms which had generally been held to be basic to Aristotle's classificatory interests, namely *analogon*, *genos*, *eidos*, are all used at every level of generality and simply do not correspond to the distinctions between genera and species of standard taxonomies.[5] Lennox in turn is persuaded that the *HA* is not natural history, that no Linnaean-style taxonomy is to be found, indeed that classification is not one of Aristotle's interests although demonstration is. Lennox sees the zoology as carrying through a programme sketched out in *APo.*, namely one of giving causal explanations, for which is it essential to determine the widest class of which a differentia is true.

Much that is of great value has emerged from these and other detailed studies of Aristotle's zoological methods and his actual practice. Two points that are relevant to the theses of my *Phronesis* article – both of which would imply modifications to those theses – may readily be agreed. First it has to be acknowledged as a matter of fact that a detailed taxonomy of the Linnaean type is nowhere presented by Aristotle in his zoological treatises. Meyer's account of the classification is a systematisation that goes far beyond the materials in the Aristotelian texts from which Meyer claimed to extract it. The fundamental point urged by Balme against Meyer is that intermediate level groupings – between the main families (such as birds and fish) and the infimae species – are extremely rare,[6] and without them the organisation of the species of animals into a family tree of ordered rankings is inconceivable. Here then I would say that – writing in 1961, the same year as the Balme article first appeared – in my enthusiasm to claim (pp. 19f.) that the main groups of animals in Aristotle *are clear* (as indeed they are), I ignored problems to do with these intermediate levels.

Secondly the combined result of the work of Balme and Pellegrin on some of the key terms used in the zoology in connection with animal groupings is to have shown that in general – though with one important qualification – *eidos*, *genos* and *analogon* are all used in respect of *different* levels of generality. However the qualification is – and it is one that they recognise while minimising its importance – that there are texts, especially methodologically or theoretically loaded texts,[7] in which those same terms *are* ordered hierarchically and indeed the hierarchy is consistent. Sameness and difference may be between individuals (numerical identity), between *eidē*, between *genē*, and only 'by analogy', where in each case a difference at one level is compatible with a sameness at the next level up. What Balme and Pellegrin have shown, then, is not that Aristotle always uses these terms in a way that

[5] However Pellegrin acknowledges (1982: ch. 3 and conclusion) that Aristotle still classifies animals, even if not in a taxonomic fashion.

[6] How the data concerning birds collected in *HA* VIII, ch. 3 especially could be used as the basis for their classification, and how they were indeed so used by some later writers, are the subject of a forthcoming study by J. J. Hall.

[7] Apart from such classic statements outside the zoology as *Metaphysics* 1016b31ff., 1018a12ff., 1054a32ff., see, for example, *PA* 644a16ff., 645b26ff., *HA* 497b10ff.

suggests an indifference to the level of generality in question, but that he *often* does: though against that must be set those methodological passages in which he sets out, with some care, how these terms correspond to an ordered hierarchy.

Claims that Aristotle had elaborated a Linnaean style taxonomy are unjustified: but to argue, as some have, that Aristotle is not interested in animal classification at all is to go to the opposite and equally mistaken extreme. That a via media between those two extremes should be adopted becomes clear, I believe, from a consideration of Aristotle's criticisms of the use of dichotomous division in *PA* I, chh. 2–4 especially. Plato, the originator of Division, had himself used it both for the purposes of defining a single item and for classifying several, and while Aristotle need not have Plato himself in mind in his criticisms of the method, those criticisms are directed not just at the method used as a method of arriving at a definition, but also as a method of classification. He clearly presupposes that when applied to animals, the method *should* yield a result in which every animal kind appears and appears only once. The key texts that express this point are *PA* 642b31ff. and 643a13ff.,[8] and they received less attention that they might have done in my *Phronesis* article since I there assumed that the point that follows from them was not in dispute.

This then is an issue on which I would still maintain a point of view closer to my *Phronesis* article than to that of those modern studies which deny a classificatory interest in Aristotle at all. The concession that needs to be made is that the positive suggestions that Aristotle explores in various texts in the zoological works are not so much a sequence of determinate solutions separated chronologically (as I tended to conclude) as a number of not necessarily chronologically separated tentative essays. But even though there is no definitive comprehensive classification of animals anywhere in the Corpus, the criticisms of the dichotomists themselves show that this interest is not just confined to single, one-off definitions, nor just to establishing differentiae. The point that should be urged against any such downgrading of Aristotle's interests is that a lack of a final or definitive solution to a problem is no indication of a lack of interest in the problem itself.

So to my mind it seems misguided to resist the conclusion that Aristotle *remained* concerned with that part of his Platonic inheritance. He is certainly concerned (all are agreed) with forms and essences. He is certainly also concerned with definition, even though adequate definitions of animal kinds are far harder to secure than some Academic examples allow one to imagine.[9] A concern with definition certainly in turn implies a concern with establishing the genera and the differentiae of the various definienda. While there is much that is tentative and flexible about Aristotle's terminology in this connection

[8] See also other texts that indicate the aim of grasping animals according to their *genē*, *PA* 643b10ff., 645a36ff. (cf. 640a14). The inadequacies of dichotomous division as a method of securing the infimae species not just of animals, but in any field or *genos*, are mentioned at *PA* 643a16ff.

[9] See further below (pp. 372–97).

and in his substantive suggestions in relation to particular animal species or families, the object of the exercise is not restricted to a survey of differentiae for its own sake, nor to a series of piecemeal one-off definitions. As in the politics, so too in the zoology, his long-term aims included giving a comprehensive classification of animals, at least in the sense of an overall account of the animal kingdom and of the relations between different groups and kinds. That this eventual goal was not one that Aristotle actually attained is not an argument against its being *one* of his aims: it is rather a further argument for the tentativeness of an Aristotle still at work on the problems and exploring various approaches to their resolution.

REFERENCES

I list below the most important contributions, since 1961, to the discussion of the problems raised in this article.

Atran, S. (1985) 'Pre-theoretical aspects of Aristotelian definition and classification of animals: the case for common sense', *Studies in History and Philosophy of Science* 16: 113–63

Balme, D. M. (1961) 'Aristotle's use of differentiae in zoology', in *Aristote et les problèmes de méthode*, ed. S. Mansion (Louvain), 195–212

(1962) '*Genos* and *eidos* in Aristotle's biology', *Classical Quarterly* N.S. 12: 81–98

(1987a) 'The place of biology in Aristotle's philosophy', in *Philosophical Issues in Aristotle's Biology*, edd. A. Gotthelf and J. G. Lennox (Cambridge), 9–20

(1987b) 'Aristotle's use of division and differentiae', revised and expanded version of Balme, 1961, in *Philosophical Issues in Aristotle's Biology*, edd. A. Gotthelf and J. G. Lennox (Cambridge), 69–89

Düring, I. (1966) *Aristoteles: Darstellung und Interpretation seines Denkens* (Heidelberg)

Granger, H. (1984) 'Aristotle on genus and differentia', *Journal of the History of Philosophy* 22: 1–23

(1985) 'Deformed kinds and the fixity of species', *Classical Quarterly* 37: 110–16

Kullmann, W. (1974) *Wissenschaft und Methode* (Berlin)

Lennox, J. G. (1980) 'Aristotle on genera, species and "the more and the less"', *Journal of the History of Biology* 13: 321–46

(1987a) 'Divide and explain: the *Posterior Analytics* in practice', in *Philosophical Issues in Aristotle's Biology*, edd. A. Gotthelf and J. G. Lennox (Cambridge), 90–119

(1987b) 'Kinds, forms of kinds, and the more and the less in Aristotle's biology', revised version of Lennox, 1980, in *Philosophical Issues in Aristotle's Biology*, edd. A. Gotthelf and J. G. Lennox (Cambridge), 339–59

Pellegrin, P. (1982) *La Classification des animaux chez Aristote* (trans. A. Preus, *Aristotle's Classification of Animals*, Berkeley, 1986) (Paris)

(1985) 'Aristotle: a zoology without species', in *Aristotle on Nature and Living Things*, ed. A. Gotthelf (Pittsburgh), 95–115

(1987) 'Logical difference and biological difference: the unity of Aristotle's thought', in *Philosophical Issues in Aristotle's Biology*, edd. A. Gotthelf and J. G. Lennox (Cambridge), 313–38

Pratt, V. (1984) 'The essence of Aristotle's zoology', *Phronesis* 29: 267–77

Preus, A. (1975) *Science and Philosophy in Aristotle's Biological Works* (Hildesheim)

THE DEVELOPMENT OF ARISTOTLE'S THEORY OF THE CLASSIFICATION OF ANIMALS[1]

Many aspects of the development of Aristotle's thought have been studied and elucidated by scholars since Jaeger's book on Aristotle published in 1923. Yet comparatively little work has been done on possible developments in Aristotle's biological theories. Jaeger originally assumed that all the main biological works belong to Aristotle's second period of residence in Athens.[2] But this interpretation has been generally rejected. A detailed examination of the development of Aristotle's psychology led Nuyens[3] to place all the biological works, with the exception of *GA*, in the middle period (i.e. between the two periods of Aristotle's residence in Athens). And following a suggestion made by D'Arcy Thompson,[4] Lee[5] established a relationship between the place-names mentioned in *HA* and the areas where Aristotle lived between 347 and 335 (Troad, Lesbos, Macedon). But though the relation of the main biological works to the rest of the Aristotelian Corpus is now fairly || clear,[6] the possibility of tracing developments in Aristotle's biological theories has hardly been considered. Probably the most important contribution in this field is that of I. Düring, who made a number of fertile suggestions concerning possible developments in Aristotle's biological theories, in his edition of *PA*.[7] The aim of the present article is to take a single theme, the classification of animals,[8] and to examine and compare a number of passages, both in the biological works and outside them, which deal with this problem or imply an attitude towards it. The evidence points to a development in Aristotle's ideas, and it seems possible to establish the probable order in which these passages were written. It is not, of course, my view that the date of a book may be determined on the basis of a single

[1] The translations which I have adopted for the groups of 'bloodless' animals recognised by Aristotle are those used by Ogle, 1882, i.e. 'Cephalopods' (μαλάκια), 'Crustacea' (μαλακόστρακα), 'Testacea' (ὀστρακόδερμα) and 'Insects' (ἔντομα).

[2] Jaeger, 1923: 352f. (transl. 1948: 329f.). Jaeger thought 'It can scarcely be true, as has sometimes been asserted, that the History of Animals would be conceivable apart from the discoveries made by Alexander's expedition', while he also said, of *HA*, 'As a collection of material its relation to [*PA* and *GA*] . . . is exactly the same as that of the collection of constitutions to the late, empirical books of the *Politics*.'

[3] Nuyens, 1948: see esp. ch. 4 paras. 23–5 and 32, and ch. 6 para. 48.

[4] In his Prefatory Note (p. vii) to the Oxford translation of *HA* (1910).

[5] Lee, 1948: 61–7.

[6] Nuyens' results, in so far as they concern the biological works, have been accepted, in the main, in such recent works as Bourgey, 1955: 17ff, P. Louis' edition of *PA* (Paris 1956, xxiiiff.) and Ross, 1957: see esp. 66.

[7] Düring, 1943: see esp. 22ff. The problem of the development of Aristotle's classification of animals is dealt with on pp. 109ff. Though on several points I disagree with Düring's analysis of those passages which he considers, I agree with his interpretation of their relative chronology. In my own interpretation of this aspect of Aristotle's development, I have used a larger body of evidence than Düring considers, and I have also attempted to trace that development beyond the stage of the rejection of Division, where Düring leaves the problem.

[8] The standard work on this subject is Meyer 1855, but see also esp. Ogle, 1882: xxiff. and Thompson, 1921. The most recent article is Louis, 1955: 297ff.

passage. But much evidence has still to be collected and assessed before a definitive account of the development of Aristotle's thought can be given, and the evidence of a development in his theory of the classification of animals should, I suggest, be added to the other evidence which is at present more widely known.

First, I shall deal with a number of passages which are not in the biological works themselves, but which nevertheless throw light on Aristotle's attitude to the problems of zoological classification. It is true that some of the theories, and, indeed, several of the specific zoological examples, which are contained in these passages, are borrowed or adapted from Plato or the Academy. And for this reason, perhaps, the significance of the passages which I shall consider has sometimes been missed, because || they have been contrasted with Aristotle's 'own' theories to be found in the biological works. But while it is true that the biological works contain Aristotle's mature, or final, theory on many important problems, it seems very unlikely that he would, at any stage, have introduced and applied theories which he knew *at the time* to be based on false distinctions. Rather, a close examination of the passages in question usually reveals Aristotle's own beliefs fairly clearly, and we may infer the extent to which he himself agrees or disagrees, at any particular stage, with the Platonists.

First, then, there is a chapter in *Top.* VI.[9] At *Top.* 141a24ff., Aristotle gives a number of rules for examining proposed definitions, to find out whether they give the essence or not. In ch. 6 he considers how the differentiae should be examined, and at 143a34ff. he suggests 'You must see also whether the proposed differentia has a coordinate opposite to it in the division; for otherwise, clearly it would not be a differentia of the genus. For every genus is divided by opposed coordinate differentiae, as, for example, "animal" by "walking" and "flying" and "aquatic" and "biped".'[10] A number of other rules follow, and then at 144b13ff. he goes on. 'It is generally accepted that the same differentia may not be used of two non-subaltern genera. Otherwise, the result will be that the same species will be in two non-subaltern

[9] Cf. Düring, 1943: 109ff. Düring concludes from this passage that 'Aristotle is honestly endeavouring to show up the inutility of the dichotomic system from a practical point of view and to release himself from its fetters', but this is, I think, to exaggerate the extent to which Aristotle dissociates himself from the users of dichotomy. At two points (144b20ff., 35ff.) he explicitly defends their view-point, and, indeed, their whole method is presupposed to be valid.

[10] I translate Bekker's text as it stands. ὁρᾶν δὲ καὶ εἰ ἔστιν ἀντιδιῃρημένον τι τῇ εἰρημένῃ διαφορᾷ. εἰ γὰρ μὴ ἔστι, δῆλον ὅτι οὐκ ἂν εἴη ἡ εἰρημένη τοῦ γένους διαφορά· πᾶν γὰρ γένος ταῖς ἀντιδιῃρημέναις διαφοραῖς διαιρεῖται, καθάπερ τὸ ζῷον τῷ πεζῷ καὶ τῷ πτηνῷ καὶ τῷ ἐνύδρῳ καὶ τῷ δίποδι. Trendelenburg omitted καὶ τῷ δίποδι, and Düring goes further (1943: 110 n. 1) and omits καὶ τῷ ἐνύδρῳ as well (with some MSS authority). This makes an attractive simplification of the text, and I should be inclined to accept Düring's reading but for the evidence of *Cat.* 1b18f. where the same four differentiae are mentioned (see p. 11). It may be that, as in *Cat.* 1b18f., Aristotle mentions these typical differentiae with little regard for arranging them into coordinate pairs. Cf. the use of these differentiae in Plato, see *Plt.* 264 D–E, 266E, *Sph.* 220A–B.

genera.'[11] The fact that each differentia implies its own genus is then illustrated with another zoological example – 'walking' and 'biped' imply the genus 'animal'. Yet having arrived at || this conclusion, Aristotle corrects himself (144b20ff.).[12] 'Or perhaps it is not impossible for the same differentia to be used of two non-subaltern genera ... For "walking animal" and "flying animal" are non-subaltern genera, and "biped" is a differentia of both of them.' So the original statement is qualified: the same differentia may not be used of two non-subaltern genera 'except if they are both subordinate members of the same genus'. A third passage in which a zoological illustration appears follows at 144b31ff. 'See, too, if he has given "being in" something as the differentia of the essence ... For people raise objections to those who divide "animal" into "walking" and "aquatic" on the grounds that "walking" and "aquatic" merely indicate place.' But having expressed this view, Aristotle again goes on to correct himself. 'Or perhaps in this case their objections are unjustified. For "aquatic" indicates a quality, rather than "being in" something, or place. For an aquatic animal is still aquatic even on dry land; and similarly a land-animal is still a land-animal and not aquatic, even in water.'

It is true that in this chapter of the *Topics*, Aristotle has the Platonists particularly in mind, and it may be expected, then, that he will use a number of arguments 'ad hominem'.[13] Yet his own attitude to the use of division in zoology is apparent. (I) At 143a34ff., he makes use of a method of dividing the genus by opposed differentiae, and it is clear that he assumes its validity. So far from suggesting that a differentia should be objected to if it implies the division of the genus into opposites, Aristotle proposes that it should be objected to if such is *not* the case. And it is clear that he mentions the zoological example, the division of 'animal' by such differentiae as 'walking' and 'flying', as an instance of the *validity* of the method. (2) The problem of how 'biped' can be the differentia both of 'walking animal' and of 'flying animal' occurs to Aristotle at 144b22ff., but the solution to this difficulty which he proposes is not to reject this method of classification as a whole, but to concede, tentatively, that the same differentia may be used of two such genera, provided that these are both subordinate to the same higher genus.[14] (3) Certain people who || divide animals by the differentiae 'walking' and 'aquatic' are referred to at 144b32ff. Aristotle does not identify himself with them, but neither does he side with their critics and opponents. Rather, he is

[11] I borrow the term 'non-subaltern' to translate μὴ περιεχόντων ἄλληλα from Pickard-Cambridge, Oxford trans., vol. I.

[12] Düring fails to mention this passage (144b20ff.) in which Aristotle qualifies his earlier statement. But it is important evidence of the extent to which Aristotle himself was prepared to accept the method of Division as applied, in particular, to zoology.

[13] Besides the reference to 'those who divide "animal" into "walking" and "aquatic"' at 144b33 (cf. Plato, *Sph.* 220A–B), the τόπος at 143b23ff. is said to be 'useful against those who postulate the existence of the Ideas', indeed against them alone, see 143b29ff.

[14] Contrast *PA* 643a11ff., where it is shown that no indivisible differentia can be common to different species, and *PA* 643a3f., where the 'two-footedness' of birds and men is explicitly stated to be different.

of the opinion that one particular, and, surely, important, criticism which had been made of the division into 'aquatic' and 'land-animals', is unjustified.[15]

We may conclude that, in this chapter of the *Topics* at least, Aristotle found no serious criticisms to make either of the method of division as a whole, or of its particular application to problems of zoological classification. On the contrary, his arguments depend on the assumption that such a method is valid; he is prepared to endorse the procedure of sub-dividing the genera 'walking animals' and 'flying animals' by such a differentia as 'biped'; and he even appears to defend the Platonic division into 'aquatic' and 'land-animals'. That this is no freak theory of a single chapter of the *Topics*, but represents, rather, the first stage in the development of Aristotle's thought on the problems of the classification of animals, can be shown from other passages where similar divisions are accepted without criticism and even endorsed by Aristotle himself.

The best parallels to *Top.* 143a34ff. come from two passages in the *Categories*. At *Cat.* 1b18f., Aristotle mentions as differentiae of 'animal' '"walking" and "biped" and "flying" and "aquatic"' (oddly enough, precisely the four differentiae given at *Top.* 143b1ff., but see p. 9, n. 10 on the text of that passage), and at *Cat.* 14b33ff., he again refers to 'flying' and 'walking' and 'aquatic', to illustrate 'simultaneous' species which are 'opposed to one another in the same division'. He goes on to state, unequivocally, that '"animal" is divided into these, into "flying" and "walking" and "aquatic"'.[16] It is true that the definition of man as 'walking || biped animal' was probably a stock Academic example,[17] and even those passages[18] in which it is referred to explicitly as a correct definition of essence, are, perhaps, of little value as evidence of Aristotle's own beliefs.[19]

[15] Contrast, e.g., *HA* 589a10ff., 590a13ff., where the ambiguity of the terms 'walking' and 'aquatic' as applied to genera of animals is analysed.

[16] It is true that this passage implies a tripartite division of animals, rather than the use of a dichotomy. It seems likely that Aristotle insisted on the rule that division must be by exclusive contraries, only after he had analysed the method from the point of view of syllogistic proof (see *APo.* 97a14–22. At *APo.* 96b26f. he refers to his previous discussion of Division as proof, i.e. in *APo.* II.5 and *APr.* I.31. See pp. 12ff). Before that, it may be that Aristotle allowed other types of division as well (cf. also Plato, *Plt.* 287c2ff.). That the classification give here in *Cat.* 14b37f. is, in any case, an early one, is shown by the terms employed. The type of classification by means of 'functions common to body and soul' (e.g. πορευτικά and πτηνά) is definitely rejected at *PA* 643a35ff. (see p. 19), and see n. 15 above on analysis of the terms 'walking' and 'aquatic' in *HA* 589a10ff.

[17] This is suggested by a number of passages in the *Metaphysics* where this definition of man is mentioned in connection with the problem of how the *Forms* 'animal' and 'biped', or 'animal itself' and 'two-footedness itself' can constitute a unity. See esp. *Metaph.* A. 9 991a28f., Z.14 1039a30ff., b2ff., H.6 1045a15ff., M.4 1079b8ff., 5 1079b31ff.

[18] See *Top.* 132a1ff., 132b35–133a5, 140b33ff. It may also be noted that in one of the chapters (*Metaph.* A.9) in which Aristotle discusses the problem of how 'animal' and 'biped' can make a unity, he is speaking as a Platonist himself (see the use of the first person plural 'we' at 990b9, 991b7 etc.).

[19] Aristotle is not entirely consistent in his analysis of this definition in the *Topics*. Thus, although at 132a1–4 and 133a3–5 he implies that 'walking biped' is not the *property* of man,

But the argument at *Top.* 133b7ff. at least, is of interest: having first given a rule of argument by which the property of 'bird' ('flying biped') is established on the basis that 'walking biped" is the property of man, Aristotle goes on to point out that in some cases this rule is fallacious, and he gives 'walking quadruped' as an example of a property which belongs to a number of species. It is remarkable, then, that he apparently *accepts* the first instance of the argument (referring to 'bird'), and it is clear that he has no *general* objection to the use of such differentiae as 'walking biped', 'flying biped', to distinguish groups of animals. We may conclude that several passages in the *Topics* and the *Categories* are evidence that at one stage Aristotle accepted, without serious criticism, a method of classifying animals by dividing them by opposed differentiae, similar to the method adopted in the Academy; and this conclusion is borne out by some evidence in *HA*, which I shall consider later.

The second stage in the development of Aristotle's attitude to the problem of the classification of animals is marked by his criticisms of the method of Division. In *APr.* I.31, the main criticisms are (1) that Division begs what it ought to prove (46a33, cf. b11, 17ff., 32f.), and (2) that what Division in fact establishes is not the essence of the thing defined, but a disjunctive proposition of the type 'man must be either mortal or immortal' (46b10f.). The main example taken is, at least apparently, a problem of zoological classification. To arrive at a definition of man, living beings are divided first into 'mortal' and 'immortal' (46b3ff.) and then into 'footed' and 'footless' (b12ff.). Aristotle's conclusion, then, is that the method of division does not prove the definition. ||

At *APo.* II.5, Aristotle again considers Division, and his main criticism is, again, that it does not demonstrate its conclusion (see 91b14ff.). Again, the example taken is the definition of man, which is given at 92a1 in the form 'animal, mortal, footed, biped, wingless'. Two points of interest arise from the discussion of division in this passage. (1) The divider is described as proceeding as follows: 'Is man an animal or inanimate? Then he assumes the answer "animal" (he has not proved it). Again, all animals are walking or aquatic. He assumes the answer "walking"' (91b18ff.). To this, Aristotle's objection is *not* that such a division as 'all animals are walking or aquatic' is not exhaustive, *nor* that such divisions as a whole are artificial and unsatisfactory, but merely that the answer taken by the divider is assumed rather than proved. (2) At 91b28ff., Aristotle gives the defence which the user of Division might offer to his criticisms (that they should take only elements in the essence, in order; and that they should see that what is divided is all within the division, and omit nothing). To this further defence of Division, Aristotle replies that it still does not prove its conclusion, though it *may give*

at 133b8 and at 136b20ff. he seems to imply that it is. It is clear that he sometimes uses such stock examples to illustrate slightly different points in the course of the discussion of various topics.

knowledge in another way (91b33f.). He then compares it with induction, which equally does not prove anything ἀλλ' ὅμως δηλοῖ τι. It appears then, that Aristotle's objection to the definition of man at 92a1 (quoted above) is not on the grounds that it represents a series of false divisions, but merely on the grounds that it should not be considered to have been proved.[20]

A further assessment of the method of Division is given in *APo.* II.13, and this affords further evidence on Aristotle's attitude to the problem of zoological classification at this stage. He refers back (96b26f.) to his previous discussion of the claims of division to be proof, but the purpose of this passage is to point out the usefulness of this method in defining. Division is recommended for two main purposes in defining, (1) to ensure that the predicates are taken in the right order, e.g. 'animal, tame, biped' rather than 'biped, animal, tame' (96b30ff.), and (2) to avoid omissions. Indeed, for this latter purpose, Aristotle says that to use Division is the *only* way (see 96b35f., 97a4ff.). But to achieve this end, the division should be into opposites which exclude a middle term – a point which Aristotle emphasises several times.[21] He concludes 'It is || clear that when, proceeding in this way, one reaches subjects incapable of further differentiation, one will have the definition of the essence' (97a18f., cf. 37ff.). The relevance of this whole passage to the problem of zoological classification is evident: indeed, all the examples given are zoological ones.[22] It is clear that, at this stage, Aristotle believed that the infimae species could be determined by the method of dividing and subdividing genera into opposites, and he insists on dividing into exclusive contraries in order to ensure that nothing is omitted in the process of division. Although he refers to such natural groups as birds (97a3) and fish (a4), he apparently holds that the method of division can be applied to them too.[23] We must conclude that when Aristotle came to review the Platonic method of Division, he rejected it, certainly, as a method of demonstration, but retained it as a useful method in defining; he laid down that division should be into exclusive contraries, but he held that by such a method the infimae species would be revealed; finally, to judge from his constant use of

[20] With this passage *APo.* II.5, cf. also *APo.* 92a27–33, where a similar criticism of Division is made, namely that the conclusion is not demonstrated, and where the definition of man as 'animal, biped, walking' is again taken as an example.

[21] See esp. 97a14ff. εἶτα ὅταν λάβῃ τἀντικείμενα καὶ τὴν διαφορὰν καὶ ὅτι πᾶν ἐμπίπτει ἐνταῦθα ἢ ἐνταῦθα...and a19ff. τὸ δ' ἅπαν ἐμπίπτειν εἰς τὴν διαίρεσιν, ἂν ᾖ ἀντικείμενα ὧν μή ἐστι μεταξύ, οὐκ αἴτημα, but cf. also 96b38f., 97a1ff. and a36. It may be noted that in the discussions of Division in *APr.* I.31 and *APo.* II.5, all the examples given, with the exception of πεζόν ἔνυδρον at *APo.* 91b19, in fact use exclusive contrary terms (see *APr.* 46b4, 13f., 30, *APo.* 91b18, 92a3). And from *APo.* 91b19 πάλιν ἅπαν ζῷον ἢ πεζὸν ἢ ἔνυδρον it is clear that the division into πεζόν and ἔνυδρον too was considered to be exhaustive, for the purposes of the division.

[22] ζῷον ἥμερον δίπουν at 96b30ff., ὁλόπτερον and σχιζόπτερον as the division of πτηνὸν ζῷον at 96b38ff. At 97a1ff. (see n. 23 below). Aristotle refers to the differentiae of 'animal' (cf. also 97a36) and of the genera 'birds' and 'fish'.

[23] πρώτη δὲ διαφορά ἐστι ζῴου, εἰς ἣν ἅπαν ζῷον ἐμπίπτει. ὁμοίως δὲ καὶ τῶν ἄλλων ἑκάστου, καὶ τῶν ἔξω γενῶν καὶ τῶν ὑπ' αὐτό, οἷον ὄρνιθος, εἰς ἣν ἅπας ὄρνις, καὶ ἰχθύος, εἰς ἣν ἅπας ἰχθύς (97a1ff.).

zoological examples, he apparently hoped to apply this method particularly in that field. The net result of his analysis of Division in the *Analytics* was, then, for him to insist on the application of a set of rules to govern the use of the method (see *APo.* 97a23ff.), and in particular to emphasise that division should be into exclusive contraries.[24]

The next evidence to be considered is that from various passages in the *Metaphysics*. First, there are two passages which imply an attitude to Division similar to the one just revealed in passages in the *Analytics*. In *Metaph.* I 8, Aristotle discusses 'otherness in species', and shows (1058a26f.) that the difference between things which differ in species must be a contrariety. At each stage of the division down to the infima species, things are divided into contraries (1058a19ff.), and, indeed, the general || rule is stated that 'all things are divided by opposites' (a9f.). No detailed zoological examples are given, but that Aristotle had in mind the application of this method in zoology is clear from the references to the genus 'animal' at 1057b36f., 1058a2ff. and 5ff. Again, in the next chapter of *Metaph.* I, discussing why difference in sex does not amount to a difference in species (although male and female are contraries), Aristotle illustrates the fact that some contrarieties *do* make things different in species with the example of 'walking' and 'flying' animals (1058a35f.). It seems that in both these passages in *Metaph.* I, he assumes the validity of the method of Division and applies it to zoology; and as in the passages from the *Analytics* considered above, so too here he recognises the rule that division should be by contraries.

The analysis of Division is taken a step further in the discussion in *Metaph.* Z. 12,[25] where the problem of the unity of the elements in a definition is considered. First, some the ideas which had appeared in *APo.* II.13, are restated here with greater clarity and precision. Where it had been merely noted, in passing, at *APo.* 96b39f., that 'whole-winged' and 'split-winged' are the proper differentiae of 'winged animal', in *Metaph.* Z.12 Aristotle lays down the general law that you must divide by 'the differentia of the differentia', explaining with examples what is meant (see 1038a9ff., 25ff.), and he points out the inappropriateness of dividing by accidental qualities (1038a26f.). But three new points are also introduced in *Metaph.* Z.12: (1) the definition will consist of the genus and the last differentia (1038a19ff., 25f., 28ff.); (2) the infimae species will be the same in number as the differentiae (1038a17f.); and (3) the remark that τάξις δ' οὐκ ἔστιν ἐν τῇ οὐσίᾳ (1038a33) seems to imply a correction of his earlier ideas. (In *APo.* II.13,[26] and

[24] Another passage in *APo.* in which Aristotle shows his interest in zoological problems is II.14 98a1ff. (cf. Düring, 1943: 113f.), where he describes how to set about proving that certain common properties inhere in certain species of animal. But this is not, strictly speaking, relevant to the question of classification.

[25] Cf. Düring, 1943: 112f.

[26] See 96b30ff. διαφέρει δέ τι τὸ πρῶτον καὶ ὕστερον τῶν κατηγορουμένων κατηγορεῖσθαι..., 97a23ff. εἰς δὲ τὸ κατασκευάζειν ὅρον διὰ τῶν διαιρέσεων τριῶν δεῖ στοχάζεσθαι, τοῦ λαβεῖν τὰ κατηγορούμενα ἐν τῷ τί ἐστι, καὶ ταῦτα τάξαι τί πρῶτον ἢ δεύτερον..., cf. 97a28ff.

elsewhere,[27] he held that the order in which the differentiae are taken will contribute to the successful outcome of the procedure of division). This correction, and the other slight differences in the two treatments of division in *APo*.II.13 and *Metaph*. Z.12, suggest that the discussion in *Metaph*.Z.12 may well be somewhat later. Nevertheless, Aristotle still believes that the infimae species will be revealed by a process of dividing and sub-dividing genera || into opposites,[28] and the zoological examples taken (1037b32f., 1038a4, 10–18, 22f., 27, 31f.) indicate that he still sought to apply this method particularly in that field.

The bulk of the evidence discussed so far concerning Aristotle's attitude to the problem of zoological classification has come from passages where he deals with the method of Division. One final passage may be considered (before I turn to the evidence from the biological works themselves) where this is not the case. This is the comparison, in *Politics* IV.4, between the method of classifying constitutions and that of classifying animals.[29] At *Pol.* 1290b21ff., Aristotle tackles the problem of the number of different types of constitution, and at b25ff. he considers what they would do if they chose to arrive at the species of animal:

> first, we should define the parts which are necessary to every animal (for example, some of the sense-organs, the organs for digesting food, and for taking it into the body, e.g. mouth and stomach, and in addition to these, the organs of locomotion of each species). If these were *all* the necessary parts, there would be variations in them (I mean several sorts of mouth...). The number of combinations of these varieties will necessarily produce many different kinds of animals..., so that when all the possible combinations of these parts have been arrived at, they will comprise the species of animals. And there will be as many species of animals as there are combinations of the necessary parts.

The comments which I would make on this passage are: (1) Aristotle clearly has in mind a theoretically complete enumeration of all the species of animals; though he does not imply that such a complete classification existed. (2) The method by which such a classification should be arrived at, apparently makes no use of Division.[30] (3) The method is, however, deductive. Once the necessary parts of animals, and their variations, || have

[27] See *Top*. 144b10f. τοῦ μὲν γὰρ γένους ὕστερον, τοῦ δ' εἴδους πρότερον τὴν διαφορὰν δεῖ εἶναι and cf. Düring, 1943: 113.

[28] Though, in this passage, there is no explicit recommendation to use exclusive contraries in dividing, we may judge from the examples πτερωτόν, ἄπτερον (1038a12) and σχιζόπουν, ἄσχιστον (a14) that Aristotle had this type of division particularly in mind.

[29] Many passages in the *Politics* testify to Aristotle's interest in biology (cf. Barker, 1948: xi, xxx etc.), e.g. 1253a7ff., 1254b10ff., 1262a21ff., 1335a12ff. At 1256a21ff., he notices the different feeding habits of animals, and at 1256b10ff. he refers to the three modes of reproduction, viviparous, oviparous and 'larviparous', although he does not imply any classification of animals according to these differences.

[30] There is no suggestion that the possible combinations of the varieties of necessary organs will conform to a strict schema such as is produced by using the method of dividing and sub-dividing genera by exclusive contraries.

been established, the number of species may be inferred.[31] (We may compare the passage in *Metaph*. Z.12 1038a17f. dealing with Division, where Aristotle pointed out that there will be as many species as there are differentiae.) Finally, (4), it seems that nowhere in his own biological works did Aristotle use the method which he describes here. The variations, between different species, in such organs as the mouth and the stomach are, of course, frequently noted, and he does make an important distinction between the organs that are necessary to all animals, and those that are present only in some.[32] But there is at least one major disagreement between his theory on the necessary organs in the biological works, and the theory put forward here,[33] and, in any case, there is no suggestion, in the biological works, that the number of species may be inferred from the variations in their necessary organs *alone*.[34] It should be noted, then, that though in this passage in the *Politics*, the method of Division has been supplanted, and a method of classifying species according to the combinations of the varieties of necessary parts has been put in its place, yet this latter method does not correspond with anything which we find in the biological works themselves.

To summarise the conclusions reached so far. From the evidence outside the biological works, three main stages in the development of Aristotle's attitude to the problems of zoological classification may be distinguished. First (in passages in the *Topics* and *Categories*), there is a somewhat uncritical acceptance of the method of Division and of some || of the particular differentiae used by the Platonists to distinguish groups of animals. Second (in passages in *APr.*, *APo.* and the *Metaphysics*), there is the analysis of Division, which led Aristotle to reject it as proof, but to retain it as a useful method for definitions, and to formulate certain rules for its application to the problem of establishing the infimae species of each genus. And third (in *Pol.* 1290b25ff.), there is the substitution, for the method of Division, of a method of classifying species according to the combinations of the varieties of their necessary parts. I must now turn to the biological works

31 The point of the zoological comparison in the context in *Pol.* IV is that it shows how a complete classification may be given once the variable factors have been determined. Yet it must be noted that although Aristotle lists the 'parts' of the State at 1290b38ff., the method which he uses when giving the varieties of democracies and oligarchies at 1291b15ff. is not strictly parallel in fact to the one proposed with the help of the zoological analogy.

32 The 'necessary organs' to which Aristotle usually refers in the biological works are the organ for admitting food, that for discharging residue, and the central area (containing the stomach and, especially, the heart or its analogue), see *PA* 655b29ff., 678b1ff., 681b12ff., *HA* 488b29ff., cf. *Juv*. 468a13ff.

33 Nowhere in the biological works is it suggested that the organs of locomotion might be necessary to every animal (cf. *Pol.* 1290b28f., and 31, and see ἅπερ ἀναγκαῖον πᾶν ἔχειν ζῷον 1290b26). On the contrary, it is often pointed out that some animals do not have the faculty of locomotion (see e.g. *GA* 715b16). Again, though the list of necessary parts given at *Pol.* 1290b26ff. is not stated to be complete, it is surprising that no mention is made of the heart or its analogue, the primary importance of which is frequently emphasised in the biological works, see e.g. *PA* 647a21ff., 678b1ff., *GA*. 741b15ff., etc.

34 Aristotle's actual classification of animals in the biological works, and the complex principles of differentiation which he uses there, are described below, pp. 19ff.

to consider what evidence they contain which would support or modify such an interpretation of Aristotle's development.

The first passage in the biological works in which Aristotle deals with the problem of the classification of animals, is *HA* I.1–6. At *HA* 487a11ff., he says that he will first describe the differences between animals 'in outline' (τύπῳ), and at 491a7ff. he repeats the point that he has only given an outline description and that they must later discuss these matters with greater accuracy.[35] Yet the first chapter of what Aristotle calls his 'outline' description is revealing. (1) He refers to a great many pairs of contrary groups, such as 'aquatic' and 'land-animals' at 487a15ff., 'gregarious' and 'solitary' (487b34ff.), 'with dwellings' and 'without dwellings' (488a20ff.), 'nocturnal' and 'living in daylight' (488a25f.), 'tame' and 'wild' (488a26ff.), 'salacious' and 'chaste' (488b3ff.) and so on.[36] (2) It is true that Aristotle seems clearly aware that many of these distinctions do not apply as differentiae of groups of animals.[37] But there is also evidence that suggests that his own attitude to these distinctions may, at one time, have been somewhat different. At 488a26f., he distinguishes between tame and wild animals, and notes 'some are at all times tame, as man and mule, or wild, as leopard and wolf, while some can be quickly tamed, like the elephant'. But after this || statement of the distinction, he goes on: 'Again [we may look at them] in another way. For all tame species are also found wild, for example, horses, oxen, pigs, sheep, goats and dogs.' This later assertion clearly contradicts the earlier remark that 'some [species] are at all times tame'.[38] It seems likely, then, that we have evidence, here, of Aristotle correcting himself, and the first statement may represent his ideas at a stage when he had not entirely rejected such Platonic dichotomies as the division into 'tame' and 'wild' animals (and we saw from evidence in the *Topics* and elsewhere that such a stage existed). The presence of this contradiction, and the great frequency with which contrary groups appear in *HA* I.1, suggest that Aristotle may, at one stage, have attempted a classification of animals

[35] ταῦτα μὲν οὖν τοῦτον τὸν τρόπον εἴρηται νῦν ὡς ἐν τύπῳ, γεύματος χάριν περὶ ὅσων καὶ ὅσα θεωρητέον· δὶ ἀκριβείας δ' ὕστερον ἐροῦμεν...Cf. also 488b27f.

[36] See further the divisions at 487b6ff., 488a23f., 24f., 31–4, and cf. on the characters of animals at 488b12ff. Each half of the division into 'aquatic' and 'land-animals' is sub-divided into two main groups: those that live in the water into those that also take in water (487a16ff.), and those that do not (a19ff.); and those that live on land into those that take in air (a28ff.), and those do not (a30ff.). Of the pairs mentioned in *HA* I.1, two at least ('aquatic' and 'land-animals', and 'tame' and 'wild') may be paralleled in Plato, see *Plt.* 264D (cf. *Sph.* 220A) and *Sph.* 222B (cf. *Plt.* 264A).

[37] Thus, for example, at 488a1f. he says that some animals are both gregarious and solitary, and at 487b3ff. he points out that some animals begin by living in water, but afterwards change, and live outside.

[38] The assertion that all tame species are also found wild, and the examples given in *HA* 488a29ff., may be compared with a very similar assertion, and an almost identical list of examples, at *PA* 643b4ff., in a passage where Aristotle argues explicitly against the division into 'tame' and 'wild'. It may be, then, that *HA* 488a29ff. was added in the light of the ideas expressed at *PA* 643b3ff.

into contrary groups. It seems likely that the first 'outline' description of the differences between animals in *HA* I. 1–6 is based, in part at least, on such a classification; though certainly by the time that these chapters were put together in the form in which we have them now, some of the contrary groups had been modified, and the whole preliminary description was treated by Aristotle as of little scientific value.[39]

Aristotle's main discussion of the method of classifying animals is, of course, in *PA* I.2–4, which is largely devoted to a criticism of the method of Division. He repeats a number of the points which had been made elsewhere. Thus, at *PA* 643a27ff., he says that division must be made according to elements in the essence (cf. *APo.* 91b29, 97a24f., b1f.); at *PA* 643a31ff., he repeats the rule which he had insisted on before (particularly at *APo.* 97a14ff., see p. 13 n. 21) that division must be by contraries; and at *PA* 643b16ff., he stresses that the 'differentia of the differentia' should be taken (see *Metaph.* Z 1038a9f., 25). But new objections to the method of Division are also made, and these show that in so far as Aristotle's attitude to this method is concerned, *PA* I.2–4 represents a later stage of development than any of the passages from the Organon or the *Metaphysics* considered above. The fact that the number of species will be the same as the number of differentiae, which had been || mentioned, incidentally, at *Metaph.* Z 1038a17f., is now used to show the absurdity of applying this method to the classification of species (*PA* 643a7–24).[40] The fact that a definition will consist of the genus and the last differentia had been pointed out, e.g., at *Metaph.* Z 1038a19f., but this fact is now used as an objection to Division because each species requires more than one differentia (see *PA* 643b28–644a11). And finally, as a quite new and fundamental objection, Aristotle now complains that dichotomy splits up the natural groups, such as birds and fish (see *PA* 642b10ff, 643b10ff., and contrast *APo.* 97a1ff., 35ff., where it was assumed that both the genus 'animal' and the groups 'birds' and 'fish' could be divided dichotomously). In contrast, then, with the discussions of division in *APo.* II.13 and *Metaph.* Z.12, in which dichotomy was held to represent a valid method whereby the infimae species may be defined, in *PA* I.2–4 there is a total rejection of this method as applied to zoology.[41] Further, some of the examples which are now given of false dichotomies, may be compared with divisions which Aristotle himself had used and accepted at an earlier stage. At *PA* 642b32f., 643b20ff., he specifically rejects the division into πτερωτόν and ἄπτερον, which had been mentioned as an example of a possible type of division at *Metaph.* 1038a12f. (cf. the use of ἄπτερον at 1037b22, 33). At *PA* 643a35ff., division by

[39] See *HA* 488b27f. and 491a7ff., quoted above, p. 17 n. 35. It should be added that in ch. 6 (490b7ff.) at least, Aristotle gives a preliminary sketch of the γένη μέγιστα of animals, and this corresponds, in the main, with the classifications given elsewhere in *HA* and *PA*, see p. 19 and n. 44.

[40] Because it can hardly be expected that the number of species will, in fact, be 'four or some other power of two' (*PA* 643a22f.).

[41] *PA* 642b6f., 644b19f. διότι τὸ διχοτομεῖν τῇ μὲν ἀδύνατον τῇ δὲ κενόν, εἴρηται.

'functions common to body and soul', e.g. πορευτικά and πτηνά, is rejected. Yet previously, Aristotle himself had referred to, and accepted, the categories 'walking animal' and 'flying animal' (*Top.* 144b22ff., 133b7ff.) and τὸ πεζόν and τὸ πτερωτόν are mentioned as contrary species at *Metaph.* I. 1058a35f. (cf. also the differentiae of 'animal' given at *Top.* 143b1f., *Cat.* 1b18f., 14b37ff.).[42] Aristotle's criticisms of Dichotomy as a whole, and of specific divisions, in *PA* I.2–4, are, no doubt, directed primarily against his opponents in the Academy;[43] yet it is clear that they may also be applied, to some extent, to || Aristotle's own earlier theory and practice of zoological classification. The complete rejection of the usefulness of dichotomy in *PA* I.2–4 contrasts sharply with the modified acceptance of that method in such passages as *APo.* 96b25ff. and *Metaph.* Z.12, and represents an important development in Aristotle's thought on the problems of the classification of animals.

The total rejection of dichotomy in *PA* I marks a new stage in the development we are studying, but we must now consider the method which is used in its place and the actual classification of animals which is proposed in *PA* and elsewhere in the biological works. We may begin with the actual zoological classification which Aristotle puts forward. This has sometimes been thought to be in doubt, but several passages in *HA* and *PA*[44] distinguish, quite clearly, between the main groups of animals. These are as follows: man and the viviparous quadrupeds, the oviparous quadrupeds and footless animals, birds, fish, cetacea (the sanguineous animals); cephalopods, crustacea, testacea, insects (the bloodless animals). There are sometimes minor variations in this schema,[45] and Aristotle occasionally has difficulty in fitting into it various intermediate species.[46] But he follows the general lines

42 Again, the division into 'tame' and 'wild' is rejected specifically at *PA* 643b3, 8 and 21. Yet cf. p. 17 above on *HA* 488a26ff., and cf. also *APo.* 96b30ff. where 'tame' appears in a definition reached by division, and where Aristotle's purpose is to point out the usefulness of the method. On the use of 'biped' as a differentia, contrast *PA* 643a3f. with *Top.* 144b22f. (see p. 10).

43 He refers to his opponents as οἱ διχοτομοῦντες (642b21f.) and mentions certain 'published divisions' (642b12, cf. 643a36f. in connection with the division into πορευτικά and πτηνά). (Some take this to refer to a work of Speusippus, see e.g. Stenzel, 1929: 1636ff. Others, however, have taken the reference to be to Plato's *Sophist* and *Politicus*, see Ogle, 1882: 148.) Yet these repeated references to Aristotle's current or past opponents in the Academy are somewhat misleading; at least, they should not blind us to the fact that Aristotle himself had, at one stage, recommended the use of Division in seeking definitions, and frequently applied the method in zoological examples.

44 See *HA* 505b25–32, 523a31–b21, 534b12–15, 539a8–15, *PA* 678a26–31, and cf. *HA* 490b7ff.

45 Though the cetacea are usually mentioned as a genus on their own (*HA* 490b9, 505b30), they are sometimes dealt with among the species of fish, see *HA* V.5 540b21ff., VI.12 566b2ff. And though the snakes are recognised as a species on their own at *HA* 505b31 and *PA* 690b14, they are more frequently referred to under the class of τὰ φολιδωτά ('scaly reptiles'), see *HA* 594a4f., 599a30f., 600b23, *PA* 671a21.

46 E.g. the ape (see *HA* 502a16ff., *PA* 689b31ff.) and the bat (see *PA* 697b7ff., cf. *HA* 490a8). Cf. further Meyer, 1855: 146ff. At *HA* 532b18ff., Aristotle talks of a number of sea-animals which cannot be classified because of their rarity. There are also several species intermediate between animals and plants, see esp. *PA* 681a9ff., *HA* 588b4ff. (in both passages, Aristotle points out that there is no clear demarcation between animals and plants). Cf. further Meyer, 1855: 165ff.

of this classification closely, not only in those passage in which he lists the main genera of animals, but also in his organisation of the subject-matter in *HA* and in *PA*, in that he usually deals with the genera of sanguineous, and the genera of bloodless, animals, separately and in turn.[47] ||

But if Aristotle's classification of animals is fairly clear, the problem of the principle or principles by which he arrives at it, is much more complex. The recommendations in *PA* I.2–4 on the correct method of classification may be given briefly: (1) animals should be taken according to their natural groups, e.g. birds, fish (*PA* 643b10ff., 642b10ff., cf. 15ff. where it is pointed out that these groups do not necessarily have a regular name,. e.g. 'sanguineous' and 'bloodless'); and (2) these groups will be marked off from one another by several differentiae (643b12, 23f.). Unfortunately, Aristotle nowhere specifies what all these differentiae are. There are many passages in which he refers to the essential or defining characteristics of species, but an analysis of these shows that a wide variety of principles of differentiation is used.[48] It is impracticable to undertake a complete review of all such differentiae here, but some of the more important passages must be mentioned briefly. (1) The essence of a group is often defined in terms of a function of the soul, particularly of the locomotive soul, e.g. 'flying' or 'swimming'.[49] (2) Sometimes the possession of an important organ, such as the lungs, is said to be a defining character.[50] (3) Similarly, a general differentiating mark between groups is the presence or absence of blood,[51] and the quantity and the quality of the blood is related to the 'natural heat' of the animal, and so to other factors, the posture of the animal, its size and its vitality.[52] (4) Aristotle also differentiates || species by considering, simply, the form or arrangement of their organs or of the whole body. Thus, at *PA* 644b7ff., he says σχεδὸν δὲ τοῖς σχήμασι τῶν μορίων καὶ τοῦ σώματος ὅλου...ὥρισται τὰ

[47] The internal parts of the sanguineous genera are dealt with in *PA* III.4–IV.4, those of the bloodless genera in *PA* IV.5. Aristotle then turns to the external parts of the bloodless genera (*PA* IV.6–9) and deals with those of the sanguineous genera in *PA* IV.10–14. Similarly, in *HA*, the external parts of the sanguineous genera are dealt with in II.1–14 (after the organs of man have been described in I.7ff), and their internal parts in II.15–III.22. The external and internal parts of the bloodless genera are then dealt with in IV.1–7.

[48] The main passages are collected by Meyer, 1855: 331ff.

[49] See *PA* 693b5–13, on the birds, 695b17ff., on fish, and cf. *IA* 708a9ff., on snakes. See Meyer, 1855: 332. Generally speaking, there is a correlation between the variety of activities an animal is capable of, and the number of organs it possesses, see *PA* 683b5ff., 656a1ff., and cf. *Juv.* 468a18ff. (on organs of locomotion, in particular).

[50] See esp. *PA* 669b8–12, καὶ ἐκείνων (i.e. the animals that have lungs) ἐν τῇ οὐσίᾳ ὑπάρχει τὸ πλεύμονα ἔχειν (b11f.). The connection between the possession of lungs, and the heat of the animal, is pointed out, e.g., at *PA* 697a26ff., 669a24ff., cf. *Resp.* 477a14ff., *de An.* 420b24f.

[51] See *PA* 678a31–4, esp. 33f. ὅτι γάρ ἐστι τὰ μὲν ἔναιμα τὰ δ' ἄναιμα, ἐν τῷ λόγῳ ἐνυπάρξει τῷ ὁρίζοντι τὴν οὐσίαν αὐτῶν. 'Those genera that are "bloodless" have, nevertheless, what is analogous to blood', see e.g. *PA* 645b8ff., 648a19ff. On the varieties of blood in different genera, see e.g. *PA* 647b29ff., 651a12ff. In the course of the discussion of Division in *PA* I.3, Aristotle implies that the blood of each of the sanguineous genera must be different (see 643a3f.).

[52] On the connection between the quantity of the blood and the heat of the animal, its size, and its posture, see esp. *PA* 669b3ff., cf. 652b25ff., *GA* 732a16–23, *Resp.* 477a20f. See also p. 23 on *PA* 686a27–687a2.

γένη.[53] This is how, in practice, he distinguishes the groups of bloodless animals, for example,[54] and the reason why some species are intermediate often seems to be because they appear to share the parts or organs of two different genera.[55] To summarise, then, very briefly: no *one* criterion is adopted to differentiate all the species of animals; sometimes differences in function are referred to, sometimes differences in form, and under the latter heading come differences in the external and internal parts, the presence or absence of certain organs, the quantity and quality of the blood, and so on. The names which are given to some of the main genera suggest that the organs of locomotion (e.g. quadrupeds) and the mode of reproduction (e.g. vivipara) may be included in the essential distinguishing marks. But on the other hand, although Aristotle continues to refer, loosely, to 'aquatic' or 'walking' animals, for example, it is clear that such differentiae have no part in his classification of genera.[56]

Aristotle's theory and practice of zoological classification in the main body of the biological works can be sharply distinguished, both from the method of division recommended in *APo.* II.13 and *Metaph.* Z. 12, for example, and from the deductive method described in *Pol.* IV.4. There is, I suggest, one further modification in Aristotle's theory, in *GA* II.1. When the problem of Aristotle's classification of animals is discussed, the || evidence in *GA* is usually considered alongside that in *HA* and *PA*. Differences between the theory in *GA* II.1 and that of the other main biological works may be noted, but it has not been suggested that these may represent a modification or development of Aristotle's earlier views. Yet, as we shall see, the differences are such that they may hardly be explained on the assumption that he changes his classification of animals according to the point of view in which he is interested in any particular passage,[57] and some such theory of a modification of his earlier ideas would seem to offer the most satisfactory interpretation.

[53] Cf. also *HA* 491a14ff., ληπτέον δὲ πρῶτον τὰ μέρη τῶν ζῴων ἐξ ὧν συνέστηκεν. κατὰ γὰρ ταῦτα μάλιστα καὶ πρῶτα διαφέρει καὶ τὰ ὅλα, ἢ τῷ τὰ μὲν ἔχειν τὰ δὲ μὴ ἔχειν, ἢ τῇ θέσει καὶ τῇ τάξει, ἢ καὶ κατὰ τὰς εἰρημένας πρότερον διαφοράς, εἴδει καὶ ὑπεροχῇ καὶ ἀναλογίᾳ καὶ τῶν παθημάτων ἐναντιότητι.

[54] See *HA* IV.1 523b1–21, where the four bloodless genera are distinguished, at first, entirely in terms of the differences in their shapes and structures. Cf *PA* 684b16ff.

[55] This is the case, e.g., with the bat (*PA* 697b7ff.: ὡς μὲν πτηνὰ ἔχουσι πόδας, ὡς δὲ τετράποδα οὐκ ἔχουσι, καὶ οὔτε κέρκον ἔχουσιν οὔτ' οὐροπύγιον, διὰ μὲν τὸ πτηνὰ εἶναι κέρκον, διὰ δὲ τὸ πεζὰ οὐροπύγιον), the ape (*PA* 689b31ff., see 33f.: οὔτε οὐρὰν ἔχει οὔτ' ἰσχία, ὡς μὲν δίπους ὢν οὐράν, ὡς δὲ τετράπους ἰσχία), the ostrich (*PA* 697b13ff.) and cf. on the seal, *PA* 697b1ff., *HA* 501a21ff. On the other hand, the question of species intermediate between animals and plants is settled by their possessing or not possessing the faculty of sensation, see *PA* 681a19f., 27f., b4, *HA* 588b16f., *GA* 731b4ff.

[56] The ambiguities of the division into πεζά and ἔνυδρα are analysed, e.g., in *HA* 589a10ff., esp. 590a13ff., and cf. in the discussion of Division, *PA* 642b13, 19f. Yet Aristotle continues to refer to these 'classes' throughout the biological works, see e.g. *HA* 504b13, 536b32, 542a25f. etc, *IA* 707b28, *PA* 668b33, 697b2 etc., *GA* 761b13f., 771b10, 775b17, cf. the note to *HA* 589a11 in D'Arcy Thompson's Oxford Transl.

[57] See the suggestion made by Thompson, 1921: 158f.

There are still, of course, important similarities between the classification used in *GA* as a whole, and that of the other main biological works: the division into sanguineous and bloodless animals, and the main genera of each group, are still referred to throughout *GA*. But in considering animals from the point of view of their modes of reproduction, in *GA* II.1, Aristotle comes across an apparent difficulty – overlapping between the genera. It is true that in his first discussion of the generation of animals in *HA* V–VII, and indeed, throughout *HA* and *PA*, the fact that some fish are oviparous, some ovoviviparous, for example, is clearly recognised.[58] But in *GA* the problem of this overlapping is discussed explicitly: συμβαίνει δὲ πολλὴ ἐπάλλαξις τοῖς γένεσιν (732b15). In particular, Aristotle points out that there is no correlation between 'biped' 'quadruped' 'footed' and 'footless' on the other hand, and the vivipara and the ovipara on the other, and he concludes (732b26ff.) that differences in the organs of locomotion cannot be used to account for the different modes of reproduction. So far it seems that he is merely criticising this particular division[59] of animals by their organs of locomotion, but he then proceeds to give a detailed alternative classification of animals according to their degrees of 'perfection', as indicated by the degree of perfection of their offspring at birth. In this classification (732b28–733b16) there are five main groups: (1) the most perfect animals, described as hot and wet and not earthy, bring forth their young in a perfect state (vivipara); (2) the second class (cold and wet) is externally viviparous, but internally oviparous (cartilaginous fish and vipers); (3) the next class (hot and dry) produces, not a perfect animal, but at least a || perfect egg (birds and scaly reptiles); (4) the fourth class (cold and dry) produces an imperfect egg (scaly fish, crustacea, cephalopods); and (5) the fifth class (coldest of all) produces, not an egg, but a 'larva' (insects).[60] First, then, the division of animals according to their organs of locomotion is definitely rejected, because the groups (e.g. quadrupeds) are found to be split up. But then a similar criticism would seem to apply also to such 'natural' groups as fish (which are partly oviparous, partly ovoviviparous, as also are the serpents). Aristotle is led to give a new classification which cuts across the lines of the old. The problem is to what extent does this mean that the old classification has been modified, or even abandoned? Perhaps no final answer to this question is possible, but some facts, at least, are clear. (1) As I said before, the same main groups and genera of animals continue to be used throughout *GA* (e.g. 'sanguineous' and 'bloodless' animals, although the fourth class in the new classification contains both sanguineous and bloodless members –

[58] See *HA* 564b15ff., *PA* 676b1ff., etc.

[59] See the use of the verb διελεῖν at *GA* 732b26f.: ταύτῃ μὲν οὖν οὐκ ἔστι διελεῖν, οὐδ' αἴτιον τῆς διαφορᾶς ταύτης οὐθὲν τῶν πορευτικῶν ὀργάνων, which suggests, of course, that Aristotle has Platonic Divisions particularly in mind.

[60] Aristotle's classification stops at this point, though there is, in effect, a sixth class, the testacea, which reproduce spontaneously (see *GA* III.11, esp. 763a25f.). The testacea are, however, described as being intermediate between animals and plants (see 761a15ff., cf. 731b8ff.).

both fish and crustacea).[61] (2) The new classification affords no means of differentiating, e.g., the various classes of vivipara, man, the viviparous quadrupeds, and the cetacea, and it seems, then, that it cannot be meant to be sufficient and complete. On the other hand, (3), it does imply certain modifications in Aristotle's theory. A tendency to define species in terms of their methods of locomotion can be seen in several passages in *PA* and *IA*.[62] And in one instance, at least, (*PA* 686a27–687a2) the genera || of animals are stratified according to their natural heat *as indicated by* their posture and *organs of locomotion*. In that passage, a correlation is assumed between the number of feet of a group, and the amount of its natural heat, which diminishes from man and the quadrupeds downwards to the many-footed animals, then to the footless animals, then to the animals which are 'upside down' and finally to the plants.[63] In *GA* II.1, too, the genera are stratified according to their natural heat (combined with their wetness or dryness), but the test of this natural heat is not their organs of locomotion, as it had been in *PA* 686a24ff., but the state of perfection of their offspring at birth. The theory in *GA* II.1, then, not only displaces Platonic division, but also contrasts with the idea, which Aristotle himself had used in *PA*, that the differences in the organs of locomotion of the various species of animals correspond, generally, to differences in natural heat. The force of the new classification is, then, not to supplant the old classification completely, but to introduce a new criterion of 'natural heat' and to apply it systematically to give a classification of animals according to their degrees of perfection.[64] The

[61] See esp. *GA* 720b2ff., 743b9ff. Cf. the continued references to the groups 'oviparous quadrupeds' (e.g. 752b32) and 'viviparous quadrupeds' (718b3).

[62] Thus, on birds, Aristotle says (*PA* 693b13) τῷ δ' ὄρνιθι ἐν τῇ οὐσίᾳ τὸ πτητικόν ἐστιν, and on their organs of locomotion δίπουν δ' ἐξ ἀνάγκης ἐστίν· τῶν γὰρ ἐναίμων ἡ τοῦ ὄρνιθος οὐσία, ἅμα δὲ καὶ πτερυγωτός, τὰ δ' ἔναιμα οὐ κινεῖται πλείοσιν ἢ τέτταρσι σημείοις (b5ff.). Cf. on fish (*PA* 695b20ff.), ἐπεὶ δ' ἔναιμά ἐστι κατὰ τὴν οὐσίαν, διὰ μὲν τὸ νευστικὰ εἶναι πτερύγια ἔχει, διὰ δὲ τὸ μὴ πεζεύειν οὐκ ἔχει πόδας. On snakes, he says at *IA* 708a9ff. τοῖς δ' ὄφεσιν αἴτιον τῆς ἀποδίας τό τε τὴν φύσιν μηθὲν ποιεῖν μάτην, ἀλλὰ πάντα πρὸς τὸ ἄριστον ἀποβλέπουσαν ἑκάστῳ τῶν ἐνδεχομένων, διασώζουσαν ἑκάστου τὴν ἰδίαν οὐσίαν καὶ τὸ τί ἦν αὐτῷ εἶναι. In *IA*, especially, he attempts to establish correlations between the various genera and groups of animals, and their organs of locomotion, as, for instance, that sanguineous animals do not move at more than four 'points', i.e. that no sanguineous animal is many-footed (*IA* 704a11 etc., cf. *PA* 693b7f. above). His realisation that differences in the organs of locomotion do not correspond with differences in the modes of reproduction of the various genera (see esp. *GA* 732b26f., see above, p. 22 n. 59) must, then, be considered in the light of his earlier tendency to refer particularly to the organs of locomotion in defining the essences of genera.

[63] See esp. *PA* 686b28ff. ἔτι δ' ἐλάττονος γινομένης τῆς αἰρούσης θερμότητος καὶ τοῦ γεώδους πλείονος, τά τε σώματα ἐλάττονα τῶν ζῴων ἐστὶ καὶ πολύποδα, τέλος δ' ἄποδα γίγνεται καὶ τεταμένα πρὸς τὴν γῆν. The testacea are mentioned separately at 686b31ff., as the animals which have their ἀρχή below (cf. 683b18ff.). So the footless animals referred to at 686b30f. as 'stretched out on the ground' must be the snakes. According to this classification, then, the snakes are considered to be less hot than the many-footed animals (e.g. crustacea, cephalopods, insects). But according to the classification given in *GA* II.1, the snakes, which are oviparous or ovoviviparous (the viper, see *GA* 732b21), belong to the third or second class ('hot and dry' or 'cold and wet') above the crustacea and cephalopods in the fourth class ('cold and dry') and the insects in the fifth ('coldest of all').

[64] As we saw above, p. 20 and notes 50 and 52, certain marks, such as the possession of a lung,

contrast between *GA* II.1 and *PA* 686a24ff. suggests that the classification in *GA* II.1 represents a new stage, or at least an important modification, in Aristotle's theory: (1) classification by the organs of locomotion is rejected; (2) even some of the natural, or conventional, groups (such as 'fish') are || found to be split up (contrast *PA* 643b10ff.); (3) a new criterion of the 'natural heat' of species is introduced, which refers to the degree of perfection of the offspring at birth; and (4) this criterion is used to give a new classification of animals according to their degrees of perfection.

The evidence in the biological works suggests three stages in the development of Aristotle's theory of the classification of animals. (1) Certain indications in *HA* I suggest that he may, at one stage, have attempted a classification of animals into contrary groups. (2) In *PA* I.2–4, Division is analysed and rejected (and the criticisms of this method go far beyond anything we found in passages in the *Analytics* or *Metaphysics*). Several passages in the biological works give the main groups and genera of animals, but these are marked off from one another by a wide variety of differentiae (differences in the external and internal parts, in faculties of the soul, etc). (3) This theory is modified, in *GA* II.1, when classification by the organs of locomotion is rejected, and a new test (by the degrees of perfection of the offspring of the various genera at birth) is introduced. The same main groups and genera continue to be referred to, but the new test is used to give a systematic classification of the genera according to their degrees of perfection.

It remains to formulate the results of this study, and to consider what conclusions may be reached on the general problem of the chronology of Aristotle's works. First, I must repeat that the date of a book cannot, usually, be established merely on the basis of the date of a single passage. But the main passages dealing with the classification of animals may be arranged, roughly, in the following order:[65] *Top.* VI.6 (perhaps with the very first stratum of *HA* I), *APo.* II.13 (contemporary with or just after *APr.*I.31, *APo.*II.5), *Metaph.* Z.12, *PA* I.2–4 and the other main passages in *HA* and *PA* giving Aristotle's usual classification of animals, and finally *GA* II.1. In addition, *Pol.* 1290b25ff. must be included, presumably after *Metaph.* Z.12 (Division is not used), but before the bulk of the biological works (which do

or the quantity of blood, which are related to differences in 'natural heat', were used elsewhere in the biological works to differentiate groups of animals (cf. also Ogle, 1882: xxiiff.). But while the classification in *GA* II.1 still makes use of these marks (see *GA* 732b29, 32ff., 733a3f.), it is exceptional in that it offers a *complete* and *systematic* analysis of the different genera of animals in terms of hot and cold, and the related pairs of opposites, wet and dry. By considering the differences in their offspring at birth, Aristotle is able to analyse the various genera in terms of the four opposites, and so to classify animals according to a scale of perfection (because the animals which are 'hotter' are more perfect, see e.g. *GA* 732b31ff.).

[65] There is not sufficient evidence to place *Metaph.* I. 8 and 9 (see above p. 14) definitely in this table. But both passages express a similar attitude to the use of Division to that found in *APo.* 96b25ff., and it seems likely that they may both fall before *Metaph.* Z. 12.

not use the deductive method recommended there). Some of the conclusions which this order suggests agree with generally accepted views of the chronology of whole treatises: for instance, that the *Topics* are earlier than *APr.* or *APo.*; that the Organon as a whole is earlier than the biological works or the *Metaphysics*; that *GA* may be later than the rest of the biological works. || On the other hand, some of the conclusions suggested are in apparent contradiction with commonly accepted interpretations of the date of various treatises. *Metaph.* Z.12 definitely seems earlier than *PA* I.2–4, or indeed the bulk of biological works. Therefore, either the opinion[66] that *Metaph.* Z is a late work must be wrong, or (as I think much more likely)[67] it must contain at least some material which was written at an early stage (i.e. perhaps early in the middle period). Again, *Pol.*IV.4 contains a theory of zoological classification which, though not dependent on Division, does not correspond with Aristotle's practice in the biological works. So either *Pol.*IV as a whole is a work of the middle period at the latest,[68] or (as, again I think is not improbable) it must contain some material, at least, from that period.[69] One final note may be added, and that concerns the problem of whether Aristotle's development may be viewed in terms of an increasing tendency towards empiricism.[70] To judge from the developments in his attitude towards the problem of zoological classification, it is true that he began by accepting, with few reservations, the dogmatic method of Division, and then progressed towards a more complex and empirical system in the biological works themselves. Yet the interpretation of a continual advance towards empiricism can hardly || be accepted, when we consider the elements of teleology, and of dogmatic analysis in terms of the opposites hot, cold, wet and dry, which we find in *GA* II.1, in what is probably the last major passage in which he dealt at length with the problems of classification.

[66] Nuyens, 1948: 176ff., cf. Jaeger, 1948: ch. 8. Contrast Düring, 1943: 114, who is of the opinion that *Metaph.* Z.12 (at least) 'seems prior to *PA* I'.

[67] None of the passages which Nuyens used to reach his conclusion that *Metaph.* Z cannot have been composed before the *De Anima*, comes, in fact, from ch. 12. This chapter is, indeed, part of a digression from the main subject of Book Z (see the beginning of ch. 13, 1038b1f.).

[68] Jaeger, 1923: 269ff., considered that Books IV–VI represent the latest stratum in the *Politics*, to be dated to the last decade of Aristotle's life. Barker, 1948: xliff., and Ross, 1957: 70f., both held that *all* the books of the *Politics* belong to the last period of Aristotle's second residence in Athens. On the other hand, Nuyens, while accepting Jaeger's view of the relative chronology of the strata of the *Politics*, held that 'if...books I, IV, V and VI are placed in the last period of Aristotle's activity, it must be maintained that...they are notably anterior to the *De Anima*' (1948: 197). It is interesting to note that Jaeger referred to *Pol.* IV 1290b25ff. particularly (1948: 270f.) and considered that it marked 'a revolution in method'. This may be the case, but it still does not describe the method which Aristotle actually uses in classifying animals in the biological works.

[69] It has already been noted (see p. 16 n. 31 above) that the method proposed at *Pol.* 1290b25ff. is not, in fact, adhered to in the description of the varieties of democracy and oligarchy at 1291b15ff. On the discrepancies between 1290b22–1291b13 and what follows, see further Barker, 1948: 164 n. 1, 167 n. 1.

[70] This was Jaeger's general interpretation (1948: esp. ch. 13) which has been challenged, e.g., by Nuyens, 1948: 10, and Ross, 1957: 72f., 77.

REFERENCES

Barker, E. (1948). *The Politics of Aristotle*, 2nd edn (Oxford)

Bourgey, L. (1955) *Observation et expérience chez Aristote* (Paris)

Düring, I. (1943) *Aristotle's De Partibus Animalium, Critical and Literary Commentaries* (Göteborg)

Jaeger, W. (1923) *Aristoteles, Grundlegung einer Geschichte seiner Entwicklung* (Berlin)

(1948) *Aristotle: Fundamentals of the History of his Development*, transl. by R. Robinson of Jaeger, 1923, 2nd edn (Oxford)

Lee, H. D. P. (1948) 'Place-names and the date of Aristotle's biological works', *Classical Quarterly* 42: 61–7

Louis, P. (1955) 'Remarques sur la classification des animaux chez Aristote', in *Autour d'Aristote, Recueil d'Etudes...offert à M. Mansion* (Louvain)

Meyer, J. B. (1855) *Aristoteles Thierkunde, ein Beitrag zur Geschichte der Zoologie, Physiologie und alten Philosophie* (Berlin)

Nuyens, F. (1948) *Ontwikkelingsmomenten in de zielkunde van Aristoteles* (Nimègue–Utrecht, 1939), Fr. transl. by A. Mansion, *L'Evolution de la Psychologie d'Aristote* (Louvain)

Ogle, W. (1882) *Aristotle On the Parts of Animals* (London)

Ross, W. D. (1957) 'The development of Aristotle's thought', *Proceedings of the British Academy* 43: 63–78

Stenzel, J. (1929) 'Speusippos', in *Pauly–Wissowa Real-Encyclopädie der classischen Altertumswissenschaft* IIIA (Stuttgart): 1636–69

Thompson, D'A. W. (1921) 'Natural science', in *The Legacy of Greece* (Oxford), 137–62

2

RIGHT AND LEFT IN GREEK PHILOSOPHY

INTRODUCTION

'Right and left in Greek philosophy' was first published in the *Journal of Hellenic Studies* in 1962. As I note at the outset, the inspiration for it came from the French anthropologist Robert Hertz, whose classic study 'La prééminence de la main droite' was a model for a whole series of inquiries into the use of right/left distinctions in a wide variety of ancient and more especially modern societies. Rodney Needham, who translated Hertz's study in *Death and the Right Hand* in 1960, and who had himself undertaken several detailed studies of right/left distinctions, in relation to the ethnographic evidence for the Meru and Nyoro in particular, collected and edited a group of discussions, including my own article, in *Right and Left* in 1973, and it is this version that is reprinted here.

In his introduction to that collection, Needham surveyed the status quaestionis in what had by then become a hotly disputed area of anthropological research. Apart from specific objections to particular interpretations of the field data, two main types of criticism have been levelled at these investigations. (1) Those who discuss right/left distinctions in comparative studies exaggerate their importance and assume incorrectly that the use of such distinctions is a general, if not indeed universal, phenomenon. (2) Such studies fail to distinguish sufficiently between actors' and observers' categories and in particular distort the views of the members of the societies in question by representing them over-schematically.

Thus to take up the first type of criticism, it has been argued that right/left distinctions may be important only in certain societies, notably those in which hierarchical differentiations are prominent, and again that more often than not a supposed dualistic belief system symbolised by the use of right and left conceals an essentially triadic or otherwise more complex structure of thought. On the question of social structure, at least, the validity of a dualistic analysis had already been challenged in many cases by Lévi-Strauss (1956/1968). Again Tcherkézoff (1983/1987), following Dumont (1967/1980), attacked right/left studies both on the grounds of oversimplifying the data and more particularly for ignoring the essentially hierarchical and asymmetrical features of classifications that can be interpreted as based on right and left.

Secondly and even more fundamentally it has been objected that right/left studies often owe more to the styles of thought of the interpreters than to those of the members of the societies under discussion. In particular Goody (1977) has argued that the common use of Tables of Opposites in this context distorts the original data. Such Tables, he insists, are a familiar device in proto-literate societies and indeed presuppose a certain level of literacy: but if so, then their use in relation to predominantly oral cultures is problematic. 'The construction of a Table of Opposites reduces oral complexity to graphic simplicity' (Goody 1977: 70).

First in his Introduction to *Right and Left* and then in subsequent studies (especially in *Counterpoints*, 1987) Needham has replied to these and other criticisms both of his own work and of that of his co-authors, while taking further his own analysis of the underlying logic of dualist classifications. He has defended his own interpretation of the Meru and Nyoro data and rebutted the claim that right/left polarities are specific to hierarchically oriented societies and convey an essentially asymmetrical relationship. To the objection that dualist classifications impose schemata that distort by oversystematising the actors' own views, the first step in his counter is that in the diagnosis of collective representations the observer has inevitably to go beyond the actors' own reports and can, in certain circumstances at least, legitimately do so. In his most recent far-reaching study of opposition Needham examines critically both the idea that it stems from some innate faculty of the mind and that it merely 'reflects' pairs given in nature (a point pressed home in relation to right and left in particular). The conceptual *complexity* of the relations treated as dyadic pairs or as modes of opposition of one type or another is given full weight. But these are now seen not as a set of variations on some essentially simple basic relationship: rather opposition is inherently polyvalent, 'an odd-job notion seductively masked by the immediacy of a spatial metaphor' (1987: 228).

So far as the data for ancient Greece go, some of those had been cited and commented on long before Hertz's essay, and Hertz himself made use of some of them. Further work on Homer and on Plato was undertaken by Cuillandre and by Schuhl, both of whom refer directly to Hertz's study, as also does the paper by Lévêque and Vidal-Naquet on Epaminondas published in 1960 but regrettably not mentioned in the 1962 version of my article.[1] My own discussion attempted a more general survey of the problem of right and left in Greek philosophy, and it was followed by a further article on the use of hot and cold, dry and wet (published in *JHS* in 1964) and then by the monograph *Polarity and Analogy* (1966). The first part of that book took an even broader canvas and attempted an analysis of the use of opposites in Greek thought in general.

My own forays in this area attracted further criticisms over and above

[1] My article, which was written during the course of 1960, was originally submitted to *JHS* in January 1961.

those directed at the Needham collection. In particular *Polarity and Analogy* was criticised on the grounds that no one could fail to make use of the kind of relationships that I had represented as particularly important in Greek thought. After all every use of language implies the recognition of similarities and differences: every application of a general term lumps the items it covers together and splits them off from all other items. There was, so it was argued, nothing exceptional about the Greek material, and even, some objected, some doubt as to whether *Polarity and Analogy* had a subject to investigate at all – a surprising view to anyone familiar with the comparative data discussed by anthropologists.

In relation both to that reaction and to both the main types of criticism made of general ethnographic studies in this area that I mentioned at the outset (p. 27) it can be argued that the data concerning right and left in ancient Greece are of particular interest and importance, for we can use them to test both claims as to the hierarchical nature of the antithesis and objections based on the distinction between actors' and observers' categories. Right and left are undoubtedly used in ancient Greece to convey hierarchical distinctions in many contexts, notably in certain authoritarian philosophical systems. However, to that must be added two fundamental points: (1) there is no uniformity, no orthodoxy, in the application of right/left polarities in Greek philosophy and science, let alone in Greek thought and culture more generally; (2) as I showed in *Polarity and Analogy* it is far from being the case that all uses of opposites in Greek thought convey a hierarchical differentiation or fall under the rubric of what I called (following Hertz) religious polarity. On the contrary, the evidence from ancient Greece bears out Needham's view that the use of oppositions and dyadic pairs takes a great variety of forms. They are not confined to cases where an underlying asymmetrical structure is detectable. Moreover so far as correlations between ancient Greek social structures and thought patterns go, whatever interpretation is given of the former the very variety of the latter undermines any claim that they simply reflect, let alone are determined by, the structure of the society that produced them.

As to distinctions between actors' and observers' categories, it is a notable feature of the Greek material that some of the Greeks themselves comment on their own use of opposites. There is no question of saying, here, that Tables of Opposites are the product of modern commentators' pre-occupations. Aristotle himself sets out the *sustoichia*, viz. Table of Opposites, he ascribes to the Pythagoreans (see p. 38 and n. 15). Of course Aristotle has to some extent systematised those Pythagorean beliefs and to that extent may be said to have acted in ways similar to those objected to in modern ethnographers. Yet the fundamental point remains: this is *ancient Greek* interpretation of ancient Greek beliefs. Here the development of the categories is the work of members of the society themselves, not that of modern observers.

On a number of points of detail the interpretations proposed in my study of right and left have been challenged. Thus Kember (1971) offered a different view of the evidence for Parmenides' sexual theories – criticisms I attempted to meet in a note in *JHS* in 1972. Again Byl challenged my account of Aristotle's views on the position of the heart (Byl 1968 and again 1980): the key factor at work, in Byl's view, is not a preoccupation with right/left polarity, but the special importance attached to the centre. That that factor is important in this context must undoubtedly be agreed even though polarities *also* remain in play in Aristotle's discussion of why the heart is not in the exact centre of the body.

However, these criticisms of detail do not seriously affect the strategic importance of the issues I focused on in this study. If anything I would now say that their importance is even greater than I claimed in 1962. I concentrated attention, in my article, on cases where right and left were used by philosophers and scientists in what might appear to be unexpected ways and I claimed that part, at least, of the key to understanding those uses lay in widespread assumptions in Greek thought of a kind that can be extensively paralleled in the ethnographic evidence – and for which there was abundant evidence in Greek literature and religion as well as in the philosophic or scientific authors in question.

But the additional point that I made above, that the Greeks were themselves self-conscious in the use of these categories, did not receive, in my original paper, the emphasis it now seems to deserve. What is exceptional, and exceptionally important, in the Greek material, is this self-consciousness, the *explicit analysis* of their own conceptual schemata and of the logic they presuppose. Preference for the right hand is for the Greeks as for many other peoples a deep-seated assumption that surfaces in a wide variety of contexts, in religious beliefs and practices, in techniques of divination, in social observances and so on. Right/left polarity comes to be a model for the use of many other pairs of opposites and the vehicle for the expression of the basic organisation of a wide variety of phenomena. In cosmology, in would-be scientific theories – in embryology, anatomy and physiology, for instance – in particular types of argument, the right/left model frequently provides part of the explanatory or theoretical framework.

Yet this deep-seated assumption became, with the Greeks, the object of analysis and criticism. On the one hand particular religious or social observances were challenged – as when Plato protested that it was ridiculous for Greek children to have their left hand swaddled to discourage its use (p. 47 and n. 43) – a practice that no doubt continued long after Plato. On the other Aristotle rejected an embryological theory based on right/left distinctions explicitly on the grounds that it conflicted with the evidence of dissection (pp. 40–1), and as I pointed out in *Polarity and Analogy* he was the first to give a formal analysis of the logic of opposition as such, distinguishing its different modes and setting out the conditions of validity of different schemata of argument based on opposites.

Both the antecedents and the consequences of those developments raise issues of considerable general significance. In what circumstances can and does any society investigate the fundamental categorial assumptions on which the very ordering of the society itself may be said to rest? How can and do such assumptions become visible to the members of the society itself? This might seem to be merely a matter of taking thought, a problem in the history of intellectuality. Yet clearly there are more than just intellectualist features in play when deep-seated religious and social assumptions are made the subject of explicit challenge. The self-conscious analysis of right/left and other oppositions in Greece provides a test case for the study of those circumstances and conditions in an ancient society. As I have argued elsewhere[2] the factors that might be invoked to explain such conditions include economic, technological and especially socio-political ones, to which must be added features to do with the technology of communication, especially the influence of modes of writing and the spread of literacy. This is not the place to attempt to summarise these complex arguments: but that there is indeed something that needs and requires explanation, in the development of self-consciousness on the question of fundamental assumptions, should be emphasised more strongly than I did in 1962.

Then so far as the consequences of that developed self-awareness go, it is again important to stress the wide-reaching implications of the Greek material. Self-consciousness concerning the validity of certain schemata of argument based on opposites may or may not influence the actual practice of argumentation. The identification of various types of fallacious reasoning does not, of itself, of course, mean an end to the use of fallacies of those types, let alone of fallacious reasoning in general. Yet once rules of formal logic have been set out they *can* be appealed to, precisely in order to challenge certain types of argument. When the underlying logical structure of opposition was rendered explicit, this was not just the outcome of the existence of a certain possibility of challenge, but itself thereafter contributed to the extension of those possibilities.

Yet the fundamental issue at the heart of that set of problems is one that lies deeper still. The formalisation of logic was an achievement of Greek philosophy, one to which Aristotle's contribution was basic. But Aristotle assumed that his analysis is valid for all discourse. His axioms, the Laws of Non-Contradiction and of Excluded Middle, are represented as the conditions of intelligibility of all communication. But that assumes that formal logic is no more than the setting out of the rules implicit in informal discourse. While there is some truth in that characterisation, the important issues that that way of putting it leaves unexplored are the relations between the implicit and the explicit, the ways in which the formal analysis of a speech act itself modifies its content or character, in short the disparity between the formalisable elements in communication and those that resist formalisation.

[2] In Lloyd, 1979: ch. 4, and most recently in Lloyd, 1990.

Formal logic, to be sure, represents an idealisation of the conditions of communication and an abstraction from certain features of it: but much actual communication depends on conditions and assumptions to do with the context of discourse that are themselves not captured by Aristotle's – or by anyone else's – *formal* logic. Thus on this score, the tendency to criticise pre- or non-formal uses of oppositions as symptomatic of a pre- or non-logical stage of thought represents a fundamental misconception of the pragmatics of communication.[3]

The uses to which the right/left distinction is put, in ancient Greece and elsewhere, stretch far beyond a mere deployment of a convenient set of symbols, far beyond the use of such distinctions to convey value judgements, and indeed to convey the very notion of a distinction in values itself. Implicated in those uses are questions to do with the constitution of meaning and intelligibility itself. This is not just a matter of the convenience of presenting complex material in schematic form: the way in which this and other pairs are used can be taken as an indicator of the types of intelligibility pursued and of the implications of their acceptance. This is no part of some attempt to uncover some universal features either of the human mind, or of language, or of the world. All such endeavours face the objection, in this context, that the uses of right and left, and of other pairs, widespread though they are, are not universal. Rather the challenge of the material discussed under this heading is to study how the human imagination puts to use what it represents as given distinctions in different ways and for different purposes, how it converts what is socially and culturally mediated and determined into what it accepts as natural and again how it may (though only may) become self-conscious of its very doing so.

[3] Lloyd, 1990 reviews critically the grounds for identifying divergent mentalities in this and other connections.

REFERENCES

Byl, S. (1968) 'Note sur la place du coeur et la valorisation de la ΜΕΣΟΤΗΣ dans la biologie d'Aristote', *L'Antiquité Classique* 37: 467–76

(1980) *Recherches sur les grands traités biologiques d'Aristote: sources écrites et préjugés*, Académie Royale de Belgique, Mémoires de la Classe des lettres 2nd ser. 64.3. (Brussels)

Dumont, L. (1966/1980) *Homo Hierarchicus*, revised transl. by M. Sainsbury of French edn (originally 1966, Paris) (London)

Goody, J. (1977) *The Domestication of the Savage Mind* (*Cambridge*)

Kember, O. (1971) 'Right and left in the sexual theories of Parmenides', *Journal of Hellenic Studies* 91: 70–9

Lévi-Strauss, C. (1956/1968) 'Les organisations dualistes existent-elles?' (originally publ. in *Bijdragen tot de taal-, land- en Volkenkunde*, Deel 112 (1956), 99–128, repr. in *Anthropologie structurale* (Paris, 1958), 147–80, transl. as *Structural Anthropology* by C. Jacobson and B. G. Shoepf (London, 1968), 132–63

Lloyd, G. E. R. (1964) 'The hot and the cold, the dry and the wet in Greek philosophy', *Journal of Hellenic Studies* 84: 92–106 (repr. in *Studies in Presocratic Philosophy*, ed. D. J. Furley and R. E. Allen, vol. I (London, 1970), 255–80)

(1966) *Polarity and Analogy: Two Types of Argumentation in Early Greek Thought* (Cambridge)

(1972) 'Parmenides' sexual theories: a reply to Mr Kember', *Journal of Hellenic Studies* 92: 178–9

(1979) *Magic, Reason and Experience* (Cambridge)

(1990) *Demystifying Mentalities* (Cambridge)

Needham, R. (1973) Introduction to *Right and Left*, ed. R. Needham (Chicago), xi–xxxix

(1987) *Counterpoints* (Berkeley)

Tcherkézoff, S. (1983/1987) *Dual Classification Reconsidered*, transl. by M. Thom of *Le Roi Nyamwezi, la droite et la gauche* (Cambridge, 1983) (Cambridge)

RIGHT AND LEFT IN GREEK PHILOSOPHY

The purpose of this article is to consider how the symbolic associations which right and left had for the ancient Greeks influenced various theories and explanations in Greek philosophy of the fifth and fourth centuries B.C. The fact that certain manifest natural oppositions (e.g., right and left, male and female, light and darkness, up and down) often acquire powerful symbolic associations, standing for religious categories such as pure and impure, blessed and accursed, is well attested by anthropologists for many present-day societies.[1] Robert Hertz, in particular, has considered the significance of the widespread belief in the superiority of the right hand, in his essay 'La prééminence de la main droite: étude sur la polarité religieuse' (Hertz, 1909; cited according to the translation by R. and C. Needham, 1960). It is, of course, well known that the ancient Greeks shared some similar beliefs, associating right and left with lucky and unlucky, respectively, and light and darkness with safety, for example, and death. Yet the survival of certain such associations in Greek philosophy has not, I think, received the attention it deserves. I wish to document this aspect of the use of opposites in Greek philosophy in this paper, concentrating in the main upon the most interesting pair of opposites, right and left. Before I turn to the evidence in the philosophers themselves, two introductory notes are necessary. In the first, I shall consider briefly some of the evidence in anthropology which indicates how certain pairs of opposites are associated with, and symbolise, religious categories in many present-day societies. The second contains || a general summary of the evidence for similar associations and beliefs in pre-philosophical Greek thought.

I

The superiority of the right hand might be thought to rest on purely anatomical factors. That there is a functional asymmetry of the brain – the left cerebral hemisphere being more developed, in some respects, than the right – is agreed (though whether this is the cause, or an effect, of the superior development of the right hand, is still an open question).[2] Yet even if we assume that there is a definite anatomical basis for the superiority of the right hand, this does not determine why many societies insist that the difference between the two hands should be not only maintained, but emphasised. The mutilation of the left arm is a practice which is reported in a number of societies. Evans-Pritchard, noting how Nuer youths put their left arm out of

In this article *CMG* refers to the several volumes of *Corpus Medicorum Graecorum* (ed. Heiberg and others, Leipzig); DK refers to *Die Fragmente der Vorsokratiker*, edited by Diels, revised by Kranz, 6th edn, 1951–2; L refers to Littré's edition of the Hippocratic treatises (Paris 1839–61).

[1] I must express my gratitude to Professor Meyer Fortes and Dr Edmund Leach, Professor and Reader in Social Anthropology in the University of Cambridge, for their help on several questions of anthropology connected with this paper.

[2] See Hertz, 1960: 90, and Needham's note *ad loc.*

action for long periods by binding it with metal rings, said the belief that underlies this and other Nuer practices is that 'the right side is the good side and the left side the evil side'.[3] According to Hertz (1960: 100), the right is often thought to be the seat of sacred power, 'the source of everything that is good, favourable and legitimate', while the left is the profane side, 'possessing no virtue other than ... certain disturbing and suspect powers'. It is interesting to note that the right is not invariably the sacred side. Although the great majority of societies hold the right to be the honourable side, there are some instances of peoples who are predominantly right-handed, but who nevertheless consider the left the nobler side: among the Zunis[4] the left and right sides are personified as brother gods, of which the left is the elder and wiser, and among the ancient Chinese,[5] the left was *yang* and therefore superior, the right *yin* and inferior. This reversal of the usual associations indicates, to my mind, the part played by social, rather than purely physiological, factors in determining the attitude to right and left.

Many primitive peoples identify the right-hand side with what is sacred and pure, the left with the profane and the impure, and other pairs of opposites also acquire similar associations. Hertz (1960: 97) has already discussed the associations which male and female have for the Maori, for example. The association of day, light, and east with the powers of life and strength, and of night, darkness, and west with the contrary powers of death and weakness, || is very common. Further, as perhaps the natural resultant of this tendency to identify certain pairs of opposites with the sacred and the profane, we find that such pairs as day/night, right/left, and male/female are often themselves correlated or identified, even where there is no manifest connection between them. A single example of this may be mentioned.[6]

[3] Evans-Pritchard 1956: 234ff., where a number of other practices illustrating this belief are given.

[4] As Evans-Pritchard notes (1960: 22), Hertz mentions this example only to dismiss it as a 'secondary development'. The fact that the Zuni are a peaceful agricultural people no doubt contributes to the relative estimation in which they hold the right, or spear, hand, and the left, or shield, hand.

[5] See Granet, 1934: 361ff., and 1953: 263ff. The Chinese attitude to this antithesis is complex, for while the left is generally superior and *yang*, and the right inferior and *yin*, yet in the sphere of what is itself common or inferior, the right in some sense has precedence over the left. Thus the right hand is used for eating (Granet, 1934: 364) and the right side is the appropriate side for women (while the left belongs to men, Granet, 1934: 368).

[6] Many primitive societies appear to classify things generally into groups of opposites (often corresponding to opposite groups in the society itself). A number of notable examples of such classifications are given by van der Kroef (1954: 847ff.), among them that of the people of Amboyna in Indonesia who, according to this authority, correlate pairs of opposites in the following way:

Right	Left
Male	Female
Land or mountain-side	Coast or sea-side
Above	Below
Heaven or sky	Earth
Worldly	Spiritual

Evans-Pritchard notes that for the Nuer there are two sets of opposites, the one comprising the left side, weakness, femininity, and evil, and the other the right side, strength, masculinity, and goodness: east is associated with life, and west with death, but then east is also identified with right and west with left 'thus bringing into the left–right polarity the polar representations not only of life and death but also of the cardinal points east and west'.[7]

II

The evidence in anthropology shows quite clearly that in many present-day societies certain natural oppositions (especially right and left) are often associated with, or symbolise, important spiritual categories, e.g. 'sacred' and 'profane', 'pure' and 'impure'. Some of the associations which various natural oppositions had for the ancient Greeks are, no doubt, well known and need little comment. One antithesis of great importance is that between *sky* and *earth*, for with these are associated two fundamental religious distinctions, (1) the distinction between Olympian and chthonian deities,[8] and (2) the general distinction between gods and men, between the *epouranioi* (heavenly ones) and the *epichthonioi* (earthly ones).[9] Another important pair of opposites is *light* and *darkness*. As has been shown by Bultmann (1948) especially, light, for the ancient Greeks, was the symbol of well-being, happiness, success, and glory in life, and of life itself (while darkness and night were generally associated with the contraries of these). Among other pairs of opposites connected with sky and earth, or with light and darkness, *up* and *down* and *white* and *black* certainly have important symbolic values from an early stage.[10] Although there appear to be no good grounds for

Upwards	Downwards
Interior	Exterior
In front	Behind
East	West
Old	New

[7] Evans-Pritchard, 1956: 234f.

[8] These two categories of gods are often referred to in invocations, e.g. Aeschylus, *A*. 89. *Supp*. 24f.; Euripides, *Hec*. 146f.; Plato, *Lg* 717A–B. The importance of the distinction between them has been particularly stressed by Guthrie, 1950: chhs. 8 and 9, e.g. p. 209: 'The distinction between Olympian and Chthonian, aetherial and sub-aetherial, or to put it more simply, between gods of the heaven and gods of the earth, is one which I hold to be fundamental for the understanding of Greek religion.'

[9] On this distinction, see Guthrie, 1950: 113ff.

[10] White is associated with good luck: a white vote was used, in classical times, for acquittal (e.g. Luc. *Harm*. 3) and the expression *leukē hēmera* (literally 'white day') is used for a lucky day. Conversely, black is the colour of death (e.g. *Il*. 2.834) and is associated with various things and personifications of evil omen: in Aeschylus, for instance, it is used of the Furies (e.g. *A*. 462f.), of misfortune (*Supp*. 89), of Recklessness (*A*. 770) and of a curse (*Th*. 832). It may be that as a general rule the colour of the victim sacrificed to an Olympian deity was white, that of the chthonians' sacrificial victims black (cf. *Il*. 3.103ff., where a white ram and a black ewe are sacrificed to the sun and to the earth). Other general distinctions between the rites associated with the Olympians and those of the chthonian deities have been collected by Guthrie (1950: 221f.), and several of these reflect the symbolic associations of such pairs of opposites as up and down, high and low.

believing that in early Greek religious practices *male* and *female* stood in an unvarying relationship of 'sacred' and 'profane' to one another (as Hertz suggested is the implication of Maori cults), it may be noted that women are usually thought of as inferior; and Hesiod, at least, repeatedly describes the first woman, || Pandora, as an evil (e.g. *Th.* 570, 585, 600; *Op.* 57, 89), and even implies that she is the source of all evil for mankind.[11]

The associations which *right* and *left* themselves have in Homer and Hesiod may be considered in a little more detail. The fact that the right is the lucky, the left the unlucky, side for the Greeks, is well known: omens on the right are auspicious, those on the left inauspicious, in Homer, for example (e.g. *Il.* 24.315–21; *Od.* 2.146–54).[12] But then the lucky direction, from left to right, was observed in many different activities, such as in the serving of wine round a group of guests (*Il.* 1.597; cf. Plato, *Smp.* 223C, etc., and *Od.* 21.141ff., where the suitors try Odysseus' bow, going from left to right of their company), and in the drawing of lots (at *Il.* 7.181ff., the lot which has been cast is taken around the group of warriors from left to right until it is claimed by its owner). The right hand is used to greet people (e.g. *Od.* 1.120f.), to pour a libation (e.g. *Il.* 24.283ff.) and to give a solemn pledge (e.g. *Il.* 4.159).[13] Conversely the left hand is unlucky. Two of the words for left (*euōnumos* and *aristeros*) are euphemisms, and a third (*skaios*) comes to mean 'ill-omened' (as in Sophocles, *Aj.* 1225) and 'awkward' (e.g. Aristophanes, *V.* 1265f.), like the French 'gauche', the opposite of *dexios* meaning 'clever' or 'skilful' (literally 'right-handed').

Many natural oppositions had strong symbolic associations for the ancient Greeks. Although we cannot, of course, speak of any developed or systematic Table of Opposites in Homer or Hesiod, it is interesting to consider the correlations which are made between the positive poles of many of these pairs of opposites on the one hand, and between their negative poles on the other. The identification of light and east and white, and sky and up, on the one hand, and of darkness and west and black, and earth and down, on the other, corresponds to certain facts of observation. Again the conception of the earth as female (or a mother), and of the sky as a generating male, is based on an obvious analogy between the growth of plants and sexual reproduction. On the other hand, at *Il.* 12.238ff. we find

[11] At *Th.* 591ff. the whole race of women – Pandora's offspring – is called 'deadly', a 'great bane' to men, and at *Op.* 90ff. it is said that before Pandora, men lived on earth free from evils, suffering, and disease. The idea of the innate inferiority of women recurs, of course, in Greek philosophy: in the *Timaeus* 90Eff., it is suggested that cowardly and unjust men become women in their second incarnation, and Aristotle considers the female sex a deviation from type, a 'natural deformity', *GA* 767b6ff., 775a14ff.

[12] This is the general rule. But that Greek diviners disagreed among themselves on this and other questions is clear, for example, from a passage in the Hippocratic treatise *On Regimen in Acute Diseases*, ch. 3, L II 242.4ff.

[13] These usages are reflected in the use of the verb *dexiousthai* for 'to greet' and of the noun *dexia* for 'pledge'.

that *right* is identified with *east* and the sun, and *left* with the 'misty *west*'. This identification seems more arbitrary,[14] though, as was noted above, there are parallels for it in other societies.

III

Having considered very briefly the symbolic associations of certain pairs of opposites in early Greek literature as a whole, I must next || discuss how some of these beliefs may have influenced the theories of the Greek philosophers; and here I refer not only to religious or ethical doctrines, but also, and more especially, to some of the explanations which they put forward to account for various complex natural phenomena. In this context, the use of the opposites right and left is particularly remarkable.

The pairs right and left, male and female, light and darkness appear, of course, in the Pythagorean Table of Opposites (*sustoichia*) given by Aristotle at *Metaph.* A.5 986a22ff.[15] It is not certain which group or groups of Pythagoreans may have held this doctrine, nor can we date the table in the form given by Aristotle with any great degree of assurance. One thing which is clear, however, is that the arranging of right, male, and light on one side, the side of the good, and of left, female, and darkness on the other, the side of the bad, corresponds to notions which are implicit, to a greater or lesser extent, in the earliest Greek writers. This feature of the Pythagorean table could be seen as the explicit expression, or rationalisation, in ethical terms, of very early Greek beliefs.[16] Elsewhere too in Greek philosophy some of these pairs of opposites are correlated together in passages which have a religious or mystical context. In the eschatological myth in the *Republic* (614cff.), for example, the souls of men are imagined as divided by their judges into two groups: the just travel to the *right*, *upwards* through the *sky*, carrying tokens of their judgement on their *fronts*, and the unjust go to the

[14] It has been suggested that Hector's words at *Il.* 12.238ff. ('Nor do I trouble myself or care at all whether the birds of omen fly to the right, towards the dawn and the sun, or to the left, towards the misty west') refer simply to the position of the Trojan lines, which happen to face north, but it is surely much more likely that they describe the usual method of interpreting omens, in which 'to the right' is identified with towards the east. The theory (taken up more recently by Cuillandre, 1943) that right is identified with light because the worshipper faces the rising sun, which then passes to his right on its transit westwards, was rightly dismissed by Hertz (1960: 159n. 86). A decisive argument against the theory is that we should expect the *opposite* correlation to be made by many peoples in the *southern* hemisphere (for if they face the sun at its rising, it passes, of course, to their left) whereas this is not found to be the case: for the Maori and Australian aborigines, for example, right is the good side and is associated with life and light, as for the ancient Greeks.

[15] The complete list of opposites is: limit/unlimited, odd/even, one/plurality, right/left, male/female, at rest/moving, straight/curved, light/darkness, good/evil, square/oblong.

[16] See Hertz, 1960: 158n. 50. Several of the sayings known as the *akousmata* or *sumbola* which are attributed to certain Pythagoreans emphasise a ritual distinction between various pairs of opposites, e.g. 'Putting on your shoes, start with the right foot; washing your feet, start with the left' (Iamblichus, *Protr.* 21, *VP* 83); 'Do not sacrifice a white cock' (Iamblichus, *VP* 84, and cf. the gloss on this in Diogenes Laertius VIII 34, 'white is of the nature of the good, and black of evil'). Diels–Kranz, 58C, provide a selection of such sayings.

left, *downwards* (into the *earth*) bearing their tokens on their *backs*.[17] But some of these opposites also figure in Greek philosophy in contexts where the purpose of the writer is to account for certain phenomena: we must now consider to what extent the theories and explanations based on these opposites are influenced by earlier beliefs and associations of ideas.

First we may deal with a group of theories which aim to account for the differentiation of the sexes at birth.[18] The theories which are attributed to Parmenides and to Anaxagoras were both based on the idea of a correlation between male and right, and between female and left. Parmenides apparently held that the sex of the child is determined by its position on the right or left side of the mother's womb (males are on the right, females on the left). Galen quotes Fr. 17 'on the right, boys; on the left, girls' and interprets it in this sense (*in Epid.* VI 48, *CMG* V 10.2.2, 119.12ff.; cf. Aristotle, *GA* 763b34–764a1, where, however, no specific author is mentioned). Of Parmenides' immediate successors, Empedocles held || that the determining factor was the heat of the womb,[19] but Anaxagoras again referred to a difference between right and left, though, unlike Parmenides, he suggested that the determining factor is the side of the body from which the father's seed comes (Aristotle, *GA* 763b30ff.; cf. *GA* 765a3ff.). A variant of this theory appears in the Hippocratic treatise *On Superfetation*, which implies quite specifically that the right testicle is responsible for male children, and the left for females (ch. 31, Littré VIII 500.8ff.).[20] Other Hippocratic treatises

[17] Cf. *Laws* 717AB, where 'even' and 'left' are assigned as honours to the chthonian deities, and their superior opposites 'odd' and 'right' to the Olympians.

[18] Cf. the excellent monograph by Lesky, 1951, especially pp. 39ff.

[19] Galen, who quotes Fr. 67 (*in Epid.* VI 48, *CMG* V 10.2.2, 119.16ff.), probably took Empedocles' theory to be that males are formed in the hotter parts of the womb, females in the colder (he compares it directly with Parmenides' theory which also referred to different *parts* of the womb). But Aristotle, who quotes the equally ambiguous Fr. 65 at *GA* 723a24ff., took Empedocles to be referring to variations in temperature in the womb as a whole over the monthly cycle (the womb is hotter at the beginning of the cycle just after menstruation has occurred, cf. 764a1ff.). Censorinus' interpretation, 6.6, DK 31A81 – that Empedocles, like Anaxagoras, held that males were formed by seed from the right-hand side of the body, females by seed from the left – should probably be ruled out: Aristotle clearly differentiates the two types of theories referring to 'hot and cold' and 'right and left' respectively and attributed the former to Empedocles, cf. *GA* 765a3ff.

[20] Cf. also the theory attributed to a certain Leophanes and others by Aristotle at *GA* 765a21ff. This text appears to suggest that Leophanes' theory was that if the *right* testis is tied up, *males* will be produced. Yet either we should transpose the words *arrenotokein* and *thēlutokein*, or they have been mentioned in that order (males first) without due regard for their correlation with what has gone before (right mentioned before left at 765a23). That the theory in question was that the right testis is responsible for males (which are, then, produced when the *left* testis is tied up) is clear not only from the passage in *Superf.* L VIII 500.8ff., and other texts in ancient writers in which the right testis is connected with male offspring (e.g. *Epid.* VI, sec. 4, ch. 21, L V 312.10f., and Pliny, *HN* 8.72.188), but also from Aristotle's own subsequent remarks. At *GA* 765a34ff., he says that the earlier theories which took hot and cold, or right or left, to be the causes of male and female, were not altogether unreasonable, and it is clear that he correlates male with right (and hot), female and left (and cold) and not vice versa: seed from the right side will be hotter, more concocted, and therefore more fertile than seed from the left.

make use of Parmenides' version of the theory,[21] or suggest other correlations between the male embryo and the right-hand side of the mother's body.[22] This is, surely, a remarkable series of theories. Although alternative suggestions are made on which part of the body, or which parent, determines the sex of the child, all these writers assume that *male* and *right* are connected, and so too *female* and *left*. We noted above the tendency to identify the positive poles of various pairs of opposites on the one hand, and their negative poles on the other (for which there is evidence not only from the ancient Greeks but from other peoples as well). It is interesting, then, that these attempted explanations of sex took the form of different applications of the theory that male and female derive from right and left respectively. It is impossible to determine what evidence (if any) Parmenides and others may have appealed to, in order to confirm their theories (it may well be that fictitious evidence was sometimes claimed to corroborate them, see below on Aristotle *GA* 765a25ff.), but it seems likely that the earlier symbolic associations of these pairs of opposites contributed to fortify the belief in a connection between the positive or superior terms, male and right. In contrast to the Greek theory, it may be noted that among the ancient Chinese (who held the left to be more honourable than the right) there were theorists who believed that an embryo on the left of the womb would be a boy, one on the right, a girl, proposing a theory opposite to that of the Greeks but in keeping with their own associations for left and right.[23]

One group of theories put forward by some Presocratic philosophers and Hippocratic writers consists of attempted correlations between male and right, female and left. But we may now show how similar theories continued to appear in fourth-century philosophy, in Aristotle himself. Aristotle, it is true, rejects the idea that right and left in some way determine the sex of the child. He criticises the theory that the two sexes are formed in different parts of the womb || in *GA* IV.1,[24] and in so doing, he refers to the decisive evidence of anatomical dissections: 'moreover male and female twins are often found in the same part of the uterus: this we have observed sufficiently by dissection in all the Vivipara, both land-animals and fish' (*GA* 764a33ff.). His criticisms of the theory that sex is determined by whether the seed comes from the right or the left testicle are also interesting. He says at *GA* 765a25ff. that some theorists claimed that when one of the testicles of a male parent animal was excised, certain results followed (i.e. their offspring were all of the same sex):

[21] E.g. *Epid.* II, sec. 6, ch. 15, L V 136.5ff; *Epid.* VI, sec. 2, ch.25, L V 290.7f.: *Aph.* sec. 5, ch. 48, L IV 550.1ff. *Prorrh.* II, ch. 24, L IX 56.19ff. [22] E.g. *Aph.* sec. 5, ch. 38, L IV 544.11ff.

[23] See Granet, 1934: 370 and 1953: 273f.

[24] The evidence from dissections is first introduced at *GA* 764a33ff. when Aristotle is criticising Empedocles' theory (that hot and cold are the causes of male and female), but it is also relevant to Parmenides' theory that males are produced on the right of the womb, females on the left, and Aristotle refers to it again when criticising that theory later, at *GA* 765a3ff. (cf. 16ff.).

'but they lie; starting from what is likely, they guess what will happen, and they presuppose that it is so, before they see that it is in fact so'. These passages clearly mark an important step forward. Aristotle here insists on the careful use of evidence to verify or falsify the theories which were put forward. Where others had been content to assume that males were formed in the right side of the womb, and females in the left, Aristotle uses dissection to prove that this does not hold as an absolute rule.[25] It might be thought, on the basis of these passages, that Aristotle himself was free from preconceptions on the subject of right and left and other such opposites. But in point of fact, this is certainly not the case. His use of the pairs right and left, above and below, and front and back, in particular, is worth considering in detail.

In Aristotle's theory, right and left, above and below, front and back are not merely relative terms. Right, above, and front are said to be the *archai*, the starting-points or principles, not only of the three dimensions, breadth, length, and depth, respectively (*Cael.* 284b24f.), but also of the three types of changes, locomotion, growth, and sensation, in living beings (*Cael.* 284b25ff.). In *IA* ch. 4, 705b29ff., for example, Aristotle attempts to establish that all locomotion, in animals, proceeds from the right. The main evidence for this which he brings is (1) that men carry burdens on their left shoulders, (2) that they step off with the left foot – in both cases, according to Aristotle, the right is the side which initiates movement – and (3) that men defend themselves with their right limbs.[26] Because he assumes that the motion of the heavenly sphere (which he thinks of as alive) must be 'from the right' and *epi ta dexia* ('to the right' or 'rightwards'),[27] he infers at *Cael.* 285b22ff. that the northern hemisphere, the one in which we live, is the lower of the two hemispheres. Again, because 'upwards' is defined in relation to the place from which food is distributed and from which growth ‖ begins (e.g. *IA* 705a32f.), the 'upper' portion of plants will be where their roots are, and Aristotle accordingly speaks of plants as 'upside down' (e.g. *PA* 686b31ff.;

[25] A passage in *HA* VII.3 (583b2ff.) is interesting, for there Aristotle says that the first movement of male embryos usually takes place on the right side of the womb on the fortieth day, that of females on the left on the ninetieth, although he goes on to qualify or correct this statement: 'yet it must not be supposed that there is any exactness in these matters'. If authentic, this passage might, perhaps, be taken as evidence that, at one stage, Aristotle may have been rather less critical of the theory that males are on the right, females on the left, of the womb.

[26] Aristotle also notes (*IA* 705b33) that it is easier to hop on the left leg, and elsewhere (*PA* 671b32ff.) he says that men raise their right eyebrows more than their left. Some of his evidence seems to be contradictory: while he states that men step off with the left foot (*IA* 706a6ff.), he believes that horses step off with the off-fore (712a25ff.). His interpretation, too, of much of the evidence which he adduces appears to be quite arbitrary.

[27] On the complex problems of the meaning of the phrase *epi ta dexia* as applied to circular motion in general, and of its interpretation in *Cael.* 285b20 in particular, see especially Braunlich, 1936: 245ff., and cf. Boeckh, 1852: 112ff., Darbishire, 1895: 65ff., and Heath, 1913: 231ff. Whether 'to the right' applied to circular motion meant the direction which we call 'clockwise', or the direction we call 'counterclockwise', the association with *right* marks it clearly as the *more honourable* direction.

IA 705b6; cf. *PA* 683b18ff. on the Testacea). Right, above, and front are, then, defined by certain functions, but Aristotle holds that these are *more honourable* than their opposites. Thus at *IA* 706b12f. he says that 'the starting-point is honourable, and above is more honourable than below, and front than back, and right than left'. Furthermore, this notion becomes an important doctrine in anatomy, for Aristotle believes that 'as a whole, unless some more important object interferes, that which is better and more honourable tends to be above rather than below, in front rather than behind, on the right rather than on the left (*PA* 665a22ff.). He uses this principle to explain such facts as the relative positions of the windpipe and the oesophagus (*PA* 665a18ff.), and of the 'great blood-vessel'[28] and the aorta (*PA* 667b34ff.),[29] as also to give an account of the function of the diaphragm (to separate the nobler, upper parts of the body from the less noble, lower parts, *PA* 672b22ff.). The faithfulness, one may almost say stubbornness, with which Aristotle adheres to his conception of the essential superiority of right to left, can be seen in his account of the position of the heart. This organ he considers to be the principle of life and the source of all movement and sensation in the animal (*PA* 665a11ff.) At *PA* 665b18ff., he says that the heart, in man, 'lies about the middle of the body, but rather in its upper than in its lower half, and more in front than behind. For nature has established the more honourable part in the more honourable position, where no greater purpose prevents this.' Faced with the obvious difficulty that the heart lies on the left side of the body, and not on the more honourable right, Aristotle argues that this is to 'counterbalance the chilliness of the left side' (*PA* 666b6ff.). On this occasion, when he encounters an obvious and important fact which apparently runs counter to his theory of the superiority and greater nobility of the right-hand side, he does not abandon that theory but refers to a second arbitrary assumption, the (purely imaginary) general distinction between the temperature of the two sides of the body.

In explaining the position of the heart in man, Aristotle refers to a difference in heat between the right and left sides of the body. In man, the heart is slightly inclined towards the left because the left side of the body is particularly cold in his case (e.g. *PA* 666b9f.). Elsewhere too, he refers to differences in the heat and purity of the || blood in accounting for the general

[28] The 'great blood-vessel' corresponds to the superior and inferior Venae Cavae: whether we take it also to include the right auricle of the heart itself will depend on how we interpret the three chambers of the heart which Aristotle recognises. See further n. 32.

[29] Cf. also *HA* 496b35ff., and *PA* 671b28ff., on the relative position of the two kidneys: Aristotle believes that the right kidney is always higher than the left (although in fact this is not so, for example, in man himself, where the left kidney is usually higher), and he gives the reason that motion starts from the right, and organs on the right push upwards above their opposites. He also believes that the right kidney is less fat than the left (*PA* 672a23ff.) and again explains this by referring to the right side being better suited for motion. Several more instances in which he explains the relative positions of organs, and other phenomena, by referring to the superiority of right, front, and above over their opposites, are given by Ogle (1912: note to *PA* 648a11).

superiority of the upper parts of the body over the lower, of the male animal over the female, and of the right side of the body over the left (*PA* 648a2–13). At *PA* 670b17ff., he accounts for the 'watery' quality of the spleen in some animals partly by referring to the generally 'wetter and colder nature of the left side' of the body.[30] He then goes on: 'Each of the opposites is separated according to the column (*sustoichia*) which is akin to it, as right is opposite left and hot opposite cold: and they are co-ordinate (*sustoicha*) with one another in the way described' (i.e. right and hot are in one column, left and cold in the other) (*PA* 670b20ff.). It is interesting that this theory that the right side of the body is hotter than the left is mentioned in *GA* IV.1 where Aristotle discusses what determines the sex of the embryo. Although, as already noted, he argues strongly in that chapter against earlier theories that the sex of the child is determined by the part of the womb in which it is conceived, yet at the end of his discussion of his predecessors' ideas, at *GA* 765a34ff., he grants that 'to suppose that the cause of male and female is heat and cold, or the secretion (*apokrisis*, i.e. seed) which comes from the right or the left side of the body, *is not unreasonable* (*echei tina logon*)': the right side of the body is hotter than the left, and hotter semen, being more 'concocted', is more fertile than cold and therefore more likely to produce males. Though he goes on to say (b4ff.) that 'to speak in this way is to seek the cause from too great a distance', he does, to some extent, accommodate earlier views to his own theory.[31] Yet if we examine this theory of the greater heat of the right-hand side of the body more closely, the weakness of Aristotle's argument is apparent. At *PA* 666b6ff., the heart is said to be on the left, in man, to counteract the chilliness of the left-hand side of the body. Yet elsewhere Aristotle suggests that the factor on which this difference in temperature depends is the heart itself. According to the account in *HA* and in *PA*,[32] the heart, in most of the large animals, has three chambers, of which the right-hand chamber is the largest and contains the most abundant and

30 Aristotle believes that the spleen on the left in some way balances the liver on the right, e.g. *PA* 669b26ff., 36ff.

31 According to Aristotle's own theory, stated at *GA* 765b8ff., male and female are distinguished by their ability or inability to concoct and discharge semen, yet because concoction works by means of heat, males must be hotter than females (b15ff.). Moreover it is due to a lack of heat that females are formed (the male element is too weak to master the female, 766b15ff.: Aristotle believes that young people, those in old age, and people of a 'wet' or 'feminine' constitution are all more likely to produce female children, *GA* 766b27ff., and these are all people in whom the 'natural heat' is weak, b33f.).

32 There is some doubt as to which are the three chambers of the heart to which Aristotle refers (e.g. *HA* 513a27ff.; *PA* 666b21ff.; cf. *Somn.* 458a15ff.). Ogle (1912: note to *PA* 666b21ff.) took them to be the two ventricles and the left auricle (he thought the right auricle was taken to be part of the 'great blood-vessel', see n. 28 above). Thompson (1910: note to *HA* 513a27ff.), on the other hand, took 'the largest of the three chambers' (*HA* 513a32; cf. *PA* 666b35f.) to refer to the right auricle and ventricle combined, which would account for the statement that the other two chambers are 'far smaller' (*HA* 513a34f.) than the third. The suggestion that traditional or mystical ideas have influenced Aristotle in ascribing three chambers to the heart cannot be ruled out, although many features of his account show, as Thompson said, 'clear evidence of minute inquiry'.

hottest blood,[33] and at *PA* 667a1f., for example, he refers to this fact as the reason for the whole of the right-hand side of the body being hotter than the left. There would seem to be an anomaly in arguing (1) that in man the heart is on the left to counteract the excessive chilliness of that side, when (2) the difference in temperature between the two sides of the body is itself seen as the result of a difference in the temperature of the blood in the left and right chambers of the heart. Man is far || from being the only species which is said to have a heart with chambers of unequal sizes, yet in man alone (Aristotle believes) the heart is displaced towards the left. Other things being equal, we should expect that the effect of the heart being displaced from the central position which it occupies in all other species of animals would be to *warm* that side towards which it was displaced. Yet so far from concluding that in man the left-hand side is rather *hotter*, relative to the right-hand side, than is the case in a horse or an ox, Aristotle believes that the left-hand side, in man, is *particularly cold*. He holds that the difference in temperature between the two sides of the body is especially great in man, but while this idea is in line with his general doctrine that right/left distinctions are pronounced in humans, it remains, of course, an unfounded assumption.

Aristotle takes right, above, and front to be starting-points or principles, and so superior to, and nobler than, their opposites. He believes, further, that the right-hand side is naturally more active and stronger than the left, not only in man, but also, as a general rule, throughout the animal kingdom. At *PA* 684a27f., he generalises: 'all animals naturally tend to use their right limbs more in their activities'.[34] We may now consider to what extent Aristotle qualified his theory of the distinction between right and left in the light of his detailed observations of various biological species, or how far he went beyond, or misrepresented, the facts, in stating his conclusions. Although he states it as a general rule that limbs on the right are stronger than those on the left, he notes certain exceptions. He remarks at *PA* 684a32ff. that in the lobsters it is a matter of chance whether the right or the left claw is the bigger; but he goes on to say that the reason for this is that lobsters are deformed and do not use the claw for its natural purpose but for locomotion (a 35–b1).[35] Again, such passages as *IA* 714b8ff. show that he recognises the fact that right and left are not clearly distinguished in such

33 Ogle (1912: note to *PA* 666b35f.) pointed out that 'in an animal, especially one killed by strangulation, as recommended by Aristotle..., the right side of the heart and the vessels connected with it would be found gorged with dark blood and contrasting strongly with the almost empty left side and vessels'. (At *HA* 511b13ff., Aristotle discusses the difficulties involved in making observations of the vascular system, and at 513a12ff., he recommends that the animal to be examined should be starved and then strangled.)

34 From *PA* 671b30f. and 672a24f., it appears that Aristotle held that the right side is naturally stronger than the left. But in several passages he notes that the degree to which right and left are differentiated varies in different species, e.g. *HA* 497b21f.; *IA* 705b21ff.

35 Cf. *HA* 526b16f., and a description of the two claws (chelae) at 526a15ff. It is not true that the chelae are used solely for locomotion (*PA* 684a35f., see Ogle's note *ad loc.*): indeed Aristotle himself remarks at *HA* 526a24f. that they are naturally adapted for prehension.

classes as the Testacea (although he does attempt to establish a *functional* distinction between right and left in his analysis of their method of locomotion);[36] but again the reason which he gives for the lack of differentiation between right and left in the Testacea, is that they are a deformed class (e.g. *IA* 714b10f.). However, some of Aristotle's statements on the subject of the distinction between right and left in animals are in need of qualification. Ogle noted that the remark at *PA* 684a26f. that 'in all the Crawfish and the Crabs the right claw is bigger and stronger' (than the left) is 'too absolute a statement'.[37] Perhaps more important is Aristotle's || failure to recognise that the heart inclines to the left-hand side of the body in other species besides man, for he firmly believes that this is so in man alone (*PA* 666b6ff.; cf. *HA* 496a14ff., 506b32ff.). Aristotle undoubtedly had detailed first-hand knowledge of the internal organs of a number of species of animals. Nevertheless there are several species, including some with whose internal anatomy he claims to be acquainted,[38] in which the heart inclines to the left, as it does in man.[39]

Aristotle's knowledge of both the external and internal organs of animals, and of their behaviour, is vastly greater than that of any of his predecessors. One of the results of the many dissections which he carried out was to establish that male and female embryos are formed in either part of the uterus, right or left, in all the Vivipara. His observations of many lower species (especially of the Crustacea) are remarkably accurate and detailed. Yet one of the theories which he constantly maintains is that right is naturally and essentially superior to left. He believes that this is true in man, and man is the norm by which he judges the rest of the animal kingdom. As he puts it at *IA* 706a19f., for example, man is 'of all animals, most in accordance with nature', and at *PA* 656a10ff. in man alone, 'The natural parts are in their "natural" positions, and his upper part is turned towards that which is upper in the universe.'[40] The reason that he gives for the

[36] In some animals, right and left are distinguished not in form, but in function alone (cf. *Cael.* 285a15f., b3ff.). As regards the stromboid Testaceans, he says that they are 'right-sided' (*dexia*) because they do not move in the direction of the spire, but opposite to it (*IA* 706a13ff.; cf. *HA* 528b8ff., and Thompson's note). He appears to argue that because they move in the direction opposite to the spire, *therefore* the spire must be assumed to be on the right-hand side.

[37] Cf. *IA* 714b16ff. Elsewhere, however, Aristotle is somewhat more cautious in his statement of the difference between right and left in the crabs, at least, e.g., *HA* 527b6f. '*for the most part* they all have the right claw bigger and stronger', and cf. 530a7ff., 25ff.

[38] At *HA* 502b25f., Aristotle remarks that the monkey and suchlike animals (e.g. ape and baboon, cf. 502a16ff.) are found *on dissection* to have similar internal organs to those of man. Yet in these animals (as also, for example, in the mole) the heart is on the left. Cf. Ogle, 1912: note to *PA* 666bff.

[39] Aristotle's statement that in all animals which have kidneys the right one is higher is another inaccuracy; see n. 29 above.

[40] Cf. *HA* 494a26ff. It is interesting that elsewhere Aristotle states that man alone of all the animals can learn to be ambidextrous (*HA* 497b31f.; cf. *EN* 1134b33ff.; *MM* 1194b31ff.), yet he continues to believe that the right is 'most right-sided' in man (*IA* 706a21f.) and that the right is naturally better than the left and separated from it (*IA* 706a20f.).

absence of any marked distinction between right and left in some species is, then, that they are imperfect or 'deformed' animals. He believes not only that there is what we might call a physiological distinction between right and left – the right side is hotter than the left – but also that in making this distinction nature fulfils an important purpose. The distinction between right and left is an *ideal* which is most fully exemplified in man: as he puts it at *IA* 706a21f. 'the right is "most right-sided" (*malista dexia*) in man'. It might be said, then, that Aristotle's great knowledge of different biological species served rather to confirm than to weaken his belief in the natural superiority, and the greater nobility, of the right-hand side.

The history of this belief in the inherent superiority of the right-hand side has now been described with evidence from a variety of Greek thinkers down to Aristotle.[41] The Pythagoreans placed right on the side of limit and good, left on the opposite side of the unlimited and evil. Parmenides, Anaxagoras, and several Hippocratic writers assumed that the difference between male and female || was to be derived from a difference between right and left, correlating the superior, and the inferior, poles of these two pairs of opposites. Aristotle explicitly states that right is the origin of locomotion, and is better and nobler than its opposite, and he uses this theory quite extensively in accounting for such facts as the position of various organs in the body. Not all the theorists who appear to have assumed the essential superiority of the right-hand side are normally thought to have been influenced by Pythagoreanism. Though Parmenides' relation to the Pythagoreans may well have been close, Anaxagoras' theories bear few signs of direct Pythagorean influence. The Hippocratic treatises *On Epidemics* II and VI are generally free from Pythagorean conceptions. Aristotle's use of the word *sustoicha*, 'co-ordinate,' in connection with his own theory of the pairs right and left and hot and cold at *PA* 670b22 is obviously reminiscent of the way in which he refers to the Pythagorean principles as arranged in co-cordinate columns (*kata sustoichian*, *Metaph*. 986a22f.), and yet on several occasions he explicitly contrasts his own account of these and other related opposites with that of the Pythagoreans;[42] and many of his detailed biological theories based on the distinction between right and left are clearly original. It seems,

[41] Lesky, 1951: 62ff., has traced the survival of beliefs in various connections between the right-hand side and male children in later writers. Although there were other theorists besides Aristotle who were sceptical about certain such connections (for example Soranus, *Gyn*. I 45, *CMG* IV 31.26ff.), several writers subscribed to them in late antiquity, including Pliny (HN 8.70.176; 8.72.188), Varro (*RR* 2.5.13), and Galen (*UP* XIV, ch. 7, Kühn IV 172–5: *De Semine* II, ch. 5. K IV 633f.). Pliny, in particular, is a mine of information concerning the survival of superstitions involving right and left.

[42] This is so especially in *Cael*. II.2, where Aristotle agrees with the Pythagorean idea that right and left apply to the universe as a whole (284b6ff.), but adopts the opposite view to theirs, saying that we live in the lower of the two hemispheres, and on the 'left', not, as the Pythagoreans said, in the upper hemisphere and on the 'right' (285b23ff.). He also criticises the Pythagoreans for not having recognised above and below, and front and back, as principles, as well as right and left (285a10ff.; cf. his own view, expressed at 284b20ff.).

then, that the belief in the inherent superiority of the right-hand side is not an exclusively Pythagorean doctrine. Indeed in some of its elements the Pythagorean Table of Opposites itself merely defined and made explicit extremely old, and no doubt widespread, Greek beliefs.

Whether or not we accept Hertz's general theory that in primitive thought certain natural oppositions often stand for the categories of the 'sacred' and the 'profane', it will be granted that for the ancient Greeks, as for many other peoples, such antitheses as sky and earth, light and darkness, up and down, right and left, have powerful symbolic associations. The values which attached to the opposites right and left in particular seem to influence some of the theories in which they figure in fifth- and fourth-century Greek philosophy. It was often assumed that right is essentially different from, and superior to, left, the one good, the other evil; or the one connected in some way with masculinity, the other with femininity; or the one thought to be honourable, the other not honourable. The social factors which are involved in the greater development of the right hand itself do not pass unnoticed by Greek philosophers: Plato, especially, remarked how childhood training contributes to || the greater usefulness of the right hand.[43] But the belief persisted that right is 'naturally' superior to, stronger and nobler than, the left. In Aristotle, the distinction between right and left is conceived not merely as a physiological fact, but as an *ideal*, to which the animal kingdom aspires, but which is most fully exemplified in man. Even a detailed knowledge of different biological species, in many of which there is no distinction, or no marked distinction, between right and left, did not uproot Aristotle's belief that right is naturally stronger and more honourable than left: on the contrary, that knowledge led him to conclude that the differentiation between right and left is a mark of man's superiority to the animals, and of his greater perfection.

The two elements, of dogmatic belief, and of empirical observation, are closely interwoven in the history of theories based on right and left. The element of dogmatic assumption appears first of all in the superstitious belief that right is 'lucky' and left 'unlucky', but we have seen that the assumption that right is essentially different from, and nobler than, left persists in Greek philosophy right down to Aristotle. Yet many Greek philosophers and medical theorists carried out extensive observations,

[43] A radical view of the effects of training and habit on the use of the two hands is expressed in the *Laws* (794D–795D) where Plato recommends that children should be taught to use both hands equally. He criticises the view that right and left are naturally different in their usefulness, pointing out that this is not the case with the feet and the lower limbs (794D5ff.). He says that it is 'through the folly of nurses and mothers' that 'we have all become lame, so to speak, in our hands'. He notes that athletes can become quite ambidextrous, and he says that the Scythians are in fact so. Cf. further Schuhl, 1948: 174ff., and Lévêque and Vidal-Naquet, 1960: 294ff., especially 302ff., who also compare the recommendation of the Hippocratic treatise *In the Surgery* (*Off.*) that the surgeon should learn to use either hand equally (ch. 4, L III 288.1ff.). With Plato's view, contrast that of Aristotle, who also recognises that we can become ambidextrous, but says that the right side is still *naturally* stronger than the left (texts in n. 40).

particularly in biology. Sometimes these observations led to the rejection of a particular theory based on the belief in the superiority of the right-hand side, as when Aristotle's dissections established that males and females are not always formed in the right and left sides of the womb respectively. More often, however, when the results of observations did not tally with preconceived opinions (for example, when it was seen that the heart inclines to the left side of the body in man), those opinions were not abandoned: on the contrary, they were retained, and further dogmatic assumptions were introduced in order to account for the phenomena. It is, perhaps, particularly remarkable that Aristotle, who conducted the most extensive and rigorous biological investigations in antiquity, should nevertheless have firmly and constantly maintained a theory of the distinction between right and left which owes much to the traditional symbolic associations which those opposites had for the ancient Greeks.

REFERENCES

Boeckh, A. (1852) *Untersuchungen über das kosmische System des Platon* (Berlin)

Braunlich, A. F (1936) '"To the Right" in Homer and Attic Greek', *American Journal of Philology* 57: 245–60

Bultmann, R. (1948) 'Zur Geschichte der Lichtsymbolik im Altertum', *Philologus* 97: 1–48

Cuillandre, J. (1943) *La Droite et la gauche dans les poèmes homériques* (Rennes)

Darbishire, H. D. (1895) *Reliquiae philologicae* (Cambridge)

Evans-Pritchard, E. E. (1956) *Nuer Religion* (Oxford)

(1960) Introduction to Hertz 1960

Granet, M. (1934) *La Pensée chinoise* (Paris)

(1953) 'La Droite et la gauche en Chine', *Etudes sociologiques sur la Chine* (Paris), 263–78

Guthrie, W. K. C. (1950) *The Greeks and their Gods* (London)

Heath, T. L. (1913) *Aristarchus of Samos* (Oxford)

Hertz, R. (1960) 'La Prééminence de la main droite: étude sur la polarité religieuse', *Revue philosophique* 68 (1909): 553–80; transl. by R. and C. Needham in *Death and the Right Hand* (London, 1960), 89–113 and 155–60

Kroef, J. M. van der (1954) 'Dualism and symbolic antithesis in Indonesian society', *American Anthropologist* 56: 847–62

Lesky, E. (1951) *Die Zeugungs- und Vererbungslehren der Antike und ihr Nachwirken* (Wiesbaden)

Lévêque, P., and Vidal-Naquet, P. (1960) 'Epaminondas Pythagoricien ou le problème tactique de la droite et de la gauche', *Historia* 9: 294–308

Ogle, W. (1912) *Aristotle, De Partibus Animalium.* Vol. v of *The Works of Aristotle Translated into English* (Oxford)

Schuhl, P. M. (1948) 'Platon et la prééminence de la main droite', *Cahiers Internationaux de Sociologie* 4: 172–6

Thompson, D'A. W. (1910) *Aristotle, Historia animalium.* Vol. IV of *The Works of Aristotle Translated into English* (Oxford)

3

WHO IS ATTACKED IN *ON ANCIENT MEDICINE*?

INTRODUCTION

The problem this article addresses is the quite specific one of the opponents attacked by the author of the Hippocratic treatise *On Ancient Medicine* (*VM*), but the implications of the underlying issues are wide-ranging, indeed more so than I explicitly indicated when I published this paper in *Phronesis* in 1963. *On Ancient Medicine* is unique among the extant writings in the Hippocratic Corpus in deploying a sophisticated terminology in attacking the methods of the author's rivals (whoever they may be). In particular it uses the term *hupothesis* not in any of its ordinary meanings (p. 55) but in the sense of preliminary assumption or postulate – a sense otherwise unattested in extant Greek literature before Plato.

The use of that and other terms, and the notable command of methodological points displayed in *VM*, were among the reasons cited by Diller (1952, see p. 54 n. 10 below) to suggest that the author was writing after Plato had introduced the term *hupothesis* in the sense of 'assumption' in the *Meno* (p. 56), though Diller's thesis has found few supporters. I agreed with the opponents of Diller that the author of *VM* does not have Plato himself in mind, nor is he reacting directly to a Platonic use of that particular term. However, I sided – and still side – with Diller and against the great majority of Hippocratic scholars in thinking that the use of that term in this treatise constitutes a major obstacle to the view, still commonly held, that the work was written some time around 440–420 B.C. One scholar who appreciated that *VM* provides evidence of interactions between philosophy and medicine is J. Longrigg, whose 'Philosophy and medicine, some early interactions' appeared in the same year as my own piece, as is mentioned in my final note (p. 68 n. 54).[1] However, Longrigg argued, quite implausibly, not just that *VM* belongs to the mid-fifth century, but that it antedates, and was an influence on, Anaxagoras. The use of an indefinite number of elements – which Longrigg took to be an idea that Anaxagoras took over from *VM* – is common to many philosophical and medical writers in a form similar to that in *VM*, and so too is the idea that, for health, those elements should be mixed. Many of Longrigg's arguments are directed to showing that

[1] Longrigg, 1983 is a restatement of his position without substantial modifications or additions.

the similarities between *VM* on the one hand and Anaxagoras and Protagoras on the other are not *necessarily* to be accounted for by the supposition that *VM* is later: yet that remains the more probable, and the more economical hypothesis. Meanwhile Longrigg does not himself offer any comment on the difficulty presented by the use of the term *hupothesis* although he remarks that other scholars have rejected Diller's dating.[2]

The gaps in our evidence for early Greek medicine are considerable and for other areas of Greek scientific inquiry even greater. We can appreciate this where medicine is concerned from the fact that of the twenty-two early (fifth- or fourth-century) medical theorists mentioned in the history preserved in the papyrus known as Anonymus Londinensis, some seven were *totally unknown* before that papyrus was discovered in 1892. What *On Ancient Medicine* does – whenever it is to be dated – is to provide precious insight into a methodological dispute that is otherwise quite unattested. Moreover this is not just a controversy between physicians about medical method (although it is true that the author of *VM* is principally concerned with medicine) but also one that also involves philosophers and those engaged in inquiries concerning 'things in the heaven and things under the earth' (p. 56). Modern scholars who approach *VM* merely with questions of medical history in mind are liable, therefore, to miss the opportunity it presents for investigating the interactions between different disciplines at a point where (to judge from the internal evidence from *VM* itself alone) methodological issues had begun to be debated with some sophistication and in earnest. The question of its exact date aside, *VM* is important evidence of cross-discipline methodological controversy: and given the interest of the development of that methodological self-awareness, the need to give some estimate of its date is the greater, even though precision and certainty on that problem are – in the state of our evidence – beyond reach.

VM itself attests that questions of method were being debated both in medicine and in philosophy. The method the author rejects involves basing medicine on a small number (one or two) of fundamental assumptions and thereby 'narrowing down the causal principle of diseases'. That, he implies, is typical of certain natural philosophers, but if we bear in mind that the term used of those fundamental assumptions – presumably by the opponents of *VM* themselves – was *hupothesis*, a term that Plato tells us had a particular role in mathematics, then that raises the question of a possible further influence in these methodological debates from that quarter.

The particular conjecture that I pursue in this article is that the Pythagorean Philolaus combined a set of interests in cosmology, in mathematics and in medicine in such a way that he would make a particularly appropriate target for some of the criticisms mounted in *VM*. The arguments are set out on pp. 62–8 and involve an analysis of the

[2] Longrigg, 1963: 174 n. 62, with reference to J.-H. Kühn and F. Heinimann, and again Longrigg, 1983: 249 n. 5, with reference to the same two scholars.

evidence (1) for Philolaus' medical theories (based on the hot), (2) for his cosmological, astronomical and 'geological' theories (his speculations about things in the heaven and things under the earth) and (3) for his work in mathematics. There is, to be sure, no direct evidence that Philolaus himself used the term *hupothesis* in precisely the way that the author of *VM* objects to: but then, as I have remarked, there is no evidence of *anyone* doing so before Plato – which is precisely where our problem starts. On the other hand the most sustained modern analysis of all the evidence for Philolaus, the regrettably as yet unpublished doctoral dissertation of C. Huffman, has suggested that the unifying thought that links several of Philolaus' investigations is the generation of order, cosmos, by the interaction of limit (the limiters) and what there is to be limited – the unlimiteds. These are the twin principles, *archai*, posited at the start of his cosmology. Moreover Huffman has also pointed out that such a methodology fits the use of *hupothesis* assailed in *VM* well enough.[3] While my original suggestion failed to gain much agreement from fellow historians of medicine, it is at least a conjecture that has won a measure of support from a scholar approaching the problems from outside the field of Hippocratic scholarship.

But whatever may be thought about this particular conjecture concerning Philolaus, the evidence of Plato clearly shows that *hupothesis* had a role in early Greek mathematics. Much of the history of the development of mathematics before Euclid remains highly controversial and set beside the comparatively rich evidence for medicine, that for mathematics is meagre indeed. However there is no dispute about one important fact, namely that a series of mathematicians, beginning with Hippocrates of Chios (some time around 430 B.C.), contributed to the systematisation of mathematical knowledge that was to culminate in Euclid's *Elements* itself. Although the first steps were hesitant, it is clear that systematic deductive arguments and demonstrations were the goal in one important strand of mathematical work from the 430s onwards.

On these important collateral developments my brief discussion in this paper could have been considerably expanded.[4] Already in the late fifth century it was mathematics that provided the chief model of an inquiry that proceeds deductively from self-evident axioms or hypotheses – even though the attested fifth-century vocabulary for describing these is vague and meagre. The opponents of *VM* are not mathematicians. Yet mathematics (I would now state more emphatically) is surely relevant to the methodological dispute in which *VM* engages. While I disagree with the view that has been expressed by Wasserstein (1972: 9) that the author of *VM* might consider the use of *hupothesis* acceptable in such a domain as astronomy, I entirely agree

[3] Huffman argued this in a paper presented to a conference on the history of Greek mathematics held at King's College, Cambridge in May 1984.

[4] Some aspects of these developments are taken up in Lloyd, 1979: ch. 2, and in Lloyd, 1990: ch. 3.

with Wasserstein that the model of deductive reasoning that the Hippocratic work criticises fits mathematical procedures well enough. The doctors and philosophers to whom that work objects proceed from certain starting-points (the author calls them unverifiable) and they narrow down the principles of diseases. Evidently the procedures they adopt bear a close resemblance to those that were being used in mathematics, even though (to repeat) it is not mathematics itself that the author has in his sights.

The gaps in our evidence are such that many questions are bound to remain unanswered and at points unanswerable. As I remarked (p. 68) certainty and precision are impossible on all the major issues discussed in this article, the exact date of *VM*, the precise identity of his opponents, the early history of the method of *hupothesis*. However, the interest and importance of the evidence in *VM* itself increase the more one appreciates its exceptional character, the way in which it provides glimpses of otherwise unattested developments.

At the most general and abstract level, the issue may be expressed like this. Two main methodological models came to be developed in Greek philosophy and science, the variations on which provide the chief articulation for much Greek speculative thought and form the key topics in explicit debates in ancient philosophy of science. On the one hand there is the model of a deductive, axiomatic system – the model set out by Aristotle in the *Posterior Analytics* and the one actually exemplified in most Greek mathematics from Euclid's *Elements* onwards. In this, certain starting-points are set out that have the status of self-evident premises, incontrovertible truths, or assumptions whose validity is, in one way or another, guaranteed. Once those starting-points are taken, the investigation proceeds deductively to conclusions often represented not just as internally consistent, but as true of the world.

On the other hand there are models of scientific inquiry that insist on their empirical nature, on the elements of conjecture involved, on the impossibility of grounding any science that is true of the world on axioms claimed to be self-evident.

These two competing models have a long and fascinating history in Greek philosophy and science, and so far as Greek medicine goes the issue of the extent to which proof *more geometrico* is possible and appropriate remains a live issue down to the second century A.D. – to Galen – and beyond (cf. Barnes, forthcoming; Hankinson, forthcoming). It would, of course, be extravagant to represent the positions either of the author of *VM* or of his opponents as fully elaborated philosophies of science comparable with Aristotle's *Posterior Analytics*. Nevertheless *VM* may be said to provide our very first concrete extant evidence for the initial steps in formulating opposing models of medicine. Against those who were for attempting to proceed deductively and to base medicine on *hupotheseis*, the author of *VM* insists on the 'tried and tested' methods of what he calls traditional medicine, conceding that medicine is conjectural, but claiming nevertheless that it *is* a *technē*.

REFERENCES

Barnes, J. (forthcoming) 'Galen on logic and therapy', in *Proceedings of the Second International Galen Conference*, ed. F. Kudlien (Kiel, 1982)

Hankinson, R. J. (forthcoming) 'Galen on the foundations of science', in *Galeno; Obra, Pensamiento y Influencia* Proceedings of the Madrid Galen Conference, March 1988), ed. J. A. Lopez Ferez

Huffman, C. (n.d.) 'Philolaus of Croton', unpublished Ph.D. dissertation, University of Austin, Texas

Lloyd, G. E. R. (1979) *Magic, Reason and Experience* (Cambridge)

(1990) *Demystifying Mentalities* (Cambridge)

Longrigg, J. (1983) '[Hippocrates] *Ancient Medicine* and its intellectual context', in *Formes de pensée dans la Collection hippocratique* (Actes du IVe Colloque International Hippocratique, Lausanne, 21–26 September 1981), edd. F. Lasserre and P. Mudry (Geneva), 249–56

Wasserstein, A. (1972) 'Le rôle des hypothèses dans la médecine grecque', *Revue Philosophique de la France et de l'Etranger* 162: 3–14

WHO IS ATTACKED IN *ON ANCIENT MEDICINE*?

On Ancient Medicine[1] is generally acknowledged to be a document of the first importance for our understanding of the development of early Greek thought. Yet the problem of its relation to the medicine and philosophy of its time is still a very open one. In their editions of the treatise both W. H. S. Jones[2] and A. J. Festugière[3] discuss some of the conflicting opinions of earlier writers who tackled this question. H. Wanner,[4] for example, following Wellmann,[5] thought that the author showed Pythagorean and Cnidian influences, although W. A. Heidel[6] asserted, on the contrary, that the treatise 'bears none of the marks of the Cnidian school'. Jones himself[7] considered the writer an eclectic 'ready to adopt views from any thinker or school of thought that appeared likely to prove of value to a practising physician'. He mentioned Dexippus, Philolaus, Petron and the authors of *On Generation*, *On Diseases* IV, *On Affections* and *On Diseases* I as theorists who held views similar to those attacked in *VM* ch. 1, and concluded[8] that 'it is quite likely that the author had no single individual in mind, but was combating all thinkers who attached undue weight to the effect of the four traditional opposites on bodily health.' Festugière[9] also thought that *VM* is attacking a whole medical school, rather than any particular individual, but he referred to a rather different group of writers to illustrate the school in question, namely Philistion, the authors of *On Regimen* I and *On* || *Breaths*, and the doctors who are criticised in the treatise *On the Nature of Man*. More recently, H. Diller[10] has proposed a radically different interpretation of the date and significance of *VM*, suggesting that the author is directly influenced by Plato, whom indeed he is opposing. 'Wir gewinnen in seiner Schrift,' as Diller puts it,[11] 'ein Zeugnis zeitgenössischer Auseinandersetzung mit platonischer Lehre.' Since Diller wrote, the problem has been further discussed by J. H. Kühn,[12] who rejects Diller's view of the date of *VM* and considers that the treatise *On Breaths* is representative of the type of work which the author is attacking. In the present article I shall re-examine the problem of the relation of *VM* to extant medical works and to known medical writers of the fifth and fourth centuries B.C. The main question to be

[1] Except where noted, the text of *VM* I is I. L. Heiberg's (*Corpus Medicorum Graecorum*, vol. I 1 Leipzig, 1927). Other Hippocratic treatises which are not included in *CMG* 1, are cited according to the edition of E. Littré (10 vols., Paris, 1839–61, referred to with the initial L followed by the number of the volume in Roman numerals). I quote the text of Anonymus Londinensis as given by Diels (*Supplementum Aristotelicum*, vol. III 1 Berlin, 1893) including his signs for uncertain letters (dots underneath), abbreviations (round brackets), his own restorations (square brackets) and so on.

[2] Jones, 1946: 45ff.

[3] Festugière, 1948: xxxif.

[4] Wanner, 1939.

[5] Wellmann, 1930: 299ff.

[6] Heidel, 1941: 83.

[7] 1946: 45.

[8] 1946: 48.

[9] 1948: xxxii.

[10] Diller, 1952: 385ff.

[11] 1952: 409, cf. 393 'Die Vorstellungen, die der Verfasser von Techne, Methode, Hypothese hat, und darüber hinaus sein methodisches Bewusstsein als solches sind ohne Platon nicht denkbar'.

[12] 1956: 46ff. Kühn's work was largely completed by 1949 (see his Preface), but he has added an independent chapter (pt 1, ch. 5) in which he discusses Diller's views on the date of *VM*.

discussed is the identity of the theorists whose ὑποθέσεις are attacked in *VM* chh. 1 and 13ff. In those chapters the author condemns what he calls a 'new' or 'new-fangled' method in medicine (καινόν ch. 13, *CMG* I 1.44.8, cf. καινῆς ch. 1, 1.36.16) and he illustrates this method by referring to certain doctrines which he specifies quite clearly. How far is it possible to determine whom precisely the author of *VM* has in mind in those chapters, and whether, in particular, the method of hypothesis which he attacks is a pre- or post-Platonic development?

The opening words of *VM* describe the theories which the writer opposes quite specifically: 'Ὁκόσοι μὲν ἐπεχείρησαν περὶ ἰητρικῆς λέγειν ἢ γράφειν ὑπόθεσιν αὐτοὶ αὑτοῖς ὑποθέμενοι τῷ λόγῳ θερμὸν ἢ ψυχρὸν ἢ ὑγρὸν ἢ ξηρὸν ἢ ἄλλο τι, ὃ ἂν θέλωσιν, ἐς βραχὺ ἄγοντες τὴν ἀρχὴν τῆς αἰτίης τοῖσιν ἀνθρώποισι νούσων τε καὶ θανάτου καὶ πᾶσι τὴν αὐτὴν ἓν ἢ δύο ὑποθέμενοι ... (*CMG* I 1.36.2ff.). In ch. 13 the writer returns to the attack with the words: ἐπὶ δὲ τῶν τὸν καινὸν τρόπον τὴν τέχνην ζητεύντων ἐξ ὑποθέσιος τὸν λόγον ἐπανελθεῖν βούλομαι (44.8f).[13] The use of the terms ὑπόθεσις and ὑποτίθεσθαι in these and other passages is striking. The noun occurs six, and the verb three, times in *VM* and the writer clearly assumes that his readers are familiar with these terms and with their use in the context of medical theories in particular. Yet as ‖ several scholars have noted, the word is very rare indeed in extant literature before Plato. It occurs once, probably, in the treatise *On Breaths*,[14] but otherwise (apart from in *VM*) nowhere before Plato and his contemporaries (e.g. Xenophon, Isocrates). The main meanings of the word may be summarised: (1) a proposal or suggestion (e.g. Xen. *Cyr.* 5.5.13); (2) the subject under discussion (often in Isoc., e.g. 4.63); (3) a thesis, i.e. a proposition to be proved (as in *Flat.* ch. 15)[15]; and lastly (4) an assumption or postulate, i.e. something which is itself not proved, but which is used as a basis for inferences or theories. This last is, of course, the meaning which the word has in a number of important passages in Plato where the method of inquiry by a ὑπόθεσις is developed and discussed. Plato's use of the term in this sense is complex, and the interpretation of some of the key passages is disputed.[16] But it should be noted that the term ὑπόθεσις in the

[13] I retain Kühlewein's τὸν λόγον (with Jones, Festugière, cf. Littré's λόγον) in preference to Heiberg's λόγων.

[14] Reading ὑπόθεσις rather than Heiberg's ὑπόσχεσις in ch. 15, *CMG* I 1.101.21 (see Festugière, 1948: n. 1, p. 26).

[15] The ὑπόθεσις here is not an *assumption* from which deductions will be drawn, but a *thesis* which the writer aims to establish. In ch. 5 (94.5ff) he says that he will show that all diseases are the 'offspring' of air, and in ch. 15 he concludes his discussion by saying ἤγαγον δὲ τὸν λόγον ἐπὶ τὰ γνώριμα τῶν ἀρρωστημάτων, ἐν οἷς ἀληθὴς ἡ ὑπόθεσις ἐφάνη (101.20f.).

[16] On the whole subject of Plato's use of ὑπόθεσις in *Meno*, *Phaedo*, *Republic* and *Parmenides*, see especially Robinson, 1953: chh. 7–10 and ch. 12. On ὑπόθεσις in the *Phaedo*, in particular, compare Hackforth (1955: 133 and 136ff.) who describes the method of hypothesis as 'the establishment of some proposition through deduction from a hypothesis, or proposition assumed to be true', with Bluck, (1955: Appendix 6, 160ff.) who contends that 'hypotheses' are not propositions, but 'provisional notions' of Forms (see also Bluck, 1957: 21ff., and 1961: 75ff. and Appendix, and cf. Stahl, 1960: 409ff.).

sense 'assumption' probably occurs first in the *Meno* in a passage in which an apparently new method of argument is introduced, and in which the term itself is carefully explained. At *Meno* 86E3ff. Socrates uses the expression ἐξ ὑποθέσεως...σκοπεῖσθαι and then immediately explains this, for Meno's benefit, giving an example from geometry: λέγω δὲ τὸ ἐξ ὑποθέσεως ὧδε, ὥσπερ οἱ γεωμέτραι πολλάκις σκοποῦνται...

In *VM* itself ὑπόθεσις means neither a proposal, nor a subject under discussion, nor yet a thesis to be proved. The writer gives as examples of ὑποθέσεις 'hot or cold or wet or dry or whatever they like', which certain theorists held to be the causes of diseases and death (ch. 1, 36.3ff., cf. ch. 13, 44.8ff., ch. 15, 46.18ff.). He complains that medicine has no || need for a ὑπόθεσις like other subjects ὥσπερ τὰ ἀφανέα τε καὶ ἀπορεόμενα, περὶ ὧν ἀνάγκη, ἤν τις ἐπιχειρῇ τι λέγειν, ὑποθέσει χρῆσθαι, οἷον περὶ τῶν μετεώρων ἢ τῶν ὑπὸ γῆν (ch. 1, 36.16ff.). There can be no doubt that the ὑποθέσεις referred to in *VM* are postulates or assumptions used as the basis of philosophical and medical theories. It is generally agreed that the term has a similar meaning in *VM* and in some of the passages in Plato in which 'hypothetical method' is discussed,[17] and yet it is difficult, or rather, as I believe, impossible, to parallel this usage in extant fifth-century literature.[18] Diller argued, then, that in his use of the term the author of *VM* is directly influenced by Plato. But even if we were to accept this suggestion, it would not solve all our difficulties. Diller maintains that the author of *VM* sometimes has *Plato himself* in mind when he criticises the use of ὑποθέσεις, but this seems very unlikely. *VM* specifically attacks the use of hot, cold, wet and dry, and these were, of course, never adopted as postulates by Plato himself. We should have to assume, then, that Plato's use of ὑπόθεσις influenced certain contemporary medical theorists, and that it was *these latter* whom the author of *VM* was attacking in chh. 1 and 13ff.[19] *Meno* 86E4ff. suggests quite strongly that ὑπόθεσις may have been used before Plato in the sense 'preliminary assumption' in the field of geometry.[20] If this was

[17] E.g. *Phaedo* 100Aff. where what is postulated is the beautiful 'itself' (καλὸν αὐτὸ καθ' αὑτό) and other Forms (100B5f.), and *Republic* 510C2ff. where ὑποθέσεις are illustrated with examples drawn from mathematics 'the odd and even and the figures and the three sorts of angles and so on'.

[18] Kühn, 1956: 5 n. 1, compares the use of ὑπόθεσις in *VM* with that in *Flat.* ch. 15, *CMG* 1 1.101.21, but there is an important difference in the meaning of the term in the two treatises. In *VM* the ὑποθέσεις are assumptions on the basis of which deductions were made concerning the causes and cures of diseases. In *Flat.*, on the other hand, the ὑπόθεσις is a thesis which the author tries to prove (see above p. 55 n. 15). In this latter sense a pair of ὑποθέσεις would be a pair of propositions to be demonstrated, not a pair of postulates such as 'the hot' and 'the cold' (cf. *VM* ch. 1, 36.5f. ἐν ἢ δύο ὑποθέμενοι).

[19] Cf. Kühn, 1956: 47ff., where he rejects what he calls the modified Diller interpretation.

[20] In the *Meno*, when the geometrician tackles the problem in hand, that of inscribing a given area as a triangle in a circle, 'by means of a hypothesis', he suggests that if certain conditions are fulfilled, then one result follows, but if they are not, then the result is different. Bluck (1961: 92) has, however, suggested that 'if Socrates' geometrician can say that he wants to make ὥσπερ τινὰ ὑπόθεσιν' (87A2), 'the word ὑπόθεσις can hardly have been a well-established technical term in mathematics'. It should also be noted that ὑποθέσεις are again illustrated with

the case, it seems at least as likely that the term was introduced into medicine || from geometry, as that its introduction was a reflection of the influence of Plato's own hypothetical method. And of course a third alternative is also possible, namely that the use of the term in medicine developed quite independently.[21] The author of *VM* uses ὑπόθεσις freely and without explanation in the sense 'postulate' or 'assumption'. Yet we have no good independent evidence by which to date the introduction of the term in this sense into medicine.

We must now examine more closely the *content* of the theories which *VM* criticises so strongly. It has, I think, generally been assumed that *VM* refers to a wide range of medical theories in his attacks on the use of ὑποθέσεις. The fact is, however, that the actual ὑποθέσεις which he mentions are always the same, namely hot, cold, wet and dry. These are the examples which are given not only in ch. 1 (36.3f.) but on each subsequent occasion when ὑποθέσεις are considered. In ch. 13 the writer returns to the theories of 'those who conduct their researches in the art according to the new method, by a hypothesis', and goes on εἰ γάρ τί ἐστιν θερμὸν ἢ ψυχρὸν ἢ ξηρὸν ἢ ὑγρὸν τὸ λυμαινόμενον τὸν ἄνθρωπον...(44.9ff.). In ch. 14 he says that the 'original discoverers' of medicine never thought that dry or wet or hot or cold or any such thing injured a man, or that a man had any need of those things (45.18ff.). In ch. 15 he mentions a further ἀπορίη which faces those who make use of a ὑπόθεσις, and again hot, cold, dry and wet are the examples he cites: οὐ γάρ ἐστιν αὐτοῖσιν, οἶμαι, ἐξευρημένον αὐτό τι ἐφ' ἑωυτοῦ θερμὸν ἢ ψυχρὸν ἢ ξηρὸν ἢ ὑγρὸν μηδενὶ ἄλλῳ εἴδει κοινωνέον (46.20ff.).[22] He goes on to explain that one sort of hot thing is astringent, another insipid, another causes flatulence, and so on (46.27ff.). In ch. 16 (47.12ff.) he asserts that cold and heat are the least potent of all the 'powers' in the body, and he devotes four whole chapters to dealing with this particular pair of opposites. Although the philosopher Empedocles is mentioned, in another connection, in ch. 20, 51.10,[23] the writer never refers to earth, || air, fire or water as examples of

examples taken from 'geometry and calculation' in the *Republic* 510cff., but that here the ὑποθέσεις are quite different, 'the odd and even and the figures and the three sorts of angles', i.e. certain fundamental notions of mathematics.

[21] Festugière, 1948: n. 1, p. 25, notes that the verb ὑποτίθεσθαι is already used in the sense 'suggest' (to someone, to say or do something) in Homer. Yet for my part, I can find no clear instance of the verb with the meaning *assume* before Plato, other than in *VM* itself.

[22] On the use of the terms εἶδος, αὐτὸ ἐφ' ἑωυτοῦ and κοινωνεῖν in this passage (which led Taylor, 1911: 215, to conclude that 'the technical phrases of the *Phaedo* are not Plato's invention but belong to fifth century science') I have nothing to add to the full discussion in Festugière, 1948: n. 54, pp. 47–53.

[23] Festugière, 1948: n. 69, pp. 58ff., uses this reference to Empedocles as his chief evidence for the date of *VM*, which he puts between 440 and 420 B.C. on the grounds that this was when Empedocles' philosophy was particularly influential. But though this reference fixes a *terminus post quem* for the treatise, it establishes no *terminus ante quem* for it. It does not even necessarily imply that Empedocles was an important influence at the time, for his *theories* are not referred to. The point at issue in *VM* ch. 20 is whether a doctor needs to know what a man's constituent elements are in order to be able to cure patients, and in Jaeger's view (1939–45: III 19 and n. 40) the mention of Empedocles serves merely to illustrate the meaning

ὑποθέσεις, nor does he refer to blood, bile, black bile or phlegm as such.[24] As for such other things as bitter and sweet, astringent and insipid, salt, acid and so on, these are not rejected as unwarranted ὑποθέσεις at all: the writer acknowledges, and indeed emphasises, their importance as bodily constituents, and as possible causes of disease (ch. 14, 45.26ff.).[25] Although he adds the words ἢ ἄλλο τι, ὃ ἂν θέλωσιν to the examples 'hot or cold or wet or dry' in ch. 1 (36.3f., and cf. ἄλλο τούτων in ch. 14, 45.19), the evidence definitely suggests that it was these four opposites (and especially hot and cold) that were the particular objects of his attack. We may, perhaps, be even more precise. To judge from the remark ἓν ἢ δύο ὑποθέμενοι in ch. 1 (36.5f.) the *main* theorists whom the author of *VM* had in mind were pathologists who held either one, or a pair, of these opposites to be the sole cause of diseases.

Whatever other opponents the author of *VM* may have wished to criticise, he concentrates his attack on theorists who had postulated the hot, the cold, the wet and the dry as the cause of diseases, and particularly on those who had referred to just one, or a pair, of these opposites. Bearing in mind that *VM* criticises certain quite specific theories in chh. 1 and 13ff., and that this affords us the best means of judging his main or immediate opponents, we may now consider the evidence in the Hippocratic Corpus and elsewhere to see how closely the criticisms of *VM* relate to any extant medical works or known medical theorists.

At first sight it seems possible to suggest that one of the thinkers whom *VM* was attacking was Alcmaeon, since according to Aetius ‖ v 30.1, DK 24B4, at least, Alcmaeon held that τῆς μὲν ὑγιείας εἶναι συνεκτικὴν τὴν ἰσονομίαν τῶν δυνάμεων, ὑγροῦ, ξηροῦ, ψυχροῦ, θερμοῦ, πικροῦ, γλυκέος καὶ τῶν λοιπῶν, τὴν δ' ἐν αὐτοῖς μοναρχίαν νόσου ποιητικήν. Though the mention of wet, dry, cold and hot suggests the type of theory that *VM* particularly attacks, there are two major objections to the view that the author of *VM* had Alcmaeon's own theory specifically in mind. (1) Alcmaeon can hardly be said to have 'narrowed down the causal principle of diseases' (*VM* ch. 1, 36.4f.). According to the same source, Aetius, Alcmaeon attributed diseases to several other causes besides the μοναρχία of one or other of the 'powers' in the body, viz. to the excess or deficiency of a diet, and to certain external causes, e.g. blows. (2) Again, if Alcmaeon used 'postulates' at all, it is quite clear that he referred to many more than 'one

of the word φιλοσοφίη in 51.10 where it is already used in its restricted sense to refer to natural philosophy.

[24] Yet we know from *Nat. Hom.* ch. 2 (L vi 34.8ff.) that certain medical theorists, presumably of the late fifth century, asserted that man is composed of one of these humours, e.g. blood or bile, alone. cf. the theory ascribed to a certain Thrasymachus of Sardis in Anon. Lond. xi 42ff., that diseases arise from the blood.

[25] ἔνι γὰρ ἐν ἀνθρώπῳ καὶ ἁλμυρὸν καὶ πικρὸν καὶ γλυκὺ καὶ ὀξὺ καὶ στρυφνὸν καὶ πλαδαρὸν καὶ ἄλλα μυρία παντοίας δυνάμιας ἔχοντα πλῆθός τε καὶ ἰσχύν. ταῦτα μὲν μεμειγμένα καὶ κεκρημένα ἀλλήλοισιν οὔτε φανερά ἐστιν οὔτε λυπέει τὸν ἄνθρωπον, ὅταν δέ τι τούτων ἀποκριθῇ καὶ αὐτὸ ἐφ' ἑωυτοῦ γένηται, τότε καὶ φανερόν ἐστι καὶ λυπέει τὸν ἄνθρωπον.

or two'. He believed in the importance of a great many 'powers' besides hot, cold, wet and dry: this is clear not only from the words of Aetius, who mentions 'bitter, sweet and the rest', but also from the evidence of Aristotle, who implies that, unlike those Pythagoreans who adopted the συστοιχία, Alcmaeon held an indefinite number of pairs of opposites as principles (*Metaph.* A.5 986a31ff., DK 24A3). In some respects, indeed, Alcmaeon's theory *corresponds* to that which the author of *VM* himself puts forward in ch. 14, 45.26ff.,[26] although Alcmaeon apparently attributed greater importance to hot, cold, wet and dry than the author of *VM* was prepared to concede.

There are, of course, several Hippocratic treatises which state theories concerning the elementary constituents of man. *On Breaths* puts it that air, which is the most powerful thing in the world as a whole (ch. 3, *CMG* I 1.92.21f.) is also the sole cause of diseases (ch. 4, 93.18ff., cf. ch. 2, 92.13ff.). *On Regimen* I states that man is composed of fire and water (ch. 3, L VI 472.12ff.), and these two substances play an important part in the writer's theory of health and disease (e.g. ch. 32, 506.14ff.). Setting aside for the moment the difficult problem of the date of these treatises, we might suppose that either of them was the particular object of the criticisms of *VM*, since they both base theories of disease on a postulate or postulates. Yet on no occasion does the author of *VM* refer to air, or to fire or water, as examples of ὑποθέσεις. *On Breaths* and *On Regimen* I undoubtedly 'narrow down the causal principle of diseases', || in the words of *VM* ch. 1, 36.4f.; yet the author of *VM* never refers to the use of such postulates as air, fire or water, which is strange if he had either of these works *specifically* in mind.[27] *If* the author of *VM* knew either or both of these works (though this must be considered rather doubtful),[28] it is possible that his general attack on the use of unwarranted assumptions in medicine refers to them, among others. But it seems very difficult to hold that either of them was the *immediate* object of his criticisms in chh. 1 and 13ff., where the typical ὑποθέσεις mentioned are the hot and the cold, the wet and the dry themselves.

Are these particular opposites used in any other Hippocratic treatise in a way which corresponds more precisely to the theory attacked in *VM*? Two

26 Both Alcmaeon and the author of *VM* share the admittedly very common Greek medical theory that health depends on a balance of certain opposed factors in the body, and they agree on the importance of the bitter and the sweet (see *VM* ch. 14, 45.26ff., quoted above p. 58 n. 25).

27 The four primary opposites are, however, brought into association with the two elementary substances in *Vict.* I: fire is hot and dry, but has some moisture, and water is cold and wet, but has some dryness (ch. 4, L VI 474.8ff).

28 *Flat.* was probably written near the end of the fifth century at the earliest (there seems to be an echo of Eur. *Tr.* 884ff. in ch. 3, *CMG* I 1.93.16, which would date that passage after 415 B.C.). As regards *Vict.* I, I should agree with Jaeger (1939–45: III 40) that 'the language of the book is more reminiscent of the middle of the fourth century than of its beginning or of any earlier period'. On the date of *VM* itself, see below p. 68. Unless we hold, with Diller, that it shows Platonic influence (and this I believe to be unnecessary), it is unlikely that the author knew *Vict.* I, and not even very probable that he knew *Flat.*

of the works which Jones[29] cited as belonging to the general group which *VM* was criticising, propose quite complex pathological theories in which many other factors besides hot, cold, wet and dry are taken into account. In *On Affections* ch. 1 (L VI 208.7ff.) diseases are attributed to bile and phlegm when they become too dry or too wet or too hot or too cold in the body, but these changes are brought about by a variety of causes among which the writer mentions food and drink, exercise, wounds etc, as well as 'the hot and the cold' themselves. In *On Diseases* I, ch. 2 (L VI 142.13ff.) excessive heat, cold, dryness and moisture are mentioned among the 'external' causes of disease, but the writer makes it clear that diseases are also caused by other factors, both external (e.g. exercise and wounds) and internal (bile and phlegm). These Hippocratic writers are among the many who ascribe a certain importance to hot, cold, wet and dry in their pathological theories, but they are hardly likely to be the theorists who are referred to in *VM* ch. 1 as reducing the causes of diseases and death to these opposites alone.

Three other treatises ascribe a more fundamental role to hot, cold, wet and dry, or to one of these opposites. In *On the Nature of Man* ch. 3 || (L VI 36.17ff.) the writer[30] says that generation cannot take place unless hot and cold, wet and dry are evenly balanced; he goes on to say that on death, the wet, the dry, the hot and the cold in a man's body return to their respective counterparts in the world at large. In subsequent chapters, however, the body is said to be composed of the four humours, blood, phlegm and the two sorts of bile, yellow and black: indeed in ch. 5, 40.15ff., the author goes to some lengths to prove that these are the constituents of the body. Moreover in ch. 4, 38.19ff., we are told that it is these *humours* which cause health and disease. Each humour is thought of as either hot or cold, and either wet or dry (e.g. ch. 7, 46.9ff.), but it is clear that the pathological theory in this treatise is rather more complex than that which is attacked in *VM* ch. 1. The doctrine of *On Diseases* IV[31] seems to come quite close to the type of theory criticised in *VM*, for all diseases except those caused by physical violence are ascribed to the four forms of 'the wet' (ch. 32, L VII 542.6ff.). Yet these four forms of 'the wet' (ὑγρόν, elsewhere the writer uses the term ἰκμάς), turn out to be phlegm, blood, bile and water (ὕδρωψ), which have distinct origins and effects in the body, as the writer shows at length in chh. 35ff. (548.11ff.). Here too, then, the theory of disease is based on humours, rather than on the opposites themselves. Finally, there is the treatise *On Fleshes* which puts forward a

[29] 1946: 48.

[30] *Nat. Hom.* is a composite work, but parts of it may be ascribed, with some probability, to Polybus, the son-in-law of Hippocrates. The account of the veins in ch. 11 (L VI 58.1–60.9) is quoted at length by Aristotle at *HA* 512b12ff. and assigned to Polybus. The account of Polybus in Anon. Lond. XIX 1ff. is very corrupt, but Diels' reconstruction, giving many echoes of *Nat. Hom.*, especially chh. 3 and 4, must be considered likely, and on these grounds it is possible to attribute the first part of the treatise, chh. 1–8, to Polybus as well.

[31] The same theory is expressed very briefly in *Genit.* ch. 3, L VII 474.7ff. This treatise is certainly closely connected with *Morb.* IV and Littré suggested, with some plausibility, that the two, together with *Nat. Puer.*, form a single continuous work.

four-element theory.[32] 'What we call the hot' (which 'the ancients seem to have called αἰθήρ') is the most important element; the others are earth, air || and 'that which is nearest the earth' (ch. 2, L VIII 584.10ff.).[33] The aim of this treatise is to describe the formation of the different parts of the body, in his account of which the writer refers repeatedly to the four main opposites, hot, cold, wet and dry, as well as to such other factors as sweet and bitter, the fatty (λιπαρόν) and the glutinous (κολλῶδες). Unfortunately, we know very little about the author's theory of disease (though in ch. 19, 612.10ff., he makes use of a doctrine of critical days). It is possible, or even likely, that he attributed some diseases to the same elements and opposites that he used in his account of the formation of the parts of the body.[34] But even if we could assume that *On Fleshes* was definitely written before *VM* (and this is by no means certain[35]), we should hesitate before concluding that the author of *VM* was attacking this treatise especially in those chapters where he criticises those who based their theories of disease on a ὑπόθεσις.[36]

Among the many different theories of disease which are found in the Hippocratic Corpus, there are several to which the author of *VM* || would have objected, either because they were based on a postulate, or because they

[32] In the introductory ch. 1 of *Carn.*, L VIII 584.3, we find the verb ὑποθέσθαι used with ἀρχή, but the sense is not 'postulate a principle' so much as 'suggest a beginning' (for the idea, cf. *De Arte* ch. 4, *CMG* I 1.11.5f. and Diogenes of Apollonia, Fr. 1). ἀρχή should not, in any case, be taken to refer to θερμόν and the other elements mentioned in ch. 2, since the writer expressly distinguishes ch. 2, which, he claims, contains his own original ideas (νῦν δὲ ἀποφαίνομαι αὐτὸς ἐμεωυτοῦ γνώμας 584.8) from ch. 1, where he presents 'common opinions' (κοιναὶ γνῶμαι).

[33] As in *Vict.* 1, so too in *Carn.*, certain opposites are associated with the elements, though the schema in *Carn.* is less neat: earth is 'cold and dry and full of movement, and there is much hot in it'; air is 'hot and moist'; and 'that which is nearest the earth' is 'moistest and thickest' (ch. 2, 584.13ff.).

[34] A passage in ch. 16, 604.16ff. shows that this was at least sometimes the case: there the writer refers to catarrhs which come from the brain, and calls these a τροπὴ τῷ θερμῷ.

[35] Like most other Hippocratic treatises, *Carn.* cannot be dated with any degree of precision, but Deichgräber (1935: 27 n. 4) concluded that it belongs to the end of the fifth century. Littré put the treatise much later (not before Aristotle), but it should be noted that his main argument for doing so is invalid. He argued that Aristotle was the first to hold that the heart is the source of the veins (though he observed that the generalisation, at *HA* 513a10ff., that *all* previous writers regarded the head as the starting-point of the veins, is incompatible with the account which Aristotle himself gave of the theory of Diogenes of Apollonia), and that treatises such as *Carn.* that contain this view must be posterior to the work of Aristotle. Yet quite apart from the doubtful assumption that Aristotle's knowledge of the medical theories of his predecessors was exhaustive, it is certain that he was not the first to suggest that the heart is the origin of the veins since this view occurs quite unmistakably in the *Timaeus* of Plato (70A–B).

[36] The treatise *On Sevens* (Roscher, 1913) should also be mentioned, though the date of this work, too, is disputed. The hot plays an important part as the cause of at least one type of disease (fevers, chh. 19f., 24ff.; at ch. 53 the author promises, but does not give, an account of other kinds of disease). However if chh. 1–11 should be considered as part of the same work (though this has sometimes been doubted), both the theory of the components of the body and the general pathological doctrine expressed there are complex and refer to other factors besides the hot. There are seven constituents in the body (among them, the hot and the cold) and pain is said to be caused by the disharmony of these as a whole (ch. 10, cf. ch. 15).

laid too great an emphasis on hot, cold, wet and dry. The criticisms of *VM* are certainly relevant, in part, to a number of Hippocratic writers. But to judge from the particular form which those criticisms take, it seems unlikely that any of the other extant treatises of the Hippocratic Corpus is the *immediate* and *specific* object of his attack. It remains to consider whether the account of early Greek medical theorists in Anonymus Londinensis helps to define the opponents of *VM* more precisely.

In Anon. Lond. IV 26ff., medical theorists are divided into two groups, those who held that diseases arise from what the writer calls the 'residues', περισσώματα, of nourishment, and those who held that they come from the elements in the body (though in the account which follows, some theorists seem to be misplaced).[37] Among the latter, three theorists are named who held that the primary constituents of the body are the hot and the cold (or the hot alone). These are Philolaus, Polybus and Petron of Aegina.[38] The account of Polybus is, unfortunately, particularly corrupt, and though Diels' reconstruction of the text, based on *On the Nature of Man* chh. 1–8, is probable enough, the passage can tell us little more than *On the Nature of Man* itself, whose doctrines have already been discussed. The theory ascribed to Petron of Aegina (XX 1ff.) is that our bodies are composed of a pair of elements, the cold (with which the wet is ἀντίστοιχον) and the hot (with which the dry is ἀντίστοιχον), and he apparently attributed diseases both to a disproportion between these elements, and to the effects of the residues of nourishment. But the most important evidence concerns Philolaus himself. At XVIII 8ff. we are told that 'Philolaus of Croton says that our bodies are composed of the hot', and there then follows an account of the argument which led Philolaus to infer that our bodies 'do not share || in the cold'. It may be noted that though initially, in the womb, the living creature has no share in the cold, immediately on birth it inhales the air, which is cold, and thereafter 'discharges it again, just like a debt' (XVIII 23f.). Some of the details of this theory are reminiscent of the cosmological doctrine attributed to the Pythagoreans by Aristotle, which began when 'the one' (or the heaven) 'draws in' or 'inhales' 'breath and the void' from 'the unlimited',[39] and there seems little reason to doubt the accuracy of the report in Anon.

[37] One of the theories which is included, somewhat strangely, in the first section, is worth noting especially. This is the doctrine attributed to 'Hippon of Croton' (XI 22ff., the name is uncertain, see Diels' note *ad loc.*), that 'the moisture' in our bodies causes diseases when it changes through excessive heat or cold. It is clear from remarks at XI 32 and 41f., however, that, to the writer's knowledge, at least, Hippon had no detailed theory of disease.

[38] The doctrines attributed to Philistion and to Menecrates also make use of opposites in connection with a theory of the elements in the body. For Philistion (XX 25ff.) our bodies consist of four elements, fire, air, water and earth, and each of these has its own 'power', hot, cold, wet and dry. Menecrates (XIX 18ff.) held that we are composed of four humours, two of which are hot (blood and bile) and two cold (breath and phlegm). Cf. the type of theory which we find in *Vict.* I (p. 59 n. 27, above) and in *Carn.* (p. 61 n. 33, above).

[39] *Ph.* 213b22ff. and Stob. *Ecl.* I 18.1c (quoting Aristotle's lost work on the Pythagoreans), and see also Simplicius, *in Ph.* 651.26ff.

Lond. which attributes an analogous biological theory to the Pythagorean Philolaus.

Here, then, is one thinker who apparently held that we consist originally of a single substance, the hot, who might seem just the type of theorist who is attacked in *VM* ch. I for 'postulating hot or cold or wet or dry or whatever they like'. But what of Philolaus' theory of disease? We are told at Anon. Lond. XVIII 30ff. that he held that 'diseases arise through bile and blood and phlegm' (cf. also 48ff. where 'excesses and defects of heat and nourishment and cold and suchlike' are mentioned as συνεργά 'contributory causes'), and this report seems incompatible with the suggestion that Philolaus himself was one of those attacked in *VM* for narrowing down the causal principle of diseases and of death to one or two opposites. However the statement that bile, blood and phlegm and the cause (ἀρχή) of diseases (XVIII 31f., cf. 47f.) must be interpreted in the light of further observations which are made in Anon. Lond. concerning Philolaus' theory of these humours. What we have in Anon. Lond. XVIII 32ff. is not an account of how diseases come from the three humours mentioned, so much as certain rather sketchy information about how these humours themselves arise in the body, and what causes the changes to which they are subject. We are told at 37f. that Philolaus held that bile, for example, is an ἰχώρ of the flesh (and certain changes in the blood are also due to the compression and dispersion of the flesh, 32ff.), and we hear more about Philolaus' theory of bile in the account of Petron of Aegina. There it is reported that Petron thought that bile is a product, not a cause, of diseases, and the passage continues (XX 21ff.): καὶ σχεδὸν [οὗτος ὡ]ς | ὁ Φιλόλαος οἴεται μὴ (εἶναι) ἐν ἡμῖν χολὴ[ν ἢ] | ἀ[χρ]ε̣ία̣ν. Although this passage is corrupt the gist of the report is fairly clear: both Petron and Philolaus held that bile is a useless residue in the body. Again Philolaus' theory of the origin of phlegm is very briefly reported at XVIII 36f.: τὸ δὲ φλέγμα συνίστασθαι ἀπὸ τῶν ὄμ|βρων φ(ησίν). It seems, then, that though Philolaus || may have derived certain diseases from bile, blood and phlegm, he certainly did not consider these humours as elementary constituents of the body, but rather as the products of certain admittedly very obscure physiological changes. Furthermore at XVIII 41ff. we are told that while the majority of thinkers held that phlegm is *cold*, Philolaus asserted that it is essentially *hot*: τό τ' α̣ὖ φλέγμα | ... θερμὸν τῇ φύσει ὑπ[ο]τί- | θεται· ἀπὸ γ(ὰρ) τοῦ φλέγειν φλέγμα εἰρῆσθ(αι). Now it was a generally accepted opinion that blood and bile are hot.[40] It could well be that this was also Philolaus' view, but that no reference is made to this in Anon. Lond. because the writer is simply concerned, at this point, to draw attention to what he calls the 'paradoxical' theories of Philolaus (XVIII 38ff.). It is possible to conjecture, then, that he believed that each of the three humours, bile, blood and phlegm, and not just phlegm alone, is by nature hot, and if this was the case, 'the hot' may have held

[40] E.g. *Nat. Hom.* ch. 7, L VI 46.22ff. and 48.7ff. and *Morb.* I ch. 24, L VI 188.19ff.

almost as important a place in Philolaus' pathological theory as in his embryological doctrine. We know that he held that 'the hot' is the sole substance of which our bodies are originally composed: it may also have been the case that he reduced the principal causes of diseases to different manifestations of 'the hot'. This conjecture cannot, however, be confirmed, since the evidence for Philolaus' theory of the origin of bile, blood and phlegm is defective at what is, for our purposes, the most important point. We are told that bile and phlegm come from flesh and water respectively, but we do not know how these and all the other substances in the body arose, whether they were derived from the hot alone, or from the hot in conjunction with the cold which is inhaled after birth, or whether some other account of their origin was given. If Philolaus held that diseases were caused by different forms of 'the hot', then his pathological theory came close to the type which is specifically mentioned and condemned in *VM*, and the case for considering that Philolaus was among those against whom that attack is particularly directed, would be very strong. Yet our evidence certainly suggests that the immediate causes of diseases are three distinct humours, and not 'the hot' *per se*, and in this respect, Philolaus' pathological doctrine seems to have been more complex than those which are the particular object of the criticisms of *VM*.

The evidence in Anon. Lond. does not permit us to identify with certainty those who held the specific doctrines referred to in *VM* chh. 1 and 13ff. Just as there are several Hippocratic treatises which emphasise the importance of hot, cold, wet and dry either as elements, i.e. primary || component substances (as in *Nat. Hom.*), or as causes of disease (e.g. *Morb.* 1), so there are several theorists who are reported in Anon. Lond. to have held similar views. Yet the author of *VM* refers to pathologists who apparently reduced the causes of diseases to such opposites alone, and this extreme form of the doctrine is found neither in the Hippocratic Corpus nor in the account of medical theories in Anon. Lond. But if we are unable to name the particular theorists who are the immediate object of the attack in *VM* ch. 1, it is nevertheless possible to make certain suggestions concerning the origin of the type of doctrine criticised there. Of those who are reported in Anon. Lond. to have stressed the role of opposites as elements in the body, the first and most important is Philolaus, who maintained that we are composed originally of the hot alone. It is, then, worth investigating further the possibility that it may be Philolaus' influence on medical theory, if not Philolaus himself, that *VM* is attacking especially in chh. 1 and 13ff. Two features of Philolaus' work are worth considering in this context, his interest in cosmology, and his interest in geometry.

The author of *VM* (writing, as we know, after Empedocles) attacks those who confuse medicine with philosophy both in ch. 20 and, indirectly, in ch. 1. No one would deny that there are many writers of the fifth or early fourth century who combined an interest in medicine with an interest in cosmology.

But the criticisms of *VM* seem particularly relevant to Philolaus, whose medical and cosmological speculations appear to have been closely interrelated. True, some have seen Empedocles as not only an eminent cosmologist, but the founder of a medical school,[41] but while his theory of pores was certainly a major influence on subsequent physiological doctrines, it is, to my mind, very doubtful whether he put forward any detailed theories of disease.[42] Again, Alcmaeon's medical, physiological and psychological theories are well known, but the evidence for his interest in cosmological problems is limited: apart from such vague general pronouncements as that δύο τὰ πολλὰ τῶν ἀνθρωπίνων (quoted by Aristotle at *Metaph.* A.5 986a31) only a few astronomical ‖ doctrines are attributed to him, and none of these seems to have been original.[43] Philolaus, however (who came, of course, from the same city as Alcmaeon), seems to have been responsible for important contributions in both medicine and cosmology. As usual when dealing with the Pythagoreans, Aristotle describes the doctrines of the Central Fire and the Counter-Earth without attributing them to any specific thinker (*Cael.* 293a21ff.), but there seems no good reason to doubt Aetius[44] when he ascribes these theories to Philolaus, and elsewhere[45] he reports Philolaus' doctrines of the sun and moon. The likelihood is, surely, that Philolaus himself originated some, if not all, of the theories which are associated with his name. But we may remember that in *VM* ch. 1 (36.15ff.) the writer refers ironically to the use of a ὑπόθεσις in such fields as τὰ ἀφανέα τε καὶ ἀπορεόμενα, περὶ ὧν ἀνάγκη, ἤν τις ἐπιχειρῇ τι λέγειν, ὑποθέσει χρῆσθαι, οἷον περὶ τῶν μετεώρων ἢ τῶν ὑπὸ γῆν, where, he says, it would not be evident either to the speaker himself, or to his audience, whether his statements were true or not. He rejects the study of 'things in heaven and things under the earth' altogether, but his *irony*, in *conceding* that this is the proper place for the use of a ὑπόθεσις, would (I suggest) have particular point if it were directed against such a writer as Philolaus, for (1) Philolaus appears to have put forward theories based on what must have seemed quite arbitrary assumptions in both astronomy and biology, and (2) in both these fields 'the hot', in particular, probably figured in an important role, in astronomy as the Central Fire in the Universe, and in biology as the primary substance of which our bodies are composed.

Then, like several Pythagoreans, Philolaus is reported to have laid great

[41] See Burnet, 1948: 200f., who based this judgement on Galen, *MM* 1 1: (DK 31A3): οἱ ἐκ τῆς Ἰταλίας ἰατροί, Φιλιστίων τε καὶ Ἐμπεδοκλῆς καὶ Παυσανίας καὶ οἱ τούτων ἑταῖροι.

[42] In Fr. 112.10ff. Empedocles refers to those who sought to hear from him the word of healing for all manner of diseases. But the fact that this passage comes in the *Purifications*, and in a fragment in which he also claims to be a seer, and, indeed, an 'immortal god', might suggest that Empedocles' approach to medical problems was mystical rather than empirical (Burnet, 1948: 201f., himself suggested that a 'characteristic of the medicine taught by the followers of Empedokles is that they still clung to ideas of a magical nature'.)

[43] The evidence is collected in DK 24A4 (Aet. II 16.3; 22.4; and 29.3).

[44] Aet. II 7.7 and III 11.3 (DK 44A16 and 17), on which see Kirk and Raven, 1957: 257ff., and, most recently, Guthrie, 1962: 282ff.

[45] Aet. II 20.12 and 30.1 (DK 44A19 and 20).

stress on the study of geometry.[46] As I have already remarked, the use of the term ὑπόθεσις in *VM* is unparalleled in extant fifth-century literature, and any attempt to trace its development must, then, be highly conjectural. However one possibility, which is suggested by *Meno* 86E4ff., is that the term may have been used in the sense 'assumption' first in the field of geometry (other examples of its use in mathematics || are found in Plato, *Republic* 510C and in Aristotle, e.g. *EN* 1151a16f., *Metaph.* 1086a10f.). We have no reliable means of determining which fifth- or fourth-century mathematician (if any) may have been responsible for introducing the term in this sense.[47] But one admittedly quite inconclusive piece of evidence seems slightly to increase the possibility that Philolaus was among those who used it. In the *Phaedo*, on the first occasion when the word ὑπόθεσις is used (92D6) the speaker is not Socrates, but Simmias. Of course Plato's readers knew the term from the *Meno*, where its meaning had been explained and illustrated at some length, and as a general rule we should certainly not try to press the historical accuracy of terms which Plato puts into the mouth of different persons in his dialogues. Yet perhaps it may not be entirely fortuitous that Plato represents Simmias, the pupil of Philolaus,[48] as being familiar with the term ὑπόθεσις: furthermore Simmias is made to use it in a passage (92C11ff.) in which he draws a distinction between an argument based on a 'ὑπόθεσις which is worthy of acceptance' and merely probable arguments, which he says he knows are deceptive '*both in geometry* and in every other field'.[49] The evidence is far from proving that Philolaus himself did, in fact, use the term ὑπόθεσις in mathematics or in any other context.[50] But if the term was used before Plato by certain mathematicians or geometricians in particular, the

[46] Plut. *Quaest. Conv.* 8.2.1, 718e (DK 44A7a): γεωμετρία κατὰ τὸν Φιλόλαον ἀρχὴ καὶ μητρόπολις ... τῶν ἄλλων (μαθημάτων). Cf. especially *Theolog. Arithm.* 82.10 (DK A13) and Procl. *in Euc.* 130.8 (DK A14).

[47] Festugière, 1948: n. 1 p. 26, suggests that the use of the term ὑπόθεσις in geometry before Plato may, perhaps, be confirmed by three texts in Aristotle, Simplicius and Themistius concerning the geometrical ὑπόθεσις of the quadrature of the circle of Antiphon (DK 87B13), though he goes on to note that in those passages the word ὑπόθεσις is still not found as a textual quotation of Antiphon himself.

[48] At *Phd.* 61D6f. (cf. E6f.) we are told that both Simmias and Cebes had associated with Philolaus. True, in that passage Cebes disclaims definite knowledge of the doctrine that it is wrong to commit suicide, which Socrates suggests he may have learnt from Philolaus, but as Hackforth (1955: 35 n. 3) has suggested, Cebes' disclaimer, at this point, seems 'no more than a device to allow Socrates to explain the point'.

[49] Simmias uses the term ὑπόθεσις with reference to Socrates' argument about reminiscence and learning (δι' ὑποθέσεως ἀξίας ἀποδέξασθαι εἴρηται), which he contrasts with arguments which proceed from probabilities (τοῖς διὰ τῶν εἰκότων ἀποδείξεις ποιουμένοις λόγοις) which he says he recognises as deceptive καὶ ἐν γεωμετρίᾳ καὶ ἐν τοῖς ἄλλοις ἅπασιν.

[50] It may also be noted that the second time that ὑπόθεσις is used in the *Phaedo* (94B1, cf. Simmias' use of the verb at 93C10) Socrates applies it to Simmias' suggestion that the soul is an 'attunement', ἁρμονία, a doctrine which has often been taken to have been Philolaus' own, though this is not certain. Macrobius (*S. Scip.* I 14.19, DK 44A23) attributes it to both Philolaus and Pythagoras himself, but Aristotle reports the doctrine without naming its author or adherents (*De An.* 407b27ff.) and elsewhere (*De An.* 404a16ff.) ascribes other views on the soul to the Pythagoreans as a whole.

possibility || that Philolaus was among those who employed it, remote though this may be, seems to be slightly strengthened by the fact that in the *Phaedo* Plato represents a pupil of Philolaus using the term in a passage in which he parades his knowledge of mathematical methods of argument.[51]

I may now recapitulate the argument of this article and summarise such conclusions as our evidence appears to warrant. In *VM* chh. 1 and 13ff. the writer condemns the use of ὑποθέσεις in medicine, mentioning hot or cold or wet or dry in particular. Several theorists who referred to these opposites either as elements in the body, or as causes of disease, are known to us from the Hippocratic Corpus and Anonymus Londinensis. Yet the writer of *VM* refers to certain pathologists who evidently reduced the causes of diseases and death to such opposites alone, and even though our sources of information about Greek medicine of the fifth and fourth centuries are comparatively extensive, we cannot (as it seems to me) say with certainty who those theorists are. However the writers whose doctrines come closest to those attacked in *VM* are Philolaus, Polybus (the probable author of parts of *On the Nature of Man*) and Petron of Aegina: each of these thinkers based his theory of the elements in the body on those opposites whose importance is so strongly denied in *VM*, although each of them seems to have adopted pathological doctrines which are rather more complex than those that *VM* particularly condemns in ch. 1. The criticisms of *VM* seem especially relevant to Philolaus, in particular, and it may tentatively be suggested that one of the main purposes of those criticisms was to oppose Philolaus' influence or the example he set for medical theorists. (1) Philolaus was, so far as we know, the first medical writer to have argued explicitly that the body is originally composed of the hot (which is tempered, as it were, by the cold inhaled by the living creature on birth): in *VM*, chh. 16–19 are || dedicated to disproving the idea that the hot and the cold are important 'powers' in the body. (2) In ch. 1 the author of *VM* concedes, ironically, that ὑποθέσεις have a place in the study of 'things in heaven and things under the earth' which are beyond empirical verification, while at the same time strenuously maintaining that they should be excluded from the study of medicine, and once again his strictures seem especially relevant to such a writer as Philolaus: little as we know about Philolaus' work, his cosmological and biological speculations

[51] It is also just worth mentioning that the verb ὑποτίθεσθαι occurs twice in the sense 'suppose' or 'assume' in the account of Philolaus in Anon. Lond., with reference to his theories that phlegm is hot (XVIII 43f.) and that bile, blood and phlegm are the ἀρχαί of diseases (48). The verb in this sense is, of course, common enough in the fourth century, yet the fact that it occurs only once elsewhere in Anon. Lond. (IV 29) suggests that it was not a particular favourite of this writer. To judge from his account at XVIII 8ff. the writer of Anon. Lond. had fairly good evidence concerning some, at least, of Philolaus' medical and biological theories, even though the passage in which he reports them is quite brief, and it might be suggested that such a term as ὄμβροι used, apparently, to mean 'water' (XVIII 36f.) may be a direct quotation from a text which the writer (or his source) took to be a genuine work of Philolaus. It is just possible, then, that the term ὑποτίθεσθαι may also be an echo of Philolaus, though I should grant that this possibility is only a slender one.

seem closely interrelated, and in particular he appears to have ascribed a primary role to 'the hot' in certain theories in both these fields, in cosmology postulating the 'Central Fire' in the universe, and in biology asserting that 'the hot' is the original substance of which the body is composed.

The problem of determining the relation of *VM* to its contemporaries is a difficult one, and our evidence does not permit us to reach positive or precise conclusions. There are a number of striking concepts and usages in this work, notably the recurrent use of the terms ὑποτίθεσθαι and ὑπόθεσις, which are quite exceptional in extant pre-Platonic literature. Yet the suggestion that *VM* is directly influenced by Plato does not solve our problem: it is not Plato's use of ὑποθέσεις that *VM* attacks, but their use by certain medical theorists, and we are still faced with the question as to who these may be. If we cannot name the authors of the particular theories specified in ch. 1, the type of doctrine to which *VM* principally objects has close affinities with those adopted by such thinkers as Polybus and Petron, and earlier still by Philolaus. Assuming that the writer is trustworthy when he describes the method of his opponents as 'new' or 'new-fangled' (καινόν), and that this provides our best means of deciding the approximate date of the treatise, it seems more likely that *VM* is a product of the late fifth or of the early fourth century, than that it is as late as, say, the middle dialogues of Plato (though we have, in my opinion, no reliable evidence by which to fix the date precisely within the broad limits to which I refer).[52] We may remember that until the discovery of the text of Anonymus Londinensis, Philolaus' own medical and physiological theories were unknown and unsuspected. To my mind, much of the significance of *VM* lies in the evidence which it affords of certain important, but otherwise largely unknown, developments in scientific method and terminology. As Festugière, Diller and others have noted, the writer already uses φιλοσοφίη (51.10) in the restricted sense 'natural philosophy', ἀναφέρειν || (36.20f and 41.21) in the sense 'refer to' as evidence or as a standard of judgement, and he has a developed notion of medicine as an art, τέχνη.[53] And most valuable of all are the references to, and criticisms of, the use of ὑποθέσεις, for *VM* is the only extant work which indicates that already in the period before Plato (in all probability) medical theorists were familiar with the concept of a postulate, i.e. something which has itself not been proved, but which is assumed as a basis for theories and explanations, and had discussed the legitimacy of making use of such assumptions in different fields of inquiry.[54]

[52] On the reference to Empedocles at 51.10 which Festugière used as his main evidence to date *VM* between 440 and 420, see above p. 57 n. 23.

[53] On the notion of τέχνη in *VM* see Festugière, 1948: xvff. and Heinimann, 1961: 105ff.

[54] A discussion of the relation between *VM* and contemporary philosophy, particularly Empedocles and Anaxagoras, has now been published by J. Longrigg, 1963: 147ff., especially 152 and 159ff. (an article which unfortunately reached me only when this paper was already in proof). It is impossible to deal here with all the points that Longrigg raises, but I should express my disagreement with his thesis that the similarities between *VM* and Anaxagoras are due to the former having influenced the latter (rather than, as is generally thought, the other way round).

REFERENCES

Bluck, R. S. (1955) *Phaedo* (London)

(1957) 'ὑπόθεσις in the *Phaedo* and Platonic dialectic', *Phronesis* 2: 21–31

(1961) *Meno* (Cambridge)

Burnet, J. (1948) *Early Greek Philosophy*, 4th edn (London)

Deichgräber, K. (1935) *Hippokrates, Über Entstehung und Aufbau des menschlichen Körpers* (Leipzig)

Diller, H. (1952) 'Hippokratische Medizin und attische Philosophie', *Hermes* 80: 385–409

Festugière, A. J. (1948) *Hippocrate, L'ancienne médecine, Etudes et commentaires*, IV (Paris)

Guthrie, W. K. C. (1962) *A History of Greek Philosophy*, I (Cambridge)

Hackforth, R. (1955) *Plato's Phaedo* (Cambridge)

Heidel, W. A. (1941) *Hippocratic Medicine, its Spirit and Method* (New York)

Heinimann, F. (1961) 'Eine vorplatonische Theorie der τέχνη', *Museum Helveticum* 18: 105–30

Jaeger, W. (1939–45) *Paideia*, 3 vols. (Oxford)

Jones, W. H. S. (1946) *Philosophy and Medicine in Ancient Greece*, Supplement to the Bulletin of the History of Medicine 8 (Baltimore)

Kirk, G. S. and Raven, J. E. (1957) *The Presocratic Philosophers* (Cambridge)

Kühn, J. H. (1956) *System- und Methodenprobleme im Corpus Hippocraticum*, Hermes Einzelschriften 11

Longrigg, J. (1963) 'Philosophy and medicine, some early interactions', *Harvard Studies in Classical Philology* 67: 147–75

Robinson, R. (1953) *Plato's Earlier Dialectic*, 2nd edn (Oxford)

Roscher, W. ed. (1913) *Die hippokratische Schrift von der Siebenzahl in ihrer vierfachen Überlieferung* (Paderborn)

Stahl, H.-P. (1960) 'Ansätze zur Satzlogik bei Platon', *Hermes* 88: 409–51.

Taylor, A. E. (1911) *Varia Socratica* (Oxford)

Wanner, H. (1939) 'Studien zu "περὶ ἀρχαίης ἰητρικῆς"', Diss. (Zürich)

Wellmann, M. (1930) 'Die pseudo-hippokratische Schrift "περὶ ἀρχαίης ἰητρικῆς"', in *Sudhoffs Archiv für Geschichte der Medizin* 23

4

EXPERIMENT IN EARLY GREEK PHILOSOPHY AND MEDICINE

INTRODUCTION

The use of – or the failure to use – experiment has been a favourite topic among those who have attempted to compare and contrast ancient Greek, and modern, science. On the one hand there have been those who have dismissed Greek science as a whole as not proper science at all on the grounds of the lack of any appreciation – in principle or in practice – of the fundamental importance of the experimental method. Against them, on the other hand, have been ranged those who have protested that the Greeks were perfectly well aware of, and practised, the experimental method, and that on that score there is no call to criticise their science as essentially flawed. The article I published on 'Experiment in early Greek philosophy and medicine' in the *Proceedings of the Cambridge Philological Society* in 1964 joins the debate and criticises both extreme views for attempting grand generalisations on a topic where the actual performance of different ancient Greek scientists on different subjects and at different periods varied considerably.

The main thrust of my argument is that each subject-area, and indeed each problem, has to be considered on its own merits. When that is done it becomes obvious that both generalisations (that they failed to experiment, and that they practised it systematically) are untenable. It is important to recognise that in some areas, such as astronomy, direct experiment is impossible, and in others (such as meteorology) impracticable – or was so for the ancient Greeks with the technology at their disposal. In other fields, such as optics and acoustics, the record of Greek scientists shows that they could, and did on occasion, conduct experiments, including some that involve the construction of special apparatus. However, in other areas (such as those we call dynamics and chemistry) it is not difficult, with the benefit of hindsight, to suggest tests that were within the range of ancient scientists and that they did *not* carry out, or at least not as early as they might have done. The reasons are complex and one recurrent factor is that the theories the Greeks entertained were themselves not formulated in such a way as to permit decisive refutation or confirmation by such experiments, even though if they had been carried out they would certainly have extended the data that any theory would have had to take into account.

Subsequent work on these issues has, in the main, accepted my main line of argument – that global generalisations are out of the question – but has gone further than I did in that article by elaborating and modifying certain points and by bringing a wider range of examples to bear. In my original paper I concentrated, as its title suggests, on *early* Greek philosophy and medicine, though some of my examples, for instance in optics, came from Hellenistic writers. In an important study published in 1975 Heinrich von Staden discussed 'experiment and experience in Hellenistic medicine'. Von Staden accepted my argument for the need for case-by-case studies and investigated a series of experiments, including experimental dissections and vivisections, from Hellenistic medicine, especially from the Alexandrian anatomists Herophilus and Erasistratus and the second-century A.D. polymathic physician Galen. These men are indeed responsible for some of the most impressive ancient examples of delicate and difficult experimental interventions brought to bear to throw light on fundamental theoretical problems such as the functioning of the valves of the heart, the processes of digestion, the functioning of the nervous system including the particular roles of specific nerves, and so on. However, von Staden showed very clearly how inconclusive many of the experiments in question were, owing to the reliance on inappropriate analogies and the frequent over-statement of the results. While such criticisms apply less to some other experiments in other fields, von Staden drew attention to the fact that even in some of the most impressive tests there are certain recurrent flaws which help to illuminate the aims and expectations of the experimenters, and he further showed how some features of Hellenistic scientific methodology – including, paradoxically, the appeal to experience in the so-called Empiricist school – militated against the conduct of deliberate experimentation.

The aims and expectations of experimenters were also the target of my own further study of the problems in *Magic, Reason and Experience* in 1979. Chapter 3 of that work attempts a general investigation of the role of appeals to empirical evidence in Greek science and several features that emerge from that investigation go beyond points that I drew attention to in my 1964 article on experiment in particular. The role of the data obtained from many tests is not so much to *decide between* theories judged antecedently to be of equal standing, as *either* to corroborate the author's own view *or* to refute that of an opponent. In the first type of case 'experimental data' are used – like any other data of observation – to confirm a hypothesis: and in many instances that eagerness to confirm the author's own hypothesis shows through in the way in which the data are already interpreted in the light of just that hypothesis. Many of the cases where the results of an experiment are overinterpreted may be put down to such overeagerness – as indeed is also the case in a variety of instances where the ancient scientist has not so much over-interpreted his results as fudged them (see the supplementary note on Ptolemy, p. 81 n. 25, asterisked sentence, below).

In the second type of case – experiment used to refute an opponent's position – overinterpretation also occasionally occurs, but is less frequent. This is understandable in the light of the well-known asymmetry in the difficulty of refuting, and in confirming, a theory: it is enough to refute one to give a single counter-example, while the coincidence of the results of an experiment with what a theory predicts tells us no more than that the theory has *not* been refuted.

In both cases appeal to experiment, in ancient science, is a straightforward extension of the appeal to observation, the observational data here being obtained by deliberate intervention designed to investigate the phenomena under artificial conditions (see further 'Observational error', ch. 13 below). However the situation is in some respects analogous to that which obtained in courts of law in early times, where witnesses were brought in specifically to corroborate a point of view (or to refute one) and there was little or no deference to any idea that the prior responsibility of the witnesses themselves was to tell the truth. Of course the extent to which modern scientific experiments are, in practice, devised to perform the role of neutral adjudicators between theories antecedently held to be of equal standing is a matter of some doubt. But the *ideal* incorporated in the experimental method is that that should be their role, and even if the ideal does not always correspond to actual practice, the very fact that the ideal exists is a factor that cannot be discounted and indeed *has* to be taken into account given the further principle that experimental results have to be repeatable.

In my original article I investigated the similarities and differences between the element theories in the philosophers and in some of the Hippocratic writers (pp. 94ff.) and I criticised many of the tests set out in the latter as indecisive or even irrelevant. In this and other contexts (cf. pp. 83f.) I mentioned a number of examples from the embryological treatises *On Generation*, *On the Nature of the Child* and *On Diseases* IV (which had been the subject of an exaggeratedly positive evaluation by Senn, see p. 96 n. 72). The methodology of these works has more recently been analysed in an important and comprehensive study by Iain Lonie (1981). Lonie insisted that the 'experiments' described have to be understood against the background of certain fundamental assumptions. A crucial difference between these tests and those that would meet the criteria of modern scientific experiments is that the Hippocratic authors generally intervene not directly on the substances in the human body but on others outside it deemed to possess the same or similar properties or otherwise to behave in the same way. There is, in other words, an essential element of analogy in the Hippocratic procedures (as von Staden also pointed to in Hellenistic experiments, and cf. Lloyd, 1966). Moreover no *justification* is attempted for the *assumption* that the analogy indeed holds, although reference *is* sometimes made to the general law of which both items compared in the analogy are asserted to be instances. This point corresponds, of course, to one element in the inconclusiveness of some early Greek tests to which I drew attention in my original study (e.g.

p. 95). But Lonie's work took further the analysis of the explicit and implicit methodological assumptions made in these treatises (1981: 72–86).

Further study of individual cases can be expected to illuminate other features of the aims, assumptions and claimed results of Greek scientists working within one or other of the branches of the 'inquiry concerning nature'. Differences in performance relate not just to the difficulty of the practical circumstances of experimental intervention, but also to the degree of elaboration of the theories in consideration. While in my original study (p. 94, pp. 97f.) I countered the argument that the key to differences in the attention paid to experimentation lies in the contrasts in the background and training of the doctors and engineers, on the one hand, and those of the mathematicians or the philosophers on the other, that is not to say that such factors can entirely be discounted. But such further complications all go to underline not just the importance of this issue as a central issue in Greek scientific methodology, but also the fatuity of attempting the grand generalisation on their aims or their practice. That such grand generalisations have so often been proposed tells us more about the temptations that beset a certain style of history of science, than about ancient Greek science itself – in particular (as I concluded by noting, p. 98) the temptation to exaggerate the continuities in the history of science and to represent it as a matter of a single, linear development. While there is no way, of course, in which judgements and evaluations can be *avoided* in the history of science, this aspect of Greek science is a good example that *defeats* most attempts to generalise such evaluations.

REFERENCES

Grmek, M. D., and Gourevitch, D. (1985) 'Les Expériences pharmacologiques dans l'antiquité', *Archives Internationales d'Histoire des Sciences* 35: 3–27

Lloyd, G. E. R. (1966) *Polarity and Analogy* (Cambridge)

(1979) *Magic, Reason and Experience* (Cambridge)

(1987) *The Revolutions of Wisdom* (Berkeley)

Lonie, I. M. (1981) *The Hippocratic Treatises 'On Generation' 'On the Nature of the Child' 'Diseases IV'*, Ars Medica Abt. 11 Bd 7 (Berlin)

Staden, H. von (1975) 'Experiment and experience in Hellenistic medicine', *Bulletin of the Institute of Classical Studies* 22: 178–99

EXPERIMENT

Anyone who attempts to tackle the question of the role of experiment in Greek science must first come to terms with the extensive modern literature on the subject, and what strikes one first about this literature is that ever since the *Novum Organum* of Bacon (1620) much of it has been highly polemical in tone. Bacon's judgement is well known:

> Atque ex philosophiis istis Graecorum, et derivationibus earum per particulares scientias, jam per tot annorum spatia vix unum experimentum adduci potest, quod ad hominum statum levandum et juvandum spectet, et philosophiae speculationibus ac dogmatibus vere acceptum referri possit.[1]

Against Aristotle in particular Bacon adopts a different line of attack, for he concedes that in some of Aristotle's works references to experiments are to be found, but accuses Aristotle of twisting the data of experience to fit his preconceived opinions. According to Bacon, then, Aristotle was more blameworthy than his modern adherents who neglected the data of experience entirely:

> Ille enim prius decreverat, neque experientiam ad constituenda decreta et axiomata rite consuluit; sed postquam pro arbitrio suo decrevisset, experientiam ad sua placita tortam circumducit et captivam; ut hoc etiam nomine magis accusandus sit, quam sectatores ejus moderni (scholasticorum philosophorum genus) qui experientiam omnino deseruerunt.[2]

Now there were, of course, good reasons why a seventeenth-century scientist should react strongly against contemporary Aristotelianism. But similar exaggerations mar much of what was said about Greek science in general, and Aristotle's contribution in particular, by nineteenth-century historians of science. G. H. Lewes[3] quotes John Playfair's Dissertation, prefixed to the 1842 edition of the *Encyclopaedia Britannica*, as typifying the view prevailing in the mid-nineteenth century on the subject of the physical science of the Greeks and the reasons for its shortcomings:

> Extreme credulity disgraced the speculations of men who, however ingenious, were little acquainted with the laws of nature, and unprovided with the great criterion by which the evidence of testimony can alone be examined. Though observations were sometimes made, experiments were never instituted; and philosophers who were little attentive to the facts which spontaneously offered, did not seek to increase their number by artificial combinations.[4]

In more modern discussions of this topic, too, the view has often been

Where a note is preceded by an asterisk, here and in ch. 6, it indicates that a supplementary note has been added to the original sequence.

[1] *Novum Organum* I 73. [2] *Ibid.* I 63. [3] Lewes, 1864: 49.
[4] Playfair, 1842: 453ff.

expressed that there is a fundamental distinction between ancient and modern science in that the ancients failed to employ the experimental method. J. O. Thomson, for example, put it that

> the Greeks were nearly always too ready to theorize, and had little of the modern will to collect and sift facts, or of the instruments and techniques necessary for this purpose: they tried to explain things without first studying and describing them properly, preferring instead to || analyse their own words and notions. So they initiated science but failed to sustain it, and never disengaged 'physics' from the general philosophy in which it began. There was a fatal neglect of detail and experiment and practical application, partly because most craftsmanship was left to slaves. Thus modern science, which rests on experiment, is in a sense not really continuous with ancient.[5]

Many other commentators have laid a similar emphasis on the failure of the Greeks to use experiment, or at least on their failure to use it systematically.[6] On the other hand what one may call the 'positivist' school of interpretation has adopted a very different view on this question. Burnet, as is well known, attempted to defend the Greeks against the charge that they made no use of experiment. 'The rise of the experimental method dates from the time when the medical schools began to influence the development of philosophy, and accordingly we find that the first recorded experiment of a modern type is that of Empedocles with the *klepsydra*.'[7] 'It is inconceivable', Burnet went on, 'that an inquisitive people should have applied the experimental method in a single case without extending it to other problems', and elsewhere he argued that the reason why we have so little information about their observations and experiments is that 'nearly all that we know on this subject comes from compilations and manuals composed centuries later, by men who were not themselves interested in science, and for readers who were even less so'.[8] According to Burnet, then, 'if we can point to indubitable examples of the use of experiment and observation, we are justified in supposing that there were others of which we know nothing because they did not happen to interest the compilers on whom we are dependent', and a similar line of argument has been used both by Heidel[9] and, in more recent years, by Blüh.[10]

[5] Thomson, 1948: 94.

[6] A number of authorities are cited by Thomson, 1948: 94 n. 1 and *addenda* p. 401. More recently H. D. P. Lee, for example, in his introduction to the Loeb edition of Aristotle's *Meteorologica* (1952: xxvii) puts it that the experimental method eluded the Greeks: 'They observed but they did not experiment, and between observation and experiment there is a fundamental difference, which it is essential to recognize if the history of Greek thought is to be understood.' Compare the rather more cautious judgement of Sambursky, 1956: 2: 'With very few exceptions, the Ancient Greeks throughout a period of eight hundred years made no attempt at systematic experimentation.'

[7] Burnet, 1948: 27.

[8] Burnet, 1929: 253f. (cf. Cornford's remarks, 1952: 4).

[9] Heidel, 1933: 78f., and later 1941: 96ff.

[10] Blüh, 1949: 384ff. On the topic as a whole cf. also Edelstein, 1952: 573ff.; Farrington, 1957: 68f.; and Zubov, 1959: 223ff.

Several of the theses which have been maintained by either side in this controversy seem implausible or exaggerated, but to examine these in further detail would serve no useful purpose. There is, however, one important point which I hope emerges from the quotations I have given, and that is that modern commentators have shown a remarkable tendency to *generalise* on the question of whether or not the Greeks || experimented. Much of the discussion has been carried on as if the important thing was to decide the answer to this *global* question, and in attempting to settle this question one way or the other it has too often been forgotten that experimentation is of varying usefulness and relevance in different fields of scientific investigation, or even on different problems within the same field: indeed the role of experimentation may also be said to vary (in certain respects) at different levels of scientific development, that is according to the level of knowledge attained in a particular field at a particular time. To my mind, then, the question that needs to be asked is not the global one 'did the Greeks experiment?', nor even 'how far did the Greeks recognise the value of the experimental method?' Rather we should ask the more concrete, and at the same time much more difficult, questions 'what experiments were open to the Greeks on different problems or in different branches of science which they did not perform?' and on the other hand 'what tests did they actually carry out, in different fields, and with what success?' To these questions there is, of course, no simple yes or no answer. Rather we must try to assess the Greek performance in each department of science, indeed on each problem, independently, and to do this generally requires a thorough knowledge not merely of the contributions made in a particular field at different stages in antiquity, but also of the history of subsequent developments, that is of how thought developed on the subject in modern, post-Renaissance times.

Of course the extent of the subject I have outlined precludes anything like a full, let alone an exhaustive, treatment here, and I shall confine myself to making certain tentative suggestions concerning some of the problems which occur when we consider the earliest period of Greek science, that is, roughly speaking, from the sixth to the fourth century B.C. I shall take in turn each of the main departments of inquiry on which the earliest Greek investigators were engaged, and consider what evidence there is in our extant sources (principally the Presocratics, the Hippocratic Corpus and Aristotle) which will enable us to answer the two questions I have propounded.

The first point that may be made is the obvious one that much of the speculative effort of the earliest Greek natural philosophers was concentrated on a department of science which, strictly speaking, is not experimental at all: I mean, of course, astronomy. Astronomers can and do attempt to verify, by further observations, the predictions they make on the basis of theories or hypotheses, but in the nature of things they cannot conduct experiments, that is they cannot vary or govern the conditions of the objects they are observing. Ancient astronomy is, no doubt, in certain respects less rigorously empirical, more aprioristic, than modern, but how far we can talk of a *fundamental* difference in method between the two is more difficult to decide. While many of the explanations which Aristotle, for instance, put forward are, we should say, highly arbitrary, it is worth recalling that on more than one occasion he draws on the results obtained from many years of observations by Egyptian and Babylonian astronomers,[11] that a passage in the *Meteorologica* suggests that his own observations extended, in some cases, over a period of fifty years,[12] and that in a striking passage in the *De Caelo*, where he introduces one of his more fanciful explanations of a highly || obscure problem,[13] he prefaces his account with this disclaimer: 'Perhaps to try to give an explanation about some things, or about everything without exception, may seem to indicate a high degree of simple-mindedness or a high degree of zeal. But', he goes on, 'this objection is not always just: one should consider the reason for speaking, and also what kind of conviction is being aimed at, whether merely human or something stronger. Whenever anyone lights upon more exact proofs, then we must be grateful to the discoverer, but for the present we must state what seems plausible'.[14] However, my immediate point is not that in assessing the work of early Greek astronomers we should weigh against the obvious dogmatic and teleological features their use of empirical data[15] and certain passages in which they draw attention to the tentative nature of some of their theories, but rather this, that to speak of a 'failure to conduct experiments' in this field would be quite inappropriate.

One may, perhaps, go further. If in astronomy it was physically impossible for the Greeks to carry out experiments, the same also applied for them, at least, in a large part of what they called 'meteorology'. Nowadays, it is true, it is possible to manufacture a lightning-flash artificially. But that the Greeks did not attempt to do so is hardly surprising (they got no further than noticing certain examples of static electricity, such as the attraction of amber when rubbed). For the Greeks most of the problems of 'meteorology', the nature and causes of lightning and thunder, meteors, winds, earthquakes and so on, were beyond the reach of direct experimental investigation. But if the theories put forward in this field by the Presocratics and later writers are generally highly dogmatic and speculative, this is not to say that no attempt whatsoever was made to adduce empirical support for some such doctrines.

11 *Cael.* 292a7ff.; *Mete.* 343b9ff. and 28ff., and cf. also *Cael.* 270b13ff.

12 *Mete.* 372a28f. (referring to the rare occurrence of moon rainbows).

13 *Cael.* II, ch. 5, 287b22ff. The problem in question is why the heavens revolve in one direction rather than the other, or, as we should put it, why the earth revolves on its axis in one direction rather than the other (so far as I know, the problem has still not been solved).

14 *Cael.* 287b28ff. There is a similar disclaimer at *Cael* II, ch. 12, 291b24ff., where Aristotle discusses the problem of why some of the heavenly bodies have 'complex', others 'simple' motions.

15 Sambursky, 1956: 50ff., has drawn attention to the improvement of astronomical measurements that took place in the Greek period, instancing the increasing accuracy of the approximations which were made of the length of the solar year.

I have in mind the occasions when the explanation of an obscure natural phenomenon was illustrated or supported by an appeal to an analogy drawn from familiar experience. The comparison between the flash of lightning and the flash made by an oar or some such object on striking the water, which is mentioned by Aristotle at *Mete.* 370a10ff., seems to have been used by Anaximenes to back a theory originally advanced by Anaximander concerning the nature of lightning (namely that it is due to a cloud being split by the force of wind).[16] Aristotle himself, in his account of thunder, compares it with the crackling of logs in a fire, attributing both phenomena to the 'dry exhalation'.[17] And when he tackles the question of whether shooting-stars are actual projectiles, or whether this phenomenon is due to a train of fire passing rapidly from one thing to another, he draws on two analogies: either, he suggests, it may be like what happens when an unlit lamp is placed below another one which is alight and the || lower lamp is lit by a flame travelling rapidly downwards from the upper one, or else the shooting star may be a solid body forced downwards under pressure, and here he compares them with such objects as the stones of fruit being shot out from between the fingers, in order to illustrate how things may move, under pressure, in a direction contrary to their natural tendency.[18] Now many of the illustrations used by Greek writers to suggest or support explanations of meteorological phenomena might strike us as rather far-fetched, though this is not always the case: one might cite, for example, the passage in which Aristotle explains why we see the flash of lightning before we hear the sound of the thunder by referring to the experience of watching a ship at sea, where the oars are already going back again by the time the sound of their striking the water reaches us.[19] But the point I should like to suggest is that in 'meteorology', where direct experimental investigation was often physically impossible, the appeal to analogies drawn from more familiar experience served the Greeks as a δεύτερος πλοῦς, a next best method, indeed in many cases the only empirical method open to them. Moreover some of the illustrations they use refer not to well-known facts or common experience, but to quite rare phenomena, and in certain instances it seems that the analogy may even have involved the deliberate undertaking of a piece of research. If we take the illustration of the two lamps which Aristotle uses to suggest one of two possible explanations for the phenomena of shooting-stars, it is fairly clear that Aristotle himself had observed quite closely the way in which one lamp may be lit from another: 'the speed with which this happens', he notes at *Mete.* 342a5ff., 'is extraordinary, and it resembles the projection of a missile, rather than fire passing from one thing to another'. And a second passage which shows how fine may be the distinction between an illustration drawn

[16] *Aet.* III 3.1–2; DK 12A23, 13A17.

[17] *Mete.* 369a29ff.

[18] *Mete.* 342a3ff., cf. 344a25ff. on comets.

[19] *Mete.* 369b8ff. The expression that sight προτερεῖν τῆς ἀκοῆς might be thought rather odd in view of the fact that elsewhere Aristotle flatly denies (against the opinion of Empedocles) that light travels at all (e.g. *Sens.* 446a25ff., b27ff.).

from familiar experience, and a deliberate piece of research, comes in Aristotle's discussion of the rainbow (*Mete.* III, ch. 4): there one of the illustrations which he adduces to support his suggestion that the rainbow is due to a reflection caused by minute drops of water is what happens when a man sprinkles water in a room which is so placed that it faces the sun and is partly illuminated by it and partly in shadow. 'Then if one man sprinkles water in the room, another standing outside sees a rainbow at the place where the sun's rays stop and the shadow begins.'[20] The invention of prisms was necessary before the spectrum could be fully investigated under strict experimental conditions.[21] But it is apparent that at an early stage the Greeks exploited their knowledge of rainbows formed under other, artificial conditions, in trying to explain the meteorological phenomenon.

In astronomy, then, and in much of what the Greeks called 'meteorology', we are at liberty to suggest that the early theorists were often uncritical, or that they seriously underestimated the complexity of the phenomena; but where experiment is impossible for objective, physical reasons, the criticism that they failed to use the experimental || method is, clearly, wide of the mark. But we have now to deal with the more interesting and more difficult problems of the role of experiment in other fields, and first of all in the sciences we know as physics and chemistry. First physics, and I may begin by considering briefly those departments of physics, such as optics, acoustics, statics and hydrostatics, in which the achievements of Greek science are by no means negligible. Concerning the Greek contribution to the study of optics, in particular, we have comparatively good information, since there are several treatises extant either in the original or in Latin translations which are specially devoted to the subject, the most important being Euclid's *Optics*, the *De Speculis* (presumed to be a digest of the *Catoptrics* of Hero of Alexandria) and a Latin translation of an Arabic version of another Greek treatise on optics which there is no good reason to doubt is the work of Ptolemy.[22] These works make it abundantly clear not only that the Greeks were successful in their application of geometry to the study of reflection and refraction, but also that some investigators undertook quite extensive experiments to corroborate the principles of optics which they formulated. Some passages from Ptolemy's *Optics* are worth quoting to illustrate one investigator's methods. At the beginning of Book III (ch. 3, 88.9ff. Lejeune) the writer sets out three elementary principles or laws of reflection. These are (1) that objects that are seen in mirrors are seen in the direction of the visual ray which falls on them when reflected by the mirror; (2) that things that are seen in mirrors are seen on the perpendicular which falls from the object to the surface of the mirror and is produced; and (3) the position of the reflected

[20] *Mete.* 374b3ff. He refers, also, to the rainbows formed under certain conditions when an oar is raised out of the water (374a29ff.).

[21] This was first achieved by Newton in his *Opticks* (1704), following on the work of Descartes and Marci.

[22] This is the conclusion of the most recent editor, Lejeune, 1956: Introduction, 13–26

ray, from the eye to the mirror and from the mirror to the object, is such that each of its two parts contains the point of reflection and makes equal angles with the perpendicular to the mirror at that point.[23] The truth of these principles, he goes on, is confirmed by the phenomena, and he proceeds to cite a series of simple experiments to corroborate his laws. Thus to confirm his first principle he remarks (III, ch. 4, 89.5ff.):

> in the case of all mirrors [that is plane, convex and concave] we find that if we mark the points on the surface through which the images are seen, and cover these points, then the image of the object will certainly no longer be visible. But then when we uncover the points one by one and look at the uncovered points, both the points and the image of the object will be seen together on the straight line drawn to the summit of the visual ray [i.e. the eye].

Further experiments follow: one which is particularly remarkable involves the use of three mirrors, one plane, one convex and one concave, ‖ and confirms very neatly that the angle of incidence is equal to the angle of reflection in each case.

These are simple, but generally very effective, tests undertaken to corroborate the elementary laws of reflection, but elsewhere the author carries out experiments of a greater complexity, notably in his discussion of refraction in Book V. There (V, ch. 3, 224.10ff.) he first points out that as in reflection, so too in refraction, the image is seen at the intersection of the line of the visual ray and the perpendicular drawn from the object to the reflecting or refracting surface, and here he refers to an experiment which goes back at least as far as Archimedes,[24] in which a coin is put into an opaque vessel in such a position that it is just hidden by the lip of the vessel, but comes into view when water is poured into the vessel. But not content merely to state certain general principles of refraction, he undertakes detailed investigations to measure the amount of refraction which takes place at different angles of incidence, and in different media. First (V, ch. 7, 227.1ff.) he describes the setting of his apparatus. To measure the angles he uses a circular disk, each quadrant of which is divided into ninety parts (i.e. like a

[23] With reference to the diagram where *MR* is the mirror, *A* the eye, *B* the object, *B′* the image, *O* the point at which the visual ray strikes the mirror, and *TO* and *BP* perpendiculars to the mirror, these three principles are: (1) *B′* lies on *AO* produced, (2) *B′* lies on *BP* produced, (3) $\angle TOA = \angle TOB$. (After Cohen and Drabkin, 1948: 269, n. 1.)

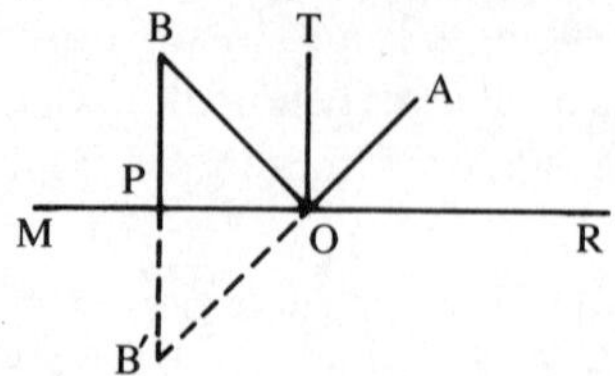

[24] See Lejeune, 1956: n. 9 to 225.9.

protractor): this disk is set up in a bowl of clean water so that the water just covers the bottom half of the circle. He then describes how a coloured marker is to be placed at different points along the circumference of one or other of the two quadrants which are above the water level, and how sightings are to be taken so that the coloured marker and the centre of the disk are aligned with the eye. The next operation is to move a small, thin rod along the circumference of the opposite quadrant which is under the water until the extremity of the rod appears in line with the coloured marker and the centre of the disk. This enables one to determine both the angle of incidence and the angle of refraction, and when these are measured, we find that the angle of incidence is always greater than the angle of refraction, and that as the angle of incidence increases the amount of refraction becomes progressively greater. The results obtained by Ptolemy are given in detail: when the angle of incidence is 10 degrees, the angle of refraction will be about 8 degrees; when the angle of incidence is 20 degrees, the angle of refraction will be 15½ degrees, and so on for angles of incidence up to 80 degrees. Concluding the passage with the remark that 'this is the method by which we have discovered the amount of refraction in the case of water', Ptolemy adds the note: 'we have found no perceptible difference in this respect between waters of different densities or rarities' (ch. 12, 230.4ff.). It is worth drawing attention to the point that Ptolemy evidently tried the same experiment with different kinds of waters to see whether this gave different results, and elsewhere in the *Optics* we find set out in detail the results of his investigations of the refraction of other media, namely from air to glass and from water to glass.[25]

In investigating the problems of reflection and refraction Ptolemy carried out extensive experiments to corroborate his general laws and in particular to establish that there is a definite quantitative relationship between the angle of incidence and the || angle of refraction. Both the problems in question, and the experiments used to study them, are, of course, quite elementary. But I have chosen this example deliberately in order to indicate that where the circumstances were favourable, that is where the problems are relatively simple and where they could be investigated empirically without too great difficulty, we do find evidence that detailed experiments were sometimes carried out in antiquity. But is this the case, perhaps, only in quite late antiquity? Are we to consider the experiments of a Ptolemy in optics, or of a Philo or a Hero in pneumatics, as quite exceptional, as marking, in fact, a radical break with the methods of investigation used in earlier periods? Or is what distinguishes Ptolemy from earlier writers on optics merely the

[25] It should be noted that Ptolemy considers the ray from the eye, not that from the object, the incident ray. For his results, which are expressed to within half a degree, compare the tables given by Brunet and Mieli, 1935: 825ff. *On the elements of 'fudge' in Ptolemy's statement of his results, that is on the way in which the purported observations have been interpreted *before* they are recorded in order to get them to tally with the underlying general theory, see below, chapter 13 (pp. 320f.).

success or thoroughness with which he applied techniques of investigation which had been used, though not fully exploited, before? Without entering into the various problems raised by the development of each one of the branches of physics in antiquity, I may briefly consider the question in so far as it concerns the earliest period of Greek science, for poor though our information is, there are grounds for believing that some problems of physics had already begun to be investigated with the help of simple tests in the Presocratic period or in the early fourth century. Some of this evidence is well known. We are all acquainted with the legends that purport to describe the experiments which led Pythagoras to discover the numerical relations between the musical intervals of the octave, fifth and fourth. One story has it that he made this discovery by measuring the weights of hammers which made different notes when struck, another that he did so as a result of experiments in which he attached different weights to a string and observed a relationship between tension and pitch, a third that he filled jars with varying amounts of water and noted a relation between the quantity of water and the sounds the jar made when struck, a fourth that he measured the lengths of string or pipe which gave various notes. These accounts, as is well known, contain much that is pure fantasy:[26] in the majority of cases when the test is carried out in the manner described in our sources, it does not, in fact, reveal the simple relations between the various musical intervals. Nevertheless we should not dismiss these stories as entirely worthless, for all their obvious inaccuracies. For one thing the very fact that such legends circulated about this discovery in antiquity suggests some recognition (if only a theoretical recognition) of the value of the experimental method, for example in determining which are the causative factors governing a particular effect.[27] Secondly, if most of these supposed tests do not, in fact, yield the results reported, exceptions must be made of two of the investigations referred to, those with the monochord and with the columns of air in pipes, for here, of course, other things being equal (e.g. the thickness, material and tension of the string) the relations between the musical intervals are readily determined with reference to the lengths of the string or pipe. We have other evidence, too, || besides the stories which refer to Pythagoras himself, which tends to confirm that the early Pythagoreans carried out certain empirical investigations in acoustics. There is the interesting, though admittedly obscure, report that Hippasus constructed bronze disks of varying thicknesses to produce certain harmonies,[28] and in a fragment preserved by Porphyry, Archytas

[26] See, for example, Guthrie, 1962: 220ff., esp. 223ff., who gives the Greek sources and comments on the various difficulties which these stories contain. Guthrie concludes that if the discovery of the relations between the intervals is indeed Pythagoras', it was no doubt on the monochord that he carried out his experiments.

[27] Cf. the judgement of Zubov (1959: 224): 'Allein die Tatsache, dass eine solche Legende in der Antike aufkam, zeugt von dem Verständnis des Wesens des Experimentes als einer rationalen Untersuchung der Wirklichkeit.'

[28] A scholium on Plato, *Phaedo* 108D (DK 18A12) contains a report of Aristoxenus which refers

refers to a variety of phenomena in an attempt to establish his theory relating the pitch of a note to its 'speed', and some of the evidence he cited seems to derive from first-hand investigations (e.g. the variations in the pitch of the sound produced when a stick is moved at different speeds, and the notes produced by different lengths of pipe).[29] Finally it is worth recalling that Plato too provides evidence of early empirical investigations in acoustics, for in the *Republic* Socrates is made to refer (with disapproval) to those who 'measure the harmonies and sounds they hear against one another' (531 A1ff.) and who 'look for numbers in these heard harmonies' (C1f.).

Acoustics, then, is one field in which the Greeks both observed and conducted rudimentary empirical tests from a very early period, and the same may be said of pneumatics and of what was later to become (with Archimedes) the science of hydrostatics. Beginning with Empedocles and Anaxagoras we find a whole series of Greek theorists who investigated the phenomena of air pressure by observing the behaviour of air enclosed in the clepsydra and other vessels, both repeating and modifying the simple experience described by Empedocles himself (Fr. 100). The author of the pseudo-Aristotelian *Problemata*, for example, objects against Anaxagoras that it is not enough simply to say that air is the cause of the water not entering the bulb of the clepsydra when the tube at the top is blocked, for in some circumstances, viz. when the clepsydra is immersed obliquely in the water, this does not happen (914b9ff.). In the Hippocratic Corpus there are several texts which refer to simple investigations of air and water pressure, as for example the creation of what we should call a partial vacuum by inverting a narrow-necked vessel containing water or oil, and the release of the vacuum by piercing a hole in the vessel.[30] But two rather more elaborate tests are worth mentioning particularly. One writer describes a test which demonstrates that water finds its own level: this involves setting up an apparatus of three or more intercommunicating vessels on level ground (this point is stressed), and the writer describes how the whole system may be filled or emptied by filling or emptying any one of the vessels (though he then uses this piece of information to support a highly speculative theory of the interplay of the humours in the body).[31] || And another quite ambitious test is described in the treatise *On the Nature of the Child* (ch. 17, L VII 498.17ff.). This involves putting three different substances (earth, sand and lead-filings)

to Hippasus' construction, and it seems possible that this may have been designed (as Burnet suggested in a note in his edn of the *Phaedo ad loc.*) to provide a model to illustrate the harmony of the spheres.

29 Fr. 1. The significance of this fragment for our understanding of the role of experiment in Presocratic, particularly Pythagorean, philosophy, has been discussed by Senn, 1929: 271ff.

30 *On Diseases* IV, ch. 57, L VII 612.6ff. (on which see Senn, 1929: 248ff.) and ch. 51, 588.17ff. Cf. also *On the Nature of the Child*, ch. 18, 502.2f., and ch. 25, 522.20ff. (on which see Senn, 1929: 245ff.).

31 *On Diseases* IV, ch. 39, L VII 556.17ff., on which Senn commented (1929: 232): 'wieder eine anschauliche Beschreibung eines einwandfrei durchgeführten physikalischen Experiments'.

into a bladder full of water and agitating them by blowing on them through a tube let down into the vessel. The author refers to this test to support his theory that the various parts of the body are formed by the action of like coming to like, but it seems probable that this test was originally designed not to illustrate the action of like-to-like, but to study the reactions of substances of different specific gravities in partial suspension in water, and that the author of *On the Nature of the Child* attempted to adapt this experiment to suit his own purposes.[32]

Further examples of simple physical experiments might be mentioned not only from the Hippocratic Corpus but also from Aristotle,[33] but it is apparent from those we have considered that in some branches of physics, where the problems are fairly elementary and where tests could be carried out without any great difficulty, certain rudimentary experiments were conducted even as early as the fifth or the fourth century B.C., even if these are neither so precise nor so complex as those conducted later by Philo and Hero in pneumatics, for instance, or by Ptolemy in optics. In some fields, then, there is a definite (if only a quite slow) progress, in antiquity, in the application of experimental methods to the study of certain physical phenomena, and in some cases the beginnings of this development can be traced already in the Presocratic period or shortly afterwards. But is it not the case that in dynamics, at least, the efforts of the earliest Greek scientists, and indeed of Greek scientists as a whole, were quite vitiated by their failure to experiment? It is all very well, I shall be told, to point to a few exceptional cases where the Greeks did conduct some simple tests, but the significance of these pales by comparison with the manifest failure to investigate the problems of motion experimentally. Can we deny that the main reason why Aristotle in particular failed to formulate adequate laws of motion, and why Galileo was so much more successful in this field, was simply this, that the first quite ignored the experimental method, while the second was indefatigable in devising and conducting practical tests to corroborate his theories? To assess how much truth there is in these judgements, we should first consider the early history of dynamics and the relation between Aristotle's theory of motion and earlier views. It is hardly an exaggeration to say that before

[32] Senn, 1929: 242ff., concludes that the test described was probably in origin a 'Sedimentierungsversuch', which the Hippocratic author applied to support his theory of the action of the 'breath' causing like substances to come together in the developing embryo.

[33] Perhaps the best known example in the Hippocratic Corpus is the test described in *On Airs, Waters, Places* ch. 8, *CMG* I 1.63.12ff., in which a bowl of water is left out of doors to freeze and when the water is thawed it is found on being remeasured to be less than the original quantity (a test which the writer supposes supports his contention that freezing causes the 'lightest and finest' part of the water to be dried up and disappear). In Aristotle we find, for example, two references to the fact that if a vessel is heated and then inverted over water, as the air in the vessel cools it contracts and some of the water is drawn up into the vessel, though it may be thought unlikely that Aristotle himself originated this test (*Cael.* 312b13ff.; *GA* 739b10ff., reading κωνικά with Platt, for ἀκόνιτα).

Aristotle himself there is nothing that can be called dynamics at all in Greek science. The Presocratics refer in various contexts to the attraction of like things to one another, but this generalisation embraces a very wide range of phenomena. The || action of gravitational forces may be included under this heading, but so too may the behaviour of animals: in a fragment quoted by Sextus Empiricus, Democritus refers explicitly to both animate and inanimate examples to illustrate how like is drawn to, and known by, like, that is on the one hand to certain gregarious species of animals (pigeons and cranes are mentioned in particular) and on the other to the separation of seeds according to their kinds in a winnowing-basket, and to that of pebbles according to their different shapes on the sea-shore.[34] It is Aristotle himself, then, who makes the first serious attempt to formulate general theories in dynamics in which the relevant factors governing the velocity of a moving object are interrelated.*[35] In various passages in the *Physics* and the *De Caelo* he isolates two main factors which govern the speed of a moving object, namely its weight (which in the case of objects of the same kind varies directly with the size) and the 'density' of the medium.[36] And he puts forward theories concerning the relation between these factors and velocity in 'natural', and in 'forced', motion. Thus in natural motion, that is in the case of freely falling or freely rising bodies, velocity is said to be directly proportional to the weight of the body and inversely proportional to the density of the medium, while in forced motion velocity is said to be directly proportional to the force applied and inversely proportional to the mass of the body moved[37] (and Aristotle also suggests that whereas in natural motion the speed of the object increases the nearer it comes to its 'natural place', in forced motion the velocity decreases as the object progresses further away from the propelling agent[38]).

These, the main theories of Aristotelian dynamics, represent, then, the first attempt to formulate abstract 'laws' of motion, to establish the relation between the various factors which determine the speed of moving objects,

[34] Sext. *M.* VII 117 (DK 68B164), cf. also Aet. IV 19.13 (DK A128). Plato uses a similar model to illustrate the separation of like to like in the Receptacle at *Ti.* 52E-53A.

*[35] My discussion of this issue on this and the following page underestimates, I should now say, the problem posed by the disparity between the issues with which Aristotle is concerned, in the various texts in *Ph.* and *Cael.* that refer to natural and forced motion, and a modern, or at least post-Galilean, preoccupation with the 'laws' of motion as such. For a more qualified statement, paying greater attention to the contexts in which Aristotle's remarks are introduced, and with references to recent studies, see Lloyd, 1987: 217–22.

[36] He also notes, e.g. at *Cael.* 313a14ff., that the speed of an object is influenced by its shape.

[37] E.g. *Cael.* 273b30ff.; 277b3ff.; *Ph.* 215a25ff. (on natural motion) and *Ph.* 249b27ff. (on forced motion).

[38] *Ph.* 230b24ff. and *Cael.* 277a27ff. At *Cael.* 288a19ff. it is suggested that in some cases the highest speed is attained not at the point from which flight begins nor where it ends but ἀνὰ μέσον, but if this means what it appears to mean, namely that the highest speed is attained in the middle of the flight, it is hardly possible to interpret it consistently with Aristotle's known doctrines. See the notes of Stocks in the Oxford Translation and of Guthrie in the Loeb edition of the *De Caelo*.

while discounting irrelevant considerations. Aristotle assumes, for example, that the medium is completely homogeneous, although it is never so in fact,[39] and while he notes that the speed of an object is influenced by its shape, he leaves this too out of account when proposing his general doctrines of natural and forced motion. But then the next point that should be made is that the theories he suggests correspond to observed phenomena much more closely than might at first sight seem likely in view of the discrepancy between Aristotelian and Newtonian dynamics. Aristotle has often been taken to task for assuming that the velocity of a freely falling body varies directly with its weight, but it is as well to be clear where his mistake lies. The fact is that in air heavier bodies do fall more rapidly than lighter ones of the same shape and size (though this is not true, of course, in a vacuum). Aristotle was correct in assuming that there is some || relationship between weight and velocity in motion that takes place in a medium, although the relationship is not a simple one of direct proportion. Then too it is an obvious fact of experience that motion through a dense medium is slower than through a rare one, but again Aristotle's theory oversimplifies the relationship between the density of the medium and velocity. Moreover the consequences of this were especially unfortunate, for it led him to deny that motion through a void is possible (the velocity would be infinitely great),[40] and here the contrast between Aristotelian and modern dynamics is most pointed, for while we should say that the effects of the resistance of the medium should be discounted in considering the relationship between force, mass and velocity, Aristotle assumes throughout his discussion that motion must take place through a medium.

The 'laws' of motion which Aristotle proposes are not utterly at variance with experience: rather they are hasty generalisations based on superficial observations. His discussion of the problems of motion in the *Physics* and *De Caelo* is highly theoretical (it is not often that he explicitly refers to empirical evidence in this connection at all), but even so it is at least arguable that in assuming that motion necessarily takes place through a medium, he stayed too close, rather than not close enough, to the data of experience. Yet this does not alter the fact that he quite failed to verify his theories experimentally, for if empirical evidence is only seldom referred to in this context in the *Physics* and *De Caelo*, experiments, whether his own or those of his predecessors or contemporaries, are mentioned even more rarely.[41] Fur-

[39] See Cohen and Drabkin, 1948: 203, n. 1. [40] *Ph.* IV, ch. 8, esp. 215a24ff.; 216a11ff.

[41] A notable exception is the passage at *Cael.* 311b9ff., where he says that each of the elements, except fire, has weight in its own 'natural place' and adduces as proof of this that a bladder weighs more when inflated than when empty. This experiment has been sharply criticised, e.g. by Ross, Introduction to his edn of the *Physics*, pp. 26ff., on the grounds (1) that the supposed experimental fact is not correct, and (2) that Aristotle's theory is not true to the experimental facts he thought he had at his command. But whether or not a bladder will weigh more when inflated will depend on, among other things, (1) whether it is inflated with atmospheric air or

thermore, nothing precluded the carrying out of certain simple tests which would have indicated the falsity of his general theories of natural and forced motion (even if they would not necessarily have suggested a better alternative account). In the *Discorsi* published in 1638, Galileo describes in detail his experiments with a pendulum and with an inclined plane (down which he rolled bronze balls) and he also refers to the more famous experiment of dropping balls of different weights from a considerable height (though several scholars doubt Viviani's report that he carried out this experiment from the Leaning Tower of Pisa). None of these tests was beyond the range of what was technically possible for the ancient Greeks,[42] and any of them might have been used to || demonstrate the inadequacies of Aristotelian dynamics (and in particular the doctrine that in natural motion velocity is directly proportional to weight). Here, then, it seems that we have a clear case in which the earlier Greek investigators might have carried out certain tests in conjunction with their theories, but quite failed to do so; but if this judgement is true in the main, two reservations should be added. First we must repeat that what Galileo understood, but Aristotle failed to appreciate and indeed would have denied, was that in studying the conditions of uniform or accelerated motion, the effects of friction and of the resistance of the medium should be discounted. Thus while it was certainly open to Aristotle to perform the three types of experiment I have mentioned, yet so long as the necessary corrections were not made to offset the effects of friction and air resistance, the actual results obtained from such experiments would certainly be difficult to interpret and perhaps even positively misleading. Second, and more important, while it is undoubtedly the case that Aristotle himself failed, in general, to undertake practical tests in connection with his theory of motion, this is much less true of some of his successors. Some of the examples of objects in motion which are discussed in the *Problemata* appear to derive less from common experience than from deliberate investigations,[43] and Strato too carried out certain tests in this field, for

with breath (which contains a higher proportion of carbon dioxide), (2) whether it is inflated under pressure or not, and (3) the amount of water vapour in the gas with which it is filled. At least three different attempts were made to carry out this test in antiquity (by Aristotle, by Ptolemy and by Simplicius, see Simp. *in Cael.* 710.24ff. and cf. also Anon. Lond. XXXI 33ff.), but that three different results were obtained is, perhaps, hardly surprising, considering the lack of precise weighing instruments and the number of factors which might influence the outcome of the test.

42 The Greeks had no precise means of measuring time, but no more had Galileo. In the *Discorsi* he describes the method he employed for measuring time in his dynamical experiments, namely that of weighing the amounts of water which percolated through a thin jet, a simple adaptation of the principle of the water-clock.

43 E.g. the account of objects rebounding from a plane, and that of the figures described by certain solids, namely the cylinder and the cone, when these are revolved (*Pr.* XVI 4 and 13, 913b6ff. and 915b18ff., and XVI 5, 913b37ff.). A passage in the *Mechanics* (858a13ff.) is worth quoting as it illustrates the difficulty which the writer experienced in tackling the problem of 'why objects which are hurled come to a standstill'. 'Does it stop when the force which started it fails, or because the object is drawn in a contrary direction, or is it due to its

example to establish the fact that falling bodies undergo acceleration.[44] Such empirical investigations as are recorded are all quite rudimentary (Strato apparently observed the impact made by stones dropped from different heights, and the way in which when water falls from a considerable height, its flow is continuous at the top, but broken at the bottom of its fall), but they may be taken to indicate that the possibility of carrying out practical tests to illuminate the problems of dynamics was not wholly ignored by Aristotle's immediate successors. Nor should we fail to note that this method was used with much greater success in later antiquity. Philoponus, for example, challenged the fundamental assumptions of Aristotelian dynamics on both theoretical and empirical grounds. Arguing against the doctrine that the speed of a falling body is proportional to its weight, he says 'but this is completely false. And this may be confirmed more forcibly by actual observation than by any sort of verbal demonstration', and he then proceeds to adduce (as a thousand years later Galileo was to adduce) the evidence of what happens when you drop two different weights from the same height: 'you will see that the ratio of the times required for the motion does not depend on the ratio of the weights, but that the difference in time is a very small one.'[45]

The next field we must discuss is chemistry, or rather what passes for chemistry in antiquity, that is, the study of the constituent elements of substances and their || interactions. Here the Presocratics made several very important contributions, though nearly all of them relate to the conceptual framework of 'chemical' theory, rather than to the discovery of facts. Thus it was one of Empedocles' most striking achievements that he explained how a variety of different substances may be derived from a limited number of primary elements by suggesting that the elements combine with one another in different proportions:[46] something like the modern 'law of fixed proportions', which states that chemical compounds always contain their constituent elements in fixed and invariable proportions by weight, was in fact assumed long before it could be demonstrated experimentally. Aristotle, in turn, succeeded, for example, in distinguishing various modes of mixture and combination, including σύνθεσις (i.e. an aggregation of different substances in what we should term a mechanical mixture, for example a pile of barley and wheat grains) and μίξις (in which the component substances are fused and the resulting compound acquires new properties, for example when tin and copper combine to form bronze – though it should be noted that not all of the examples which Aristotle uses to illustrate μίξις refer to what we should class as chemical compounds).[47] But then one asks, how far is it the

downward tendency, which is stronger than the force which threw it? Or is it absurd to discuss such questions while the principle escapes us (ἢ ἄτοπον τὸ ταῦτ' ἀπορεῖν, ἀφέντα τὴν ἀρχήν;)?' (transl. E. S. Forster).

[44] See Simplicius, *in Ph.* 916.10ff. (Wehrli, 1950: Fr. 73).

[45] Philoponus, *in Ph.* 683.16ff.

[46] See Frr. 96 and 98 on the formula or composition of bone, blood and 'other forms of flesh'.

[47] Under μίξις Aristotle includes the κρᾶσις of liquids such as wine and water, for here too an

case that early Greek theories concerning the constituent elements of things were merely a series of conjectures which they never attempted to verify or falsify by means of experimental investigations? Now as in the early history of dynamics, so too in the development of theories about the constituent elements of things, attempts were made to formulate systematic general theories before much empirical research had been undertaken. But by the time of Aristotle or shortly afterwards detailed empirical investigations had begun to be carried out in this field. Aristotle's discussion of the nature and number of the elements in the *De Generatione et Corruptione* is largely dogmatic,[48] but if we turn to the *Meteorologica*, the extent of the knowledge which it displays concerning the reactions of different substances to various simple tests is remarkable.[49] It is true that Aristotle tends to present his results in the form of generalisations, for example 'of things which are solidified by heat or cold, those that are soluble are dissolved by their opposites. For those that are solidified by dry heat || are dissolved by water (which is wet and cold) and those that are solidified by cold are dissolved by fire' (*Mete.* IV 382b33ff.). But much detailed knowledge underlies these generalisations. Aristotle evidently collected a good deal of information concerning the physical properties of a wide variety of substances (i.e. which substances are ductile, which malleable, which fissile and so on) and also concerning their reactions to fire and to water, to being burned, boiled or dissolved in various types of liquid. Much of what is contained in *Meteorologica* IV was no doubt common knowledge. Some of his more specialised information comes from an acquaintance with such contemporary industrial*[50] processes as iron-making.[51] But some of his knowledge clearly derives from deliberate investigations (whether or not is was Aristotle himself who originally undertook these). Thus he says that salt and soda are soluble

interaction may take place and the resultant compound may be ὁμοιομερής (*GC* I, ch. 10, esp. 328a26ff. and b3ff.). On Aristotle's theory of different types of mixture and combination, see esp. Joachim, 1904: 72ff.

[48] Thus in *GC* II, chh. 1ff. when he sets out to determine the nature and number of the elements, he argues (1) that coming to be and passing away are impossible without perceptible bodies (328b32f.), which in turn cannot exist apart from contrarieties; for a body must be either heavy or light, either hot or cold (329a10ff.), (2) that the principles of perceptible body will be tangible contrarieties (329b7ff.), and (3) that the tangible contrarieties may be reduced to two pairs of opposites, hot and cold, and wet and dry, but these cannot be resolved any further (329b24ff.; 330a24ff.).

[49] For the purposes of this paper I shall include the fourth book of the *Meterologica* as this is clearly evidence for the work of Aristotle's immediate school, even if some have denied that it is an authentic text of Aristotle himself (e.g. Hammer-Jensen, 1915: 113ff., and Gottschalk, 1961: 67ff., and contrast Düring, 1944: 17ff. and Lee, 1952: xiiiff. and 1962: vii, who have argued that there are no good reasons for not accepting the book as a whole, or in the main, as the work of Aristotle).

*[50] This term has misleading and anachronistic associations and I would now characterise the processes in question more simply as technological.

[51] See *Mete.* 383a32ff. (with Lee's useful note) and cf. 383a24f. on the manufacture of pottery and 383b7ff. on that of millstones.

in some liquids, such as water, but not in others (he specifies olive oil, *Mete.* 383b13ff.). Among the substances which he says freeze solid with cold are not only urine, vinegar, whey and lye (κονία, the alkaline solution used as a detergent), but also ἰχώρ (serum) (389a9ff.). And he distinguishes between different types of wine according to their combustibility and their readiness to freeze (387b9ff; 388a33ff.).

Sometimes, indeed, Aristotle explicitly claims to have discovered or proved something by a practical test, although the experiments which he does describe in the *Meteorologica* have often been severely criticised by modern scholars.[52] In one case these criticisms are probably quite justified. At 358b34ff., when he wishes to show that the saltness of the sea is due to an admixture, he describes an experiment in which a wax jar is let down into the sea with its top securely fastened, and he says that when the jar is recovered, fresh water will be found to have percolated through the wax walls.[53] But, as many scholars have pointed out, this does not, in fact, occur, and they have concluded that Aristotle never undertook this experiment himself but is simply repeating the story on hearsay. This is, no doubt, the most probable explanation, and yet it seems just possible that he did carry out the test, and that he found a small quantity of fresh water inside the jar which was the result of the condensation of water vapour which the jar had contained before it was let down into the sea (though this would not, of course, alter the fact that his theory as to how the water came to be there is quite incorrect). Another passage in which he claims to have carried out some experiments occurs in the same chapter at 358b16ff. 'We have proved by experiment (πεπειραμένοι)', he says, 'that salt water when evaporated becomes fresh and the vapour does not form sea water when it condenses again.' So far so good, and Aristotle clearly deserves full marks both for the method he used and the results he obtained. But he then goes on: 'and the same is true in other cases. For wine and all other χυμοί (flavoured liquids) that evaporate and condense into liquid again, become water.' But it is far from being the case, as editors of the *Meteorologica* and others have pointed out, that when wine is evaporated in a still it becomes water, and Lee, || for one, concludes that 'Aristotle had apparently only performed the experiment with water'. But in this instance, too, another explanation is possible, and even, I think, more likely. It is commonly assumed, I believe, that if Aristotle tried these experiments at all, he used some sort of still or condenser, but I wonder whether this was the case. The vapour driven off a boiling liquid could be collected in small quantities on any cold flat surface held directly over the vessel (the author of the Hippocratic treatise *On Breaths* refers to the phenomenon in question and uses it to suggest an account of how sweat is

[52] E.g. Diels, 1905: 310ff.

[53] Cf. *HA* 590a24ff. Aristotle's statement was apparently accepted on trust by Pliny (*HN* 31.37) and by Aelian (IX 64).

formed)[54] and it should also be noted that the most primitive method of distillation employed in antiquity seems to have made no use of a condenser, the vapour being collected in an absorbent material (such as wool) which was held over the boiling liquid.[55] But if wine is evaporated and the vapour collected on a plate or some such object held over the boiling wine, the liquid which condenses is a colourless, almost flavourless fluid of low alcoholic content which would pass for 'water' as naturally as the liquid collected from evaporating sea-water. To my mind, then, it seems probable enough that this is what Aristotle is referring to when he says that 'wine and flavoured liquids' become water, and we should not necessarily conclude that he is simply repeating something on hearsay.[56]

The *Meteorologica* itself is the first extant work which deals in any great detail with the properties of different substances or their reactions to certain simple tests,[57] but thereafter Aristotle's work in this field was followed up and extended by other investigators. Theophrastus' book *On Stones*, in particular, is an important collection of data concerning the properties and kinds of mineral substances, and *On Fire* contains a quite detailed discussion concerning the species of fire and the effects of different forms of heat. It appears, indeed, that in the latter part of the fourth century certain inquiries were undertaken in the field we should call chemistry which were parallel to, though less intensive than, the researches carried out in zoology and botany. But why, then, one may ask, did these investigations into the properties of substances not lead to any radical advance in doctrine, or at least to the overthrow of the four-element theory of Aristotle? Now the fact is that the research that was done did lead both to an increase of factual knowledge and to the suggestion of certain modifications in the Aristotelian doctrine. Aristotle himself conceded that his method of classifying compounds according to whether earth or water predominated in them left certain problems which he found difficult to resolve.[58] But then the work of Theophrastus raised two major difficulties: first there was his detailed analysis of different types of || 'earth' (*On Stones*, ch. 48ff., especially) which implicitly raised the problem of the basic nature of this 'simple body', and then in *On Fire* (chh. 1ff.) he explicitly raised the question of the nature of fire

[54] *Flat.* ch. 8; *CMG* I 1.96.15ff.

[55] This method of distillation is described in Dioscorides I 72.3.

[56] It may be noted that elsewhere in *Mete.* IV different sorts of wine are distinguished according to their reactions to being heated or frozen: new wine, for example, is said to thicken most under the influence of heat and to solidify least under the influence of cold (388a33ff.; cf. also 384a4ff. and 387b9ff.).

[57] *Mete.* IV does, however, owe a good deal to Plato's *Timaeus*, particularly to the account of the varieties of water and of earth and of their compounds, 58D-61C.

[58] In general, Aristotle considers most compounds to be composed of water and earth (those that are solidified by cold and melted by fire are said to have a greater proportion of water, those that are solidified by heat to contain more earth), but olive oil and semen, in particular, both present difficulties which he attempts to resolve by suggesting that these are compounds of water and air or πνεῦμα (*Mete.* 383b20ff.; *GA* 735a29ff.).

and drew attention to certain important respects in which it differs from the other 'simple bodies' (notably in that it always exists in a substrate). If the four-element theory as a whole survived these and other challenges in antiquity, this was due to a complex of reasons, partly no doubt because the methods of investigation used were still fairly rudimentary (in particular insufficient use was made of quantitative measurements, even though the Greeks were accustomed to distinguish different types of waters, and indeed also different solids, by their weight[59]), but partly also because of the nature of the four-element theory itself: this provided at once an extremely comprehensive, and a quite imprecise, theory embracing each of the different states of matter, solid, liquid and gaseous, so that the effect of much of the research that was undertaken was to modify the application of the theory in detail rather than to show that a more adequate general theory was needed.[60]

So far I have dealt entirely with the physical sciences, bearing in mind that it is to these that reference is usually made to substantiate the view that there is a radical difference in method and outlook between ancient and modern science. My remarks on biology and medicine must be even more compressed than my discussion has been so far. In the biological sciences, the key method of research, from Alcmaeon onwards, was dissection, including not only the dissection of dead adult animals, but also (as time went on) the dissection of embryos and vivisection.[61] Now dissection is always an experimental procedure in the weak sense in that it involves not simply direct observation, but 'observations provoquées', that is, a piece of research deliberately undertaken to discover facts. But sometimes we find dissections used not merely to uncover facts but to prove or disprove suggested theories. At *GA* 764a33ff., Aristotle is able to refute the doctrine which we find expressed in various forms in earlier writers, that the sex of the embryo is determined by the side of the womb on which it is conceived. 'Male and female twins are often found together in the same part of the uterus', he says. 'This we have observed sufficiently by dissection in all the Vivipara, both land-animals and fish.'[62] And in another passage (*GA* 746a19ff.) he again refers to the evidence

[59] The author of *On Airs, Waters, Places* (ch. 1, *CMG* I 1.56.7ff.) for example, notes that waters differ a good deal from one another both in taste (ἐν τῷ στόματι) and *in weight* (ἐν τῷ σταθμῷ), while in *On Stones* (chh. 22 and 39) Theophrastus refers to differences in 'density' (πυκνότης) and weight (βάρος) as methods of distinguishing between different types of 'stones' (including, e.g., ores).

[60] I have dealt solely with the four-element theory. But it may be noted that its main rival in the fourth century, the atomistic theory, was equally comprehensive and vague, and equally incapable of being corroborated or falsified by means of practical tests.

[61] The history of the use of dissection in antiquity has been described by Edelstein, 1933: 100ff.

[62] At *GA* 765a21ff., Aristotle refers to those who held that the sex of the embryo is determined by whether the seed of the male comes from the right or the left testicle, and who apparently thought that if one of the testicles is tied up or excised, the offspring produced are all of the same sex – a passage which indicates that some earlier writers were aware of the possibility of putting this theory to the test, even if they evidently assumed the results of such a test to be a foregone conclusion.

of dissections to disprove the notion that the || embryo derives nourishment from sucking the side of the womb.[63] From the Hippocratic texts one may mention first a passage in *On the Sacred Disease* where the writer refers to the evidence of post-mortem dissections of goats to establish that the 'sacred' disease has a natural, that is a pathological, origin. But two experimental dissections described in *On the Heart* are especially worth noting. In ch. 2 (L IX 80.9ff.) the writer considers the question of whether any drink passes from the oesophagus via the trachea into the lungs. He remarks that the epiglottis covers the larynx exactly, but suggests nevertheless that a small part of what we drink penetrates by this route into the lungs. This he proves, to his own satisfaction at least, by an experiment in which he stains some water, gives it to a pig to drink, and then cuts open the pig's windpipe as it drinks: 'you will find it stained with the drink', he says, although he notes that 'this is not an operation that the man in the street can undertake'. The theory the writer believes he has proved is in fact incorrect (if the pig's throat was stained, this was no doubt because the animal choked), but the method he uses to verify his theory is exemplary. Nor is this use of the experimental method an isolated example in this work. Later on he refers to another more complicated experiment which met with greater success. Having described the general structure of the heart (where he notices, among other things, that the ventricles and the auricles do not contract simultaneously)[64] he turns in ch. 10 to its 'hidden membranes', giving a brief but exact description of the semi-lunar valves which lie at the base of the aorta and the pulmonary artery. But he not only describes their structure: he investigates their function, showing that if on removing the heart you attempt to force water down either the aorta or the pulmonary artery, the semi-lunar valves will prevent any fluid passing into the ventricles of the heart, and he even notices that the seal formed by the valves is more effective on the left side of the heart (i.e. at the base of the aorta) than on the right (at the base of the pulmonary artery).[65] It is perhaps not out of place to note that this demonstration of the irreversibility of the flow of the blood out of the heart was an essential (if only a preliminary) step towards the discovery of the circulation of the blood.[66]

Many other experiments (whether involving the use of dissection or not)

[63] This theory is advanced in *On Fleshes*, ch. 6, L VIII 592.11ff., for example, where it is supported by various arguments, e.g. that the new-born baby instinctively knows how to suck.

[64] Ch. 8, L IX 86.4ff.

[65] Ch. 10, 86.13–88.9. At 88.6, the writer asserts that not even air can be pumped back through the aorta or pulmonary artery into the heart, but he qualifies this in ch. 12, 90.14—92.1, by suggesting that a little air can and does penetrate into the heart through the pulmonary artery.

[66] It is notable that in the *De Motu Cordis et Sanguinis in Animalibus* (1628) Harvey refers frequently not only to Galen, but also to Aristotle and to Hippocrates (mentioning *On the Heart* in particular in ch. 17) and among the passages he cites is a text of Galen in which the latter observed that the three semilunar valves placed at the opening of the aorta prevent the return of the blood into the heart.

might be cited from early Greek investigators in the biological sciences.[67] But while the extent || of the researches which had been carried out in such fields as anatomy, zoology and botany by the end of the fourth century B.C. is generally recognised, it is often argued that this is, as it were, the exception that proves the rule – that the fact that men who were mostly trained in the practical art of medicine successfully applied empirical methods to the study of biology shows up all the more dramatically the failure of other Greek theorists to do the same in other fields. Now it is well known that some of the most rigorously empirical texts of early Greek science come from the medical writers (the collections of case histories presented almost without interpretative comment in the *Epidemics* are the most obvious examples), though equally some of the physiological and pathological treatises of the Hippocratic Corpus are as dogmatic and speculative as any of the cosmological writings of the philosophers. But that some medical theorists, at least, believed there were important differences between their own methods of research and those used in such fields as 'meteorology' is clear from *On Ancient Medicine*, even though it should be pointed out that in practice, in his own physiological and pathological doctrines, this writer hardly lives up to his expressed ideal of excluding all unwarranted assumptions from the study of medicine.[68] Yet notwithstanding the evidence of *On Ancient Medicine*, the differences between Greek medicine and Greek philosophy in the matter of the attitude towards, and the use of, empirical verification and experimentation may not be so great as is sometimes made out. On the one hand I have already suggested that we should not underestimate the extent to which simple practical tests were carried out in some branches of the physical sciences: the early Greeks took some, if not all, of the most obvious opportunities for experimentation that presented themselves. Nor, on the other hand, should we overestimate the extent to which the medical theorists were able to devise experiments to illuminate the more difficult problems that faced them.[69] We have seen that some problems

[67] Aristotle, for instance, refers quite often to specimens of different species of animals which were, apparently, deliberately mutilated in order to investigate such questions as whether they can survive without certain organs, whether certain tissues will grow again when excised, or the method of locomotion of different species, e.g. *Resp.* 471b19ff.; 479a3ff.; *HA* 519a27ff.; *IA* 708b4ff.

[68] Thus although the writer attacks those who based their pathological theories on the hot, the cold, the wet and the dry, he himself numbers such things as the salty, the bitter, the sweet, the acid and so on among the constituents of the body (ch. 14, *CMG* I 1.45.26ff.), and while he criticises his opponents for oversimplifying the causal principles of diseases (ch. 1, 36.2ff.) a similar criticism might also be levelled against his own pathological theories, in which he refers, for example, to the diseases which arise from 'depletion' (κένωσις) and from 'repletion' (πλήρωσις) (ch. 10, 42.11ff.).

[69] One notable instance where the Greek biologists might have carried out systematic experiments without great difficulty, but failed to do so, is in investigating hybrids (although it should be remarked that for all the interest in heredity in post-Renaissance times the simple experiments of crossing pea-plants which led Mendel to the discovery of the law of the

in the biological sciences were investigated experimentally with a good deal of success at an early period. But there were, of course, whole areas of physiology, embryology and pathology where the Greeks posed major questions which could not be resolved by the use of dissection or the carrying out of simple tests. It is instructive, then, to consider the methods used, and the results obtained, by the medical theorists in attempting to determine the constituent elements of the body, for example, and to compare these with the work of men who were primarily || cosmologists on the similar, though more general, problem of the elements of physical substances as a whole.

Several Hippocratic writers cite practical tests in conjunction with their theories concerning the elements of the body, although the tests in question are generally quite inconclusive. The author of *On Fleshes*, for instance, held that we are composed of various substances among which 'the glutinous' (κολλῶδες) and 'the fatty' (λιπαρόν) are particularly important, but he suggests that the way we may detect the presence of these in any part or organ of the body is to cook it (when what is 'glutinous' will not readily cook, while what is 'fatty' will).[70] This seems to be strictly comparable with the type of observations which appear in the fourth book of the *Meteorologica*, where the reactions of different substances to being boiled, burned, frozen, etc., are noted down. Then the author of *On the Nature of Man* refers to certain rather more ambitious tests carried out with drugs to back his theory that the primary constituents of the body are the four humours. First he says that one may discover that these exist as different substances in the body by giving a man different types of drugs, which will draw out phlegm, bile and black bile respectively (ch. 5, L VI 42.6ff.). But then he says that the 'clearest proof' that the humours alternate in the body in a cycle according to the seasons is that 'if you will give the same man the same drug four times in the year, his vomit will be most phlegmatic in winter, most liquid in spring, most bilious in summer, and blackest in autumn'.[71] Now it is unlikely that the results of the various tests to which this writer refers would correspond at all precisely with those which he describes. Yet even if the tests produced the results he mentions, they would not, of course, prove what he was attempting to establish, for he assumes what is the point at issue, that the humours he had observed, or thought he had observed, in a man's vomit, are elemental. Many other ingenious, but quite undemonstrative, tests are found in the Hippocratic Corpus relating to such topics as the formation of the parts of

segregation of characters were not performed until the mid-nineteenth century). Equally when the dogma of spontaneous generation was challenged by Redi in the seventeenth century, the experiments he undertook to show that the worms found in decaying meat derive directly from the droppings of flies and not from the putrefaction of the meat itself, were the kind of procedures that were not technically impossible in antiquity.

[70] Ch. 4, L VIII 588.25–590.4.

[71] Ch. 7, esp. 50.9ff. Elsewhere too this writer describes the effects of different drugs, e.g. ch. 6, 44.11ff.; 46.3ff.

the body or the pathogenesis of various diseases.[72] Sometimes simple tests are carried out directly on organic substances from the body: one example has been given from *On Fleshes*, and elsewhere the same author describes tests on blood taken from a sacrificial victim in connection with his theory that the liver is formed by a process of coagulation.[73] But more often attempts were made to derive information concerning the behaviour of substances in the body by undertaking tests on other, generally simpler, substances outside the body under conditions which were (very roughly) similar. The tests with the intercommunicating vessels, and with different substances put into a bladder full || of water and blown on, have already been mentioned, but the Hippocratic writers used these in the former case to illustrate a theory concerning the passage of the humours from one part of the body to another,[74] and in the latter case to suggest how the parts of the body are formed by the breath causing like substances to come together.[75] Similarly we find the author of *On the Diseases of Women* I, for example, illustrating his theory that the flesh of women in more absorbent, because rarer, than the flesh of men, by referring to a test in which equal quantities by weight of unwoven wool and a made-up garment are left suspended over a bowl of water, and the greater absorbency of the unwoven material is shown when the two are collected and reweighed.[76] A number of medical writers undoubtedly recognized the desirability of undertaking tests to corroborate their theories, and indeed tried to do this in practice (even though the accuracy of their observations often leaves much to be desired). In investigating the structure of the body, for example, they used empirical techniques such as dissection most successfully. Yet on such intractable problems as the constituent elements of the body, the formation of the different organs, the origin of diseases and so on, their attempts to make use of practical tests met with little success, for the tests to which they refer were at best inconclusive, and at worst quite irrelevant. Yet if they failed to devise crucial experiments on the more complex problems of physiology, bio-

[72] Several examples from the treatises *On Generation*, *On the Nature of the Child* and *On Diseases* IV are discussed by Senn, 1929: 219ff., and cf. also Regenbogen, 1931: 131ff.

[73] Ch. 8, L VIII 594.9ff. He notes that so long as the blood is hot it does not coagulate, but then he also observes that it does not coagulate if it is beaten. Cf. also ch. 9, 596.9ff., where he remarks that when the 'skin' is removed from blood which is left to clot, another 'skin' forms shortly afterwards (an observation which he uses to support his account of how the skin of the body itself is formed).

[74] *On Diseases* IV, ch. 39, L VII 556.15ff., suggests that as all the vessels may be filled or emptied by filling or emptying any one of them so the reservoirs (πηγαί) of the humours in the body are filled or emptied by the stomach being filled or emptied.

[75] *On the Nature of the Child* ch. 17, L VII 496.17ff., argues that growth takes place when the breath, πνεῦμα, in the body separates the different substances according to their kinds (the dense, the rare and so on), just as the substances put into the bladder (earth, sand, lead-filings) will be found to be sorted according to their kinds when the bladder is left to dry and opened.

[76] Ch. 1, L VIII 12.9ff. It is worth remarking that this test, like that in *On Airs, Waters, Places* ch. 8, mentioned above, p. 84, n. 33, involves the use of quantitative measurements.

chemistry and pathology, this was evidently not always for lack of trying: rather their failure must be considered to a large extent inevitable, given that the successful experimental investigation of many of the questions they raised had to wait for (among other things) the development of chemistry.

In conclusion I should summarize the main points I have tried to make in this very compressed discussion of certain features of the role of experiment in early Greek philosophy and medicine. First it seems to me that the question of whether the Greeks experimented cannot be meaningfully discussed in global terms: what we must try to do is to assess the achievements and failures of the Greeks in each branch of scientific inquiry and at each period independently. Secondly, I suggested that even where the failure of the Greeks to experiment is most notorious, that is in the physical sciences, we find that in such fields as acoustics, optics, pneumatics and hydrostatics, quite successful experimental investigations were carried out in antiquity, and if the most striking successes are all the products of the Alexandrian period or later, the first attempts to undertake simple tests in those fields can be traced back to the fifth or fourth century B.C. Here where the problems investigated are relatively elementary, and where tests can often be carried out without great difficulty, the Greeks were far from ignoring the experimental method. The early history of mechanics and what we should call chemistry seems to tell a rather different story, but in chemistry the latter || part of the fourth century B.C. sees the first detailed collections of data concerning the different properties of substances and their reactions to various simple tests, and such collections of factual information were no negligible achievement, even if they did not lead to the founding of chemical science on a firm basis. And even in mechanics, whatever the apparent shortcomings of Aristotle himself, it is clear from such scanty information as we have concerning his immediate successors that they carried out a number of empirical investigations in this field (and we cannot doubt the success with which these were used for destructive purposes by some of those who opposed the doctrines of Aristotle in late antiquity). Finally, I considered the biological sciences, and here an increasing, and increasingly successful, use of experiment can be traced from the Hippocratic writers and Aristotle, through the Alexandrians Erasistratus and Herophilus, down to Galen.[77] This is, indeed, generally acknowledged, but it has often been suggested that the use of experimental methods in this field is quite exceptional and due to the fact that these men were, for the most part, trained in the practical discipline of medicine, and this argument (I should submit) has often been exaggerated. On the one hand we should not underestimate the extent to which simple experiments were performed in other fields of science besides

[77] I may mention especially the remarkable experiment, described in Anon. Lond. XXXIII 43ff., in which Erasistratus showed that there are invisible effluvia from animals by keeping a bird in a vessel without food for a given period of time and weighing the animal together with the visible excreta and comparing this with its original weight.

biology, and on the other, while there are certainly important differences in outlook and training between some medical theorists and the majority of the philosophers (differences to which *On Ancient Medicine* draws attention), this is not the only factor to be borne in mind when considering the relative success with which the Greeks applied experimental methods to biology: a more obvious point, but one that may tend to be ignored, is the relative ease with which some theories can be submitted to a practical test in certain branches of the biological sciences (for example in anatomy or embryology, by means of dissections). It will be remembered that the relative ease with which information can be gained in biology is a point which Aristotle stresses in a famous passage in the *De Partibus Animalium* where he contrasts the study of plants and animals with astronomy. 'We have better means of knowledge', he says, 'concerning the things that perish, that is plants and animals, since we live among them. And anyone who is willing to take sufficient trouble can learn much concerning each one of their kinds.'[78]

A final question arises which must, however, be dealt with summarily. Having suggested that the view prevalent in the nineteenth century, at least, that the Greeks completely failed to experiment, is false, I should say something about how this opinion may have gained currency. Here one might refer to the emphasis often laid on the passages in the *Republic*[79] in which Plato argues for the mathematisation*[80] of astronomy, acoustics and so on, and decries empirical investigation, for while || Plato's view was no doubt influential in antiquity, it did not act as the deterrent that some commentators have supposed. But more important, there is a tendency in several nineteenth-century works on the history of science to assume a constant, linear development of science, and it might be suggested that it was for this reason (among others) that there is a certain reluctance, in many such works, to allow the claims of Greek science whether in respect of methods or of results. That Whewell, for one, experienced a certain difficulty in giving credit where credit is due, may, I think, be seen from a passage from the *History of the Inductive Sciences* where he discounts the claim of Aristotle to have formed a systematic classification in zoology: 'it would be difficult', Whewell says,[81]

> to reconcile such an early maturity of zoology with the conviction which we have had impressed upon us by the other parts of our history, that not only labour but time, not only one man of genius but several, and those succeeding each other, are requisite to the formation of any considerable science.[82]

[78] *PA* I, ch. 5, 644b28ff. Aristotle suggests that our meagre acquaintance with the heavenly bodies gives us greater joy, but that our knowledge of plants and animals is superior in that we can acquire more and better information about them. [79] E.g. 529Aff. and 531Aff.

*[80] Some of the complexities of Plato's position on this topic are, however, discussed below (chapter 14). [81] Whewell, 1837: III 344.

[82] I must express my gratitude to Dr M. B. Hesse, who read and criticised an earlier draft of this paper, and to Dr H. B. F. Dixon and Mr F. H. Sandbach for their advice and comments on particular points.

REFERENCES

Blüh, O. (1949) 'Did the Greeks perform experiments?', *American Journal of Physics* 17: 384–8

Brunet, P., and Mieli, A. (1935) *Histoire des sciences: antiquité* (Paris)

Burnet, J. (1929) *Essays and Addresses* (London)

(1948) *Early Greek Philosophy*, 4th edn. (London)

Cohen, M. R., and Drabkin, I. E. (1948) *A Source Book in Greek Science* (New York)

Cornford, F. M. (1952) *Principium Sapientiae* (Cambridge)

Diels, H. (1905) 'Aristotelica', *Hermes* 40: 300–16

Düring, I. (1944) *Aristotle's Chemical Treatise, Meteorologica, Book IV* (Göteborg)

Edelstein, L. (1933) 'Die Geschichte der Sektion in der Antike', *Quellen und Studien zur Geschichte der Naturwissenschaften und der Medizin* 3.2: 100–56

(1952) 'Recent trends in the interpretation of ancient science', *Journal of the History of Ideas* 13: 573–604

Farringon, B. (1957) 'The Greeks and the experimental method', *Discovery* 18: 68–9

Gottschalk, H. B. (1961) 'The authorship of *Meteorologica*, Book IV', *Classical Quarterly* N.S. 11

Guthrie, W. K. C. (1962) *A History of Greek Philosophy*, I (Cambridge)

Hammer-Jensen, I. (1915) 'Das sogenannte IV. Buch der *Meteorologie* des Aristoteles', *Hermes* 50: 113–26

Heidel, W. A. (1933) *The Heroic Age of Science* (Baltimore)

(1941) *Hippocratic medicine, its Spirit and Method* (New York)

Joachim, H. H. (1904) 'Aristotle's conception of chemical combination', *Journal of Philology* 29: 72–86

Lee, H. D. P. (1952) *Aristotle, Meteorologica*, Loeb edn (Cambridge, Mass.)

(1962) *Aristotle, Meteorologica*, 2nd Loeb edn (Cambridge, Mass.)

Lejeune, A. (1956) *L'Optique de Claude Ptolémée* (Louvain)

Lewes, G. H. (1864) *Aristotle: A Chapter from the History of Science* (London)

Playfair, J. (1842) 'Dissertation... Exhibiting a general view of the progress of mathematical and physical science, since the revival of letters in Europe', *Encyclopaedia Britannica*, 7th edn

Regenbogen, O. (1931) 'Eine Forschungsmethode antiker Naturwissenschaft', *Quellen und Studien zur Geschichte der Mathematik, Astronomie und Physik*, Abt. B.I

Sambursky, S. (1956) *The Physical World of the Greeks*, transl. M. Dagut (London)

Senn, G. (1929) 'Über Herkunft und Stil der Beschreibungen von Experimenten im Corpus Hippocraticum', *Archiv für Geschichte der Medizin* 22: 217–89

Thomson, J. O. (1948) *History of Ancient Geography* (Cambridge)

Wehrli, F. (1950) *Straton von Lampsakos* (Basel)

Whewell, W. (1837) *History of the Inductive Sciences from the Earliest to the Present Times* (London)

Zubov, V. P. (1959) 'Beobachtung und Experiment in der antiken Wissenschaft', *Das Altertum* 5: 223–32

5

POPPER VERSUS KIRK: A CONTROVERSY IN THE INTERPRETATION OF GREEK SCIENCE

INTRODUCTION

The article I published in the *British Journal for the Philosophy of Science* in 1967 discussed a controversy between Popper and Kirk that had important implications for the interpretation of Greek science. The issue that divided these two scholars had both a philosophical and a historical component. The philosophical one related to the correct analysis of scientific theories and of what marks them out as scientific. The historical one concerned the nature of early Greek speculative thought and its contribution to the development of science. Popper argued that scientific theories stem essentially from problems – certainly not from collections of observations – and he saw the importance of the Presocratic philosophers as having nothing to do with observations, and everything to do with the questions and problems they raised and the critical debate they originated. Kirk countered by protesting that (1) observations are the true ultimate origin of science since they are prior to the perception of problems, and (2) in particular the theorising of the Presocratic philosophers is notable for how close they stuck to the data of experience and to what Kirk called 'common sense': they departed from this only when they believed themselves constrained to do so by overwhelmingly powerful arguments.

In my own comments on this controversy I concentrated mainly on its historical aspects. There can or should, to be sure, be no divorce between the philosophy, and the history, of science. Philosophy of science that ignores how science actually is and has been conducted risks being merely aprioristic and sterile, although decisions about what precisely counts as science themselves involve taking positions in philosophical disputes. Again, whether or not historians make explicit their views on the philosophy of science, the history they write will inevitably incorporate judgements, on the nature of science itself, on what demarcates it from other inquiries, on scientific methodology. My own historical investigations were no exception, for they both incorporated a certain conception of the nature of science and carried certain implications for the study of the philosophical issues to do with the starting-points of science. I was perhaps less explicit about those implications in my original article than I might have been and so will devote some comments on them here.

The principal aims I set myself in the article were twofold, to comment on the disputed aspects of Presocratic speculation, and to broaden the scope of the discussion. The ideas we associate with those whom we group together, for convenience, under the title 'Presocratic philosophers', are only one part of the early Greek contributions to science, and the question of whether or not they are characteristic of those contributions as a whole should not be begged. I turned my attention to a second principal area of Greek inquiry, namely medicine, where the documentary evidence for developments in the fifth and early fourth centuries is far richer than it is for the Presocratic philosophers. I might have remarked at the time, but do so now, that any comprehensive study of early Greek science would have to take a third main field into account as well, namely mathematics and the exact sciences, though for these the documentation is even more impoverished than for philosophy. But, as I hope some of my other articles in this collection illustrate, the question of the interrelations of mathematics, medicine, natural philosophy and epistemology is one of the most important topics that any study of early Greek thought must consider.

On the Presocratic philosophers themselves, the room for possible disagreement about the elements of observation and abstract speculation, as also about the primary motivations of the philosophers concerned, remains very large. In my article I protested, first, against the application of an unexamined notion of 'common sense' to the ancient Greeks (p. 107), underlining the dangers of subjective assumptions in evaluating what may have passed as unproblematic *to them* from the standpoint of what *we* might judge to be matters of common sense to us. I note in passing that these dangers are not avoided in a recent ambitious cross-cultural study that takes common sense as some kind of more or less universal category: the failure to confront the question of the diversity of matters that can, in different societies and at different times, pass as commonsensical seriously undermines, in my view, the value of Scott Atran's recent monograph (forthcoming).

But it is worth giving some indication of the range of interpretations that have subsequently been put forward concerning the work of the Presocratic philosophers – whether or not those interpretations have taken issue directly with the views expressed by Popper or by Kirk. Among notable recent contributions, those of Hussey (1972), Barnes (1979), Vlastos (1955/1970, 1975) and Furley (1987) will serve to illustrate the point. Thus Hussey revives a thesis originally propounded by Jaeger to the effect that a major preoccupation of the early Greek philosophers was with notions of the divine: one of their chief concerns is, indeed, to propose what has been called a reformed *theology* or several different ones. Barnes in his important two-volume study focuses especially on the philosophical *arguments* proposed, and is quite clear that that is what, for him, makes the period worth studying. Vlastos, who had earlier (1955/1970) criticised Cornford's views contrasting the empirical medical writers with the dogmatic philosophers, argued forcefully that the speculations of the Presocratics were, in the main, beyond verification or falsification. As with the element theory of Plato (with whom Vlastos was chiefly concerned in his 1975 study) their doctrines were not empirically testable but should be evaluated rather with regard to such criteria as simplicity and coherence. Finally in his recent synoptic survey of early Greek cosmology Furley has drawn attention to a recurrent feature of those controversies. Most early – and later – Greek cosmological thought falls into one or other of two opposing camps. On the one side there were those who held that the world is finite, who adopted continuum theories of matter (and of time and space) and who were teleologists. On the other side were ranged those who saw the world as infinite (or who believed that there are infinite worlds), who adopted atomist, that is indivisibilist, theories of matter, time and space, and who ignored or explicitly rejected teleology. While, in Furley's view, the arguments of teleology did not *entail* a continuum theory, in *practice* these two are in constant conjunction.

To pursue the issues raised by these and other important contributions to our understanding of early Greek philosophy here would take us too far afield. But I mention them to point out the extreme diversity of points of view from which the study of the Presocratics can be approached – and the variety of conclusions which can claim to be supported by evidence available to us. That argument was their forte, not empirical research, is a common feature of most modern interpretation: as I put it in my article, precisely the evidence that Kirk invoked to suggest that they did not depart from what he called common-sense positions gratuitously could serve to support a very different conclusion from the one he himself drew – namely that in one instance after another, in Heraclitus, Parmenides, Democritus and many others, they felt constrained precisely by *arguments* to suggest theories that run counter to ordinary assumptions. The readiness of Greek philosophers early middle and late to countenance radical and radically counter-intuitive solutions – driven by arguments – is indeed a recurrent phenomenon distinctive of what the Greeks themselves understood by rationality. In this respect the position broadly advocated by Popper continues to receive more endorsement than the more empiricist picture of the early philosophers proposed by Kirk.

However, so far as the primary *motivations* of the philosophers in question go, I would now say that greater caution is needed than I showed in my article on the issue of whether it makes sense to attempt to *generalise* the answer. I accepted too readily the assumption that *both* disputants adopted, namely that it should be possible to arrive at some global characterisation of the primary concerns of those whom we call the Presocratic *philosophers*. My own chief line of argument was to insist that the philosophers were not the *only* figures who had to be taken into account in evaluating early Greek science: the medical writers too had to be included and they presented a rather different picture on the points in dispute. But I might have extended a similar objection and applied it critically to the category of 'philosophy' itself.

The very fact that there are those theological interests that Hussey emphasises, the interest in abstract argument forms that Barnes studies, the conflict between opposed camps on the question of explanations in terms of the good, all helps to show that even within those who are traditionally grouped together as 'philosophers' the diversity on the fundamental question of the nature of the inquiry they were engaged in is very considerable (see further below, chapter 6). What many of them – though not all – share is an interest in epistemological questions, the foundations of knowledge: and again many (not all) engage in speculation on the basic constituents of physical objects, even though the *kinds* of answers they offer differ widely: for Parmenides this is just the Way of Seeming, but for the Pythagoreans the answer lies in mathematics, and so on. But while more or less dogmatic streaks are to be found in all those whom we label philosophers, we can never afford to forget that that label – philosopher – is *our* categorisation (even if we could say it has some authority in Aristotle). The individuals concerned would not have recognised themselves as all engaged in the same kind of investigation.

On the question of the role of observation, in particular, it is hardly surprising that widely divergent conclusions have been proposed – hardly surprising if we look, for example, at the Pythagoreans on the one hand, and at Parmenides on the other. The Pythagoreans certainly carried out observations, in harmonics for instance, but these were clearly motivated by the overarching doctrine that 'all things are numbers'. But for Parmenides the world of change belongs to the Way of Seeming. Nor does that exhaust the possible positions adopted, for others again are to be found in Empedocles, for example, or Anaxagoras, or Democritus.

In this respect, then, my own original discussion was not critical enough of the assumptions made by both opposing parties. However, I was clear that generalisation to Greek science on the basis of natural philosophy alone was out of the question. Certainly the early Greek medical writers had important contributions to make to the development of science and there should be no question of attempting to treat any one of the different areas of early Greek speculative thought as typical of the whole. This is all the more important when we are dealing with a period when the very categories – of philosopher, doctor, sophist, mathematician, let alone 'wise man' – were themselves fluid and disputed: none of these, not even 'doctor', corresponds to a profession in the fullest modern sense. Moreover given that some of the medical writers explicitly take issue with the natural philosophers on how to study nature, the idea of hiving off the latter from the former can be said to run directly counter to ancient perceptions themselves.

The outcome of my brief survey of early Greek medicine was to suggest a very different picture from philosophy with regard to the elements of observation and of theory. The medical writers provide some of our best early examples of sustained empirical research. In many cases this was research directed by clearly identifiable theoretical assumptions – as for instance by the doctrine of critical days, which served as the guiding idea motivating the day-by-day recording of medical symptoms in the *Epidemics*. But while research was sometimes directly led by *theories*, that was not the only type of case that the evidence for Greek science suggests. In some instances research was prompted principally if not solely by the notion of the importance of research itself – for one of the ideas that comes to be made explicit in early Greek science is the very idea that inquiry into the phenomena is important. Moreover in the case of the development of the use of dissection – when that occurred (see below, chapter 8) – we have a third type of relationship, namely one where the research is stimulated, in part, by the desire to exploit a new technique.

A moral of some philosophical interest emerges, then, from the historical inquiry I briefly surveyed. Due weight must be given to the actual diversity in the given historical situation. That diversity takes at least three forms, first in relation to the epistemological and methodological assumptions made by the participants themselves. Secondly there is diversity in their extra-scientific preoccupations and motivations, for example in their views on the moral relevance – or lack of it – of scientific activity itself and on the values – or lack of them – that science uncovers in what it investigates. There is, thirdly, diversity in the views expressed on the nature of science itself, on what marks it out from other disciplines, and on the requirements to be met for it to claim to *be* science. But in these circumstances the bid to systematise and to generalise, either about the original stimulus to science, or about the relations between theory and observation, has to be resisted. It must be recognised that to privilege the experience in one field of inquiry and to make it the basis for such general characterisations is likely to be quite arbitrary. A historically well-informed philosophy of science may be altogether less neat and tidy on fundamental questions to do with the origins of science but has the argument for historicity on its side.

REFERENCES

Atran, S. (1985) 'Pre-theoretical aspects of Aristotelian definition and classification of animals: the case for common sense', *Studies in History and Philosophy of Science* 16: 113–63

(forthcoming) *Cognitive Foundations of Natural History*

Barnes, J. (1979) *The Presocratic Philosophers*, 2 vols. (London)

Furley, D. J. (1987) *The Greek Cosmologists*, 1 (Cambridge)

Hussey, E. (1972) *The Presocratics* (London)

Vlastos, G. (1955/1970) Review of Cornford, F. M., *Principium Sapientiae* (Cambridge, 1952) in *Gnomon* 27: 65–76, repr. in *Studies in Presocratic Philosophy*, 1 edd. D. J. Furley and R. E. Allen (London) 42–55

(1975) *Plato's Universe* (Oxford)

POPPER VERSUS KIRK: A CONTROVERSY IN THE INTERPRETATION OF GREEK SCIENCE

It is a minor scandal that specialists in the interpretation of early Greek thought have, in general, paid so little attention to Professor Sir Karl Popper's provocative foray into their territory in his Presidential Address to the Aristotelian Society (Popper, 1958). That paper was answered by Professor G. S. Kirk in an article in *Mind* (Kirk, 1960), and since then both scholars have contributed a second paper which develops parts of their respective views (Kirk, 1961, Popper, 1963). But subsequently the debate has fizzled out. Nor, so far as I know, has any other classical scholar besides Kirk taken part (though Mr J. E. Raven repeated some of Kirk's criticisms of Popper in a paper read to the joint conference of the Hellenic and Roman Societies in 1965). And yet their controversy raises two fundamental issues, first the major philosophical question of the logic of scientific discovery, and secondly the historical question concerning the characteristics and methods of Greek natural philosophy. It is this latter question that I wish to take up here.[1] In particular I wish to broaden the field of the discussion to take the whole of early Greek speculative thought (and not merely the work of the philosophers) into account. And I shall suggest where certain generalisations which may apply to those writers whose interests were primarily cosmological should be modified when we take all the available evidence for the period down to Plato into account. I shall, however, begin by rehearsing briefly the main arguments that have been advanced by Popper and Kirk concerning the Presocratic philosophers.

Popper's original paper was entitled 'Back to the Presocratics'. 'What I want to return to', he said 'is the simple straightforward *rationality* of the Presocratics. The simplicity and boldness of their questions is part of it, || but more important still is the critical attitude which, as I shall try to show, was first developed in the Ionian School' (Popper, 1958: 1). But Popper's purpose was not merely to praise Thales, Anaximander, Anaximenes and the rest, but also to draw lessons from their work for the history of science as a whole. In particular he used the evidence relating to the work of the Presocratics in order to attack, as he had done on previous occasions, the 'Baconian myth according to which science starts from observation and then slowly and cautiously proceeds to theories' (Popper, 1958: 3). 'Western science', as he put it, 'did not start with collecting observations of oranges, but with bold theories about the world' (Popper, 1958: 3). He argued that most of the ideas

[1] An earlier version of this paper was read to the History and Philosophy of Science Seminar at Cambridge and to Professor Sir Karl Popper's Seminar at the London School of Economics. I am most grateful to those who have criticised my paper on those occasions and in correspondence and especially to Sir Karl Popper and Professor Kirk. The defects that remain are, of course, entirely my own responsibility, but I am conscious that they would have been far greater but for the patient and courteous criticisms I have received.

of the early Presocratics, and the best of them, 'have nothing to do with observation', and to support this claim he referred to such examples as Thales' notion that the earth floats on water, and Anaximander's idea of the earth's free suspension in space. He dealt in some detail with other Presocratics too, particularly with Heraclitus, where he argued strenuously against the view taken by Kirk (1957) according to which Heraclitus himself held not the strong thesis that every single thing is constantly and invariably in change, but merely the much weaker thesis that the world as a whole undergoes continuous change.

Popper presented his theses in what can only be considered a provocative manner, saying that 'the exciting story of the development of the problem of change' (for example) appeared to be 'in danger of being completely buried under the mounting heap of the minutiae of textual criticism' (Popper, 1958: 9f.). 'In this paper', he put it,

> I speak as an amateur, as a lover of the beautiful story of the Presocratics. I am not a specialist, nor an expert: I am completely out of my depth when an expert begins to argue what words or phrases Heraclitus might have used, and what words or phrases he could not possibly have used. But when the experts replace a beautiful story, based on the oldest texts we possess, by one which – to me at any rate – makes no sense any longer, then I feel that even an amateur may stand up and defend an old tradition. (Popper, 1958: 2)

When Kirk (1960) came to reply, he defended the practice of minute textual criticism against Popper's somewhat indiscriminate attacks.[2] And he put forward a different interpretation of certain specific Presocratic doctrines from that which Popper had advanced. In particular he corrected Popper's suggestion || that in Anaximander winds were responsible not only for the weather but for 'all other changes within the cosmic edifice' (Kirk, 1960: 332).[3] And thirdly where Popper had argued that Presocratic philosophy contained some 'staggering anticipations of modern results', Kirk advanced a more sceptical and seemingly more judicious view of the extent to which such anticipations are to be found.

But if on these mainly peripheral issues Kirk made a number of telling points, he was less successful in his criticisms of the central thesis of Popper's paper, the anti-Baconian argument. The first part of Kirk's paper was a critique of Popper's theory of scientific methodology. There he began by considering why, that is for what historical and personal reasons, Popper arrived at his – as Kirk thought – utterly mistaken view.[4] But on the main

[2] Popper (1963: 157) has since protested that he neither said nor suggested that consideration of the words or phrases Heraclitus might have used was irrelevant: he merely disclaimed competence in the field of linguistic criticism. Nevertheless some of his remarks can be construed as attacks not on a particular expert nor on particular conclusions reached on the basis of a close study of the text, so much as on the experts, and the practice of textual criticism, in general.

[3] When he came to reprint his original paper Popper (1963: 136ff.) modified some of his statements and introduced an explanatory note to meet Kirk's criticisms at this point.

[4] In his reply Popper (1963: 154ff.) has protested that Kirk has misrepresented his position,

point at issue Kirk simply stated that 'science ultimately does start from observation'.

> Naturally, most attempts to extend scientific knowledge start immediately from an idea or intuition, which is then tested 'scientifically' and accordingly approved, modified, or rejected. But the idea or intuition which acted as the starting-point of any such particular process is itself the culmination of a previous process or series of processes which must have been 'inductive' in some valid sense because it must ultimately have been based on an indefinite number of particular observations...What Popper has done, then, in his description of the process of scientific discovery, is to ignore the essential preliminary stage of making observations, of building up a complex structure of experience out of which, by some kind of inductive process, come intuitions or universal theories. (Kirk, 1960: 321f.)

But Kirk's notion of this 'essential preliminary stage' in the process of scientific discovery seems not only true but a truism:[5] and it may be remarked that it does not help us to discriminate between what is and what is not science.

But apart from the general question of the nature of scientific method, there is a substantial disagreement between Popper and Kirk on the place of observation, and of what Kirk calls common sense, in Presocratic philosophy. In his Presidential Address Popper took Kirk to task for his remark that 'it cannot be too strongly emphasised that before Parmenides and his apparent proof that the senses were completely fallacious...gross departures from common sense must only be accepted when the evidence || for them is extremely strong' (Kirk, 1957: 197; Popper, 1958: 16). In his reply Kirk made a small but perhaps important change in the formulation of his position: 'Naturally many of the conclusions of the early Presocratics were contrary to common sense; but they were not gratuitous departures from it ("gratuitous" expresses my meaning better than "gross") since they appeared to be entailed by arguments which themselves depended on observation and common sense' (Kirk, 1960): 335f.). Kirk devoted a paragraph to this in the 1960 paper, but a whole article (Kirk, 1961) entitled 'Sense and common-sense in the development of Greek philosophy' was published the next year,[6] in which he went through not only the Presocratics but the whole of classical Greek philosophy considering which of their theories could be accounted exceptions to his rule that the Greek philosophers did not gratuitously depart from, or overstep the bounds of, common sense. 'Common sense' is at the best of times a dangerously vague

particularly by suggesting that his, Popper's, view of scientific methodology is an intuitionist one.

[5] Compare Popper's recognition of the role of 'experience', including observational knowledge, in the origin of problems (Popper, 1963: 1955), quoted p. 109, n. 10.

[6] This paper originated in one read to a classical conference in 1958, that is to say it was based on ideas which Kirk had developed before Popper's first paper (1958) had appeared.

and subjective term. In his opening paragraphs Kirk gave various examples to explain the distinction between a notion allowed by common sense and one precluded by it, but the examples he gave suggest that he would be reluctant to concede that these categories may be culture- or society specific.[7] At least when he draws a general contrast between Greek myths and those of their ancient Near Eastern neighbours he appears to discount the possibility that some of the 'symbolist extravagances' of the Egyptians may have seemed just as commonsensical to *them* as the Greek beliefs about the sun or the sky or the origin of things did to the Greeks.

But Kirk's chief concern was with the philosophers. He granted that there are quite a number of their theories that offend common sense, but he suggested that, in general, the philosophers took refuge in such theories only when they believed themselves to be compelled to do so by the demands of logic. He offered, in effect, two types of explanation for the theories in question. First such a theory may be a generalisation arrived at by over-bold induction from a single observation or set of observations. The Pythagorean doctrine that the world is somehow made out of numbers is the prime example. But this number-physics, as Kirk pointed out, seems to have resulted from an important new observation – that the musical scale is basically numerical. Secondly there are cases where a startlingly || improbable theory arose directly as the result of following an initial axiom to its apparently logical conclusions (see, e.g., Kirk, 1961: 111). Here Parmenides provides the clearest example. Kirk allowed that from the point of view of common sense Parmenides' doctrine of Being is 'completely improbable and indeed utterly nonsensical'. But, he went on, 'the Eleatic conclusion about Being was the direct result of a logical process of inference – admittedly an incorrect one – and...it was logic alone that led Parmenides to overthrow the world of common-sense' (1961: 110f.).[8] He dealt similarly with Empedocles, for example, arguing that certain of his 'rather quaint' cosmological ideas were 'initially imposed upon' him 'by the demands of symmetry in working out his cyclical scheme, itself necessitated by his premises of essential unity and no becoming' (1961: 111). As for Anaxagoras, Kirk agreed that his physical theory 'must have seemed inherently improbable, as well as intolerably complex, to the common-sense view of interested amateurs', but went on: 'we must recognise that a degree of improbability was inevitably entailed by the attempt to retain the sense-world at all' (1961: 112). The Atomists too he saw as taking a 'momentous step away from the phenomenal

[7] 'Common sense', he said (Kirk, 1961: 105), 'might not prevent a man from believing that the sun is a large ball of fire...On the other hand the belief that the sun is made out of triangles, or is rowed across the sky with oars, may be felt to offend common sense, because there are no obvious elements of our experience that can be combined without contradiction to form such a picture.'

[8] In his first paper Kirk had stated emphatically that those of the Presocratics' theories that are contrary to common sense are not gratuitous departures from it 'since they appeared to be entailed by arguments which themselves depended on observation and common sense' (1960: 335f.). But it would seem impossible to claim this to be true of Parmenides' doctrine of Being.

world of common-sense'. But again their theory 'depended from a chain of reasoning, one which owed much to that of the Eleatics. It was the apparent cogency of this reasoning', Kirk concluded, 'that gave Democritus the confidence to proceed beyond the senses' (1961: 112).

Kirk continued with Plato and Aristotle , the Epicureans and the Stoics, but failed there too to find gratuitous departures from common sense. Indeed considering his idea of what would constitute such a gratuitous departure and his explicit statement that 'philosophers normally avoid hypotheses that are gratuitously contrary to common-sense' (1961: 105), it would have been quite surprising if he had found many such theories. He did, in fact, cite two possible examples in the history of classical Greek philosophy,[9] Xenophanes' obscure idea that eclipses are caused by the sun 'wandering off into a region of the earth uninhabited by men', and the doctrine of innumerable worlds attributed to Anaximander. But the former he saw as an ironical parody of the 'excessive dogmatism and naive theorisation of the Milesians' (1961: 108), and the latter he pointed || out, may well be a doxographic misrepresentation of Anaximander. Yet to show that the early Greek philosophers avoid theories that are purely whimsical does not seem particularly interesting (even if it serves to counteract a certain tendency, on the part of some commentators, to assume that many of their theories are quite arbitrary). And one might draw a rather different conclusion from the one Kirk suggested from the material on which he commented. What might be thought remarkable about that material is not the point that Kirk draws attention to, that there are so few *gratuitous* departures from 'common sense', so much as that there are so *many departures* from 'common sense' – not that when they suggested theories that offend against the evidence of the senses, the Greek philosophers thought they had good reasons for doing so, but rather that they felt themselves constrained to do so so often.

Subsequently Popper (1963), too, has made a second contribution to the debate, where he argued that Kirk had misrepresented his view of scientific methodology[10] and reaffirmed his general thesis on the Presocratics, and then concentrated most of his attention on two specific points in the interpretation of Heraclitus.

The main issue between Popper and Kirk is a general one in the philosophy of science. At the same time they have expressed divergent views on the role of observation in the early Greek natural philosophers, and this raises a historical issue concerning the methods of early Greek science. It is this issue

[9] Kirk noted that Heraclitus would be another instance if he held the strong thesis that every individual thing is in perpetual flux (though Kirk denies, of course, that this was Heraclitus' thesis) (1961: 109).

[10] Popper (1963: 155) briefly restated his position on the question of the starting-point of science as follows: 'I do not say that science starts from intuitions but that *it starts from problems*; that we arrive at a new theory, in the main, by trying to solve problems; that these problems arise in our attempts to understand the world as we know it – the world of our "experience" (where "experience" consists largely of expectations or theories and partly also of observational knowledge – although I happen to believe that there does not exist anything like *pure* observational knowledge, untainted by expectations or theories).'

that I wish to follow up in the rest of this paper. While Popper and Kirk have confined their attention, so far, to figures who appear in the histories of Greek *philosophy*, I wish to extend the area of the discussion to take the evidence for other parts of early Greek science into account. There are interesting and important differences both between the practice of different early Greek scientists, and between the theories some of them entertained on the subject of the methods to be used in the investigation into nature. A study of the medical writers, for example, can, of course, in no way invalidate generalisations that are meant to apply to the cosmologists alone: it may, however, help us to discover where the methods favoured by particular philosophers are typical or atypical of early Greek science taken as a whole. ||

Apart from the philosophers the other major strand to Greek science in the pre-Platonic period is represented by certain of the Hippocratic writings. It is true that this material is difficult to handle because very few of the texts can be assigned to a specific author and the dates of most of them cannot be determined at all precisely. But against this it must be said that the *general* period within which almost all of them fall can be fixed reasonably certainly, that is from the mid fifth to the late fourth century B.C., and secondly that they have one enormous advantage (from our point of view) over the remains of the Presocratic philosophers, namely that we possess not just a series of isolated fragments quoted by later writers, but a considerable number of quite extensive treatises. These constitute, in fact, one of our main sources not merely for Greek medical theory and practice (that is obvious), but also for Greek biology in general and even for certain aspects of contemporary Greek physics and cosmology. What is more, they provide some striking early examples of the painstaking collecting and reporting of particular facts. In attempting to assess how far there are any signs of inductivist tendencies in early Greek science taken as a whole we should, then, consider such works as the Hippocratic treatises *On Epidemics*.

Books I and III of the *Epidemics* probably form a single work which appears to date from some time in or around the last decade of the fifth century B.C. (Deichgräber, 1933: 16; Bourgey, 1953: 32). These books contain first what are known as the 'constitutions', that is general descriptions of the climatic conditions accompanying certain outbreaks, and then a number of detailed case histories in which the daily progress of a particular patient's illness is set out. The entries under each day vary in length from a single remark to a fairly detailed description,[11] and the observations continue until the patient either dies (as happens in the majority of cases) or recovers, in some cases as late as the 120th day from the onset of the disease. These treatises have always

[11] E.g. *Epid.* III, Case 3 (First Series): 'Fourth day. Vomited scanty, bilious, yellow vomits, and after a short interval, verdigris-coloured ones; slight flow of unmixed blood from the left nostril; stools unaltered and urine unaltered; sweat about the head and collar-bones; spleen enlarged; pain in the direction of the thigh; tension, soft underneath, of the right hypochondrium; no sleep at night; slight delirium' (trans. Jones, 1923: 223).

been famous for their cool, professional attitude to clinical medicine, and their careful and methodical observations of the symptoms of various conditions. One may also remark the absence of any dogmatic overall theory of the origins of diseases such as we find often enough elsewhere in the Hippocratic Corpus (an extreme example is provided by the work *On Breaths* which calmly states that the cause of all diseases is one and the same, namely 'air', chapters 2, 4 and 5, ‖ *Corpus Medicorum Graecorum* I 1.92.13ff.). We might ask, then, how far it would be justified to see the case histories of the *Epidemics* as serving the purpose of preliminary collections of observations prior to the proposal of pathological doctrines. How far would it be right to represent this writer as proceeding inductively from particular case histories to general theories?

First of all we must be clear about the writer's motives for undertaking and setting out his case histories in the way he does. Like most of the Hippocratic medical writers, he attaches greater importance to prognosis than to diagnosis. The object of assembling the collections of case histories is not so much to provide information which would enable the causes of diseases to be established, as to provide information which would help doctors to predict the outcome of particular diseases (especially, of course, whether the patient would die or recover). But a further point concerns the way in which the observations are set out, that is the way in which the writer begins with the first day of the disease and makes an entry for each subsequent day on which any significant change was observed until death or recovery. The observations are methodical and even meticulous. But the writer has an additional motive for presenting these observations in the way he does, and indeed for carrying out his *daily* check, *over and above* any laudable desire to be thorough in his work, that is he adheres to the common Greek medical theory that the course of acute diseases is determined according to what are called 'critical days'. Thus in the third Constitution in Book I (ch. 22) we find several such passages as the following:

> Most cases had a crisis on the fifth day from the outset, then intermitted four days, relapsed, had a crisis on the fifth day after the relapse, that is, after thirteen days altogether. Mostly children experienced crises thus, but older people did so too. Some had a crisis on the eleventh day, a relapse on the fourteenth, and a complete crisis on the twentieth. But if rigour came on about the twentieth day the crisis came on the fortieth. (trans. Jones, 1923: 179–81)

And later in the same book (ch. 26) the writer produces a detailed table of critical periods for diseases that had crises on even, and for those that had crises on odd, days.

It is clear that these books of the *Epidemics*, for all their appearance of being a set of systematic observations carried out in a spirit of 'disinterested' inquiry, owe something of their overall form to the writer's preconceived idea of the importance of critical days. But to this two points should be added. First one should not underestimate the experiential basis for the notion of 'critical' days. Jones, for example, remarked that it is a commonplace that some diseases tend to reach a crisis on a fixed day from the commencement, although the day is not absolutely fixed, nor is it the same for all diseases, and he went on to suggest a particular connection || between the theory of critical days and the periodicity of malaria (Jones, 1923: liv–lv). And secondly we should note the relation between theory and observation in *Epidemics* I and III. The writer is certainly disposed to believe that 'critical' days follow certain patterns. But the specific rules he suggests are evidently based on his particular observations, that is the case histories, including, no doubt, many others besides those recorded in our texts. Thus in chapter 21 of the third Constitution, having noted that 'when there was a crisis on the seventh day, with an intermission of six days followed by a relapse, there was a second crisis on the seventh day after the relapse', he mentions an example: 'in the case of Phanocritus, for example, who lay sick at the house of Gnathon the fuller' (transl. Jones, 1923: 179). And in the same chapter he refers by name to two patients whom we may assume to be identical with the subjects of the first and second case histories in the series that immediately follows (although if the Silenus mentioned is the same man, this example shows that the writer is capable of careless mistakes in using the case histories, in this instance concerning the day on which the patient died). It is not, then, that the writer conducted his observations simply in order to confirm rules *that he had already formulated in detail*. Rather those detailed rules are, for the most part at least, generalisations which he made on the basis of his particular observations (cf. Deichgräber, 1933:20f.).[12] And although the writer only rarely makes suggestions relating to the causes of the diseases he was studying, when he does so he is again clearly building on the evidence of the detailed case-histories, as for example in the third Constitution when he remarks on the predominance of the humour blood and several times notes the connection between loss of blood and recovery (chh. 14 and 15, cf. Deichgräber, 1933: 13).

Not all Greek science, even in the period before Plato, is as heavily inclined towards abstract theorising, and as impatient of empirical investigation, as most of the Presocratic philosophers appear to have been. *Epidemics* I and III, in particular, report detailed observations which served as the basis for generalisations concerning the periodicities of diseases. But it is not only their actual practice that suggests that different attitudes were taken by different early Greek scientists on the question of the proper method of conducting the inquiry into nature. We should next consider what the Greek authors themselves have to say on the subject of || the aims of science and on the nature of scientific method. It is true that most of the important texts relating

[12] Most of these rules take the form of generalisations which (he claims) apply 'for the most part' or 'in the majority of cases', and he notes instances where the pattern of critical days for similar conditions was dissimilar. Thus in chapter 20 of the third Constitution he remarks that two brothers fell ill at the same time but had their first crises on different days. Cf. also *Prognostic*, ch. 20, the author of which observes that critical periods cannot be calculated in whole days any more than the solar year or the lunar month can.

to these questions come not from the pre-Platonic period, but from the fourth century. Aristotle is obviously our most important single source if we try to investigate what the Greeks thought they were doing when they were doing science, or what ideas they had on the nature of the method of inquiry to be used in science. And yet it would be wrong to assume that the Aristotelian doctrine of *epistēmē* is the only, even if it may be the most representative, Greek notion of what 'science' is. Again the anonymous medical writers supply interesting evidence relating to the period from the mid-fifth to the mid-fourth century B.C.

The author of *On Ancient Medicine*, for example, who was probably writing around the end of the fifth century, shows what, for his time, is a quite surprising grasp of problems of method and of the distinctions between different types of inquiry. In chapter 1, particularly, he distinguishes different inquiries not merely by their subject-matter, but by their method, especially by whether or not they need to employ what he calls *hupotheseis* – postulates or assumptions. Medicine, he claims, has no need of such assumptions, differing in this from 'obscure and problematic subjects, concerning which anyone who attempts to hold forth at all is forced to use a postulate, as for example about things in heaven or things under the earth: for if anyone were to speak and declare the nature of these things, it would not be clear either to the speaker himself or to his audience whether what was said was true or not, since there is no criterion to which one should refer to obtain clear knowledge' (CMG I 1.36.15ff.). The writer distinguishes, then, between those inquiries where some sort of 'postulate' is necessary, and those like medicine (as he believes) where it is not. But when he cites astronomy, meteorology and geology as examples of inquiries where a postulate *is* necessary, it is not that he approves of the use of a postulate in these subjects but not in others. On the contrary, the very fact that they have to make use of a postulate is enough, in the writer's opinion, to condemn those inquiries as worthless – for that surely is the implication of the remark 'it would not be clear either to the speaker himself or to his audience whether what was said was true or not, since there is no criterion to which one should refer to obtain clear knowledge'. This is in effect, a statement of the need for scientific theories to be testable: speculation about what goes on in the sky and under the earth is worthless because unverifiable, at least according to the author's standards of verifiability. And yet when we turn to the theories concerning the component substances in the body and the origins of diseases that are proposed by the author himself, there is perhaps little need to point out || that they are similar in kind to, and almost as arbitrary as, the doctrines that he refuted with such damaging arguments.[13]

[13] He criticises medical theorists who had postulated 'the hot' 'the cold' 'the wet' or 'the dry' as the component substances in the body, but in his own admittedly rather more complex doctrine (chapter 14) he mentions as components such things as 'the sweet' and 'the bitter' (see further, Lloyd, 1966: 69f.).

Chapter 1 of *Ancient Medicine* provides important evidence of what one writer in the period before Aristotle thought on certain methodological issues. At first sight his demand for 'clarity' (*to saphes*) might seem comparable with the Aristotelian insistence on certain, unshakable knowledge. But the two ideas are quite different. Aristotle speaks of two types of cognitive state as unfailingly true, *nous*, the understanding of the primary self-evident premises or starting points of knowledge, and *epistēmē*, 'scientific' knowledge based on the demonstrative syllogism (see, e.g. *APo.*100b.5ff.). *Ancient Medicine*'s idea of 'clear knowledge' is much less sophisticated, but clarity appears to belong, in his view, only to notions for which there is overwhelming support in the direct evidence of the senses, and he certainly rejects conjecture for the sake of conjecture as worthless.

What is more *Ancient Medicine* also sets out certain ideas on the origins of medicine, and these too are worth comparing with the later, more influential notions of Aristotle on the development of different kinds of knowledge. The views expounded on this subject in *Metaphysics* A, chapters 1–2, are well known. There Aristotle distinguishes between 'experience', 'art' and 'science', but he makes no secret of his preference for those branches of knowledge that are purely speculative and unproductive, and he suggests that the highest form of knowledge, wisdom, arises from the sense of wonder (982b11ff.). *Ancient Medicine* deals, it is true, mainly with the origin of one specific 'art', medicine, but his views on this are striking. He treats medicine as a development of dietetics. He traces its origin to the trial and error experiments that men in their primitive state must (he believes) have carried out on their food in order to make it digestible. 'Trying many other things out on their food,' he says in chapter 3 (38.16ff.), 'they boiled and roasted and mixed it... adapting it all to the nature of man...But what juster or more fitting name could one give this discovery and inquiry than medicine?' And when he comes in a later chapter (20, 51.6ff.) to talk about the inquiry into nature more generally, he says, 'I think that clear knowledge about nature can only be gained from medicine, and from no other source.' Unless one studies medicine, he goes on, one cannot know 'what a man is, by what causes he comes to be and so on exactly'. His view, then, is that the 'arts' (and his || term *techne* is one that covers not only technology, but also inquiries that we should classify as scientific rather than technological) develop as a response to practical human needs.[14]

Much more could be said on the theme of the variety of the ideas on the nature, aims and origins of 'the inquiry into nature' that are developed by different Greek writers in the fifth and fourth centuries. But while the basis of my approach has been that the evidence for the cosmologists is only a part (though the best known and in many ways the most important part) of the total material available in a study of early Greek science, it is now time to

[14] Compare the views on the origin of civilisation and the arts reported in Diodorus I 8.1ff. (which are generally associated with Democritus).

return to the general problem of the relation between, and the relative importance of, conjecture and observation in early Greek science, bearing in mind the differing views that have been expressed by Popper and Kirk on the Presocratics, Popper maintaining that the best of the Presocratics' ideas have nothing to do with observation, and Kirk on the other hand insisting on the part played by observation (and common sense) in their theories. In part the disagreement between Popper and Kirk at this point seems to be a disagreement on values or emphasis, rather than on facts, and to reflect the different aspects of Presocratic speculation they have chosen to stress, and indeed to some extent one may, without contradiction, agree with what each of them has suggested. At the same time the evidence of the medical writers introduces certain new factors into the assessment of the balance between the dogmatic and the empirical strains in early Greek science as a whole, and I may now attempt to summarise the general conclusions that I think can be drawn on this issue.

First several of the theses concerning the origins of Greek science that Popper has developed (with some, at least, of which Kirk too is in agreement) must surely be accepted. The first is that Greek science begins with global questions, not with detailed, specific ones, let alone with collections of observations. It begins with such problems as how things began and what they are made of. And of course the question of origins, particularly, had always been a favourite subject of myths, so that the Milesian philosophers' theories of the beginnings of things may be seen as rationalistic answers to a question that had already been posed, and answered, in mythical terms in, for example, Hesiod's *Theogony*.

Secondly the role of rational criticism and debate in the early stages of Greek science is amply demonstrated by an impressive body of evidence. Whether or not Anaximander developed some of his doctrines in reaction to those of Thales, and Anaximenes to those of Anaximander, with later philosophers we have texts in which they refer unmistakably to the theories || of their predecessors, often mentioning them by name. Xenophanes evidently satirises Pythagoras (Fr. 7), besides criticising Homer and Hesiod for their anthropomorphism. Heraclitus criticises both Pythagoras and Xenophanes by name (Fr. 40). Whether Parmenides had Heraclitus, among others, in mind in Fr. 6 is disputed, but the remains of Empedocles and of Anaxagoras contain obvious echoes of Parmenides. And here the medical writers provide supplementary evidence which tells a similar story. Besides the many Hippocratic treatises which criticise the theories of other medical writers, *On the Nature of Man* (ch. 1) refers explicitly to the philosopher Melissus,[15] and *On Ancient Medicine* (ch. 20) to Empedocles. Although our information on the dates and places of residence of many writers is imprecise,

[15] *On the Nature of Man* (ch. 1) refers to the debates that took place on cosmological issues. The writer complains that given the same speakers and the same audience the same man never wins in the debate three times in succession.

we have enough evidence to be sure that at the end of the fifth century theorists working in widely separated parts of the Greek world were quite often acquainted with one another's doctrines in some detail. The ease with which ideas seem to have travelled, in a period when there were still formidable barriers to the passage of men and goods, is remarkable and deserves to be more fully investigated.

Then quite early in the history of the 'inquiry into nature', indeed not long after the Milesians themselves, there are second-order disputes, debates not between one particular theory or explanation and another, but on such questions as the bases of knowledge in general.[16] This particular problem is, of course, largely the province of the philosophers.[17] But what is especially striking and noteworthy is that even though there is no fully articulated doctrine of 'scientific method' until Aristotle, we find preliminary sketches, if no more, of various notions of how the investigation of natural phenomena should be conducted in several earlier writers, and here the evidence from the medical theorists is particularly valuable.[18] The extant texts of the period to the end of the fourth century B.C. provide, I || believe, no example of the most extreme inductivist thesis, the idea that a theory or explanation can simply be *read off* from collected observations. Such a thesis is not stated, so far as I know, nor for that matter does it appear to have been assumed in practice by any early Greek scientist.[19] But one view that practising 'inquirers into nature' *do* express is a distrust of speculation that is not capable of being verified (even if their idea of what would constitute a verification may be rather crude). Historically the emergence of this idea may be associated with the reaction of certain medical writers against what they represent as an invasion of medicine and biology by the assumptions and methods of the cosmologists. The writer of *On Ancient Medicine* considered that the geological and meteorological theories of his contemporaries suffered from one fundamental flaw, there was no evidence to confirm or refute them, and

[16] Cf. Popper's comments on the importance of different epistemological theories in antiquity (1963: 164ff., cf. 9ff. and 236ff.).

[17] By the end of the fifth century (or not long after) various positions had been stated by different writers on the question of the basis of knowledge, ranging from the pure intellectualism of Parmenides, to the crude sensationalism associated with Protagoras, via the complete scepticism that Gorgias professed: 'nothing exists, but if it exists, it is unknowable, and if it exists and is knowable, it still cannot be indicated to others' (*De Melisso*, *Xenophane*, *Gorgia*, 979a12f.). And that 'phenomena' or observed facts may be used as the basis for inferences concerning 'what is obscure' is the thesis of several writers beginning with Anaxagoras (Fr. 21a, see Lloyd, 1966: 338ff., 353ff.).

[18] *On Regimen* I, ch. 2, for example, states a view diametrically opposed to that of *On Ancient Medicine*: 'I say that he who intends to write correctly about human regimen must first know about the nature of man in general..., that is know from what things he is originally composed...'

[19] The nearest the Greeks came to expressing such a thesis is, perhaps, the equation of knowledge with sensation associated with Protagoras: but one should note first that Protagoras himself was no scientist, no inquirer into nature, and second that we know this doctrine mainly from Plato (e.g. *Theaetetus* 152Aff.) and it may well be that Plato has exaggerated it for his own polemical purposes.

the question of the methods proper to medicine and to cosmology is one that concerned other theorists at this period.[20]

The medical writers provide, as we saw, some of the most remarkable early examples of the systematic collection of data, although their investigations were evidently carried out in the light of, and clearly reflect, their theoretical preconceptions. At the same time some of the Hippocratic authors had become aware that the problem of how to proceed in the inquiry into nature is *a problem* and took issue with the cosmologists over it. The dogmatic nature of much Presocratic speculation is a feature that had struck the writer of *On Ancient Medicine*, who explicitly rejected the use of arbitrary postulates such as 'the hot' and 'the cold'. It is clear to us that he too made certain quite arbitrary assumptions in his own pathological doctrines, for instance. But this does not diminish the importance of the fact that he attempted to distinguish the methods proper to medicine from those of cosmology. In judging the dogmatic elements of Presocratic thought, then, we should not forget that those very elements provoked a reaction among the medical writers who attempted to set up an alternative ideal of how the inquiry into nature should be conducted.

It is tempting to offer sweeping generalisations about the nature of science in antiquity, and particularly about where it differs from science as we know it today. But many of the favourite generalisations of the textbooks, || helpful as they may be as very broad generalisations, often disregard quite a substantial body of evidence. It is often said, for instance, that Greek science is coloured, or rather tainted, by an all-pervasive teleology. Yet by the mid-fourth century, at any rate, the Greeks themselves were well aware of this issue, that is they could and did distinguish between different types of causes, 'teleological' or otherwise, and of course they took different sides on the substantive point, the atomists denying as strenuously as Plato and Aristotle maintained the relevance of teleological causation. Then it is often said that Greek science is unduly influenced by mathematical models, and again this may be true as a very broad generalisation, but again we should note that mathematics was not the only model for knowledge that was adopted. And I have argued elsewhere (Lloyd, 1964) that the failure of the Greeks to devise and carry out experiments has been greatly exaggerated.

Generalisation appears equally hazardous on the question of the relation between theory-construction and empirical research in antiquity, as here too the situation varies from one branch of science to another, depending on the subject-matter investigated and the means available to investigate it. Thus if we take the chief question that preoccupied Greek natural philosophers in the earliest period, that of the ultimate constituents of matter, empirical

[20] Thus *On the Nature of Man* (ch. 1) also contrasts his own approach to the study of man with that of the cosmologists. Like the author of *Ancient Medicine* he criticises certain theorists for suggesting as the original constituents of man such things as air, or fire, or water, or earth, which do not obviously exist *in* man.

investigations of the properties of different substances were almost certainly not undertaken at all extensively until the late fourth century, long after the theoretical debate had been initiated by the Presocratic philosophers. And in that instance the first such investigations that we know of (the fourth book of the *Meteorologica*, Theophrastus' *De Lapidibus*) were the work of men who adopted the Aristotelian four-element theory as the basis of their inquiry.[21] In dynamics, too, it is evident that the first recognisable dynamical theories in antiquity (those of Aristotle) precede any attempt to conduct deliberate investigations to throw light on the factors which govern the speed of a moving object.[22]

In astronomy, however, the situation is more complex. First there is a series of rather crude models for the heavenly bodies (Anaximander's incorporates the idea that the fixed stars are lower, that is closer to the earth, than either the sun or the moon). But by the fourth century the Greeks certainly had access to the work of some Egyptian and Babylonian astronomers (see Aristotle, *De Caelo* 292a7ff.) and had already produced || some observational astronomers of note themselves. In several cases we can trace how improvements in observational astronomy led to criticism of existing theories or indeed to new theoretical problems. The *Ars Eudoxi* provides information on the increasingly accurate estimates of the length of the seasons made from Euctemon and Meton in the late fifth century to Callippus in the latter part of the fourth. But this apparent irregularity in the movement of the sun constituted a difficulty for Eudoxus' theory of concentric spheres, and was, it seems,[23] one of the reasons that led Callippus to modify that theory in certain respects. Then to take an example from later Greek astronomy, it was by conducting his own detailed observations of the stars and by comparing these with those of earlier astronomers that Hipparchus was led to discover the precession of the equinoxes, and the observations in question (which are reported in Ptolemy, *Syntaxis* VII, chh. 1f.) need not have been, and probably were not, carried out with any idea of confirming or refuting a particular theory of the motion of the heavenly bodies.

In biology, some important problems, including, for example, the question of whether the seed comes from the whole of the body or not, had begun to be discussed before Aristotle. The so-called 'pangenesis' theory is associated with Democritus and may have originated with him, and it appears in the Hippocratic treatises *On Generation* (ch. 3) and *On Diseases* IV (ch. 32), which belong to the group of embryological works which also, interestingly enough, provide us with the first extant record of systematic investigations of the development of the hen's egg (*On the Nature of the Child*, ch. 29). But biology

[21] This remains true whether or not it was Aristotle himself who composed *Meteorologica* IV.

[22] While Aristotle himself, so far as we can judge, seems, in his dynamics, to have relied almost entirely on common experience, we may take it from Simplicius, *in Ph.* 916.12ff., that Strato undertook certain tests in this field relating, for example to the phenomena of acceleration.

[23] This is the view of Eudemus reported in Simplicius, *in Cael.* 497.18.ff.

also provides some good examples of problems which were only recognised as problems after quite extensive research had been done, in particular after the method of dissection had begun to be used fairly widely. Thus it was only after dissection been carried out on the heart that biologists began to discuss how precisely the blood moves into and out of the vessels of the heart and in the blood-vessels of the body generally.[24] And some of the typical problems debated by the Alexandrian biologists not only required the use of dissection and vivisection to || be studied, but only emerged as questions to be investigated as a result of knowledge obtained in the first place by the use of those methods.[25]

These few examples already show (I suggest) that there are variations in the relationship between problem-appreciation, theory-construction and programmes of empirical research in different contexts in ancient science. In particular we can distinguish between programmes of empirical research (if we may call them that) that were fairly clearly undertaken with a view to providing data that would confirm or refute a particular theory, and those programmes that reflect not a desire to test a theory so much as a desire to exploit a new scientific technique, such as dissection. Thus when the method of dissection was used systematically, this revealed problems that had not been dreamed of previously, and here it seems to me to make more sense to talk of the observations (not the problems themselves) as the starting-point of scientific progress. But whether or not that is accepted, I may end by observing that even a rapid survey such as this serves to indicate some of the quite striking differences to be found in early Greek science both in the conception of 'the inquiry into nature' and in its practice, and that so far as the historical issues arising out of the controversy between Popper and Kirk are concerned, what are needed are more, and more detailed, case-studies of specific scientific problems in antiquity, to throw further light on the intricate questions of the methods, and methodological assumptions, of early Greek scientists.

[24] Of course even before dissection of the heart had been attempted, there are certain writers, such as Empedocles, who refer to movements of the blood in the body, but they do so in the vaguest terms. The first extant text to refer to the valves of the heart in the context of a description of its general structure is *On the Heart* (ch. 10) which also makes some obscure and fanciful suggestions about the contents of the various vessels of the heart. Thereafter the questions of the functions and contents of the arteries and veins and of the possible intercommunications between them were evidently debated by Herophilus and Erasistratus, although it is Galen who provides us with our first surviving texts in which these problems, together with that of the movement of the blood into and out of the vessels of the heart, are set out and discussed at length (e.g. *Nat. Fac.* III, chh. 14f., Kühn II 204ff.).

[25] E.g. the investigation of the nervous system (both Herophilus and Erasistratus seem to have distinguished between motor and sensory nerves and to have attempted to trace particular nerves back to their origins) and the debate on the nature of digestion (where Erasistratus, having observed the peristaltic movement of the stomach and intestines, apparently maintained that this was solely responsible for the process of digestion). In both cases the investigation of the problem was taken much further by Galen, who provides the evidence concerning the work of the Alexandrians (e.g. *Loc. Aff.* III, ch. 14, *Nat. Fac.* III, ch. 4).

REFERENCES

Bourgey, L. (1953) *Observation et Expérience chez les médecins de la Collection Hippocratique* (Paris)

Deichgräber, K. (1933) *Die Epidemien und das Corpus Hippocraticum* (Berlin)

Jones, W. H. S. (1923) *Hippocrates*, I, Loeb edn

Kirk, G. S.(1960) 'Popper on science and the Presocratics', *Mind* N.S. 69:318–39

(1961) 'Sense and common-sense in the development of Greek philosophy', *Journal of Hellenic Studies* 81: 105–17

Kirk, G. S. and Raven, J. E. (1957) *The Presocratic Philosophers* (Cambridge)

Lloyd, G. E. R. (1964) 'Experiment in early Greek philosophy and medicine', *Proceedings of the Cambridge Philological Society* 190 (N.S. 10): 50–72

(1966), *Polarity and Analogy* (Cambridge)

Popper, K. R. (1958–9) 'Back to the Presocratics', *Proceedings of the Aristotelian Society* N.S. 59: 1–24 (reprinted with slight alterations and additions in Popper, 1963: 136–53)

(1963), *Conjectures and Refutations* (London) ('Historical conjectures and Heraclitus on change', pp. 153–65)

6

THE SOCIAL BACKGROUND OF EARLY GREEK PHILOSOPHY AND SCIENCE

INTRODUCTION

'The social background of early Greek philosophy and science' is a contribution to a multi-volume work, edited by Daiches and Thorlby, entitled *Literature and Western Civilisation* (vol. I, 1972). The three main questions the essay raises are nothing if not ambitious. The first relates to the self-perception of those whom we represent as the early Greek 'philosophers' or 'scientists' and how *they* saw the inquiries on which they engaged. The second concerns the general economic and political factors in the background to the rise of early Greek speculative thought and the particular question of when 'philosophy' provided a living. The third group of questions has to do with the mode of publication of philosophical works, the audiences to which they are addressed and how far the nature of the audience has any bearing on the character of those works themselves (p. 128). I drew attention, naturally, to the difficulty of these questions and to the limitations in the evidence available to us to suggest answers to them. However, undeterred, I set out the main data and attempted an overview of each problem at least so far as the early period, comprising the fifth and fourth centuries, goes.

In the nature of the exercise, qualifications were kept to a minimum, footnotes were altogether excluded, and the bibliography with which the essay was provided includes only a few of the essential items and is limited to works written or available in English. What needs now to be added to my account is some indication of the controversial nature of the issues and of the current state of debate. It is not that the main data (as I have just called them) need revision – although on some topics that are relevant to the problems, such as the invention of the alphabet, more evidence has subsequently become available.[1] Nor is that the *kinds* of explanatory factors that might be appealed to in order to account for the Greek experience are in serious doubt. But where controversy has been intense is on the *relative* weight to be attached to different factors. On the first of my three questions, the self-images of philosophy and science, little needs to be added. The observations I concluded with, concerning the wide divergences between different individuals and groups in interests, style, medium, attitude towards, and role

[1] Among recent surveys of the problem are the studies of Coldstream, 1977: 295ff.; Driver, 1976; Isserlin, 1982.

in, society, still stand (p. 133). Indeed this diversity might have been further illustrated extensively with more evidence from medicine and from mathematics. However, on my other two questions, both the general economic and political factors at work in the background, and the possible influence of the modes of publication, are at the centre of heated debate.

One of the articles listed in the bibliography is an early paper by Havelock on 'Pre-literacy and the Presocratics' (1966), and already at the time I wrote the question of the degree of literacy of ancient Greek society at different periods was a much contested issue. In this and an impressive array of other specialised and general publications Havelock and his associates have argued that the development of literacy in Greece was indeed a *revolution*, one with massive consequences for the whole subsequent history of literature and of science.[2] Indeed without that change, Havelock argues, *our* notions of *literature* and of *science* would themselves be unthinkable. Moreover this revolution can be dated, he believes, fairly precisely to the decades of the 440s and 430s. Before then what we have is not, of course, illiteracy, but, precisely, pre-literacy, and many of the most famous and influential works of Greek literature down to and including Euripides testify to the gradually increasing tension between orality and literacy, both in the writing and in the reception of the works in question. By Plato's day, in the early and mid-fourth century, the change had been effected, though it still leaves its marks on Plato's works as well.

Many specific points of interpretation on which Havelock's thesis rests, and his overall conclusion, have been contested by classical scholars, locked in dispute on such questions as the oral nature of the Homeric poems, the role of the Pisistratid 'edition', the components of Greek primary education, the extent of the penetration of knowledge of letters at different periods, the differences between Athens and other city-states, and many other problems.[3] But so far as our understanding of the development of early Greek philosophy and science goes, even more important contributions have come from a new comparative dimension introduced especially by the work of Goody. Goody's original paper, written in collaboration with Watt, was published in 1963, and should, despite its general nature, have been included in the bibliography to my article. Subsequently in three further studies (1977, 1986, 1987) Goody has modified and refined his thesis.

Goody agrees with Havelock on one basic point, namely the fundamental importance of the rise of literacy. But Goody has been concerned not so much with the comparison between different periods in Greece, as with that between Greece, the ancient Near East and modern 'traditional' societies. Whereas Havelock argued that within Greek philosophy the Presocratics come before, Plato after, the great revolution, Goody sees as the fundamental factor in the Greek development of philosophy at all the rise of literacy that

[2] Apart from Havelock's collected essays, 1982, see also Havelock and Hershbell, 1978 and Robb, 1983, especially.

[3] Thomas, 1989 reviews the problems.

followed from the invention of the alphabet: whenever precisely that is to be dated, it certainly antedates by some centuries the decades Havelock identifies as the turning-point. Goody focuses on the major differences in the circumstances of literacy in Greece on the one hand, in Egypt and Babylonia on the other. In the latter literacy was very largely confined to a tiny elite of specialists, who alone underwent the long and arduous education necessary to master cuneiform or the hieroglyphic script. While Goody has always allowed some – greater or smaller – place to other factors as well, and has certainly disavowed monocausal explanations, the chief thrust of his argument has been that in any attempt to explain the major differences between the main intellectual products of various ancient civilisations the *most important* group of factors relates to the technology of communication. The key points to consider include both the method of writing and the degree of literacy of readers and writers. The refinements that Goody has incorporated relate to such matters as the gradualism in the transition from (comparatively) illiterate to (comparatively) literate, the importance of the use of tables, lists, maps, and *aides-mémoire* of various kinds in proto-literacy, and the degrees of literacy present in a predominantly literate society, where some individuals may be fully fluent in reading and writing but others able merely to write their names.

As with Havelock, so too with Goody, the theses I have just outlined have proved controversial, and several of his principal points have been challenged by anthropologists and others. Thus Goody emphasised the liberating effects of increased literacy, and the way in which, once the word is written down, it can be made the subject of critical analysis in a manner that is impossible in oral exchange. But against that Parry (1985) for one has pointed rather to the inhibiting influence of the book, certainly when it takes the form of a sacred text deemed to be the repository of all-time truths.

However, so far as our understanding of early Greek philosophy and science goes, it is not so much the evaluation of the advantages and disadvantages of increasing literacy that is important, as the assessment of the relative weight to be attached to literacy as against other factors. In my article I referred very briefly and in general terms to economic factors (pp. 131, 139) and more especially to political ones (the connection of a new critical spirit in philosophy with the habit of free debate in politics and the law, p. 131, the influence of debates on the growth of logic and ethics especially, p. 139). The pioneering work there was that of J.-P. Vernant, P. Vidal-Naquet, M. Detienne and their associates, several of whose fundamental studies date from the early 1960s, although their publication in English translation did not get seriously under way until the late 1970s.

In subsequent studies (1979, 1987) that I have myself undertaken, following their lead, I have set out the arguments that suggest that while several different kinds of factor have no doubt to be brought into account in attempting any 'explanation' of the rise of philosophy and science of the

Greek kind in ancient Greece, it is above all the political factors that have primary importance. No doubt the existence of books and of a reasonable number of people able to read them is a contributory factor. Yet if we are to understand the growth of the kind of critical and open discussion that is characteristic of so much early Greek speculative thought, the key consideration is the political experience associated with the institutions of the Greek city-state. Those institutions created an audience of people who had extensive experience of evaluating evidence and arguments in the context of legal and political debates, and it is that audience that is crucial to the deployment of the particular styles of reasoning characteristic of early Greek speculative thought.

This is not the place to rehearse the theses that I have propounded at length elsewhere, the more so on points that remain controversial. It is more fruitful and constructive to attempt now to evaluate where the debate has got to in the sense of where the opposing parties are in basic agreement, and to consider the way forward in the sense of the most promising avenues for future work that may help to resolve or clarify the issues.

We must begin by repeating that on many points uncertainty is inevitable. On the extent of literacy in Greece and other ancient civilisations there is no question of our ever being able to give answers as precise as those that can be offered for the later development of literacy in modern Europe. Data such as those used by Furet and Ozouf (1982) in that connection will never be available for ancient civilisations. While further evidence is not inconceivable, and may well come to light, that will help to clarify the relation between various Semitic proto-alphabets and the earliest Greek ones, and the dates at which these were severally developed or interacted, here too problems are bound to remain.

However, it is agreed on all sides first that the stabilisation of the earliest Greek alphabets had already occurred by about 700 B.C. There is consensus, too, on a second, important point: whatever may be believed about the extent of literacy in different sections of the Greek population in the fifth and fourth centuries B.C., it is clear that the role of books was principally as *aides-mémoire* and that the medium of most intellectual exchanges was oral (as such evidence as that from Plato's *Parmenides*, set out in my article, p. 137, suggests). At that time Greek culture was still a culture mediated *chiefly* by the spoken word. Thirdly so far as the role of *debate* in both politics and emerging Greek speculative thought goes, the evidence from several fifth- and fourth-century writers (set out in Lloyd, 1987: ch. 2) shows that they recognised the parallelism and moreover that they saw the development of free speech in politics as having a crucial influence on other aspects of Greek culture.

But these and other reasonably well-established points do not, of course, enable us to resolve questions to do with the relative weight to be given to factors of different types in assessing the causes for the distinctive intellectual products of different ancient and modern societies. For these purposes it seems essential to carry the debate into areas that have remained comparatively neglected so far. First it is desirable to distinguish between different areas of speculative thought – for example between mathematics, natural philosophy and medicine – to test whether the same or different factors are at work in each. Secondly the range of societies taken into account could profitably be extended.

Thus on the first head one possible line of inquiry is to consider the comparison and contrast between Greek mathematics and other areas of speculative thought in the fifth and fourth centuries. While the general level of literacy is a factor affecting the culture as a whole, issues specifically to do with the availability of an alphabetic system of writing are naturally a good deal less important in mathematics than in philosophy, at least where mathematics is concerned with the manipulation of numbers and the use of diagrams rather than with words. Conversely the nature of the mathematics investigated may well be influenced both by the notations adopted and by the styles of presentation favoured. Again if socio-political factors are held to be influential in the background, that might be expected to be detectable across the board. A preliminary study (1990) suggests to me that the latter point can be confirmed in one respect at least: one feature that is to be found in Greek natural philosophy, in Greek medicine and in Greek mathematics, is a recurrent concern with foundations and with the explicit justification of a position, a concern that has striking analogues in both the theory and the practice of politics and the law.

The second desideratum – the extension of the range of societies considered – is more difficult to achieve since no comparison or contrast is of any value unless it is based on detailed, specialist, analysis. To date, much of the debate has focused on the similarities and differences between the Greeks and their main Near Eastern neighbours where issues to do with debts, borrowings and independent developments have often been discussed in very general terms and in relation to evidence that is sometimes tenuous in the extreme.[4] But the intellectual products, the technology of communication and the political situations, of both ancient India and of ancient China offer further opportunities to test hypotheses concerning the relevance of the last two to the first.

Of these two civilisations the data for China are especially promising, being both fuller and on the whole more securely datable. In particular the advanced technology of ancient China, combined with its development of competing philosophical groups, provides certain at first sight remarkable parallels with ancient Greece. Moreover the circumstances of the technology of communication are markedly dissimilar in these two civilisations, for ancient China is as much a culture of the written word as Greece is of the

[4] See for example Renfrew, 1987; Bernal, 1987.

spoken. There can be no question of arguing that Chinese philosophy and science depended, for their initial growth, on an increase in literacy that stemmed from the adoption of a simpler mode of writing. Moreover the impact of the advent of printing in ancient China shows certain dissimilarities from the experience of the West in that regard. Conversely so far as the political circumstances of ancient China go, the crucial difference from ancient Greece is the absence of the characteristic institutions of the city-state. It thus appears that we have a possibility to pursue, in greater detail than has been attempted so far,[5] the relative importance of different types of factor at different stages in the histories of these ancient civilisations. While we cannot, of course, anticipate the outcome of such a detailed study, we can, with some confidence, identify the opportunity presented and outline the agenda.

[5] Studies to be grouped as vol. VII of Needham's *Science and Civilisation in China*, elaborating and modifying views expressed in earlier volumes, will provide a useful basis for further work.

REFERENCES

Bernal, M. (1987) *Black Athena* (London)
Coldstream, J. N. (1977) *Geometric Greece* (London)
Detienne, M. (1967) *Les Maîtres de vérité dans la grèce archaïque* (Paris)
ed. (1988) *Les Savoirs de l'écriture en grèce ancienne* (Lille)
Driver, G. R. (1976) *Semitic Writing*, revised edn (London)
Finnegan, R. (1988) *Literacy and Orality. Studies in the Technology of Communication* (Oxford)
Furet, F., and Ozouf, J. (1982) *Reading and Writing: Literacy in France from Calvin to Jules Ferry* (Cambridge)
Gentili, B. (1988) *Poetry and its Public in Ancient Greece*, transl. by A. T. Cole of *Poesia e pubblico nella Grecia antica* (Rome, 1985) (Baltimore)
Goody, J. (1977) *The Domestication of the Savage Mind* (Cambridge)
(1986) *The Logic of Writing and the Organization of Society* (Cambridge)
(1987) *The Interface between the Written and the Oral* (Cambridge)
Goody, J., and Watt, I. P. (1962–3/1968) 'The consequences of literacy' (originally in *Comparative Studies in Society and History*, v, 1962–3, 304–45), in *Literacy in Traditional Societies*, ed. J. Goody (Cambridge, 1968), 27–68
Havelock, E. A. (1982) *The Literate Revolution in Greece and its Cultural Consequences* (Princeton)
(1986) *The Muse Learns to Write* (New Haven)
Havelock, E. A. and Hershbell, J. P., edd. (1978) *Communication Arts in the Ancient World* (New York)
Humphreys, S. C. (1986) 'Dynamics of the Greek breakthrough', in *The Origins and Diversity of Axial Age Civilizations*, ed. S. N. Eisenstadt (New York), 92–110
Isserlin, B. S. J. (1982) 'The earliest alphabetic writing', in *Cambridge Ancient History*, 2nd edn. vol. III, edd. J. Boardman et al. (Cambridge), 794–818
Lloyd, G. E. R. (1979) *Magic, Reason and Experience* (Cambridge)
(1987) *The Revolutions of Wisdom* (Berkeley)
(1990) *Demystifying Mentalities* (Cambridge)
Needham, J. (1954–) *Science and Civilisation in China* (Cambridge)

Parry, J. P. (1985) 'The Brahmanical tradition and the technology of the intellect', in *Reason and Mortality*, ed. J. Overing (London), 200–25

Renfrew, C. (1987) *Archaeology and Language* (Cambridge)

Robb, K. ed. (1983) *Language and Thought in Early Greek Philosophy* (La Salle, Ill.)

Santirocco, M. S. (1986) 'Literacy, orality, and thought', *Ancient Philosophy* 6, 153–60

Svenbro, J. (1988) *Phrasikleia* (Paris)

Thomas, R. (1989) *Oral Tradition and Written Record in Classical Athens* (Cambridge)

Vernant, J.-P. (1962/1982) *The Origins of Greek Thought*, transl. of *Les Origines de la pensée grecque* (Paris, 1962) (London)

Vidal-Naquet, P. (1981/1986) *The Black Hunter*, transl. by A. Szegedy-Maszak of *Le Chasseur noir* (Paris, 1981) (Baltimore)

THE SOCIAL BACKGROUND OF EARLY GREEK PHILOSOPHY AND SCIENCE

The idea that Thales invented or discovered a new inquiry, 'philosophy', goes back to Aristotle, as also does the notion that a more or less continuous development can be traced in certain branches of speculative thought from Thales onward. Aristotle is our main source of information about early Greek philosophy, but when he comments on his predecessors, as he does at length in *Metaphysics* A and elsewhere, it is not in order to write a history of Greek thought so much as to consider what light they had thrown on the philosophical and scientific problems (such as that of causation) that he himself was investigating. In this context he naturally emphasises the continuity and homogeneity of Presocratic speculation. He represents many of the first philosophers, particularly the group he calls the 'physicists' (*phusikoi* or *phusiologoi*), as if their investigations had the same aims and the same clearly defined subject-matter as his own physical treatises. Yet the circumstances under which they conducted their inquiries, and indeed their conceptions of the nature of the inquiries they were undertaking, were in many respects very different from what we know about Aristotle and other fourth-century philosophers.

The general history of early Greek cosmological, physical, and ethical theories can be reconstructed reasonably confidently from the information in Aristotle and our other sources, the most useful of our later sources being those that preserve quotations from the original works of the philosophers themselves. The social background against which philosophy and science developed among the Greeks raises a series of questions that are much more difficult to answer, because our earlier and more reliable sources largely neglect this aspect of their subject. First, what conception || did the thinkers have of the activity they engaged in? We may choose to represent them as 'philosophers' or scientists', but what view did they themselves have of their inquiries? Second, what economic and political factors were involved in the rise of philosophy and science in Greece, and what, in particular, was the social role of the men who pursued these inquiries? When, for example, did philosophy become a profession in the sense that it provided a livelihood? And third, how were their ideas published or made known? Can we identify the audiences to which philosophical or scientific compositions were addressed, and does the nature of the audience tell us anything important about the nature of the compositions?

Let us begin where our evidence is most solid – that is, with Aristotle at the end of the period under consideration. Here we can answer the first question fairly definitely. Aristotle often discusses the relations between 'physics', 'mathematics', 'first philosophy' (the study of being), 'politics', and so on, and he generally draws clear distinctions between these main departments of inquiry, although his classification does not coincide exactly with our own. His conception of the value of philosophy is vividly expressed in *Nicomachean Ethics*, book X, where he claims that the life of theoretical inquiry is superior to the practical life of the statesman and is supremely happy. We also have a good deal of information about the circumstances under which he worked, and this helps us to answer our other two questions, concerning the social role of the philosopher and the transmission of his ideas. The main events of his life are established, even though many of the details are obscure, and we know that quite apart from whatever private fortune he enjoyed (his father was court physician to King Amyntas of Macedon) he did not lack powerful connections. When he left Athens on Plato's death (347 B.C.) he was invited to go to Assos by Hermeias, the ruler of Atarneus, and he was later engaged by Philip of Macedon to teach the young Alexander. When he returned to Athens in 335 and began to teach in the Lyceum, he evidently had the approval and support of Antipater, Alexander's regent in Athens. When news of Alexander's death (323) reached Athens, Aristotle's position became sufficiently difficult to make him leave Athens for Chalcis, on the west coast of Euboea.

The importance of the Lyceum is obvious. Originally the relation between master and pupils was probably quite informal: it was only under Aristotle's successor, Theophrastus, that the Lyceum acquired extensive property and had (like Plato's Academy) the legal status of a *thiasos*, or religious association. But however informal the school may have been || under Aristotle, it enabled him to co-ordinate the work of a number of philosophers and scientists and to begin an unprecedentedly ambitious programme of research in many different subjects, notably biology and the social sciences. The school was also important for more mundane and materialistic reasons. Although we have no direct evidence on the point, we may presume that fees were charged for attending the lectures, as they were in other schools, and in the third century, at least, the pupils were certainly expected to make financial contributions towards the general upkeep of the school. Furthermore, it was for the lectures that Aristotle gave in the Lyceum and elsewhere that most of his extant treatises were prepared, and this has direct bearing on their style and content. Their lack of literary polish is evident: they are often highly compressed, obscure, and repetitious. On the other hand it is worth bearing in mind that several Greek philosophers distrusted the written word and confined their most important doctrines to oral teaching. In Aristotle's case the treatises contain many tentative ideas that served as the basis for discussions in the Lyceum, and he might well have been reluctant to present them to a wider public in the form in which we have them. Above all, the treatises allow us to observe the philosopher at work. His thought has often been described as a fixed, dogmatic system, but this is a gross misrepresentation. It is abundantly clear that he conceived the business of philosophy to lie as much in the defining of problems, the debating of alternative views, and the exploring of difficulties, as in the propounding of solutions. Although not cast in the dialogue form, his treatises at points retain something of the tone of actual philosophical discussions.

We can give a comparatively detailed account of the organization of the Lyceum in the fourth century and of the place it occupied in Greek society. But this account is inapplicable to the earlier Presocratics. Philosophy and science as activities conducted in well-established and well-organised institutions were the end-products of long, complex social and intellectual developments. How far can we reconstruct the circumstances under which the men who are considered the founders of philosophy and science actually worked?

A note on Thales will illustrate the magnitude of the problem. It is well known that before Aristotle there is almost no evidence to suggest that Thales engaged in natural philosophy or speculative inquiry of any kind. In popular belief he ranked among the Seven Wise Men, along with Solon, Pittacus, and so on. The exact list varies, but the Seven were in most cases men whose main role in society was as statesmen, law-givers, || and constitutional reformers. Their teaching was supposedly expressed, as a general rule, in the form of pithy, oracular statements. Plato (*Protagoras* 343AB) tells us that the maxims 'Know thyself' and 'Nothing too much', which were inscribed on the temple of Apollo at Delphi, were derived from them. Later writers attribute a set of such statements to Thales, but it is more important to remark that there is good early evidence of his engaging in political activity. Herodotus (I.170) praises the advice that he says Thales gave to his fellow Ionians, namely to federate and set up a common council. Other stories refer to his success in practical affairs. Herodotus (I.75) reports how he diverted the River Halys; Plato (*Republic* 600A) says he was responsible for many ingenious inventions (although Plato also has a laugh at his expense when, in the *Theaetetus* (174a), he tells the story of Thales falling down a well while he was looking at the stars); and Aristotle (*Politics* 1259a6ff.) tells how Thales made a fortune by cornering the market in olive-presses. To be sure, we also hear from Herodotus (I.74) that Thales predicted a total eclipse of the sun to within a year (this would have been the eclipse of 585 B.C.); yet whatever the truth behind this story, it does not allow us to attribute any definite astronomical model to Thales, and even knowledge of eclipses was not a purely theoretical achievement, but had important (if rare) practical applications. None of this proves, or even suggests, that Aristotle's view of Thales as the first natural philosopher is incorrect. But it is important to recognise that Thales impressed his contemporaries and immediate successors not for any remarks about water as an originative substance (whatever these were, they are not mentioned in any extant source before Aristotle), but for his superior skill in a wide range of fields where that skill had practical applications.

Although our testimonies are conflicting, it seems most likely that Thales left nothing in writing and that his teaching was entirely oral. The evidence for Anaximander's and Anaximenes' writings is much more definite. Simplicius (*in Ph.* 24.20f.) comments on the poetical diction of the one quotation from Anaximander that has been preserved, and Diogenes Laertius (II 3) tells us that Anaximenes used a plain Ionic style. Even so, we must be cautious. Both these thinkers evidently discussed certain cosmological topics. In particular, Anaximander apparently described the development of the world and the origin of living creatures. But it is far from clear how extensive their compositions were; nor indeed can we be certain that their primary purpose was what we should call cosmological. The references to style and the extant fragments themselves prove that both men wrote in prose, and this is in itself quite remarkable, || because it makes Anaximander not merely the first philosophical writer, but one of the very first *prose* writers, in Greek literature. But beyond this, on such questions as the relative importance of oral teaching and written text in spreading their ideas, we are reduced to guesswork.

Aristotle was the first to connect the rise of theoretical inquiry with the leisure afforded by affluence (*Metaphysics* A, chh. 1f.), and certainly Miletus – the home of Thales, Anaximander, and Anaximenes – was the most important and prosperous Greek city in Asia Minor until its destruction by the Persians in 494 B.C. It was famous for its trade, its industries, and especially its colonies (it was said to have founded 90). Moreover, thanks to alliances first with Croesus and then with Cyrus, it retained more political independence during the greater part of the sixth century than most of its Greek neighbours. Internally it was far from enjoying a settled constitution. Herodotus (5.28) refers to the party strife it suffered, and it was ruled intermittently by tyrants. But these upheavals did not prevent, and may even have done a good deal to encourage, the development of political institutions and political awareness. The growth of a new critical spirit in philosophy in the sixth and fifth centuries may be seen as a counterpart and offshoot of the contemporary development of the habit of free debate and discussion of politics and law throughout the Greek world.

We cannot determine what part either Anaximander or Anaximenes played in the social and political life of Miletus. Important though they are in the early history of philosophy, they are simply not mentioned by any extant source before Aristotle. Anaximander was said to have been responsible for the first Greek map, for which some of the Milesian colonists may have been grateful, and it is reasonable to assume that (like Thales) he took an active part in the affairs of the city. Again, we may infer *some* association between Thales, Anaximander, and Anaximenes, though what form that association took we do not know. Late sources speak of a teacher–pupil relationship in each case, but with their love for cut-and-dried philosophical genealogies the doxographers are notoriously unreliable on such a point, and it would be quite unjustified to infer from their association the existence of a formal school, a prototype Academy or Lyceum. Very likely, speculative inquiry, at this stage, was at most the avocation of a few private citizens.

The next figures who appear in the histories of philosophy – Pythagoras, Xenophanes, Heraclitus, and Parmenides – are all quite different from what we can judge of the three Milesians, and indeed from one another, and the contrasts between them are instructive. Although the evidence || for early Pythagoreanism is hazy, we can be reasonably certain about some very important points. (1) Pythagoras was partly, perhaps primarily, a religious and moral leader. One of the few doctrines that can be traced back to Pythagoras himself is the transmigration of souls, and Plato (*Republic* 600B) tells us that he taught his followers a way of life. (2) The Pythagoreans, from early on, formed a distinct group or sect that had a reputation for exclusiveness and secrecy.*[1] (3) Pythagorean associations were a political force in several cities in Magna Graecia in the late sixth century B.C. The Cylonian conspiracy at the end of that century was an anti-Pythagorean 'counter-revolution' and marks the end of a period during which the Pythagoreans had apparently been a major political influence in western Greece. It is true that the term 'Pythagorean' came to be applied to fifth-century thinkers whose association with the sect was quite loose. Nevertheless it is significant that the most prominent and numerous group of philosophers and scientists in the pre-Platonic period was one that had been originally founded – and was still in certain places kept together – at least as much for religious, ethical, or even political motives, as for the purpose of conducting what we should call philosophical and scientific investigations. Furthermore the religious nature of the group influenced the work of its members profoundly. One reason why it is so difficult to establish the individual authorship of early Pythagorean doctrines is that Pythagoras himself was held in such awe, and where the authority of the founder counted for so much, criticism and discussion of his views were slow in developing. Mathematics was considered the key to the secrets of the universe, but mathematical discoveries were, to begin with at least, guarded from outsiders as jealously as were the details of the mystery rites from those who had not been initiated.

Our next philosopher, Xenophanes, belongs as much to the history of lyric poetry as to that of cosmology. True, several of his verses are important for the development of speculative thought, particularly those in which he expresses ideas about god in opposition to the anthropomorphism of Homer and Hesiod. But these fragments were composed by a poet who was as much

*[1] That reputation is, however, largely the product of the views expressed by late and often unreliable sources. Here and at the end of this paragraph the opinions I expressed about early Pythagoreanism should have been more cautious. Secretiveness is, however, as I note (p. 139), a feature of some medical writings in the Hippocratic Corpus: see also Lloyd, 1979: 41 and cf. 228 for a more qualified statement concerning the Pythagoreans.

an entertainer as a philosopher, as we can see from the two complete poems of his that are preserved. One of these (Fr. 1) describes a banquet; in the other (Fr. 2) Xenophanes claims that his 'wisdom' is more valuable to the city than the skill of any athlete, and this poem is especially interesting because it is not as a cosmologist or as a natural scientist that Xenophanes makes this claim, but as a poet and moral leader.

Heraclitus and Parmenides are speculative thinkers of a very different || calibre. Heraclitus is the first philosopher from whom we have more than just one or two prose fragments. His reported statements have a very distinctive elliptical style, which justly won him a great reputation for obscurity, but is also undeniably memorable; many of his statements owe their preservation to their very obscurity. If Xenophanes may in some respects be compared with an Anacreon or a Theognis, Heraclitus, like the Wise Men before him, invites comparison with an oracle. Indeed he refers approvingly to the Delphic oracle in one fragment (Fr. 93), where he says that Apollo 'neither speaks nor conceals but indicates' his meaning. In other ways, too, Heraclitus is exceptional among the early Greek thinkers. Although some of his fragments convey a political message, he apparently refused to take an active part in politics, and expresses his contempt for the common run of his fellow citizens in many of his sayings.

Heraclitus produced a series of oracular pronouncements, and bluntly described his method of approach to the truth (Fr. 101) as 'I searched myself', a dictum that may echo the Delphic 'Know thyself.' When we turn to Parmenides, the contrast could hardly be greater, whether we consider the content of his thought, or his style and method. First, he chose verse as his medium. Second, his 'Way of Truth' is introduced with a proem in which he describes how he is borne toward the light, how he passes through the gates of the paths of night and day and is greeted by an unnamed goddess who remarks that the road he has travelled is 'far from the footsteps of men'. Third, the whole of the rest of the poem, both the 'Way of Truth' and the 'Way of Seeming', is the speech of this goddess. In all this, Parmenides was far from merely following literary convention, but was claiming for his philosophy the status of a revelation. It is striking that the first closely argued discussion of the central philosophical problem of being is in verse, and was composed by a man who considered himself divinely inspired.*[2]

We may now pause to take stock of the earlier Presocratics. The thinkers I have mentioned are usually considered to form a single fairly continuous 'history of early Greek philosophy'. From the point of view of their physical and cosmological theories this line of interpretation can largely be justified. At the same time we should recognize how different these thinkers were from one another: different in their *interests*, in the *style* and *medium* they used in communicating their ideas, and in their *attitude toward* and *role in* society. Neither the phrase *peri phuseos historia* (inquiry concerning nature) nor the

*[2] The actual conclusions of the Way of Truth are, however, the outcome of the first tight deductive argument of its kind in Western philosophy.

term *philosophia* (philosophy) itself can be dated precisely. Our later sources regularly use the former as the || title of early philosophical works, but this evidence is untrustworthy. The term 'philosophy' is sometimes said to have been invented by Pythagoras and may have acquired a special sense applied to the Pythagoreans, but it almost certainly had earlier non-technical usages in Ionic Greek. It is not until the later part of the fifth century that we find reliable texts in which these terms are used to refer specifically to 'natural philosophy'; and several of the texts in question occur, interestingly enough, not in the philosophers themselves, as one might expect, but in the medical writers, who were often highly critical of the cosmologists and who resisted what they represented as an invasion of medicine by the methods of natural philosophy. So far as the earlier Presocratics down to Parmenides are concerned, it is fairly clear that none of them placed himself in any category of 'philosopher' or 'inquirer concerning nature' that included all the others. It is even uncertain how far any of them saw themselves as part of a single developing investigation, despite the fact that they were often aware of one another's ideas. Thus Xenophanes pokes fun at Pythagoras in one poem (Fr. 7), and Heraclitus (Fr. 40) criticises both Pythagoras and Xenophanes. But it is significant that in the fragment in which Heraclitus does this, he lumps the two philosophers together with the poet Hesiod and the geographer Hecataeus: 'Much learning does not teach sense; for otherwise it would have taught Hesiod and Pythagoras and again Xenophanes and Hecataeus.' The earlier Presocratics competed with one another and with others, particularly the poets, for the attention of their fellow-Greeks, but 'philosophy' provided as yet no clearly defined role. Besides their interest in cosmology, those whom we know as the first Greek philosophers all had one or more of the further roles of sage, religious teacher, statesman, moralist, and entertainer.

Until after Parmenides there is little evidence of prose works on natural philosophy – indeed, little evidence of prose composition of any sort. During the course of the fifth century, certain major changes take place. First, the sheer quantity of work produced on philosophical, scientific, and technological subjects increases markedly. Second, prose overtakes verse as the dominant medium. And third, alongside the successors of the philosopher-sages of the sixth century, two new kinds of authors appear: professional educators who write on any subject that people will pay them to teach; and (not always clearly distinguished from the former group) professional practitioners who write on technical subjects mostly for other practitioners.

These generalisations must be qualified. Empedocles, for instance, || wrote in verse and combined the roles of religious leader, mystic, and prophet with those of physicist and cosmologist. As Parmenides had addressed the goddess at the beginning of his 'Way of Truth', so Empedocles, apparently in direct imitation, invoked the Muse in his poem *On Nature* (Fr. 3). More interestingly, his other work, the *Purifications*, is (as its title suggests) a religious poem in which he describes the fall, transmigrations, and redemption of the *daimon*. And this begins (Fr. 112) with a passage in which Empedocles coolly describes himself as 'an immortal god, no longer mortal', and says that people throng to him 'asking the path to gain, some desiring oracles, while others seek to hear the word of healing for all kinds of diseases'. There is something of the magician in Empedocles, alongside the natural scientist who could produce quite detailed accounts of the physiological processes of respiration and vision.

Yet Empedocles was the last great Presocratic cosmologist to write in verse. After Parmenides the usual medium of philosophical writers was prose: this is true of the later Eleatics Zeno and Melissus, of the natural philosophers Anaxagoras, Diogenes of Apollonia, Leucippus, and Democritus, and of the later Pythagoreans Philolaus and Archytas, as well as of a host of lesser cosmologists. And prose is also the usual medium both of the Sophists and of the authors of technical treatises on such subjects as medicine and music.

Although almost all their writings are lost, we know a good deal about the rise of the Sophists, a movement*[3] that had far-reaching consequences over the whole field of Greek education as well as specifically in the development of philosophy. Plato (*Protagoras* 349A) tells us that Protagoras of Abdera was the first to demand a fee for teaching virtue. But he was soon followed by many others, the most famous of whom were Gorgias, Hippias, Prodicus, Thrasymachus, Antiphon, and Critias. Some of these specialised in a particular branch or branches of learning: for example, Thrasymachus chiefly taught rhetoric, and Prodicus was mainly known as a philologist. Others, such as Hippias, claimed to be able to teach almost any subject from mathematics and astronomy to mythology. But what all these men had in common, and what marks them out from the earlier generations of philosophers, was that they taught for money and were prepared to travel all over the Greek world to do so.

They acquired and built up their reputations primarily, it seems, by giving public performances at the great pan-Hellenic festivals. Hippias, we are told, went regularly to the festival at Olympia to give exhibition speeches and to answer questions from the crowd that gathered. In some || cases we know how much the Sophists charged to attend their courses. Prodicus apparently gave two courses on philology: the beginners' costing 1 drachma (that is, as much as Anaxagoras' treatise *On Nature*), and the advanced costing 50 drachmas. Hippias is said to have earned 20 minae from a visit to a single small town in Sicily, which was about 2,000 times the current daily wage for a skilled worker. Even when we allow for some exaggeration in our sources, it is clear that several fifth-century Sophists grew rich from their profession,

*[3] The term 'movement' – I would now wish to add – should not, in this context, be taken to imply doctrinal or indeed any other kind of unity. Those whom we conventionally label Sophists were teachers with often highly developed individualistic characters and quite diverse interests.

which continued to be well paid in the fourth century too. For example, Isocrates (*Antidosis* 158ff.) tells us that he made a considerable fortune as a teacher, although he also indicates (*Against the Sophists* 3ff.) that there were plenty of minor Sophists in Athens in his day who barely scraped a living from their lectures.

In the late fifth century a new kind of learning began to challenge the old education, which consisted largely of grammar, music and poetry, and gymnastics. Starting with the sons of the richest citizens, who had time and money to spare, the Sophists eventually attracted a wide clientele. Apart from bringing about a general broadening of education, they helped to introduce two other important developments. First, one of the main subjects they professed was rhetoric, and skill in public speaking was becoming increasingly important in many different contexts: in the law-courts, in political assemblies, and on diplomatic missions from one city-state to another. In teaching rhetoric as an art the Sophists undoubtedly helped to make their contemporaries more conscious not only of literary style, but also of the whole question of techniques of persuasion and methods of argument, and thus contributed both directly and indirectly to the development of logic.

Second, the challenge to the old education was seen as a challenge to traditional morality. The new interest in ethics in the late fifth century is associated particularly with Socrates. But he did not bring about this major shift in interest single-handed. It is clear that the Sophists did much to stimulate debate on ethical issues, for example in the controversy between 'nature' and 'convention'. Indeed, had the teaching of Protagoras, Gorgias, and the rest not had an obvious moral significance, Plato would hardly have taken such pains to attack what they said.

Some Sophists were prepared to lecture on a wide range of topics, including technical subjects of which they had little or no practical knowledge. But such subjects (particularly music and medicine) were also taught more professionally, by actual – and to intending – practitioners. The Greeks were careful to distinguish between learning an art for the sake of general education, and learning it in order to practise as a || professional. In music, for instance, there was an important difference between learning the lyre as part of one's education as a gentleman, and learning it in order to become a professional lyre-player: the first was allowed and encouraged, the second severely frowned upon, by the higher echelons of society.

By far the most important 'technical' subject for the development of science was medicine, and the treatises of the Hippocratic Corpus provide excellent examples of the different ways in which this subject was treated. Some works were evidently composed for rhetorical performances by men who were probably not themselves medical practitioners. One such piece is *On Breaths*. Another treatise, *On the Nature of Man*, refers directly to the debates on medicine and other subjects. The writer says (ch. 1) that the best way to discover how ignorant his opponents are is to attend their discussions.

'Given the same debaters in front of the same audience, the same speaker never gains the advantage three times in succession, but now one man wins, now another, now whoever happens to speak most fluently before the crowd.' These and other texts prove that medicine was among the subjects on which public debates were held. On such occasions, where the contest was adjudicated either by a lay umpire or by the audience itself, what counted was rhetorical skill, not the technical knowledge that a speaker revealed; and this goes a long way to explaining the superficial quality of the discussion in some of the medical treatises that have survived. On the other hand, the Hippocratic corpus also contains works of a very different kind. The surgical treatises and the collections of case-histories known as the *Epidemics* were written by professional practitioners for their colleagues. These works pay no attention to style. Their aim was simply to convey useful medical knowledge, and this they do most effectively.

Fifth-century writers differ considerably in the extent to which they cultivate literary style. Yet in most cases their works were read aloud, usually before an audience. This is true not only of the exhibition speeches of the Sophists, but also of the cosmological works, whether in prose or in verse, and even of such a sophisticated treatise as Zeno's arguments against the pluralists. The beginning of Plato's *Parmenides* (127Aff.) provides useful evidence on this point, for there we are told that Socrates, having heard that Parmenides and Zeno were in town for the Great Panathenaea, called on Zeno at his lodging to hear him read from the treatises that they had just brought to Athens for the first time. These were definitely written compositions (the term used in Plato is *grammata*) and Zeno interestingly remarks of one piece that no sooner had he || composed the work than someone stole it and (as we should say) pirated an edition. But Socrates does not ask to borrow Zeno's book or to read it for himself: he asks Zeno to read it out and they then debate its contents. Even complex philosophical works were more commonly recited and discussed than studied alone and in silence.

The evidence concerning the manufacture and publication of books in the fifth century is poor. Yet by the end of that century it is clear that in Athens one could obtain not only editions of Homer and the poets, but also some highly specialised works. A famous passage in the *Apology* (26Dff.) indicates that Anaxagoras' cosmological treatise could be bought for one drachma at most, from the stalls in the Orchestra. The increasing availability of texts obviously contributed a great deal both to the preservation and to the spread of philosophical and scientific ideas. Although private libraries were still quite rare, certain individuals acquired considerable collections of books. Thus, according to Xenophon (*Memorabilia* 4.2.8ff.), Euthydemus owned large numbers of medical treatises and works on architecture, mathematics, astronomy, and other subjects, as well as editions of the most famous poets. Such a collection was exceptionally large, but we may presume that the medical schools and the Pythagoreans had their own libraries. Indeed the extant Hippocratic treatises probably derive, in the main, from the library of one fourth-century medical school.*4

The rise of the Sophists, the growth of such professional groups as the medical schools, and the increasing availability of books, were all important factors in the development of philosophy and science in the fifth and fourth centuries B.C. Yet these changes were far from being always and everywhere approved. Plato's distrust of the written word is well known, and although his own magnificent writings seem to give him the lie, all of them (with the exception of some doubtfully authentic letters) are dialogues purporting to represent actual conversations. Even his favourite word for the activity of the philosopher, *dialektikē*, has as its root sense the art of conversation. Again, although several Hippocratic authors emphasise the value and importance of the art of medicine and the difference between the professional practitioner and the layman, doctors were still mere craftsmen, even though in the hierarchy of craftsmen they ranked among the highest. Finally, Aristophanes and Plato were certainly not the only Athenians of their respective generations to disapprove strongly of the profession of paid Sophist.

Despite the hostile reception the Sophists met in some quarters, much of the new learning they taught was taken over into 'liberal' education || during the course of the fourth century. The era of the great 'polymath' Sophists, Protagoras and Hippias, who travelled from city to city gathering pupils as they went, gave way to a period dominated by more stable, and more respectable, schools. Of these the most famous were Isocrates' school of rhetoric and Plato's Academy. Isocrates' school, where the emphasis was laid on useful knowledge, particularly on skill in public speaking, may be considered the direct successor to the fifth-century Sophists. Plato's Academy owed more to the model of the Pythagorean fraternities, and in turn it provided the chief model for Aristotle's Lyceum and for countless other educational institutions. The programme of education Plato prescribes for his statesmen-philosophers in the *Republic* is a long and elaborate one. The student begins as a child with music and gymnastics and proceeds to dialectic, at the age of 30, only after an intensive course in mathematics; a further 20 years pass before the best minds graduate to the highest study of all, the contemplation of the Good. We do not know how closely Plato tried to keep to this scheme in the actual curriculum of the Academy. But we may be sure of two things at least: first, that, unlike Isocrates, Plato placed great emphasis on the role of the mathematical sciences in higher education; and second, that his object was to produce not academic intellectuals, but statesmen-philosophers, men who could and would influence the course of events in their cities and in the Greek world at large.

Much as one might like to represent what we call philosophy and science as

*4 I should now wish to qualify this statement: such a library may possibly be the origin of our Hippocratic treatises, but to put it more strongly than that is mere conjecture.

the products of a single, continuous development in Greece, the available evidence suggests a very different and far more complex story. We are used to recognising the variety of political institutions that the Greeks produced – a variety that contrasts strongly with, and was only possible in the absence of, the monolithic authoritarian regimes of the Near Eastern super-powers Egypt and Persia. But equally, and not unconnectedly, the Greeks developed a variety of different conceptions of education. In the sixth and fifth centuries B.C. philosophers and scientists with very different ideas, interests, and ambitions competed with one another, and with the poets and religious leaders, as educators. Even in the fourth century, although competing schools agreed in their claim to teach *philosophia*, what was meant by that term differed from one school to another: it was not only Plato, but also Isocrates, who professed to practise and teach 'philosophy'. Furthermore, this very variety of competing models of education and philosophy was an important factor, both in making the Greeks more aware of the distinctions between different || intellectual disciplines, and in stimulating discussion of fundamental ethical issues. As Plato saw, the question of right education could not be settled except in conjunction with the question of the good life as a whole.

Aristotle's view of philosophy as the product of natural curiosity in a leisured society is helpful as far as it goes. Clearly, it was only because he was comparatively free from anxiety concerning his livelihood that the Greek citizen was able to devote so much of his time and energy to the activities he enjoyed so much – political affairs and the social life of the city-state, including its festivals and entertainments. The economic conditions allowed individuals to engage in theoretical studies without regard to any useful outcome they might have. Moreover the political circumstances in Greece positively favoured the growth of free discussion, so important for the development of philosophy and science. Both logic and ethics may, without too much exaggeration, be said to derive ultimately from the debates of the market places, law courts, and assemblies of the city-state. But the development of science and mathematics required other factors as well, particularly the idea of co-operation in research. Here both the Pythagoreans and the medical schools (in their very different ways) had important contributions to make. But in neither case was the chief motive for these associations any idea of the value of scientific research for its own sake. Religious and political ties helped to keep the Pythagorean groups together, and the medical schools were exclusive associations formed from professional motives, like a medieval guild or a modern trade union. Moreover the doctors, like the Pythagoreans, were on occasion secretive about their discoveries.

We noted at the beginning that the first extensive philosophical and scientific investigations were undertaken in the Lyceum. It may now be suggested that the success of the Lyceum was in part the result of its combining the tradition of free discussion with the idea of corporate research that goes back to the Pythagoreans and to the early medical schools. Although the Museum at Alexandria later surpassed even the Lyceum in the range of its researches, the institutions where extensive scientific investigations were carried out were rare throughout antiquity. The ancients lacked the idea that dominates our own society, that scientific research holds the key to material progress. Indeed, although there were many who recognised that civilisation had developed in the past, there were few who imagined that it would or could progress much further in the future. The *raison d'être* of the Lyceum and Museum and of the many minor schools modelled on them was not any idea of the usefulness of scientific research, but the ideal of a 'liberal' higher education. The || physical or the biological sciences were part of philosophy in the widest sense of that term, and with two main exceptions little attention was paid to the possibility of turning scientific discoveries to practical advantage. The first main exception was the application of technology to improving weapons of war – siege engines, catapults, and the like. The second was medicine. Many of the most famous biologists were doctors, who were motivated in their research partly by the desire to improve the treatment of the sick, and sought to apply their knowledge to this end. Yet not even the most famous and successful doctors in antiquity entirely escaped the disdain usually felt for the craftsman. In the Greek scale of values the theorist was always superior to the technologist, and although this ideology did not completely prevent the practical application of scientific discoveries, it certainly inhibited it, and acted as an important barrier to the cross-fertilisation of different intellectual disciplines.

REFERENCES

Cherniss, H. (1945) *The Riddle of the Early Academy* (Berkeley and Los Angeles)

Davison, J. A. (1962) 'Literature and literacy in ancient Greece', *Phoenix* 16: 141–56 and 219–33

Farrington, B. (1961) *Greek Science*, rev. 1-vol. edn (London)

Guthrie, W. K. C. (1962–9) *A History of Greek Philosophy*, I-III (Cambridge)

Harvey, F. D. (1966) 'Literacy in the Athenian democracy', *Revue des études grecques* 79:585–635

Havelock, E. A. (1966) 'Pre-literacy and the pre-Socratics', *Bulletin of the Institute of Classical Studies* 13: 44–67

Jaeger, W. (1946) *Paideia: The Ideals of Greek Culture,* 3 vols., 3rd edn (Oxford)

Kenyon, F. G. (1951) *Books and Readers in Ancient Greece and Rome*, 2nd edn (Oxford

Lloyd, G. E. R. (1970) *Early Greek Science, Thales to Aristotle* (London)

Marrou, H. I. (1956). *A History of Education in Antiquity*, transl. by G. Lamb (London)

Pfeiffer, R. (1968) *History of Classical Scholarship from the Beginnings to the End of the Hellenistic Age* (Oxford)

Reynolds, L. D. and Wilson, N. G. (1968) *Scribes and Scholars* (Oxford)

Turner, E. G. (1951) 'Athenian books in the fifth and fourth centuries B.C.' (inaugural lecture, University College London)

7

GREEK COSMOLOGIES

INTRODUCTION

In 1972 the Faculty of Oriental Studies in Cambridge organised a set of lectures on ancient cosmologies which were later published as a book with that title. Among the contributors were, for example, Joseph Needham on China, R. F. Gombrich on India, W. G. Lambert on Sumer and Babylon. My own task, as I remark at the outset, was a daunting one, the vast field of Greek cosmology from Mycenae to Byzantium, from which I tried to select some of the most interesting or important topics. I concentrated, as I explain (p. 146), first on the transition from pre-cosmological mythology to cosmology itself, defined strictly, following the Greek sense, as a comprehensive view of the universe as an ordered whole: second on the pluralism of Greek cosmological notions and their dialectical nature: and third on the development of critical methods, both the development of argument and the appeal to the data of observation.

While I still stand by most of what I wrote, in the second and third cases especially it now seems to me that my discussion did not go far enough. Two points in particular are now worth not just further exemplification, but some conceptual elaboration.

Following the analysis in Part II of *Polarity and Analogy* I identified three recurrent Greek cosmological models, broadly those that represent the cosmos as a living organism, as an artefact, and as a political entity (of various types: kingship, an oligarchy of balanced powers, anarchy). In each case I endeavoured to show both what the cosmological model owed to myth and where it departed from the patterns of earlier Greek mythology, notably in the systematisation of ideas to produce, precisely, an overall or comprehensive view of the cosmos *as such*. That was not the only possible way to organise the complex material that Greek cosmological thought comprises. As I have already noted (above, p. 102) Furley's recent important study (1987) suggests that Greek cosmologists divide into two clearly demarcated camps, where those who believe in teleology, continuum theory and a finite universe, are ranged against those who maintain anti-teleology, atomism and the doctrine of infinite worlds. But both Furley and my own discussion emphasise, from different perspectives, the debates engaged in by those who attempted to produce comprehensive cosmological systems.

However, there was more to the use of the three models I focused on than I indicated. Subsequent work in the history of science and in anthropology has drawn attention to aspects of the pervasiveness of dominant models or metaphors that have a bearing on the ancient Greek material. I have in mind work in the history of science developing Kuhn's ideas on the roles of paradigms in scientific crises and in normal science, Goodman's study (1978) of the factors that go towards the constitution of a world-picture, and the work of Lakoff and Johnson (1980) and others on dominant metaphors in our own ordinary speech. In addition a large number of ethnographic studies, such as that of Rosaldo on Ilongot metaphors and models for the self (1980), have, from their different points of view, also drawn attention not just to the presence of dominant images in explicit forms, but also to their influences on deeper assumptions and conceptualisations. Both at the explicit and at the implicit levels the metaphors deployed by a given society or group will be among the crucial constitutive elements of world – views, value-systems or ideologies, and of attitudes to or beliefs about the self and the other. The ancient Greeks are certainly remarkably explicit about the models they invoke in their cosmologies and elsewhere – which made my task of identifying the prominent analogies all the easier – and this explicitness stems, no doubt, in part from the argumentative nature of cosmological debate, a point mentioned in my essay and to which I shall return here. However, the implicit repercussions of these preferred models and metaphors are far-reaching.

For example, a common feature of all three models is the idea of the interconnectedness of the parts that make the whole. They are indeed three different ways of expressing that notion, of interconnectedness, the very notion, as I remarked, that lies at the heart of the Greek conception of the cosmos *as* an *ordered whole*. But at a higher level of generality than I explored in my essay, this very notion that the cosmos *is* or is *like* an ordered whole makes certain assumptions that themselves merit further reflection – even if they were assumptions that did not go completely unchallenged by and were not totally invisible to the ancient Greeks themselves. I mentioned aspects of the prevailing anthropocentricity of much Greek cosmological speculation, as also the positive side to this, its confident humanism. But the momentousness of the expectation that the cosmos is *intelligible to us* (which is part of that anthropocentricity) deserves more emphasis.

There are, to be sure, as I pointed out, sceptical traditions – on which as on many other topics much fruitful work has since been done (e.g. Burnyeat, 1983). One such tradition denies that the world *is* knowable and another suspends judgement on that question. However, they did not become well-worked-out philosophical positions until the Hellenistic period: nor did they ever represent the dominant view in Greek antiquity. Certainly a feature shared by the main positive schools of cosmology – and both of Furley's opposing camps can be included here – is that of the intelligibility, to human reason, of the cosmos, however much humans may differ about how they do understand the cosmos. Certainly that underlying feature reflects a measure of confidence in the viability of the exercise of cosmological speculation. It is not that the ancient Greeks inhabited a world the workings of which were, and were bound to remain, a mystery, a world where there were no laws or regularities to be discovered, that just played games with its inhabitants, that was bound to defeat any attempts at understanding. But the very fact that *we* share – *mutatis mutandis* – some such belief, may make the Greek assumption less visible to us: it is then all the more important to draw attention to it, by contrast to its alternatives. For it is far from being the case that all ancient and all modern peoples have shared the belief in the intelligibility, to mere humans, of the world they inhabit. So while the particular vehicles the Greeks used to express one or other modality of that idea, the cosmos as a living organism, as an artefact, as a society, all received some attention in my essay, it was the further analysis of what these ideas themselves presuppose that I now feel should be added to the account.

The second point where some conceptual elaboration is necessary is linked to the first and concerns the relationship between the pluralism of Greek cosmology and the development of critical methods. While I drew some comparisons between early Greek mythology and the myths of Egypt and Babylonia, I might have embarked on more explicit comparisons between the Greek cosmological material and that discussed by some of my co-authors in the original volume.

Pluralism in cosmological notions is not particularly exceptional, as the Indian material illustrates especially. What is important, or at least distinctive, about the Greek experience is not so much alternative cosmological pictures or models, as the dialectical nature (as I called it) of their cosmological thought. Here too I might have been more explicit. Rivalry or competitiveness in philosophical systems, including in the cosmological doctrines they present, is one factor, but, as again the Indian material illustrates, not a factor that is unique to ancient Greece. Rather the key is the attempt at evaluation: it is not the mere fact of competition, but the nature of the competition and in particular how it is to be adjudicated that are important. Quite how superiority in wisdom is to be judged is often left quite unexplicit in Indian culture, at least by contrast with the Greeks. The Greeks – or most of them – had no hesitation at any rate about the first stage reply: they identified *logos* as the arbiter. Between competing cosmological, philosophical or scientific theories, the winner will be the one for which the best account, *logos*, can be given, and that is to be judged, not by a closed group, of experts, sages or the initiated, but by people in general. The fact that, in *practice*, the authority of acknowledged experts and of past tradition counted for a good deal in Greek debates, especially in the Hellenistic period (Lloyd, 1987: ch. 2), does not alter the point that *in principle* what was to be preferred was what had the best grounds, the theory for which the best rational account could be given.

The dialectical character of Greek cosmological thought is, then, a feature that affects not just the types of cosmological doctrine on offer, but the very style of considering cosmological questions, the conception of what it is to do cosmology. The pluralism of Indian cosmological systems enables one contrast to be set up: that of ancient Chinese cosmologies a second. In the development of a plurality of philosophical schools in the Warring States period (fifth to early third centuries B.C.) the Chinese experience resembles that of the Greek. In the Chinese case too a number of leading or pervasive cosmological notions can be identified that permeate a great deal of philosophical and scientific work, the notions of the balance between the opposed forces of Yin and Yang, that of the constancy of process, the notions of energy (Qi) and of immanent order (Li). Whatever disagreements there were between Confucians, Daoists, Mohists, Logicians and others, much of the physical thought of all of them was mediated by the use of such conceptions. They often differed too on the question of the possibility of attaining understanding and on the comparative importance of the investigation of nature and of human society (although the notion of the Unity under Heaven comprehended *both*, and a marked division between nature and culture was alien to much Chinese thought).

But while at a first level certain comparisons – and contrasts – are possible between Chinese cosmological models and Greek ones, it is more important to focus on the second level, on the conditions for the resolution of cosmological questions. Here it is not so much that the Chinese were less aggressive in debate than the Greeks (though they were) nor that they often sought reconciliation and compromise (though that is a generalisation that needs substantial qualification). Rather it is that the supremacy of *logos* is *not* assumed. The Greeks were ready to follow, as Plato makes Socrates say, wherever the *logos* or the argument leads, and that sometimes meant the granting, or maintaining, of extreme, radical, even totally counter-intuitive, positions – as is the case with Parmenides' denial of change and plurality. Against this, by contrast, the Chinese stance was very different. It is certainly not the case that they lacked critical methods of evaluation: but appeal to what was represented as the pure dictates of reason was generally subject to well-defined provisos and limits. In particular what reason suggested had to prove its pragmatic usefulness: theorising for theory's sake alone was ruled out, or rather simply did not enter in. Moreover if and when reason suggested a view that runs counter to ordinary experience, then it would have been reason, not experience, that was to be rejected.

No doubt to do justice to the comparative aspects of the problems of ancient cosmologies would have required a further volume of essays to itself. Yet to appreciate the distinctive contributions of different ancient and of modern societies a comparativist perspective is essential. From some points of view, to be sure, ancient Greek philosophy and science strike us nowadays as themselves sufficiently alien for us to be able to resist the temptation to identify them with our own, and they may even help us to uncover aspects of our own culture that might otherwise pass unscrutinised. But from another point of view, the very depth of our indebtedness to classical antiquity makes it the more important not to be content with those Eurocentric comparisons, but more boldly to adopt a more comprehensive, world-wide, diachronic perspective.

REFERENCES

Burnyeat, M. F. ed. (1983) *The Skeptical Tradition* (Berkeley)

Furley, D. J. (1987) *The Greek Cosmologists*, 1 (Cambridge)

Goodman, N. (1978) *Ways of Worldmaking* (Hassocks, Sussex)

Kuhn, T. S. (1962/1970) *The Structure of Scientific Revolutions* (1st end 1962), 2nd edn Chicago

(1977) *The Essential Tension* (Chicago)

Lakoff, G., and Johnson, M. (1980) *The Metaphors We Live By* (Chicago)

Lloyd, G. E. R. (1987) *The Revolutions of Wisdom* (Berkeley)

Rosaldo, M. Z. (1980) *Knowledge and Passion: Ilongot Notions of Self and Social Life* (Cambridge)

The field of Greek cosmological thought, from Mycenae to Byzantium, is immense. I can only select some features of it that I believe to be particularly interesting or important, but my selection is partial, certainly in one, and probably in two senses of that term.[1]

I shall concentrate, to begin with, on three interrelated themes, the transition from mythology to philosophical cosmology, the pluralism of Greek cosmologies, and the development of critical methods. The transition from mythology to philosophical cosmology is, of course, a well-worn and much-abused topic. Studies still appear on the theme, and sometimes with the title, 'from myth to reason', many of them arguing, or at least assuming, that the two are directly comparable, and that the one simply supplanted the other. One associates with the 'Greek miracle' view of ancient history the tacit assumption – and sometimes it is not just tacit – of a contrast in kind between the Greeks and their Near Eastern neighbours. To begin with (so this view has it) there were those charming, but childish, Egyptians and Sumerians with their weird and fantastic notions about the cow-goddess in the sky, the sweet waters under the earth, and so on, and then along came the Greeks, who were adult rational people like ourselves. The notion that there is or was a mythological or pre-rational or pre-logical mentality, different in kind from a scientific, rational or logical mentality is at best grossly oversimplified and at worst a piece || of dangerously misleading propaganda.[2] When we study what actually happened in the sixth and fifth centuries B.C. in Greece (and I am not denying, of course, that certain important changes did take place), the picture that emerges is very different. Indeed one of the main reasons why the study of Greek thought of that period continues to be rewarding is that it provides us with an opportunity to discover what actually happened, and check some of the sometimes wildly exaggerated theses that have been put forward.

I am speaking as if one *can* reconstruct what actually happened, but of course there is a good deal we do not know and many questions we cannot hope to answer. Even the principal doctrines of the three earliest philosophers, Thales, Anaximander and Anaximenes (who worked in the sixth century B.C. in Miletus) are a matter of controversy. Nevertheless one can, I believe, be reasonably confident about some points. First I would maintain a negative proposition, that in Greece there is nothing we can describe as cosmology in the strictest and fullest sense before the philosophers: by the strictest sense I mean a comprehensive view of the cosmos as an ordered whole (*kosmos* being, indeed, the Greek for 'order' or 'ordered whole'). There are, to be sure, plenty of ideas mentioned by Homer

[1] This is printed here as delivered in lecture form except for some minor alterations of phraseology and slight additions.

[2] I have discussed the problems from one particular point of view in Lloyd, 1966.

and other sources that are relevant to the question of what the early Greeks believed about themselves, their environment, the origins of certain things and so on. Homer speaks of a river of Ocean running round the world and says that Ocean is the begetter of the gods or of all things.[3] Much more interestingly, Hesiod's *Theogony* provides an account of the origins of 'the gods and the earth and the rivers and the immense sea ... and the shining stars and the wide heaven above'.[4] This begins with Chaos, in the Greek sense of 'gap'; then Earth, Tartaros and Eros; Erebos and Night, Aither and Day; then Earth produces the Sky (Ouranos), the tall mountains and the sea.[5] Once Earth and Sky mate and produce Kronos, Rhea and the Titans, we join up with the usual genealogies of the major Olympian gods: Kronos and Rhea are the parents of Zeus and Hera. Outside Hesiod, again, other origin myths involving || Time (Chronos), Night, an original egg, and so on, are known from the evidence for the so-called Orphic and related cosmogonies.[6] These stories include not only theogonical, but also more generally cosmogonical, ideas. One may contrast the ordinary births of the anthropomorphic gods from anthropomorphic parents on the one hand, with, on the other, less straightforwardly anthropomorphic generation, where the figures involved, while undoubtedly divine, are less obviously conceived in human form, or not conceived in human form at all, and where their coming-to-be may or may not be conceived as a birth. When, in Hesiod, Earth bears the Mountains or Dawn brings forth the stars,[7] the words used are still those of human generation (γείνατο, τίκτεν) though what is born (the mountains and the stars) may not be conceived anthropomorphically. But, as is well known, there are other early texts relating to an original splitting of Earth and Sky, where there is no question of intercourse or birth, but of a separation of two originally united beings.[8] Yet my main point is this: while these pre-philosophical myths contain a variety of stories of origins, none of them constitutes a cosmology in the strict sense I have defined. None of them, that is, presents a comprehensive account of the world as we know it as an ordered system. Even to say that everything else comes from an egg (or Time or Chaos) does not tell us how the world as we know it is regulated. Cosmology, in the sense of theories concerning how the world as we know it forms an ordered whole, manifesting physical regularities, is a product of Greek philosophy.

One important strand in early Greek cosmological speculation relates to the question of the material constitution of the world. Attempts to give an account of the material constituents of the world may go back to Thales himself. That at least was Aristotle's view, although I am one of those who

[3] See *Il.* 14.201 and 246. [4] *Th.* 108ff. [5] *Th.* 116ff.

[6] See, for example, Aristotle, *Metaph.* 1091b4ff.; Aristophanes, *Av.* 693ff.; Damascius, *De Principiis* 123ff. The evidence is evaluated in Kirk and Raven, 1957: ch. 1.

[7] *Th.* 129, 381f. [8] See, for example, Euripides, Fr. 484 Nauck.

have reservations about fully accepting his interpretation on this point. The controversy turns on what questions one believes Thales had formulated, and my own view would be that while he may well have considered the problem of what things came from (on which, in an unsystematic way, the myths had already || pronounced), there is some doubt about whether he also asked the question of what things as we know them are made of. Yet this dispute is of minor importance for our purposes, since by the time we come to the third of the Milesian philosophers, Anaximenes, we can be fairly confident that he believed that all things are made of the same substance, namely air, which changes into other things by processes which he conceived as condensation and rarefaction.[9]

Early on in Greek philosophy, then, we have evidence of the world conceived as a unity in this sense, that all material objects are varieties of a single substance. But doctrines of how the plural world is an ordered whole take many other forms. Three common types of model in particular throw light on the discontinuities, and continuities, between the philosophers' ideas and what went before. First, the cosmos was conceived as a living organism, second as an artefact, and third as a political entity.[10] In each case the idea incorporated in the model has certain mythological uses, and in each case *particular* applications of the idea appear early on in Greek philosophy. Yet *generalised* applications of the idea (the idea pressed into service to give an account of the world-order as a whole) are in two of the three cases, at least, comparatively late – to judge, that is, from the extant texts.

Take first the use of craftsman images. This idea has obvious pre-philosophical antecedents in, for example, the myth of the creation of Pandora, the first woman, by Hephaestus from earth and water in Hesiod (not to mention even earlier Egyptian and Babylonian parallels).[11] Yet in myth what is described in these terms is the creation of particular objects. Moreover, they are the work of a personal god. Hephaestus makes Pandora on Zeus's instructions to spite Prometheus, who had stolen fire and given it to mankind. In cosmology, by contrast, personalities are irrelevant, indeed excluded. We have a number of examples of craftsman images used in particular contexts in Presocratic philosophers: the notion of a force that guides or pilots or steers the world is particularly common,[12] and Empedocles especially has a wealth of craftsman images to describe || the role of his cosmic force Philia (Love).[13] But the first clear extant general statement of the world as a whole as the product of a craftsmanlike agency comes in Plato:

[9] There is a full analysis of the evidence for Milesian cosmology in Guthrie, 1962: ch. 3. For a brief statement of one interpretation, see Lloyd, 1970: ch. 2. Another sharply differing view has recently been put forward by Stokes, 1971.

[10] These three types of models are discussed in some detail in Lloyd, 1966: ch. 4. Cf. especially Vlastos, 1953: 337–66, and Solmsen, 1963: 473–96.

[11] *Th.* 570ff., *Op.* 59ff.

[12] See Aristotle, *Ph.* 203b10ff.; Heraclitus, Frr. 41 and 64; Parmenides, Fr. 12; Diogenes of Apollonia, Fr. 5.

[13] For example, Frr. 73, 87 and 96.

the work of the Craftsman is depicted in vivid metaphors in the *Timaeus*, many of them being metaphors that had been used of Zeus and Hephaestus in Homer or Hesiod. But the important point in Plato is the underlying message, and this, put baldly, is that the world as a whole is the product of design.

Similar points can be made concerning the other two types of models I mentioned. The notion that the primary physical elements are alive and divine is as old as Greek philosophy itself. While we can connect the living earth and air of the early cosmologists with earlier ideas of a divine Gaia in Hesiod, for instance, the more important point is again that in cosmology earth and air, while still divine, are not personal gods. They have no will. They are left with one and only one of the properties of the living, namely the capacity for self-movement. But so far as general cosmological applications of vitalist ideas go, it is again Plato who supplies us with our first definite extant text ('this world is in truth a living creature, endowed with soul/life and reason'),[14] although vitalist notions are important much earlier in accounts of how the world developed from an undeveloped, undifferentiated state,[15] and even though the idea that the world is a living creature may already be implicit in the comparison that Anaximenes drew between the role of air in the world and that of breath in man.[16]

Thirdly, with political images, the earliest use of the model of political and social relations in cosmology may be in the very first philosophical fragment we possess, the quotation from Anaximander to the effect that certain things 'pay the penalty and recompense to one another for their injustice, according to the assessment of time'.[17] The problem of what the things in question are is disputed, but they appear to be cosmological factors of some sort, conceived as equal opposed forces. There is no question of a *conscious* selection of the political sphere to provide a model for cosmology. Rather political, or in this case more precisely legal, terms provide the || metaphors in which the idea of the stable interrelation of different things is conveyed. Again the similarity to, and contrast with, pre-philosophical beliefs are evident. In the Olympian religion, Zeus the sky-god rules over the other gods, though Poseidon, the sea, and Hades, the underworld, claim equal rights with him.[18] The notion of the gods forming a society like that of man is worked out in the fullest detail in Homer, and described so vividly that we almost forget that the gods in question are gods of the sky, the sea, fire and so on. But in philosophy the factors that are now related together are not personal deities, autocratic, touchy, unpredictable, but depersonalised factors, physical elements such as earth, air, fire and water, or opposite

[14] *Ti.* 30B.

[15] This idea was probably already present in Anaximander: see ps.-Plutarch, *Strom.* 2. Some of the Pythagoreans are reported as believing that the original 'one' from which the complex cosmos developed was composed of seed, see, for example, Aristotle, *Metaph.* 1091a15ff.

[16] Aetius I 3.4 ('fragment' 2). [17] Fr. 1, from Simplicius, *in Ph.* 24.19ff. [18] *Il.* 15.185ff.

qualities such as the hot, the cold, the dry and the wet. And the variety of political, social and legal metaphors used in early Greek cosmology is remarkable. The notions of justice, ἰσονομία (equality), war, strife, rule, contract, are used by one Presocratic after another to convey different conceptions of how the world as we know it, made up of a variety of different things, is nevertheless an ordered whole.

The evidence suggests, I believe, that the notion of the world as a unity of interrelated parts was achieved only as a result of a good deal of speculative effort. As was to be expected, and as happens frequently in myth, of course, the philosophers drew on familiar conceptions, for example of living things, of technology, of politics and society, for their ideas. But although the links with pre-philosophical beliefs are in many cases striking, the achievement of the philosophers was to arrive at *generalised* and *depersonalised* notions of the world-whole as a unity.

This takes me to my second theme, what I called the pluralism of Greek cosmology. I have mentioned three common types of model: but each of these is used to express more than one cosmological doctrine. The same type of model may be, and in fact was, used to convey widely different conceptions of the world-whole. Thus the political analogies used in early Greek cosmology comprise at least three main kinds: (1) a view || of the cosmos as ruled by a single supreme principle (Plato provides the chief example: in the *Philebus* (28C), for instance, Socrates is made to say that 'all wise men agree...that reason is king of heaven and earth'. In Plato, especially, this idea is connected with the conception of the world as an artefact: the benevolent designing agency acts now as king of a state, now as master-craftsman);[19] (2) a view of the cosmos as a balance of equal but opposed forces (for example, Anaximander, Parmenides in the *Way of Seeming*, and Empedocles);[20] and (3) a view of the cosmos as a place where war and strife are universal. Heraclitus criticised Homer for a line in which the wish was expressed that strife should be abolished from among gods and men, and he also probably implied a criticism of Anaximander when he remarked that justice *is* strife.[21] The message is that the interaction of opposites, described as war or strife, is universal: what is 'right' and 'just' and normal or usual *is* just this constant interaction of opposites. The conception of the world in political terms can, then, take many forms, depending on whether the conception is of the world as a kingdom, as an oligarchy of balanced powers, or as an anarchy, and if we were dealing with Greek political philosophy rather than with Greek cosmology, we could trace how different cosmological views of the world as a state are related in turn to different political theses or doctrines.

[19] Cf. also Heraclitus, Fr. 53, Anaxagoras, Fr. 12 and Diogenes of Apollonia, Fr. 5.

[20] See Anaximander, Fr. 1, Parmenides, Fr. 9.4 and Empedocles, Fr. 17.20 and 27ff.

[21] Aristotle, *EE*, 1235a25ff., and Heraclitus, Fr. 80 ('war is common and justice is strife and everything happens through strife and necessity').

There is no such thing as *the* cosmological model, *the* cosmological theory, of the Greeks. One is hard put to it to describe the *predominant* notion or notions in Greek cosmology, though I shall make an attempt to identify some important themes later. Indeed, one can and must go further: one of the remarkable features of Greek cosmological thought is that for almost every idea that was put forward, the antithetical view was also proposed. For every cosmology, there is, one might say, a counter-cosmology, suggested by the Greeks themselves.

Let me illustrate.

One of the principal ideas that the model of the cosmos as an artefact was used to convey is that the world is the product of, || or under the guidance of, a rational, usually benevolent, intelligence. In the fourth century B.C. this idea had the full weight of the authority of Plato and Aristotle, although Plato and Aristotle differ in their expression of it: for Plato the Craftsman is, or at least is described in terms that appear to imply that it is, transcendent, while Aristotle's view is of an immanent force, in that nature herself is purposeful. But the idea that the universe is the product of design had been denied, in the late fifth century, by the atomists Leucippus and Democritus, and it was so again by Epicurus and later Epicureans.[22] If teleologists often dominated the argument, anti-teleologists also had a hearing. Though little of the work of Leucippus and Democritus remains, the anti-teleological view-point is forcefully expressed in the letters of Epicurus and by Lucretius, who make clear their belief that the world is the result not of design, but of necessity, that is the mechanical interactions of atoms.

Secondly, it was, as I have remarked, commonly assumed that the physical elements are alive. Here we can trace argument and counter-argument through several generations of philosophers. Aristotle criticised his predecessors severely for believing that soul is intermingled in the whole universe, and also for the opinion that the elements themselves are alive (why does not the soul which exists in air or fire form an *animal*?).[23] Yet despite the scorn that Aristotle poured on the idea, in the fourth century and later we find the Stoics confidently reaffirming the doctrine that the cosmos as a whole is a living creature.[24]

A third example from physical theory, involving some of the thinkers that have already been mentioned, is the debate between atomism and continuum theory.[25] This dispute goes back before Aristotle, but it is after him that it becomes most vigorous. The Stoics worked out a sophisticated continuum theory of matter, picturing the world as a plenum, and conceiving movement as the transmission of a disturbance in an elastic medium, in opposition to

[22] See, for example, Aristotle, *Ph.* 196a24ff., *GA* 789b2ff., Epicurus, *Letter to Herodotus* 76f., *Letter to Pythocles* 88ff.

[23] *De An.* 411a9ff.

[24] For example, Sextus Empiricus, *M.* IX 104 (on Zeno), Diogenes Laertius VII 142ff. (on Chrysippus).

[25] The evidence is collected and discussed in Sambursky, 1959 and 1961: 376–81.

the fourth-century proponents of atomism, the Epicureans, who held that matter, space and time || all exist in the form of discrete individual units and who interpreted movement in terms of the transport of material particles through a void.

A fourth and a fifth debate concern the questions of whether the world is eternal or created, and one or many. We can find proponents for no less than five different views: (*a*) the universe is one and eternal (for example, Aristotle);[26] (*b*) the universe is one and created (Plato, at least on one construction of his views);[27] (*c*) the universe is one and alternately, and everlastingly, created and destroyed (Empedocles, again according to one interpretation);[28] (*d*) there are innumerable worlds that exist (*d*1) in succession (a view attributed to Anaximander in Simplicius, for example)[29] or (*d*2) co-existent (the atomists: thus Democritus' pupil Metrodorus of Chios is reported to have said that it is as unlikely for one ear of corn to be produced in a great plain, as for one world in the boundless void).[30]

I have concentrated so far on physical and cosmological theories, and their counter-theories, but if we broaden the field of discussion for a moment, we find the same pattern elsewhere. In theology, alongside the various versions of polytheism and what one may call, with some reservations, monotheism, both agnosticism and atheism are expressed. God does not exist, or we cannot know whether he does or not. As the fifth-century sophist Protagoras put it:' ...concerning the gods I am unable to discover whether they exist or not, or what they are like in form; for there are many hindrances to knowledge, the obscurity of the subject and the brevity of human life'.[31] And although it is notoriously difficult to be sure quite what is meant when men like Prodicus and Critias were labelled atheists, it is obvious enough from the castigation of those who believed that there are no gods in Plato's *Laws* (book X) that Plato, at least, took seriously the threat of the denial of the existence of the gods.

Again, on the question of the sources of knowledge in general, the dispute that begins with Heraclitus and Parmenides continues right through the history of Greek philosophy. Parmenides, especially, must be mentioned, for not only was || he the first philosopher explicitly to deny the validity of the senses,[32] but beginning with the statement 'it is and it cannot not be' he

[26] Aristotle presents arguments for the unity and eternity of the world in, for example, *Cael.* I, chh. 8–12.

[27] As is well known, the question of whether Plato intended his account of the coming-to-be of the cosmos in the *Timaeus* to be taken literally, or whether he gave his account that form merely for the sake of convenience of exposition, is one that was disputed already by Plato's own immediate successors in the Academy. See Aristotle, *Cael.* 279b17ff., 32ff.

[28] See, for example, Fr. 17. The details of Empedocles' cosmology have been subject to widely differing interpretations. See especially Hölscher, 1965: 7–53; Solmsen, 1965: 109–48; Bollack, 1965–9; and O'Brien, 1969.

[29] See especially Guthrie, 1962: Additional Note, pp. 106–15.

[30] Aetius I 5.4. Cf. Diogenes Laertius IX 31, Epicurus, *Letter to Pythocles* 89.

[31] Fr. 4 quoted, for example, by Diogenes Laertius IX 51.

[32] Fr. 7.

produced not, of course, a cosmology, but what he calls a Way of Truth, leading to the conclusion that what is is ungenerated, indestructible, unchanging, present and continuous.[33] After Parmenides' denial that change and coming-to-be take place, the status of γιγνόμενα, 'things that come to be', was a major problem in Greek philosophy. The central dispute in epistemology ranged round the arguments for and against reason on the one hand, and sensation on the other, and we find quite early on indications of the growth of scepticism. The weakness, or limitations, of human knowledge is expressed by Xenophanes: '...no man knows or ever will know the clear truth about the gods and about everything I speak of...seeming is wrought over all things'.[34] And Democritus has this: '...in reality we know nothing, for truth is in the depths' (Fr. 117). In another passage Democritus represents the senses saying to the mind: '...wretched mind, do you take your evidence from us and then throw us down? That throw is your overthrow.'[35] In the fifth century a statement of an extreme position is found in Gorgias, *On What is Not, or On Nature*, although this is another text whose interpretation is highly disputed. It began: '...he says that nothing exists, but that if it exists, it is unknowable, and that if it exists and is knowable, it still cannot be indicated to others'. From the fourth century onwards we can trace a dispute, or at least differences of opinion, among the sceptics themselves, in that some denied that knowledge is possible, while others took the view that such a denial was itself a dogmatic assertion, and that as any sort of dogmatic assertion must be ruled out, the true sceptic must on this, as on every other question, withhold judgement. Some sceptics did not allow themselves to *assert* the key doctrine of scepticism, that knowledge is not possible.[36]

Many other examples could be given, but I have said enough to illustrate the theme of the pluralism of Greek cosmology. But I have so far merely indicated *what* different theorists believed, and not *why* they believed it, and I must now turn to || the question of criteria and methods. In the great majority of cases, the cosmological ideas I have mentioned were worked out in direct opposition to the views of other theorists. There are two points here. First, the actual *evidence* adduced in connection with general cosmological theories down to the fourth century amounted, in most cases, to no more than a few well-known data, and the main support and justification for cosmological doctrines came from rational *argument*. Secondly, criticism of other cosmologists' views is a constant characteristic of Greek cosmological speculation. This begins, probably, very early: there is some evidence that Anaximander implies criticisms of views that can be attributed to Thales, for

[33] Parmenides goes on to present a cosmology in the *Way of Seeming*, but he makes it clear that he does not consider this account to be true. At Fr. 8.52ff., introducing it, he says, 'listen to the deceitful ordering of my words', even though he includes the account 'so that no judgement of mortals shall outstrip you' (Fr. 8.61). [34] Fr. 34. [35] Fr. 125.

[36] See, for example, Sextus Empiricus, *P.* I, for example, 236–41. For a recent account of the history of scepticism, see Stough, 1969.

example. Where it seems that Thales held that the earth floats on water, Anaximander is reported to have held that it 'hangs freely', 'remaining where it is because of its equal distance from everything'.[37] But it is typical that Anaximander's view is not supported by, and was presumably not suggested by, empirical evidence of any sort. The impulse to put forward this theory came rather (one may suppose) from Anaximander's realisation of the force of the argument that Thales' view, and all views like it, runs into one obvious difficulty: if water holds the earth up, what holds the water up?[38]Throughout the Presocratic period, and despite the fact that the men concerned often inhabited widely separated parts of the Greek world, Greek philosophers were remarkably well informed about each other's ideas. The extant fragments bear witness to the impact that Parmenides' arguments had on Empedocles and Anaxagoras, as well as on his own followers Zeno and Melissus.[39] Later we can trace the disputes between the atomists and Plato, between Plato and Aristotle, between the Stoics and the Epicureans, and so on, right down to the controversies between the Christian and pagan commentators of Aristotle in the sixth century A.D.

Greek cosmology is nothing if not dialectical. And this is not an accidental or contingent feature of Greek cosmology, but of the essence of the Greek contribution. What marks out philosophical cosmology from mythology is first that the former || proposes definite and comprehensive accounts of the world as an ordered whole, where the order does not depend on the arbitrary will of gods or divine beings, and second that the former is, in a sense that does not apply to the latter, critical. It is no part of the mythologist's purpose to produce a better, in the sense of a *truer* account than that of other myths. If he is in competition with his contemporaries and predecessors at all, it is not, generally speaking, on the matter of who produces the most rational, or best argued, or most consistent account. The cosmologists, on the other hand, *were* in competition with one another in that way. The demand is for the best explanation, the most adequate theory. They are obliged to consider the grounds for their own ideas, and the evidence and arguments in their favour, and they do their best not only to strengthen their own case but also to undermine their opponents'. The *means*, as I have said, consisted mostly of *argument*: in early Greek cosmology the evidence that was adduced, indeed the evidence that could be adduced, consisted of a few well-known facts, and in some cases the same familiar data were used on both sides of a cosmological debate. Nevertheless from the beginning there is an awareness of the need to examine and assess theories in the light of the grounds adduced for them.

As time goes on, both the range of evidence taken into account broadens – at least in certain fields – and the handling of deductive argument becomes

[37] Aristotle, *Cael.* 294a28ff., 295b10ff., Hippolytus, *Haer.* I 6.3.

[38] Cf. the argument for postulating the Boundless as ἀρχή reported by Aristotle at *Ph.* 204b24ff.

[39] See Empedocles, Frr. 12–14, Anaxagoras, Fr. 17.

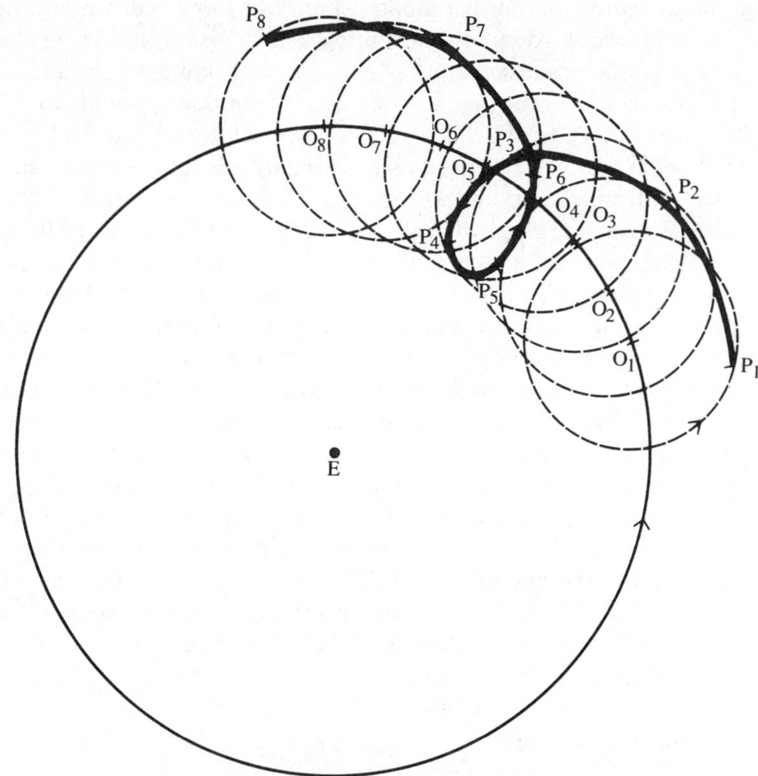

The epicyclic model used to explain the retrogradation of the planets.

increasingly sophisticated. One contrast between earlier and later cosmology relates to the availability of more detailed knowledge of astronomical phenomena, that is of such problem-posing facts as the irregularity of the seasons, the anomalies of the moon's movement, the stations and retrogradations of the planets. But while the range of data to hand increases, so too does the ambitiousness of the doctrines evolved to account for them. Astronomy provides one of the best, certainly the best-known, example of one of the great strengths of Greek science, the application of mathematical methods to the explanation of natural phenomena. This begins with the doctrine of concentric spheres put forward by || Eudoxus in the fourth century, and continues in the doctrine that superseded it, that of epicycles and eccentrics, originally proposed by Apollonius in the third century. The theories are complex, too complex to attempt to describe here, although I should remark that it is sometimes forgotten that the data these theories were designed to explain are themselves highly complex. But the fundamental point is that the strength of both types of model lies in the rigour of their geometry. Here too we have the phenomenon of model and counter-model, of modification and further modification. But from Eudoxus onwards, while argument raged round the advantages and disadvantages of one model against another, that *some geometrical* || model would provide the solution to the problem of celestial motion was common ground to all Greek astronomers. After Euclid especially, the *Elements* provided a model of method, in particular a model of an axiomatic, deductive system, not only for other mathematicians and astronomers, but also for work in other physical sciences, as for example that of Archimedes in statics and hydrostatics.[40]

I have remarked how difficult it is to generalise about Greek cosmology. It is quite impossible to talk of *the* cosmological theory of the ancient Greeks. Yet if we concentrate on dominant trends, and if we stand back and compare common Greek assumptions with the assumptions that influence our own attitudes to the world we live in and man's place in it, certain broad contrasts stand out. Much of Greek cosmological thought is anthropocentric. True, the rejection of anthropomorphic gods occurs early in Greek thought. Xenophanes in the late sixth century B.C. remarks, in a famous fragment, that 'if oxen and horses and lions had hands and could draw with their hands and produce works of art like men, horses would draw the forms of the gods like horses, and oxen like oxen, and they would make their bodies such as each of them had themselves'.[41] Nevertheless, throughout Greek cosmological thought it remains true, as a general rule, that man's position in the universe is a privileged one. First, man is the highest member of the animal kingdom. Secondly, the earth we inhabit holds a privileged position in that it occupies the centre of the universe.

The first doctrine was never seriously questioned, and it had some strange manifestations: Aristotle, no mean biologist, asserts that man of all animals is most in accordance with nature, and that the parts of the body are, in man, in their natural position – it is natural to be upright.[42] The second theory, however, was contested. First there were those, as we have seen, who believed in innumerable worlds, although they did not necessarily deny geocentricity, especially when their innumerable worlds were successive, not co-existent. Democritus is reported to have believed that

> there are innumerable worlds of different sizes. In some there is neither sun nor moon, || in others they are larger than in ours and others have more than one. These worlds are at irregular distances, more in one direction and less in another, and some are flourishing, others declining. Here they come into being, there they die, and they are destroyed by collision with one another. Some of the worlds have no animal or vegetable life nor any water.[43]

This opens the possibility of worlds being arranged in different ways, though it does not pronounce on the question of the position of the earth in our world: in fact other evidence suggests that both Leucippus and Democritus

[40] There is a brief account of the theories mentioned in this paragraph in Lloyd, 1970: ch. 7 and 1973: chh. 4–5. [41] Fr. 15. [42] For example, *IA* 706a19ff., *PA* 656a10ff.

[43] Hippolytus, *Haer*. I 13.2, translation from Guthrie, 1965: 405.

assumed geocentricity. But then there were those who denied that the earth is at the centre of the solar system. The first to do so were some of the Pythagoreans in the late fifth century: the evidence is in parts confused, but it is reasonably certain that one Pythagorean theory (associated with the name of Philolaus) was that neither the earth nor the sun occupied the centre, which was the place of an invisible centre fire. But interestingly enough, one of the reasons for displacing the earth from the centre, and it may have been the chief reason, was a religious or symbolic one: the earth is not *noble enough* to occupy the centre.[44] But while these were the first to deny geocentricity, the first astronomer to put forward an astronomical theory based on heliocentricity was Aristarchus of Samos in the third century B.C. Although the evidence is indirect, it is incontestable. Archimedes, a close contemporary of Aristarchus, reports that

> Aristarchus brought out a book of certain hypotheses, in which it follows from what is assumed that the universe is many times greater than that now so called. He hypothesises that the fixed stars and the sun remain unmoved; that the earth is borne round the sun on the circumference of a circle...; and that the sphere of the fixed stars, situated about the same centre as the sun, is so great that the circle in which he hypothesises that the earth revolves bears such a proportion to the distance of the fixed stars as the centre of the sphere does to its surface.[45]

Here then was a fully fledged heliocentric theory, combining the two doctrines of the daily axial rotation of the earth and the || yearly revolution of the earth round the sun. But, as is well known, Aristarchus' views found little favour, not merely with the man in the street, but with other astronomers. Only one other ancient astronomer, the Babylonian Seleucus of Seleucia, maintained the heliocentric theory. The most important Greek astronomers after Aristarchus, Hipparchus (second century B.C.) and Ptolemy (second century A.D.) both denied it. The reasons are complex, and in the case of the astronomers, at least, religion had little or nothing to do with it.[46] But although Ptolemy agrees that axial rotation enabled the phenomena relating to the stars to be explained, he believes that the physical and astronomical arguments against axial rotation and heliocentricity are overwhelming.[47] First, there was the physical argument from the observed effects of gravity on earth. Second, there was the physical objection that the speed of the rotation of the earth must be enormous, and yet this movement had no observed effect on objects moving through the air. Third, the main

[44] See Aristotle, *Cael.* 293a21ff., 30ff., b23ff.

[45] Archimedes, *The Sandreckoner*, introduction (II 244.9ff. Heiberg).

[46] We hear, however, from Plutarch (*On the Face of the Moon*, ch. 6, 923a) that the Stoic philosopher Cleanthes 'thought that the Greeks ought to indict Aristarchus of Samos on a charge of impiety for putting in motion the Hearth of the Universe [that is, the earth]'.

[47] See *Syntaxis* book I, ch. 5 and 7. He remarks, however, concerning the hypothesis of the axial rotation of the earth, that 'so far as the phenomena relating to the stars are concerned, perhaps nothing might prevent things from being in accordance with the simpler [form of this] theory' (book I, ch. 7, I 24.14ff. H).

astronomical argument against heliocentricity was the apparent absence of stellar parallax, the change in the relative positions of the stars observed from the earth at different points on the earth's orbit. And to these considerations one may add, fourthly, that on one problem that had taxed astronomers since the mid-fourth century B.C., and where quite exact data were available, namely on the irregularity of the lengths of the seasons, it was evident that heliocentricity by itself was inadequate as an explanation. And finally heliocentricity was also inadequate, and indeed irrelevant, to the solution of the problem of the irregular movements of the moon. The fact that in the case of the movements of the sun and the moon eccentricity and/or epicycle motion had (it was assumed) to be postulated must, one supposes, have weakened the attractions of heliocentricity in the case of the movements of the planets. Yet, so far as we can judge from Ptolemy, the main counter-arguments to heliocentricity that weighed with him were the two physical ones, the doctrine of natural places and the absence of any observed effects of axial rotation. For all the mathematical or geometrical character of Ptolemy's system || (and elsewhere he is prepared to ignore certain quite major physical objections to his theories when he believes those theories to be adequate mathematical solutions),[48] on the question of the position of the earth and whether it is at rest, he is not prepared to abandon certain fundamental physical principles, despite the increased simplicity and economy that would have resulted.

Heliocentricity was known, but for a complex of reasons, some of them, in the state of knowledge at the time, apparently good ones, geocentricity was preferred. The common assumption, by laymen and astronomers alike, was that the earth is at the centre of the universe. It is interesting, next, to consider the development of an awareness of the *dimensions* of the universe. To begin with, Anaximander appears to have believed that the sun is further away than the stars. The sun is at twenty-seven earth-diameters, the moon at eighteen and the stars at nine from the earth, the earth itself being pictured as a flat-topped cylinder three times as wide as it is deep.[49] Here the multiples of three give the game away: it is *symmetry* that counts, and the dimensions in question are not the result of observation or measurement. The second stage is represented by Aristotle. He records the first precise estimate of the dimensions of the earth (the figure he gives for the circumference of the earth is almost twice the actual one) and he also remarks that 'the bulk of the earth is as it were nothing compared with the surrounding universe'.[50] A *general* idea that the earth is tiny compared with the heavens thereafter becomes a commonplace, and from the fourth century B.C. a good deal of attention was

[48] The classic example of this is in his theory of the moon, where the values he assigned to the radii of the moon's epicycle and deferent circle had the consequence that the angular diameter of the moon should appear to vary by nearly a factor of 2. See Lloyd, 1973: 127f.

[49] The evidence is, however, fragmentary, and its interpretation highly disputed. See, for example, Kahn, 1960: 58–63; Guthrie, 1962: 93ff., and Dicks, 1970: 45f.

[50] *Cael.* 298a6–20. *Mete.* 340a6ff., cf. 352a27f.

paid by astronomers to the topic of the sizes and distances of the sun and moon. The nature of their work on this problem is, however, rather different from what we might expect. One astronomer who tackled the subject is Aristarchus. His treatise *On the Sizes and Distances of the Sun and Moon* is the one complete work of his that is extant. It is a fascinating document that raises many thorny problems of interpretation, not least among them why Aristarchus should have assumed a figure of two degrees for the angular diameter of the moon, when the || fact that the angular diameter is approximately one-half a degree was well known to the Greeks before Aristarchus, and when indeed we are told by some of our sources that Aristarchus himself adopted that value. Why, then, should he have chosen a figure so wide of the mark in his treatise *On the Sizes and Distances*? Various explanations have been put forward, but part of the answer, at least, lies, I believe, in the point that in that treatise, despite its title, Aristarchus is interested not so much in arriving at concrete results – figures for the sizes and distances in question – as in the solution of the geometrical problems that the topic posed. He was not interested, that is, in setting out his estimates, in stades, for the values in question: in fact there are no concrete results set out in *that* form in the work at all, since the conclusions of the work are expressed as proportions, stating the *relations* between different diameters and distances.[51] His chief concern appears to be in the mathematical exercise, the solution of the geometrical problem, and for this purpose the accuracy of the figure he assumed for the diameter of the moon was unimportant.

It would, however, be wrong to leave the impression that Greek astronomy is merely theoretical, or merely interested in the solution of mathematical problems, although that is undoubtedly its forte. Important work was also done in observational astronomy, and some of this is relevant to the world-picture of the scientist, if not to that of the man in the street. Of course, Greek observational astronomy owes an enormous debt to the Babylonians. Ptolemy, for example, draws on Babylonian eclipse records going back to the eighth century B.C., and Hipparchus had probably done the same before him. But it is important not to exaggerate the contrast between Babylonian and Greek astronomy at this point, by representing the Babylonians as observers while the Greeks were theorists. At least one must recognise the solid observational achievements of the Greeks themselves. One of the more striking discoveries that resulted from detailed observation, and that was relevant to cosmology, was Hipparchus' discovery of the phenomenon || known as the precession of the equinoxes. The positions of the

[51] For example, 'the distance of the sun from the earth is greater than 18 times, but less than 20 times, the distance of the moon from the earth' (Proposition 7). T. L. Heath, following Hultsch and others, gives an account of the later history of the problem, 1913: part 2, ch. 4. It should be noted that despite the title of this chapter in Heath ('later improvements on Aristarchus' calculations') it was not always the case that later astronomers improved on their predecessors' results.

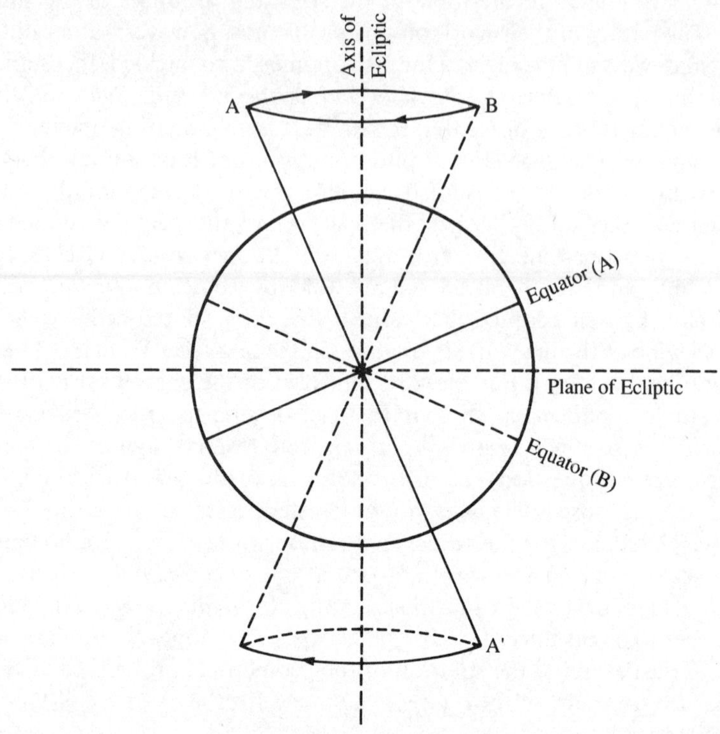

The precession of the equinoxes.

equinoctial points, defined as the intersection of the ecliptic and the celestial equator, do not remain constant in relation to the fixed stars, but are displaced from east to west very slightly each year. Indeed, Hipparchus not only detected this phenomenon by comparing his observations with those of Greek astronomers working some 160 years earlier, but he also gave an astonishingly accurate estimate of the *rate* of precession. A passage in Ptolemy[52] implies that he set a figure of 1° in a hundred years as the lower limit, but the actual figure he adopted may have been 2° in 160 years, or 45 seconds of angle a year, within six seconds of that determined by modern astronomers. ||

This example shows the power of the Greeks in observational astronomy, but it also serves to illustrate the gap between astronomers and laymen. Hipparchus' discovery had very little impact on the common notions about the unchanging nature of the heavens. Even though Ptolemy discusses the phenomenon at some length in the *Syntaxis*, references to precession are rare thereafter. Indeed, when it is mentioned, it is often for the writer to express his own disbelief. It was referred to several times in late antiquity as an

[52] *Syntaxis* book VII, ch. 2, II 12.21ff. H.

instance of the *absurdity* of the views of the astronomers, along with the hypotheses of epicycles and eccentrics that constitute the core of the Ptolemaic system. In the fifth century A.D., Proclus, for example, remarks that these hypotheses 'do not have any probability, but some are far removed from the simplicity of divine things, and others, fabricated by more recent astronomers, suppose the motion of the heavenly bodies to be as if driven by a machine'.[53] And in the sixth century, Philoponus, the commentator on Aristotle, mentions the different periods of revolution of the heavenly bodies, and the precession of the equinoxes, only to go on to say: 'who would be able to state the cause of these things?... This only we can say, that God has made everything well and as is needed, neither more nor less.'[54] Each in his own day, Proclus and Philoponus were among the foremost theorists who were interested in the investigation into nature. If one turns to other writers, particularly among the Christian fathers, it is sometimes not just the precession of the equinoxes that is flatly disbelieved, but also the sphericity of the earth.[55] The discovery of precession shows, then, the problem of the lack of penetration of scientific ideas: it must be remembered that the numbers of those who progressed beyond an elementary knowledge of mathematics, astronomy and biology were always – even in the heyday of Greek science in the third century B.C. – very small. And this example also illustrates the problem of the loss of knowledge during the decline of Greek science, although that is beyond my brief in this paper.

The history of early Greek cosmology is one of argument and counter-argument with a paucity of references to empirical || data, and those mostly familiar ones. Yet in the natural sciences, if not in cosmology as such, the use of, on the one hand, deductive methods, and, on the other, of observation, measurement, even, on occasion, controlled experiment, was, in the hands of certain scientists at least, highly developed. The Greek speculative imagination was extraordinarily fertile in ideas, some of them strongly suggestive of a point of view opposed to the prevailing anthropocentric emphasis, such ideas as heliocentricity, innumerable worlds, and the precession of the equinoxes. Nevertheless, despite the fertility in ideas, and despite the development of criteria and methods, the dominant cosmological view remained anthropocentric. The victory of geocentricity over heliocentricity was both a symptom and a cause of this. The observations of the biologists meanwhile (which included the use of human dissection and vivisection in Alexandria in the third century B.C., and the extended use of experimental animal dissections and vivisections by Galen in the second century A.D.)[56] were often used to confirm the proposition of the privileged

[53] *In Ti.* III 56.28ff. Diehl. [54] *De Opificio Mundi* III 4.117.15ff. Reichardt.

[55] An extreme example is provided by the fantastic cosmology of the *Christian Topography* of Cosmas Indicopleustes of Alexandria in the sixth century, but Lactantius, too, in the fourth, had rejected the sphericity of the earth (*Divinae Institutiones* III, ch. 24).

[56] The evidence (e.g. from Celsus, *De Medicina*, proem 23ff.) concerning the use of human dissection and vivisection by Herophilus and Erasistratus in the third century B.C. has,

place of man among the animals. Notions of the development of natural species, or at least of changes in existing species, the survival of the fit, and the extinction of the unfit, the development of man from a primitive to a more civilised state, can be traced back into the Presocratic period;[57] but the prevailing view was that of the fixity of natural species. Moreover, whether one believed in fixity or change, it was common ground to both sides of the argument that man is supreme among the animals.

The anthropocentrism of Greek cosmology and science is in certain respects at least, a weakness. Harsher critics would say a symptom of a failure of nerve. Yet from another point of view this characteristic of the dominant (but, I repeat, not the only) strain in Greek cosmological thinking has, perhaps, a moral for us today. We live in a world that is far stranger than anything the Greeks dreamed of. If the names of astronomy and physics have not changed, their contents have, almost totally. Yet while, at the frontiers of knowledge, the pure scientist is engaged in an activity which, while it is quite different in || content, yet remains similar in spirit to that of the ancients, the role of science in society, and the expectations that society entertains of science, are nowadays very different from the ancient situation. The notions of applying knowledge to practical ends, and of controlling nature, can be found in ancient writers, despite what has been written by some modern critics. But even among those ancient writers who are aware of the possibility of applying science to practical ends, the chief motive for the investigation of nature generally remains the non-practical one. The ancients explored nature not to dominate her, certainly not exploit her, but to become wise. The aim was understanding: and the view was often expressed that without understanding and knowledge, peace of mind and happiness are unattainable. Science had no need to be uneasily defensive in relation to a society, or to governments, that demanded concrete material benefits in return for a massive expenditure. There was simply no massive expenditure, and the scientist felt no more obliged to defend or justify his activities than did the poet or the philosopher. Science was, indeed, a part of philosophy, and it was treated by some ancient writers as an aid to improving the character. Ptolemy has this to say about astronomy:

> ...of all studies this one especially would prepare men to be perceptive of nobility both of action and of character: when the sameness, good order, proportion and freedom from arrogance of divine things are being contemplated, this study makes those who follow it lovers of this divine beauty, and instils, and as it were makes natural, the same condition in their soul.[58]

however, been disputed. See, for example, Edelstein, 1967: 247–301, and Kudlien, 1968: cols. 38–48. Among the most remarkable of Galen's vivisections of animals are those in which he investigated the effects of severing one side, or the whole, of the spinal cord at different points on the spinal column, described in his *On Anatomical Procedures* book IX, chh. 13ff.

[57] The most important evidence relates to Anaximander (Hippolytus, *Haer.* I 6.6, Plutarch, *Quaest. Conv.* 8.8.4, 730e–f, ps.-Plutarch, *Strom.* 2, and Aetius V 19.4) and Empedocles (Frr. 57 and 61, Aristotle, *Ph.* 198b29ff., Simplicius, *in Ph.* 371.30ff). Cf. also Diodorus I 7.1ff., 8.1ff.

[58] *Syntaxis* book I, ch. 1, I 7.17ff. H.

And again, in an epigram attributed to him:

> I know that I am mortal, a creature of a day: but when I search with my mind into the multitudinous revolving spirals of the stars, my feet no longer touch the earth, but beside Zeus himself, I take my fill of ambrosia the food of the gods.[59]

We may smile at the idea of Ptolemy supping with the gods: but we cannot, I think, fail to be struck by the ideal of science as an inquiry to be pursued as an end in itself, as part of the good life, and indeed of moral education. Greek cosmology and science are anthropocentric. But the other side of || that coin is that they are also confidently humanist, confident that the primary justification of the inquiry is not practical applicability, but knowledge. Science should be useful, but the criterion of usefulness is not material welfare, but understanding.

[59] *AP* IX 577.

REFERENCES

Bollack, J. (1965–9) *Empédocle*, 3 vols. in 4 (Paris)
Dicks, D. R. (1970) *Early Greek Astronomy to Aristotle* (London)
Edelstein, L. (1967) 'The history of anatomy in antiquity', in *Ancient Medicine* (Baltimore)
Guthrie, W. K. C. (1962) *A History of Greek Philosophy*, I (Cambridge)
(1965) *A History of Greek Philosophy*, II (Cambridge)
Heath, T. L. (1913) *Aristarchus of Samos* (Oxford)
Hölscher, U. (1965) 'Weltzeiten und Lebenszyklus', *Hermes* 93: 7–33
Kahn, C. H. (1960) *Anaximander and the Origins of Greek Cosmology* (New York)
Kirk, G. S., and Raven, J. E. (1957) *The Presocratic Philosophers* (Cambridge)
Kudlien, F. (1968) 'Anatomie', in *Pauly–Wissowa Real-Encyclopädie*, Suppl. Bd 11: 38–48
Lloyd, G. E. R. (1966) *Polarity and Analogy* (Cambridge)
(1970) *Early Greek Science, Thales to Aristotle* (London)
(1973) *Greek Science after Aristotle* (London)
O'Brien, D. (1969) *Empedocles' Cosmic Cycle* (Cambridge)
Sambursky, S. (1959) *The Physics of the Stoics* (London)
(1961) 'Atomism versus continuum theory in ancient Greece', *Scientia* 96: 376–81
Solmsen, F. (1963) 'Nature as craftsman in Greek thought', *Journal of the History of Ideas* 24: 473–96
(1965) 'Love and Strife in Empedocles' cosmology', *Phronesis* 10: 109–48
Stokes, M. C. (1971) *One and Many in Presocratic Philosophy* (Center for Hellenic Studies, Washington, DC)
Stough, C. L. (1969) *Greek Skepticism, A Study in Epistemology* (Berkeley and Los Angeles)
Vlastos, G. (1953) 'Isonomia', *American Journal of Philology* 74: 337–66

8

ALCMAEON AND THE EARLY HISTORY OF DISSECTION

INTRODUCTION

The article I published on 'Alcmaeon and the early history of dissection' in *Sudhoffs Archiv* in 1975 had two related aims, (1) the analysis of the evidence for Alcmaeon's work in the life sciences and especially for the claim that he was the first Greek to practise anatomical dissection, and (2) to study the early history of the development of that practice. On the first topic the suggestion I made was that at most Alcmaeon may have excised the eyeball to reveal what we call the optic nerve leading off from the back of the orbit to the brain (intracranial cavity). On the second I reviewed the – scanty – evidence concerning the use of dissection in the treatises in the Hippocratic Corpus: this yields a largely negative result, the one main exception being the work *On the Heart* which belongs to the Hellenistic period. I focused on Aristotle's use of the method and the possible reasons that led him to apply it more systematically than any earlier investigator – reasons that relate, I argued, to his doctrine of the causes and to his expressed view of the need to study every kind of animal, however lowly, in order, precisely, to reveal the formal and final causes that are there to be found. Finally I emphasised the difference in scope between Aristotle's work in this area and that of later Greek anatomists, the Alexandrians Herophilus and Erasistratus in the late fourth and early third century B.C., and Galen in the second century A.D. especially.

At the time these theses challenged commonly accepted views: but in neither case have they proved controversial and I can limit my remarks here to noting some important further studies.

An article published in the same year as mine (1975) came, independently, to similar conclusions with regard to the principal role and interests of Alcmaeon. This was Jaap Mansfeld's 'Alcmaeon: "Physikos" or Physician?', which undertook a careful analysis of the evidence associating Alcmaeon with the Presocratic natural philosophers on the one hand and the tradition of medical writers on the other, and concluded that Alcmaeon belongs rather to the former than to the latter category. On the specific question of the reliability of Chalcidius as an authority for Alcmaeon's supposed dissections Mansfeld too argued that the utmost caution is necessary in evaluating his evidence, not least because the interest in his sources focuses on establishing that the rational principle is located in the brain. This was welcome confirmation, from a scholar approaching the problem from a different starting-point from my own, of the scepticism that I had expressed on that score, although Mansfeld did not proceed to an examination of the possible procedures to which the ambiguous report in Chalcidius may refer.

So far as later dissection goes, I confine myself here to drawing attention to some of the most outstanding contributions to our understanding. With the exception of Galen, the most brilliant Greek anatomist was Herophilus of Chalcedon. But his work had always been difficult to evaluate since his own writings do not survive. Although there are extensive reports – and criticisms – of his ideas and discoveries in later writers, especially Galen, these 'fragments' had never been systematically collected and edited. This situation has now been transformed with the publication of von Staden's magnum opus (1989). Where my own comments were limited merely to mentioning some of the most notable features of Herophilus' work in this area (e.g. pp. 170, 191f.) this part of the later story can now be studied in far greater detail thanks to von Staden's authoritative survey.

Secondly, and from a very different perspective, aspects of the later use of dissection have been illuminated also by the work of Vegetti and others (especially Vegetti, 1979, cf. 1983). Thus Vegetti has studied the use of the knife from a variety of points of view, discussing the type of intervention that its use implies, the occasions when dissection may be used, and its diverse aims and purposes. These occasions include, for example, not just attempts to undertake research and to educate and instruct intending medical practitioners, but also as a public or semi-public spectacle to increase the reputation of particular doctors (an aim that Galen explicitly allows). In some Greek states there were official contests between doctors including in relation to surgery (Nutton, 1988: V p. 205, VIII pp. 27 and 37, cf. Keil, 1905: 129, 132). The element of spectacle is prominent in several reports in Galen which refer to doctors being challenged concerning the results of a dissection, and even to bets being laid by spectators on the outcome. In the notable case of the dissection of an elephant's heart, described by Galen in *On Anatomical Procedures* VII, ch. 10, he claims he predicted what would be found (cf. Scarborough, 1985), and in VII, ch. 16 he mentions the stake put up by those who challenged an Erasistratean to show that Erasistratus' theory of the contents of the arteries is correct, namely that they contain no blood but air alone. While my 1975 article focused especially on the importance of dissection as a technique of research, the studies of Vegetti and others show very usefully that it was not just *simply* as a technique of research that dissection was employed.

Finally I may note that while at the end of my article I did not refer directly to my discussion of problems to do with the origins of scientific ideas in the controversy between Popper and Kirk (above, ch. 5, pp. 100–20), the early history of dissection is one instance that illustrates two points very clearly. First there is the importance of theories and problems to guide the investigator: if investigators have no theory to test, no problem to try to resolve, then what they will discover from the use of the knife is very little. Secondly, however, once the value and usefulness of the technique had been established (in some quarters at least) its more general application itself led to the *discovery* of further *problems*. One excellent example that illustrates this is the shift in problems that occurred once the valves of the heart had been investigated. Whereas the role of the heart as the seat of various vital functions had been much discussed in early natural philosophy – in the debate between heart-centred and brain-centred theories of the location of the controlling principle – once the valves of the heart had been described, a further set of issues of great importance had to be resolved, namely the relationship between the right heart and the left, and between the venous system and the arterial.

REFERENCES

Duminil, M.-P. (1983) *Le Sang, les vaisseaux, le coeur dans la collection hippocratique* (Paris)

Keil, J. (1905) 'Ärzteinschriften aus Ephesos', *Jahreshefte des österreichischen archäologischen Institutes in Wien* 8: 128–38

Kollesch, J. (1965) 'Galen und seine ärztlichen Kollegen', *Das Altertum* 11: 47–53

Longrigg, J. (1988) 'Anatomy in Alexandria in the third century B.C.', *British Journal for the History of Science* 21: 455–88

Mansfeld, J. (1975) 'Alcmaeon: "Physikos" or Physician?', in *Kephalaion: Studies ... offered to C. J. de Vogel*, edd. J. Mansfeld and L. M. Rijk (Assen), 26–38

Manuli, P., and Vegetti, M. (1977) *Cuore, sangue e cervello* (Milan)

Nutton, V. (1988) *From Democedes to Harvey* (London)

Scarborough, J. (1985) 'Galen's dissection of the elephant', *Koroth* 8: 123–34

Staden, H. von (1989) *Herophilus: The Art of Medicine in Early Alexandria* (Cambridge)

Triebel-Schubert, C. (1984) 'Der Begriff der Isonomie bei Alkmaion', *Klio* 66: 40–50

Vegetti, M. (1979) *Il coltello e lo stilo* (Milan)

(1981) 'Modelli di medicina in Galeno', in *Galen: Problems and Prospects*, ed. V. Nutton (London), 47–63

(1983) *Tra Edipo e Euclide* (Milan)

THE EARLY HISTORY OF DISSECTION

Alcmaeon is generally recognised as a figure of considerable importance in the development of the biological sciences in ancient Greece. Yet there is little agreement among scholars about his work in that area or on the methods he used – where he has been variously represented as the first truly experimental biologist and as an *a priori* theorist in the mould of the main Presocratic cosmologists.[1] He has often been hailed as the father of anatomy, of physiology, of embryology, of psychology, of medicine itself[2]: yet such enthusiasms are, to say the least, premature when the interpretation of the handful of texts that provide our evidence remains so disputed. The aim of this article is (in I) to re-examine the evidence concerning his use of dissection and (in II and III) to discuss some more general issues relating to the early history of this method.

I

Two interrelated preliminary points, both much discussed in the scholarly literature, must first be raised, namely Alcmaeon's relationship with the Pythagoreans and his date. On the first question there is a discrepancy between the evidence in Aristotle and in our later sources. When the latter call him a pupil of Pythagoras (Diogenes Laertius VIII 83) or list him as one of the Pythagoreans (Iamblichus, *VP* 104 and 267, Philoponus *in de An.* 88), little weight can be attached to their testimony.[3] At *Metaph.* 986a27ff. Aristotle distinguishes the || dualist theory of Alcmaeon from that of some of the Pythagoreans, and although he speaks only of one group of Pythagoreans (986a22), his expression would have been most odd if Alcmaeon had been known as a member of the school himself. On this question, then, it is usually, and in my view rightly, thought to be more probable that Alcmaeon was not a Pythagorean.[4] But in any event it is clear that on the issue of

Acknowledgement: My warmest thanks are due for the patient help and advice I have received from my former colleague, Professor Gabriel Horn, Professor of Anatomy in the University of Bristol, who has allowed me to consult him on a wide range of anatomical questions. The use I have made, in this study, of the information that he has provided remains, of course, purely my own responsibility.

1 Olivieri 1919, Stella (1938–9), Erhard (1941) and Ebner (1969) especially have emphasised the empirical and experimental character of Alcmaeon's work, Magnus (1878 and 1901) and Schumacher (1963) its theoretical inspiration.

2 See, for example, Philippson, 1831: 188, Unna, 1832: 55f., Gomperz, 1896: ch. 5, para. 5, Wellmann, 1929a: 159, Stella, 1938–9: 247, Erhard, 1941: 88.

3 References to master–pupil relationships in the doxographers are notoriously untrustworthy, and Iamblichus' list of Pythagoreans includes such names as Parmenides, Melissus and Empedocles, none of them, in their mature philosophy, orthodox Pythagoreans. When in the opening words of his book (D.L. VIII 83, DK 24B1) Alcmaeon addresses Brotinus, Leon and Bathyllus, this does not, of course, prove that he belonged to the same school as they, even if we could be sure that they were all Pythagoreans (on Brotinus or Brontinus, see DK 17; Leon and 'Bathylaus' are in Iamblichus' list of Pythagoreans, *VP* 267).

4 Contrast, however, Timpanaro Cardini, 1958–64: I 118ff.

whether or not he practised dissection, no conclusion can be drawn from his alleged association with the Pythagoreans.[5]

On the question of the date of his main activity,[6] the direct evidence is meagre. As is well known, the MSS and the ancient commentators are divided on the question of the inclusion of the words ἐγένετο τὴν ἡλικίαν and ἐπὶ γέροντι Πυθαγόρᾳ at Arist. *Metaph.* 986a29f.[7] The value of Iamblichus' report (*VP* 104) that Alcmaeon was taught by Pythagoras in his old age, is negligible since he also includes Leucippus, Philolaus, Eurytus and Archytas in his long list of Pythagoras' pupils. The fact that Aristotle expresses doubt as to whether Alcmaeon influenced the Pythagorean dualists or vice versa (*Metaph.* 986a28f.) shows that Aristotle himself is uncertain of the precise dates of these theories, but the general context of his discussion in *Metaph.* A, ch. 5 makes a sixth-century date unlikely.[8] Within the period from say 490 to 430 different scholars will have different preferences, but the *arguments* for a more precise dating are quite tenuous. ||

Our first chief problem is the evidence concerning his use of dissection, where our most important text is an extended passage in Chalcidius' *Commentary on Plato's Timaeus* which must be quoted in full (ch. 246, 256.16 to 257.15, ed. Waszink).[9]

> Quare faciendum, ut ad certam explorationem Platonici dogmatis commentum uetus aduocetur medicorum et item physicorum, illustrium sane uirorum, qui ad comprehendendam sanae naturae sollertiam artus humani corporis facta membrorum exectione rimati sunt, quod existimabant ita demum se suspicionibus atque opinionibus certiores futuros, si tam rationi uisus quam uisui ratio concineret. Demonstranda igitur oculi natura est, de qua cum plerique alii tum Alcmaeo Crotoniensis, in physicis exercitatus quique primus exectionem aggredi est ausus, et Callisthenes, Aristotelis auditor, et Herophilus multa et praeclara in lucem protulerunt: duas esse angustas semitas quae a cerebri sede, in qua est sita potestas animae summa et principalis, ad oculorum cauernas meent naturalem spiritum continentes; quae cum ex uno initio eademque radice progressae aliquantisper coniunctae sint in frontis intimis, separatae biuii specie perueniant ad oculorum concauas sedes, qua superciliorum obliqui tramites porriguntur, sinuataeque illic tunicarum gremio naturalem humorem

[5] Thus when, for example, Hirschberg (1921: 130) argues that Alcmaeon cannot have dissected human beings on the grounds that he was a Pythagorean, the argument is unsound even though we may agree with the conclusion.

[6] For an early date (born around 540, floruit 500 or earlier) see, for example, Wachtler, 1896: 16, Olivieri, 1919: 15ff., Hirschberg, 1921: 129, Stella, 1938–9: 237 and 246, Ebner, 1969: 34. For a floruit in the middle of the fifth century, see Deichgräber, 1935: 37, Sigerist, 1961: 101 and 114, n. 50, Heidel, 1941: 43, while Edelstein, 1942: 371, entertained the possibility of an even later floruit.

[7] A[b] omits them and they do not occur in Alexander, but they appear in E Γ and are read by Asclepius: see Ross, 1924: I 152 and cf. Wachtler, 1896: 5ff. Diels conjectured νέος before ἐπὶ γέροντι. The meaning of ἐγένετο by itself is ambiguous ('was born' or 'lived'), see Wachtler, 1896: 9ff.

[8] The chapter begins ἐν δὲ τούτοις καὶ πρὸ τούτων (985b23) where 'these' refers, presumably, to the Atomists whom he has just been considering. Vague though this is, it leaves the impression that the theorists he is about to discuss were approximate contemporaries either of Empedocles and Anaxagoras on the one hand, or of Leucippus and Democritus on the other. Cf. Guthrie 1962: 357f.

[9] The passage from 'Demonstranda' (256.22) is quoted by Diels–Kranz as DK 24A10.

recipiente globos complent munitos tegmine palpebrarum, ex quo appellantur orbes. Porro quod ex una sede progrediantur luciferae semitae, docet quidem sectio principaliter, nihilo minus tamen intelligitur ex eo quoque, quod uterque oculus moueatur una nec alter sine altero moueri queat. Oculi porro ipsius continentiam in quattuor membranis seu tunicis notauerunt disparili soliditate; quarum differentiam proprietatemque si quis persequi uelit, maiorem proposita materia suscipiet laborem.

Extravagant claims have been made on the basis of this passage, and astonishingly some of those who have commented on it have failed to record that the account of the eye it contains is not attributed to Alcmaeon alone or have otherwise skirted the problem posed by the mention of Callisthenes and Herophilus, namely how much of the account is to be ascribed to them.[10] Chalcidius, whose date is given by Waszink as around 400 A.D., does not mention his source of information; nor can this now be determined with any degree of assurance.[11] In general, the accuracy of his comments on earlier || philosophers and scientists, where they can be checked, is very variable.[12] Yet, late as Chalcidius is, we cannot reject the testimony of this passage out of hand.[13] The question is, rather, what positive conclusions does it entitle us to draw concerning Alcmaeon's work? The text poses three main problems, the reference to human dissection at 256.19, the direct attribution of 'exectio' to Alcmaeon at 257.1 and the detailed account of the eye that begins at 257.2.

The first issue is whether such investigations as Alcmaeon carried out were done on human or animal subjects. In the sentence that precedes the mention of Alcmaeon[14] Chalcidius refers expressly to human dissection in the words 'artus humani corporis facta membrorum exectione rimati sunt'. Yet the idea that Alcmaeon himself used human subjects has usually, and surely rightly, been rejected.[15] The propriety of human dissection and vivisection became a matter of controversy in the third century B.C. This is clear from the Proem of Celsus' *De Medicina* which summarises the arguments on both

[10] An uncritical attitude on this problem vitiates, to a greater or lesser degree, the discussions in Stella (1938–9), Erhard (1941) and Ebner (1969).

[11] Switalski (1902) suggested Posidonius as the ultimate source of Chalcidius' commentary, a view repeated by Taylor (1928: 465), and Wellmann (1929a: 159 n. 7) for example. Yet Switalski's position has latterly been severely criticised: see the full discussion of the question of sources in Waszink 1962: xxxvff.

[12] It is not surprising that although there are some 30 references in Chalcidius to other major Presocratics, not including the exceptional case of Pythagoras, Diels–Kranz include only two of these texts in addition to 24A10 on Alcmaeon. Compare, for example, Chalcidius ch. 280, 284.14ff. on Thales with Aristotle, *Metaph.* 983b20ff.

[13] It does not inspire confidence, however, that Chalcidius introduces various extraneous notions in his translation and interpretation of Plato's theory of vision – on which he is commenting at this point. Thus where the text of the *Timaeus* (45B–C) speaks merely of the particular denseness of the centre of the eye, Chalcidius refers to what he calls the 'angusta medietas' of the eye and interprets this as equivalent to the passages that the anatomists had found leading into the back of the eye. It is this view of Plato's theory that leads him to find authorities among the anatomists for what he takes to be Plato's own idea, see, e.g., 258.11ff. and 20ff.

[14] 256.16ff., a sentence not included in Diels–Kranz.

[15] See, for example, Hirschberg, 1921: 130, but for a contrary view, Timpanaro Cardini, 1938: 241f., and Stella, 1938–9: 246.

sides of the dispute (paras. 23ff., 40ff. and 74f.). Reporting the views of those who defended human dissection (paras. 23ff.) Celsus says that they approved the practice of Herophilus and Erasistratus who not only dissected, but also vivisected, human subjects whom 'they obtained out of prison from the kings', and although doubts continue to be expressed in some quarters, it is now generally agreed that the dissection (if not vivisection) of human subjects was practised in Alexandria in the third century.[16] On the other hand there is no || shred of evidence that this had happened in the Greek world before. Indeed the terms in which Aristotle (who certainly dissected animals) refers to the problem of studying the internal parts of the human body show that the possibility of dissecting a man just did not occur to him. At *HA* 494b21ff. he says that 'the inner parts of man are for the most part unknown, and so we must refer to the parts of other animals which those of man resemble, and examine them'.[17] Yet Aristotle was familiar enough with the work of Alcmaeon[18] and must surely have known if he had dissected human subjects. The conclusion we must draw is clear: whereas the reference to human dissection in Chalcidius tallies with what we know of the work of Herophilus and Erasistratus, it is Herophilus alone, of the three anatomists named in ch. 246, of whom this can be said.[19]

Our next problem is the interpretation of the statement that Alcmaeon 'primus exectionem aggredi est ausus', which some scholars take to refer specifically to work on the eye, while others hold that it has quite general force and implies that according to Chalcidius Alcmaeon was the first to employ dissection as a general method. The reference to Alcmaeon's interest in natural science ('in physicis exercitatus') had been thought to tell for the general interpretation.[20] Yet the fact that the reference to 'exectio' is firmly embedded in the context of the discussion of the structure of the eye ('demonstranda igitur oculi natura est') would seem to tell more strongly for the opposite conclusion.[21] While it would be premature to reach a definite || conclusion, we may for the moment remark that while some investigation of the eye at least is referred to, that may be all that is involved.

[16] See, for example, Edelstein, 1967: 247ff., Kudlien, 1968: 42f. Some support for Celsus comes from Tertullian, *De An.* ch. 10. In Galen's day human subjects were still used at Alexandria in the teaching of osteology (*De Anat. Admin.* I, ch. 2). Rufus, too, refers to human dissection without, however, specifying where or by whom this was carried out (*Onom.* 134, Daremberg–Ruelle). On the arguments recently brought by Fraser (1969: 518ff. and 1972: I 347ff.) against the view that Erasistratus worked at Alexandria and that he practised human anatomy, see Lloyd, 1975

[17] Cf. also *HA* 511b13ff., 513a12ff., on which see below pp. 179–80.

[18] Apart from the reference to Alcmaeon at *Metaph.* 986a29f., there are three others in the zoological treatises (*HA* 492a14, 581a16, *GA* 752b25) and one in the *De Anima* (405a29).

[19] The reference to Callisthenes at 257.1 is obscure. We have no other evidence for Callisthenes' interest in anatomy and no means of knowing what Chalcidius' source of information was, unless indeed he was referring to the zoological works in the Aristotelian Corpus itself.

[20] The phrase 'facta membrorum exectione' in the sentence before (256.19f.) is, admittedly, quite general, but there other investigators besides Alcmaeon are clearly involved.

[21] Cf. the careful, and non-committal, discussion in Wachtler, 1896: 17f.

The more difficult question here is the meaning of 'exectio' itself, where scholars have differed first on whether a surgical or an investigative procedure is involved, secondly on whether living or dead subjects were used, and thirdly and more fundamentally on the nature of the procedure itself, where a measure of disagreement is already indicated by the different translations of 'exectio' as, for example, 'excision' and 'dissection'. The most we shall attempt to achieve at this stage is to narrow down the possibilities. First, if Chalcidius had meant to refer to a surgical operation, that is one undertaken not to reveal the anatomy of the eye but for therapeutic purposes,[22] he would surely have had to make this clear. Again, although Hirschberg[23] conjectured that 'exectio' refers to vivisection on the grounds that Chalcidius would not have said 'est ausus' if it had been a question of Alcmaeon merely cutting out or dissecting the eye, this depends on a questionable assumption concerning what Chalcidius (or his source) would have considered daring. Whether or not Koelbing is right to refer to Chalcidius' Christian beliefs at this point,[24] the way in which Aristotle feels obliged to justify the study of internal anatomy in *PA* I, ch. 5[25] already suggests that there is nothing surprising in Chalcidius considering the first person to cut open an animal for an anatomical inquiry an adventurous man.

But how far can we go towards defining the meaning of 'exectio' itself in this passage? So far as investigations of the eye and neighbouring structures are concerned, it is essential to distinguish between three quite different procedures, namely (*a*) cutting out the eyeball – with or without the further step of dissecting the structures thereby revealed || behind the eye; (*b*) dissecting the eye itself; and (*c*) cutting open the skull to investigate the structures communicating with the eye within the skull itself. These are three quite separate investigations, directed to different questions and able to reveal quite different sets of facts. Thus (*a*) cutting out the eyeball – an investigation confined to the orbit – would simply reveal the structures leading off from the back of the eye passing through the optic foramen towards the intracranial cavity, the most prominent of these structures (in the 'stalk' of the eye) being what we call the optic nerve. (*b*) Dissection of the eye itself would reveal its internal structure and in particular its several membranes. But only if (*c*) the skull itself were opened, would it be possible to trace the course of the optic nerves, for example, including the optic chiasma, within the brain. Clearly

[22] Harris, 1973: 6 n. 3 remarks: 'might not this operation have been undertaken in the case of severe cranial injury involving an eye "hanging out" and crushed or mangled? In such a situation Alcmaeon may very well have "dared" to sever the optic nerve.' But so far as the text of Chalcidius goes, 'exectio' relates not to any surgical procedure, but to the problem of 'demonstrating the nature of the eye': cf. also 256.20 and 258.12.

[23] 1921: 132f., followed by Diels–Kranz, Wellmann, Erhard and others: but cf. the doubts expressed by Olivieri 1919: 41 n. 1, Sigerist, 1961: 114 n. 51 and Koelbing, 1968: 8f.

[24] 'ausus' would express a reaction to Alcmaeon's 'curiositas'; Koelbing, 1968: 9.

[25] Cf. below pp. 190–1. Aristotle probably had Platonists chiefly in mind, but his defence of empirical investigation has a general relevance: as we shall see, dissection was still far from being a well-established method in Aristotle's day.

the term 'exectio' itself will bear any of these three interpretations.[26] A decision between them will, then, depend on our view of the scope of Alcmaeon's inquiries, the problems he was interested in and the results he reached, and it must therefore be deferred until we have analysed such other evidence as we have that bears on these questions.

The last problem posed by the text of Chalcidius is how much of the detailed description of the eye from 257.2 ('duas esse angustas semitas...') should be ascribed to Alcmaeon himself among the authorities mentioned. At this point Chalcidius gives what he takes to be an accurate anatomical description of the eye in so far as this is relevant to the understanding of the text of Plato he is commenting on. But many features of that description relate, fairly clearly, to ideas and theories that became current only in the Hellenistic age.[27] In particular, although we find references to membranes in the eye in earlier texts,[28] it was, almost certainly, only after the work of Herophilus that the view that there are four such membranes became canonical.[29] This is ‖ the account given in Rufus, *Onom.* 136f. and 154, in Ps.-Rufus, *Anat.* 170ff. and in Celsus, *De Medicina* VII 7.13 and in all three cases we find references to the work of Herophilus, for example to the anatomical terms he introduced. Thus according to Rufus he compared the retina with a net, ἀμφίβληστρον, from which the term ἀμφιβληστροειδής was later coined, the origin of the Latin 'retina' and so of our own term. There can be little doubt, then, that it was Herophilus who was responsible for the first detailed account of the internal structure of the four membranes of the eye as also for that of the ventricles of the brain,[30] and the probability is that much of Chalcidius' description ultimately derives from him.[31] That is not to

[26] Neither 'exectio' nor 'sectio' (used by Chalcidius at 257.10 where he is talking about the root of the 'light-bearing paths') was confined to 'dissection'.

[27] 'Naturalem spiritum' (257.4) may also be an idea of Hellenistic origin, but since air in some form had played a part in earlier beliefs about the function of the brain (for example in Diogenes of Apollonia and *Morb. Sacr.*), this cannot be proved.

[28] Especially *Loc. Hom.* ch. 2 and *Carn.* ch. 17, on which see below pp. 184–5.

[29] Cf. Chalcidius' reference to 'quattuor membranis seu tunicis' (257.12f.), though it is notable that he draws back from a detailed description of each and his phrase 'disparili soliditate' (257.13) is characteristically vague. The early development of views of the number of membranes in the eye (from two in 'Hippocrates' to three or four) is outlined in ch. 11 of the *Introductio seu Medicus*, XIV 711ff. K, ascribed to Galen. In what became the usual view, the four membranes are (1) κερατοειδής (corresponding to the sclera and cornea), (2) χοριοειδής or ῥαγοειδής (the chorioid), (3) ἀραχνοειδής or ἀμφιβληστροειδής (the retina) and (4) κρυσταλλοειδής (the capsular sheath of the lens).

[30] Herophilus' work on the brain – distinction of the main ventricles, identification of the chorioid concatenations, naming of the *Torcular Herophili* and *calamus scriptorius* – is often referred to in our sources. We must repeat that the optic chiasma (possibly, but by no means certainly, referred to in Chalcidius' words 'progressae aliquantisper coniunctae sint in frontis intimis', 257.5f.) would only be revealed by inspecting a brain that had been exposed either deliberately by opening the skull or in an extensive injury. Although such investigations were possible before Herophilus (and Aristotle has been thought to refer to what we call the optic chiasma when he speaks of certain ducts from the eye meeting behind it at *HA* 495a11f.), Herophilus was evidently the first to give a detailed account of the brain.

[31] The repeated reference to a single root ('uno initio' 257.4f., 'eademque radice' 257.5, 'una sede' 257.9) to the paths of the eye is problematic: it is neither anatomically true of the optic

say that all of that description is of Hellenistic origin. Given that there are some references not only to membranes in the eye (μήνιγγες, δέρματα or χιτῶνες) but also to channels of some sort leading to it (whether πόροι or φλέβες) in the Hippocratic writings and in Aristotle, to attribute similar ideas to Alcmaeon cannot be ruled out as hopelessly anachronistic. Yet we clearly need independent evidence to confirm that any item in Chalcidius' account relates to Alcmaeon. ||

On two points, then, the results of our inquiry into the evidence of Chalcidius must be negative: (1) the reference to *human* dissection at 256.19 must be taken to refer to Herophilus and is most unlikely to apply to Alcmaeon; (2) equally, the detailed description of the eye primarily applies to, or derives from, Herophilus. All that is positively ascribable to Alcmaeon, on the basis of Chalcidius' report, is the first use of 'exectio': but even here the text of Chalcidius by itself does not enable us to give firm answers to our two most important questions, the precise method that Alcmaeon used in investigating the eye and the extent to which he applied similar methods to other anatomical inquiries.

Fortunately a text of Theophrastus, *De Sensu* (25f., DK 24A5) provides invaluable evidence on these problems. Here is an authority who is, of course, far more reliable than Chalcidius. The passage is not only one of our earliest but also one of our most extensive pieces of information about Alcmaeon, and since it deals with, among other things, his theory of vision, it can be used both to supplement and to modify what we learn from Chalcidius. Theophrastus reports Alcmaeon's view on sight in particular as follows: ὀφθαλμοὺς δὲ ὁρᾶν διὰ τοῦ πέριξ ὕδατος. ὅτι δ' ἔχει πῦρ, δῆλον εἶναι· πληγέντος γὰρ ἐκλάμπειν. ὁρᾶν δὲ τῷ στίλβοντι καὶ τῷ διαφανεῖ, ὅταν ἀντιφαίνῃ, καὶ ὅσον ἂν καθαρώτερον ᾖ, μᾶλλον. Although several of the details of this report are unclear,[32] we can be confident on some points. First the contents of the eye are imagined as fire and water. Though we cannot assert, on the basis of this text, that Alcmaeon had no idea of the internal *structure* of the eye, that is of its various membranes, there is no evidence in Theophrastus to confirm that he had, and such evidence as there is strongly suggests that the chief question that interested him was that of the elemental

tracts nor an idea that such later anatomists as Herophilus and Galen seem to have entertained (Galen indeed clearly describes the separate terminations of the optic tracts at *De Anat. Admin.* XIV, ch. 2). Either Chalcidius (or his source) had some quite different structure in mind – for example among the blood-vessels in the brain, or even the stalk of the pituitary gland – and was not referring to the optic tracts here at all, or – more probably – the idea of the single termination of the optic paths is a mere conjecture. Although he claims that it is shown by 'sectio', he also says that it is proved by the fact that the eyes move together: it seems possible that it was this observation that suggested the doctrine in the first place.

[32] τὸ στίλβον is generally taken to refer to the fire in the eye, and τὸ διαφανές to the water (Wachtler, 1896: 48f.): but Beare and Stratton take καί to be epexegetic here (Stratton translates: 'vision is due to the gleaming – that is to say, the transparent – character of that which [in the eye] reflects the object'). While most scholars take τὸ πέριξ ὕδωρ to refer to water in the eye, Taylor (1928: 282) suggested it might mean the atmosphere surrounding our body.

substances in the eye. It is with this in mind, clearly, that he inferred the presence of fire from what happens when the eye is struck.

Thus far Alcmaeon's theory is comparable with that of other Presocratic philosophers who conjectured doctrines about the elements || in the eye in broad agreement with their general physical speculations.[33] But Theophrastus goes on to report a doctrine of πόροι: evidently Alcmaeon believed that, with the possible exception of touch, where Theophrastus says that he had no definite theory, all the sense-organs are connected by πόροι to the brain which, as we know from other information,[34] he considered to be the seat of consciousness.

Those who have commented on this theory have disagreed sharply on the elements of observation and conjecture in it. The principal problem that concerns us, however, is whether the doctrine of πόροι implies the use of dissection. Take first the senses of smell and hearing. Theophrastus says that according to Alcmaeon 'we smell by drawing in the breath (πνεῦμα) to the brain through the nostrils at the same time as we breathe', and that in his account of hearing he spoke of a void (κενόν) in the ears. Here as elsewhere Alcmaeon evidently imagined the process of sensation as involving the transport of πνεῦμα to the brain, and in these two cases the outer entrances for the πνεῦμα can be clearly identified as the nostrils and the ears (i.e. the external auditory meatus). Now just how far Alcmaeon may have tried to trace the pneuma-carrying channels back from the external sense-organs towards or into the brain is not at all clear. In both cases it is possible to suggest several different candidates for the channels he might have observed, that is *if* he investigated the matter empirically and did not simply postulate the existence of such links.[35] Thus if he explored the back of the nostrils with a probe, he might either have discovered the many small holes or perforations in the cribriform plate, or indeed have pierced that plate itself (and the fracturing of the cribriform plate *may* be accompanied by the oozing out of brain matter: if he had seen that, he would no doubt have taken it as clear confirmation of his theory of the link between nose and brain);[36] or alternatively he may have mistaken one of the sinuses (sphenoidal or frontal) for a link with the brain. So far as the sense of hearing goes, it is possible || that he had discovered the pharyngo-tympanic (or Eustachian) tubes and supposed them to provide a communication between the ear and the brain;[37] or he may have pierced, with a probe introduced through the

[33] Cf. e.g. Empedocles, Fr. 84 (see below pp. 181–2) and Diogenes of Apollonia 64A19.

[34] E.g. Aet. IV 17.1 and V 17.3 and cf. Plato, *Phaedo* 96B (where however the originator of the doctrine is not named).

[35] Cf. below p. 176 on his doctrine concerning the sense of taste.

[36] A passage in Herodotus (2.86), noted for example by Wachtler (1896: 52, n. 3), describes Egyptian embalmers drawing out part of the brain through the nostrils by means of an iron hook, and this would probably be through a fracture in the cribriform plate. But how far the Greeks were acquainted with such procedures before Herodotus' history became known is not at all clear.

[37] According to Aristotle, *HA* 492a14f., Alcmaeon held that goats breathe through the ears, which might be taken to confirm that he had discovered the pharyngo-tympanic tubes. Yet

external auditory meatus, the roof of the middle ear, the tegmen tympani (a thin plate of bone separating the intracranial and middle ear cavities). Thus *if* Alcmaeon had carried out an empirical investigation, several different links can be suggested between the external sense-organs and the brain.[38] Yet on the question of the method that he is likely to have used, it is clear that – whether he took a human or an animal subject – by far the simplest and most effective way of attempting to demonstrate channels leading from the ear and nose in the brain would be to use a probe. Dissection in the strict sense is neither a necessary nor a particularly appropriate technique for the job of work Alcmaeon needed to do.

As regards vision and taste, Theophrastus does not help us to determine the channels or communications in question. But so far as the eye is concerned, it seems much more likely that these were what we call the optic nerves[39] than that they were, for example, the arteries, veins or muscles of the eye. The reason for this is simply that the optic nerves are by far the most obvious and distinct structures that an observer would remark behind the eye.[40] The fact that Alcmaeon took the role of these connections to be to transport air or pneuma to the brain and || so presumably held them to be hollow does not tell against their identification with the optic nerves:[41] when we turn to later Greek anatomists whose descriptions refer unambiguously to what we call the optic nerves, we find that many of them inferred that these are hollow and some even assert that their lumina are clearly visible.[42] But if this identification is correct, how far back did Alcmaeon attempt to trace the structures he saw? As we have pointed out, the investigation of the structures behind the eye *within the orbit* is quite distinct not only from a dissection of the eye itself but also from an investigation of the structures communicating with the eye *within the skull* itself. Our examination of the evidence of Chalcidius has already suggested that Alcmaeon may have done

that is not necessarily the case, since he may have believed that the air in question (like that necessary, in his view, for the sense of hearing) passed first to the *brain* (i.e. rather than to the pharynx), a theory which can be paralleled e.g. in *Morb. Sacr.* ch. 16. It is striking that our first definite reference to the pharyngo-tympanic tubes comes in the passage that immediately follows in Aristotle, *HA* 492a19f., where, however, there is no mention of Alcmaeon. But just as *HA* 492a14f. does not prove that Alcmaeon knew the pharyngo-tympanic tubes, so a19f. does not prove that he did not. Cf. Wachtler, 1896: 43ff.

38 The suggestions in the text, for which I am indebted to Professor Horn, are far from exhausting the possibilities for an investigation carried out on a human subject and others could be added for other species of animals.

39 This is not to say that Alcmaeon had any clear idea of their function as nerves: cf. Solmsen, 1961: 151ff.

40 Thus in humans the optic nerve is a prominent structure some 3 to 4 mm in diameter, containing within it a much smaller blood-vessel, the central artery of the retina, a branch of the ophthalmic artery: in most other species, too, the optic nerves are, as a general rule, appreciably larger than the central artery of the retina.

41 Despite Magnus, 1901: 80, Hirschberg, 1921: 130f. and Schumacher, 1963: 75.

42 This view is ascribed to Herophilus and his followers by Galen at *UP* x, ch. 12 (II 93 Helmreich, III 813 K) and *De Sympt. Caus.* I, ch. 2 (VII 88f. K), and it is one adopted by Galen himself (e.g. *PHP* VII, ch. 4, V 612f. K, and *UP* VIII, ch. 6, I 463 H, III 639 K) although at *De Anat. Admin.* XIV, ch. 2 he admits to some difficulty in demonstrating the hollow passage within the nerve.

no more than cut out the eyeball: and precisely *that* investigation is all that is necessary to have convinced him of the existence of channels from the eye to the brain. As for the other possibility, that he investigated the course of the optic nerves within the skull (and this would have been necessary if he had discovered the optic chiasma and the optic tracts), there is no evidence in Theophrastus to suggest that he carried this out. Indeed the balance of probability is that he did not, for if he had explored the cranial cavity, then other aspects of his theories are surprising, for example that he continued to hold both that there are channels leading directly from the ear to the brain[43] and that there are similar channels in the case of the sense of taste.

Finally there is the problem of taste itself, and here, unlike the other three senses we have considered, there are no obvious structures that lead from the tongue to the brain. Yet here – and in the case of touch as well, if he extended his theory to it[44] – he seems simply to have || inferred the existence of πόροι of some sort on the basis of what he believed he had established in the case of the other three senses. He had seen the beginnings (at least) of the channels of hearing and smell leading off towards the brain and (if we are right) knew that the eyes too are connected (by the optic nerves) to the brain. Just as Aristotle was to argue that links that were manifest in the case of two of the senses should be inferred for the other three,[45] so Alcmaeon too may have inferred his πόροι of taste by a similar analogical argument.

What conclusions, then, does our analysis of Theophrastus' evidence suggest concerning Alcmaeon's use of dissection? There can be no doubt that the view that there are connections between the brain and the sense-organs of hearing, smell and sight could have been based on, or confirmed by, quite straightforward investigations. There is no need to assume, and indeed it is highly improbable, that Alcmaeon had discovered what we know as the olfactory and auditory nerves, for example. The channels that he referred to evidently included such gross structures as the passages of the nostrils and the external auditory meatus. The chief aim of his inquiry was, it seems, to reveal the existence of *some* connection leading from the sense-organs to the brain, and once this had been achieved, his investigation may well not have been pursued further. True, if our interpretation of the 'channels' of the eye is correct, the observations he had carried out in this case were not *purely* of external or surface structures: that much would be implied by a knowledge of structures behind the eye. Yet even in that case his investigation may have

[43] It is, however, possible (as Prof. Horn has kindly pointed out to me) that someone looking for channels between the ear and the brain might mistake the large intracranial internal auditory meatus for the inner opening of such a channel.

[44] Theophrastus says that Alcmaeon did not state how touch took place, but also reports that Alcmaeon held that *all* the senses are somehow connected with the brain. The former phrase would tell against, the latter for, the suggestion that Alcmaeon postulated πόροι in the case of touch as well.

[45] See *Juv.* 469a12ff., cf. *Sens.* 439a1f., *PA* 656a29ff. For Aristotle, the heart is the common sensorium. Claiming, admittedly rather obscurely, that the links between the senses of taste and touch and the heart are manifest, he argues that the other sense-organs too must similarly be supposed to be connected with the heart.

been – and I suggest probably was – no more than a matter of the excision of the eye to reveal the structures behind it leading off to the brain.

How far does Theophrastus enable us to answer the two questions we posed above (p. 173) in considering the evidence in Chalcidius? The reported theories of sensation in general provide us with a good opportunity to judge how extensive Alcmaeon's use of empirical methods is likely to have been. The evidence in Theophrastus, so far from leading us to conclude that Alcmaeon used dissection as a regular method, tells, if anything, for the opposite conclusion. The empirical investigations he conducted in connection with the sense-organs seem || to have been quite limited in scope and may not have involved dissection proper[46] at all.

Such other, admittedly very limited, evidence as we have about Alcmaeon's biological work, namely his theory of sleep and certain embryological ideas, tends to bear out these conclusions. Thus Aetius (V 24.1, DK 24A18) reports that he held that sleep comes about through the retreat of the blood to (or into) the blood-carrying veins, αἱμόρρους φλέβας; that waking is its dispersion through them, and that a complete retreat is death. Once again large claims have been made on the basis of this passage, for example that Alcmaeon must have observed that in a dead animal the arteries are drained of blood, and accordingly distinguished the arteries and the veins (the latter termed αἱμόρρους φλέβας)[47] But this is far from being the only, and is not the most likely, interpretation. The terms φλέβες and φλέβια with or without qualifying adjectives were used, both in the Presocratic period and later, of a wide variety of ducts and vessels.[48] The term αἱμόρρους is not specifically ascribed to Alcmaeon by Aetius,[49] and even if we assume that he used it, the implied contrast could be between any major blood-vessels on the one hand, and any other vessels imagined as holding less, or no, blood on the other, for example one between the larger blood-vessels mostly in the interior of the body (e.g. the superior and inferior venae cavae and the aorta) and the smaller, mostly superficial, blood-vessels. Indeed since the idea that sleep is due to, or accompanied by, a reflux of blood towards the interior of the body appears to have been a common one,[50] it seems much more likely that Alcmaeon had some such contrast in mind rather than that he had observed, and been misled by, bloodless arteries in a dead subject. ||

[46] That is as opposed to the use of the knife or scalpel to excise the eye, or to the use of the probe to explore the back of the ear and nose.

[47] E.g. Wachtler, 1896: 71f., Fredrich, 1899: 67, Kayserling, 1901: 177f., Olivieri, 1919: 22f., Stella, 1938–9: 273, Timpanaro Cardini, 1958–64: I 146f.; but caution is expressed, for example, by Tannery, 1930: 223 and Harris, 1973: 8.

[48] Of passages carrying air, e.g. *Morb. Sacr.* chh. 3f., *Flat.* chh. 10 and 14; of spermatic ducts, Diogenes of Apollonia, Fr. 6; and of channels of sensation, e.g. *Loc. Hom.* chh. 2f., *Carn.* ch. 17 and in Theophrastus' accounts of Diogenes of Apollonia (DK 64A19) and of Democritus (DK 68A135).

[49] It is indeed an emendation of Reiske's where the MSS read ὁμόρους.

[50] E.g. *Epid.* VI 5.15 (V 320.6f. Littré), cf. *Epid.* VI 4.12 (V 310.6f.) and Aristotle (*Somn.* 457a33ff., cf. *HA* 521a15ff., *PA* 653a10ff.) – where one may note that the theory is not connected with any contrast between arteries and veins.

Finally there are several brief, and sometimes conflicting, testimonies about his embryological ideas. (1) At *GA* 752b25ff. (DK 24A16) Aristotle remarks that he held that the white of the egg is its 'milk' or nourishment. Although Stella (1938–9: 271) claimed on this basis that Alcmaeon undertook a detailed study, using vivisection, of the development of the chicken embryo, this assumption is unwarranted.[51]

(2) Aetius V 16.3 (DK 24A17) reports that Alcmaeon held that the embryo takes in food through its whole body like a sponge. However a different theory is attributed to him by Rufus quoted in Oribasius (III 156, *CMG* VI 2.2 136.28ff.),[52] namely that the embryo already takes in food through its mouth while still in the womb. We need not enter here into the question of which of these two testimonies to accept, since neither implies that he had carried out dissections in this context.[53]

(3) Nor need we decide between the conflicting testimonies on Alcmaeon's view of which part of the embryo is formed first, since again neither of our sources implies that he used dissection in this context. While Censorinus (*De Die Nat.* 5.5, DK 24A13) suggests that he thought the problem beyond the range of observation, Aetius (V 17.3) says that he held that the head was formed first: but even that would seem to imply that if he investigated the matter empirically (as opposed to proposing a conjecture in line with his doctrine of the brain as the ἡγεμονικόν) he confined his observations to surface anatomy.

Our analysis of the remaining evidence for Alcmaeon shows how important it is to qualify references to his use of dissection. To attribute to him, quite baldly, the invention of the method of dissection as such is potentially highly misleading for it might be taken (and indeed in some cases is meant to be taken) to imply that he applied that method generally, self-consciously and systematically. But that is to go far beyond what our direct evidence allows us to conclude. We may be reasonably confident that he used the knife in one context, in examining the structures connecting the eye and the brain: even here, however, and in his work on the sense-organs in general, his interest was in certain theoretical problems (such as the common seat of sensation) not in the || method of dissection as such. Beyond this, we enter the field of conjecture. Admittedly our direct evidence for Alcmaeon is very limited, and given that this is so, and that the vague reference to 'exectio' in Chalcidius may be taken in a general sense, it has often been argued that the probability is that Alcmaeon used the method elsewhere. We have already expressed doubts about this thesis in connection with specific aspects of his work: our next task is to review briefly the chief texts relevant to the broader issue of the early history of dissection as a whole.

51 Such inquiries are, however, recorded in *Nat. Puer.* and Aristotle (see n. 77).

52 Reading στόματι. Olivieri, 1919: 34, however, suggested emending to σώματι to bring this testimony into line with Aetius.

53 Cf. Aristotle, *GA* 746a19ff. who remarks – somewhat optimistically – that the idea that embryos are nourished in the womb by suckling could easily be refuted by carrying out dissections on animals.

II

In a subject as obscure as the development of dissection, it is as well to begin where our evidence is fairly solid, namely with Aristotle. Widely different estimates have been given of the extent to which Aristotle himself dissected. Certainly some surprising and gross errors and confusions remain in his anatomical descriptions,[54] due either to a failure to observe or more often to his observations being hasty or coloured by theoretical interests and preconceptions. We have already seen that the possibility of dissecting human subjects was not entertained,[55] and his use of vivisection was generally confined to observing the effects that maiming had on an animal's vital functions.[56] Yet the || references in the extant zoological works to the results of dissections are frequent and explicit[57] (whether these dissections were carried out by Aristotle himself or by his assistants and fellow-workers) and they include instances where he draws attention to the mistakes that may arise from faulty or careless dissection.[58] Even more important, for our present purposes, he sometimes refers to his predecessors' use of the method. By far the most valuable text is *HA* III, ch. 2, 511b13ff., where he criticises earlier studies of the blood-vascular system:[59]

> The reason for their ignorance is the difficulty of carrying out observations. For in dead animals the nature of the most important blood-vessels is unclear because they especially collapse immediately the blood leaves them...And in living animals it is impossible to investigate the nature of the blood-vessels because they are internal. And so those who have examined dead bodies[60] by dissection have not observed the principal sources of the blood-vessels, while those who have examined very emaciated living men have inferred the sources of the blood-vessels from what could then be seen externally.[61]

[54] To mention just two of the best-known examples, there are his obscure and apparently inconsistent accounts of the heart as having three vessels in *HA* 513a27ff., *PA* 666b21ff. and cf. *Somn.* 458a16ff. (on which see, most recently, Shaw, 1972 and Harris, 1973: 123ff.), and his account of the brain, where he says that the brain itself is bloodless, cold and devoid of φλέβες and that the back of the skull is empty (*HA* 494b33ff.).

[55] Cf. above p. 170 on *HA* 494b21ff. Some commentators (e.g. Ogle in his translation of *PA* and most recently Shaw) have, however, suggested that he may have dissected a human embryo. Despite his considerable knowledge of mammalian embryos, this seems doubtful. One striking passage is *HA* 583b14ff. where he records what happens when a male human embryo aborted on the fortieth day is put into water: it holds together in a sort of membrane, and if this membrane is pulled to bits, the embryo is revealed inside. On this occasion he appears not to have proceeded to a dissection, since his subsequent brief remarks are confined to surface anatomical details. Cf. below p. 186 on *Carn.* ch. 19.

[56] See e.g. *IA* 708b4ff., *GA* 774b31ff. and many references to insects living when cut up, *De An.* 411b19ff., 413b19ff., *Long.* 467a18ff., *Juv.* 468a23ff., *Resp.* 471b20ff., 479a3ff., *PA* 682b29ff. Many of his observations must have been carried out on animals that had become mutilated naturally, but the frequency of these references suggests some deliberate human intervention.

[57] Aristotle also wrote a work, now lost, entitled the 'Dissections' ('Ανατομαί): he refers to the anatomical diagrams in this book at *HA* 497a31f. for example.

[58] E.g. *HA* 496a9ff.: 'in all animals alike...the apex of the heart points forwards, although this may very likely escape notice because of a change of position while they are being dissected'; cf. *HA* 510a21ff.; *PA* 676b33ff. is one passage that draws attention to the dangers of generalising concerning the whole species on the basis of observations of one or a few specimens. [59] Cf. also *HA* 496b4ff. [60] I.e. of animals, as the context makes plain.

[61] Aristotle himself recommends combining both methods: 'it is only in animals that have been

This text shows both that dissection had been used by those who had attempted to describe the blood-vessels before Aristotle and that it was not their only method, since some investigators relied on observation of emaciated human subjects. Aristotle notes the drawbacks of both methods and indeed his criticisms of earlier theories on this topic are, in the main, borne out by what we know of them. He himself cites three accounts at some length, those of Syennesis of Cyprus,[62] Diogenes of Apollonia and Polybus,[63] and all three are, to a large || extent, fanciful.[64] An over-fondness for bilateral symmetry – seen particularly in the supposed criss-crossing of major blood-vessels from right to left and left to right – is a feature of all three accounts, and to judge from the references to blood-letting in the theories of Diogenes and Polybus their views were partly based on, and no doubt served in turn to justify, current practices in venesection.[65]

If we turn to other late fifth- or early fourth-century accounts of the blood-vessels, not quoted by Aristotle, some, at least, appear to be based on little or no use of dissection.[66] Thus *On the Sacred Disease* presents some quite detailed anatomical theories in the course of its discussion of the causes of epilepsy. The author holds that the φλέβες are responsible for conveying blood, air and, in certain conditions, humours round the body and that they communicate directly with the outer air,[67] and in ch. 3 especially he gives an account of the main φλέβες that is no less fanciful than those of Diogenes or Polybus.[68] How the author arrived at his ideas is obscure, but elsewhere in the work (ch. 11) we find him referring to opening the heads of goats in order to confirm the natural origins of epilepsy. He claims that the disease arises when the brain is unnaturally moist and flooded with phlegm, and adds: 'the truth of this is best shown by the cattle that are attacked by this disease, especially by the goats, which are the most common victims. If you cut open the head you will find the brain moist, very full of dropsy and of an evil

first starved to emaciation and then strangled that the facts can be discovered sufficiently' (*HA* 513a12ff., cf. 515b1 and *PA* 668a21f.).

62 Nothing is otherwise known of this man. The report in *HA* III, ch. 2 corresponds to part of ch. 8 of the composite treatise *Oss.*

63 Aristotle's report corresponds to the longer accounts in *Oss.* ch. 9 and *Nat. Hom.* ch. 11.

64 Thus none of these authors recognises the heart as the centre of the blood-vascular system. The identification of the particular pairs of φλέβες they refer to is, in most cases, quite conjectural and complicated by the fact that, as already noted, φλέψ is applied to other vessels besides what we should term blood-vessels. See the full discussion in Harris, 1973: 20ff.

65 Thus Polybus describes his first pair of veins as follows: 'one pair runs from the back of the head through the neck on the outside past the backbone on either side till it reaches the loins and so to the legs, and after that through the shins to the outer part of the ankles and to the feet. That is why surgeons make incisions in the hams and outer parts of the ankles to relieve pains in the back and loin' (transl. Peck).

66 Some other, more accurate, accounts will be discussed below, pp. 184–6.

67 This seems to be implied in ch. 4 (VI 368.1ff. Littré, 68.40ff. Grensemann). The φλέβες also get air via the lungs, see ch. 7.

68 Thus as in Diogenes and Polybus great importance is attached to a pair of φλέβες called 'hepatic' and 'splenetic', which are thought to connect the liver with the right side of the body and the spleen with the left.

odour, whereby you may learn that it is not a god but the disease which injures the body.'[69] This passage is important because it shows that the idea of conducting a || post-mortem examination on animals had occurred.[70] At the same time the inspection that was made (assuming one was indeed carried out) was, clearly, a quite cursory one. Once the author had satisfied himself on the particular point at issue, the dropsical state of the animal's brain, his inquiry was pursued no further. In particular, it is apparent that he did *not* take the opportunity to check his theories on the routes of the main φλέβες communicating with the brain, let alone attempt a detailed investigation of the structure of the brain and its ventricles.

On Aristotle's authority we may accept that dissection was used by some of his predecessors in inquiries concerning the blood-vessels, and *On the Sacred Disease* provides us with evidence concerning the use of dissection in another context, that of a post-mortem examination. But whether we turn to the remains of the Presocratic philosophers or to the Hippocratic writers, the occasions when we can definitely confirm the use of dissection for the purposes of a scientific inquiry in fifth- or fourth-century texts are rare.[71] Let us consider, first, the later Presocratic philosophers, Empedocles and Democritus.

Thus Empedocles certainly proposes quite complex theories concerning eyesight and respiration in the well-known fragments (84 and 100) in which he presents the analogies of the lantern and the clepsydra. Yet although the lantern and the clepsydra themselves have obviously been carefully observed, there is no suggestion that he sought to follow up his theories of the internal functionings of the eye and of respiration by carrying out dissections on either human or animal subjects.[72] In the case of sight, although Fr. 84 refers to fire 'enclosed in membranes (μήνιγξιν)' trapping or giving birth to the pupil in 'delicate tissues (ὀθόνῃσι)' which are pierced through with 'marvellous passages || (χοάνῃσι)', no attempt is made to describe the precise structure and relations of the parts of the eye (retina, cornea, sclera etc), and the passages within the tissues, like the fire in the eye itself, are arrived at by inference, not observation. Again, although the detailed interpretation of the clepsydra is controversial,[73] it is clear that his ideas concerning the interplay of blood and air in the body are based on conjecture and inference: they were

[69] VI 382.6ff. L, 78.78ff. G = ch. 14 Jones: transl. Jones.

[70] One may compare Plutarch's story (*Pericles* ch. 6) of Anaxagoras having the skull of a one-horned ram opened to show that this phenomenon had a natural cause.

[71] The infrequency of dissection for the purposes of research may seem more surprising in that in another context, divination by the inspection of entrails or haruspicy, animals were regularly opened and their parts examined, even if that examination was usually no more than an inspection of *surface* features of, for example, the liver (see, e.g., Cicero, *De Div.* 2.12.28ff., cf. Plato, *Ti* 71Aff.). But although we find occasional references to anatomical data learned from sacrificial victims in our 'scientific' authors (e.g. Aristotle, *HA* 496b24ff., *PA* 667b1ff. and cf. *Carn.* ch. 8 which refers to blood taken from sacrificial animals), the contrast in the context and aims of divination and those of anatomical studies was no doubt sufficiently marked to act as an effective barrier to communication.

[72] Cf. Lloyd, 1966: 327 and 333.

[73] The secondary literature is very extensive: see most recently Seeck, 1967 and O'Brien, 1970.

not ideas that he had arrived at as a result of the use of dissection – or thought to check by such a method.

The evidence for Democritus looks at first sight more promising. Theophrastus devotes more space to his theory of sensation than to that of any other writer (*Sens*. 49ff., DK 68A135) and Democritus' account of the eye, in particular, was quite complex, distinguishing the 'outer membrane' (ὁ ἔξω χιτών), the 'inner parts' (τὰ ἐντός) and the φλέβες round the eyes. Yet how far his ideas were based on direct observation is doubtful. At least we are put on our guard by the reference, in Theophrastus, para. 56, to an apparently similar theory of a χιτών and φλέβια in the case of hearing, where we may be in some doubt as to what precisely (if anything) Democritus had *seen* to lead him to speak of empty φλέβια in this case.[74] It looks, in fact, as if he was applying a general model to both these senses at some cost to the accuracy of his description of either. Although we have a good deal of evidence in Aristotle and other sources that demonstrates the wide range of biological questions that Democritus tackled, none of our testimonies can be said to establish *conclusively* that he had dissected.[75]

Whereas the fragmentary nature of our information is a major disability in judging any aspect of the work of the Presocratic || philosophers, original texts of the medical writers of the fifth and fourth centuries exist, of course, in some quantity. Yet with a few exceptions – and we shall be considering the three main texts, *The Heart*, *Places in Man* and *Fleshes* shortly – the method of dissection is almost entirely ignored in the Hippocratic Corpus. Such surgical treatises as *Fractures* and *Joints* show a fair degree of anatomical knowledge, but this was, we must assume, gained very largely in the actual treatment of fractures, dislocations and wounds of different types: there is nothing in those works to suggest that their authors attempted to increase their anatomical knowledge by dissecting animals or men.[76] Elsewhere in the Hippocratic writers descriptions of internal anatomy are, in the main, very weak. We have already considered some of the speculative notions of the

[74] Thus if, as seems possible, the χιτών here is the tympanic membrane, the φλέβια might be *either* the pharyngo-tympanic tube, *or* the cavities of the middle and/or inner ear, *or* blood-vessels behind the ear – or any combination of these.

[75] E.g. Aristotle, *GA* 740a13ff. and *PA* 665a31ff. (DK 68A145 and 148) on his theories on the formation of the embryo and on the invisible viscera of bloodless animals. Yet *if* Aetius (V 5.1, DKA142) is correct in ascribing a knowledge of the prostate gland to him as well as to Epicurus (though this has with reason been questioned by Lesky, 1951: 73) this would undoubtedly suggest what would be, for the time, advanced anatomical knowledge on that point. References to him dissecting in the spurious correspondence of Hippocrates (IX 356.4ff. L, DK C3) are untrustworthy, as also are the stories recorded by Aelian (DK A150a to 155a and 156).

[76] Two passages in *Art*. are especially revealing. In ch. 46 (IV 196.19ff. L, II 174.17ff. Kühlewein) the writer speaks of reducing a dislocation by opening a patient and inserting a hand in his body in order to illustrate the *impossibility* of carrying out such a procedure. In ch. 1 (IV 80.1ff. L, II 112.4ff. K) he refers to cutting away the flesh of the arm of a patient suffering from forward projection of the humerus in order to demonstrate that no dislocation had occurred: this too, however, is a 'thought experiment', not a procedure that could ever be contemplated in practice.

blood-vascular system to be found in such works as *On the Nature of Man* and *On the Sacred Disease*. In other treatises we find equally, or even more, bizarre ideas concerning the interrelations of the main organs in the body. Examples of this are the doctrine in *On Regimen* I chh. 9f. of the three περίοδοι or circuits in the body corresponding to the author's idea of the three main circuits of the heavenly bodies, and the theory in *On Diseases* IV, ch. 39 that there are four main 'sources' (πηγαί) of the humours in the body, heart, head, spleen and liver, all of which communicate directly with the stomach. It is true that elsewhere in the embryological treatises we find one of our rare references to the possibility of dissection. In *On the Nature of the Child* ch. 29 (VII 530.10ff. L) the writer suggests incubating a batch of 20 or more hen's eggs and opening one each day to observe the embryo chick's development. Yet even here the writer does not *in fact* set out the results of the investigation he suggests in any detail but confines himself to a single observation concerning the membranes extending from the umbilicus.[77] Moreover texts in two other treatises provide direct evidence concerning || how their authors thought one should proceed to gain insight into the internal functionings of the body – and in neither case is there any mention of dissection. *On the Art* ch. 12 (CMG I 1.18.3ff.) suggests that nature may be forced to yield information by the administration of certain foods and drinks, for example, and *On Ancient Medicine* ch. 22 (*CMG* I 1.53.1ff.) notes the difficulty of obtaining knowledge about the internal structures in the body but recommends doing so by studying objects such as cupping glasses outside the body.[78]

So far as most of the treatises in the Hippocratic Corpus are concerned, references to dissection are rare, and their absence in some contexts where the authors in question are discussing how to investigate certain anatomical and physiological problems suggests that those authors, at least, were not familiar with the method. We have, however, so far left out of consideration the three works, *The Heart*, *Places in Man* and *Fleshes*, each of which merits special attention.

The Heart is something of an exception to prove the rule. The writer of this treatise does refer to both dissection and, in one passage at least, vivisection.[79] Although brief and in parts obscure, the account he gives of the anatomy of the heart is quite detailed and it contains unmistakable references to two of the valves of the heart, where both the structure and the function of these

[77] It is notable that when Aristotle undertakes a similar investigation of the development of a hen's egg at *HA* 561a4ff., his account of his observations is much more detailed than that in *Nat. Puer*.

[78] The vagueness of this writer's classification of internal structures can be judged from the fact that the bladder, head and womb are said to be similar, namely 'broad and tapering', like a cupping glass.

[79] In ch. 2 (IX 80.13ff. L) the author suggests an experiment with a pig, in which the animal is given dyed water to drink and its throat then cut, in order to establish the theory that some drink passes to the lungs. Although this theory is incorrect, this does not show that he did not try the experiment.

valves are correctly understood.[80] Yet it is now generally agreed that this treatise is much later than most of the Hippocratic collection, that is that it is approximately contemporary with the work of Herophilus and Erasistratus. The conclusions of Abel's analyses (1958) have now been endorsed in the main, but modified and made more precise, by the careful study made by Lonie (1973). This treatise is evidence of the use of dissection, to be sure, but of its use in the third century, not the fifth or fourth.

Our other two treatises, *Places in Man* and *Fleshes*, are, however, much more likely to have been composed before the end of the fourth || century, even though their dates cannot be fixed at all precisely.[81] Both works deal with the two topics that we have found discussed at some length in other texts, namely the blood-vascular system and the sense-organs. Thus on the latter *Places in Man* ch. 2 (VI 278.14ff. L) speaks, for instance, of 'voids' in the region of the ears (κενεά cf. κενόν in Theophrastus' account of Alcmaeon) and the writer holds that the sounds we hear pass through a hole in the membrane round the brain.[82] Turning to the eyes, he writes of communications, here called φλέβια, from the brain through the 'enveloping membrane' to the eyes. These φλέβια 'nourish the sight by means of the purest part of the fluid from the brain', and he distinguishes three membranes (μήνιγγες) in the eye itself, a thick outer one, a thinner middle one and a third inner one 'that guards the moist element'. The description is brief and the identification of his three membranes with the sclera, chorioid and retina, though attractive, cannot be said to be certain. Like other writers before Herophilus, he lacks anatomical terms for the various membranes. Nor is it clear how he gained his information. He refers to lesions of the eye, suggesting in particular that when the middle membrane is broken it 'comes out like a bladder' (ἐξίσχει οἷον κύστις).[83] The extent of his anatomical knowledge[84] is such that we should probably assume some dissection, but it is striking that no explicit reference is made either here or elsewhere in the treatise to the method.

Fleshes contains an even more surprising mixture of wild conjecture and detailed, and in places quite accurate, anatomical descriptions. Thus the account of the formation of the parts of the body, based on a version of the four-element theory in which the 'glutinous' (associated with 'the cold' and

[80] See chh. 10 and 12 (IX 86.13ff., 90.11ff.) on what we call the aortic and pulmonary valves. Although he also speaks of other membranes within the ventricles that may be identified with what we call the atrio-ventricular valves, he evidently did not understand their function *as valves*, see Lonie, 1973: 11ff.

[81] With Littré's view that *Carn.* is not before Aristotle, contrast the discussion in Deichgräber, 1935: 54f. (the age of sophistic).

[82] Two such membranes (μήνιγγες) round the brain are distinguished at the end of ch. 2 (VI 280.7ff.) and it is tempting to see these as corresponding to the dura and the pia mater. The clear reference to a hole through the membrane round the brain at 278.17f. is, however, on any interpretation, obscure.

[83] It does not do so, presumably, by itself, at least not if the chorioid is meant, for this cannot 'come out' without the retina also becoming detached.

[84] Cf. also his account of the main φλέβες in the body in ch. 3, on which see, for example, Harris, 1973: 47f.

the brain) and the 'fatty' (associated with 'the hot' and the heart) play prominent roles, is almost entirely speculative, and much play is made of the special significance of the number seven at the end of the treatise (ch. 19). On the other hand || chh. 5f. (VIII 590.5ff. L) contain an account of the blood-vascular system in which two main blood-vessels communicating with the heart are distinguished, one called ἀρτηρίη (which appears to correspond to the aorta and its branches), the other the hollow φλέψ, and all the other φλέβες in the body are said to branch off from these two.[85]

The account the writer gives of the organs of hearing, smell and sight in chh. 15–17 (602.19ff.) is equally striking. He describes the auditory channels ending in a 'hard and dry bone, like a stone' and says that next to this bone there is a skin (δέρμα, i.e. membrane) which is 'thin as a spider's web, and the driest of all skins'. As for the relation between the brain and the organs of smell, he says that here there is no bone, only a 'soft cartilage, like a sponge' and the brain 'reaches to the hollows of the nostrils'.[86] As for sight, he says that from the membrane (μῆνιγξ) of the brain a φλέψ reaches each eye through the bone, and he claims that 'the thinnest part of the glutinous' reaches the eye by this route. As in Alcmaeon, vision takes place in part by reflection,[87] and he recognises that there are membranes in the eye, although his description of these is vague. He merely identifies 'many transparent skins' (δέρματα) in front of the part that sees: he describes the 'white flesh' about the eye, notes that the pupil (κόρη) appears black (although it is transparent) because it is deep-set in the eye and says that this has many black 'tunics', where he uses the term χιτών and suggests a distinction between two kinds of membrane, internal χιτῶνες and external δέρματα.

Like that in *Places in Man*, this account is clearly based in part on careful observation and we have interesting texts that throw light on the methods the author used. Thus in ch. 17 (606.10ff.) he says 'the moist element in the eye is glutinous: for we have often seen glutinous moisture oozing out of an eye that has ruptured', adding that when this fluid is hot, it is liquid, but when it is cold, it becomes dry 'like transparent incense' and that 'it is the same in men and in animals'. This text suggests observation of both animal and human subjects, but it is significant that – like *Places in Man* – he cites the || evidence from lesions, rather than that to be obtained from dissection, to confirm his ideas about the nature of the contents of the eyeball.

Elsewhere too[88] we find him making use of the information yielded by lesions and perhaps our most important and revealing text comes in ch. 19

[85] He also holds that the heart 'has most of the hot where the hollow vein lies' and that it dispenses or controls (ταμιεύει) the pneuma, 590.11ff.

[86] Here, as elsewhere in these chapters on sensation, the author is concerned to distinguish what facilitates or impedes sensation, interpreting the relevant factors usually in terms of such pairs of opposites as wet and dry.

[87] τούτῳ γὰρ τῷ διαφανεῖ ἀνταυγέει τὸ φῶς καὶ τὰ λαμπρὰ πάντα· τουτέῳ οὖν ὁρῇ τῷ ἀνταυγέοντι, 606.4ff., cf. above p. 173 on Alcmaeon.

[88] Cf. in his discussion of voice in ch. 18, 608.16ff.

(608.22ff.). There he is concerned to establish that all the parts of the embryo are formed in seven days, and he refers to what he says he has often seen, namely a human foetus, deliberately aborted by a public prostitute.[89] It comes out, he says, like flesh, and 'if you put this flesh in water and inspect it, you will find that it has all the members, and the places for the eyes and the ears and the limbs: the fingers of the hands, the legs, the feet and the toes, the genitals and all the rest of the body are clearly visible' (610.6–10). The passage is remarkable not only for what it contains, but also for what it omits. Evidently the idea of examining an aborted human foetus had occurred to this writer: equally evidently there is no suggestion that the foetus might be dissected, and no reference to any *internal* organs. The author of this treatise is exceptional both for the energy he showed in collecting information relevant to his theoretical concerns, and for the ingenuity he displayed in thinking of possible new ways of obtaining such information.[90] It is all the more interesting, therefore, that he appears not to have considered the possibility of dissecting the aborted human embryo.[91] As with *Places in Man*, it would be too simple and hasty to conclude straightforwardly that he had never dissected.[92] On the other hand, while he mentions certain lesions from which he gained particular information, he never refers to dissection as such, and the fact that he suggests merely an external examination of the aborted embryo shows that – to put it at the very least – dissection was not, for him, an obvious or an automatic procedure. ||.

III

We may now try to summarise the main results of this rapid survey. Aristotle's zoological works show that he was familiar with the method of dissection and that he or his associates used it on a number of animal species, though not on human subjects: it was not until Herophilus and Erasistratus that human dissection was practised, only to decline once again after a short period. On Aristotle's authority we may accept that some of his predecessors had also dissected. But in the extant evidence for the fifth and fourth centuries we find only quite rare references to the method and this indicates that its use before Aristotle was unsystematic, sporadic and tentative. *On the Sacred Disease* and Plutarch's story concerning Anaxagoras refer to cutting open an animal to see what disease it suffered from, and *On the Nature of the*

[89] He implies that the foetus was aborted very soon after conception since he uses this as evidence for his theory of the formation of the embryo within seven days. But to judge from his description of what he claims to have seen, the foetus must have been much older than that.

[90] Thus in chh. 8 and 9 he refers to tests that he claims to have made on blood to show, for example, that it does not coagulate so long as it is warm, or when it is beaten, but does so when allowed to cool.

[91] No more is there any question of dissection in the reference to the product of an abortion in *Nat. Puer.* ch. 13 (VII 488.22ff. L).

[92] His knowledge of the blood-vessels, especially, suggests that he either had inspected animal specimens closely himself, or had access to the work of others who had.

Child mentions cutting open eggs to observe the growth of the embryo chick. But even where we can be fairly confident that an animal was cut open, the inspection that was made often appears to be quite cursory. Certain advances in anatomical knowledge, for example of the blood-vascular system, were made in the period before Aristotle, and we may believe that these were partly attributable to the use of dissection. Yet hazy and indeed fantastic notions of internal anatomy were still prevalent, and there are many occasions where we would expect our texts to refer to dissection, if it had been commonly used, where they singularly fail to do so.

What, then, should be our conclusions so far as Alcmaeon is concerned? It is, of course, not necessarily the case that because an idea or method was generally ignored at a particular period, it was universally so. The history of science provides plenty of examples of exceptional individuals employing what were, not only for their own day, but also for some time afterwards, exceptional procedures. Yet in our case, it must be thought exceedingly unlikely that Alcmaeon undertook extensive and systematic dissections six decades at the very least before Aristotle was to do so.[93] It is far more probable that Alcmaeon's use of the knife was, if not confined to, at least not much more || extensive than, the one area we have discussed, namely his investigations of the eye.

But if this statement of the facts is broadly correct, it suggests two main problems that need to be discussed in conclusion. First why, once dissection had begun to be used to however limited an extent, were the Greeks so slow to apply and extend the method? Secondly and conversely, can we say what led to the eventual development of the method in the fourth century, notably by Aristotle? Both issues are obscure and any suggestions that we put forward must be conjectural. But both problems should at least be aired, and it seems possible to go some way towards elucidating them.

First Aristotle implies that some Greeks felt a certain squeamishness concerning the investigation of the parts of the body and indeed himself says that 'it is not possible to look at the constituent parts of human beings, such as blood, flesh, bones, blood-vessels and the like, without considerable distaste' (*PA* 645a28ff.).[94] But we should not exaggerate the importance of this factor. There can be no doubt that the general public felt a certain revulsion from the study of internal anatomy: nor is there anything special about the ancients here, since the same holds true today. But how far that provides an answer to our problem is hard to judge. After all, Aristotle

[93] That is a minimum estimate, using the lowest possible date for Alcmaeon (*c.* 430) and assuming (what is unlikely) that Aristotle embarked on extensive anatomical researches as soon as he arrived at Athens as a pupil of Plato in 367. A more probable (but still conservative) estimate of the gap between the main anatomical work of the two men would be 100 years, and much higher figures cannot be ruled out.

[94] Although Aristotle refers to the parts of *human beings* in the quotation, his point is a general one. There were, of course, other religious factors inhibiting the dissection of humans: but we are concerned here purely with that of animals.

himself was successful in overcoming his own feelings of distaste so far as animals are concerned, and we have no reason to believe that as a general rule the medical practitioners (at least) would have been more inhibited than Aristotle in this respect.

Some possibly more fundamental factors should be mentioned. First, it is easy for a modern researcher – who takes dissection for granted and has a wealth of received learning to draw on – to underestimate the difficulties of pioneer work in this field. For a dissection to be carried out successfully requires not only patience, attention to detail and practical skill, but also and more importantly a clear conception of how to proceed and what to look for. We know that in many contexts the Greeks were able observers: one has only to think of the painstaking clinical observations recorded in the *Epidemics* or – outside the domain of 'the inquiry into nature' – of the marvellously well-observed representations of both men and animals in classical Greek sculpture. || But progress in anatomical research depends as much on the development of theories and models as on any other factor, although theory and practice are, no doubt, *inter*dependent. To advance beyond a merely superficial account of, say, the contents of the skull or the heart requires above all an idea of what there is to find. In fact in both our earliest recorded references to the skull being opened as part of a 'scientific' inquiry, the aim was the strictly limited one of determining the state of health or disease of the brain. But even if these investigators had attempted a more general examination, it is doubtful how much they would have *seen* – that is, how much of what they saw they would have understood. Again, after dissections had begun to be made on the heart, it was some time before the valves, for instance, came to be recognised *as such*, as can be seen from a comparison between Aristotle and *The Heart*, and similar examples can be multiplied from both ancient and modern times. In the earliest history of anatomy experience in dissection undoubtedly contributed to the development of both anatomical and physiological doctrines: but practice itself – the nature of the dissections that were carried out – always depended on, in the sense that it was guided by, theory.

Before the method was accepted as a more or less routine procedure of investigation, the immediate stimulus to carry out a dissection had to come from a problem – a phenomenon to be explained or a controversy to be resolved. One of the keys to the slow development (as *we* see it) of the use of dissection lies, indeed, in the nature of the problems the Greek theorists were interested in and in the way in which those problems were formulated. Thus one of the topics that both philosophers and medical writers tackled was sensation in general and the functioning of each of the special senses individually. Yet as we have seen, so far as the problem of sight was concerned, what interested the earliest Greek investigators was not so much the question of the precise interrelations of the various membranes of the eye (sclera, chorioid, retina and so on), as the question of the elemental constituents it was composed of. It was commonly assumed that vision was to be explained in terms of some relationship or interaction (for example the process of 'like-to-like' or the interaction of unlikes) between fundamental physical elements such as earth, water, air and fire. Yet with the exception of 'water', none of these elements could be directly observed in the eye. If they were not simply assumed to exist in the eye, their presence was inferred, as we can see from the argument about fire ascribed to Alcmaeon by Theophrastus (above p. 173). || The fire in the eye was, in fact, a theoretical construct, as also were, for example, the pores in the eye postulated by Empedocles. Their function could be illustrated by the analogy of the lantern, but both in the eye *and in the lantern itself* the pores whose existence Empedocles inferred were *below the level of direct observation*. While theorists were concerned to bring their doctrines of sight into line with their general physical and psychological theories, they gave accounts of the functioning of the eye that were often not capable in practice – indeed in some cases not even in principle[95] – of direct verification. In these circumstances dissecting the eye to examine its structure was irrelevant. The contrast with the controversy concerning the claims of different parts of the body to be the common seat of sensation is illuminating. Here too there were plenty of theorists who were content with purely speculative accounts. Yet here there was an opportunity for advocates of both the brain and the heart to support their views of the common sensorium by direct reference to visible structures in the body, and, as we have seen, some early investigators took that opportunity, even though for the purposes of this controversy all that was *necessary* was to show *some* communication between sense-organ and common sensorium and this may well have been, in fact, where their demonstration ended.

The way in which the problems were formulated is also relevant to the scope of the use of dissection on the second topic that is much discussed by early writers, namely the blood-vascular system. Here too some of the early accounts of the blood-vessels were far from being simply and solely descriptive: at least the references to venesection in the texts quoted by Aristotle suggest that these accounts were partly based on, and used in turn to justify, current therapeutic procedures. It is true that in this case the way lay open (and was eventually taken) to gain a far clearer knowledge of the blood-vessels by means of direct inspection. But in so far as some early writers may have been preoccupied less with the question of the exact structure of the body than with the problems of therapy, this may help to explain both some of the fantastic theories they proposed and one factor that may have inhibited a more careful and thorough inquiry, for the links they postulated between particular parts of the body seemed to be implied by current practices in venesection. ||

The evidence indicates that for a long time after Alcmaeon dissection was not carried out for its own sake as part of a routine procedure of

[95] Thus for the atomists the ultimate explanation of sensation lies in the interaction of atoms that differ in shape, size and position but are not, in principle, observable.

investigation. Such dissections as were performed were evidently undertaken for a particular and quite definite purpose, to explain strange phenomena, to support a theory or settle a controversy. Moreover a powerful specific motive was a necessary, but not a sufficient, condition for recourse to dissection. Although on several topics where we might have expected dissection, the problems were formulated in such a way that the evidence that dissection might have provided was irrelevant or incapable of resolving the issue, it is not hard to think of other occasions when opportunities to dissect were not taken.[96]

These remarks on our first problem lead naturally to our second, the factors that helped the more widespread application of dissection in the fourth century. It was, we may suggest, in no way fortuitous that the first reasonably extensive use of dissection – by Aristotle – is found associated with a fully worked out epistemology and methodology. Aristotle's doctrine of causes sets out the types of question to be explored, and the programme outlined in *PA* I not only justifies, but also obliges him to undertake, the study of the whole of the animal kingdom. Although animals are inferior to the heavenly bodies as objects of study, animals too exhibit form and finality: moreover 'we have much better means of obtaining information' about them and 'anyone who is willing to take sufficient trouble can learn a great deal concerning each one of their kinds [i.e. animals and plants]' (*PA* 644b28ff.). The investigator should seek the causes of the individual parts (both uniform and non-uniform) and of the vital functions not only of man, but also of every other species of animal. Although the direct investigation, by dissection, of the internal parts was still limited to animals, Aristotle set himself the ideal of collecting all the differences between the various species of animals (e.g. *HA* 491a7ff.).

The later history of dissection raises many problems that are beyond the scope of this study. But it should be noted that the method always || remained, to some extent at least, controversial. Although there is nothing in extant later writings to match Aristotle's passionate apologia for a programme of biological research in *PA* I,[97] the proponents of dissection used two arguments, especially, in its support: first the practical one of the value to the clinician and surgeon of the knowledge that was thereby gained, and second the theoretical one that the study of anatomy reveals the beauty and purposefulness of nature.[98] Even so, Celsus reveals that of the three chief

[96] Thus one of the controversies which goes back to Alcmaeon and which seems positively to invite the use of dissection was on which part of the embryo is formed first. Censorinus, for instance, cites the theories of Empedocles, Hippon, Anaxagoras, Diogenes of Apollonia, Democritus, Aristotle and Epicurus on this (*De Die Nat.* 6.1–2, cf. Aet V 17.1–6). Yet there is no evidence that any of these except Aristotle tried to determine the answer by dissection – even though, as we saw, an investigation of hens' eggs is proposed in another context in *Nat. Puer.*

[97] We have, however, Erasistratus' classic statement of the persistence that scientific research demands, quoted by Galen: *Consuet.* ch. 1 (*Scr. Min.* II 17.11ff. Müller).

[98] Cf. Galen: *De Anat. Admin.* II, ch. 2 (II 286 Kühn, trans. after Singer): 'anatomical study has one use for the natural scientist who loves knowledge for its own sake, another for him who

medical sects of the late Hellenistic period, one, the Empiricists, rejected not only vivisection, but also dissection, as irrelevant and superfluous for medical practice.[99] In fact, however, the method continued to be used, and to produce notable results, down to Galen at least.[100]

Even though Aristotle provides the first sustained rationale of biological research, his use of dissection is primitive and crude compared with that of some of his successors.[101] To turn from the vague and obscure descriptions of the eye, the brain or the heart in all earlier || writers, Aristotle included, to the work of Herophilus and Erasistratus – difficult as this is to reconstruct – is to enter a new world. Where earlier investigators, again Aristotle included, had been content with only a very general account of the transmission of movement and sensation, the Hellenistic biologists began to draw fundamental distinctions both between the different kinds of nerve, and between the nerves proper and other tissues that had also been called νεῦρον.[102] And if this is one example where the Hellenistic biologists transformed a problem which they had inherited, in other instances, such as the discovery of the valves of the heart, the use of dissection itself brought to light new problems that had not been dreamed of before.

We see, therefore, that it was only after Aristotle that dissection came to be fully exploited, and the history of its use before him is one of a very slow growth indeed. If one may agree that the first use of the knife in the interests of natural inquiry goes back to Alcmaeon, the assumption that the method of dissection thereafter and straightforwardly came to be accepted as a regular part of the armamentarium of the biologist is quite mistaken. Indeed dissection was never *universally* approved by ancient natural scientists, and it came to be used confidently and systematically only after a complex process of development whose history we have attempted to outline.

values it not for its own sake but rather to demonstrate that nature does nothing without an aim, a third for one who provides himself from anatomy with data for investigating a function, physical or mental, and yet another for the practitioner who has to remove splinters and missiles efficiently, to excise parts properly, or to treat ulcers, fistulae and abscesses'.

99 *De Medicina*, Proem, paras. 27ff. The Empiricists argued that the inquiry about obscure causes and natural actions is superfluous because nature cannot be comprehended. Thus we have no need to inquire how we breathe, but what relieves laboured breathing, nor what moves the blood-vessels, but what the various types of movement signify (para. 39); and if dissection is superfluous, vivisection should be rejected on the further grounds that it is cruel (paras. 40ff.).

100 Among his most notable uses of vivisection are the investigations carried out on the processes of digestion (e.g. *Nat. Fac.* III, ch. 4) and on the nervous system (e.g. *De Anat. Admin.* IX, chh. 13f.), see Lloyd, 1973: ch. 9. Although there is some evidence, for example in Theophilus, that dissection continued to be practised long after Galen, this was not for the purposes of original research, but, at most, as a part of medical education, and principally to confirm the facts as Galen had set them out.

101 According to Galen (*De Anat. Admin.* II, ch. 1, II 282 K) it was Diocles who wrote the first technical handbook on anatomy. Even though the controversy over his date still continues, and his detailed contributions to anatomical research are even more difficult to reconstruct than those of Herophilus, Diocles probably provides a bridge between Aristotle and the Alexandrian biologists.

102 See Solmsen's classic study (1961), especially 184ff.

REFERENCES

Abel, K. (1958) 'Die Lehre vom Blutkreislauf im Corpus Hippocraticum', *Hermes* 86: 192–219

Andreae, A. (1841) *Zur ältesten Geschichte der Augenheilkunde* (Magdeburg)

(1846) *Grundriss der gesammten Augenheilkunde*, 3rd edn, pt I (Leipzig)

Andriopoulos, D. Z. (1971) 'Alcmaeon re-examined', *Studii Clasice* 13: 7–14

Beare, J. I. (1906) *Greek Theories of Elementary Cognition from Alcmaeon to Aristotle* (Oxford)

Codellas, P. S. (1931/32) 'Alcmaeon of Croton: His Life, Work and Fragments', *Proc. of the Royal Soc. of Med.* (Sec. Hist. of Med.) 25: 1041–6

Deichgräber, K. (1935) *Hippokrates, Über Entstehung und Aufbau des menschlichen Körpers*, ΠΕΡΙ ΣΑΡΚΩΝ (Leipzig)

Diels, H. – Kranz, W. (1951/2) *Die Fragmente der Vorsokratiker*, 6th edn (Berlin)

Dörrie, H. (1970) 'Alkmaion', in *Pauly–Wissowa Real-Encyclopädie*, Supp.-Bd 12: 22–6

Ebner, P. (1969) 'Alcmeone Crotoniate', *Klearchos* 11: 25–77

Edelstein, L. (1942) Review of Stella, 1938/39, *American Journal of Philology* 63: 371–2f.

(1932) 'Die Geschichte der Sektion in der Antike', *Quellen und Studien zur Geschichte der Naturwissenschaften und der Medizin* 3.2. Reprinted as 'The history of anatomy in antiquity' in *Ancient Medicine* (Baltimore (Johns Hopkins), 1967), 247–301

Erhard, H. (1941) 'Alkmaion, der erste Experimentalbiologe', *Sudhoffs Archiv für Geschichte der Naturwissenschaften und der Medizin* 34: 77–89

Fraser, P. M. (1969) 'The career of Erasistratos of Ceos', *Rendiconti del istituto Lombardo* (Classe di Lett. e Sci. Mor. e Stor.) 103: 518–37

(1972) *Ptolemaic Alexandria*, 3 vols. (Oxford)

Fredrich, C. (1899) *Hippokratische Untersuchungen*, Philologische Untersuchungen 15 (Berlin)

Gomperz, T. (1896) *Griechische Denker*, I (Leipzig)

Grensemann, H. (1968) *Die hippokratische Schrift 'über die heilige Krankheit'* (Ars Medica Abt. II Bd. I, Berlin)

Guthrie, W. K. C. (1962) *A History of Greek Philosophy*, I (Cambridge)

Harris, C. R. S. (1973) *The Heart and the Vascular System in Ancient Greek Medicine from Alcmaeon to Galen* (Oxford)

Heidel, W. A. (1941) *Hippocratic Medicine: Its Spirit and Method* (New York)

Hirsch, A. (1864) *Commentatio historico-medica de Collectionis Hippocraticae Auctorum Anatomia* (Berlin)

Hirschberg, J. (1921) 'Alcmaion's Verdienst um die Augenheilkunde', *Albrecht von Graefe's Archiv für Ophthalmologie* 105: 129–33

Kayserling, A. (1901) 'Die Medicin Alcmaeons von Kroton', *Zeitschrift für klinische Medicin* 43: 171–9

Koelbing, H. M. (1968) 'Zur Sehtheorie im Altertum: Alkmeon und Aristoteles', *Gesnerus* 25: 5–9

Kudlien, F. (1967) *Der Beginn des medizinischen Denkens bei den Griechen* (Zürich)

(1968) 'Anatomie', in *Pauly–Wissowa Real-Encyclopädie*, Supp.-Bd 11: 38–48

Lackenbacher, H. (1913) 'Beiträge zur antiken Optik', *Wiener Studien* 35: 34–61

Lesky, E. (1951) *Die Zeugungs- und Vererbungslehre der Antike und ihr Nachwirken*, Akad. d. Wiss. u. d. Lit. Mainz, Abh. d. geisteswiss. u. sozialwiss. Klasse, 1950 (Wiesbaden)

(1952) 'Alkmaion bei Aetios und Censorin', *Hermes* 80: 249–55

Littré, E. (1839–61) *Œuvres complètes d'Hippocrate*, 10 vols. (Paris)

Lloyd, G. E. R. (1966) *Polarity and Analogy* (Cambridge)
(1970) *Early Greek Science, Thales to Aristotle* (London)
(1973) *Greek Science after Aristotle* (London)
(1975) 'A note on Erasistratos of Ceos', *Journal of Hellenic Studies* 95: 172–5
Lonie, I. M. (1973) 'The Paradoxical Text "On the Heart"', *Medical History* 17: 1–15, 136–53
Magnus, H. (1878) *Die Anatomie des Auges bei den Griechen und Römern* (Leipzig)
(1901) *Die Augenheilkunde der Alten* (Breslau)
Michler, M. (1962) 'Das Problem der westgriechischen Heilkunde', *Sudhoffs Archiv für Geschichte der Naturwissenschaften und der Medizin* 46: 137–52
O'Brien, D. (1970) 'The effect of a simile: Empedocles' theories of seeing and breathing', *Journal of Hellenic Studies* 90: 140–79
Olivieri, A. (1919) 'Alcmeone di Crotone', *Memorie della reale Accademia di Archeologia, Lettere e Belle Arti* (Società Reale di Napoli) 4: 15–41
Philippson, L. (1831) ΥΛΗ ΑΝΘΡΩΠΙΝΗ (Berlin)
Ross, W. D. (1924) *Aristotle's Metaphysics*, 2 vols. (Oxford)
Schumacher, J. (1963) *Antike Medizin*, 2nd edn (Berlin)
Seeck, G. A. (1967) 'Empedokles B 17, 9–31 (= 26, 8–12), B 8, B 100 bei Aristoteles', *Hermes* 95: 28–53
Shaw, J. R. (1972) 'Models for Cardiac Structure and Function in Aristotle', *Journal of the History of Biology* 5: 355–88
Sigerist, H. E. (1961) *A History of Medicine* II (Oxford)
Solmsen, F. (1961) 'Greek philosophy and the discovery of the nerves', *Museum Helveticum* 18: 150–67, 169–97
Souques, A. (1935) 'Connaissances neurologiques d'Hérophile et d'Erasistrate', *Revue Neurologique* 63: 145–76
Stella, L. A. (1938–9) 'Importanza di Alcmeone nella storia del pensiero greco', *Atti della reale Accademia Nazionale dei Lincei*, Memorie ser. 6, 8: 237–87
Stratton, G. M. (1917) *Theophrastus and the Greek Physiological Psychology before Aristotle* (London)
Switalski, B. W. (1902) *Des Chalcidius Kommentar zu Plato's Timaeus*, Beiträge z. Geschichte d. Philosophie d. Mittelalters 3, 6 (Münster)
Tannery, P. (1930) *Pour l'histoire de la science hellène*, 2nd edn (Paris)
Taylor, A. E. (1928) *A Commentary on Plato's Timaeus* (Oxford)
Timpanaro Cardini, M. (1938) 'Originalità di Alcmeone', *Atene e Roma*, ser. 3.6: 233–44
(1940) 'Anima, vita e morte in Alcmeone, *Atene e Roma*, ser. 3.8: 213–24
(1958–64) *Pitagorici, Testimonianze e frammenti*, 3 vols. (Firenze)
Unna, M. A. (1832) 'De Alcmaeone Crotoniata eiusque fragmentis, quae supersunt, in *Philologisch-historische Studien auf dem akad. Gymnasium in Hamburg*, ed. C. Petersen (Hamburg), 41–87
Wachtler, J. (1896) *De Alcmaeone Crotoniata* (Leipzig)
Waszink, J. H. (1962) *Plato Latinus* IV. *Timaeus a Calcidio translatus commentarioque instructus* (London)
Wellmann, M. (1901) *Die Fragmente der sikelischen Ärzte Akron, Philistion und des Diokles von Karystos* (Berlin)
(1929a) 'Alkmaion von Kroton', *Archeion* 11: 156–69
(1929b) 'Die Schrift περὶ ἱρῆς νούσου des Corpus Hippocraticum', *Sudhoffs Archiv für Geschichte der Medizin* 22: 290–312

9

THE HIPPOCRATIC QUESTION

INTRODUCTION

In the article I devoted to the Hippocratic Question in the *Classical Quarterly* in 1975 I undertook a review of the evidence that had been used to identify the genuine works of Hippocrates of Cos himself among the extant treatises of the Hippocratic Corpus. We hear about Hippocrates' fame as a doctor from Plato and from Aristotle, and about the method he is supposed to have used or recommended from Plato; and there is a brief but maybe garbled report ascribing certain theories to him in the history of medicine preserved in the papyrus Anonymus Londinensis that derives from Aristotle's pupil Meno. In antiquity and in modern times Hippocratic scholarship has expended massive efforts to identify the authentic works, although conclusions on that issue have often been based not on evidence nor on argument so much as on subjective impressions about what is most admirable in the Corpus as we have it.

Taking my lead in the main from Edelstein, I arrived at a sceptical conclusion: that the evidence we have allows us in *no* case to be confident that a work is by Hippocrates himself. And I embarked, further, on a discussion of the nature of these treatises and their interrelations. Once it is no longer assumed that the Corpus represents the work of a single great man, or chiefly consists of his work, the apparent inconsistencies between one work and another, and even between different parts of the same work, can be given due weight. Comparing some of the extant treatises with modern scientific textbooks, I suggested (p. 211) that they should, in several cases, be deemed to be multi-author works to which additions had been made at different stages by successive hands – by people who were less concerned with such questions as the unity and authorship of a work, than with the useful medical information it contained. These are practical handbooks, not works of grand literature, and the literary criteria we bring to bear on their study have to be adjusted accordingly.

The desire at once to be able to name the author of notable early medical treatises, *and* to rescue Hippocrates from the fate of being 'a name without a work', remains remarkably deep-seated. Although my arguments have been accepted in some quarters, it cannot be said that they have in any sense won the day. Scholars continue to engage in the search for the genuine works of Hippocrates, sometimes with, but sometimes without, serious attention to the principal counter-arguments. I shall limit myself here to three of the most prominent recent discussions, those of Smith, Joly and Mansfeld.

The most sustained analysis of the Hippocratic Question since my article has been Wesley Smith's *The Hippocratic Tradition* (1979). This includes in particular a masterly survey of the steps whereby the myth of Hippocrates came to be promulgated. Once a collection of works had become associated with his name in Alexandria it became the subject of extensive commentary of a literary as well as medical character. It is not that what Hippocrates was taken to stand for, in medicine, was always and everywhere revered: the criticisms made of him and his followers by Soranus (second century A.D.) adequately testify to that. However, he was often held up as the supreme ancient authority in medical matters, even before this attitude received canonical form at the hands of Galen.

Galen himself is a special case – in more ways than one. The prestige of Galen himself helped to secure that his view of Hippocrates would dominate right down to the seventeenth century, and Galen's view is clear. As he puts it, Hippocrates is his guide in all that is fine (see further below, chapter 17 p. 398 at n. 4). Galen is well aware of a Hippocratic question in his own day: but he believes that Plato's account of Hippocrates' method tallies with the method actually found used in the treatise *On the Nature of Man* (cf. below, p. 201, no. 8). Although that by itself would not *prove* that Hippocrates wrote that work (because after all a method advocated by Hippocrates might be imitated by any number of other medical writers), Galen is convinced that *Nat. Hom.* chh. 1–8 at least are by Hippocrates himself. Building on this, in the way that so many others have done (pp. 199, 208), Galen believes he is justified in seeing a substantial body of other works in the Corpus as genuine.

However Galen's reconstruction is, of course, not neutral. He himself *agrees* with the theories he ascribes to 'Hippocrates', not just the element theory of *Nat. Hom.*, but also the main features of its pathological doctrine, as well as many particular medical ideas and practices to be found scattered through the Corpus, and even the psychological theory he associates with Hippocrates on the basis of certain remarks in such treatises as *Epidemics* II. But it is not just that Galen agrees with Hippocrates: it is rather that Hippocrates serves as a key authority for the views that he, Galen, favours. Moreover where Galen is highly critical of many of his own contemporaries for the arrogance with which they claimed to introduce new theories and practices into medicine, he can defend himself against a similar criticism on the grounds that he faithfully follows the principles laid down by the great Hippocrates (see further, chapter 17).

On many aspects of the later reception of Hippocratism, Smith's work provides a comprehensive and authoritative guide which serves substantially to supplement the brief discussion, in my article (pp. 207, 220), on aspects of the question of Hippocrates' reputation. However, when it comes to the substantive issue of identifying, within the Corpus, the genuine works of Hippocrates, Smith takes a far less sceptical, indeed far more traditional, line, although the work he favours, *On Regimen*, is not one that has usually been thought a plausible candidate.

Smith relies in the main on the account of Hippocrates' method in Plato's *Phaedrus*, and in my own brief comments on that (p. 201, n. 8) I had acknowledged that there was a better fit between the account of that method in Plato and *Vict.* I than there was (for example) with the treatise Galen favoured, *Nat. Hom.* Nevertheless I concluded then – and would still conclude now – that the fit between *Phaedrus* and *Vict.* I is still nothing like *good enough* to permit the identification Smith makes. The general argument, that *Vict.* I is an eclectic work, containing, for example, quotations or near quotations from Heraclitus, Parmenides, Empedocles and especially Anaxagoras (see p. 211 and n. 52) may not be an overwhelming objection: yet the more that treatise is found to side with, even directly imitate, the type of natural philosopher whom Plato castigates in *Laws* X, for instance, the more difficult it would be to conceive of Plato wishing to be complimentary about its author. But the second argument I used is stronger. Even though aspects of the method used in *Vict.* I show some similarity to that ascribed to Hippocrates in the *Phaedrus* (for *Vict.* identifies the primary constituents of the human body and discusses their *dunameis*) there is still this very marked dissimilarity, that while the Hippocrates of the *Phaedrus* is represented as insisting on being *methodical* and *systematic* in the orderly division-like presentation of the material, the author of *Vict.* is far from practising what the *Phaedrus* preaches in *those* respects.

I remain unconvinced, therefore, by Smith's positive conclusion – nor has he persuaded many with his arguments, even among those scholars who themselves favour ascribing *some* writings to Hippocrates himself. Thus Joly (1983a) believes that the case for *Epidemics* I and III, *Fractures* and *Joints* is persuasive, and that round them cohere a further group of works, *Prognostic*, *Humours*, *Surgery*, *Mochlicon*, *On Airs*, *Waters*, *Places*, *On the Sacred Disease* and *On the Nature of Man*. But while Joly agreed that if those works (or some of them) are by Hippocrates, then *Vict.* I cannot be, he remained unmoved by the arguments I presented to the effect that, even within the most favoured group of treatises, there are deep-seated inconsistencies that rule out single authorship. Thus little weight, he thought, can be attached to the divergences, within *Prognosis* and *Epidemics* I, on the topic of critical days, 'variations on the same theme', as he put it (Joly, 1983a: 41), 'that should not be overly dramatized'. Excesses of precision are, one may agree, a feature of all the theories in question. Yet that obsession with precision does nothing to help account for the total disregard for consistency (if they are all by the same author), an inconsistency not just on the relevant numbers, but on the underlying principles by which they are to be determined.

Mansfeld (1980, 1983) who wrote in reply to Joly, though one of his papers was published before Joly's, was as unhappy with Joly's solution as they both were with Smith's. As for his own positive conclusions, Mansfeld resuscitates the claim that *Airs, Waters, Places* is in Plato's mind in the *Phaedrus* and even toys with the idea that Hippocrates himself may have collected the earlier works in the Corpus. He challenges, for example, the description of the method actually used in *Aër.* as broadly observational and empirical (see below, pp. 202f.) and claims that Plato was, in any case, more tolerant towards empirical research in his later period (Mansfeld, 1980: 359). Yet if that latter point may be conceded, the fundamental difficulty remains. The method Plato associates with Hippocrates is a formal one and one that corresponds closely enough to Plato's own method of division for him to be able to assimilate the two. Whatever label we attach to the method actually used in *Aër.*, it dramatically fails to meet the requirements of the *Phaedrus*, for *Aër.* certainly does not proceed systematically by first determining the nature of the subject, whether it is simple or complex, and then either (if simple) analysing the capacities or (if complex) enumerating the parts and then giving such an analysis. If, however, those requirements are *not* taken strictly, and Plato is seen as making only a very general and unspecific recommendation as to medical method, then the difficulty with that line of argument (as I pointed out, p. 201) is that that provides at best only a *very weak* basis for identifying any one of a number of treatises in the Corpus as the one that Plato had in mind.

Whether any more convincing thesis on the genuine works of Hippocrates will ever be propounded, time alone will tell, but the studies undertaken since 1975 have not advanced that prospect. The cautious and sceptical arguments adduced first by Edelstein and then by myself are often dismissed with the assertion that they are *unduly* sceptical. Yet the efforts of the non-sceptical to identify the genuine works continue to be characterised – and indeed undermined – by fundamental disagreements. The thrust of the arguments of the second part of my paper was that Hippocratic scholarship is more fruitfully deployed in examining some of the far-reaching implications of questions to do with the nature of these early medical writings, how they were constituted, what their audience was, and how they were used. Here indeed some more solid progress has been made, in, for example, Lonie's study (1983) of the effects of increasing literacy in Hippocratic medicine, and Kudlien's work (1967, 1968) on the relations between Hippocratic and early Greek popular medicine (cf. also Joly, 1966). Among others Harig and Kollesch too have opened up new lines of research on questions to do with the status of doctors and their education (Kollesch, 1979, Harig and Kollesch, 1977). Ever since the days of Alexandrian scholarship the Hippocratic Corpus has been mined for interesting lexical, philological and linguistic points – and indeed these works have further lessons to teach us in that regard. But far more important are the insights their study can afford about the early constitution, training and self-perception of a medical elite.

REFERENCES

Cambiano, G. (1966) 'Dialettica, medicina, retorica nel "Fedro" platonico', *Rivista di Filosofia* 57: 284–305

Di Benedetto, V. (1980) 'Cos e Cnido', in *Hippocratica*, ed. M. D. Grmek (Paris), 97–111

(1986) *Il medico e la malattia* (Torino)

Harig, G., and Kollesch, J. (1977) 'Neue Tendenzen in der Forschung zur Geschichte der antiken Medizin und Wissenschaft', *Philologus* 121: 114–36

Herter, H. (1976) 'The problematic mention of Hippocrates in Plato's *Phaedrus*', *Illinois Classical Studies* 1: 22–42

Joly, R. (1966) *Le Niveau de la science hippocratique* (Paris)

(1983a) 'Hippocrates and the School of Cos', in *Nature Animated*, ed. M. Ruse (Dordrecht), 29–47

(1983b) 'Platon, Phèdre et Hippocrate: vingt ans après', in *Formes de pensée dans la Collection hippocratique*, edd. F. Lasserre and P. Mudry (Geneva), 407–21

Jouanna, J. (1977) 'La *Collection Hippocratique* et Platon (*Phèdre*, 269c–272a)', *Revue des Etudes Grecques* 90: 15–28

Kollesch, J. (1979) 'Ärztliche Ausbildung in der Antike', *Klio* 61: 507–13

Kudlien, F. (1967) *Der Beginn des medizinischen Denkens bei den Griechen* (Zurich)

(1968) 'Early Greek primitive medicine', *Clio Medica* 3: 305–36

(1977) 'Bemerkungen zu W. D. Smith's These über die knidische Ärzteschule', in *Corpus Hippocraticum*, ed. R. Joly (Mons), 95–103

Lonie, I. M. (1978) 'Cos versus Cnidus and the Historians', *History of Science* 17: 42–75, 77–92

(1983) 'Literacy and the development of Hippocratic medicine', in *Formes de pensée dans la Collection hippocratique*, edd. F. Lasserre and P. Mudry (Geneva), 145–61

Mansfeld, J. (1980) 'Plato and the method of Hippocrates', *Greek, Roman and Byzantine Studies* 21: 341–62

(1983) 'The historical Hippocrates and the origins of scientific medicine', in *Nature Animated*, ed. M. Ruse (Dordrecht), 49–76

Smith, W. D. (1979) *The Hippocratic tradition* (Ithaca, New York)

Vegetti, M. (1969) 'La medicina in Platone, IV Il Fedro', *Rivista critica di storia della filosofia* 24: 3–22

THE HIPPOCRATIC QUESTION

The question of determining the genuine works of Hippocrates, a topic already much discussed by the ancient commentators, still continues to be actively debated, although the disagreements among scholars remain, it seems almost as wide as ever.[1] In comparatively recent times, Edelstein's ΠΕΡΙ ΑΕΡΩΝ and two subsequent studies of his written in the 1930s (Edelstein, 1935 and 1939) marked a turning-point in that they presented a particularly clear and comprehensive statement of the sceptical view, according to which Hippocrates is, as Wilamowitz put it long ago,[2] 'ein berühmter Name ohne den Hintergrund irgend einer Schrift'. But Edelstein's book was soon followed by studies by Deichgräber (1933), Pohlenz (1938 and 1939) and Nestle (1938), each of whom put forward positive, although quite widely differing, suggestions concerning the Hippocratic treatises that could be considered genuine, and since the end of the 1930s there have been more than twenty major, as well as a host of minor, contributions to the debate, the most important being those of Jones (1945), Bourgey (1953), Diller (1959a), Joly (1961), and Knutzen (1964).[3] Despite the arguments of Edelstein and other sceptics, fresh attempts continue to be made to establish the probable, if not the certain, genuineness of particular treatises in the Hippocratic Corpus. The line of attack is generally the same. Once the authenticity of one or a few treatises has been shown, to the author's satisfaction at least, on the basis of the external evidence (the references to Hippocrates in Plato, Aristotle, Anonymus Londinensis, and so on), the range of works that may be considered to be by Hippocrates is then extended by using arguments based on the internal evidence, that is on the connections between different treatises in the Corpus. The aim of this article is twofold, first to re-examine the strength of the external evidence, and secondly to analyse the assumptions underlying arguments based on the internal evidence and in particular to consider the criteria for establishing the common authorship of different treatises.

I

The main external evidence has often been discussed and our review can accordingly be quite brief. As is well known, there are four main pre-Alexandrian references to Hippocrates, namely those in Plato's *Phaedrus* (270C) and *Protagoras* (311B–C), in Aristotle's *Politics* (1326a14ff.), and in the account of Hippocrates' medical doctrines that is attributed to 'Aristotle'

[1] The bibliography at the end of this article includes the most important contributions from 1930 to 1975 and provides bibliographical details of other works that will also be referred to by the author's name and the date. Abbreviations for Hippocratic works are those in Liddell–Scott–Jones.

[2] Wilamowitz, 1901: 22. He was, however, later to change his mind; see Wilamowitz, 1929: 480ff.

[3] Joly (1961) and Flashar (1971), especially, provide full surveys of the recent literature.

in Anonymus Londinensis (V 35–VI 42, ed. Diels) – that is, as is generally agreed, the account given in Meno's history of medicine. To these may be added three more doubtful references ascribed to Ctesias and Diocles by Galen and by the scholiast Stephanus Atheniensis.

Of these testimonies, the passage in Aristotle's *Politics* tells us only that || Hippocrates was known as a great doctor, and Plato's *Protagoras* 311B–C that he taught medicine for a fee, both interesting pieces of information, but neither able to help us in any way to identify Hippocrates' writings.

The two main testimonies that have been used for that purpose are those in the *Phaedrus* and in Anonymus Londinensis. In both cases the interpretation is, in places, controversial, but certain points can be said to be by now well established. First, the *Phaedrus* passage provides us with information about, at most, Hippocrates' methods, not his specific medical theories. Phaedrus and Socrates agree, at this point in the dialogue, that Hippocrates held that the correct method in medicine is to study the 'nature of the whole'.[4] What 'the whole' means here is disputed – as it already was in antiquity – and at least four interpretations are possible, namely that it means (1) the whole of nature or the universe, (2) the whole of the body, (3) the whole of the body–soul complex, or (4) the whole of whatever subject happens to be under discussion.[5] Nor is it clear, when at 270C9–D7 Socrates proceeds to elaborate what 'Hippocrates and the true account' have to say 'on this matter concerning nature' and suggests that the correct method consists in (1) first deciding whether a thing is simple or complex, and then (2*a*) if it is simple, asking what its capacity for acting or being acted upon is, or (2*b*) if it is complex, enumerating its parts and then asking the same question of each of them, how much of this method is supposed to have been made explicit by Hippocrates himself.[6] Yet so far as the Hippocratic question goes, these uncertainties are comparatively unimportant, for *whatever view we take* on the main disputed points, this text provides insufficient grounds for asserting the genuineness of any of the treatises in the Corpus.[7]

Thus if we assume that the complete method set out at 270C9ff. is Hippocrates', we can certainly be clear about what that method consists in: it is indeed a quite formal one, and one that corresponds closely to Platonic

[4] ΣΩ. Ψυχῆς οὖν φύσιν ἀξίως λόγου κατανοῆσαι οἴει δυνατὸν εἶναι ἄνευ τῆς τοῦ ὅλου φύσεως; ΦΑΙ. Εἰ μὲν Ἱπποκράτει γε τῷ τῶν Ἀσκληπιαδῶν δεῖ τι πιθέσθαι, οὐδὲ περὶ σώματος ἄνευ τῆς μεθόδου ταύτης (*Phaedrus* 270C1–5). The passage has, of course, to be taken in the whole context of the discussion from 269E to 270E.

[5] The problem has been very extensively discussed: for an analysis of both ancient and modern views see Kucharski (1939) and Joly (1961) especially.

[6] Cf., e.g., Hackforth, 1952: 151: 'I strongly suspect that when the question is asked τί ποτε λέγει Ἱπποκράτης καὶ ὁ ἀληθὴς λόγος, Plato is about to read into Hippocrates what he wants to find there; it is analogous, I suggest, to what Protagoras told his disciples in secret (*Tht.* 152C) or the real meaning of what Heraclitus expressed badly (*Smp.* 187A).'

[7] The principal, though far from the only, attempts to mount such a thesis have been those of Galen (who saw the passage as proof of the authenticity of *Nat. Hom.*), of Littré (arguing for the authenticity of *VM*), and of Pohlenz, 1938 (arguing for that of *Aër.* and other treatises).

division. Yet although there are plenty of Hippocratic texts that show an interest either in determining whether a thing is simple or complex, or in what effect something has on something else, there is no treatise that either advocates, or exactly puts into practice, the full formal two-stage method outlined at 270c9ff.[8] ||

On the other hand, if, with the majority of scholars, we assume that all that Plato means to ascribe to Hippocrates at 270c1–5 is the *general* recommendation of the study of 'the nature of the whole' (in whatever sense of whole), then the main problem about using that as evidence for the authenticity of any given Hippocratic work lies in its very vagueness and generality. Thus if we take 'whole' to refer to the whole body, all that Hippocrates may be represented by Plato as recommending is that the doctor should study the whole patient. This is, of course, consistent with what is commonly assumed and quite often stated in the medical works, namely that the doctor should proceed to his diagnosis and prognosis only after a careful and thorough examination of all the patient's signs and symptoms.[9] But the difficulty here is that the idea of examining the patient thoroughly is not only so common, but also so obvious, that we can hardly take the text of Plato to establish the authenticity of any of the works in which it is introduced.[10]

It is true that if we take 'whole' at 270c1–5 to refer to nature or to the universe in general, the recommendation there ascribed to Hippocrates has

[8] Although Galen (*in Hipp. Nat. Hom.*, *CMG* V 9.1.8.31ff. and 54.26ff.) saw a reference to *Nat. Hom.* here, the writer of that treatise can hardly be said to proceed in the way Socrates describes at 270c9ff. Although the opening polemic against those who assert that man is one thing can be represented as addressed to the question of whether man is one or many, once the writer has stated his own view that there are four main constituent substances in the body (blood, phlegm, yellow and black bile) he does not then proceed – as according to the methodology of *Phaedrus* 270c9ff. he would have been expected to – to ask concerning each of these substances in turn what its capacity for acting and being acted upon is. There are, moreover, reasonable grounds for supposing that the author of *Nat. Hom.* chh. 1–8 and 11 is Polybus (see below, p. 210). There is a closer, though still not perfect fit between *Phaedrus* 270c9ff. and *Vict.* I, chh. 2ff., where the writer says that anyone who intends to write correctly about regimen must first study the nature of man in general, that is, such questions as his primary constituents, and he goes on not only to identify these as fire and water but also to consider their δυνάμεις in the body. But although this covers the subject-matter that Socrates says should be dealt with at 270c9ff., the correspondence is still not exact in this respect, at least, that the Hippocratic writer does not set out his arguments in the clear, logical order that Socrates' method suggests. Moreover the possibility that *Vict.* I itself is referred to in the *Phaedrus* is generally dismissed on other grounds: it is clearly an eclectic and derivative work, and its claims to be a genuine work of Hippocrates were generally considered weak even in antiquity.

[9] The fullest statements of what the doctor should look for in examining the patient come in *Prog.* (ch. 1 and *passim*) and *Epid.* I, ch. 10 Littré (23 Kühlewein): but the idea that the doctor should pay attention to all the factors relating to a patient's condition, his age and constitution, the season of the year, and so on, appears in many other contexts and works, e.g. *Nat. Hom.* ch. 9, *Salubr.* ch. 2, *Aph.* I 2 and 17, II 34, *Hum.* chh. 1, 2, 4 and 5, *Vict.*I, chh. 2 and 32, *Morb.* I, ch. 16, *Nat. Mul.* ch. 1, *Mul.*II, ch. 111, and *Prorrh.* II, ch. 39.

[10] Alternatively, if 'whole' is taken to refer not to all a patient's signs but to his physical constituents, the problem is again that such a recommendation could be said to tally with any of a large number of treatises in the Corpus that discuss the elements of which a man is composed and propose different theories on that subject (see further below, p. 213).

a more definite content, or at least greater point, that is, that the physician should study 'natural science', and on this interpretation the passage in the *Phaedrus* has often been taken to refer to (and therefore establish the authenticity of) one or other of the treatises in the Corpus that bear on this point, the favourite candidates being *On Ancient Medicine* and *Airs, Waters, Places*. Thus in *On Ancient Medicine* ch. 20 the writer says that the only way to study nature (that is, for example, such problems as the constituent substances of man) is through medicine. If 'whole' in the *Phaedrus* passages is taken in the sense of nature as a whole, then a point of similarity between the two texts is that both suggest a connection between medicine and natural inquiry in general. Yet in this case a far more important contrast lies in the fact that – as has often been pointed out || – whereas the *Phaedrus* passage would imply that medicine depends on natural science, in *On Ancient Medicine* the reverse is asserted, that the study of nature depends on medicine. As Festugière and many others have said, the position ascribed on this view to Hippocrates at *Phaedrus* 270C is closer to that *criticised* by the author of *On Ancient Medicine* when at the beginning of the same chapter he attacks certain doctors and sophists who had suggested that the study of man in general is prior to medicine proper.[11]

As for the other main suggestion, that *Phaedrus* 270C may allude to *Airs, Waters, Places*,[12] it is true that that treatise recommends that the doctor should study, among other things, the seasons of the year, the winds, the locations of cities, and the properties of waters for the purpose of prognosis, and in ch. 2 meets the objection that this smacks of 'meteorology' by saying that the contribution of ἀστρονομίη to medicine is no small one.[13] But here too the similarities are quite general and they fall far short of establishing, or even making it likely, that Plato had *Airs, Waters, Places* in mind in this passage in the *Phaedrus*. Moreover there is a well-known difficulty in this or any other view that sees the method ascribed to Hippocrates as one that involves the detailed empirical study of natural phenomena in general, and this lies in the implausibility of representing *Plato* as agreeing with, let alone recommending, any such method.[14] This point comes out quite clearly in the

[11] *VM* ch. 20, *CMG* I 1.51.6–17. On the text of 51.6–12 see Dihle, 1963: 145ff.

[12] See especially Pohlenz, 1938: 77ff., and cf. Edelstein, 1940: 226ff.

[13] εἰ δὲ δοκέοι τις ταῦτα μετεωρολόγα εἶναι, εἰ μετασταίη τῆς γνώμης, μάθοι ἄν, ὅτι οὐκ ἐλάχιστον μέρος συμβάλλεται ἀστρονομίη ἐς ἰητρικήν, ἀλλὰ πάνυ πλεῖστον (*CMG* I 1.57.7ff.). An additional point of similarity has been found in that at *Phaedrus* 269E4ff. Socrates said that all the greatest τέχναι need ἀδολεσχίας καὶ μετεωρολογίας φύσεως πέρι: yet the sense of μετεωρολογία there may be simply high-flown speech, and the reference to Anaxagoras at 270A4 seems to be rather to his doctrine of νοῦς (see A5) than to his explanations of natural phenomena.

[14] We can gain some idea of what Plato thought a theory of diseases should look like from *Timaeus* 81Eff. Three features of that account that should be noted are: (1) the form that the discussion takes is to give a classification of diseases; (2) consideration is given not only to diseases of the body, but also to those of the soul arising διὰ σώματος ἕξιν (86B): the discussion relates not just to the body, but to the whole individual, that is, the complex of

continuation in the *Phaedrus*, in that what Socrates chooses to attribute to 'Hippocrates and the true account' at 270C9ff. turns out to be, not a broadly observational or empirical method at all, but, as we should expect from Plato, a formal, analytic method of classification. Those who wish to argue for the authenticity of any Hippocratic work that employs or advocates an empirical methodology on the basis of what we have in the *Phaedrus* have, then, a problem in that they must also argue that at 270C9ff. Socrates does not so much develop or elaborate Hippocrates' actual methods as ignore them, substituting his own, quite different, procedure.

In sum, an examination of the evidence in the *Phaedrus* leads to negative conclusions. (1) That evidence relates only to methods, not to medical theories. (2) If the method is taken to include Socrates' elaboration at 270D1–7, we do not find that adopted or recommended in any of the Hippocratic treatises. || (3) If not, although several different constructions of the sense of 'whole' are possible, we again find that the correspondences that can be suggested between the *Phaedrus* and particular treatises in the Corpus are tenuous.

But if one of the principal limitations of the evidence in the *Phaedrus* is that the information it provides concerns Hippocrates' methods, not his actual medical doctrines, the testimony of Meno's account, preserved in Anonymus Londinensis,[15] suffers from no such drawback. Rather, the description of Hippocrates' views on the causes of diseases is both quite clear and quite definite. The problem here is – as has been recognised ever since the papyrus was first discovered[16] – that the particular theory ascribed to Hippocrates, namely that diseases are caused by φῦσαι, does not correspond exactly to anything in the Corpus. The closest approximation to it is in the treatise *On Breaths*, a sophistic ἐπίδειξις which sets out simple-mindedly to prove that the origin of all diseases is the same, that is, air or breath, and which may well not have been composed by a practising physician.[17] Even here, although both Meno's account and *On Breaths* share the idea that φῦσαι

body and soul; and (3) the whole theory forms part of an account of nature where the emphasis is on final causes. Despite what has sometimes been claimed, Plato did not hope to determine the causes of diseases, or of any other natural phenomena, by using purely *a priori* methods, to the total neglect of observation and experience: yet nothing in the *Timaeus* modifies his usual view of the superiority of reason to sensation, and indeed at 29C–D he emphatically reasserts the distinction between *certain* accounts of *Being* and *probable* accounts of *Becoming*.

15 The writer of Anonymus Londinensis himself disagrees with 'Aristotle' and goes on to put forward an alternative account of Hippocrates' medical doctrines (VI 43ff.). This appears (although the papyrus is particularly fragmentary at this point) to correspond with views found in *Nat. Hom.* The value of this evidence is, however, small, since the author of Anon. Lond. was probably not writing before the first century A.D.; see Diels, 1893a: 412ff.

16 Diels, 1893a: 422ff. The most important recent discussions are those of Edelstein, 1939: 135ff., 1940: 221ff., Pohlenz, 1938: 66ff., Steckerl, 1945: 166ff., Bourgey, 1953: 84ff., Diller, 1959a: 276f., and Schumacher, 1967: 143ff.

17 See, e.g., Jones, 1923–31: II 221ff., Bourgey, 1953: 116ff.

are the causes of disease and hold that πνεῦμα is a or the most important factor in the body,[18] they differ at certain points, notably in that whereas in Meno the breaths that cause diseases arise from residues (περισσώματα) in the body, in *On Breaths* there is no mention of residues: the breaths there come into the body direct from the outside air.[19]

This provides an argument in support of the view that Meno did not have *On Breaths* itself in mind, and indeed there are few, if any, scholars who would wish to conclude that it is a genuine work of Hippocrates. Yet attempts to take the evidence of Meno as establishing the authenticity of *any other* Hippocratic treatise have been quite unsuccessful. There is, for instance, nothing in Meno's account to justify the claim that he was referring to the doctrine of *Airs, Waters, Places* that atmospheric air is a major contributory factor in disease. Although at VI 14ff. he says that πνεῦμα in us is connected with the (outside) air, he refers quite unmistakably to the air produced by residues *within the body* when he reports Hippocrates' theory of diseases. Again, although air is assigned an important function in the body, particularly as the vehicle of consciousness, in *On the Sacred Disease*, that treatise develops a much more elaborate theory of diseases than that ascribed to Hippocrates by Meno.[20] Finally Meno does not || provide any support for the view that *On Ancient Medicine* is an authentic work of Hippocrates.[21] It is true that a minor role in disease is ascribed to breaths in chh. 10 and 22 in that treatise. But it is a *minor* role, and the general theory of diseases put forward by the author in ch. 14 refers to a wide variety of factors (salt, bitter, sweet, acid, astringent, insipid, and so on) an imbalance in which may cause disease. To say of this author, what Meno says of Hippocrates at V 35f., that 'breaths are the causes of disease', would be a grossly misleading caricature of his views.

Here too, then, as with the evidence in Plato and Aristotle, the conclusions we must reach are negative ones. Although Meno provides our earliest evidence of Hippocrates' medical theory,[22] and although the range of medical

[18] Compare Anon. Lond. V 35f. with *Flat.* ch. 4, *CMG* I 1.93.18f. and Anon. Lond. VI 30f. with *Flat.* ch. 3, 92.21f. These and other parallelisms, including certain similarities in phraseology, are set out by Diels, 1893 (b): 8f. and Jones, 1947: 34ff.

[19] Contrast Anon. Lond. VI 11f. ἐγ δὲ τῶν περισσωμάτ(ων) ἀναφέρονται φῦσαι with *Flat.* ch. 3, 92.20f. πνεῦμα δὲ τὸ μὲν ἐν τοῖσι σώμασιν φῦσα καλέεται, τὸ δὲ ἔξω τῶν σωμάτων ἀήρ. In *Flat.* ch. 7 the breath that causes flatulence when food is taken into the body is not the product of residues from the food itself, but is clearly said to enter the body (i.e. from outside) at the same time as the food: μετὰ δὲ πολλῶν σιτίων ἀνάγκη καὶ πολὺ πνεῦμα ἐσιέναι (95.6f.).

[20] Thus in ch. 18, VI 394.9ff. L, the writer refers especially to changes in the winds and weather and to the imbalance of hot, cold, wet and dry, as well as to 'what enters and leaves' the body. In chh. 2 and 5 (364.15ff., 368.10ff.) bile and phlegm represent innate constitutional differences: they are not residues that produce breaths that in turn produce diseases.

[21] *Pace* Steckerl, 1945: 176f.

[22] There have, of course, been scholars who have taken Meno to be mistaken about Hippocrates in whole or in part (e.g. Diels, 1893a: 424ff.). It is, however, only possible to diagnose his mistakes if we have *better independent* evidence concerning Hippocrates' medical theories – and this is not forthcoming.

doctrines contained in the Corpus is remarkable, we cannot establish the authenticity of any treatise on the basis of this report. Indeed if the evidence of Meno is accepted, it provides a strong argument *against* the authenticity of those passages – and there are many of them[23] – that suggest alternative pathological doctrines which are incompatible with the account attributed to Hippocrates at Anonymus Londinensis V 35ff.

Having exhausted our four earliest and most reliable testimonies, we may now turn to some of the evidence from other pre-Alexandrian writers whose views are recorded in later sources. (1) In Book IV, ch. 40 of his Commentary on *Joints* (*in Hipp. Art.* XVIII A 731.5ff. Kühn), Galen reports that Ctesias of Cnidos,[24] among others, criticised Hippocrates for attempting to reduce a dislocation of the thigh at the hip.[25] Now an account of how to effect this reduction certainly appears in ch. 70 of *Joints* (IV 288.11ff. L, II 224.18ff. Kühlewein) in the passage on which Galen is commenting at this point. But to claim that the testimony of Ctesias establishes the authenticity of that treatise is to underestimate two major difficulties. First, we may not presume that Hippocrates was the only fifth-century doctor to suggest this surgical procedure. Secondly and more fundamentally, even if we assumed that Ctesias was criticising this very passage in *Joints*, we could still not be certain that he took it to be by Hippocrates. When Galen writes that Ctesias was one of several authors who criticised Hippocrates' procedure, we must take into account the fact that Galen himself of course assumed that Hippocrates was the author of *Joints*.[26] This being so, the reference to Hippocrates may well have been supplied by Galen himself.[27] Given that Galen does not actually quote Ctesias || at this point, but merely records a view that he attributes to him, the status of the direct reference to Hippocrates is in serious doubt, and so too, therefore, must be the value of this text as evidence for his work.

(2) Precisely similar difficulties confront us concerning the passage in *in Hipp. Epid. I*, Book III ch. 2 (*CMG* V 10.1,112.31ff.) where Galen records a criticism of Diocles.[28] Here the Hippocratic doctrine criticised is that there are quintan, septan, and nonan fevers, a theory which is clearly stated in the

[23] See below, pp. 213–214.

[24] Ctesias was physician to Artaxerxes and so a close contemporary of Hippocrates.

[25] κατεγνώκασιν Ἱπποκράτους ἐπεμβαλεῖν τὸ κατ' ἰσχίον ἄρθρον, ὡς ἂν ἐκπῖπτον αὐτίκα, πρῶτος μὲν Κτησίας ὁ Κνίδιος συγγενὴς αὐτοῦ, καὶ γὰρ αὐτὸς ἦν Ἀσκληπιάδης τὸ γένος, ἐφεξῆς δὲ Κτησίου καὶ ἄλλοι τινές. The passage has been discussed by, among others, Littré, 1839–61: I 69ff., Schöne, 1910: 466, Diels, 1910: 1148, Edelstein, 1931: 139, n. 1, Deichgräber, 1933: 161ff., Pohlenz, 1938: 80, Bourgey, 1953: 99f., and, most recently, Knutzen, 1964: 66ff.

[26] Indeed Galen counts *Art.* and *Fract.* among the 'most genuine and most useful' Hippocratic treatises, *in Hipp. Epid. III*, book II intro., *CMG* V 10.2.1, 60.15ff.

[27] Elsewhere in his commentaries Galen commonly refers to the author of the treatises he is discussing as Hippocrates, even where he knows that the authenticity of the treatise is in doubt, and sometimes does so even when (as with *Epid.* II and VI, see, e.g., CMG V 10.2.2, 5.7ff. and 272.5ff.) he himself suspects that the text has been subject to later editing.

[28] πρὸς δ' οὖν τὸν Ἱπποκράτην τάχα καὶ λογικὴν ἄν τις ἀπόδειξιν εἴποι, καθάπερ ὁ Διοκλῆς· ἐπὶ τίσι γὰρ ἐρεῖς [τίσι] σηπεδόσιν ἢ χυμοῖς τὴν πεμπταίαν ἢ ἑβδομαίαν ἢ ἐναταίαν γίνεσθαι περίοδον, οὐχ ἕξεις. See, e.g., Deichgräber, 1933: 160, Edelstein, 1935: 1308f., and Bourgey, 1953: 100f.

text of the *Epidemics* (I, ch. 11, II 672.2f. L = ch. 24, I 200.5f. Kühlewein) on which Galen is commenting at this point. But again (*a*) we should probably not presume that Hippocrates was the only pathologist to hold that theory, and (*b*) even if we could be sure that Diocles was referring to this particular text in the *Epidemics* we could still not be certain that he took it to be by Hippocrates: once again the reference to Hippocrates does not itself come in a verbal quotation of Diocles and may well have been supplied by Galen.[29]

(3) Finally there is the evidence of another report of an objection that Diocles made to a Hippocratic doctrine, namely that contained in *Aphorisms* II 34 (IV 480.7ff. Littré) to the effect that those suffering from a disease related to the season of the year (e.g. fevers in summer) run less danger than when the disease is not so related. Our evidence for Diocles' objection comes from two sources, Galen and the scholiast on the *Aphorisms* whose identity is not certain but who is generally taken to be Stephanus Atheniensis.[30] But of these two Galen merely records, at this point in his Commentary (*in Hipp. Aph.* II, ch. 34, XVII B 530.9ff. Kühn), that both Diocles and the author of *On Sevens* contested the aphorism in question, without stating that either of these writers directly ascribed the doctrine to Hippocrates.[31] It is only Stephanus who reports Diocles' objection as an objection to Hippocrates and gives what purports to be a verbatim quotation of Diocles which begins with a direct invocation of Hippocrates.[32] If we could accept this quotation as reliable, this would provide good evidence that a particular text in the Hippocratic Corpus corresponds to something that Hippocrates believed.[33] Unfortunately, however, the reliability of the quotation is in serious doubt. First there is the minor point that Galen || does not record this text of Diocles, despite his fondness for quoting earlier sources. Secondly and more importantly, we must ask what source of Diocles' own words could have been available to the scholiast other than the fragments to be found in such writers as Galen himself. The date of Stephanus, the most likely author, is most uncertain, but he has been thought to belong to the eleventh century A.D.,[34] that is, nine centuries after Galen and fourteen after Diocles, and the chances of his having access to otherwise unknown texts of Diocles must be thought remote. Moreover when we add that it seems to be a particular stylistic feature of this

[29] That Diocles knew the treatise of *Art.* does seem likely from the evidence of another passage in Galen (*in Hipp. Art.* III, ch. 23, XVIII A 519.11ff. Kühn) which reports that in his work *On Bandages* Diocles paraphrased a text from that treatise containing the term τύρσις. But in that passage in Galen there is no mention of who Diocles thought was the author of *Art.*

[30] Or, alternatively, Meletius: see Dietz, 1834: I xviff., II ixff., and 236f.

[31] He does, however, say that they argued that the doctrine contradicted the view of 'Hippocrates himself' that 'opposites are cures for opposites'. Whether the ascription of that dictum to Hippocrates comes from Diocles or Galen is again not clear: the doctrine in question is common in Greek medicine, but the dictum in that precise form occurs in *Flat.* ch. 1, *CMG* I 1.92.8 (on which see above, pp. 203f.).

[32] καὶ ἀπορεῖ ὁ Διοκλῆς πρὸς τὸν Ἱπποκράτην λέγων, τί φῄς, ὦ Ἱππόκρατες...; Dietz, 1834: II 326f.

[33] Even so, it would not prove that *Aph. as a whole* is a genuine work of Hippocrates, since it is clearly a composite treatise (see below, p. 209).

[34] See Dietz, 1834: I xix.

writer to make his points in the form of an exchange of questions and answers in which a doubt or difficulty concerning the Hippocratic view is first raised and then resolved or elucidated,[35] it must be thought more likely that this text is the result of the scholiast's embroidering Diocles' objection, rather than a genuine fragment of that writer.[36]

None of the evidences we have considered can be said to establish with a reasonable degree of probability, let alone with certainty, the authenticity of any treatise in the Hippocratic Corpus. Although many different attempts have been made to mount such arguments, none can offer convincing proof, and the very variety of the theses that different scholars have put forward testifies to the weakness of the evidence on which they have to depend. Nor can arguments for authenticity be reliably based on the later evidence, that is, from the Hellenistic period, when a collection or collections of medical treatises began to be the subject of commentaries by scholars working mainly in Alexandria. It is clear that a collection of medical treatises – indeed the core of our own Hippocratic Corpus – was already in existence *as a collection* in the early third century, when the first commentaries, glossaries, and scholarly editions were made.[37] Now precisely what association the earliest collection or collections had with the name of Hippocrates we cannot say for certain: but the evidence of the terms commented on by Bacchius about the middle of the third century shows that at that period a collection already existed that contained quite heterogeneous and disparate works.[38] But if this, the earliest collection we can attempt to reconstruct, already contained works that could not conceivably be by Hippocrates, since they could not all be by the same man, it follows that the presence of any particular treatise among those commented on cannot be used as sound, || let alone conclusive, evidence for Hippocrates being the author. From the time when a group of treatises came to be the subject of scholarly commentaries in Alexandria, it appears that a considerable variety of medical works already passed as

[35] Cf., e.g., Dietz, 1834 II 279 n. 2, 282 n. 4, 304 n. 1.

[36] See Diels, 1910: 1144f. and Deichgräber, 1933: 160 n. 2 (who also argues against authenticity on the grounds of hiatus) and contrast Littré, 1839–61: I 321ff., Bourgey, 1953, 100f.

[37] A list of the early commentators is given by Erotian, who is responsible for our first extant glossary dating from the first century A.D. He names Xenocritus of Cos (probably early third century) as the first grammarian to write a Hippocratic commentary. He was soon followed by Bacchius, who edited *Epid.* III (see Galen, *CMG* V 10.2.1, 87.10ff.), commented on a number of other works, and wrote a lexicon, many of his glosses being preserved by Erotian. But individual terms that appear in Hippocratic treatises had begun to be commented on and explained earlier still: see above, p. 206 n. 29 on Diocles, and Herophilus appears to have commented on terms from *Prog.* and *Aph.*, see Galen, XVIII A 186.14ff. Kühn, and Erotian 10, 10 Nachmanson. Cf. Littré, 1839–61: I 80ff., Bourgey, 1953: 27f.

[38] Cf. Diller, 1959a: 281. Some sixty of Bacchius' glosses are mentioned by Erotian, and although, where the term in question occurs in several Hippocratic texts, there is some uncertainty as to which of these Bacchius was commenting on, he appears to have known some twenty or more treatises. These include such works as *Morb.* I (which is generally thought to be Cnidian), *Liqu.*, *Loc. Hom.*, *Oss.*, and possibly also *Mul.* I and *de Arte*, as well as treatises such as *Prog.*, *Art.*, *Epid.* I and III, and *Acut.*, which are among those that modern scholars have usually preferred to consider genuine.

'Hippocratic' or at least belonged to that corpus: but this in turn means that the evidence of such collections and commentaries can hardly be used to establish the authenticity of any particular treatise or treatises.

II

Each of the main pieces of external evidence that have been used to support hypotheses concerning the genuine works of Hippocrates should, then, be described as at best inconclusive. It might, however, be thought that, weak as each item of evidence is on its own, jointly they would establish the authenticity of a group of treatises provided there were good grounds for holding that the Corpus contains a recognisable body of work that can be ascribed to the same writer. This takes us to our second problem, that of the interrelations of the treatises within the Corpus, which are at issue throughout what may be called the second stage of arguments for authenticity, where the list of works that may be considered genuine is extended by suggesting connections between them (see above, p. 199). Many detailed studies, analysing the similarities and differences in the terminology, contents, and methods of different groups of treatises, have been carried out in recent years. Thus, following Schleiermacher (1929), Knutzen (1964) and Grensemann (1970) have examined the relations between the surgical works, Kahlenberg (1955) those of the embryological treatises, and Lonie (1965b) and others those of *On Diseases* I and II, *On Affections*, and other works that have been held to be of 'Cnidian' origin. But it is one thing to point to similarities in terminology or doctrine between various treatises: it is, of course, quite another to establish that they were composed by the same man. It is with the criteria for identity of authorship that we are chiefly concerned here.

Some general points concerning the nature of the Hippocratic collection as a whole are fundamental. This differs from the Platonic and (though to a lesser extent) the Aristotelian Corpus in two main ways. First, with Plato and Aristotle we have a central body of work accepted as by the author in question which can, accordingly, be used as a yardstick when judging whether other works are also his: in the case of the Hippocratic collection the existence of such a body of work is, at best, problematic. Secondly (though here we may compare parts of the Aristotelian Corpus), many of the Hippocratic treatises do not form a clearly defined unity. Both points are important and need elaboration.

So long as it was generally believed that the major, or at least a substantial proportion of the Hippocratic Corpus was by Hippocrates, it could be assumed that, other things being equal, a treatise was by him unless shown otherwise. But while the possibility that particular groups of treatises are by a single author remains open, it is agreed on all sides that the Corpus contains the work of a considerable number of hands. An analysis of, for example, the pathological and physiological doctrines in the Corpus immediately reveals their extraordinary variety (see below, pp. 212–14). And if this does not prove different authorship in every case (since the same man may have held different views on the same problem at different stages in his career), that remains, nevertheless, in most cases, the most likely explanation. While the heterogeneity of the || Corpus is generally acknowledged, the full implications of this for the Hippocratic question are not always recognised. In the circumstances, the burden of proof lies on those who wish to assert the unity of authorship of any group of treatises.

Secondly, in many, indeed perhaps in most, cases we are not dealing with works that form a clearly defined unity. No one fails to recognise this in such instances as *Aphorisms*, *Coan Prognosis*, *Prorrhetic* I, *Nutriment*, *Dentition*, *Crises*, and *Critical Days*. But apart from those works that consist of collections of aphorisms, other treatises too comprise several more or less distinct parts. The treatises we know as *On the Nature of Man* and *On Regimen in Health* sometimes passed as a single work in ancient times, as we learn from Galen.[39] But not only does *On Regimen in Health* evidently deal with a different topic from those tackled in *On the Nature of Man*, but the latter treatise itself (as is commonly acknowledged) is not a unity. Chapters 1–8 form a coherent discussion of the fundamental constituents of man and their role in disease, but in the subsequent chapters (9–15) we have a series of disconnected discussions of quite separate subjects. *On the Nature of Man* provides a particularly clear-cut case.[40] But the unity of such other treatises as *Airs, Waters, Places*[41] and *On Ancient Medicine*[42] is also a matter of some doubt.

Where a treatise does not form a well-defined whole, the risks of interpolations, additions, and disruptions to the text are, of course, increased. In the case of such works as the *Epidemics*, for instance, particular case-histories would be easy to interpolate, as has been suspected with regard to some of those included at the end of *Epidemics* III.[43] Again, not only does the same material often figure in different treatises, but some treatises consist largely of excerpts from other works. As is well known, *Aphorisms* and *Coan Prognosis* not only have more than sixty aphorisms in common, but also contain dicta that appear in other treatises in substantially the same terms.[44]

[39] *In Hipp. Nat. Hom.*, *CMG* V 9.1.57 4–21 (Galen, remarking on the unscrupulous practices of those who sold books to the Attalid and Ptolemaic kings, suggests that since both books are short, someone may have joined them together to make a more imposing article for sale). Cf. the ancient dispute as to whether *Art.* and *Fract.* form one work, Galen, *in. Hipp. Art.* XVIII A 300ff. Kühn.

[40] We have another in *Acut.* and what is known as its 'Appendix', which have been studied by, for example, Blum, 1936, Regenbogen, 1953, Lonie, 1965a, and Joly, 1972.

[41] That the treatise falls into two main parts (chh. 1–11, 12–24) has been generally recognized at least since Fredrich (1899: 32 n. 2) and Wilamowitz (1901: 16ff.), though differing views continue to be taken on whether the parts are or are not by the same author: for unity of authorship see, e.g., Deichgräber, 1933: 113ff., Pohlenz, 1938: 3ff., 31ff., Heinimann, 1945: 170ff., against Edelstein, 1931: 57ff., Diller, 1934: 89ff. (but cf. 1942: 65ff.)

[42] It has, for example, been suggested that *VM* proper ends with ch. 19; see Jones, 1946: 91f. and cf. Festugière, 1948: xxxf.

[43] e.g. Jones, 1923–31: I 270 n. 1.

[44] E.g. *Aph.* contains passages identical with, or similar to, ones that appear in *Aër.*, *Epid.* II, IV,

The treatise *Instruments of Reduction* consists very largely of passages, often abridged, from *Joints* and *Fractures*,[45] and the work known as *On the Nature of Bones* contains chapters that also appear in other treatises.[46]

Now the fact that a work is a composite one does not mean that its various || parts are necessarily by different authors. Indeed in one notable case, *On the Nature of Man*, we have good grounds for believing that both chh. 1–8 and ch. 11, at least, are by the same man, namely Polybus.[47] On the other hand we cannot, in such cases, ignore the possibility that the different parts are the work of several hands. Thus with parts of *On the Nature of Bones* this can actually be shown by referring to the evidence of Aristotle, who ascribes passages that appear in different chapters to different authors.[48]

Moreover although several Hippocratic authors refer to themselves in the first person singular, some works may well have been the result of a collective effort. It is noteworthy that when the work called *Cnidian Sentences* (now lost) is referred to in *On Regimen in Acute Diseases* it is ascribed not to a single man, but to (several) *authors*, οἱ ξυγγράψαντες, ch. 1, II 225.1 Littré, I 109.2 Kühlewein. Indeed in this case a distinction is drawn between the original author*s* and the later reviser*s* of the work, οἱ...ὕστερον ἐπιδιασκευάσαντες, 226.8 Littré, 110.3 Kühlewein, where again the plural shows that more than one man is involved. As the context indicates,[49] the aim of such later revisers was not to preserve or restore an original text, but to improve the contents of the treatise. We do not know how common either joint authorship or later revisions of medical treatises were, but these passages from *On Regimen in Acute Diseases* show that both sometimes occurred, and we may draw a lesson from this concerning some of the works in the Corpus. Many of the Hippocratic treatises are practical manuals, and those who used them in the fifth and fourth centuries were, no doubt, less concerned with such questions as the exact original text or the identity of the author or authors, than with the substance of their contents, the useful medical knowledge they conveyed. We may presume that many such treatises were subject to frequent minor additions, adjustments, and improvements. The conception of authorship we apply to a philosophical dialogue, to a lyric poem, or to a tragedy would be quite inappropriate to such works. We might

VI, *Hum.*, *Nat. Hom.*, *Liqu.*, *Morb.* I and II; *Coac.* contains passages that are identical with, or similar to, ones that appear in *Epid.* II, VI, *Morb.* I, III, *VC*, and *Prog.*

[45] The relations between *Fract.*, *Art.*, and *Mochl.* have been analysed by, for example, Littré, 1839–61: I 248ff., IV 328ff., and Withington, 1928: 84ff.

[46] E.g. *Oss* ch. 9 corresponds to *Nat. Hom.* ch. 11, *Oss.* ch. 10 to *Epid.* II 4.1.

[47] That Polybus is the author of *Nat. Hom.* chh. 1–8 is likely from Anon. Lond. XIX 1ff. (even though this section of the papyrus is in a very damaged state); that *Nat. Hom.* ch. 11 is also by him appears from Aristotle, *HA* 512b12ff.

[48] At *HA* 511b23ff. Aristotle ascribes an account of the veins that also occurs at *Oss.* ch. 8 to Syennesis of Cyprus; at *HA* 512b12ff. he ascribes other views on the same topic, which also occur at *Oss.* ch. 9, as well as at *Nat. Hom.* ch. 11, to Polybus.

[49] *Acut.* refers to the 'more medical' approach to the subject of the remedies to be used that was shown by the 'later revisers'.

think rather of the way in which some standard textbooks, including modern medical and scientific textbooks, are subject to revisions and improvements, though there is still this point of difference, that in their case, unlike the ancient medical treatises, the various contributors are identified by name.[50]

All these points are relevant to arguments that set out to establish that the || same author – be it Hippocrates or anyone else – composed a number of different treatises. In judging theses based on the correspondences in the ideas or style of different texts, we must first take into account the nature of the treatises in which the texts in question occur. Given that the collections of aphorisms are composite works, it would, for example, certainly be unjustified to infer from a similarity between a given aphorism and a text in another treatise that the treatise and the collection of aphorisms in question were by the same man.

That indeed is obvious: but we must go further. It has been a recurrent weakness in arguments for authenticity based on the interrelations of treatises that alternative explanations for the similarities between particular texts have been too easily discounted, or even totally ignored. Yet one such alternative explanation often lies to hand in the common background of ideas and methods shared by groups of medical writers. Thus no one would wish to argue from similarities between medical or biological doctrines that we find in Aristotle and those in a particular Hippocratic treatise that Aristotle wrote the latter.[51] Yet some arguments for the common authorship of different Hippocratic works have been based on evidence that is little stronger than this.

A second possibility is the deliberate borrowing by one writer of another's ideas. There are some particularly obvious examples of this where the medical writers imitate – without acknowledgement – the theories of the philosophers. Several passages in *On Regimen* I, for instance, follow well-attested fragments of Heraclitus, Parmenides, Empedocles, and Anaxagoras closely.[52]

[50] Thus the ninth edition (Oxford, 1952) of Samson Wright's textbook *Applied Physiology* (originally written in 1926) was ascribed to him 'with the collaboration' of M. Maizels and J. B. Jepson and described in the *Introduction* as follows: 'this edition of *Applied Physiology* is virtually a new book; more than half the text has been rewritten and the rest has been carefully revised to reflect the present state of knowledge'. After Samson Wright's death in 1956, the revisers of the tenth and subsequent editions were C. A. Keele and E. Neil (the latest edition being that of 1971). One may also compare the later revisions of Sir William Osler's *The Principles and Practice of Medicine*, first written in 1892, then revised for subsequent editions by Osler himself, then by Osler working with T. McCrae, then (after Osler's death in 1919) by McCrae, and finally by H. A. Christian (the last edition, the sixteenth, came out in 1947).

[51] Compare *PA* 655a32ff. with *Aph.* VII 28 and *Coac.* 495 (cartilage and bone when cut off do not grow again), *PA* 657b3f. and *HA* 493a29f. with *Aph.* VI 19 and *Coac.* 494 (the prepuce when cut does not grow together), *PA* 670b4f. and *Morb.* IV 37 and 39 (the spleen draws excess fluids from the stomach).

[52] Compare for example, *Vict.* I, ch. 4, VI 474.12ff. L (οὕτω δὲ τούτων ἐχόντων, πουλλὰς καὶ παντοδαπὰς ἰδέας ἀποκρίνονται ἀπ᾽ ἀλλήλων καὶ σπερμάτων καὶ ζῴων, οὐδὲν ὁμοίων ἀλλήλοισιν οὔτε τὴν ὄψιν οὔτε τὴν δύναμιν) with Anaxagoras, Fr. 4 (τούτων δὲ οὕτως ἐχόντων χρὴ δοκεῖν ἐνεῖναι πολλά τε καὶ παντοῖα ἐν πᾶσι τοῖς συγκρινομένοις καὶ σπέρματα πάντων

And we may presume that medical writers borrowed from medical sources even more freely. Even when we are dealing with two reasonably coherent and unified discussions, the existence of a closely similar, or even identical, passage in both does not necessarily mean that the same author has chosen to use the same passage in different contexts, and in assessing the likelihood of that being the case, it is clearly essential to take *all* the evidence into account, that is, points of difference as well as of similarity between the texts in question.

That a large number of medical writers was at work in the fifth and fourth centuries is not only obvious from the heterogeneity of the extant texts but also confirmed by the testimony of Anonymus Londinensis.[53] The onus of proof, we said, lies with those who would assert that a group of treatises is by a single author. It is difficult enough to establish this from correspondences of style and content where we have a recognisable body of work from the author concerned: it is far harder to do so when we are dealing with texts such as those that || make up the Hippocratic collection. For such arguments to be acceptable, we must specify first that the treatises, or parts of treatises, in question should be fairly clearly defined unities, and secondly that the correspondences between them should be such as to render alternative explanations either in terms of a shared background of ideas, or in terms of a deliberate borrowing, unlikely. The strongest evidence is provided by explicit cross-references, where a writer says that he has discussed, or will discuss, a particular problem elsewhere. Yet even here caution is in order. As is well known, the chances of such references being later editorial insertions are often high; and in fact the number of such cross-references in the Corpus is small, the most notable being, perhaps, those in the embryological treatises.[54]

After these methodological remarks, we may turn to consider some particular points of comparison between treatises in the Corpus. A full investigation is far beyond the scope of this study. Some test cases may, however, illuminate aspects of our problem, even though definite conclusions are usually out of the question.

We may begin with two examples where the opportunities to make direct comparisons are most favourable, that is, between passages that deal with the same subject-matter. Two general problems that are repeatedly discussed from different points of view in different treatises are the constituents of the human body and the origin of diseases, and in both cases the variety of ideas

χρημάτων καὶ ἰδέας παντοίας ἔχοντα καὶ χροιὰς καὶ ἡδονάς), and, later in the same ch., *Vict.* 474. 16ff. (ἀπόλλυται μὲν οὖν οὐδὲν ἁπάντων χρημάτων, οὐδὲ γίνεται ὅ τι μὴ καὶ πρόσθεν ἦν· ξυμμισγόμενα δὲ καὶ διακρινόμενα ἀλλοιοῦται) with Anaxagoras, Fr. 17 (οὐδὲν γὰρ χρῆμα γίνεται οὐδὲ ἀπόλλυται, ἀλλ᾽ ἀπὸ ἐόντων χρημάτων συμμίσγεταί τε καὶ διακρίνεται).

[53] It should be recalled that several of the medical writers referred to in Anon. Lond. were quite unknown before the discovery of that papyrus.

[54] E.g. *Genit.* ch. 3, VII 474.9ff. L, an apparent reference to *Morb.* IV (though cf. Kahlenberg, 1955: 252ff. and Plamböck, 1964: 106), and *Genit.* ch. 4, 476.15f., a possible reference to *Mul.*

expressed is great. Thus on the question of the constituents of the human body we find the following suggested as answers in different places:[55] fire (associated with hot and dry) and water (associated with cold and wet);[56] earth, air, 'the hot', and water;[57] blood, phlegm, yellow bile, and black bile (analysed in terms of hot, cold, dry, and wet);[58] blood, phlegm, bile and water;[59] an indefinite number of opposed savours;[60] and air by itself.[61] Now although some of these theories, notably those in *On the Nature of Man* and *On Regimen* I, are quite complex, they represent different, indeed unless qualified, incompatible, answers to the question of what the fundamental constituents of man are.[62] Again we must allow that the same author may hold now one theory, now another, on the same topic at different times. Yet if these major differences of view on the elements of man do not *necessarily* reflect different authors, they nevertheless constitute prima-facie evidence for that conclusion. Nor should we be in any way surprised that such a wide variety of ideas is expressed on this subject when we also find this in the doctrines reported – and explicitly attributed to different writers – by Anonymus Londinensis.[63] ||

Precisely similar conclusions emerge from an examination of the general pathological theories proposed in different Hippocratic texts, where again the variety is considerable. First there are theories that relate directly to a view of the elements in the body. Thus in *On Breaths* we find the doctrine, worked out in great detail in the bulk of the treatise, that air is the cause of disease: indeed in ch. 2 we are told that 'of all diseases the manner is the same, but the place varies...All diseases have one form and cause' (*CMG* I 1.92.13ff.). Both *On Ancient Medicine* and *On the Nature of Man* hold that disease is due to an imbalance in the constituents of the body, but the application of that idea in each case reflects a quite different notion of what those constituents are.[64] Other theories invoke other factors, for example the humours (not always conceived as elemental), or diet, or external factors such as the changes in the seasons or the winds. To give just two examples, in *On the Sacred Disease* ch. 18 (VI 394.9ff. L) it is stated that 'the disease

55 Cf. the analysis in Schumacher, 1963: 194.
56 *Vict.* I chh. 3f., VI 472.12ff., 474.8ff. L.
57 *Carn.* ch. 2, VIII 584.9ff. L.
58 *Nat. Hom.* chh. 3–7, e.g., VI 38.10ff., 40.15ff. L.
59 *Genit.* ch. 3, VII 474.7ff., and *Morb.* IV chh. 32 and 38, 542.6ff, 556.7ff. L.
60 *VM* ch. 14, *CMG* I 1.45.26ff.
61 *Flat.* chh. 3ff., *CMG* I 1.92.21ff., 93.18ff., 94.1ff.
62 Besides advocating their own theories on this topic, some of the works mentioned in the preceding notes also criticise competing doctrines. Thus monistic theories based on air, fire, water, or earth, or one of the humours, are rejected in *Nat. Hom.* chh. 1f., VI 32.3ff. L, and theories based on hot, cold, dry, or wet in *VM* ch. 1, *CMG* I 1.36.2ff.
63 E.g. the theories ascribed to Hippon (based on water, XI 22ff.), Philolaus (the hot, XVIII 8ff.), Polybus (hot and cold, XIX 1ff.), Menecrates (blood and bile, breath and phlegm, the former pair hot, the latter cold, XIX 18ff.), Petron (hot and cold, XX 1ff.), and Philistion (fire, air, water, and earth, XX 25ff.). Though there are grounds for supposing that Polybus wrote *Nat. Hom.* chh. 1–8, it should be stressed that in general the fact that the same theory appears in an account of a particular theorist in Anon. Lond. and in a Hippocratic treatise does not *prove* that the former wrote the latter.
64 *VM* ch. 14, *CMG* I 1.46.1ff., *Nat. Hom.* ch. 4, VI 40.4ff. L.

called sacred comes from the same causes as the rest, from the things that enter and leave the body, from cold, sun, and the changing and never resting winds', and in *On Affections* ch. I (VI 208.7ff. L) we find this: 'in men, all diseases are caused by bile and phlegm. Bile and phlegm give rise to diseases when they become too dry or too wet or too hot or too cold in the body.'[65] Now some treatises put forward several different suggestions concerning possible causes of diseases, and of course statements concerning the origins of *some* diseases may without contradiction be combined with other such statements. But as our quotations illustrate, we also find statements claiming to give the origins of *all* diseases that constitute *competing* theories on that subject. As before, these *may*, to be sure, have been put forward by the same man at different stages in his career. But in most cases they more probably represent the work of different authors.[66]

The frequent contrasts and occasional incompatibility between the various general physiological and pathological doctrines in the Hippocratic Corpus are well known, but several of the treatises that figure prominently in discussions of the 'genuine works of Hippocrates' put forward no such theories. Pride of place, in such discussions, has usually been given to such works as *Prognosis*, books I and III of the *Epidemics*, some of the surgical treatises (especially *Joints* and *Fractures*), and though less often, *Airs, Waters, Places, On Ancient Medicine*, and *On Regimen in Acute Diseases*. These treatises are concerned with a wide range of subjects, and direct points of comparison between texts dealing with the same topic are correspondingly harder to find. On a few occasions, however, such comparisons are possible and we may take three examples to illustrate some of the difficulties that face theses concerning the common authorship of most or all of these works.

First there is some evidence relating to doctrines of critical days. Some idea || that the courses of diseases, particularly 'acute' diseases, are governed by set periods is common ground to a large number of Hippocratic works. Indeed some such idea underlies the usual Greek classification of fevers into tertians, semi-tertians, quartans, quintans, and so on.[67] But more elaborate theories are sometimes proposed concerning the periods of acute diseases. It has often been remarked that both *Prognostic* and *Epidemics* I and III share an interest in such periodicities,[68] and it has generally been assumed[69] that this tells for the conclusion, favoured by many scholars, that both works are

[65] Cf. also *Morb.* I, ch. 2, VI 142.13ff.

[66] Another area where we can make direct comparisons between texts in different treatises is anatomy. Thus Harris has recently analysed the (widely differing) accounts of the system of φλέβες that occur in texts in *Epid.* II 4.1, *Nat. Hom.* ch. 11, *Loc. Hom.* ch. 3, *Morb. Sacr.* chh. 3f. (L), *Anat.*, *Carn.* (especially chh. 5f.), *Cord.*, *Alim.*, and *Oss.* especially.

[67] The classification was a comprehensive one when fevers that could not be assigned to a definite period were called 'irregular', πλάνητες.

[68] As has often been noted, the interest in critical periods provides one reason for the *daily* recording of changes in a patient's condition in the case-histories in the *Epidemics*.

[69] See, e.g., Wellmann, 1929: 19, Deichgräber, 1933: 20ff., but contrast Alexanderson, 1963: 19–23.

by the same man, often identified as Hippocrates himself. Yet the actual theories put forward in *Prognostic* ch. 20 and *Epidemics* I, ch. 12, at least, differ more fundamentally than has sometimes been appreciated. Thus in *Prognostic* ch. 20 (II 168.6ff. L, I 100.8ff. Kühlewein) the writer notes, cautiously, both that the periods of diseases cannot be calculated exactly in whole days any more than the lengths of the solar year or of the lunar month can be, and that it is difficult to forecast the crisis of a disease at the outset when the crisis comes after a protracted interval. But this does not prevent him from putting forward an elaborate doctrine in which he suggests the following series of critical days, the 4th, 7th, 11th, 14th, 17th, 20th, 34th, 40th, and 60th.[70]

Now at the end of the third 'constitution' in *Epidemics* I (chh. 11f.) there are some general remarks about the modes of fevers, including some specific suggestions about their periodicities in ch. 12. Yet the theory elaborated there is quite different from that in *Prognostic* ch. 20 in that it is based on a distinction between *odd* and *even* days.[71] The chapter begins (II 678.5ff. L = ch. 26, I 201.18ff. Kühlewein): 'when the exacerbations are on even days, the crises are on even days. But when the exacerbations are on odd days, the crises are on odd days', and the writer proposes two series of critical days, one of even days (4th, 6th, 8th, 10th, 14th, 20th, 24th, 30th, 40th, 60th, 80th, and 120th)[72] and the other of odd days (3rd, 5th, 7th, 9th, 11th, 17th, 21st, 27th, and 31st).[73] Although one cannot rule out the possibility that the same physician held each of these two contrasting theories at different times, the differences between the two doctrines are quite fundamental and once again they constitute prima-facie evidence that these two chapters (at least) are not from the same hand.[74] ‖

Other briefer passages in other works also bear on the same general topic,

[70] Other critical days are to be added between the 20th and 34th, the 34th and 40th, and the 40th and 60th (viz., probably 24th, 27th, 31st, 37th, 44th, 47th, 51st, 54th, and 57th). The writer says that both up to the 20th day and thereafter the periods are obtained by adding four days at a time (that is, every three days by our way of counting), but this is presumably meant only as a rough guide, since the periods concerned are not all divisible by three.

[71] Cf. also *Morb.* IV, ch. 46, VII 572.1ff., and *Acut.* ch. 4, II 250.11ff. L. Odd and even (which figure in the Table of Opposites ascribed to certain Pythagoreans by Aristotle, *Metaphysics* 986a22ff.) also occur in other contexts in medical theories: e.g. *Hum.* ch. 6 (V 486.4ff. L) says that evacuations on the odd days should be upwards, on the even days downwards.

[72] Kühlewein. Littré omits the 24th and has 100th for 120th.

[73] The writer envisages the possibility of crises occurring on other days, but remarks that, if this happens, there will be relapses. Pains or exacerbations regularly occurring on even days are noted, for example, in case I of *Epid.* I, cases 3, 10, and 12 in the second set in *Epid.* III, and cf. *Epid.* I, ch. 9 (II 652.4ff. L) and *Epid.* III, ch. 6 (III 82.1ff.).

[74] The relation between *Epid.* I, ch. 11f. and the rest of the work is problematic. The observations of crises and relapses in ch. 9 (which in some cases, e.g. Philiscus, correspond to individual case-histories in the set that follows – though there are also discrepancies, e.g. Silenus) do not tally with the theory based on the distinction between odd and even days in ch. 12. Yet many of the generalisations in ch. 9 (e.g. II 662.3ff. L) do not correspond with *Prog.* ch. 20 any more than they do with *Epid.* I, ch. 12. In fact we may have not two, but three distinct theories of critical periodicities in these works, to which a fourth, less elaborate, doctrine can be added from *Aph.* IV 36 (cf. also II 24).

and one in *Airs, Waters, Places* ch. 11 may be mentioned in particular. There the writer says that the physician should guard against the most violent changes in the seasons and against the risings of the stars, 'especially the Dog Star, then Arcturus, and also the setting of the Pleiads. For it is especially at these times that diseases have their crises' (*CMG* I 1.67.8ff.). While it would clearly be wrong to put too much weight on a single brief passage, we may observe that the view it implies is in one important respect quite different from those expressed in the texts of *Prognostic* and *Epidemics* I that we have considered. Whereas the notion of critical days found in both those texts is that fevers follow periods of crises and exacerbations that are determined *by the type of fever itself*, in *Airs, Waters, Places* ch. 11 the idea is that the crisis is influenced by a purely *external* factor, namely the changes in the seasons and the risings and settings of stars.

My second example concerns theories of prognosis. Here again there are, as is well known, many similarities between *Prognostic* and *Epidemics* I and III. Thus *Prognostic* chh. 11–14 sets out general rules for interpreting the signs to be found in a patient's stools, urine, vomit, and sputum, and there are repeated references to these in the case-histories in *Epidemics* I and III. There are, to be sure, also distinctions between the two works. Thus whereas the indications provided by the appearance of a patient's face are given great prominence at the beginning of *Prognostic* (ch. 2), very little reference is made to such indications in either the individual case-histories, or the general constitutions, of *Epidemics* I and III.[75] But in general it is clear that there is a great deal of common ground on the question of what signs the doctor should look for between the theory of *Prognostic* and the practice (and also in some cases the theory)[76] of *Epidemics* I and III. Yet *Airs, Waters, Places* also advocates the practice of prognosis and the instructions it gives about what a doctor should attend to take a very different form. Chapters 1–11 of that treatise deal with such external factors as the positions of cities in respect of the winds, the differences in the waters used, and the changes in the seasons. Now an interest in these external factors is not by itself in any way incompatible with an appreciation of the importance of the information to be gained from the indications in an individual patient's stools, urine, and so on. Yet not only does *Airs, Waters, Places* not mention those factors in prognosis, but ch. 2 (at least) appears to leave no room for them at all. There we are told that the physician 'knowing the changes of the seasons and the risings and settings of the stars...will know beforehand how the year will turn out. Carrying out his inquiry thus and knowing the times beforehand, a man will have full knowledge about each case[77] and will best succeed in securing

[75] Conversely, such signs as nausea, loss of appetite, coma, and epistaxis are all given greater prominence in *Epid.* I and III that they are in *Prog.*, where they are only occasionally mentioned (e.g. epistaxis in chh. 7 and 21, loss of appetite twice in ch. 17).

[76] E.g. *Epid.* I, ch. 10, II 668.14ff. L, which sets out what the doctor should look for.

[77] περὶ ἑκάστου at 57.6 presumably refers to the individual patient or his disease, rather than to the circumstances of the changes in the seasons.

|| health...For men's κοιλίαι change along with the seasons.'[78] The contrast between this statement and the detailed account of what the physician should consider in *Prognostic* is striking,[79] and we have what amounts to two quite different theories of prognosis in the main parts of these works.

The fact that the constitutions in *Epidemics* I and III begin by referring to seasonal factors provides a further point of comparison with *Airs, Waters, Places* ch. 10, and again the differences both in general approach and in detail are marked. The constitutions in the *Epidemics* describe the year under consideration season by season, noting whether each season was 'southerly' or 'northerly', wet or dry, and so on, and whether there were marked changes within a particular season, but no attempt is made to set up general theories covering how the occurrence of particular diseases might be deduced from the weather. Moreover the great variety of diseases, and the different reactions of different individuals to the same disease, are frequently remarked[80]. In *Airs, Waters, Places* ch. 10, on the other hand, not only is the description of the seasons more schematic,[81] but also the writer attempts an aetiology of diseases. Although differences between the sexes, the old and young, and the phlegmatic and bilious are all incorporated into his overall schema, less attention is paid than in the *Epidemics* to possible variations between individuals *within* the categories recognised. Indeed the writer presents a number of dogmatic theories concerning why (as he believes) particular changes in the seasons produce particular diseases, asserting, for example, that if the seasons have such and such a character, then such and such diseases follow of *necessity*.[82]

My third and final example concerns dietetics, where a detailed comparison is possible between two treatises especially, *On Regimen in Acute Diseases* and *On Ancient Medicine*. The similarities between *On Ancient Medicine* ch. 10 and *On Regimen in Acute Diseases* ch. 9 have often been noted. Both texts recommend studying the effects of bad diet on the sick by referring to its effects on healthy men. Both consider what happens to a man who changes his usual habits, either by taking a midday meal when he is not used to one, or by missing it when he is, and the detailed descriptions of both cases are similar not only in doctrine but also in terminology.[83] These correspondences

[78] *CMG* I 1.57.2–10 Heiberg. In the last sentence Jones reads καὶ αἱ νοῦσοι after ὥρῃσι, following Kühlewein, who, however, deleted καὶ αἱ κοιλίαι.

[79] This remains true, even though (as ch. 2 shows) *Prog.* is chiefly concerned with acute diseases.

[80] See, e.g. *Epid.* I, ch. 3, II 612.3ff. L.

[81] The writer evidently correlates southerly and rainy, northerly and dry, and appears not to allow cross-correlations (southerly and dry, northerly and wet): contrast, e.g., *Epid.* I, ch. 1, II 598.7ff.

[82] Cf. the use of ἀνάγκη at *CMG* I 1.65.5, and cf. 65.11 and 66.14.

[83] Compare especially *VM* ch. 10, *CMG* I 1.42.11f., with *Acut.* ch. 9, II 280.8f. (= ch. 28, I 122.16f. Kühlewein); *VM* 42.22–5 with *Acut.* 282.10–284.3 L (= 123.6ff. Kühlewein); and *VM* 42.27–43.7 with *Acut.* 288.3–290.4 L (= ch. 30, 124.3ff. Kühlewein). Other correspondences between the two works are also noted by, for example, Littré, 1839–61: I 314ff. and Festugière, 1948: 41, though contrast Lonie, 1965a: 60f.

are such as to leave little doubt that *either On Ancient Medicine* ch. 10 is copying *On Regimen in Acute Diseases* ch. 9, *or* vice versa, *or* both are following a common source. But if that much may be agreed, the question of authorship is still an open one, and against those who would conclude that the two works as a whole are by the same man there are strong counter-arguments. ||

(1) Thus in ch. 20[84] *On Ancient Medicine* discusses the kind of knowledge that the physician should have concerning the effects of foods and drinks and he takes as an example (*CMG* I 1.52.1ff.): 'undiluted wine, drunk in large quantity, produces a certain effect on a man'. Although the text of the next sentence is corrupt, it is clear from what follows that the writer considers wine to be an instance where the effects are clearly known. But with this one may contrast two texts in *On Regimen in Acute Diseases*. Chapter 10 L (ch. 37 Kühlewein) notes briefly that a change from white to red wine (or vice versa) or one from sweet to vinous wine (or vice versa) may produce many alterations in the body, and in ch. 14 L (chh. 50–2 Kühlewein) the writer gives a detailed account of the different effects produced by four main types of wine and uses this analysis as the basis of equally detailed recommendations about how each of them should be used in treatment. Evidently in *On Regimen in Acute Diseases* the differences between different types of wine are thought to be of great importance: yet the generalisation in *On Ancient Medicine* ch. 10 not only does not mention these distinctions, but in treating wine as a *simple* case appears to leave no room for them.

(2) In *On Ancient Medicine* chh. 5–6 the writer argues that medicine proper developed from dietetics and he suggests that the early discoverers of medicine learned how to modify diet by observing the beneficial effects of giving patients less food. Thus they gave gruel (ῥυφήματα) to those patients who were able to assimilate it, and gave only liquids to those who could not take even gruel. He clearly assumes that the treatment of these early dieticians in reducing the diet of the sick was along the right lines, and he concludes this part of his discussion by saying: 'all the causes of the pain can be reduced to the same thing: it is the strongest foods that harm a man most and most obviously, both the healthy man and the sick' (*CMG* I 1.40.9ff.). These confident pronouncements in *On Ancient Medicine* are in marked contrast to the cautious and critical position in *On Regimen in Acute Diseases*. So far as the diet for acute diseases goes, that writer castigates both the assumptions of laymen and the mistakes of physicians who disagree violently among themselves and whose treatments generally cause more harm than good.[85] He devotes several pages (chh. 4–6 L, chh. 10–20, 24–5 Kühlewein) to detailed instructions about the giving of gruel (ῥύφημα) or πτισάνη (barley-gruel), noting the difficulties of working out the right

[84] See above, p. 209 n. 42, on the relation between this chapter and the rest of *VM*.

[85] E.g. *Acut.* chh. 2 and 3 (II 234.2ff., 238. 8ff. L = chh. 6–8, I 111.12ff., 112.6ff., 19ff., Kühlewein).

treatment and the dangers that accompany mistakes, and being particularly critical of the wrong use of a reduced diet.[86]

The relations between these other passages in the two treatises have been mentioned both for their bearing on the specific problem of the correct interpretation of the obviously close correspondences between *On Ancient Medicine* ch. 10 and *On Regimen in Acute Diseases* ch. 9, and as an illustration of our general problem. Although a natural view of those correspondences, taken on their own, might be that the treatises in question were composed by the same man, that is, as we remarked, by no means the only possible explanation, and the greater the disparities between other sections of these works, the less likely it becomes that we are dealing with the same author (even allowing for the possibility that the || same author changed his mind on certain points) rather than with two (or more). The disparities, in this case, are certainly not such as to *demonstrate* different authorship: on the other hand they provide good reason for hesitating before we conclude from the similarities between the two treatises that the same author was responsible for both.

We may now attempt to summarize the conclusions of our study. First an examination of the external evidence shows that no convincing case can be mounted, on its basis, for the authenticity of any particular treatise. Secondly, theses concerning the interrelations of treatises within the Corpus face greater problems than is sometimes allowed. Arguments for identical authorship that depend on correspondences of style and content are difficult enough in the most favourable circumstances, where we have a set of demonstrably authentic works as a standard of comparison. Such arguments are far more hazardous when we are dealing with a group of texts such as the Hippocratic collection. (1) With the exception of some rhetorical ἐπιδείξεις, they are not polished literary works. (2) In many cases, the treatises do not form clearly defined unities, but are composite works, compilations consisting of several more or less disparate parts. (3) Additions, interpolations, and borrowings whether from other medical, or from non-medical (e.g. philosophical) sources can be established on many occasions and may be suspected on many others. (4) There is some evidence of joint authorship and of later revisions of medical works in the fifth and fourth centuries, and although we do not know how common either was, it would clearly be wrong to attribute our own concerns for establishing an original text and preserving it intact to those who used and transmitted practical medical manuals in this period.[87]

[86] E.g. *Acut.* ch. 4, 246.4ff. L (ch. 11, 114.6ff. Kühlewein); cf. also ch. 7, 276.9ff. L (ch. 25, 121.15ff. Kühlewein); and ch. 11, 308.2ff. L (chh. 40f., 129.3ff., 13ff. Kühlewein).

[87] Even Galen, many centuries later, is more concerned with the question of the truth of what is contained in Hippocrates' works than with the question of their authenticity (see, e.g., *in Hipp. Nat. Hom.* I ch. 42, *CMG* V 9.1 55.26ff.) – and Galen's interests, and ability, in philology and textual criticism were, comparatively speaking, highly developed.

So far as the Hippocratic question itself goes, the radical scepticism of the Wilamowitz of 1901 and of Edelstein does not seem misplaced.[88] Although the precise origin of the collection or collections that came to form our Corpus is highly problematic,[89] the evidence for the earliest such collections clearly points to the conclusion that they already contained quite disparate and heterogeneous works. It may be that some of Hippocrates' work has come down to us in the Corpus, but we cannot now prove this, nor determine which his work is; moreover our best witness for his medical theories, Meno, reports them in terms that do not tally with anything we find in the Corpus. But if little progress can be hoped for on the subject of the 'genuine works of Hippocrates', the detailed analysis of the interrelations of treatises in the Corpus is an area where – despite the many fruitful studies undertaken in recent years – much work still remains to be done. Here scholars will, no doubt, continue to disagree in their precise evaluation of the affinities and differences between || particular texts. But I hope to have given grounds for insisting on caution as regards claims for identical authorship and to have illustrated that even in some apparently promising examples (such as parts of *Prognostic* and of *Epidemics* I and III) the verdict should remain open.

[88] That is not to say, of course, that the sceptics' arguments are all sound. In particular Edelstein was clearly wrong to insist (though in 1939: 243 n. 25 he cited Deichgräber, 1933: 163 on his side on this point) that *all* of Hippocrates' known teaching should be found in any particular treatise claimed as genuine.

[89] See, for example, Littré, 1839–61: I 44ff., Jones, 1923–31: I xxixff., Edelstein, 1931: 152ff., Bourgey, 1953: 27ff., Diller, 1959a: 277ff.

REFERENCES

Alexanderson, B. (1963) *Die hippokratische Schrift Prognostikon, Überlieferung und Text*, Studia Graeca et Latina Gothoburgensia 17 (Göteborg)

Alsina, J. (1969) 'Sobre la medicina hipocrática', *Estudios Clásicos* 13: 13–24

Baisette, R. G. (1936) 'La médecine grecque jusqu'à la mort d'Hippocrate', in *Histoire Générale de la Médecine*, ed. P. M. M. Laignel-Lavastine, I (Paris) 129–277

Blass, F. (1901) 'Die pseudippokratische Schrift περὶ φυσῶν und der Anonymus Londinensis', *Hermes* 36: 405–10

Blum, R. (1936) 'La composizione dello scritto ippocrateo Περὶ διαίτης ὀξέων', *Rendiconti della R. Accademia Nazionale dei Lincei*, Classe di scienze morali, storiche e filologiche, ser. 6, 12: 39–84

Bourgey, L. (1953) *Observation et expérience chez les médecins de la collection hippocratique* (Paris)

Capelle, W. (1922), 'Zur Hippokratischen Frage', *Hermes* 57: 247–65

Davies, C. (1971) 'Hippocrates of Cos: the founder of scientific medicine', *History Today* 21: 273–9

Deichgräber, K. (1933) *Die Epidemien und das Corpus Hippocraticum*, Abhandlungen der preussischen Akademie der Wissenschaften, phil.-hist. Kl. (Berlin)

Di Benedetto, V. (1966) 'Tendenza e probabilità nell'antica medicina greca', *Critica Storica* 5: 315–68

Diels, H. (1893a) 'Über die Excerpte von Menons Iatrika in dem Londoner Papyrus 137', *Hermes* 28: 407–34

(1893b) *Anonymi Londinensis ex Aristotelis Iatricis Menoniis et aliis medicis Eclogae*, Supplementum Aristotelicum 3 (Berlin, 1893)

(1910) 'Über einen neuen Versuch, die Echtheit einiger Hippokratischen Schriften nachzuweisen', *Sitzungsberichte der königlich preussischen Akademie der Wissenschaften* (Berlin) 1140–55

Dietz, F. R. (1834) *Scholia in Hippocratem et Galenum*, 2 vols. (Königsberg)

Dihle, A. (1963) 'Kritisch-exegetische Bemerkungen zur Schrift Über die Alte Heilkunst', *Museum Helveticum* 20: 135–50

Diller, H. (1934) *Wanderarzt und Aitiologe*, Philologus Supplementband 26. 3 (Leipzig)

(1942) Review of Pohlenz, 1938, *Gnomon* 18: 65–88 (reprinted in his *Kleine Schriften zur antiken Medizin*, edd. G. Baader and H. Grensemann (Berlin, 1973), 188–209)

(1959a) 'Stand und Aufgaben der Hippokratesforschung', *Jahrbuch der Akademie der Wissenschaften und der Literatur, Mainz*, 271–87 (reprinted in Flashar, 1971: 29–51, and in *Kleine Schriften zur antiken Medizin*, 89–105)

(1959b) 'Der innere Zusammenhang der hippokratischen Schrift de victu', *Hermes* 87: 39–56 (reprinted in *Kleine Schriften zur antiken Medizin*, 71–88)

(1964) 'Ausdrucksformen des methodischen Bewusstseins in den hippokratischen Epidemien', *Archiv für Begriffsgeschichte* 9: 133–50 (reprinted in *Kleine Schriften zur antiken Medizin*, 106–23)

Dumesnil, R. (1944) 'Hippocrate', *Lettres d'Humanité* 3: 33–45

Edelstein, L. (1931) ΠΕΡΙ ΑΕΡΩΝ *und die Sammlung der hippokratischen Schriften*, Problemata 4 (Berlin)

(1935) 'Hippokrates', *Pauly–Wissowa Real-Encyclopädie*, Suppl. Bd 6, cols. 1290–1345

(1939) 'The genuine works of Hippocrates', *Bulletin of the History of Medicine* 7: 236–48 (reprinted in *Ancient Medicine*, ed. O. and C. L. Temkin (Johns Hopkins Press, Baltimore, 1967), 133–44)

(1940) Review of Pohlenz, 1938, *American Journal of Philology* 61: 221–9 (reprinted in *Ancient Medicine*, 111–20)

Festugière, A. J. (1948) *Hippocrate, L'Ancienne Médecine*, Études et commentaires 4 (Paris)

Flashar, H. ed. (1971) *Antike Medizin* (Darmstadt)

Fredrich, C. (1899) *Hippokratische Untersuchungen*, Philologische Untersuchungen 15 (Berlin)

Frenkian, A. M. (1941) *La Méthode hippocratique dans le Phèdre de Platon* (Bucharest)

Greco, E. (1966) 'La medicina nell'antica Grecia', *Atene e Roma* 11: 97–109

Grensemann, H. (1968a) *Die hippokratische Schrift 'Über die heilige Krankheit'*, Ars Medica Abt. II Bd 1 (Berlin)

(1968b) *Der Arzt Polybos als Verfasser hippokratischer Schriften*, Akademie der Wissenschaften und der Literatur, Mainz, Abhandlungen der geistes- und sozialwissenschaftlichen Klasse, Jahrgang 1968, 2 (Wiesbaden)

(1970) 'Hypothesen zur ursprünglich geplanten Ordnung der hippokratischen Schriften De fracturis und De articulis', *Medizinhistorisches Journal* 5: 217–35

Hackforth, R. (1952) *Plato's Phaedrus* (Cambridge)

Harris, C. R. S. (1973) *The Heart and the Vascular System in Ancient Greek Medicine from Alcmaeon to Galen* (Oxford)

Heidel, W. A. (1941) *Hippocratic Medicine: its Spirit and Method* (New York)

Heinimann, F. (1945) *Nomos und Physis* (Basel)

Joly, R. (1956) 'Notes hippocratiques', *Revue des études anciennes* 58: 195–210

(1960) *Recherches sur le traité pseudo-hippocratique Du Régime* (Paris)

(1961) 'La question hippocratique et le témoignage du Phèdre', *Revue des études grecques* 74: 69–92 (German version, with Nachtrag, in Flashar, 1971: 52–82)

(1966) *Le Niveau de la science hippocratique* (Paris)

(1970) *Hippocrate, De la génération, De la nature de l'enfant, Des maladies IV, Du foetus de huit mois* (Paris)

(1972) *Hippocrate, Du régime des maladies aiguës, Appendice, De l'aliment, De l'usage des liquides* (Paris)

Jones, W. H. S. (1923–31) *Hippocrates*, Loeb edn., 4 vols. (London)

(1945) '"Hippocrates" and the *Corpus Hippocraticum*', *Proceedings of the British Academy* 31: 103–25

(1946) *Philosophy and Medicine in Ancient Greece, Suppl. to the Bulletin of the History of Medicine* (Baltimore)

(1947) *The Medical Writings of Anonymus Londinensis* (Cambridge)

Junco, Y. de (1964) 'Hippocrate', *Bulletin de l'Association Guillaume Budé* 1964: 188–96

Kahlenberg, W. (1955) 'Die zeitliche Reihenfolge der Schriften περὶ γονῆς, περὶ φύσιος παιδίου und περὶ νούσων 4 und ihre Zusammengehörigkeit, *Hermes* 83: 252–6

King, L. S. (1963) 'Hippocrates and Philosophy', *Journal of the History of Medicine and Allied Sciences* 18: 77–8

Knutzen, G. H. (1964) *Technologie in den hippokratischen Schriften* περὶ διαίτης ὀξέων, περὶ ἀγμῶν, περὶ ἄρθρων ἐμβολῆς, Akademie der Wissenschaften und der Literatur, Mainz, Abhandlungen der geistes- und sozialwissenschaftlichen Klasse, Jahrgang 1963, 14 (Wiesbaden)

Kranz, W. (1944) 'Platon über Hippokrates', *Philologus* 96: 193–200 (reprinted in *Studien zur antiken Literatur und ihrem Fortwirken* ed. E. Vogt (Heidelberg, 1967), 315–19)

Kucharski, P. (1939) 'La "méthode d'Hippocrate" dans le *Phèdre*', *Revue des études grecques* 52: 301–57

Kudlien, F. (1967) *Der Beginn des medizinischen Denkens bei den Griechen* (Zürich)

Kühn, J. H. (1956) *System- und Methodenprobleme im Corpus Hippocraticum*, Hermes Einzelschriften 11

Lichtenthaeler, C. (1957) *La Médecine hippocratique II–V* (Neuchâtel)

(1959) *Deux Conférences* (Geneva and Paris)

(1960) *Leçon Inaugurale, Sixième étude hippocratique* (Geneva and Paris)

(1963) *Quatrième série d'études hippocratiques VII–X* (Geneva and Paris)

Littré, E. (1839–61) *Œuvres complètes d'Hippocrate*, 10 vols. (Paris)

Lonie, I. M. (1965a) 'The Hippocratic Treatise περὶ διαίτης ὀξέων', *Sudhoffs Archiv für Geschichte der Medizin und der Naturwissenschaften* 49: 50–79.

(1956b) 'The Cnidian Treatises of the *Corpus Hippocraticum*', *C.Q.* N.S. 15: 1–30

Martiny, M. (1964) *Hippocrate et la médecine* (Paris)

Miller, H. W. (1966) '*Dynamis* and the Seeds', *Transactions and Proceedings of the American Philological Association* 97: 281–91

Nelson, A. (1909) *Die hippokratische Schrift* ΠΕΡΙ ΦΥΣΩΝ, *Text und Studien* (Uppsala)

Nestle, W. (1938) 'Hippocratica', *Hermes* 73: 1–38 (reprinted in his *Griechische Studien* (Darmstadt, 1968), 517–66)

Petersen, W. F. (1946) *Hippocratic Wisdom* (Springfield, Illinois)

Plamböck, G. (1964) *Dynamis im Corpus Hippocraticum*, Akademie der Wissenschaften und der Literatur, Mainz, Abhandlungen der geistes- und sozialwissenschaftlichen Klasse, Jahrgang 1964, 2 (Wiesbaden)

Pohlenz, M. (1937) *Hippokratesstudien*, Nachrichten von der Gesselschaft der Wissenschaften zu Göttingen, phil-hist. Kl. Fachgr. I, N.F. II, 4 (Göttingen:

reprinted in vol. II of his *Kleine Schriften*, ed. H. Dörrie (Hildesheim, 1965), 175–209)

(1938) *Hippokrates und die Begründung der wissenschaftlichen Medizin* (Berlin)

(1939) 'Hippokrates', *Die Antike* 15: 1–18

(1953) 'Nomos und Physis', *Hermes* 81: 418–38 (reprinted in vol. II of *Kleine Schriften*, 341–60)

Regenbogen, O. (1921) 'Hippokrates und die hippokratische Sammlung', *Neue Jahrbücher für das klassiche Altertum, Geschichte und deutsche Literatur* 47: 185–97 (reprinted in his *Kleine Schriften*, ed. F. Dirlmeier (Munich, 1961), 125–40)

(1953) 'Probleme um die Hippokratische Schrift "De Victu Acutorum"', in *Studies presented to D. M. Robinson*, II, ed. G. E. Mylonas and D. Raymond (St Louis, Missouri, 1953), 624–34 (reprinted in *Kleine Schriften*, 195–205)

Rey, A. (1930–48) *La Science dans l'antiquité*, 5 vols. (Paris)

Robert, F. (1953) 'Hippocrate', *L'Information Littéraire* 5: 144–9

Schleiermacher, W. (1929) 'Die Komposition der Hippokratischen Schrift περὶ ἀγμῶν, περὶ ἄρθων ἐμβολῆς, *Philologus* 84, N.F. 38: 273–300, 399–429

Schöne, H. (1910) 'Echte Hippokratesschriften', *Deutsche medizinische Wochenschrift* 36: 418–19, 466–7

Schumacher, J. (1963) *Antike Medizin*, 2nd edn (Berlin)

(1967) 'Der Menon-Bericht zu Hippokrates im Anonymus Londinensis', in *Melemata* Festschrift W. Leibbrand, ed. J. Schumacher (Mannheim), 143–8

Sigerist, H. E. (1934) 'On Hippocrates', *Bulletin of the Institute of the History of Medicine* 2: 190–214

(1961) *A History of Medicine* II (Oxford)

Steckerl, F. (1945) 'Plato, Hippocrates, and the *Menon Papyrus*', *Classical Philology* 40: 166–80

Vegetti, M. (1963–4) 'Technai e filosofia nel *peri technes* pseudo-ippocratico', *Atti della Accademia delle Scienze di Torino*, Classe di Scienze Morali, Storiche e Filologiche 98: 308–80

(1965) *Opere di Ippocrate* (Turin)

Wellmann, M. (1929) 'Hippokrates, des Herakleides Sohn', *Hermes* 64: 16–21

Wilamowitz-Moellendorff, U. von (1901) 'Die hippokratische Schrift περὶ ἱρῆς νούσου', *Sitzungsberichte der königlich preussischen Akademie der Wissenschaften* (Berlin, 1901), 2–23 (reprinted in vol. III of his *Kleine Schriften* (Berlin, 1969), 278–302)

(1929) Lesefrüchte', *Hermes* 64: 458–90 (reprinted in vol. IV of his *Kleine Schriften* (Berlin, 1962), 476–508)

Withington, E. T. (1928) *Hippocrates*, vol. III of Loeb edn (London)

10

THE EMPIRICAL BASIS OF THE PHYSIOLOGY OF THE *PARVA NATURALIA*

INTRODUCTION

Two particularly lively areas of recent Aristotelian research have been the relation between his zoological work and his philosophy of science, and his philosophy of mind. The former is the theme of the volume edited by Allan Gotthelf and James Lennox (1987) to which reference has already been made in my notes to chapter 1. The latter is the subject of a forthcoming collection of essays edited by Martha Nussbaum and Amelie Rorty. The paper I gave to the Symposium Aristotelicum in 1975 and that was published in the proceedings, edited by myself and G. E. L. Owen, in 1978, tackles a specific problem at the intersection of Aristotle's zoology and his psychology, namely the empirical basis of the physiological theories proposed in the group of treatises we know as the *Parva Naturalia*, and the results it reached were, in some respects, surprising. My aim here is to spell out in rather more detail than I did in my article the implications of my investigation for each of the two main areas of current debate that I have identified.

First there is the general question of the relationship between the practice of science in Aristotle and his avowed methodology in statements on that topic both in the *Posterior Analytics* and in his physical treatises. From that point of view, the passages and topics I discussed in the *Parva Naturalia* may appear at first sight anomalous. On the one hand they do not exactly bear out the more empirical methodological recommendations where Aristotle insists, for example, on the importance of the preliminary survey of the phenomena in the sense of the data of observation. On the other, the Aristotelian bid to give fully fledged demonstrations or at least causal explanations of those data hardly tallies with the manner of his discussion of problems to do with the common sensorium, the structure and function of the eye and so on.

The particular problems I chose to investigate relate to the connection between the senses and the common sensorium, the function of the eye in particular, the nature and function of the brain, the relations between the lung and heart and the structure of the heart. On such problems one might expect Aristotle's empiricist inclinations to have been to the fore. His reputation for empirical research in zoology is firmly grounded, and there is abundant evidence, in the zoological works, of his actually practising what the programmatic recommendations of the *De Partibus Animalium* I, chh. I and 5 preach, namely the detailed exploration of the parts of every kind of animal, however lowly. However, in relation to the problem of the connections between the sense-organs and the common sensorium, where we might have expected him to have been particularly careful to provide detailed anatomical evidence to support his general theories (not least in view of his criticisms of his predecessors for failing to do so) the extent to which he actually does so is modest. In some cases where it would have been possible for him to have checked one of his theories empirically, he does not do so, and in others he appears, from the superficiality of his reports of his observational data, to have been impatient to find *support* for his general doctrines and ends his empirical investigation once this, quite limited aim, has been achieved. At points, in fact, he comes close to committing the mistake of which he accuses others, namely of not considering carefully the observational data themselves, but assuming in advance what observational data will be found.

At the same time, whatever may be true of other areas of his work on perception, the passages in the *Parva Naturalia* on this do not show any signs of attempted demonstrations on the model of the *Posterior Analytics*. The role of certain over-arching theories, the central common sensorium, its location in the heart, the subordinate role of the brain, these are what influence his choice of data to present, and his interpretation of them once presented. But while there are plenty of arguments to recommend these doctrines, they are not formulated to conform to the ideal of demonstration set out in the *Posterior Analytics*.

From a consideration of Aristotle's performance on the topics I analysed, two negative conclusions can be drawn. First it would be rash to exaggerate the empiricism of Aristotle's actual practice. Naturally enough there are features of his work, and problems that he investigates, where his reputation for careful empirical study is borne out. But not in these contexts in the *Parva Naturalia*. But secondly where much Aristotelian scholarship opposes the empiricism of the zoological works to the deductive structures of the Organon, the latter too do not tally closely with his procedures. Yet there was, of course, always more to Aristotle's methodology than just empirical research and demonstrative arguments. The aspect of his methodology that is in play is – broadly speaking – dialectical. Even if the *phainomena* in the sense of the data of observation are not collected with as much energy as one might have expected, he certainly surveys and takes into full account the common and recognised opinions on the topics he discusses, for example of the elementary constitution of the eye, or on the location of the common sensorium.

Indeed it is the influence of his preferred solutions to the questions that had been discussed in those long-standing debates that may be said to be chiefly responsible for some of the superficiality of his empirical work. From this perspective at least some recent attempts to minimise the dialectical aspects of Aristotle's procedures (for example Bolton, 1987) seem misplaced.

In the topics I investigated in my paper Aristotle is very clearly locked into existing debates. His deployment of anatomical data to refute rival theories is often acute, but his survey of positive data to support his own is sometimes superficial, in that it ceases once *some* support has been identified. No doubt the end results of his discussion *could* be presented in strict deductive form to match the programme of the *Posterior Analytics*, but there are no signs of his actually undertaking this in this context in the *Parva Naturalia*.

Let me now consider what lessons might be drawn from my original study with regard to current controversies in the interpretation of Aristotle's philosophy of mind. Here the issues debated include, for instance, the viability of Aristotle's solution to the problem of the relation of the mind (or rather more generally the *psuchē*) and the body, and on whether that solution can be said to be a functionalist one, incorporating the idea of so-called compositional plasticity, that is that the soul or mind can or could be instantiated in matter of quite different kinds. These in turn relate to the question of the success, or otherwise, of Aristotle's representing the soul–body relationship as one of form to matter, and to the light that his psychology may throw on his use of that key contrast. This is not the place to attempt a full discussion of these problems. However, the texts I studied are among those that have to be taken into account in any attempt to study Aristotle's views on the relationship between the physiological and the cognitive aspects of perception.

On this topic I would now wish to emphasise an apparent indeterminacy in Aristotle's positions, one that encourages a verdict of not proven on the issue separating such scholars as Burnyeat and Sorabji, but one that itself raises further questions as to why Aristotle – apparently – left certain aspects of the question open.

One important disputed topic concerns whether or not Aristotle is committed to the view that the eye-jelly actually becomes red when it sees a red object, the nose actually becomes smelly (in Burnyeat's phrase) when it smells something, the hand actually becomes hot or hard when it perceives something hot or hard. To be sure the data *we* have to take into account on this question extend beyond the material from the *Parva Naturalia* that I surveyed in my article, particularly texts in the *De Anima* that lie outside the scope of my remarks here. However, that material from the *PN* is among the evidence that underlines the difficulty of *generalising* Aristotle's solution to the problem. One major reason for this is that the properties normally and naturally possessed by different sense-organs vary. The nose is not naturally smelly nor the ear possessed of an audible quality, in the way in which in the case of touch the sense-organ always *has* a certain temperature. Being aware of something hotter can hardly, in Aristotelian physics, be separated from being affected, i.e. qualitatively, by its heat. Moreover (as I noted, p. 237 n. 31 and p. 238) Aristotle hesitates on the question of precisely what the role of the flesh is, in touch, whether it is the medium, or the organ, of that sense.

On the question of the eye-jelly becoming (for example) red, this is not in any event something that could have been verified (if indeed Aristotle had been committed to it). What he does attempt to do, and succeed in doing, is to refute any theory that would have it that seeing takes place at the outer extremity of the eye. *De Sensu* 438b14, discussed on p. 234 of my article, successfully invokes the evidence of those who have suffered from lesions to the temples to disprove any such theory. At least we may say this, then, that whatever happens in the eye itself, it is not the eye that sees, in the sense of performing the cognitive act, but rather the common sensorium. The messages or stimuli (as we might say) from the eye have essentially to be communicated to the common sensorium for seeing, or any other perceiving, to take place.

Moreover the lack of any detailed description of the structure of the eye (to which I drew attention, pp. 233–6) suggests or is compatible with the view that Aristotle is *not* concerned with the details or maybe even the nature of the changes it undergoes, whether affection as distinguished from cognition (as Sorajbi holds) or affection as already cognitive (Burnyeat). This would appear to be a case where the issue between opposing modern interpretations can hardly be definitively resolved – for the simple reason that those interpretations pose a question to the Aristotelian texts that those texts do not explicitly address. That may or may not be considered a weakness in Aristotle's account of perception. But it must be recognised on either side of the dispute on the eye-jelly that there is no text that unequivocally asserts, nor one that unequivocally denies, that it becomes red. But then no more is there a text that clearly describes the anatomical structure of the eye even in the grossest terms. On that score (as I point out) Aristotle's apparent concern is merely to set up a correlation between the five senses and the four elements and to secure the conclusion that the eye is essentially 'water'.

However, a lack of interest in some of the physiological details leaves still unanswered the major question of where Aristotle's positive concerns in his account of perception lie. If we reflect on the topics on which he appears most eager to produce evidence, these relate first to the doctrine that there *is* a common sensorium, and secondly to its location in the heart (not the brain). On both topics the influence of Plato in the background is manifest, though Aristotle's reaction to that influence is complex. On the one hand Plato had insisted, in the *Theaetetus*, that what does the perceiving is not the senses, but the soul through the senses. Just what elements of awareness or noticing are to be ascribed to the senses in that dialogue continues to be hotly debated (Kanayama, 1987; Frede, 1989; Burnyeat, forthcoming). But there can be no doubt as to the fact, or as to the importance, of the doctrine of a common sensorium.

But if Aristotle agrees with Plato on that, he disagrees completely on where it is to be located. For both Plato and Aristotle, *aisthēsis* is common to all living animals (Plato would add plants as well), and reasoning, at least in the form of *logizesthai*, belongs to humans alone. But given the differences in their analysis of *aisthēsis*, what each philosopher thereby ascribes to animals differs. Plato had invoked animals and children, in the *Theaetetus*, in connection merely with a bare awareness, while Aristotle, by contrast, stresses the discriminating, judgemental, capacity of perception itself (described as a *kritikē dunamis* at *Posterior Analytics* 99b35).

Moreover for Aristotle the crucial point is that perception is the defining characteristic of animals *qua* animals and what marks them out, precisely, from plants. That in turn provides him with a very powerful motive for identifying the location of the central faculty of perception with that of the vital activities of the animal in general. Here certainly we reach an argument in Aristotle that relates to and directly reflects his zoological interests and investigations. No doubt the clinching factor in his taking the heart to be the seat of the vital functions is provided by the embryological data (referred to on p. 232 and n. 9, p. 239 and nn. 44–5), namely that (as he holds) the heart is the first part of the embryo to develop.

On this reading, Aristotle's preoccupations relate primarily to his agreements and disagreements with Plato. On the one hand the question of the role of the common sensorium (and the need for one) receives considerable attention: so too on the other is the issue of where it is to be located. The data that Aristotle musters to establish the connection between the senses and the heart suffer from the weaknesses I illustrated. But against that he shows himself entirely confident that so far as the vital activities of the animal in general are concerned, they must be located in the heart. No doubt it would be far too simple to claim that Aristotle's reasons for locating the common sensorium in the heart, rather than in the brain, stem *purely* from the embryological argument, though just as surely those reasons *include* that argument and thereby provide a striking illustration of the influence of zoological perspectives on his psychology. Where a direct influence from Plato is detectable in the doctrine of the common sensorium itself, an indirect one emerges in Aristotle's different answer to the question of its location. Certainly in his own account of the structure and function of the *brain* he is careful (as I showed) to spell out that its functions are *subsidiary* to those of the heart (pp. 239–40). Thus some of the very weaknesses (as they may seem to us) of the empirical research he undertook on this group of problems may serve indirectly to highlight *his* theoretical preoccupations, and in particular his concern to advocate a rival view to that of Plato on the location of the common sensorium. In other words the guiding thread in his discussion is not so much any idea of a comprehensive survey of all the empirical data that might be collected, nor yet one of setting out conclusions to meet the rigorous standards of his theory of demonstration, but rather his notion of what is necessary, in the dialectic of the situation, to secure his own position against rivals.

REFERENCES

Bolton, R. (1987) 'Definition and scientific method in Aristotle's *Posterior Analytics* and *Generation of Animals*', in *Philosophical Issues in Aristotle's Biology*, edd. A. Gotthelf and J. G. Lennox (Cambridge), 120–66

Burnyeat, M. F. (1976) 'Plato on the grammar of perceiving', *Classical Quarterly* 26: 29–51

(1979) 'Conflicting appearances', *Proceedings of the British Academy* 65: 69–111

(forthcoming) 'Is an Aristotelian philosophy of mind still credible?' in *Essays on Aristotle's De Anima*, edd. M. Nussbaum and A. Rorty (Oxford)

Frede, D. (1989) 'The soul's silent dialogue: a non-aporetic reading of Plato's *Theaetetus*', *Proceedings of the Cambridge Philological Society* 35: 20–49

Gotthelf, A., and Lennox, J. G., edd. (1987) *Philosophical Issues in Aristotle's Biology* (Cambridge)

Kanayama, Y. (1987) 'Perceiving, considering, and attaining being (*Theaetetus* 184–186)', *Oxford Studies in Ancient Philosophy* 5: 29–81

Sorabji, R. (1971/79) 'Aristotle on demarcating the five senses' (from *Philosophical Review* 80: 55–79) in *Articles on Aristotle*, edd. J. Barnes, M. Schofield and R. Sorabji, vol. IV (London), 76–92

(1974/79) 'Body and soul in Aristotle' (from *Philosophy* 49: 63–89) in *Articles on Aristotle*, edd. J. Barnes, M. Schofield and R. Sorabji, vol. IV (London), 42–64

THE EMPIRICAL BASIS OF THE PHYSIOLOGY OF THE *PARVA NATURALIA*

Aristotle's fame as a biologist is as firmly entrenched as any aspect of his reputation. When he is acclaimed for his work in this field, it is not only, and often not primarily, as a theorist – for example, for his acute discussion of the problems of generation and heredity in *GA* – but also, and perhaps more especially, as an observer, for his detailed zoological descriptions. The zoological treatises show a familiarity with a quite impressive range of animal species; the exactness of many of his descriptions of the external and internal parts of animals and of aspects of animal behaviour has often rightly been praised,[1] and in many cases his accounts refer to or presuppose the use of dissection, whether undertaken by Aristotle himself or by his associates. Meanwhile the famous fifth chapter of *PA* I leaves us in no doubt that he recognised the importance of detailed research in zoology and the opportunities it presented for his enquiry into causes, while he remained realistic both about the difficulties of such research and about the repugnance that some of his contemporaries would feel at the investigation of the less honourable animals and of internal anatomy.[2]

The *PN*, whose subject is certain activities that are 'common to soul and body', presupposes the study of the soul itself,[3] and the opening sentences of *Sens.* not only look back to *De An.* but also forward to the study of living beings in general.[4] This poses, as a topic for investigation, the extent to which Aristotle's practice in *PN* corresponds to the ideals enunciated in *PA* I.5, or, more generally, the relation between empirical data and theories in *PN*. How far are the theories advanced in those treatises suggested or supported by, or checked against, empirical observations? To what extent does Aristotle appear to have engaged in deliberate research relevant to the issues explored in *PN*? These are complex questions that have not received the attention they deserve.[5] In this paper I wish to consider certain aspects of these problems not so much from the point of view of the chronological question of the relative date of *PN*, as from || that of the methodological one of the role of observation in Aristotle's natural philosophy.

Given the recommendations of *PA* I.5, our initial presumption might well be to expect fairly frequent references, in *PN*, to the findings of empirical investigations, whether anatomical, physiological or zoological, in the

[1] Many of the finest descriptions occur in the later books of *HA* (e.g. VI and IX) whose authenticity is doubtful. The general point can, however, be established well enough from *PA* and *GA*.

[2] See especially *PA* 644b28–31, 645a1–4, 7–36 and cf. *PA* I.1, 640b17ff. At 645a6f. and 21–3 he recommends the study of every kind of animal, so far as possible, without exception. That this enquiry is directed to the formal and final causes especially is made clear in both ch. 5 and ch. 1.

[3] This study itself is, of course, seen as of primary importance for the study of nature, *De An.* 402a4–6.

[4] See *Sens.* 436a1–11.

[5] Much relevant material is, however, collected in Ogle, 1897.

discussion of such topics as the individual senses, sleep, respiration, life and death. Our first task, however, is to review such passages in these treatises as bear directly on the question of the relevance of such researches. Although *PN* contains no methodological programme such as we have in *PA* I, several texts allude to that question.

Thus one passage issues an explicit warning concerning the extent to which it is appropriate to enter into detail on a point of anatomy. This is *Somn.* 458a20f. where Aristotle has been discussing the causes of sleep. He notes at 458a10ff. that waking occurs when (1) digestion has been completed, (2) the heat once more prevails and (3) the more corporeal, and the purer, blood have been separated. The heart, he continues, is the ἀρχή of all the blood: the middle chamber is common to each of the other two, each of which draws from its own vessel (the great vessel and the aorta), and the separation takes place in the middle chamber.[6] But, he goes on, τὸ μὲν διορίζειν περὶ τούτων ἑτέρων ἐστὶ λόγων οἰκειότερον. What he draws back from, here, is a detailed anatomical description of the heart and its vessels. He has noted the one point that is of immediate importance for his account of sleep, namely that there is a separation of blood in the middle chamber of the heart. This passage neither states nor implies that anatomy as such is irrelevant, only that detailed consideration of the heart's anatomy is. We may compare occasions when he simply refers to other treatises, or to the results of dissection, for a more detailed or exact account on a particular point. He does this, for instance, at *Resp.* 478a26ff. on the question of the connections between the heart and the lung. Here too we may distinguish between, on the one hand, the bare fact that there is a connection (a fact that is presupposed in his explanation of the role of breath in cooling the heart) and, on the other, the detailed description of those connections. Similarly at *Resp.* 478a35ff.[7] he

[6] On the discrepancies between this and Aristotle's other accounts of the heart, see pp. 242–4.

[7] I am most grateful to J. Brunschwig for raising the question of the precise sense of the contrast at *Resp.* 478a35f. πρὸς μὲν τὴν ὄψιν ἐκ τῶν ἀνατομῶν δεῖ θεωρεῖν, πρὸς δ' ἀκρίβειαν ἐκ τῶν ἱστοριῶν, and distinguishing the two possibilities, (*a*) that Aristotle is inviting his audience to practise dissection to confirm his account, and (*b*) that he is inviting them to consult anatomical diagrams. As has been noted, e.g. by E. Heitz (who conveniently collected the relevant passages, 1865: 70ff.), when Aristotle refers to ἀνατομαί elsewhere, this is sometimes to actual dissection (e.g. *PA* 677a9, *GA* 746a22, 764a35, 771b32, 779a8), but sometimes to a work, now lost, which evidently contained, and may even have consisted in, diagrams (cf. διαγραφή at *HA* 497a32, 525a8f., cf. τὰ ἐν ταῖς ἀνατομαῖς διαγεγραμμένα at *HA* 566a14f. and *GA* 746a14f. which refers to ἔκ τε τῶν παραδειγματων τῶν ἐν ταῖς ἀνατομαῖς καὶ τῶν ἐν ταῖς ἱστορίαις γεγραμμένων; the fact that at *PA* 684b4 he refers to ἀνατομαί where he has just been describing the *external* parts of the Crustacea suggests that the work contained diagrams based on external observation as well as on dissection). Although the reference to τὰ ἀνατεμνόμενα at *Resp.* 478a27 has been taken, e.g. by W. D. Ross, to relate to dissection, I agree with J. Brunschwig that at 478a35f. it seems more likely that what is being opposed to the exact account of the 'histories' is not the practice of dissecting, but rather anatomical diagrams: what is implied is not that dissection is inexact, but that diagrammatic representations are. One may compare *PA* 680a1ff. where Aristotle contrasts what can be made clear better by a verbal account with what can to sight (τὰ μὲν γὰρ τῷ λόγῳ τὰ δὲ πρὸς τὴν ὄψιν αὐτῶν σαφηνίζειν δεῖ μᾶλλον) although elsewhere he is content enough to refer to ἀνατομαί (with or without the 'histories') for an exact (or more exact) account on an anatomical point (*HA* 511a13f., *PA* 668b28ff., 696b14ff., cf. *HA* 509b22ff.).

refers both to 'the *dissections*' and to 'the *Histories*' on the relation between the heart and the gills in fish, although he gives a summary description || of that relation here.

While it is obviously not to Aristotle's purposes, in *PN*, to present detailed records of dissections (whether his own or other people's), he cites their results, or what he claims as their results, not infrequently. At *Somn.* 456b2, for example, he does so for the point that the heart is the ἀρχή of the φλέβες.[8] At *Juv.* 468b29ff., after remarking that in sanguineous animals the heart comes to be first, he says 'this is clear from what we have observed in those cases where it is possible to see them as they come to be', and there is no need to emphasise the importance of this purported observation as support for his account of the role of the heart.[9] The passage continues: 'so necessarily in bloodless animals also what is analogous to the heart comes to be first'. Here, then, he claims that a point is established by observation in certain classes of sanguineous animals, generalises from this to all sanguineous animals, and then extends the doctrine by analogy to the bloodless animals as well.

As in the zoological treatises proper, so too in *PN*, his careful noting that certain points have not yet been observed should be interpreted against the background of his evident readiness to extrapolate from those data that he believed had been established by observation. Thus at *Somn.* 454b21ff. he calls in λόγος where αἴσθησις fails. Having remarked that almost all animals are clearly seen to sleep, and mentioned that the sleep of 'hard-eyed' creatures and insects is of short duration, he says of the testacea that κατὰ τὴν αἴσθησιν it is not yet clear whether they sleep, but if the λόγος given is trustworthy, it will be believed that they do so.[10] At *Juv.* 469a23ff., in a difficult passage to which I shall return, he states that it is established both κατὰ τὰ φαινόμενα and κατὰ τὸν λόγον that the ἀρχή of both the perceptive and the nutritive soul is in the heart and in the middle of the three main divisions of the body.[11] The λόγος he mentions is that 'we see nature bringing about what is best in all cases so far as possible'. But what counts as φαινόμενα has to be judged from the immediately preceding discussion, where he says that two of the senses evidently stretch to the heart 'so the others necessarily do so also'.[12] Yet the clearest evidence in *PN* for Aristotle recognising that it is important to take account of the data obtained by dissection comes at *Resp.*

[8] Cf. also *Juv.* 468b31ff.

[9] Cf. especially *PA* 665a33ff. and *HA* VI.3, the latter recording sustained observations of the development of a hen's egg including the heart's first appearance as a blood spot that palpitates and moves as though endowed with life (the so-called 'punctum saliens'). Cf. Ogle, 1897: 110 n. 24: 'the heart is not actually the first structure that appears in the embryo, but it is the first part to enter actively into its functions'.

[10] Reading τοῦτο at 454b23, with Bywater, W. D. Ross and others. The argument is that sleep is a necessary affection of the perceptive faculty (which every animal must have).

[11] These are (1) the part by which food is taken in, (2) that by which residues are discharged and (3) what is intermediate between them, see *Juv.* 468a13ff. That the ἀρχή of the nutritive soul is in the centre of the body is said to be established both κατὰ τὴν αἴσθησιν and κατὰ τὸν λόγον at 468a20ff.

[12] *Juv.* 469a12ff., see pp. 237–39.

470b8ff. and 471b23ff. where || he criticises his predecessors for their lack of familiarity with the facts and particularly with the internal organs of animals. In the latter passage he ascribes their mistaken belief that all animals breathe first to their lack of knowledge of internal anatomy (he has been talking about insects and fish particularly) and then to their non-acceptance of the final cause in nature.

But whilst it is not hard to cite texts in *PN*, as in his other works, that acknowledge the value of sensation in general and of dissection in particular, it is now time to consider some examples where we can test the extent to which in practice he appears to have attempted to bring the findings of empirical investigations to bear on the problems discussed in these treatises. Four topics in particular offer opportunities to do so, his accounts of the structure and function of the eye (*Sens.* 2), of the connections between the senses and the common sensorium (in *Juv.* especially), of the nature and function of the brain (*Sens.*, *Somn.*) and of the relations between the lung and the heart and the structure of the latter (*Somn.*, *Resp.*).

In *Sens.* ch. 2 he engages in a general account of the sense-organs, especially the eye. The main ἀπορίαι he mentions for consideration are (1) how the five senses are to be correlated with the four elements (437a19ff.) and (2) why the eye does not see itself (437a26ff.). During the course of his discussion he has occasion to refer to each of the three main parts he usually identifies in the eye, namely the pupil (κόρη, 438a16, b16), the 'so-called black' (τὸ καλούμενον μέλαν i.e. the iris)[13] and 'the white' (438a20, i.e. the visible white surrounding to the iris). There is a brief reference to a, or rather the, membrane (μῆνιγξ) of the eye at 438b2, and to its passages (πόροι) which he says are cut off when a man is wounded on the temple (438b12ff.). He mentions also that water or fluid (ὕδωρ) flows from decomposing eyes (438a17f.), notes that in the case of embryos this fluid is exceptionally cold and glistening (a18f.) and remarks that the eyes of bloodless creatures are σκληρόδερμοι (438a24).

The impression this list of references may give is that Aristotle has been to some pains to collect and take into account relevant anatomical and other data. An analysis of the texts in question reveals, however, how selective and restricted his use of evidence is. Take first the reference to the membrane of the eye at 438b2. Here || he is objecting to various versions of the thesis that vision consists of a coalescence (συμφύεσθαι) of light with light and he asks in particular how the internal light (i.e. within the eye) can coalesce with the external, since the membrane is in between. What is the membrane he is speaking of? In fact we should say that light[14] has to pass through (1) the

[13] 437b1, to be taken, with W. D. Ross, as the iris, not (with Beare, for example, taking καὶ as epexegetic) as 'the central part'. The main parts of the eye are identified at *HA* 491b21f. as τὸ μὲν ὑγρόν, ᾧ βλέπει, κόρη, τὸ δὲ περὶ τοῦτο μέλαν, τὸ δ' ἐκτὸς τούτου λευκόν. Cf. also 492a1ff.

[14] Aristotle himself denies both that light, which is an ἐνέργεια, travels (*De An.* 418b9ff., 20ff., *Sens.* 446b27f.) and that vision takes place because of something issuing from the eye (*Sens.*

transparent cornea, (2) the anterior chamber of the eye and (3) the lens, before it enters (4) the bulb of the eye, which is filled with vitreous humour, at the back of which lie the retina and the optic nerve. Although we have to wait until the Hellenistic biologists for what became the canonical Greek theory of the four main membranes of the eye,[15] we can trace the growth of knowledge of these membranes in earlier writers.[16] Now it is true that if Aristotle's objection to the doctrine of 'coalescence' is, as it appears to be, that it ignores the presence of a solid (even if transparent) barrier, then reference to *any such* barrier will serve his purpose. It is notable, however, that his reference is quite vague. If by 'the membrane' he means the *set of* membranes that envelop the vitreous humour, he does not make this clear. But even if – as is perhaps more likely – he means the outermost membrane (the cornea) alone, to speak of this as 'the' membrane is, to say the least, elliptical.[17]

Precisely similar remarks apply also to the references to the πόροι of the eye at 438b14, where he supports the claim that the perceptive faculty of the soul is not located at the outer extremity of the eye by referring to the case of men wounded on the temple who are blinded when the πόροι of the eye are severed. An interest in the connections between the eye and the brain can be traced back to Alcmaeon[18] and continues in some of the later Presocratics and Hippocratic writers, including some who did not endorse Alcmaeon's view that the brain is the ἡγεμονικόν.[19] In Aristotle there are several general references to the πόροι of the eye in the zoological works,[20] and at *HA*

438a25ff., cf. 437b12ff., *Top.* 105b6f.: rather, according to *Sens.* 438b3ff., it is a process, κίνησις, in the medium that causes sight). Yet dealing especially with the phenomena of reflection he often speaks of sight (ὄψις, that is the visual ray) reaching or not reaching its object (e.g. *Cael.* 290a17ff., *Mete.* III 374b13ff., 378a4ff., cf. 373b2ff.).

15 That is (1) κερατοειδής (corresponding to the cornea and sclera), (2) χοριοειδής or ῥαγοειδής (the chorioid), (3) ἀραχνοειδής or ἀμφιβληστροειδής (the retina) and (4) κρυσταλλοειδής (the capsular sheath of the lens), see, e.g. Rufus, *Onom.* 154, [Rufus], *Anat.* 170ff., Celsus, *De Medicina* VII 7.13, where in each case the work of Herophilus in particular is referred to.

16 The first fairly detailed account of the various membranes in the eye is probably that in *Loc. Hom.* ch. 2 (VI 280.2ff., L) which identifies three such membranes (μήνιγγες), a thick outer one, a thinner middle one and a third inner one 'which guards the moist part' (cf. also *Carn.* ch. 17, VIII 604.21ff.). The exact date of *Loc. Hom.* cannot be determined, nor is it certain that Aristotle knew it. But some interest in the structure of the eye goes right back to Empedocles, to the very fragment quoted by Aristotle at *Sens.* 437b26ff., even though Empedocles does not describe the 'membranes' (μήνιγγες) and 'tissues' (ὀθοναί) he refers to in the eye at all precisely; and later Democritus too not only identified the contents of the eye as water (as Aristotle tells us) but also (according to Theophrastus, *Sens.* para. 50) distinguished between the dense, thin, 'outer membrane', and the porous inner parts.

17 Cf. *De An.* 420a14f. and *GA* 780a26 (where the term is δέρμα) and *GA* 781a20.

18 Chalcidius, *in Ti.* ch. 246, 256.16ff. Waszink (on which see Lloyd, 1975: 115ff. and Mansfeld, 1975: 26ff.), and Theophrastus, *Sens.* 25f.

19 References to connections of some sort between eye and brain (generally φλέβια or φλέβες) are found in, for example, Theophrastus' accounts of Diogenes of Apollonia (*Sens.* 40ff.) and Democritus (*Sens.* 50), in *Loc. Hom.* ch. 2 (VI 278.21ff.) and *Carn.* ch. 17 (VIII 604.21ff.).

20 See especially *PA* 656b16ff., *GA* 743b35ff. At *GA* 744a6ff. he shows some knowledge of the fact that the eyes change position in relation to the brain during the course of the embryo's development (cf. *Sens.* 438b28ff. on the eye being formed from the brain).

495a11ff. three such pairs are distinguished by their sizes, and their courses described. Thus the smallest pair is situated nearest the nostril, they go to the ἐγκέφαλον, are the most widely separated and do not meet: both the other pairs go to the παρεγκεφαλίς, the largest 'run side by side and do not meet', whilst the medium-sized ones meet 'and this is particularly clear in fishes'. The precise interpretation of the details of this text is disputed,[21] but it is || at least possible that by the medium-sized πόροι which meet Aristotle is referring to the optic nerves and their chiasma, although he had, of course, no knowledge of their function *as nerves*,[22] and indeed when he refers to all three pairs of πόροι behind the eye indifferently as πόροι there is nothing to suggest that he differentiated their various functions.

The πόροι referred to at *Sens.* 438b14 might be any of a number of different passages, channels or connections behind the eye.[23] Clearly the text can be taken to refer to what we call the optic nerves (though not, let us repeat, to them understood *as* nerves) But the πόροι might equally well refer to other structures behind the eye, such as the ophthalmic arteries or veins. Whether or not *HA* 495a11ff. was written before *Sens.* 438b14, the account of three separate pairs of πόροι behind the eye provides a clear warning of the dangers of assuming that those mentioned at *Sens.* 438b14 must be identified with the optic nerves. That reference, like the mention of the membrane of the eye at 438b2, is quite vague: once he has given evidence, or what he believes to be evidence, for his immediate point – that the faculty of sensation cannot be located at the outer extremity of the eye – we hear no more of the πόροι.

The main topic around which much of the discussion in *Sens.* ch. 2 centres is what the eye is made of. Aristotle takes some trouble to refute the theory – found in Empedocles and the *Timaeus* – that the eye is fire, and adopts, or rather adapts, Democritus' view that the eye is water, correcting it by adding that vision belongs to the eye not because it is water but because it is transparent (438a12ff.). Again there is an appeal to facts (here ἔργα a17) to support his theory, chiefly the evidence of decomposing eyes and that of the eyes of embryos. Yet no attempt is made to describe the structure of the eye as a whole, although this is, of course, complex. The three main parts Aristotle identifies quite incidentally in the course of this chapter, pupil, iris and white, relate primarily to the superficial appearance of the eye. Apart from the one reference to the membrane of the eye and the one reference to certain πόροι, already mentioned, his remarks on the internal structure of the eye are confined to the point that the pupil, κόρη, consists of water. We may take it that this refers to the vitreous humour that occupies most of the bulb of the eye and which, in certain lesions, might produce || a watery discharge. But there is no mention of the membranes enveloping the vitreous humour

[21] See, e.g., Magnus, 1878: 25f., Ogle, 1882: 176f., and note to *PA* 656b17 in Ogle, 1912, Solmsen, 1961: 173 and Clarke, 1963: 3.

[22] Knowledge of the nervous system as such does not antedate the Hellenistic biologists, see Solmsen, 1961: 150ff.

[23] Cf. Ross, 1906: 143.

(retina, chorioid, sclera), nor of the lens, nor of the anterior chamber between the cornea and the lens. There is, in fact, no mention of most of the parts that seem difficult to identify straightforwardly as water,[24] and no systematic description of the internal structure of the eye as such at all. Whilst evidence is cited for his conclusion, the thesis that the eye is water is clinched by an argument from exhaustion: the eye must admit light and so be transparent; but if transparent, then either water or air; but not air;[25] so water.[26]

The adequacy, or otherwise, of Aristotle's discussion must, to be sure, be judged in relation to his particular, explicit, concerns. The problem he poses at the outset of the chapter and returns to deal with at some length at 438b16–439a1 is how the five senses are to be correlated with the four simple bodies. For these purposes identifying water as the main constituent in the eye enables some sort of answer to be given so far as that sense-organ is concerned. Even so, the impression of confidence Aristotle gives in moving to his conclusion that the eye is water is only possible because of the superficiality of his account.

To recapitulate: no attempt is made to describe the internal structure and relations of the eye, nor to investigate its functioning;[27] explicit appeals to evidence are made on a number of occasions, but references to anatomical points are generally vague to the point of serious obscurity. So far as this chapter of *Sens.* is concerned, there is no direct evidence that Aristotle had investigated the eye by dissection. Speculation about πόροι behind the eye antedates Aristotle, and his reference to them comes in a passage where he is discussing wounds sustained in battle; the evidence of water flowing from the eye also comes from the observation of lesions; and even the reference to the coldness of the fluid from the eyes of embryos could again come from observation of a lesion, rather than from deliberate dissection. Such empirical evidence as is used in *Sens.* ch. 2 could have been collected without recourse to deliberate research. We have, then, three possibilities: either (*a*) at this stage Aristotle had not attempted to dissect the eye; or if he had, then either (*b*) his dissection was confined to the confirmation of the presence of water in the eye, or (*c*) he ignored such other findings || as complicated the answer to the question of the nature of its constitution.

My second main example concerns Aristotle's doctrine that the heart is the

[24] The 'white' is, however, said to be fat and oily at 438a20f. when he speaks of its role as protection for the fluid of the eye.

[25] Air is rejected partly on the grounds that water is εὐφυλακτότερον and εὐπιλητότερον, 438a15f.

[26] See 438a15ff. and b6ff.: ἀνάγκη ἄρα ὕδωρ εἶναι, ἐπειδὴ οὐκ ἀήρ (W. D. Ross: other editors read καὶ ἀνάγκη κτλ.).

[27] Yet elsewhere Aristotle quite often refers to the effects of maiming on an animal's vital functions (e.g. *Juv.* 468b15, *IA* 708b4ff., *GA* 774b31ff., *HA* 519a27ff., and many passages referring to insects living when cut up), and although many of his observations may well have been carried out on animals that had become mutilated naturally, the frequency of the references may suggest some deliberate human intervention.

common sensorium. In a passage that has already been mentioned, *Juv.* 469a10ff. he argues that

> what is responsible for the senses in all the sanguineous animals is in this [the heart]; for the common sense-organ of all the sense-organs is necessarily in it. We see two [of the senses], taste and touch, evidently extending there,[28] so the others necessarily do so too. For it is possible for the other sense-organs to cause movement in it, but these [taste and touch] do not extend to the upper region [of the body] at all. And apart from these considerations, if life is located in this part for all animals, clearly the sensitive principle necessarily is also.

He goes on to acknowledge (469a21f.) that the organs of sight, hearing and smell are located in the brain,[29] but he emphases both at *Juv.* 469a12f. and elsewhere that taste and touch 'extend to' the heart, which is, as he repeatedly states, the ἀρχή of all sensation.[30]

Passages in the zoological treatises help to clarify some of the details of Aristotle's views on the transmission of sensation. In *GA* 743b35ff., especially, he says that the sense-organ of the eye is

> like the other sense-organs, set upon πόροι. Whereas the organ of touch and of taste is directly the body or some part of the body of animals,[31] smell and hearing are πόροι connecting with the outer air and full of connate pneuma, and ending in the φλέβια that, coming from the heart, stretch out round the brain.[32]

Again in a difficult and probably corrupt passage at *GA* 781a20ff. he appears to say that the πόροι of all the sense-organs extend to the heart and to suggest that those of hearing end at the part where the connate pneuma causes either pulsation or respiration.[33] Finally at *PA* 656b16ff. he speaks more directly of the πόροι from the eyes going to the φλέβες around the brain and of a πόρος from the ears going to 'the back part'.[34] Although there are inconsistencies between these texts, and a good deal remains uncertain, Aristotle's view of sight, hearing and smell is that all three have πόροι of some sort, and from *GA* 743b35ff. it appears to be certain φλέβια (all of which originate in the

[28] δύο δὲ φανερῶς ἐνταῦθα συντεινούσας ὁρῶμεν, 469a12f., cf. a20f. αἱ μὲν τῶν αἰσθήσεων φανερῶς συντείνουσι πρὸς τὴν καρδίαν.

[29] Cf. *Sens.* 438b25ff.: the organ of smell has its proper place near the brain, a cold organ, since cold matter is potentially hot (and smell belongs to fire, b20f.), and 444a8ff.: the ability to perceive odours that are fragrant *per se* (which he believes man alone to possess) is a safeguard to health, for man's brain is particularly cold and so particularly in need of the compensatory heat from such smells. Cf. a similar argument on the eye, *Sens.* 438b27ff. and *PA* 656a37ff.

[30] Cf. also *Sens.* 439a1f. and, e.g., *PA* 656a27ff. (which refers to a discussion ἐν τοῖς περὶ αἰσθήσεως).

[31] Aristotle sometimes says that the sense-organ of touch is flesh or what is analogous to it (e.g. *PA* 647a19ff.), though he sometimes describes flesh as the medium, not the organ, or touch (*PA* 656b34ff., *De An.* 423b22ff., cf. *PA* 653b24–30, where both suggestions are made, and see Ogle, 1912: note *ad loc*).

[32] *HA* 514a21f. also speaks of φλέβες ending in the sense-organs.

[33] The difficulties of the passage are fully discussed by Peck, 1943: 563f. The reference to the part where the pneuma causes either pulsation or respiration is, as Platt (1912: note *ad loc.*) pointed out, unintelligible, since no animal that respires lacks a heart. The doctrine concerning the pores of hearing here evidently contradicts both *GA* 743b35ff. and *PA* 656b16ff.

[34] Cf. Clarke and Stannard, 1963: 134ff.

heart) that provide the connection he needs between the sense-organs in the head and the common sensorium. The reference to the connate || pneuma in that passage suggests that it acts as the vehicle by which the movements in the sense-organs are transmitted to the heart, although, to be sure, Aristotle does not commit himself to an explicit statement to that effect.[35]

Yet if the main outlines of his doctrine are tolerably clear, the difficulties it presents are formidable. This is not one of those occasions when he was simply not aware of another, alternative view, at least on the question of the common sensorium. On the contrary, he refers to the doctrine – which goes back to Alcmaeon and was endorsed by Plato – that the brain is the seat of sensation both briefly in our passage at *Juv.* 469a21f. and at some length elsewhere, for example *PA* II.10, 656a15ff.[36] But so far as his own doctrine goes, the confidence with which he claims that touch and taste evidently support it is striking. Taste is included presumably on the assumption that it is a modification of touch.[37] But as for touch itself, in so far as flesh is either the organ or the medium of this sense, there is, we might think, no more reason for saying that touch extends to the heart than to any other part of the body. His only anatomical grounds for specifying the heart is that it is the source of all the blood-vessels, and this same point provides his main counter to the apparent difficulty that the organs of sight, hearing and smell are located in the head. Once again his scattered anatomical references are vague. Matching his remarks about the πόροι of the senses against possible structures is – beyond a certain, rather superficial, point – impossible.[38] We have already noted (pp. 234–5) the difficulty of identifying the πόροι of the eye. Similarly when he speaks of a πόρος leading back from the ear (*PA* 656b18f.) and ending in the φλέβια round the brain (*GA* 744a1ff.) it is not at all clear precisely what he may be referring to. The external acoustic meatus continues behind and below the tympanic membrane[39] into the pharyngo-tympanic or Eustachian tube, leading, of course, not to the back of the brain but down into the pharynx.[40] Nor is it easy to identify an obvious candidate

[35] The alternative would be to consider that the blood itself transmits the movements from the sense-organs (as might be thought to be suggested at *Insomn.* 461b11f., 462a8ff.). But blood itself lacks sensation (as he often says, e.g. *PA* 666a16f.) although sensation is confined to those parts that have blood (e.g. *PA* 656b20f.).

[36] Among the objections he raises to this view are (1) that the brain itself is devoid of sense (*PA* 652b4f., 656a23f.) and (2) that it has no continuity with the organs of sense (*PA* 652b2ff.) and he was no doubt influenced also by his view that the brain is cold and bloodless (its function being to counteract the heat of the heart, see pp. 239–40) and by his observation that not all animals have a brain or analogous organ (see Ogle, 1882: 172f. and 1912: note to 656a24).

[37] Elsewhere, however, he recognises the tongue as the organ of taste, for example in his discussion of the dual nature of the sense-organs, *PA* 656b36f.

[38] One major complication is that the term πόρος is so general and can refer to structures as diverse as the nostrils and infra-sensible apertures in the skin.

[39] Cf. the reference to the μῆνιγξ at *De An.* 420a14.

[40] As indeed is recognised by Aristotle at *HA* 492a19f. That he has some idea of the internal structure of the ear is clear from his comparing it with a trumpet shell (*HA* 492a16f., cf. also the reference to ἕλικες at *De An.* 420a13) and at *HA* 492a20 (cf. 514a15ff.) he speaks of a φλέψ from the brain to the ear.

for this πόρος from among the structures behind the middle or inner ear.[41] As to the sense of smell, while the passages connecting with the external air (*GA* 744a1ff.) are obviously the nostrils, it is again in no way clear what precise structure (if any) he had in mind when he implied that these πόροι too end in φλέβια round the brain. ‖

Although the question of the common sensorium and its connections with the sense-organs had been much discussed before Aristotle, and it was certainly open to him to investigate aspects of this problem by dissection, there is little enough evidence, in *Juv.*[42] or in the zoological treatises, of his attempting to do so. In this case his own doctrine was principally based on the argument that the ἀρχή of sensation must be identified with that of life itself. As he puts it at *Juv.* 469a17f., 'if life is located in this part for all animals, clearly the sensitive principle necessarily is also', and elsewhere he often claims that there must be a single principle of life, motion, sensation, nutrition and growth.[43] Now the view that the heart is the principle of life is, as we noted, given empirical support in the supposed observation that it is the first part of the embryo to develop,[44] and that it is the first part to contain blood is cited as evidence that it is the seat of sensation, for example at *PA* 666a10–b1.[45] But given first that he believed there was an overwhelming theoretical reason for holding that the heart is the seat of sensation, and secondly that *some* connection between each of the sense-organs and the heart could be found, we may suspect that even quite detailed knowledge of the structures associated with the sense-organs would not have shaken his conviction in the correctness of his doctrine.

My next example relates to Aristotle's views on the nature and function of the brain.[46] The opposition between brain and heart is one of the corner-stones of his physiology. Thus according to *Sens.* 438b29ff.[47] the brain is the 'most fluid' and the coldest part of the body (it is proportionately larger in

[41] Clarke and Stannard, 1963: 146ff., however, suggest that the idea may have originated from observations of the endolymphatic duct and sacs of a turtle or similar reptile.

[42] *Juv.* ch. 3 ends with a reference to another discussion of why some senses clearly extend to the heart, while others are located in the head. This is taken by Ogle and W. D. Ross, for example, to refer to *PA* II.10, 656a27–657a12. Yet 656a27ff. begins with a reference to 'the works on sensation' (see above, n.30) and 656b16ff. is, as we have seen (p. 237), not much fuller or clearer than *Juv.* on points of anatomy.

[43] E.g. *Somn.* 455b34ff., *PA* 647a21ff., 665a10ff., 666b13ff. Feelings of pleasure and pain and so on, as well as sense-perceptions, are located in the heart, e.g. at *PA* 666a11ff.; 669a19ff.

[44] Cf. above p. 232. At *GA* 743b25ff. he reverses the usual argument: because the heart is the seat of sensation, it comes to be first.

[45] Other factors that weighed with Aristotle are that the heart or analogous organ is present in all animals, and that it is in the central position in the body, in the place appropriate to the controlling part.

[46] Cf. Clarke and Stannard, 1963: 130ff. I am grateful to Professor P. Moraux for drawing attention to the important criticisms already mounted by Galen (e.g. *De Usu Partium* VIII 3) of Aristotle's views on the function of the brain (see Moraux, 1976: 127–46).

[47] Cf. *Somn.* 457b29f. and many other passages, e.g. *GA* 782b17.

man than in any other animal, and particularly cold),[48] and the heart as the hottest part of the body, is said at *Sens.* 439a2ff. to balance the brain. The first problem here is the account of the brain itself. Whilst in passages in *HA* especially he distinguishes two membranes, ὑμένες, that envelop the brain[49] and identifies the 'so-called παρεγκεφαλίς' (i.e. cerebellum),[50] he adopts the view that the back of the head is empty and hollow in all animals.[51] Although various conjectures have been made as to the empirical basis of this doctrine,[52] it may be that his adopting it owes more to the fact that a similar view appears in some of the medical writers[53] than to any observations he had carried || out himself. Another puzzle is his claim that the brain is bloodless and has no φλέψ in it.[54] Finally there is the doctrine of the special coldness of the brain. Even when we bear in mind the complexity of Aristotle's use of 'hot' and 'cold', and his careful distinctions between acquired and innate, accidental and essential, potential and actual, heat and cold,[55] his clear statement that the brain is cold 'to the touch' is not one that can have been based on, or checked by, an examination of a recently dead subject.[56] Yet the doctrine of the coldness of the brain is fundamental to his conception of its function, which he describes as being to preserve the whole body by counteracting the heat of the heart.[57]

One of the many contexts in which this theory is applied is in the account of sleep and waking, which he explains in terms of an interplay of hot and cold, specifically in terms of a concentration (σύνοδος) or recoil (ἀντιπερίστασις) of the hot when matter from the lower region is carried up to the brain and cooled there. While the core of his theory is not in doubt, some of its details are hazy. Thus there is some fluctuation (though perhaps

[48] *Sens.* 444a8ff., 28ff. (see above, n. 29) and cf. *HA* 494b27ff. The doctrine of a cold brain appears also in the Hippocratic works *Liqu.* ch. 2, VI 122.3ff., and *Carn.* ch. 4, VIII 588.14ff.

[49] *HA* 494b29ff. At *PA* 652b30 and *GA* 744a10, however, he speaks of a single μῆνιγξ round the brain. [50] E.g *HA* 494b31f, 495a12. [51] *HA* 491a34f., 494b33ff., *PA* 656b12f.

[52] Thompson, 1910: note to *HA* 491b1, suggested that the view may have arisen from an association of hearing with air and a recognition of the fact that the auditory region of the skull contains air-spaces. Ogle, 1882: 174ff. and 1912: note to *PA* 656b13, noted that a similar view is found in the Hippocratic writers but added that it may have derived support from an examination of the brain of cold-blooded animals (fish and reptiles) and remarked that the observation, in *GA* 744a17, that the volume of the brain changes as the embryo develops suggests that Aristotle had seen this in embryonic fish.

[53] E.g. *Morb.* II, ch. 8, VII 16.11ff., cf. *VC* ch. 2, III 188. 11f., 190.12f., 192.10ff.

[54] E.g. *HA* 495a4ff., 514a18f., *PA* 652a35f. There are, however, φλέβια in the membrane round the brain from both the 'great blood-vessel' (i.e. Vena Cava) and the aorta, e.g. *PA* 652b27ff. Cf. *Sens.* 444a10ff. which speaks of the blood in the φλέβια round the brain as 'thin', 'pure' and 'easily cooled'. [55] See especially *PA* II.2.

[56] κατὰ τὴν θίξιν *PA* 652a34f., cf. *HA* 495a6. As Payne, 1897: 39 n.1, and Ogle, 1912: note *ad loc.*, remark, the doctrine of the coldness of the brain continued to be taught by Harvey in his *Prelectiones Anatomiae Universalis, Lectures on the Whole of Anatomy* (1616), (O'Malley, Poynter and Russell, 1961) even though some thirty years previously Piccolomini (whose *Anatomicae Praelectiones* (Rome, 1586) was well known to Harvey) had recorded an experiment on a dog (whether living or dead he does not say) in which he found that the heart and the brain felt almost equally hot to the touch (O'Malley, Poynter and Russell, 1961: 275).

[57] E.g. *PA* 652b6f., 653a32ff., cf. *Sens.* 439a2ff.

no conflict) in the terms in which he describes the material cause of sleep. Sometimes he speaks of the evaporation from the food,[58] or, more loosely, of the food itself;[59] he distinguishes the liquid[60] and the bodily[61] parts of the evaporation, and from 458a2ff. he introduces a further distinction between two kinds of evaporation, the περιττωματική (responsible for catarrhs) and the τρόφιμος (responsible for sleep).[62] More importantly, although he often speaks of the φλέβες or πόροι which act as communicating links between heart and brain, these references are, with one exception, all quite unspecific. The exception is 455b6ff., which mentions the φλέβες in the neck which, when pressed, cause loss of sensation.[63] Elsewhere his references are indeterminate, and this is, perhaps, all the more surprising in view of the fact that he several times adduces the 'thinness' and 'narrowness' of the φλέβες round the brain (along with its coldness) as a contributory factor in causing sleep.[64] Yet as with his remarks on the channels of sensation, so too here Aristotle appears satisfied with the fact that links of some sort can be found between heart and brain and attempts a detailed account of their anatomy.

My final example concerns Aristotle's views on the relations between || the lung and the heart and on the structure of the latter. An impressive range of anatomical and zoological data is cited in the course of his account of respiration. He takes his examples from a wide variety of animal species, noting, for instance, that 'no animal has yet been seen' that has both lung and gills,[65] and observing a contrast between tortoises and frogs on the one hand and fish on the other in that the former discharge air when forcibly suffocated in water, while in the latter no such discharge occurs.[66] He distinguishes inspiration through the nostrils and through the windpipe (ἀρτηρία), knows that only the latter is essential for life, and specifies that in the former too the air passes through the channel beside the uvula at the back of the roof of the mouth.[67] At *Resp.* 476a31ff. he gives a clear, if brief, account of the function of the epiglottis and notes that in birds and oviparous quadrupeds, where the epiglottis is absent, this function is performed by the

[58] *Somn.* 456b19f., 33f., 457a25, 29, b14, cf. πνεῦμα at 457a12.
[59] *Somn.* 457a5.
[60] *Somn.* 456b25, reading τό τε, cf. 457a19, 24. At *PA* 653a12f. he speaks of the ἐπίρρυσις of the blood from the food.
[61] *Somn.* 456b25, cf. 457b20, 458a26.
[62] 'The hot' is sometimes what is carried up to the brain (*Somn.* 458a1, cf. 456b21f., 457b1), sometimes what causes (other) substances to rise (*Somn.* 458a27 of the connate heat).
[63] Cf. *HA* 514a2ff. where the φλέβες in question are named σφαγίτιδες.
[64] General references to the φλέβες occur at *Somn.* 457a13 (where he is comparing epilepsy with sleep) and b21. At 457a21ff. he explains why the ἀδηλόφλεβοι sleep a lot in terms of the narrowness of their φλέβες – while the φλεβώδεις do not because of the εὔροια of their φλέβες (W. D. Ross reads πόροι). Again at 458a5ff. he cites the thinness and narrowness of the φλέβες round the brain as contributing to its being kept cool and its not receiving the evaporation easily. Cf. 457b13ff. referring to the cooling of the πόροι and places in the brain.
[65] *Resp.* 476a6f. Ogle, 1897: 125 n. 106, pointed out that there are exceptions to this general rule.
[66] *Resp.* 471a31ff. This was one of the points that led him to conclude that fish do not respire, but effect the necessary cooling of their vital heat directly by the intake of water, e.g. *Resp.* 476a1f.
[67] *Resp.* 473a17ff., 474a7ff., 17ff., criticising Empedocles.

contraction of the windpipe.[68] We have seen that both in the context of the structure of the heart, and in that of the relation between heart and lung or gills, Aristotle deliberately draws back from a detailed anatomical description.[69] On the other hand it is in connection with the organs of respiration that he particularly criticises earlier writers for their ignorance of internal anatomy, and these passages suggest that he is confident enough of the accuracy of his own views on this topic even if he does not feel it necessary to go into them at length.[70] Since he believes that the function of respiration is to cool the vital heat,[71] his theory requires some connection between heart and lung or gills. So far as his account of fish goes, where he speaks of an αὐλὸς φλεβονευρώδης running from the heart to the middle 'where the gills join' (*Resp.* 478b7ff.), this can be vindicated in the main.[72] Yet when we follow up what he has to say on the links between heart and lung[73] in other sanguineous animals, we encounter problems.[74] Both at *HA* 496a22ff. and at 513a35ff. we are told that there are connections between *all three* cavities of the heart and the lung. Yet in animals with lungs, the lungs are directly connected with – at most – two vessels of the heart. Thus in man the pulmonary artery (divided into right and left branches) and the pulmonary veins (divided into right and left pairs) are connected with the right ventricle and the left atrium respectively. It is true that in both passages || Aristotle notes that the connection is distinct in only one case – which suggests that his theory of three connections is partly based on inference. Yet the reference to the distinctness of only one πόρος is itself strange since in most large vivipara the pulmonary veins are not much less prominent structures than the pulmonary arteries.

This takes us to the vexed question of his account of the heart itself.[75] Apart from *Somn.* 458a15ff., the three main texts that contain descriptions of the heart are *HA* I.17, *HA* III.3 and *PA* III.4. In each of these texts he speaks of three cavities, a right, a middle and a left, although at *HA* 513a27ff. and *PA* 666b21f. he suggests that in some smaller animals the heart has only two

[68] Cf. *HA* 495b17ff., where he rejects the view (found in some Hippocratic writers as well as in Plato, *Ti.* 70C, 91A) that drink goes to the lungs via the windpipe.

[69] See above p. 231 on *Somn.* 458a20f., *Resp.* 478a26ff., 35ff.

[70] See above pp. 232–3 on *Resp.* 470b8ff., 471b23ff.

[71] He cites as evidence for this (1) that exhaled breath is hotter than inhaled, e.g. *Resp.* 472b33ff., and (2) that we breathe more frequently in hot weather, 472a31ff.

[72] See Ogle, 1897: 131 nn. 135 and 136. Cf. also *HA* 507a5ff.

[73] A minor difficulty is his statement that the lung is single: he remarks, however, that the lung has a tendency to be double, even if he goes on to say that this is least discernible in man (*HA* 495a32ff., cf. *PA* 669b23ff. and *HA* 513b16ff.).

[74] *HA* 495b14ff. appears to suggest that when the windpipe is distended with air, the air can actually be seen entering the heart (if αὐτήν at b16 refers, as is generally thought, to the heart). *HA* 496a27ff. notes more exactly, however, that there is no common πόρος between the ducts from the heart and those from the windpipe, although the former receive air from the latter διὰ τὴν σύναψιν.

[75] The problem has been extensively discussed by, for example, Huxley, 1880: 1ff., Ogle, 1882: 197ff., Thompson, 1910: note to *HA* 513a35, Platt, 1921: 521ff., Byl, 1968: 467ff., Shaw, 1972: 355ff. and Harris, 1973: 121ff.

cavities, and in others only one.[76] Moreover the *HA* and *PA* passages agree in identifying the right hand cavity as the largest, the left as the smallest and the middle as intermediate in size.[77] Since at *HA* 513b1–5 (cf. 496a25ff.) the aorta is clearly stated to be attached to the middle cavity, and the great blood-vessel (i.e. Vena Cava) to the largest, right cavity, this has been taken to establish that the middle cavity there is what we term the left ventricle (the right atrium being either deemed to belong to this cavity, or considered as the dilated junction of the superior and inferior Vena Cava).

There can be little doubt that, as D'Arcy Thompson put it,[78] the account of the vascular system 'is so far true to nature that it is clear evidence of minute inquiry'.[79] At the same time, as Thompson also recognised, obscurities and inconsistencies remain,[80] and one apparent inconsistency between *Somn.* and the zoological treatises particularly concerns us. This relates to the identification of the three cavities themselves, for whereas *HA* 513b1ff. clearly states that the aorta is attached to the middle cavity, *Somn.* 458a16–19 no less clearly implies that the aorta is connected to the left cavity. Yet what *Somn.* has in common with the accounts in the zoological works is as revealing as what it does not. The role of the heart as ἀρχή of the blood-vessels is fundamental and maintained consistently throughout.[81] But when the heart has several cavities (and in Aristotle's view it is better to have more than one) the problem of the location of the ἀρχή arises. Now despite the evident divergence between *Somn.* and *HA* III.3 on the identity of

[76] The number of cavities in the heart is indeed less than four in some reptiles and fish, though the number does not depend on the size of the animal, see Ogle, 1882: 199.

[77] *HA* 496a20ff., 513a32ff., *PA* 666b35ff. *Somn.* is silent on the relative sizes of the three cavities.

[78] 1910: note to *HA* 513a35.

[79] Apart from his clear account of many particular blood-vessels, he draws a general distinction between the textures of the Vena Cava and aorta, describing the former as ὑμενώδης and δερματώδης, and the latter as narrower and σφόδρα νευρώδης, *HA* 513b7ff. He speaks of the sinews (νεῦρα) within the heart (though he does not identify its valves) at *HA* 496a13, 515a28ff., *PA* 666b13f.; and he knows that the heart in man is inclined to the left side of the body, e.g. *HA* 496a15f., *PA* 666b6ff.

[80] The chief difficulty in the fullest account, *HA* III.3 relates to the two sentences 513b2ff. and b7, in which he appears to say first that the great blood-vessel passes διὰ τοῦ κοίλου τοῦ μέσου, i.e. through the middle cavity (not, as Ogle translated, 'though the centre of the cavity') and then that it stretches to or towards (εἰς) the aorta from the heart. The only way to begin to square these statements with anatomical fact is to suppose that in both cases he is describing the foetal heart. Thus 513b2ff. might be taken to refer to the foramen ovale (by which blood passes direct from the right to the left atrium) and b7 to the ductus arteriosus (by which the pulmonary artery communicates with the aorta), both structures present in the foetus which close up after birth. Although it has been argued, most recently by Shaw, that Aristotle had investigated the foetal heart, what we have in these passages seems more likely to be either a mistake, or more probably, a corrupt text. Most modern editors take 513b7 at least as corrupt, and the transposition or deletion of μέσου at b3 would allow the φλέψ mentioned there to be taken to refer either, as Ogle wanted, to the pulmonary artery, or to the superior Vena Cava.

[81] E.g. *Somn.* 458a15f., *HA* 513a21f., *PA* 665b14ff., 666a6ff., 31ff. *PA* 666b24f. states that the blood comes to be first in the heart, though *Somn.* 458a17f. seems to envisage the possibility of the right and left cavities drawing from (δέχεσθαι) the great blood-vessel and aorta respectively.

the ‖ cavities, *Somn.* agrees with *PA* that the middle cavity is 'common to' the other two. At *PA* 666b32ff., having argued that it is better to have two cavities than one on the grounds that the main blood-vessels, the great blood-vessel and the aorta, are two, he goes on to say that it is better still to have three cavities, so that the middle and odd one can be the common ἀρχή for the other two. Again in *Somn.* 458a16f. the middle cavity is said to be common to the other two, and the place where the separation of the purer and less pure blood occurs – despite the fact that the middle cavity is not the same cavity as that called by that name in *HA* III.3. While there is, as we said, ample evidence of close observation, using dissection, in Aristotle's accounts of the heart, he is also concerned, especially but by no means exclusively in *PA*, with questions of value, pointing out, for instance, that the heart, as the noblest organ, occupies the noblest position in the body.[82] His doctrine of the middle cavity as common to the other two reflects this preoccupation,[83] and if, as seems likely in view of the agreement on the relative dimensions of the three cavities, the account of them in *PA* III.4 is to be equated with that in *HA* III.3, it would appear that the doctrine of the middle cavity as ἀρχή persisted even when his views on the identity of the cavities changed. In this case, what we have is not, or not only, the result of direct observation,[84] but the application of preconceived ideas concerning the superiority of the middle and its fitness to be ἀρχή.[85] Indeed one might even conjecture that concern with the question of identifying the common ἀρχή in the multi-cavitied heart was one factor that prevented Aristotle from seeing the heart as a two-sided, four-vesselled organ.[86]

The weakness of the work of Aristotle's predecessors in anatomy is apparent both from his reports and from the Hippocratic writers. We can be

[82] E.g. *PA* 665b20ff. and cf. 666b6ff. for the explanation he gives for the heart being on the (inferior) left side in man.

[83] He also says that the blood in the middle cavity is purer than in the other two, and of intermediate heat, *PA* 667a4ff.

[84] Whether we take the middle cavity as (*a*) the left ventricle (as suggested by *HA* 513b4ff.) or (*b*) the left atrium (when, as in *Somn.* 458a17ff., the aorta is deemed to be connected with the left cavity, i.e. left ventricle), the idea that the middle cavity is common to the other two faces the major difficulty that the septum of the heart acts as a solid barrier between the two sides – although the difficulty for (*b*) would be mitigated if we are prepared to believe that he may observed the foramen ovale in the foetal heart (see above, n. 80 on *HA* 513b2ff.).

[85] See especially Byl, 1968: 467ff.

[86] The question arises whether the divergence between *Somn.* 458a16ff. and *HA* III.3 is of such a kind as to support a particular hypothesis about their relative chronology. Firm conclusions are, no doubt, impossible, especially since the account in *Somn.* is so brief. But it might be argued that the connection between the middle cavity and the aorta in *HA* III.3 is an embarrassment for the doctrine of the middle cavity as common to the other two, since it associates that cavity with one of the two main blood-vessels (and indeed in contrast to *PA* III.4, that doctrine is not actually stated in *HA* III.3). If so, it might be thought more likely that the simple schema of *Somn.* represents the earlier view, later modified in the more complex account of *HA* III.3, rather than that the latter account was earlier and was later simplified to fit his preconceptions concerning the middle cavity as ἀρχή, cf. Platt, 1921: 522.

reasonably certain both that dissection had been practised before Aristotle, and that its use was very far from extensive.[87] Thus his comments on earlier views of the blood-vessels in *HA* III.2, 511b13ff., make it clear first that some of his predecessors had dissected animals in this connection, and secondly that this was not the only method they had used, since some investigators relied on what would be observed externally by examining emaciated living men. The accounts he goes on to ascribe to Syennesis of Cyprus, Diogenes || of Apollonia and Polybus in particular bear out his general strictures on their work.[88]

Aristotle's own use of dissection, and the range of his zoological researches, were undoubtedly far wider than those of any earlier writer. Nevertheless the evidence we have considered concerning some problems tackled in *PN* provides grounds for caution. Although a fair body of zoological data is deployed in *PN*, and some of his anatomical references are accurate enough, some others are extremely vague. In part this can be said to be because he deliberately omits detail that is irrelevant to his immediate concerns: but in part the vagueness of some of his accounts reflects the imprecision of his ideas or the limitations of his knowledge. Although in one case (the account of the three chambers of the heart) there is an apparent conflict between passages in *Somn.* and the zoological works, and it is possible that these texts correspond to different stages in his investigation of that problem, there are several instances where the supplementary material on anatomical points that is provided by the zoological treatises is far from removing all the obscurities or difficulties in Aristotle's views. Thus all his references to communications between the heart and the sense-organs, and between the heart and the brain, suffer from a greater or lesser degree of imprecision. In such cases a developmental hypothesis does not resolve our problem, though that is not to deny that such hypotheses may have a bearing on the issue.

PA I.5, whenever it was composed, suggests an open-ended programme of research in zoology. Yet the difficulties of implementing any such programme were immense. It is all too easy for us to assume that once the method of dissection[89] had begun to be employed on particular topics, it would rapidly be applied systematically and on a large scale. Yet not only were the practical difficulties severe,[90] but dissection had always to be guided by an idea of what to look for and what there was to find. So far as the evidence we have taken from *PN* goes, this shows the overriding importance of theoretical considerations, both in determining the problems to be investigated (as when he deals with the question of the constitution of the eye very largely in terms of the problem of correlating five senses with four elements) and in

[87] See Lloyd, 1975: 128ff.

[88] On pre-Aristotelian accounts of the blood-vessels, see Harris, 1973: chh. 1–3.

[89] That is animal dissection: human dissection where other inhibiting factors were at work, does not antedate the Alexandrian biologists, Herophilus and Erasistratus.

[90] Thus Aristotle mentions the difficulty of observing the courses of blood-vessels when the blood has drained from them in dead specimens, *HA* 511b14ff.

interpreting the findings of those investigations (as in the interpretation of the role of the chambers of the || heart, or that of the function of the various ducts he saw as the links between different parts or organs in the body). In the *PN* Aristotle cites anatomical and zoological data quite freely, and in places quite effectively, both to disprove his opponents' theories and to support his own. Yet in the latter connection the role of observation is rather to corroborate, than to test, his theories – let alone to attempt to falsify them. While some of his remarks may create the superficial appearance that he was drawing on a considerable body of fairly detailed and thorough research, an examination of how anatomical evidence is used in the cases we have discussed shows that this appearance can, on occasion, be misleading. On certain physiological problems – such as the temperature of the brain – he seems not to have attempted to check his theory directly; and on others his investigations were sometimes quite restricted, being indeed, in some cases, confined to providing the barest anatomical grounds to justify his theories.

REFERENCES

Byl, S. (1968) 'Note sur la place du cœur et la valorisation de la ΜΕΣΟΤΗΣ dans la biologie d'Aristote', *L'Antiquité Clasique* 37: 467–76

Clarke, E. (1963) 'Aristotelian concepts of the form and function of the brain', *Bulletin of the History of Medicine* 37: 1–14

Clarke, E., and Stannard, J. (1963) 'Aristotle on the anatomy of the brain', *Journal of the History of Medicine* 18

Harris, C. R. S. (1973) *The Heart and the Vascular System in Ancient Greek Medicine from Alcmaeon to Galen* (Oxford)

Heitz, E. (1865) *Die verlorenen Schriften des Aristoteles* (Leipzig)

Huxley, T. H. (1880) 'On certain errors respecting the structure of the heart attributed to Aristotle', *Nature* 21

Lloyd, G. E. R. (1975) 'Alcmaeon and the early history of dissection', *Sudhoffs Archiv* 59: 113–47

Magnus, H. (1878) *Die Anatomie des Auges bei den Griechen und Römern* (Leipzig)

Mansfeld, J. (1975) 'Alcmaeon: "Physikos" or physician?', in *Kephalaion, Studies in Greek Philosophy and its Continuation Offered to C. J. de Vogel*, edd. J. Mansfeld and L. M. de Rijk (Assen)

Moraux, P. (1976) 'Galien et Aristote', in *Images of Man in Ancient and Medieval Thought. Studia G. Verbeke ... dicata* (Louvain), 127–46

Ogle, W. (1882) *Aristotle on the Parts of Animals* (London)

(1897) *Aristotle on Youth and Old Age, Life and Death and Respiration* (London)

(1912) *De Partibus Animalium*, in *The Works of Aristotle translated into English*, edd. J. A. Smith and W. D. Ross, vol. v (Oxford)

O'Malley, C. D., Poynter, F. N. L., and Russell, K. F., edd., (1961) *Harvey, Praelectiones Anatomiae Universalis, Lectures on the Whole of Anatomy* (Berkeley)

Payne, J. F. (1897) *Harvey and Galen* (London)

Peck, A. L. (1943) *Aristotle, Generation of Animals*, Loeb edn (London and Cambridge, MA)

Platt, A. (1912) *De Generatione Animalium*, in *The Works of Aristotle translated into English*, edd. J. A. Smith and W. D. Ross, vol. v (Oxford)

(1921) 'Aristotle on the heart', in *Studies in the History and Method of Science*, ed. C. Singer, vol. II (Oxford)

Ross, G. R. T. (1906) *Aristotle De Sensu and De Memoria* (Cambridge)

Shaw, J. R. (1972) 'Models for cardiac structure and function in Aristotle', *Journal of the History of Biology* 5: 355–88

Solmsen, F. (1961) 'Greek philosophy and the discovery of the nerves', *Museum Helveticum* 18: 150–67 and 169–97

Thompson, D'A. W. (1910) *Historia Animalium* in *The Works of Aristotle translated into English*, edd. J. A. Smith and W. D. Ross, vol. IV (Oxford)

11

SAVING THE APPEARANCES

INTRODUCTION

The debates between the opposing schools of thought in philosophy of science that can be labelled, very broadly, 'instrumentalist' and 'realist', have had momentous repercussions on the interpretation of ancient Greek science. Of course these two labels have been used to characterise not just, in either case, a single well-defined thesis, but rather a broad spectrum of positions. However the fundamental issues on which they are divided may be represented as the question of the constraints on a scientific theory. Is it enough, as the instrumentalists hold, that a scientific theory should yield predictions that correspond to the observed data (indeed some hold that it is not just enough for them to do so, but the most that can be demanded)? The theories will then be calculating devices in relation to observation statements (p. 254 and n. 3). Or should they pass a further test, namely that they should be true of the underlying physical realities – as different brands of 'realism' all maintain?

Whether or not these opposed viewpoints have been named as such, and whether or not their historical antecedents have been identified, their influence can be traced in many discussions of Greek science. Indeed the interpretation of its fundamental character has often reflected the stand taken (explicitly – or merely implicitly or by default) on whether the aims of ancient science were, chiefly, instrumentalist or realist ones (I shall call this the I/R debate). One of the foremost proponents of the instrumentalist view was Pierre Duhem, who expressed the opinion not that the whole of ancient science is instrumentalist (to be sure) but that the best, and the most typical, parts of it are, and Duhem's prestige in both the philosophy and the history of science has been such as to insure that his views received wide circulation. Indeed his opinions have been echoed, with or without direct attribution, in many other studies, particularly in general handbooks. At the time I published my article 'Saving the appearances', in 1978, Duhem's instrumentalist view of ancient science still represented the usual, majority, assumption, if not orthodoxy.

Duhem had his own axes to grind and his own battles to wage, both in philosophy of science, and in the scientific debates of his own day. As a historian he did much pioneering work of the greatest value. However, on the particular set of issues that relate to the I/R debate, his line of interpretation on Greek astronomy is – as I showed in my article – well wide of the mark. In several instances he badly misrepresented what the ancient writers say and in several his interpretation rests on a straight mistranslation of the Greek texts. Moreover in other cases his conclusions discount or ignore important counter-evidence. It is particularly striking that he was so convinced of the overall line of interpretation he advocated that even when he modified some of his translations of the Greek, that did not lead him to change his view of the positions of the authors concerned (see e.g. p. 257 n. 20).

My objections to Duhem's interpretation of Greek astronomy have not, of course, meant the end of the debate – though on the whole the force of the criticisms I made has been accepted.[1] However, subsequent work on the underlying issues suggests the need now to elaborate three points mentioned, but not sufficiently emphasised, in my original article.

First the pluralism of ancient science once again needs stressing. The I/R debate relates especially to the exact sciences. But the aims and assumptions of ancient investigators in astronomy, acoustics, optics and so on, differ, not only as between one of those disciplines and another, but within each. Thus within astronomy itself the types of study engaged in, the types of treatise composed, differ. Alongside the tradition represented in the mathematical astronomical model-building of Hipparchus and Ptolemy, there is, on the one hand, more descriptive work, and on the other, work of a more purely mathematical kind exploring mathematical problems useful to the astronomer. I mentioned Aristarchus' purely geometrical study *On the Sizes and Distances of the Sun and Moon* (p. 275): such a tradition includes also Theodosius' *Spherica*, Autolycus' *On the Moving Sphere* and Euclid's *Phenomena*.

These last three works, as Mueller (1980) has stressed, are purely mathematical exercises. They are not brought to bear directly to resolve astronomical problems, though the exercises were doubtless undertaken with the eventual application to, and solution of, astronomical problems in mind. It is essential, however, not to over-interpret the aims and ambitions of the tradition that these works represent. In particular it would be quite mistaken to see these as being instrumentalist in character. The point is important and needs some explanation. The instrumentalist view has it that the proper aim of the astronomer is *limited* to producing theories that are merely (mathematical) calculating devices. Once that aim is achieved, that is all the astronomer can hope to do (Duhem's own view was that the metaphysician then took over: but that is idiosyncratic). But while a distinction is often drawn in ancient science between mathematics and physics, one has to be careful not to assume that this distinction *corresponds to* one between an

[1] See, for example, Mourelatos, 1981: 20. In other recent work on early Greek astronomy, the focus of attention has shifted away from the question of the underlying methodological assumptions entertained: see for example Aiton, 1981, Goldstein and Bowen, 1983.

instrumentalist and a realist view of science in the terms set out in the modern debate. To start with, the terms 'mathematician' and 'mathematics' are ambiguous and may indeed cover 'astronomy' (Cf. p. 271 n. 84). But more important, to engage in a mathematical study by itself tells us nothing about the position the investigator adopts on the viability or otherwise of further, physical inquiries to which the mathematical ones may be related. Thus it is only if the mathematics is engaged in to the exclusion of any ambition to do physics that we would have prima-facie grounds for describing this as an instrumentalist position. But when mathematics is engaged in as a preliminary to a further, physical investigation, that is fully compatible with a realist position – and the same can be said with even greater conviction when the mathematical inquiry takes as given or presupposes certain physical assumptions.

Thus Ptolemy, whose realist ambitions are explained in my article, undertakes some preliminary mathematical studies in the *Syntaxis* when he sets out the lemmas for his spherical trigonometry. Moreover the bulk of his development of his astronomical models in the course of that work consists of deductive geometry. However, there can be no shadow of a doubt on the question of Ptolemy's strategic aims: he sought, and gave, a physical account of the constitution and movements of the heavenly bodies in the *Planetary Hypotheses*, and even in the *Syntaxis* itself the astronomical models are firmly anchored to certain fundamental physical assumptions, for example that the earth is at rest in the centre of the universe.

Similarly – although the point is more controversial – Aristarchus' heliocentric theory was not suggested purely as an instrumentalist solution, but was intended as a realist account – though how far it was worked out is an open question. Here too it would be very rash to overinterpret the fact that *On the Sizes and Distances* is a purely mathematical exercise and take it as evidence that Aristarchus was some kind of instrumentalist.

It follows that if in these cases mathematical studies of use in astronomy do not exclude other, physical and realist investigations, the same is also true of Autolycus and Theodosius. As with many other cases, to which I drew attention, such as Eudoxus and Callippus, the evidence available to us is not definite enough for us to be able to specify precisely what views these astronomers took on the ultimate aims of astronomy itself. However, whenever we have such determinate evidence, we find realist ambitions in play. Among those who practised astronomy (as opposed to merely commenting on it) there is no clear-cut case of anyone who can definitely be identified as a whole-hearted instrumentalist.

My second point follows on from the first and can be stated briefly. The relationship between mathematics and physics cannot, I said, be held to correspond to that between instrumentalism and realism. Moreover consideration of ancient views of mathematics itself reveals that, although there were competing conceptions of what we call the philosophy of mathematics, especially those we may label, broadly, the Platonist and Aristotelian positions, both these main philosophies of mathematics are realist in their underlying claims, although the realism in either case has to be understood differently.

The Platonist in mathematics is a realist because what mathematics studies is intelligible realities (although for Plato himself mathematical objects are not themselves the Forms, but intermediate between Forms and particulars). For a study to make a claim to knowledge it has to be, for the Platonist, a study directed to intelligible objects: but that requirement is met by mathematics. The mathematician can be said to be a realist, for he can arrive at truth about the underlying *onta* when he studies the triangle itself, the circle itself and the like.

But the Aristotelian is also a realist in mathematics, but for a very different reason. Mathematics for Aristotle, does not study separate intelligible objects (as it does in Plato). Rather it studies the mathematical properties of physical objects, in abstraction from the other, physical, properties that make them the physical objects they are.[2] But mathematics is not nominalist, conventionalist or intuitionist for Aristotle, because the mathematical properties in question are the properties of *real* objects – not of course real in the way that Plato's Forms are, but real in the only way Aristotle acknowledged, namely as substances.

No doubt many ancient mathematicians took no explicit position in this philosophical debate. But it may be conjectured that in general Greek mathematicians believed that their mathematics is true, and true of the world. Certainly there is no hesitation as to truth claims. But equally the assumption that appears to underlie most Greek mathematics from Hippocrates of Chios to late antiquity is that it is true of the world. Thus it seems overwhelmingly likely that Euclid, for one, believed his geometry to be an account of physical space, not merely a construct derived from the particular set of axioms that he selected.

Thirdly, some elaboration is necessary of the point that is briefly mentioned at the end of my article (pp. 275–6 and n. 101), namely the ambiguities of the slogan of 'saving the appearances'. This did not stand for one well-defined programme, but was used in connection with several rather divergent ones.[3] First Smith has usefully drawn attention to the fact that in the exercise of saving the phenomena, there has often been a prior selection of the phenomena to be saved. The scope of the programme is limited, in other words, to what is deemed to be salvageable (Smith, 1981: 80), the movements of the planets, sun and moon, for example, but not comets or shooting-stars. Secondly, once the apparent anomalies had been brought

[2] The pioneering work on Aristotle's philosophy of mathematics is Lear, 1982. Graeser, 1987 is a collection of essays illustrating many aspects of the more recent debate.

[3] I have attempted an analysis of a number of particular cases from harmonics and optics as well as astronomy in Lloyd, 1987: ch. 6, 295ff. Cf. also Smith, 1981 and 1982.

under a general law or explained by means of a general model, they then become *evidence for* that law, not exceptions or difficulties for it.

A crucial distinction thus emerges. In two different types of case the appearances provide the starting-point for an inquiry, but the end-result may be very different. In some cases to arrive at a satisfactory theory the scientist will have to abandon the appearances, reject them as the mere appearances they are, in his efforts to arrive at the true underlying intelligible realities. This corresponds to the Platonic programme in so far as the end aimed at is an account in terms of the Forms, to which the particulars are no more than approximations expected to be only poor imitations of the true realities.[4] However, in another type of case the *anomalies* originally perceived in the appearances are themselves merely apparent, and once the theory is secure are no longer considered as such. Retrogradations, for instance, can be fully accommodated in planetary theory. Once they are understood in terms of a general theory, the appearances in the sense of the original data of observation can *themselves* be seen as conforming to laws. In this latter type of case there is no reason to hold that the phenomena have themselves to be revised, let alone rejected, to arrive at the truths the scientist seeks.

Thus it is important to recognise that, in some uses, the 'appearances' are sound enough data of observation and the 'saving' is reaching an adequate general law. Here what is 'apparent' but not 'real' is the anomalies originally perceived in the data which provide the starting-point of the inquiry, but by its end have been shown to be no longer anomalous. But in other cases the 'appearances' may be data of observation deemed or assumed – for example for Platonic reasons – to be inadequate guides to the underlying laws, and in such cases the data themselves are subject to revision or rejection, at least in part, in the bid to uncover the laws. Similarly where the 'appearances' are or include the common opinions on a particular subject – often used by Aristotle especially as the starting-point of his investigation – the same general distinction applies. Sometimes the common opinions are saved by being drastically revised or even totally rejected, but sometimes by being explained and in some sense justified.[5]

[4] However, in his 1981 paper Smith goes too far in categorising the metaphysical assumptions in the background of the programme of 'saving the appearances' as a whole as Platonic, since it is far from being the case that all who saw themselves or were seen by others as engaged in one or other type of inquiry so labelled were Platonists or influenced by Platonist metaphysics.

[5] For one interpretation of the Aristotelian use, see Nussbaum, 1982, criticising the classic paper of Owen (1961/1986). Nussbaum herself, however, underestimates, in my view, the extent to which Aristotle can and does countenance radical departures from the common opinions.

REFERENCES

Aiton, E. J. (1981) 'Celestial spheres and circles', *History of Science* 19: 75–114

Bulmer-Thomas, I. (1984) 'Plato's astronomy', *Classical Quarterly* 34: 107–12

Goldstein, B. R. (1980) 'The status of models in ancient and medieval astronomy', *Centaurus* 24: 132–47

Goldstein, B. R., and Bowen, A. C. (1983) 'A new view of early Greek astronomy', *Isis* 74: 330–40

Graeser, A., ed. (1987) *Mathematics and Metaphysics in Aristotle* (Bern)

Jardine, N. (1979) 'The forging of modern realism: Clavius and Kepler against the Sceptics', *Studies in History and Philosophy of Science* 10: 141–73

(1984) *The Birth of History and Philosophy of Science* (Cambridge)

Lear, J. (1982) 'Aristotle's philosophy of mathematics', *Philosophical Review* 91: 161–92

Lloyd, G. E. R. (1987) *The Revolutions of Wisdom* (Berkeley)

Mourelatos, A. P. D. (1980) 'Plato's "real astronomy", *Republic* 527D–531D', in *Science and the Sciences in Plato*, ed. J. P. Anton (New York), 33–73

(1981) 'Astronomy and kinematics in Plato's project of rationalist explanation', *Studies in History and Philosophy of Science* 12: 1–32

Mueller, I. (1980) 'Ascending to problems: astronomy and harmonics in *Republic* VII', in *Science and the Sciences in Plato*, ed. J. P. Anton (New York), 103–21

Nussbaum, M. (1982) 'Saving Aristotle's appearances', in *Language and Logos*, edd. M. Schofield and M. Nussbaum (Cambridge), 267–93

Owen, G. E. L. (1961/1986) '*Tithenai ta phainomena*', in *Aristote et les problèmes de méthode*, ed. S. Mansion (Louvain), 83–103, repr. in *Logic, Science and Dialectic*, ed. M. C. Nussbaum (London, 1986)

Riddell, R. C. (1979) 'Eudoxan mathematics and the Eudoxan spheres', *Archive for History of Exact Sciences* 20: 1–19

Smith, A. M. (1981) 'Saving the appearances of the appearances: the foundations of classical geometrical optics', *Archive for History of Exact Sciences* 24: 73–99

(1982) 'Ptolemy's search for a law of refraction: a case-study in the classical methodology of "saving the appearances" and its limitations', *Archive for History of Exact Sciences* 26: 221–40

SAVING THE APPEARANCES

I

'Saving the appearances', σῴζειν τὰ φαινόμενα, is a slogan that, in its time, stood or was made to stand for many different methodological positions in many different branches of ancient natural science.[1] It is not my aim, in this paper, to attempt to tackle the subject as a whole.[2] I shall concentrate on just one inquiry, astronomy. Nor, with astronomy, can I do justice to all the complexities of what was certainly one of the central methodological issues, if not *the* central issue, in the history of ancient theoretical astronomy. I have a quite limited aim, to examine the foundations, and test the applicability, of a widespread and influential line of interpretation of ancient Greek astronomy according to which it was essentially, or at least predominantly, what we may call 'instrumentalist'[3] in character – that is, broadly speaking, that Greek astronomical theories were devices or fictions put forward purely for the sake of calculations with no claims to correspond with physical reality.

Thus Duhem, one of the chief proponents of the line of interpretation in question, distinguished two views of the status of astronomical hypotheses as follows:

> On peut, en effet, regarder les hypothèses de l'Astronomie comme de simples fictions mathématiques que le géomètre combine afin de rendre les mouvements célestes accessibles à ses calculs; on peut y voir aussi la description de corps concrets, de mouvements réellement accomplis. Dans le premier cas, une seule condition est imposée à ces hypothèses, celle de *sauver les apparences*; dans le second cas, la liberté de celui qui les imagine se trouve beaucoup plus étroitement limitée; s'il est, en effet, l'adepte d'une philosophie qui prétende connaître quelque chose de la cęleste essence, il lui faudra mettre ses hypothèses d'accord avec les enseignements de cette philosophie.[4]

Although he recognised some exceptions, the most notable of which was Aristotle, Duhem ranged the major Greek astronomers and commentators on the status of astronomy under the former head. Their hypotheses were

[1] This paper stems from a question originally put to me by my colleague, Dr N. Jardine, Lecturer in the History and Philosophy of Science at the University of Cambridge, to whom my warmest thanks are due not only for raising the problem but also for many illuminating discussions both of the philosophical issue and of aspects of the historical questions treated here. I am also most grateful for the comments made on an earlier draft of this paper at a seminar at the Institute for Classical Studies, London, and especially for those of Mr M. F. Burnyeat, Professor A. C. Lloyd, Dr R. Sorabji, and Professor G. Vlastos.

[2] Apart from the work of Duhem (1908), the chief general discussion is that of Mittelstrass (1962). (The bibliography at the end of the article provides details of these and other works that will also be referred to by author's name and date of publication.)

[3] 'Instrumentalism' is defined by Hesse (1967 : 407) as follows: 'Instrumentalists assume that theories have the status of instruments, tools, or calculating devices in relation to observation statements. In this view it is assumed that theories can be used to relate and systematize observation statements and to derive some sets of observation statements (predictions) from other sets (data); but no question of the truth or reference of the theories themselves arises.'

[4] Duhem, 1908: 281. Cf. Doland and Maschler, 1969: 28.

'pure conceptions'. It was not a queston of their being true, or even probable ('vraisemblable') – and he glosses 'true' by 'in conformity with the nature of things'.[5] Their aim was simply || and solely to 'save the appearances', interpreted by Duhem as meaning that they should furnish conclusions that correspond with the observations.[6] It was possible for several different hypotheses to save the same appearances: in that case it was not a question of choosing between them on the grounds of correspondence with physical reality, but merely on the grounds of mathematical simplicity. With some modifications and developments, Duhem saw the same fundamental methodological debate running through the whole of Western science down to Galileo, and indeed on through to his own day. The tradition of the principal Greek theorists, including Geminus, Ptolemy, Proclus, and Simplicius, continues through Maimonides, Aquinas, Jean de Jandum, down to Osiander, Ursus, and Bellarmin.[7] Against them were ranged the realists, Alpetragius, the Averroists, and so on down to Kepler and Galileo. Nor does Duhem leave us in any doubt about his own position, which is that the former view is correct: 'en dépit de Képler et de Galilée, nous croyons aujourd'hui, avec Osiander et Bellarmin, que les hypothèses de la Physique ne sont que des artifices mathématiques destinés à *sauver les phénomènes.*'[8]

In the course of assessing the evidential basis of this interpretation of the main stream of Greek astronomy I shall have occasion to question the way in which the alternatives are presented by Duhem. But before turning to the evidence it is as well to point out that the 'instrumentalist' line has some formidable supporters. Even before Duhem had developed his interpretation at length in his articles in *Annales de philosophie chrétienne*, Dreyer had written that, by the time of Ptolemy, 'it had... become a recognized fact, that the epicyclic theory was merely a means of calculating the apparent places of the planets without pretending to represent the true system of the world', and again that 'it appears from many statements, not only of Ptolemy himself, but also of his commentators, that they merely considered the numerous circles as a convenient means of calculating the positions of the planets.'[9] In his *The Physical World of Late Antiquity*, Sambursky wrote of Proclus, at least, that 'he takes a decidedly positivistic view and rejects the idea that any reality can be attributed to Ptolemy's spheres or segments of spheres'.[10]

[5] E.g. Duhem, 1908: 120, 284.

[6] E.g. Duhem, 1908: 135.

[7] Duhem claimed Copernicus too for this tradition in so far as he commented (Duhem, 1908: 374): 'Copernic a essayé l'hypothèse du mouvement de la Terre à titre de supposition purement fictive'. Yet he went on to note, and to blame Copernicus for, certain realist assumptions: 'il a voulu faire davantage... il a voulu prouver la vérité de cette hypothèse...'

[8] Duhem, 1908: 592, cf. 484, 587ff.

[9] Dreyer, 1906: 196 and 201.

[10] Sambursky, 1962: 146. Cf. also Dijksterhuis, 1961: 67: 'Among later Greek philosophers Proclus is clearly in agreement with the standpoint taken by Ptolemy in the *Almagest*: the motions into which the single planetary motion observed is resolved are mere mathematical fictions, which exist nowhere but in the mind of the astronomer carrying out the resolution;... the only object pursued in framing an astronomical theory is that of making it possible to calculate the celestial phenomena.'

Finally there is a particularly clear statement of a Duhemian line, with an explicit acknowledgement to Duhem, in Wasserstein's article 'Greek scientific thought'. From Plato's time, he wrote,

> geometrical methods and procedures become predominant. By this I do not mean only that astronomical models are now conceived as geometrical constructions; I mean something quite different; namely that like the geometer or arithmetician the astronomer now starts from axioms or postulates, or whatever you like to call them, and then deduces a system from them. The important point here is this: the geometer is not concerned with the truth || of his initial axioms, just as the logician is not concerned with the truth of his initial premises – both are concerned only with the *validity* of the conclusions that are derived *deductively* from their axioms or premisses... Similarly in Greek astronomy the aim was not, at least not always, the discovery of a theory that corresponded with fact, with physical truth, with physical reality. Σῴζειν τὰ φαινόμενα is not that, at least it is not always that, in the dominant strand of the astronomical tradition, even as represented by Ptolemy, and before him by Hipparchus, by Eudoxus, and indeed, as we shall see, by Plato.[11]

After this negative statement of what one strand of Greek astronomy was not, Wasserstein went on to define it positively as follows:

> The Greek astronomer in formulating his astronomical theories does not make any statements about physical nature at all. His theories are purely geometrical fictions. That means that to save the appearances became a purely mathematical task, it was an exercise in geometry, no more, but, of course, also no less.[12]

Now the instrumentalists present a variety of ancient texts in support of their view, but the key witness is undoubtedly Proclus. Duhem's view of Proclus' position is clear:

> Tout l'effort de Proclus va à établir que les mouvements hypothétiques en des excentriques et des épicycles qui, par leur composition, reproduisent le mouvement des astres errants sont de pures abstractions.[13]
>
> Les combinaisons de mouvements proposées par les astronomes étant de pures conceptions, dénuées de toute réalité, elles n'ont pas à être justifiées à l'aide des principes de la Physique; elles doivent seulement être disposées de telle sorte que les apparences soient sauvées.[14]

He sums up:

[11] Wasserstein, 1962: 54. (The italics are Wasserstein's.)

[12] Wasserstein, 1962: 57. He had just quoted the preface to Copernicus' *De Revolutionibus* ('the task of the astronomer consists in the careful collection of observations of heavenly movements. Since, however, no reasoning can help him to attain to the true causes of these movements, he conceives and imagines any sort of hypothesis by means of which these movements can be geometrically calculated both for the past and for the future. It is not necessary that these hypotheses be *true*; it is not even necessary that they be *likely*; it suffices that they lead to a calculation that accords with the observations') where he noted 'suggestive echoes of older doctrines or rather shades of older attitudes'.

[13] Duhem, 1908: 132.

[14] Duhem, 1908: 133.

> Les artifices géométriques qui nous servent d'hypothèses pour sauver les mouvements apparents des astres ne sont ni vrais, ni vraisemblables. Ce sont de pures conceptions que l'on ne saurait réaliser sans formuler des absurdités.[15]

Duhem's discussion of Proclus is liberally interspersed with translations, even the occasional Greek phrase, from, especially, the *Hypotyposis*, and, writing in 1908, he based himself on Halma's edition of 1820[16] (Manitius' Teubner came out in 1909). The most important passages come in the final chapter of the *Hypotyposis*, where both Halma's Greek and his French translation are extraordinarily defective.[17] Thus Duhem's first quotation from Proclus runs: 'les astronomes qui ont présupposé l'uniformité des mouvements des corps célestes ignoraient que l'essence de ces mouvements est, au contraire, l'irrégularité.'[18] But the Greek is: τὰς κινήσεις τῶν οὐρανίων ὁμαλὰς ἀποφῆναι προθυμηθέντες οἱ περὶ ἀστρονομίαν δεινοὶ ἔλαθον ἑαυτούς αὐτὴν τὴν οὐσίαν αὐτῶν ἀνώμαλον καὶ παθῶν ἀνάπλεων ἀποφήναντες,[19] i.e. 'those who are clever at astronomy, || who were eager to show that the movements of the heavenly bodies are regular, tended, without realising it, to show that their substance itself is irregular and full of modifications'. Here Duhem drastically misrepresents Proclus' position. He implies that Proclus' *own* view is that the movements of the heavenly bodies are essentially irregular, and indeed full of πάθη: the astronomers did not realise this and tried to show that those movements are regular. But it is clear that what Proclus is in fact doing is criticising the astronomers for producing theories that *conflict* with the assumption of the regularity of the movements of the heavenly bodies.[20]

At this point it is not Halma's Greek text that is the source of the problem. Although printed without accents and smooth breathings, his Greek is the same as Manitius'. One suspects, however, that Duhem followed Halma's French translation, where we find: 'que les astronomes... qui ont présupposé que les mouvements des corps célestes étoient uniformes, ignoroient que leur essence est l'irrégularité et la variation', that is precisely the same misrepresentation of ἔλαθον as in Duhem.[21]

[15] Duhem, 1908: 135.
[16] As the footnote (Duhem, 1908: 132 n. 1) indicates.
[17] Thus apart from the many incoherences that Halma's Greek text contains, his translation completely omits the passage from ει δε και (*sic*) (Halma, 1820: 151, col. 1 line 12) to και διακρισεις (*sic*) (line 21) in the Greek.
[18] Duhem, 1908: 132.
[19] *Hyp.* 236.12–15 Manitius, Halma, 1820: 150f.
[20] Even though Proclus allows the movements of the planets to be complex, he insists that they are orderly, cf. further below, pp. 261ff. and n. 41. It is striking that in his later *Système du monde* Duhem gave a more accurate translation of this passage ('ils ne se sont pas aperçu qu'ils déclaraient, [par là], que l'essence même de ces corps célestes était privée d'uniformité et douée de toutes sortes de passivités', Duhem, 1954: 104), but in no way modified his general interpretation of Proclus. Wasserstein, who translated the passage correctly although he omitted the important καὶ παθῶν ἀνάπλεων, also took it that Proclus himself held the movements of the heavenly bodies to be irregular and indeed that this text showed that 'he is willing to regard not only circularity but even uniformity as expendable assumptions' (Wasserstein, 1962: 56).
[21] Halma, 1820: 150. The one point of variation is that Halma's 'leur' (p. 151, col. 2 line 3) might refer to either 'mouvements' or – more likely – 'corps célestes', whereas Duhem opts

That should already put one on one's guard. But worse is to follow. Proclus goes on to mention two different ways of construing the epicycles and the eccentrics that the astronomers postulated. Manitius' text (*Hyp.* 236.15ff.) may be translated: 'For what are we to say about the eccentrics they go on about and the epicycles? [Are we to say] that they are merely contrivances [objects of thought] or that they also have existence in their spheres in which they are fixed?'[22]

He then goes on to consider each of these two possibilities and to raise difficulties about both, that is at *Hyp.* 236.18ff. and 236.25ff. 'For if [one is to say] that they are only contrived, they have unwittingly gone over from physical bodies to mathematical concepts and given the causes of physical movements from things that do not exist in nature.'[23] This first difficulty is then followed by a second (*Hyp.* 236.22ff.) where he attacks the idea of putting these objects of thought in motion.[24] ||

Proclus then continues by considering the second alternative, the view that the epicycles and eccentrics actually exist in the spheres in which they are fixed, and here his objection is that the epicycles and eccentrics destroy the συνέχειαν – continuity or connection – of the spheres: the circles and the spheres are moved separately; 'nor do they move these [the circles] in the same way as each other, but in opposite directions';[25] and they 'confound their relative distances, if sometimes they [the circles] are brought together and are in a single plane, but sometimes are separated and cut each other. Thus there will be all kinds of divisions and foldings-up and separations of the heavenly bodies.'

Although many points of detail are obscure, the overall structure of the argument of this passage seems clear enough. Proclus mentions two possible ways of taking epicycles and eccentrics and raises objections against *both*. Where precisely that leaves Proclus himself is a question I shall postpone for the moment, because I want to consider how Duhem – and Halma – took the passage. At this point Duhem was, to some extent at least, critical of what he found in Halma. Thus he disagrees with Halma's reading ἐκ τῶν οἰκούντων

definitely for the former ('l'essence de ces mouvements'). It seems more likely, however, that it is the heavenly bodies (τῶν οὐρανίων) rather than their movements whose substance (οὐσίαν) is said to be irregular and full of modifications.

22 τοὺς γὰρ ἐκκέντρους οὓς θρυλοῦσι καὶ τοὺς ἐπικύκλους τί φῶμεν; ἆρα ἐπινοεῖσθαι μόνον ἢ καὶ ὑπόστασιν ἔχειν ἐν ταῖς σφαίραις αὐτῶν, ἐν αἷς ἐνδέδενται;

23 εἰ μὲν γὰρ ἐπινοεῖσθαι μόνον, λελήθασιν ἀπὸ τῶν φυσικῶν σωμάτων εἰς μαθηματικὰς ἐπινοίας μεταστάντες καὶ ἐκ τῶν οὐκ ὄντων ἐν τῇ φύσει τὰς τῶν φυσικῶν κινήσεων αἰτίας ἀποδιδόντες.

24 οὐ γάρ, ἐπειδὴ ταῖς ἐπινοίαις ἡμῶν κινοῦνται, διὰ τοῦτο οἱ ἐπ' αὐτῶν νοούμενοι ἀστέρες κατὰ ἀλήθειαν ἀνωμάλως κινοῦνται, 'for it is not the case that since they are moved according to our thoughts, for that reason the stars that are imagined on them truly move irregularly'. What is being denied here is not the reason (the stars truly move irregularly, but not for the reason given) but (as in Manitius's translation) the conclusion – they do not truly move irregularly at all.

25 Thus the moon and sun move on their epicycles in a sense opposite to that of the epicycles on their deferents. Each of the planets, however, moves on its epicycle in the same sense as that of the epicycle on its deferent (cf. Proclus, *Hyp.* 154.27ff.).

ἐν τῇ φύσει and suggests that a negative has dropped out: οὐκ οἰκούντων.[26] Moreover he distinguishes the two theses that Proclus considers much more clearly than Halma's translation does. Halma seems to have taken his αρα (*sic*) on p. 151, col. 1 line 3 as inferential, not as an interrogative. At least he translated: 'il faut donc les concevoir comme simplement fictifs et idéaux, ou comme attachés à des sphères'. While Duhem keeps 'simplement fictifs et idéaux', he sets out the alternatives more clearly: 'ou bien... ou bien...'[27] Yet the important point is that in the sequel both Duhem and Halma imply that *Proclus opts* for the instrumentalist alternative. After mentioning the two possibilities very sketchily in the passage just quoted, Halma proceeds: 'car puisqu'ils ne doivent être que des conceptions'.[28] Similarly Duhem went on: 'ceux qui le prétendent "oublient que ces cercles sont seulement dans la pensée"'.[29] Where they both agree, and both misrepresent the Greek, is in this: both take as an assertion what is, in the Greek, the protasis of a conditional, where the apodosis sets out an objection to the view contained in that protasis. Both represent Proclus coming down firmly for the instrumentalist option,[30] whereas in fact Proclus raises objections against that view just as much as against the alternative, according to which the epicycles and eccentrics were held to exist in the spheres in which they are fixed.

That much should be clear. But it might be thought that although Duhem (misled, perhaps, to some extent, by Halma) has misrepresented Proclus' argument || at certain points in the final chapter of the *Hypotyposis*, the main burden of his interpretation of Proclus' position is, nevertheless, one with which we must agree. For this question we have to discuss what precisely Proclus' position was, and unfortunately one can scarcely say his position was *precise*. To understand his point of view in the *Hypotyposis* it is necessary first to consider what he says at the outset of the work, where he explains its purpose:

> The great Plato, my friend, expects the true philosopher at least to say goodbye to the senses and the whole of wandering substance and to transfer astronomy above the heavens and to study there slowness-itself and speed-itself in true number. But you seem to me to lead us down from those contemplations to these periods in the heavens and to the observations of those clever at astronomy and to the hypotheses they devised from these, [hypotheses] which Aristarchuses and Hipparchuses and Ptolemies and such-like people are used

[26] Duhem, 1908: 133 n.1 on Halma, 1820: 151, col. 1 lines 7f. Yet Grynaeus' edition of 1540 already has the negative and indeed provides the same text as that in Manitius: ἐκ τῶν οὐκ ὄντων ἐν τῇ φύσει (Grynaeus, 1540: 81).

[27] 'Ou bien ces cercles sont simplement fictifs et idéaux: ou bien ils ont une existence réelle au sein des sphères des astres...', Duhem 1908: 132f.

[28] Halma, 1820: 151, col. 2 lines 7f. Proclus' criticism of the astronomers then becomes that they attribute material properties to mathematical conceptions!

[29] Duham, 1908: 133. He fudges the criticism of the astronomers that follows: 'ils font des échanges entre des corps naturels et des conceptions mathématiques.'

[30] The structure of the argument, with the two alternatives set out with εἰ μὲν and εἰ δέ, is of course, much obscured in Halma's text.

> to babbling about. For you desire indeed to hear also the doctrines of these men, in your eagerness to leave, so far as possible, nothing uninvestigated of what has been discovered by the ancients in the inquiry into the universe.[31]

He goes on to explain that he had promised to work on this 'in his own fashion' when he had some free time, and that now that he has, he is fulfilling that promise: 'Closing my eyes, for the time being, to those exhortations of Plato and to the expositions themselves of the heavenly movements both of the fixed stars and of the planets which he persuaded us to give the first rank to, I shall proceed to tell you the "absolute" truth as believed on the basis of long and endless arguments by those who love to gaze at the heavenly bodies.'[32]

Proclus thus opens his work with an explicit disclaimer. He cannot here do astronomy in the way that he believes Plato to recommend in the *Republic*, 'transferring astronomy above the heavens' and there studying 'slowness-itself' and 'speed-itself' in 'true number'. What the *Hypotyposis* contains is quite different, because he is led down from such (purely abstract) contemplations to such matters as the periods in the heavens and the observations of the astronomers. As a good Platonist – as he conceives – Proclus often mentions the inexactness of sensible objects.[33] Yet that does not deter him from giving a quite lengthy account of astronomy in the *Hypotyposis*, including not only a full, if in parts inaccurate, statement of current astronomical theories, but also a surprisingly detailed description of the main astronomical instruments and how to use and construct them.[34] He begins with a statement of the ten main problems, such as, for example, the variations in the apparent speeds of the sun, ‖ moon, and planets,[35] and he introduces this by saying that he will first identify the phenomena that caused astronomers to inquire into their causes:

> They correctly hypothesised that the movements of the heavenly bodies must be circular and orderly, even if the circular movement is not the same in all of them, nor unmixed with what is not such [i.e. not circular], yet this too is assuredly orderly. For being borne always in the same way and according to a

[31] Πλάτων μὲν ὁ μέγας, ὦ ἑταῖρε, τόνγε ὡς ἀληθῶς φιλόσοφον ἀξιοῖ τὰς αἰσθήσεις χαίρειν ἀφέντα και τὴν πλανωμένην ἅπασαν οὐσίαν οὐρανοῦ τε ὑπεραστρονομεῖν κᾀκεῖ τὴν αὐτοβραδυτῆτα καὶ τὸ αὐτοτάχος ἐν τῷ ἀληθινῷ ἀριθμῷ σκοπεῖν. σὺ δέ μοι φαίνῃ κατάγειν ἡμᾶς ἀπ' ἐκείνων τῶν θεαμάτων εἰς τὰς ἐν οὐρανῷ ταύτας περιόδους καὶ τὰς τῶν δεινῶν περὶ ἀστρονομίαν τηρήσεις καὶ τὰς ἐκ τούτων αὐτοῖς μεμηχανημένας ὑποθέσεις, ἃς Ἀρίσταρχοί τε καὶ Ἵππαρχοι καὶ Πτολεμαῖοι καὶ τοιοῦτοί τινες διαθρυλεῖν εἰώθασι. ποθεῖς γὰρ δὴ καὶ τὰς τούτων ἐπιβολὰς ἀκοῦσαι μηδὲν ἀδιερεύνητον κατὰ δύναμιν ἀπολιπεῖν τῶν τοῖς παλαιοῖς ἐξηυπορημένων ἐν τῇ θεωρίᾳ τῶν ὅλων προθυμούμενος (*Hyp.* 2.1–13). The opening sentence is, of course, an allusion to Plato, *Republic* 529D.

[32] μύσας ἐν τῷ παρόντι πρὸς τὰς τοῦ Πλάτωνος ἐκείνας παρακελεύσεις καὶ αὐτὰς τὰς περὶ τῶν οὐρανίων κινήσεων τῶν τε ἀπλανῶν καὶ τῶν πλανωμένων ὑφηγήσεις, ἃς ἐκεῖνος ἡμᾶς πρεσβεύειν ἀνέπεισεν, ἔρχομαί σοι λέξων αὐτὴν καθ' ἑαυτὴν τὴν διὰ μακρῶν καὶ ἀπεράντων ἐφόδων πεπεισμένην τοῖς φιλοθεάμοσι τῶν οὐρανίων ἀλήθειαν (*Hyp.* 4.1–7). The reference to the φιλοθεάμονες (an allusion to *Republic* V) shows that the expression αὐτὴν καθ' ἑαυτὴν τὴν... ἀλήθειαν is ironic.

[33] E.g. *in Ti.* I 351.20ff.

[34] See especially *Hyp.* ch. 3, 42.5–54.12, cf. ch. 4, 128.6–130.26 and ch. 6, 198.15–212.6, and cf. 72.20ff., 110.3ff., 120.15ff.

[35] *Hyp.* 6.12–16.16.

single formula and in one absolutely self-consistent order would, I suppose, best befit the most divine of visible things, especially for those who postulate that all these things are borne round according to reason. For reason is always the provider of order in all the things of which it has charge. Clinging to this notion, as to a safe stern-cable, they appear with reason already to be vexed at this apparent disorder, seeking which hypotheses would show them that the periods in those circles are accomplished rationally instead of irrationally, and that they are determined by numbers that befit each one instead of being borne round indeterminately and in a disorderly fashion.[36]

Once the problematic phenomena have been set out, the bulk of the *Hypotyposis* consists of a detailed analysis of each of these in turn. In the final chapter he first of all recapitulates the problems and gives their suggested solutions and then ends with the passage Duhem made so much of. It is worth noting, first, that the doubts raised in that passage do not relate to everything that has gone before. The chief question Proclus poses concerns the status of the *epicycles* and *eccentrics*. But not all his discussions of the problematic phenomena depend directly on those hypotheses.[37] More important, it would be wrong to assume that the doubts he expresses about the status of the epicycles and eccentrics apply also to the doctrine that there are *heavenly spheres* – for example, a sphere of the fixed stars.[38] Finally his doubts about epicycles and eccentrics are the more understandable when we reflect that – unlike many other late commentators – Proclus knows very well that they are not in Plato.[39] ||

[36] τοῦτο μὲν ὀρθῶς ὑποθέμενοι τὸ τὰς κινήσεις τῶν θείων σωμάτων ἐγκυκλίους δεῖν καὶ τεταγμένας ὑπάρχειν, εἰ καὶ τὸ ἐγκύκλιον οὐ τὸ αὐτὸ ἐν πᾶσιν ἐκείνοις, οὐδὲ ἄμικτον πρὸς τὸ μὴ τοιοῦτον, ἀλλ᾽ οὖν καὶ τοῦτο πάντως τεταγμένον. τὸ γὰρ ἀεὶ ὡσαύτως καὶ καθ᾽ ἕνα λόγον φέρεσθαι καὶ μίαν τάξιν αὐτὴν καθ᾽ ἑαυτὴν ὁμολογοῦσαν πρέποι ἂν που τοῖς θειοτάτοις τῶν φανερῶν μάλιστα τοῖς κατὰ νοῦν ἐκεῖνα πάντα περιάγεσθαι τιθεμένοις· νοῦς γὰρ ἀεὶ τάξεως χορηγός ἐστιν ἅπασιν, οἷς ἂν ἐπιστατῇ. ταύτης δὲ ὥσπερ ἀσφαλοῦς πείσματος ἐξεχόμενοι τῆς ὑπονοίας [καὶ] εἰκότως ἤδη δυσχεραίνειν φαίνονται πρὸς τὴν φαινομένην ταύτην ἀταξίαν [καὶ] ζητοῦντες, τίνες ὑποθέσεις αὐτοῖς ἀντὶ μὲν ἀλόγων κατὰ λόγον ἐπιτελουμένας τὰς περιόδους ἀποφήναιεν ⟨ἐπὶ⟩ τῶν κύκλων ἐκείνων, ἀντὶ δὲ ἀορίστως καὶ ἀτάκτως φερομένων ὡρισμένας ἀριθμοῖς τοῖς προσήκουσιν ἑκάστοις (*Hyp.* 4.15–6.5). Note especially ὀρθῶς at 4.15.

[37] Thus in one instance (that of the precession of the equinoxes) he resolves the problem simply by denying that the phenomenon occurs (*Hyp.* 136.4ff., 234.7ff.).

[38] Thus in *in Ti.* he follows Plato in postulating a system based on spheres of the Same and of the Other (to account for the daily movement of the heavens and the longitudinal movement of each planet on the ecliptic respectively), e.g. *in Ti.* III 73.27ff., 123.20ff., 146.1ff., 148.1ff.: the substance of which the stars and their spheres are composed is discussed at *in Ti.* III 128.14ff. (cf. below p. 264 and n. 51), cf. e.g. 96.6f. where he says that the spheres 'fill up' the whole of the heavens. Cf. also the references, at *Hyp.* 236.18 and 238.1, to the spheres in which the epicycles or eccentrics are fixed, in his account of the difficulties facing those hypotheses.

[39] This is clear from e.g. *in Ti.* III 56.31ff., 76.28f., 96.19ff. and *in R.* II 214.6ff., 227.23ff. At *in Ti.* III 146.14ff., especially, epicycles and eccentrics are again criticised as involving *either* little circles that move in a direction opposite to that of the spheres on which they are located (which will destroy the continuity of the spheres or introduce into the heavenly bodies circles belonging to another nature, φύσις) *or* movement round different centres, and Proclus objects to the latter, on the dynamical grounds that it 'does away with the common axiom of the physicists', namely that every simple movement is either round the centre of the universe or to or from that centre.

Although Proclus evidently has his overall, and as he believes Platonic, quarrel with any kind of 'phenomenal' astronomy, he certainly does not object to all phenomenal astronomical hypotheses equally. Thus he shows no signs of wavering on the question of the earth being at rest in the centre of the heavens.[40] Nor, despite Duhem and Wasserstein, can there be any doubt about his endorsing the view that the observed courses of the heavenly bodies must, so far as possible, be explained in terms of *circular* and *orderly* movements.[41] The problem was, of course, to account for the evident complexity of the movements of the planets, sun, and moon. His dilemma is acute: he knows there is no Platonic authority for eccentrics and epicycles, yet how can the complex movements of the planets, sun, and moon be explained without them? In one mood he reiterates the Platonic thesis that sensible objects are unstable, adding a contrast between human beings – who must be content with approximations to the truth – and the gods, who alone grasp the truth itself.[42] Then again, in his accounts of Plato's astronomy, especially, he certainly acknowledges that the movements of the planets, sun, and moon are, to some extent at least, irregular. In *in Ti.* III 56.31ff., for example,[43] he interprets Plato in the *Republic* to be saying that while the fixed stars are both regular and orderly, and sublunary things are both irregular and disorderly, the planets are intermediate between them, irregular but orderly, and in that work he attributes the complexity (ποικιλία) of the planet's motions to their souls.[44] Yet Proclus sometimes appears to want

[40] See e.g. *Hyp.* 28.7ff. and 21ff., *in Ti.* III 137.6ff.

[41] This is clear from *Hyp.* 4.15ff. (quoted above, n. 36). Elsewhere in *Hyp.* he says that the assumption of the regularity of the movement of the heavenly bodies is the ἀρχή of the whole of astronomy (28.15–20), that it is accepted by all astronomers that the heavenly bodies move in an orderly fashion since they are 'far from mortal troubles' (18.17–25 – note the first person plural at 18.22 – cf. 26.7ff.), and that the astronomers claimed to give an account of the phenomena that is in accord with the 'incontrovertible assumptions concerning the heavenly bodies' that they all move regularly, and that their irregularity is apparent and not true, the result of the combination of their various movements (146.4ff.). Again in his accounts of Plato's astronomy Proclus assumes the orderliness (τάξις) of the movements of all the heavenly bodies (e.g. *in Ti.* III 55.11f., 57.2f., 90.22ff., 96.21ff., 127.7ff., 146.2, 147.12, *in R.* II 230.22ff., 231.3ff.: at *in Ti.* III 117.19f. he says it is μὴ θέμις to consider their souls to be irrational); at *in Ti.* III 56.12ff. he asserts that not only the fixed stars, but also the planets have a *single*, *regular* (ὁμαλός) unceasing movement, even though he later qualifies this by introducing an element of irregularity in their movements (see below, nn. 43 and 44); and he criticises astronomical hypotheses on the grounds that they are 'far removed from the *simplicity* of divine things' (*in Ti.* III 56.29) although the 'simplicity' of the planets includes multiplicity (πλῆθος) (*in Ti.* III 127.9ff.).

[42] E.g. *in Ti.* I 352.5ff., 28ff., 353.22ff. Yet at *in Ti.* III 122.10ff. he insists that the heavenly region is as immaterial as it is possible for any sensible object to be – that is, that it is free from any unstable, ἀνέδραστος, matter, cf. 122.18ff. – and that it is free from the accidental.

[43] Cf. also *in Ti.* III 67.2ff. (the movements of the planets are regular ἑαυταῖς, but irregular πρὸς ἀλλήλας), 79.12ff., 96.21ff., 147.9ff., cf. *in R.* II 230.15–22, 234.26–235.3.

[44] E.g. *in Ti.* III 147.2ff. The planets undergo a complex of movements, (*a*) in longitude (κατὰ μῆκος), (*b*) in latitude (κατὰ πλάτος), (*c*) in 'anomaly' (κατὰ βάθος, the motion in anomaly, being represented by an epicycle, produces variations in the distance of the planet from the earth, i.e. 'in depth') and (*d*) axial rotation. The resultant movement of (*a*), (*b*) and (*c*) is spiral

more || than that – to want a determinate and detailed account of their movements.[45] In that mood, even though he is critical of epicycles and eccentrics, he comes close to accommodating himself to them in certain passages. There are, then, I suggest, certain vacillations in the line that Proclus adopts in the texts in which he comes closest to confronting the problem directly.

This can be seen by juxtaposing some of the passages in question. Take first the continuation of a text from the first chapter of the *Hypotyposis* to which I have already referred.

> I shall proceed [he has just said] to tell you the 'absolute' truth as believed on the basis of long and endless arguments by those who love to gaze at the heavenly bodies. Nor shall I be able to restrain, here, my usual testing of opinions, though I shall use it sparingly, since I believe the refutation of the hypotheses will be obvious to you from their very exposition – the hypotheses in which they unfold, with pride, the whole of the theory which they propose.[46]

That looks like a straightforward and outright condemnation, as also may *in Ti.* III 56.28ff.; for instance, where he says: 'Nor do these hypotheses [particularly epicycles and eccentrics] have any probability, but some are far removed from the simplicity of divine things, and others, fabricated by more recent astronomers, suppose the motion of the heavenly bodies to be as if driven by a machine.' Yet we may contrast with this the conciliatory tone of the beginning of chapter 7 of the *Hypotyposis* (212.9ff.): 'Since we said in the introduction from what [starting-points] especially those who love to gaze at such things have been led to investigate these things, come now, in each case, let us bring forward the resolutions of these [difficulties] from these hypotheses, approving [ἐγκρίνοντες] some of what they say, but rejecting [or testing, βασανίζοντες] other parts.' Even in the concluding section of the chapter (238.21ff.) he criticises the astronomers for, among other things, not stating ὅσα δυνατὸν προσευπορῆσαι, those things that it is possible to grasp, the problems that can be resolved, and at the very end of the chapter he again appears to hedge his bets in the final sentence of the work: 'Yet one must know this much, that among all the hypotheses these are the simplest and most fitting for heavenly bodies, and that they have been contrived to discover the manner of the movements of the stars that are really moved as they appear, so that the measure of what is in them may be grasped.'[47]

– a mean between purely circular, and rectilinear, movement. See e.g. *in Ti.* III 76.30ff., 78.29ff., 95.34ff., 128.8ff., 148.5ff., *in R.* II 232.24ff., 233.16ff.

45 Cf. the demand at *Hyp.* 238.13ff. to know the causes of the planes and distances, 'I mean the true causes, such that when the soul saw them especially it might cease all its travail.'

46 *Hyp.* 4.5–12. The text continues from that quoted above, n. 32: οὐδὲ ἐνταῦθα μὲν ἐπέχειν δυνάμενος τὴν εἰωθυῖαν ἐμοὶ τῶν δογμάτων βάσανον, σπανίᾳ δὲ ὅμως αὐτῇ χρώμενος, ἐπεὶ καὶ σοὶ καταφανῆ πέπεισμαι δι' αὐτῶν ἔσεσθαι τῶν λεγομένων τὸν τῶν ὑποθέσεων ἔλεγχον, ἐφ' αἷς ἐκεῖνοι καλλωπιζόμενοι πᾶσαν ἐξελίττουσι τὴν προκειμένην αὐτοῖς θεωρίαν.

47 *Hyp.* 238.22f. πλὴν τοσοῦτον ἰστέον, ὅτι πασῶν τῶν ὑποθέσεων αἱ ἁπλούστεραι καὶ οἰκειότεραι θείοις σώμασιν αὗταί εἰσι, καὶ ὅτι ἐπινενόηνται πρὸς εὕρεσιν τοῦ τρόπου τῶν κινήσεων τῶν ἀστέρων κατ' ἀλήθειαν οὕτω κινουμένων, ὥσπερ καὶ φαίνονται, ἵνα γένηται καταληπτὸν τὸ μέτρον τῶν ἐν αὐτοῖς.

Finally, in *in Ti.* too he says at one point[48] that epicycles and eccentrics are not in vain, since they enable one to resolve complex movements into simple ones.

There are, then, certain unresolved tensions in Proclus' position. There is evidence, in both *Hyp.* and *in Ti.*, of his desire for a simple account, not just of ‖ the movement of the fixed stars, but also of those of the planets, sun, and moon.[49] Moreover he knows, or at least the end of the *Hypotyposis* suggests that he knows, that the *simplest* hypotheses are eccentrics and epicycles.[50] Yet there are problems, not just the lack of Plato's authority, but also the question we began with, are they mere contrivances or do they have real existence? *Both* present difficulties. But when he sets out those difficulties, it is not that he intends this as a *reductio* argument, but rather as a genuine statement of ἀπορίαι. We should now reconsider the nature of the difficulties he specified. Against the assumption that the epicycles and eccentrics are real he argues by pointing to complications (such as that the continuity of the spheres is destroyed) that are themselves realist (p. 258 above). But if the epicycles and eccentrics are simply objects of thought, then one has unwittingly slipped over into mathematics and one cannot account for physical motions by appealing to things that do not exist in nature. Now why should Proclus be dissatisfied with that solution? Surely the chief problem, on that way of taking the epicycles and eccentrics, is simply that *a merely instrumentalist account will not do*. So whilst he argues against the realist way of taking these hypotheses on realist assumptions, he argues against the instrumentalist way of taking them *also* on realist assumptions. Nor is that surprising when we reflect that in *in Ti.* too his standpoint is a realist one when he discusses, for example, what the stars and the spheres in which they are carried round are made of and concludes that both consist of a special kind of fire.[51]

Duhem's interpretation of Proclus, I conclude, is open to criticism on three grounds. First he speaks quite generally of Proclus' view on astronomical hypotheses. But what is at issue in the key passage at the end of *Hyp.* ch. 7 is not the status of astronomical hypotheses in general, but only that of epicycles and eccentrics. Elsewhere, Proclus shows no inclination to consider as mere objects of thought such assumptions as that the earth is at rest or that the movement of the heavenly bodies is, in general, circular and orderly. Secondly, as far as the particular text discussing epicycles and eccentrics is

[48] *In Ti.* III 148.23ff. At *in Ti.* III 65.26ff., too, his own solution to the problem of the sun's movement appears to incorporate the epicyclic hypothesis. Cf. also *in R.* II 233.21ff.

[49] E.g. the reference to the simplicity of divine things at *in Ti.* III 56.29 and 127.9ff., and that to a single regular movement at 56.12 (see n. 41 above). At *Hyp.* 18.2ff. the Pythagorean preference for the simplest hypotheses, on the grounds that they are more fitting for divine bodies, is endorsed by Proclus himself and in that work he distinguishes between the eccentric and the epicyclic hypothesis on the grounds of simplicity at 76.17ff. and 148.18.

[50] Cf. also *Hyp.* 198.6ff. where he says he has given an outline account of the hypotheses of those who appear to have furthered (κατωρθωκέναι) the inquiry concerning the heavenly bodies most.

[51] *In Ti.* III 128.14ff., 28ff., cf. also 113.20ff., 114.15ff.

concerned, Duhem represents Proclus opting for the instrumentalist view, when in fact he criticises both that and the realist alterative. Thirdly, the assumptions at work in both cases in that text turn out to be realist ones.[52]

II

Now Proclus is not exactly one of the leading lights in the history of Greek astronomical theory: rather he is a moderately intelligent summariser and critic || of received views. Yet he does at least state and discuss a distinction between the view that epicycles and eccentrics are mere objects of thought and the view that they have real existence in the spheres in which they are fixed, and that is rare enough, indeed quite exceptional, in ancient texts of whatever period.[53] The other writers whom Duhem and others cite yield no passage in which the general contrast between 'instrumentalist' and 'realist' astronomy is debated. There are, of course, discussions of, for example, the distinction between φυσική and μαθηματική beginning with Aristotle's in *Physics* II, ch. 2, which itself provided the starting-point for other analyses, and Duhem, for one, certainly took these texts to be relevant to the issue and indeed to provide evidence to support his general view. Once again, however, we may have doubts.

The chief text is the famous passage in Simplicius, *in Ph.* 291.21ff., where he quotes Alexander, who in turn quotes Geminus' summary of Posidonius' *Meteorologica*. Duhem, who quotes the text at length, hails it as the most exact ancient Greek definition of the roles of the astronomer and the physicist, and he takes the distinction between those two to be one between two dependent, autonomous, and unconnected inquiries. His view of how that distinction was interpreted by the Greeks comes out very clearly in a passage where he summarises the Greek achievement before turning to consider Arabic astronomy:

> Leur génie logique et métaphysique s'était appliqué à ... l'examen des compositions de mouvements imaginées par les astronomes; après quelques hésitations, il s'était refusé à regarder les excentriques et les épicycles comme des corps doués, au sein des cieux, d'une existence réelle; il n'avait voulu y voir que des fictions de géomètres, propres à soumettre au calcul les phénomènes célestes; pourvu que ces calculs s'accordassent avec les observations, pourvu que les hypothèses permissent de sauver les apparences, le but visé par l'astronome était atteint; les hypothèses étaient utiles; seul le physicien eût été en droit de dire si elles étaient ou non conformes à la réalité; mais, dans la plupart des cas, les principes qu'il pouvait affirmer étaient trop généraux, trop peu détallés pour l'autoriser à prononcer un tel jugement.[54]

[52] Thus his fundamental complaint against epicycles and eccentrics is not that they do not provide a means of calculating the positions of the heavenly bodies ('save the phenomena' in Duhem's understanding of that phrase) – on the contrary, to judge from, for example, *in Ti.* III 148.23ff., he is prepared to use them in that capacity. Rather it is that these models do not yield – what Proclus ultimately demands – a consistent physical account.

[53] That is, in the context of astronomy. The notion of things that exist merely as objects of thought had, of course, long been familiar in other, philosophical, contexts, notably in debates on the nature of forms.

[54] Duhem, 1908: 277.

The astronomer, therefore, on this reading is not merely distinct from the physicist, he is not concerned with physical problems at all. Provided the hypotheses allowed the appearances to be saved, his job was done. The subjunctive used as a conditional in Duhem's penultimate sentence ('eût été en droit': only the physicist *would have had* the right) is especially remarkable, as also is Duhem's conclusion that in the majority of cases the physicists' principles were too general to authorise him to pronounce such a judgement.

But if we turn to the passage in Geminus or to that in Aristotle (on which Simplicius was commenting at that point), the contrast drawn between astronomy and physics is, in certain respects, crucially different from Duhem's version. In Aristotle, as is well known, the mathematician differs from the physicist in that he deals with surfaces, volumes, and so on in abstraction from physical objects. Optics, harmonics, and astronomy are introduced as 'the more physical of the μαθήματα': whereas geometry investigates physical lines but not *qua* physical, optics investigates mathematical lines but not *qua* mathematical, but *qua* physical. By implication astronomy does the same. When Aristotle first raises the question of whether astronomy is or is not a part of physics, he says it is absurd if the physicist should be supposed to know what the sun and moon are, || but not to know any of their essential attributes, and he remarks that in point of fact those who write on nature do discuss such questions as the shape of the moon and sun and whether the earth and the cosmos are spherical.[55]

The upshot of this passage in Aristotle is that astronomy ἐπαμφοτερίζει: it is one of the more physical branches of mathematics, and some of its subject-matter is dealt with also by the physicist. Geminus' position, in the passage quoted by Simplicius, is similar, though he is concerned more directly with the relationship between astronomy (not mathematics in general) and physics. It is the job of physics to deal with the οὐσία of the heaven and the stars, their δύναμις and quality, their coming-to-be and destruction: it is even in a position to prove facts about their size, shape, and arrangement. Astronomy, on the other hand, 'does not try to speak about any such kind of thing. It proves the arrangement of the heavenly bodies by declaring that the heaven is truly a cosmos. It speaks about the shapes and sizes and distances of the earth, sun, and moon, about eclipses and conjunctions of stars, and about the quality and quantity of their movements...It needs, accordingly, arithmetic and geometry.'[56] Geminus proceeds to give instances of the same point proved both by the astronomer and by the physicist (that the sun is of great size, and that the earth is spherical – Aristotle's example). The two approaches will differ, the physicist arguing from the οὐσία and the δύναμις, the astronomer from the properties of figures and magnitudes. When he proves facts from external properties, the astronomer is not qualified to judge of the cause, as when, for instance, he declares the earth or the stars to

[55] Aristotle, *Ph.* 193b22–194a12.

[56] Simplicius, *in Ph.* 291.26ff.

be spherical.' Sometimes he does not even seek to grasp the cause' (*in Ph.* 292.12f.), as when he speaks about eclipses. 'At other times he inquires by means of hypothesis, and exhibits certain ways, by the assumption of which the phenomena will be saved' – and the examples given are eccentrics and epicycles. Then: 'it will be necessary to go into in how many ways it is possible for these appearances to be accomplished so that the theory concerning the wandering stars may fit the explanation of causes according to the possible method'.[57] After mentioning the views of a 'certain Heraclides' to the effect that the earth moves in a certain way (a famous crux which fortunately does not concern us here), Geminus says that it is not the business of the astronomer to know which bodies naturally rest and which move, but he introduces hypotheses... and considers from what hypotheses the appearances in the heaven will follow. But he must take his ἀρχαί (starting-points or principles) from the physicist, namely that the movements of the stars are simple and regular and ordered.[58]

Here too, then, as in Aristotle, the same problem, such as the shape of the earth, can sometimes be dealt with by both the astronomer and the physicist: the distinction will be between the kinds of argument they use. Geminus further tells us (1) that in some cases the astronomer does not even seek to grasp the cause, (2) it is his business to say in how many ways it is possible to save the phenomena, (3) it is *not* his business to know which bodies naturally move and which are naturally at rest, but (4) he must take his starting-points or principles || from the physicist. (1), (2), and (3) enable one not merely to distinguish between, but to contrast, astronomy and physics. So far as these statements go, Duhem's view might seem to be the one we should prefer. Yet the introduction of the fourth point makes a crucial difference.[59] (2) certainly says that the astronomer should consider in how many different ways the phenomena can be saved: but (4) subordinates astronomy to physics in this respect, that the astronomer has to take his ἀρχαί from physics, for example the principle that the movements of the stars are simple, regular, and ordered. Geminus, following Aristotle, distinguishes, even contrasts, astronomy and physics: but he does *not* say it is legitimate to do astronomy *divorced from* physics. On the contrary, Geminus' position is clearly that astronomy *presupposes* physics. The problem here is not that Duhem mistranslates the Greek. He writes, quite correctly, 'c'est du physicien qu'il tient ses principes'.[60] It is rather that he ignores the point in question in his discussion. Where Duhem argues that Greek astronomy was concerned purely with the mathematics of their problems, to the exclusion of

[57] Simplicius, *in Ph.* 292.18–20 δεήσει τε ἐπεξελθεῖν, καθ' ὅσους δυνατὸν τρόπους ταῦτα ἀποτελεῖσθαι τὰ φαινόμενα, ὥστε ἐοικέναι τῇ κατὰ τὸν ἐνδεχόμενον τρόπον αἰτιολογίᾳ τὴν περὶ τῶν πλανωμένων ἄστρων πραγματείαν.

[58] Simplicius, *in Ph.* 292.26f. ληπτέον δὲ αὐτῷ ἀρχὰς παρὰ τοῦ φυσικοῦ, ἁπλᾶς εἶναι καὶ ὁμαλὰς καὶ τεταγμένας κινήσεις τῶν ἄστρων...

[59] Cf. also the reference to the heavens being a true κόσμος at Simpl. *in Ph.* 291.27f.

[60] Duhem, 1908: 122, lines 35f.

physics, it is clear that Geminus links that mathematical study to physical assumptions. Nor are there grounds, in the Geminus passage at least, for the subjunctive used as a conditional ('eût été en droit') in which Duhem implies that Greek physicists were not, in general, in a position to provide what they saw as sound and adequate principles on which astronomy could be based.

Two of the main authorities cited by Duhem, Proclus and Geminus, turn out to be frail supports indeed, and the same goes for our source for Geminus, Simplicius himself. Like his contemporary, Philoponus,[61] Simplicius points out critically that the astronomers have not demonstrated their hypotheses and he knows that the same phenomena were sometimes explained by different hypotheses.[62] But that is not to make him an instrumentalist. What he considers (in Duhem's terms) as 'fictitious' or 'not real' are simply the irregularities of the movements of the sun, moon, and planets. The contrast is between those irregularities – which are merely *apparent* – and the *true* circular, orderly, and regular motions in terms of which (as Plato had suggested)[63] those irregularities are to be explained.[64] Simplicius' realist assumptions come out often enough in his discussion of astronomical problems, for example in his reference to the problem of the void left between the spheres in his account of the difficulties that the eccentric hypothesis faces,[65] in his own discussion of what is in between || the stars,[66] and in his recognition that one hypothesis might be preferred to another on the grounds that it postulates fewer heavenly bodies.[67] Finally his lengthy comments on Aristotle's doctrine of the fifth element presuppose that both the stars and the spheres to which they are attached are corporeal entities, σώματα, consisting of a substance whose special property it is to move in a circle.[68]

But if the principal commentators cannot be said to support Duhem's overall thesis, it is now time to turn to his interpretation of the positions of the main astronomical theorists themselves. Of course the chief problem that confronts us is that although we have our Ptolemy, we have none of Apollonius' astronomy and very little of Hipparchus and Aristarchus. We

[61] Philoponus, *De Opificio Mundi* III, ch. 3, 114.24ff. At III, ch. 4, 117.21ff. he implies that the astronomers attempted to give a physical account of the phenomena.

[62] Simplicius, *in Cael.* 488.24ff., 492.25ff. But at 32.29ff. he dissents from Philoponus to say it is no cause for reproach (ἔγκλημα) that the astronomers save the same appearances by different hypotheses. Cf. further below, pp. 270–3, on Ptolemy and Hipparchus.

[63] Simplicius is, of course, our chief evidence for this, e.g. *in Cael.* 488.19ff., citing Sosigenes, who himself may have been following Eudemus.

[64] E.g. *in Cael.* 422.3ff., 427.10ff. Even in 488.10ff. when Simplicius says that the 'true account' not only does not accept stations, retrogradatons, and so on (even if they appear thus) but also 'does not admit the hypotheses' (eccentrics, epicycles, and reacting spheres) 'as being such', what he has in mind is Plato's stipulation that the motions of the sun, moon, and planets should be interpreted as *simple* (ἁπλᾶς, *in Cael.* 488.13, cf. μίαν ἀεὶ κύκλῳ, Plato, *Laws* 822A, a passage to which Simplicius goes on to refer, *in Cael.* 489.5ff.): he recognises, however, that astronomers had to be content interpreting the motions of the sun, moon, and planets in terms of regular, uniform, and circular movements (488.14ff.).

[65] *In Cael.* 510.15ff.

[66] *In Cael.* 461.17ff., cf. also 443.27ff., 451.10ff.

[67] *In Cael.* 509.16ff.

[68] *In Cael.* 435.12–438.26, cf. 428.26ff., 448.6ff., 455.29ff., 477.5ff., 509.30ff.

have Aristotle's *De Caelo* and *Metaphysics* Λ, ch. 8, but not Eudoxus or Callippus. So we are bound to admit that much remains indeterminate in this question. Yet if we can begin where the evidence is solid, we have, at least, our Ptolemy.

No one can doubt that the second book of the *Planetary Hypotheses* with its tambourines or segments of spheres on which the planets are carried is attempting a realist account,[69] that is an account of the actual arrangement of physical objects in the heavens. But given that Halma only edited and translated the section of book I that is extant in Greek, and that a section of what is extant only in Arabic was omitted from Nix's German translation,[70] it might be thought that Duhem had some excuse for representing Ptolemy as an instrumentalist in his articles in 1908. But the situation is more complicated. For one thing Duhem seems to ascribe several physical assumptions to Ptolemy. He began his discussion: 'Ptolémée attribue à chacun des astres errants un orbe d'une certaine épaisseur, contigue aux orbes de l'astre qui le précède et de l'astre qui le suit. Entres les deux surfaces sphériques, concentriques au Monde, qui délimitent son orbe, la planète se meut... '[71], and this is strange. He cited *Syntaxis* IX, ch. I as his authority for this, but that chapter concerns merely the order and relative distances of the planets, and says nothing about the nature and disposition of their spheres, let alone about two spherical surfaces which delimit the orbit of the planet and between which it moves.[72] Yet whatever the source of Duhem's remark, the idea that Ptolemy's astronomy presupposes physical considerations is played down in the sequel. Duhem concentrates, rather, on such texts as *Syntaxis* XIII, ch. 2 and III, ch. 4, interpreting these as support for his general thesis about Greek astronomy,[73] and indeed a modern Duhemian might still want to argue that Ptolemy was a sound instrumentalist in the *Syntaxis* even though he mistakenly adopted a naive realist position in the *Planetary Hypotheses*. But to ‖ that one must say that although most of the *Syntaxis* is undoubtedly taken up with solving purely mathematical problems, the whole discussion is set very firmly in the framework of certain physical assumptions. The two chief instances are (I) the use of physical arguments, relating to αἰθήρ, in the proof of the sphericity of the heavens in I, ch. 3, [74] and

[69] See especially ch. 6, 117.8ff.

[70] Nix, 1907. The complete Arabic text has subsequently been edited, and the missing section of book I translated, by Goldstein, 1967.

[71] Duhem, 1908: 129.

[72] He later correctly noted, however, that Ptolemy refers to the homogeneity and transparency of the medium of the heavenly region in *Syntaxis* XIII, ch. 2, II 533.I–10; Duhem, 1908: 130f.

[73] E.g. 'il faut bien se garder de croire que ces constructions mécaniques aient, dans le Ciel, la moindre réalité' (Duhem, 1908: 131.). Here as elsewhere it is not clear whether by 'constructions mécaniques' Duhem means the astronomical hypotheses, or actual scale models. On the previous page he ascribes to Ptolemy the view that it is folly to try to represent the movements of the heavenly bodies in mechanical devices made of *wood* or *metal*: yet in *Syntaxis* XIII, ch. 2 the devices (ἐπιτεχνήματα) that Ptolemy says may be found troublesome are simply the astronomical hypotheses themselves.

[74] The argument is that the heavens are composed of the finest and most homogeneous element, αἰθήρ: since the surfaces of homogeneous bodies will themselves be homogeneous, and the

(2) the fact that the two main arguments in I, ch. 7 for the absolute immobility of the earth are both physical, namely the doctrine of natural places and the absence of observed centrifugal effects on the earth's surface.[75]

What has impressed modern commentators is the problem that arises from the values that Ptolemy adopts for the diameter of the epicycle and deferent of the moon, values from which it follows that the apparent angular diameter of the moon should vary by about a factor of 2, when the observed variation is much smaller.[76] But the conclusion drawn from this by Dreyer, for example, when he says that 'it had now become a recognised fact, that the epicyclic theory was merely a means of calculating the apparent places of the planets without pretending to represent the true system of the world',[77] is simply *not* drawn by Ptolemy himself. He merely passes over the problem in silence. Even in XIII, ch. 2, when he asks us not to be dismayed by the complexity of the hypotheses that he has to use, his standpoint is not one of indifference to the question of whether his devices represent the 'true system'. Why, one might ask, should he worry over purely mathematical complexity? One might suggest that the source of his concern is, in part at least, the implications of those complexities when translated into physical terms. Certainly the justification that he offers for the hypotheses he adopts is one that appeals to the difference between the substance of the heavens and the sublunary region. At *Syntaxis* XIII, ch. 2, II 532.14ff., he says:

> It is not fitting to compare human things with divine ones,[78] nor to form beliefs concerning such great things from examples that are so unlike them. For what could be more unlike than those things that are eternal and unchanging and those that are never unchanging, or those that can be hindered by anything and those that cannot be hindered even by themselves?... For provided each of the appearances is saved as a consequence of the hypotheses, why should it still seem strange to anyone that such complications can come about in the movements of the heavenly bodies, when their nature is such as to offer no hindrance, but is exactly fitted to yield and give way to the natural movements of each of them (even if the movements happen to be contrary) so that they can all penetrate and shine through absolutely all the fluid media.

Thus he does not defend his hypotheses *solely* on the grounds that they save the phenomena: rather he adduces physical arguments from the nature of the substance ‖ of the heavenly region (which is eternal, unchanging, homogeneous, and transparent) to support the possibility of the types of motion

most homogeneous solid figure is the sphere, we may suppose that the αἰθήρ is spherical, *Syntaxis* I, ch. 3, I 13.21ff.

[75] *Syntaxis* I, ch. 7, I 21.14ff., 24.14ff.

[76] Indeed the actual values he assigns to the least and greatest distances of the moon in the *Plantetary Hypotheses* (I, part 2, ch. 3, Goldstein, 1967: 7, cf. *Syntaxis* V, ch. 13–18) are 33 earth radii and 64 earth radii respectively, ignoring fractions. Cf. e.g. Neugebauer, 1957: 195f., and Copernicus, *De Revolutionibus* IV, ch. 2.

[77] Dreyer, 1906: 196.

[78] The importance of Ptolemy's reference to the *divinity* of the objects studied by astronomy should not be underestimated. The famous epigram ascribed to him (*AP* IX 577) suggests, if genuine, a more than merely conventionally religious element in the spirit with which he conducted his investigations, and *Syntaxis* I, ch. 1, I 7.17ff. clearly states that contemplation of the good order and proportion of divine things promotes good order in the soul.

he proposes.[79] Here too, then, the influence of his underlying realist assumptions is apparent.

Apart from XIII, ch. 2, the other main passage in the *Syntaxis* that Duhem took instrumentally is III, ch. 4, where Ptolemy observes, in connection with his theory of the sun in particular, that the appearances may be saved on either an epicyclic or an eccentric hypothesis. The recognition of the equivalence of these two models is, indeed, represented by Duhem as good evidence that all that ancient astronomers were concerned with was the mathematics of the problem, not the physics. That conclusion is, however, premature. What Ptolemy actually says, after noting that both models can be used to account for the appearances in relation to the sun, is that the eccentric hypothesis is to be preferred because 'it is simple and effected by one, not two movements'.[80] That is not as clear as it might be, since the 'simplicity' in question might be either mathematical or physical or both. The issue would have been settled if Ptolemy had said either that the eccentric is superior merely because it is easier to calculate with, or that it is preferable because it requires fewer heavenly bodies.[81] But the reference to one, not two movements would appear to be compatible with either type of concern, and if that is the case, one should hesitate before concluding that Ptolemy has in mind mathematical considerations *alone*. That is, no doubt, to some extent a matter of debate. But the fundamental point remains that to represent Ptolemy in general as interested purely in the mathematics of his problems cannot be right given first the appeal to physical arguments in I, chh. 3 and 7 of the *Syntaxis* and second the straightforwardly realist account offered in the second book of the *Planetary Hypotheses*.[82]

But Ptolemy aside, how did other ancient astronomers react to the equivalence of the epicyclic and eccentric hypotheses, a feature which – as is now generally agreed[83] – was probably known and demonstrated by Apollonius himself? So far as Apollonius' own position goes, we simply have no evidence at all. But Duhem used a passage in Theon of Smyrna to suggest that Hipparchus' response, at least, contributed to the divorce of mathematics from physics in Greek astronomy. The information we have from Theon is meagre enough. First in ch. 26 he says: 'Hipparchus says that it is worthy of mathematical[84] attention to see the reason why the same results appear to follow from such widely differing hypotheses, that of the eccentric circles, and that of the concentric, epicyclic ones.'[85] Then in ch. 34,

[79] I am grateful to Professor G. J. Toomer for having emphasised this point to me.

[80] *Syntaxis* III, ch. 4, I 232.14–17 εὐλογώτερον δ' ἂν εἴη περιαφθῆναι τῇ κατ' ἐκκεντρότητα ὑποθέσει ἁπλουστέρᾳ οὔσῃ καὶ ὑπὸ μιᾶς, οὐχὶ δὲ ὑπὸ δύο κινήσεων, συντελουμένῃ. Cf. Duhem, 1908: 131f.

[81] Cf. Simplicius, *in Cael.* 509.16ff., noted above, n.67.

[82] Although as noted above, p. 269, Duhem began by noting some interest in physical principles on Ptolemy's part, he subsequently represents Ptolemy as a pure instrumentalist, e.g. 1908: 284.

[83] See e.g. Neugebauer, 1959: 5–21.

[84] μαθηματικῆς: a term which does not, of course, necessarily mean 'mathematical' as opposed to 'physical'.

[85] *Expositio Rerum Mathematicarum* 166.6ff., cf. also ch. 32, 185.17.

when, following Adrastus, he has shown that each of the two hypotheses can be represented as the *per accidens* consequence of the other, he goes on:

> Seeing this, Hipparchus praised the epicyclic hypothesis as being his own, saying that it is more plausible that all the heavenly bodies should lie symmetrically with regard to the centre of the universe and be joined together similarly. Yet since he was not sufficiently supplied from physics, not even he recognised exactly which of the planetary motions is according to nature and thus a true motion, and which is accidental and [only] apparent.[86] ||

Duhem, whose translations here were, in the main, accurate enough,[87] drew some drastic conclusions from the later passage: 'En prouvant que deux hypothèses distinctes pouvaient s'accorder *par accident* et sauver également toutes les apparences du mouvement solaire, Hipparque a grandement contribué à délimiter exactement la portée des théories astronomiques.' That 'delimination' becomes clear in the outcome, where, referring now to Theon, Duhem wrote: 'Ces propositions mettent en évidence, selon lui, l'impossibilité où se trouve l'astronome de découvrir l'hypothèse vraie, celle qui est conforme à la nature des choses.'

One may first object that the passage that Duhem goes on to quote as giving Theon's view on the subject is in fact one of his frequent quotations from Adrastus.[88] It was Adrastus who thought that the disagreement among the mathematicians was shown up as absurd because both hypotheses save the phenomena. Yet Theon himself did not believe that to be the end of the matter. On the contrary chapters 32ff. are devoted to establishing that there is *one* correct account. Although he recognises that the two hypotheses are mathematically equivalent, one account is the true natural, κατὰ φύσιν, one, the other merely *per accidens*, κατὰ συμβεβηκός. The natural account turns out to be one in which the epicycle is interpreted as a great circle on a solid sphere, this solid sphere being imagined as carried round within two hollow spheres.[89] It is only possible to say, as Duhem says, that Theon believed that the astronomer cannot discover the true hypothesis, by quoting a passage from Theon's preliminary aporetic discussion, before he came to give his own solution. Moreover Theon is not only a naïve realist himself, but he also represents Greek astronomy as a whole as founded on physics. This comes out clearly in a passage not mentioned by Duhem in which Theon contrasts

[86] *Exp. Rer. Math.* 188.15ff. ὅπερ καὶ συνιδὼν ὁ Ἵππαρχος ἐπαινεῖ τὴν κατ' ἐπίκυκλον ὑπόθεσιν ὡς οὖσαν ἑαυτοῦ, πιθανώτερον εἶναι λέγων πρὸς τὸ τοῦ κόσμου μέσον πάντα τὰ οὐράνια ἰσορρόπως κεῖσθαι καὶ ὁμοίως συναρηρότα· οὐδὲ αὐτὸς μέντοι, διὰ τὸ μὴ ἐφωδιάσθαι ἀπὸ φυσιολογίας, σύνοιδεν ἀκριβῶς, τίς ἡ κατὰ φύσιν καὶ κατὰ ταῦτα ἀληθὴς φορὰ τῶν πλανωμένων καὶ τίς ἡ κατὰ συμβεβηκὸς καὶ φαινομένη.

[87] Duhem, 1908: 119f. (Theon's expression διὰ τὸ μή ἐφωδιάσθαι ἀπὸ φυσίολογίας, 188.19f., would seem to mean 'because he was not sufficiently supplied from physics', i.e. with data or principles or both, rather than Duhem's vague 'ne connaissant pas suffisamment la Physique').

[88] See φησί at *Exp. Rer. Math.* 154.12; cf. the reference to Adrastus at 151.20.

[89] See especially *Exp. Rer. Math.* 181.12ff., 186.12ff. Cf. also the rejection of eccentrics as being remote from what is 'according to nature' and rather 'per accidens' in ch. 34, 188.13–15.

Babylonian and Egyptian astronomy with Greek in just this respect: the former were merely arithmetical and geometrical, but incomplete because lacking φυσιολογία, while the Greeks included the latter.[90] Finally at the end of the treatise Theon quotes Dercyllides to the effect that in astronomy certain principles must be agreed, and these principles turn out to include not merely the assumption that the cosmos is orderly, but also which bodies are in movement and which at rest.[91]

But then what about Hipparchus? Here Theon may well be a very unreliable witness: we must bear in mind that he attributes to Hipparchus a preference for the epicyclic hypothesis which is precisely the hypothesis that he, Theon, prefers. But so far as what Theon says goes, the reason he gives for Hipparchus' preference || is general and cosmological, not purely mathematical. He does not say that Hipparchus chose epicycles because they are mathematically simpler – more convenient for the purposes of calculation – but rather that he did so because 'it is more plausible that all the heavenly bodies should lie symmetrically with regard to the centre of the universe and be joined together similarly'.[92] The point appears to be that whereas in the case of an individual planet the eccentric hypothesis may save the phenomena, the system as a whole requires several different eccentrics, that is several different centres of motion, while on the epicyclic hypothesis, on the other hand, the concentric deferents have a single centre. The latter is clearly more easily squared with Aristotle's physical principle according to which movement must be either to, from, or round the centre of the universe,[93] and if that was Hipparchus' point, or one of them, then it would indeed be mistaken to represent him as a pure instrumentalist.

Finally we must comment very briefly on the fourth-century-B.C. evidence used by Duhem. Here the contrast between Eudoxus and Callippus on the one hand, and Aristotle on the other, is usually represented as one between a kinematic, and a dynamical, theory,[94] and indeed Aristotle's introduction of retroactive spheres is to be explained in terms of an attempt to account for the transmission of movement from the outermost sphere to the sublunary region. Yet while we can be confident that Aristotle made that much of an attempt at a dynamical theory, the fact that our evidence for Eudoxus and Callippus is limited to their kinematic theories does not of itself prove that they had no dynamical theories at all. It is as well to recognise that we simply have no reliable information on that point,[95] only at best a questionable

[90] *Exp. Rer. Math.* 177.9–178.2, especially 177.20ff: πάντες μὲν (i.e. the Babylonians, Chaldaeans and Egyptians) ἄνευ φυσιολογίας ἀτελεῖς ποιούμενοι τὰς μεθόδους, δέον ἅμα καὶ φυσικῶς περὶ τούτων ἐπισκοπεῖν· ὅπερ οἱ παρὰ τοῖς Ἕλλησιν ἀστρολογήσαντες ἐπειρῶντο ποιεῖν...

[91] *Exp. Rer. Math.* 199.14ff., 200.7ff.

[92] *Exp. Rer. Math.* 188.17ff., quoted above p. 272 and n. 86.

[93] Cf. Proclus' reference to this 'common axiom of the physicists', *in Ti* III 146.21ff., above, n. 39.

[94] I should certainly now wish to qualify too conventional statements of my own to that effect; Lloyd, 1970: 92.

[95] It is noteworthy that Simplicius refers to the concentric spheres model (common to Eudoxus,

argument from silence.[96] Nor do we have any *evidence* concerning their views on the status of the homocentric spheres they postulated, though we may of course advance certain conjectures on that question.

III

It is now time to take stock of our conclusions, and I must first repeat, with the strongest possible emphasis, that for many of the most important figures in the history of Greek astronomy we are simply not in a position to pronounce definitely on their views either on the status of the various hypotheses they used, or on the more general question of the nature of astronomy and its relation to physics. Where we do have some evidence, however, whether from practising astronomers or from the major commentators, it often contradicts the line of interpretation advocated so forcefully by Duhem and thereafter echoed by others. So far from the majority of those texts supporting the thesis that Greek astronomers were, in general, not concerned with the truth of their hypotheses and with whether they conformed to the nature of things, those texts tend to provide evidence against that thesis. In the methodological statements of || Geminus, Theon, and Proclus, and in the actual practice of Ptolemy, we find support for the opposing point of view, that so far from being indifferent to physics the astronomer must take his starting-points from the physicist, starting-points which include not only the general Platonic assumption that the movements of the heavenly bodies are regular, uniform, and circular, but also assumptions or theories concerning which bodies are at rest and which in movement, mentioned among the ἀρχαί by Theon and explicitly discussed in the first book of Ptolemy's *Syntaxis*.[97] Indeed the adverse reception of the heliocentric theory itself surely tells against the view that Greek astronomers were, in general, indifferent to the physical implications of the hypotheses they adopted.

None of this is to deny that the great strength of Greek theoretical astronomy lies in its application of mathematics to the problem of celestial motion – a point that Duhem was, of course, absolutely right to emphasise, as he was also in drawing attention, in particular, to the influence of Plato. The chief task of the astronomer *qua* astronomer was to work out mathematical models from which the observed courses could be derived, and

Callippus, and Aristotle) as the hypothesis of the *reacting* spheres, e.g. *in Cael.* 32.16ff., 488.9, 493.4ff.

96 Wright, 1973–4: 165ff. has indeed recently argued that certain features of Eudoxus' system reveal his concern for the physics of his problems and that his interest was far from being purely geometrical.

97 In Geminus, too, although it is not the astronomer's business to decide which bodies are at rest and which in movement, he takes his starting-points from the physicist, see above, pp. 266–8.

for that purpose Greek astronomers often simplify their problems, as Ptolemy, for example, does when he omits movement in latitude from his discussion of the planets until book XIII of the *Syntaxis* or when he argues that the earth has the ratio of a point to the heavens (I, ch. 6). On occasions Greek astronomical assumptions are not merely not translatable back into physical terms, but known by their proponents to be incorrect. Here I would agree with Wasserstein and others that this is the most likely interpretation of the hypothesis we find in Aristarchus' *On the Sizes and Distances of the Sun and Moon* when he takes 2° as the value of the angular diameter of the moon. One presumes he knew this value to be grossly inaccurate, but in this context any value will do since his aim is to solve the geometrical problems of the question.[98] Yet the important point is surely this: the astronomers' interest in the mathematics of their problems often *did* presuppose a concern with the physics and often again did not exclude such a concern.[99]

To conclude: some of the support Duhem claimed for his general thesis from particular texts depends on a questionable, in places I should say certifiably incorrect, understanding of them. Where it is perfectly fair to say that the Greeks distinguished, even contrasted, mathematics and physics, it is an exaggeration to claim they advocated a mathematical astronomy divorced from physics or sought to liberate astronomy from all the physical conditions imposed on it.[100] Where we may well agree that the astronomers (like other scientists) || often simplified their problems and sometimes advanced positions for the sake of argument, Duhem again exaggerated in representing Greek astronomical hypotheses in general as adopted purely for the sake of calculations. Dynamical and other physical factors, as well as considerations of mathematical simplicity, could be appealed to in deciding between theories. It was sometimes not just a matter of saving the appearances but of giving the true, κατὰ φύσιν, account, and even 'saving the appearances' sometimes meant more than just providing calculations that corresponded with the data, but 'saving' the φαινόμενα by relating them to ὄντα, with the emphasis on the distinction between the mere 'appearances' and the underlying 'realities'.[101] Duhem represented the major Greek thinkers as coming down on the side of Osiander and Ursus against Kepler and Galileo,

[98] See Wasserstein 1962: 57f. and cf. e.g. Neugebauer, 1972: 248.

[99] Even though no ancient astronomer was successful in giving an adequate *dynamical* account of the movements of the heavenly bodies, that did not preclude their being interested in the *physics* of their problems – a point sometimes obscured by Duhem's concentration on a simple contrast being 'mathématique' and 'physique' even though he was well aware of certain differences between his own 'physique' and ancient φυσική e.g. Duhem, 1908: 114. So far as attempted dynamical theories go, an important feature of some of the vitalist views that stem from Plato is their dualism: Plato himself identified the moving force as an (incorporeal) soul different *in kind* from the (corporeal) heavenly body it moves (e.g. *Laws* 898EF).

[100] E.g. Duhem, 1908: 129: 'les partisans de Ptolémée étaient tenus ... d'affranchir les hypothèses astronomiques des conditions auxquelles les physiciens les avaient, en général, asservies'. Cf. also Mittelstrass, 1962: 164.

[101] As in e.g. Simplicius (see above, p. 268 and n. 64). On the ambiguities of the expression σῴζειν τὰ φαινόμενα see Mittelstrass, 1962: 140ff.

and he thereby joined the controversy that Ursus and Kepler themselves engaged in on the nature of Greek astronomy. Yet so far as our evidence goes, it would be truer to say that the aims and presuppositions of many Greek writers on astronomy have more in common with those of Kepler than with those of Ursus – as Kepler himself suggested.[102] The question of the emergence and development of this recurrent debate in European astronomy, and that of the relevance of this for Duhem's reading of the Greeks, are, however, issues beyond the scope of this paper.

[102] In his *Apologia Tychonis contra Ursum* (*Opera Omnia*, ed. C. Frisch, vol. I, Frankfurt, 1858), referred to by Duhem, 1908: 574ff.

REFERENCES

Except where otherwise stated, ancient authors are cited according to the following editions: Philoponus, *De Opificio Mundi*, ed. W. Reichardt (Leipzig, 1897); Proclus, *Hypotyposis Astronomicarum Positionum*, ed. C. Manitius (Leipzig, 1909); *in Platonis Rem Publicam Commentarii*, ed. W. Kroll (Leipzig, 1899–1901); *in Platonis Timaeum Commentaria*, ed. E. Diehl (Leipzig, 1903–6); Ptolemy, *Syntaxis Mathematica*, ed. J. L. Heiberg (Leipzig, 1898–1903); *Opera Astronomica Minora*, ed. J. L. Heiberg (Leipzig, 1907); Simplicius, *in Aristotelis De Caelo Commentaria*, ed. J. L. Heiberg (Berlin, 1894); *in Aristotelis Physica Commentaria*, ed. H. Diels (Berlin, 1882–95); Theon of Smyrna, *Expositio Rerum Mathematicarum*, ed. E. Hiller (Leipzig, 1878).

Dijksterhuis, E. J. (1961) *The Mechanization of the World Picture*, original Dutch 1950 (Oxford)

Doland, E. and Maschler, C. (1969) *To Save the Phenomena*, (transl. of Duhem, 1908), (Chicago)

Dreyer, J. L. E. (1906) *History of the Planetary Systems from Thales to Kepler* (Cambridge)

Duhem, P. (1908) ΣΩΖΕΙΝ ΤΑ ΦΑΙΝΟΜΕΝΑ, *Annales de Philosophie Chrétienne* 6: 113–39, 277–302, 352–77, 482–514, 561–92

(1954) *Le Système du monde*, I 2nd edn (1st edn 1913) (Paris)

Goldstein, B. R. (1967) 'The Arabic version of Ptolemy's *Planetary Hypotheses*', *Transactions of the American Philosophical Society* 57.4

Grynaeus, S. (1540) *Procli Diadochi Hypotyposis Astronomicarum Positionum* (Basel)

Halma, N. (1820) *Hypothèses et époques des planètes de C. Ptolémée et Hypotyposes de Proclus Diadochus* (Paris)

Hesse, M. B. (1967) 'Laws and theories', *Encyclopedia of Philosophy*, ed. P. Edwards, vol. IV, 404–10 (New York)

Lloyd, G. E. R. (1970) *Early Greek Science, Thales to Aristotle* (London)

Manitius, C. (1909) *Proclus, Hypotyposis Astronomicarum Positionum* (Leipzig)

Mittelstrass, J. (1962) *Die Rettung der Phänomene* (Berlin)

Neugebauer, O. (1957) *The Exact Sciences in Antiquity*, 2nd edn (Providence, R.I.)

(1959) 'The equivalence of eccentric and epicyclic motion according to Apollonius', *Scripta Mathematica* 24: 5–21

(1972) 'On some aspects of early Greek astronomy', *Proceedings of the American Philosophical Society* 116: 243–51

Nix, L. (1907) Translation of book II of Ptolemy, *Planetary Hypotheses*, in Ptolemy, *Opera Astronomica Minora*, ed. J. L. Heiberg (Leipzig)

Sambursky, S. (1962): *The Physical World of Late Antiquity* (London)

(1965): 'Plato, Proclus, and the limitations of science', *Journal of the History of Philosophy* 3: 1–11

Wasserstein, A. (1962) 'Greek scientific thought', *Proceedings of the Cambridge Philological Society* 188, N.S. 8: 51–63

Wright, L. (1973–4) 'The astronomy of Eudoxus: geometry or physics?', *Studies in the History and Philosophy of Science* 4: 165–72

12

THE DEBT OF GREEK PHILOSOPHY AND SCIENCE TO THE ANCIENT NEAR EAST

INTRODUCTION

As its informal style and lack of footnotes no doubt suggest, the paper published under the title 'The debt of Greek philosophy and science to the ancient Near East' in *Pedilavium* in 1982 originated in a public lecture. An earlier version was first given in Birmingham, as the Rundle Clark Memorial lecture in 1976, and the version published corresponds fairly closely to an address to the Japanese Classical Society in 1981. In an occasionally provocative and at points deliberately oversimplifying way, the paper attempts both to suggest certain ground-rules for comparative studies and to set out some broad theses with respect to the particular problems posed by the relationship between the philosophy and science of the ancient Greeks and the theories and practice of their immediate ancient Near Eastern neighbours.

So far as the ground-rules for any such study go, there was, I would now say, little exaggeration in my emphatic insistence on the need to be wary of the grand generalisation. The validity of the point I made (p. 283) that the circumstances of influence or transmission vary importantly as between the four fields I mentioned (technology, religion and mythology, mathematics and astronomy, medicine) has not diminished. Although we can use those general characterisations of broad aspects of the culture of the ancient civilisations concerned, not only must we be prepared to draw distinctions between these four where any single culture is in question, but we also cannot afford to assume that the intellectual or social position, aims or preoccupations of any one field in one culture will be identical with those in any other. Medicine, no doubt, is always directed to healing the sick: but the conception of what it is that needs healing, the role or roles of the often diverse types of person who practise healing, may vary drastically from one culture to another. Again while broad comparisons are possible between one religion and another, one mythology and another, their place cannot be assumed to remain fixed and stable in all cultures – and the same must also be said even of mathematics and astronomy.

My particular concern, in this study, was with the archaic and classical periods when the actual communications between Greece and the Near East were limited. Of course the picture becomes appreciably more complex for later periods when there is evidence of far more extensive direct contacts, and not just between Greece and the Near East, but rather between much of the Greco-Roman world and the Middle and Far East. Yet that similar detailed investigations are possible has been shown, above all, by Joseph Needham's discussions in his *Science and Civilisation in China*. Here too it is clear that just how particular ideas, knowledge, myths, techniques travelled, and why some did easily and others only very slowly, are questions that have to be resolved case by case. There are indeed as many interesting problems relating to the *failure* of transmission, when cultural contact existed, as there are to successful transmission, as many questions that are worth raising about the presuppositions that favoured or impeded influence as about the adaptation of the ideas and techniques actually transmitted.

As for my own rapid *tour d'horizon* of what might be said, for the archaic and classical periods, about Greek philosophy and science, I would now observe that the perspective from which I discussed philosophy was very much a Greek one, as, for example, when I wrote (p. 297) that philosophical inquiry as such is a Greek invention. That is true of the style of philosophy that *we* have inherited from the Greeks – and the points I made concerning the differences between that style of inquiry, and myth, hold subject to that qualification. But of course if I had taken a wider perspective and considered modes of philosophising that take different forms, the claim concerning the Greeks rapidly becomes transparently absurd. India and China both had their distinct philosophical, as well as their religious and scientific, traditions. However, from the point of view of what the Greeks might have learnt from Egypt or Babylonia, our evidence still suggests that that would not have extended as far as philosophy, construed as the argumentative, rational or would-be rational inquiry that it was for most Greeks.

Here too much further work needs to be done, and the issues will undoubtedly prove to be more convoluted than even the complexities of the material I discussed. The analysis of the origins of science, technology and philosophy in any given culture, and of what they may or may not owe to outside influences, is just the first step towards the analysis of the culture as a whole. That first analysis takes one into problems not just of an intellectual or internalist nature, but, as I acknowledged but could not follow up in my article, into issues concerning the whole background of the social, political and ideological conditions that accompanied the development of the distinctive *styles* of science and philosophy in question. My original paper set an agenda, in other words, and does no more than outline aspects of the answers in relation to the ancient Greeks and their Near Eastern neighbours.

REFERENCES

Bernal, M. (1987) *Black Athena* (London)
Cornford, F. M. (1912) *From Religion to Philosophy* (London)
(1952) *Principium Sapientiae* (Cambridge)

Frankfort, H., ed. (1949) *Before Philosophy* (London)
Jacobsen, T. (1949) 'Mesopotamia', in *Before Philosophy*, ed. H. Frankfort (London), 137–234
Kirk, G. S., and Raven, J. E. (1957) *The Presocratic Philosophers*, 1st edn (Cambridge)
Needham, J. (1954–) *Science and Civilisation in China* (Cambridge)
West, M. L. (1971) *Early Greek Philosophy and the Orient* (Oxford)
Wilson, J. A. (1949) 'Egypt', in *Before Philosophy*, ed. H. Frankfort (London), 39–133

THE DEBT OF GREEK PHILOSOPHY AND SCIENCE TO THE ANCIENT NEAR EAST

To reopen so venerable a topic as the debt of Greek philosophy and science to the ancient Near East calls for some words of explanation. The topic goes back, after all, to the Greeks themselves. Ancient Greek attitudes towards their Near Eastern neighbours underwent several transformations – not that we should think of those attitudes as uniform or universal at any period. Two phases, in particular, stand out, very broadly speaking, a phase of discovery and one of syncretism. First there is the great upsurge of interest from the mid-sixth century, continuing through the fifth and fourth, a period when Greek knowledge of the Egyptian and Babylonian civilisations especially increased tremendously and when we find evidence of the deep impression those civilisations made upon the Greeks in one major Greek author after another. Herodotus' admiration for Egypt and Babylonia is obvious in his detailed descriptions of them (that of Egypt, at least, based on first-hand acquaintance). Nor need I remind you that there is a series of references in Plato (some more serious than others, to be sure) to the antiquity of the Egyptian race and to several of their more notable cultural achievements.

The second phase, that of syncretism, was already advanced by the turn of the millennium, as we can see from Diodorus and Strabo, for example. Even in Herodotus' day, the Egyptian priests whom he quotes claimed that Egypt was the source of much Greek religion. By the time we get to Diodorus, the list of those Greeks who – according to the Egyptians – got their ideas from Egypt has grown fantastically. It now includes Orpheus, Musaeus, Melampus, Daedalus, Homer, Lycurgus, Solon, Plato, Pythagoras, Eudoxus, Democritus and Oenopides. The priests whom Diodorus cites put it bluntly that 'all the things for which [these men] were admired among the Greeks were brought from Egypt'. The tendency to assimilate Greek and Near Eastern wisdom, and to see the latter as anticipating Greek philosophy, grows still further in the early Christian period. Thus Clement of Alexandria, who quotes Numenius for the idea that Plato is really Moses writing Attic, sets out systematically, in his *Stromateis*, to prove that Greek philosophy was anticipated by the wisdom of the prophets and that the Greek philosophers plagiarised what they present as their own ideas from the East.

But if ancient authors initiated the debate, the continuation of the controversy forms an important strand in the transmission of Greek learning through the Middle Ages down to the Renaissance and beyond. The fortunes of the two opposing views (of Greek originality, || and of Greek derivativeness) shift from one generation to another and I cannot do justice to that aspect of the question here. But Stevin, for example, was one important scientist who believed in an oral, unwritten wisdom in what he calls the Age of the Sages long before Presocratic philosophy, and Isaac Newton himself wrote a treatise on 'the chronology of ancient kingdoms amended' to establish a similar thesis. In the nineteenth century similar battle lines are drawn up. Thus a prominent section in the introduction to Zeller's classic *History of Greek Philosophy* was devoted to refuting the theses of Röth and Gladisch. According to Gladisch, for instance, 'the Presocratic systems reproduced without any material alteration the theories of the universe of the five chief Oriental nations', that is Chinese, Hindus, Persians, Jews and Egyptians.

Many of the contributions to this immensely long-drawn-out debate have been highly charged with emotive language. Indeed it has been so long drawn out partly because 'Greece' and the 'Near East' have often been used as a polar antithesis, 'Greece' being taken to stand for reason, the 'near East' for Faith, Religion, Mysticism or The Irrational – as if (apart from all the other points that such an anthithesis ignores) the Greeks did not have their own religion, indeed their mystery religions, and as if, conversely, the Egyptians and Babylonians did not excel in such hard-headed practical matters as the administration of large-scale empires. It was, on this own account, partly because he was provoked by this type of gross oversimplification that Dodds wrote the book, *The Greeks and the Irrational*, which has, ever since its appearance in 1951, been largely instrumental in producing a swing away from the earlier drastically misguided identification of the Greeks with pure reason.

But why, then, reopen a subject which has been the occasion of so much arid, prejudiced and unscholarly posturing? I am not going to claim that we have now achieved some Olympian height from which we can adjudicate on the dispute, though I would claim (I have just claimed) that we may be in a better position than many of our predecessors to see that some of this debate has not really been about what it purports to be about at all. It has not been a historical study, but a pretext for the debaters to air their own views about the relative merits of Reason and the Irrational. But when we have progressed beyond that point, and beyond the point of merely distributing compliments or criticisms to the Greeks and to their various Near Eastern neighbours, there are important issues to be discussed concerning the question of the origin or invention of philosophy and science themselves. The two fundamental problems here are first what sort of development in thought are we to suppose that they involved (and in particular should we see the origin of philosophy and science in || terms of a gradual development or of some revolutionary change or breakthrough)? And secondly (though this is not a question I shall be able to follow up today) what were the social, political and ideological conditions that accompanied this development or revolution? If we are to get clear on these questions, we must indeed try to come to terms with the problem of the relations of the Greeks to the Near East. Many aspects of those relations are – and in the absence of new evidence must remain – highly obscure, and we must acknowledge that fact.

But some detailed work recently undertaken in a number of different inquiries has made it possible to be clearer on certain aspects of the problem. I aim to collate points from some of this recent work to arrive at some provisional conclusions on some features of the question.

In considering what the Greeks may or may not have taken over from their ancient Near Eastern neighbours, we must first recognise the great variety of different fields of possible influence and the fact that each different field poses its own problems. Four of the main areas that will concern us are (1) technology, (2) religion and mythology, (3) mathematics and astronomy and (4) medicine. But what on the one hand enabled or facilitated, and what on the other impeded, the transmission of ideas varies with the field in question – a simple point that has, I fear, too often been ignored. Thus the circumstances in which a metallurgical technique may be transmitted are quite different from those of the transmission of a religious belief or myth, which differ in turn from those of a piece of astronomical lore, which differ in turn from those of a method of cure. In particular the extent to which the transmission must be mediated *through language* differs, and so too does the extent to which the transmission is effected between individuals who already possess *specialised* knowledge. Thus there may be less formidable barriers to communication between two specialists of different cultures, than between a specialist and a layman from the same culture. The English and the Russian mathematician may well communicate more freely (even without knowing each other's natural language) than the English mathematician and the man in the street: and the same may also be true, on occasion, of the English and the Russian medical man, although in considering both these examples we must be aware that the easy communication between modern specialists reflects the standardisation of much specialist knowledge – while the question of how far there was any such standardisation in the ancient world is, of course, one of our main problems.

After these preliminaries, let us consider each of the four main fields I have identified in turn, and first, briefly, technology. No one seriously doubts, I imagine, that most of the basic techniques used in the Greek world in the classical period in such areas as agriculture, metallurgy, textiles, even pottery, had arrived there as the result of a long process of diffusion whether from the Near East or elsewhere. I am thinking, for || example, of the use of the plough, of that of the potter's wheel and of the wheel for transport, of the main techniques of spinning and weaving, and of those of the extraction and working of metals (hammering, melting, casting). In some cases, of course, the hypothesis of independent development of the same or a similar technique in different parts of the Near East and eastern Mediterranean basin cannot be ruled out and may even be preferred. But that some diffusion took place is agreed on all sides, even though *how* that diffusion took place is very much a matter of guesswork: the fact that many craftsmen were itinerant may be one factor, but we must set against that their usual extreme conservatism, at least to judge from the evidence from the historical period. The process stretches back to the third millennium at least, and continues, sporadically, in the historical period, where we are sometimes in a position to date, within broad limits, the introduction of new technological devices, such as the screw-press or the water-wheel.

Yet if we ask how important the development of technology was for the growth of philosophy and science, the answer must be only slightly so. The idea that ancient natural philosophers were *never* interested in technology, *never* concerned to apply their ideas to tame and exploit natural forces, has been much exaggerated (one thinks not only of Archimedes, but of Ctesibius, Philo, Hero of Alexandria and Vitruvius). On the other hand it *is* fair to say that the dominant motive in philosophy was understanding or wisdom, and that the connections between science and technology were far less extensive in the ancient world that they are today.

The period we must focus on is that from, say, the eighth to the sixth century, the period leading up to the practice of the enterprise that we can identify reasonably confidently as *philosophy* and *science* more or less as we know them. Certainly two extremely important developments that may, on a somewhat generous acceptance of the term, be called 'technical' or 'technological' do occur in this period, namely the introduction of coinage (diffused from Lydia, according to Herodotus) and that of the alphabet (where the chief debt of the Greeks was to the West Semitic group of languages). Clearly these developments had an immense impact on the Greek world, and so indirectly on everything that happened within it. Yet it would be hard to claim that either was directly responsible for bringing about the development of philosophy and science. Literacy was, no doubt, essential for the spread of philosophical and scientific inquiry. Equally we may suppose that neither could have been produced except in a society whose economy had the sort of flexibility guaranteed by coinage. Yet even if both these factors (along with many others) may be *necessary* conditions for the development of philosophy and science, neither can by itself (nor can they jointly) be a *sufficient* condition. We have only to reflect that coinage was common to many other peoples in the ancient Near East where there was no ‖ speculative thought of the type practised by the Greek philosophers, and that the same is true (though to a much more limited degree) of the use of an alphabetic system of writing. Although there are certain exceptions, there is a striking overall *homogeneity* in the level of technology throughout the Near East and eastern Mediterranean basin in the period that concerns us. In this area, the Greeks were undoubtedly chiefly beneficiaries, receivers rather than givers. Yet that very homogeneity suggests that the topic is only of limited usefulness and relevance to our attempt to understand the growth of distinctive modes of speculative thought.

Our second field of inquiry, religion and mythology, yields, or has been thought to yield, much richer material for our debate. In recent years the case for the relevance of mythical antecedents to the earliest Greek philosophy has been argued forcefully by a series of outstanding writers, notably Frankfort (*Before Philosophy*), Cornford (*From Religion to Philosophy* and *Principium Sapientiae*), Kirk and Raven, and M. L. West. It is particularly striking that in Kirk and Raven's handbook entitled *The Presocratic Philosophers*, the longest single chapter should be devoted to 'the forerunners of philosophical cosmogony', i.e. myth. Yet the problems that any such thesis faces are formidable, and though some of these have been fully recognised by its advocates, others (particularly some that stem from recent anthropological studies of myths) have been rather neglected. A brief summary of some of the general difficulties that the thesis must face is in order before considering some particular case-histories.

First, while there is no problem in supposing that the earliest Greek philosophers were familiar with their own, Greek, mythologists (such as Hesiod), the idea that they were aware of Egyptian, Babylonian or Hittite myths is – we must remember – an *assumption*. It is one that has greater or less plausibility in different cases, depending on the answers to two questions: first how good is the evidence that the philosopher himself travelled in the Near East, and second what is he likely to have learned from Milesian or other traders who did travel? That Miletus was especially active both in trade and in founding colonies is well established. That Thales travelled to Egypt is possible. That Anaximander drew the first Greek map is probable, though we do not know how far it was based on first-hand experience. Yet when Plutarch and Simplicius, for instance, conjecture that Thales was familiar with Egyptian myths, that is, of course, simply a *conjecture*, as are modern suggestions of a similar kind. It is true that the source of a Greek idea is sometimes represented not as an Egyptian, Babylonian or Hittite myth itself, but some archetype from which all the variant versions are derived; but that still involves plenty of conjecture, indeed *more* than the thesis of direct influence.

Secondly, there is the problem of distinguishing fortuitous || from non-fortuitous parallelisms or similarities. Alongside Egyptian or Babylonian material used to interpret Greek ideas, we often find cited Maori or Scandinavian myths. Yet where the 'parallelism' is just as marked with a Maori as with an Egyptian myth, such non-Near-Eastern material provides the basis of a counter-argument to the thesis of direct influence, even though this does not always seem to be recognised. If a particular idea or belief can be 'paralleled' in a culture where it is impossible to postulate direct or indirect influence, this will tend to weaken the claim of direct influence even where there is that possibility.

This takes me immediately to a far more fundamental third point. Since structuralism has – for all its excesses – proved such a powerful tool of interpretation in the study of myths, there has been a transformation in the view taken by anthropologists on the question of the elements to be taken as the basis of comparison in cross-cultural inquiries. The essential point is that it is no good taking *individual* motifs (such as the Sky God, or the castration motif) and comparing *these* across cultures. The basis of the comparison must be not the isolated motif, but the *complex*, for it is only within a complex structure that any individual item can be understood even within a single culture. But when we accept that principle, the similarities between Greek and non-Greek mythologies begin to look far less impressive.

Fourthly and finally a distinction must be observed between the transmission of mythical ideas from one culture to another, on the one hand, and the influence of myth on *philosophy* on the other. When we are considering the Milesian philosophers and their successors, the question can and should always be asked: what did they *see* in the particular myths that are thought to have influenced them? Why did any particular Presocratic choose the particular myth he did? How did he use the idea he derived from it? This raises fundamental questions about the nature of the philosopher's activity, and of his entitlement to be called a philosopher. Yet the distinction in aim between a Hesiod and a Thales must always be borne in mind in evaluating their handling of, or response to, mythical beliefs.

Now to apply these principles to some actual examples – and I have, of course, to be highly selective – first to Thales' water, then to Anaximander's Boundless, and then to Heraclitus' fire. In assessing the suggestion that in postulating water as the origin of things Thales was influenced by ancient Near Eastern myths, and in particular by the Babylonian myth of Tiamat and the Egyptian one of Nun, we must first set those mythical figures in their respective complex, and quite different, contexts. Tiamat, as Kirk himself put it, is a primeval water goddess whom Marduk splits, making one half the sky (and the celestial waters) and one half Apsu the deep and Esharra, the 'great abode' or firmament of earth. But before this splitting takes place, we || have an account of the state of things at the beginning of the poem, *Enuma Elish*, that runs as follows: 'when on high the heaven had not been named, firm ground below had not been called by name, naught but primordial Apsu, their begetter, (And) Mummu-Tiamat, she who bore them all, their waters commingling as a single body...' Jacobsen commented on this: 'the chaos consisted of three intermingled elements: Apsu, who represents the sweet water; Tiamat, who represents the sea; and Mummu, who cannot as yet be identified with certainty but may represent cloud banks and mist'. Even accepting *that* interpretation of the text, it is obvious that we have no *simple* story. Even if we have three different aspects of water, we already have male and female principles, a begetter and a bearer – and of course neither the splitting of a Tiamat into two, nor the copulation of Apsu and Tiamat, has any analogue in our admittedly very limited information concerning Thales.

In Egypt too the myth in question is a complex one. Nun is the primeval water, but there are, as Wilson tells us, four pairs of gods 'who were before the beginning', that is not only Nun and his consort Naunet (who becomes the counter-heaven), but also Huh and Hauhet, Kuk and Kauket, Amun – Amon the hidden – and Amaunet. The eight are, no doubt rightly, seen as representatives of chaos or disorder, in contrast with the Nine, Ennead, beginning with Atum, who represent order. But again we may note a certain complexity – and one must add that Atum himself was there in Nun. It is not the case that what we have in Egypt and Babylonia are *clear, simple* and *unequivocal* statements of the idea that everything came from water – simple stories to that effect complicated merely by the addition of transparently non-essential embroidery. Tiamat and Nun are both parts of complex and rich wholes: notably in both cases the motif of sexual reproduction is there from the beginning.

So even if we assume, then, that Thales was acquainted with, and impressed by, those Near Eastern myths, we must remark that he has simplified them, and we may legitimately ask not only (1) why he did so, but also (2) why he selected these myths from among quite a wide range of creation stories current in both Egypt and Babylon (they include other examples of the idea that things are created by their being named). We are led back, then, to the question of what Thales' aims were – or rather, in the state of our evidence, what they could conceivably have been. Clearly his aim was not to produce yet another *myth*. If we accept Aristotle's account at all, it was *water*, ὕδωρ, that Thales spoke about, and not, for example, a figure such as Oceanos who already had an established place in Greek mythology – even though Aristotle does mention the possibility that Thales was impressed by the idea that Ocean was the father of gods. Aristotle, let us recall, does not claim to know *why* Thales chose water, starting his comments on this question with the words '*perhaps* he [Thales] got the idea from...', but in those || comments Aristotle begins by canvassing a variety of naturalistic factors, the observation that food is moist, that water is essential for life and so on. Although so much remains obscure, one thing does seem clear if we are to say anything about Thales' cosmogony at all, and that is that he was *not* simply *imitating* any myth, whether Greek or non-Greek. At the very most he was selecting and critically evaluating mythical ideas, and Aristotle at least would represent him (conjecturally) as having been influenced by naturalistic considerations above all. Now it may be that Thales was also influenced by myth – that he was impressed by stories involving Tiamat and Nun. That is a positive contribution to the stock of conjectures about the background to his work. Yet (1) we must be clear that there is no compelling necessity to say even that much, and (2) nor should we underestimate the *gap* that would still remain between Thales and any Egyptian or Babylonian – or Greek – mythologist.

Anaximander's Boundless, my second example, is from one point of view a more complex problem (the evidence is richer, though still sparse enough) but from another – from the point of view that concerns us here in discussing Greek debts to the Near East – a simpler one. Cornford's argument was that there is important common ground between Anaximander's cosmology and Hesiod's *Theogony*: both assume a primal undifferentiated Unity (the Boundless, in one case, chaos in *Theogony* 116); both then proceed to describe a first separation of opposites of some kind; and both then treat of the interaction or reuniting of those opposites (where the mention of *eros* in *Theogony* 120 may be compared with that of the γόνιμον in pseudo-Plutarch's account of Anaximander's cosmogony). The possibility of *Hesiod* incorporating, into the *Theogony*, mythical ideas from non-Greek sources has been mentioned before. What is probably the closest parallelism that can be cited between *complexes* of mythical elements in Greek and non-Greek sources is that between the story of the succession of Ouranos, Kronos and Zeus in Hesiod and the Hittite epic of Kumarbi (where Kirk notes the following similarities: the succession of sky-god, father of the gods, storm god; the emasculation of the sky-god; and the impregnation of the earth by the rejected member – though there are, to be sure, as Kirk also went on to note, differences between the two myths as well). Yet what we are concerned with here is not the debt of Greek *myth* to the Near East, but with that of Greek philosophy and science. In this case Anaximander's debt (such as it was) was to *Hesiod* and not (except indirectly) to such parallels as can be found for Hesiod's chaos in non-Greek material. Limited as our evidence is, I would argue that Anaximander's enterprise is quite different from Hesiod's. In addition to whatever may have impressed him in the *Theogony*, Anaximander probably has quite another kind of reason for postulating an original undifferentiated mass, one that stems from reflection on his predecessor's suggestion of water. It appears from Aristotle and Simplicius that it may have occurred to Anaximander that || Thales' account (and others like it) was open to an obvious objection. If you say water is the origin of all things, how can you account for the production of its opposite, fire? Conversely, if it were fire from which all things originate, how could water come to be? The original state of things (one might well conclude on this argument) must be undifferentiated. But leaving aside that point – which may be (and in my view is) more important for our understanding of Anaximander than the comparison with Hesiod – the relevance of Near Eastern mythology in this case is at *most* indirect. Their motifs have been mediated (at least) by Hesiod – who himself provides insight more into the background to Anaximander's ideas, than to his activity *qua philosopher*.

My third example is Heraclitus, where it has been suggested, most recently in a book by M. L. West, that Heraclitus' thought shows extensive Indo-Iranian influences. The first problem here is the nature of our evidence for Iranian or Persian religion, or of those aspects of it (such as the importance of fire, the conception of the interchange of elements) that are brought into relation with Heraclitus. Some points are known from Greek sources, but the main texts that West cites are the three Pahlavi books, the *Bundahism* (book of creation), the *Datastan-i-Denik*, and *Denkart*, which all themselves date from the *ninth* century A.D. Now first of all, *all* these works are highly obscure: Zaehner, one of the principal specialists, does not hide the ambiguity of the Pahlavi script nor the corruption of the texts and he says of the *Denkart* that it is written in an abbreviated 'note' style compared with which the *Metaphysics* of Aristotle is plain sailing. Secondly, while it is likely that much of the material they contain is older than the ninth century, how much older and which material are largely a matter of pure speculation. Zaehner believes that they contain material going back to the orthodoxy established in the fourth century A.D. under Shapur II, but there is still 1,000 years separating that orthodoxy from original Zoroastrianism. The degree of contamination possible can be illustrated by the fact that the *Denkart* refers directly to 'Roman philosophers' – that is Greek philosophers of the Byzantine Empire – and even at one point mentions Ptolemy's *Syntaxis*. When we turn to the earliest direct textual evidence, in the Avesta itself (again highly obscure at key points) the similarities with Heraclitus are far more tenuous and relate primarily to certain religious practices connected with fire. Even here caution is needed: it is well known that Heraclitus was contemptuous of many of the Greek religious practices of his day, and there is some admittedly not conclusive evidence (in our source for Fr. 14) that he actually included the Magoi in his criticisms, along with Bacchants and those who participated in the mysteries. Secondly there is, in my view, an overriding objection to seeing Heraclitus as seriously under the influence of Zoroastrianism, at any rate in his central doctrines, and that lies in the essential contrast between the *dualism* of the latter (Ohrmazd and Ahriman are opposed || implacably) and Heraclitus' doctrine of the *unity* of opposites.

What does this mean? Once again, we cannot and should not rule out the possibility of eastern influences on Heraclitus (Iranian, even Indian if you wish). Yet the question that must be put is: how important are these for our understanding of Heraclitus *as a philosopher*? Here the key factor is surely his use of paradox to stimulate reflection on the interdependence and unity of opposites. This is exemplified not only in physical phenomena (hot, cold, dry, wet, summer, winter) and in social and moral phenomena (war, peace, good, evil, pleasant, painful) but also, for instance, in the opposition between what we *call* a thing and what it *is*. By the use of paradox, especially, he directs attention beneath the surface of appearances to an underlying reality (nature loves to hide) which can, however, only be expressed in the very language the inadequacies of which he reveals. It is this, above all, that marks his chief contribution *as a philosopher*. When we consider him as such, although some of his examples are not original, his generalisation of the notion of the interdependence of opposites surely *is*.

On the difficult and controversial problem of the relation between myth and philosophy my argument, then, is this. Whatever particular themes or ideas it may take over from myth (and I would not deny that such a doctrine as the immortality of the soul comes into philosophy from religion), philosophy is a distinctive enterprise, marked out by, and indeed defined in terms of, its own aims and methods. Unlike the person inventing or recounting a myth, the philosopher offers an account that, implicitly or explicitly, claims to be true according to criteria that are subject to scrutiny. His theses are arrived at, and supported or defended, by reasoned arguments and (where appropriate) appeals to evidence. That may seem an excessively charitable view of Presocratic philosophy, much of which seems, after all, highly dogmatic. Nevertheless it can, I believe, be justified, certainly from Parmenides onwards, and if my and the usual interpretation of Anaximander is correct, then also earlier still, from him, if not from Thales himself. The adaptation of the theses and ideas from Greek and non-Greek myths and religion should (let me repeat the point yet again) certainly *not* be ruled out. But what Greek philosophy took over from such sources, it generally recast in a new, dialectical, framework. Let me give a final illustration from a later period where our evidence is more reliable. It is clear from the *Politicus* (for example) that Plato did know something of Zoroastrian dualism, the idea of two opposed cosmic forces, one good and the other evil. It so happens that Plato rejects this doctrine, though there was nothing that ruled out his accepting it and something like it may, in fact, have been maintained by Empedocles, although whether *he* knew of Zoroastrianism is more doubtful. Yet the point is that as philosophers both Empedocles and Plato were committed to explain, defend and give arguments for || such theses as they advanced. Even Empedocles did so, telling us what is meant by Love and attempting to justify the claim that it is at work in the cosmos as a whole in Fr. 17. More clearly still, Plato does not merely assert his own position as against alternative views, but provides detailed metaphysical and epistemological arguments to support it and to refute those of his opponents, not only in the *Politicus*, but also in the *Republic* and *Timaeus* and most notably of all in the tenth book of the *Laws*.

If my point about the *distinctiveness* of the philosophical enterprise is accepted, then attempts to make *direct* comparisons between philosophy and myth and to identify the debts of the one to the other (whether to Near Eastern or to Greek myths) must be subject to that all-important reservation. But we can now turn to subjects where Near Eastern and Greek work can, on the face of it, be compared directly, and first to mathematics and astronomy: I say 'on the face of it', since again certain differences of aim will emerge. In these areas, particularly in astronomy, tremendous progress has been made, in recent years, in studying both ancient Near Eastern and Greek work, and we are now in a far better position than we used to be to assess the possibilities of influence in fairly precise terms, though this can, of course, be no more than a rapid survey.

Take first arithmetic, where we must begin by noting the *heterogeneity* of the systems of notation developed in the ancient world. The Babylonians had both a decimal and a far more important sexagesimal system: the latter, based on the place-value principle, was enormously influential in astronomy, to which I shall be turning later. But outside astronomy too we may remark occasional signs of the possible influence of sexagesimal arithmetic in Greek culture, in , for example, the division of the talent into 60 minae (already in the Mycenaean period).

Yet so far as Greek arithmetic (*logistikē*) itself goes, an Egyptian influence looks more promising. Like the Greek, the Egyptian system was a decimal one. In it fractions (with the exception of $\frac{2}{3}$) were all treated as submultiples or single aliquot parts (i.e. the numerator was always one: thus 0.4 was treated not as $\frac{2}{5}$, but as $\frac{1}{3}+\frac{1}{15}$), and a similar tendency is found also in Greek numeration. Yet again there are differences. One of the two main systems of numbering in Greece (and the one that eventually predominated) was based on the alphabet, and given the presence of the digamma for 6 and of Phoenician signs for 90 and 900, it has been argued that this system must have been introduced a fair while before the first actual extant evidence for the use of such symbols on Greek inscriptions in the mid-fifth century B.C. Yet although the Greek alphabet itself is an adaptation (through intermediaries) from Phoenicia, the application of letters to numbers is distinctively Greek. That does not prove Greek autonomy, but it suggests a certain measure of independence: it tends to support the thesis that Egyptian, Babylonian and || Greek *logistikē* were, at least in part, three independent developments. Now the Greeks of the sixth or fifth centuries certainly *could* have learnt a great deal from Babylonian *logistikē*. Already in the second millennium B.C. the Babylonians showed considerable mastery in a whole range of arithmetical and algebraic techniques, for example in the solving of quadratic equations. Yet there is no solid evidence that *before* the Hellenistic period the Greeks did learn anything of importance from this source in this field. The superiority of Babylonian arithmetical manipulations to what we find in Greece is evidence *against* extensive influence in this area.

But what about geometry? It is after all geometry and astronomy that provide the two star cases of studies which the Greeks themselves said were developed by their Near Eastern neighbours and which they said they learned from them. There, were, in fact, two competing ideas current in Greece about the origin of geometry, in both of which it is located in Egypt. In one, the version we find in Aristotle, geometry (or rather the mathematical arts in general) originated in Egypt because the priestly class there enjoyed the leisure essential for theoretical pursuits. In the other, the version that goes back to Herodotus, *geometriē* arose in response to the purely practical problems of land measurement – as the etymology of the Greek term suggested. It was from the need to measure the land before and after the Nile flooding that the study arose, the Greeks thereafter deriving their knowledge of it from the Egyptians.

In what remains of Egyptian geometry, as of Egyptian arithmetic, practical exercises bulk large. One example after another deals with practical problems such as measuring areas or volumes: very important if you have to calculate the number of bricks you will need for a pyramid. This does not by itself rule out a theoretical interest as well, to be sure. Yet what was lacking, from both Egyptian and Babylonian geometry, *so far as we can tell*, was the notion of geometrical proof. An illustration may make this clearer. The truth of what we know as Pythagoras' theorem was undoubtedly known and used at a very early stage. On one cuneiform tablet from Babylonia dating from around 1600 B.C. there are fifteen rows of 'Pythagorean triplets', that is numbers (like 3, 4, 5) in which the squares of the first and the second equal the square of the third. Yet what is missing is evidence of any attempt to prove Pythagoras' theorem geometrically. Of course it can be proved, and was in fact proved by the Greeks, in a variety of other ways besides the traditional 'windmill' proof that figures in Euclid, *Elements* I 47 (which is rather *un*likely to have been the original method of demonstration). But what any proof must do, to be a proof at all, is to proceed deductively from certain premises to the required conclusion, and it is this conception of a geometrical demonstration that is, *so far as we know*, lacking from Egyptian and Babylonian, but highly developed in || Greek, geometry. There is no need to doubt that the influence of Egyptian and Babylonian geometrical knowledge (that is the propositions known by them to be true) on the Greeks may well have been considerable. But Herodotus' thesis is, by and large, endorsed by the extant evidence. There appears to be a fundamental distinction between the general aims of Egyptian and Babylonian geometry on the one hand, and those of Greek geometry on the other, in the concentration, in the latter, on demonstration. The development of geometrical proof begins some time in the fifth century, and rapid progress is made towards the full axiomatisation of geometry into a deductive system in the fourth leading up to Euclid's *Elements* around 300 B.C. But this, in the current state of our knowledge, must be said to be a purely Greek development.

The story we have to tell in astronomy is similar, though more complex. Herodotus tells us, for example, that the *polos* and the *gnomon*, the simple sighting instruments used in Greek astronomy, were introduced into Greece from Babylonia. The author of the *Epinomis* (who may or may not be Plato) says that the first to observe the planets was a barbarian and reference is made to the peculiarly favourable atmospheric conditions for astronomical observation in Egypt and Syria. Much more clearly Aristotle mentions astronomical observations carried out by the Egyptians and Babylonians 'who have watched the stars from the remotest past and to whom we owe many incontrovertible facts about each of them'.

These testimonies establish that already in the fourth century B.C. the Greeks spoke freely of the useful astronomical knowledge that they had derived from the Egyptians and Babylonians, but the question we must ask is precisely what knowledge and from whom. The references to the Egyptians (in the *Epinomis* and Aristotle) are odd, since they hardly tally with what we know of Egyptian astronomy. The extant direct evidence does not support the idea that the Egyptians carried out detailed observations of, for example, planetary positions before the Hellenistic period. *Either* that is simply due to the fragmentary nature of our extant evidence, *or* what the Greeks were speaking of are not original Egyptian observations so much as Egyptian knowledge of Babylonian work. Be that as it may, the chief lesson the Greeks could have learnt (and that Greek astronomers eventually did learn) from Egypt in this field was the value of the Egyptian solar calendar of 365 days and its superiority to their own chaotic lunisolar civil calendars. But although the conventional 365-day year is the system that late Greek astronomers such as Ptolemy used, it would be a rash person who would date its introduction into Greek astronomy before (say) Hipparchus in the second century B.C. Meanwhile the Greeks persisted in their use of the various, confused, non-standardised civil calendars, even though from about 430 B.C. onwards (after the work of Meton and Euctemon) the length of the solar year had been determined fairly accurately. ||

But astronomical observation was, of course, much more the forte of the Babylonians, and extant cuneiform tablets dating from the second millennium B.C. show that the range of phenomena they were interested in was extensive. They include eclipse data and records of the appearances and disappearances of planets. In part, these periodic tables are based not on direct observation, but on computation, that is extrapolation from the data. For our purpose, however, it is enough to note that extended observations did, nevertheless, take place. But the questions we have to ask are (1) when did knowledge of these Babylonian tables permeate into the Greek world, and (2) what relevance did they have to Greek astronomy?

Part, at least of the answer to the second question can be gained from looking, once again, at late Greek astronomy, particularly Ptolemy. Ptolemy, who uses a sexagesimal system of division of degrees into minutes and seconds which is undoubtedly derived from the Babylonians, is able to cite eclipse and planetary data going back to the eighth century B.C. He takes the first year in the reign of Nabonassar, i.e. 747 B.C., as epoch, and uses several eighth- and seventh-century eclipses. It is also clear from Ptolemy that the use of Nabonassar I as epoch and that of Babylonian eclipse records go back to Hipparchus in the second century B.C. But if by *his* time Babylonian observations clearly provided important material for Greek theoretical astronomy, how much earlier than Hipparchus did this begin? Here we must confront the thorny problem of Thales, who is reported by Herodotus to have predicted an eclipse of the sun (in 585) to within a year – where many modern commentators have supposed that his achievement must have been based on Babylonian eclipse records. Yet that conclusion is, to say the least, premature – for two main reasons. First, at no stage was anyone, whether Greek or Babylonian, in the ancient world in a position to predict solar eclipses *visible at a particular point on the earth's surface* (though they could say when an eclipse was ruled out and when it was not). Secondly Herodotus says merely that Thales foretold the eclipse to *within a year* (a qualification often omitted by later doxographers in their wish to represent Thales as a marvel). It looks as if the most we should attribute to him is some knowledge of the regularity of eclipses. Moreover *if* he had access to Babylonian eclipse data it is very strange that no other Greek astonomer made any use of them down to the fourth century.

It is there, in fact, in a study of the evidence for the fourth century, the time of Eudoxus and Aristotle, that our best hope of answering our question lies. Eudoxus, who was responsible for the first fairly detailed mathematical models of the movements of the sun, moon and planets, may well have derived his figures for the zodiacal and synodic periods from the Babylonians. Yet it is nowadays thought unlikely that he had access to detailed records concerning the retrograde arcs of the planets – or that he had himself carried out detailed observations of these. Simplicius suggests that || records of Babylonian observations only began to reach Greece in considerable quantities *after* the conquests of Alexander. But that is not the main argument. Eudoxus' model simply fails to take account of the differences in the length and shape of the retrograde arcs, from which we may conclude that either Eudoxus was not aware of these or he chose to ignore them in his model. The evidence in Aristotle tends to confirm that the Greeks were in general satisfied with rather imprecise astronomical observations in the fourth century. First he has no precise dating system (and never dates an observation more exactly than to the archon year). Secondly he had no system of locating an event or object in the heavens with precision – no system of celestial coordinates, whether polar or ecliptic. Though Aristotle is, as I noted, evidence that *some* knowledge of Babylonian astronomical observations extending over a long period had begun to penetrate into the Greek world, we may have valid doubts both about the extent of that penetration and about the use the Greeks would have put the data to in the fourth century B.C.

'The use the Greeks would have put the data to' raises, however, another and more fundamental problem, that of the aims of the two traditions of astronomy, Greek and Babylonian. As I have said, we find detailed periodic tables relating to a variety of celestial phenomena dating back to the second millennium B.C. in Babylonia. But though we can be confident that the practice of observation began at an early period, if we ask how far those early Babylonian observers were concerned with astronomical theory, that is with geometrical models, the answer is very different. We have little or no evidence of any Babylonian attempts to construct mathematical models of the heavenly bodies until the Seleucid period. Early Babylonian astronomy, to put it briefly, was not *geometrical* or *theoretical* astronomy, as that term was understood by the Greeks, at all, but *computational.* From their periodic tables certain phenomena could be predicted (much in the way that high and low tides can be predicted from periodic tables without any theory of the causes of tides). But what we lack is evidence of any interest in the question of explaining the movements of the planets, moon and sun in terms of a mathematical model, that is as the resultant of a combination of mathematically determined figures.

What then should our conclusions be, so far as the influence of Babylonian on Greek astronomy goes? First there is no need to doubt Herodotus' statement that sighting instruments were introduced into Greece from Babylonia. We can add that some Greek constellation configurations and the zodiac itself may have been influenced by Babylonian conceptions. Again there is no need to doubt that some knowledge of the results of Babylonian observational astronomy had begun to penetrate the Greek world before the end of the fourth century. The possibility that Eudoxus drew on those results is there, though the extent to || which he did so should not be exaggerated. Yet the chief point is this: the debt of Greek astronomy to Babylonian is in the *material* on which to construct theories, not in the theories themselves or in the idea of the possibilities of such theories.

I turn finally to the last of the four areas I selected for discussion, namely medicine. Here too, as in astronomy, work has been undertaken recently that helps to define and delimit the possibilities of influence much more narrowly than before. In this case it is Egypt, not Babylonia, that is important. Babylonian medicine was, to judge from the extant remains, much more straightforwardly magical than Egyptian. So far as Egypt itself is concerned, we have a range of medical papyri dating from the second and first millennia B.C. which present an interestingly complex picture from which it is clear that Egyptian medicine was far from being just a matter of magical prayers and rituals combined with some simple empirical treatments. The famous Edwin Smith papyrus (dating from about 1600 B.C. but incorporating material from a much earlier period) is remarkable for two reasons, especially, (1) it is almost (though not quite) free from references to charms and the like, and (2) it contains a systematic and quite full description of a number of surgical cases. When we turn to the Greeks – of a far later period, to be sure – we must first emphasise the heterogeneity of what we have to call 'Greek medicine'. Apart from folk-medicine, there was a strong strain of religious or 'temple' medicine, connected with a variety of gods and heroes thought of as healers, and especially, from the fifth century on, with Asclepius. Then too there was what we may call theoretical or rational medicine, and this in turn was itself highly heterogeneous. From as early as the sixth century B.C. we find a bewildering variety of theories put forward by different medical writers on such questions as the causes of diseases and their cures. The diversity of theories contained in the Hippocratic Corpus is very great, and we can confirm from the history of medicine in the Anonymus Londinensis papyrus that many other theories were produced by the Greeks in the fifth and fourth centuries.

Of these main overlapping strands in 'Greek medicine' it is the Hippocratic writers that concern us most from the point of view of the development of Greek science, and it has recently been suggested that many of the treatises that have been associated with Cnidos especially may have been directly influenced by Egyptian medicine in two main respects. The first is in the presentation or description of disease in a systematic form, in which the title of the disease comes first, followed by an examination or description and diagnosis, followed by notes on therapy, and in which diseases are dealt with in sequence 'a capite ad calcem', starting from the head and working down the body. The second respect is in the particular importance attached to 'residues' in the body as pathogenic substances. Now in neither case can we || be certain of such a direct influence. The interpretation of the Egyptian term for 'residue' is disputed. The systematic presentation of diseases does not necessarily tell for direct influence, since (1) the fit is not exact (between the Edwin Smith papyrus, for example, and the Hippocratic works in question) and (2) the sequence 'a capite ad calcem' might be one that any doctor might arrive at independently as soon as he saw the need to introduce some organisation into the account of diseases.

Nevertheless although the hypothesis of direct influence may be said to be 'not proven', a useful general lesson can be learned from the comparison between Greek and Egyptian medicine. The importance of medicine in the early development of science has often been underestimated in comparison with the more impressive results obtained in, for example, astronomy. Yet medicine was one of the chief battlefields on which the attempt to distinguish the 'rational' and the 'magical' was fought. Here too – as we have found so often elsewhere in our inquiry – there is an important distinction between the Greeks and their Near Eastern predecessors, in that Greek medical literature includes, in such works as *On the Sacred Disease*, *direct and explicit* attacks on the use of magical practices and beliefs. But if *that* cannot be paralleled in Egypt, the concentration on direct observables (on empirical factors) in the Edwin Smith paprus is suggestive. In folk medicine, and primitive medicine in the twentieth century, what *we* distinguish as 'empirical' and 'magical' beliefs and practices often coexist – without any clear distinction being drawn between them. But their very coexistence can provide occasions for reflection on their different status. Explicit attacks on 'magic' as such are, I said, a Greek phenomenon. But the Egyptian evidence shows very clearly how even before 'magic' as such became an issue – as it did in Greece – the emphasis, in practice, can be very strongly on the empirical end in the empirical–magical spectrum.

If I may claim your indulgence for a few minutes longer, I should like to try to draw some of the threads of my argument together. If we look at the eastern Mediterranean world *after the conquests of Alexander*, the situation – thanks largely to those conquests – was one where the communication and exchange of ideas were *comparatively* easy. Many of the barriers between

Greeks and non-Greeks, and among different non-Greeks, began to be eroded, even if they were far from being removed entirely. There is a symbolic significance in the fact that Alexandria itself, one of the main centres of Greek scientific activity from the third century B.C. on, was a Greek foundation in Egypt, although, to be sure, one should guard against attaching *too* much importance to that fact. The idea that Herophilus and Erasistratus learned how to dissect from Egyptian mummifiers is just one gross exaggeration among many perpetrated by those who under-estimate the gulf that still existed between the Greek community || in Alexandria and the indigenous Egyptian population. Yet in astronomy, by the time of Hipparchus, the results of Babylonian observational work were available to the Greeks, and the importance of that confluence of two traditions would be hard to exaggerate.

But *before* the Hellenistic period, if we go back to the sixth or fifth centuries B.C., the situation is a complex one. There was undoubtedly some exchange of ideas, some interpenetration, between the three main cultures. Yet there are also important differences between them, plenty of signs of independent developments in such matters as writing and numerical notation, on occasion positive barriers to, or failures of, communication (as when Babylonian skill in handling quadratic equations appears to have been confined to Babylonia).

The problem I began with was that of the origins of philosophy and science. One can argue, I think one must argue, that philosophical inquiry was a distinctive Greek invention. Philosophy took over many ideas, beliefs and attitudes from both religion and mythology, and both Greek and non-Greek religion and myths are involved. Yet in so far as the philosopher is committed to justifying his position with argument and evidence, his aims and methods are different from those of either the priest or the prophet or the mythologist. If we should recognise the debt of Greek philosophy to the cosmological ideas implicit in Greek and non-Greek religion and myths, we must also recognise the fundamental difference between the aims of philosophy and those of mythology.

In science, as I said, a far more direct comparison is possible between Greek and pre-Greek contributions. Here it is not a matter of trying to compare Greek philosophy with Near Eastern mythology, but of comparing what we rightly call Babylonian *astronomy*, Egyptian *medicine* and so on, with their Greek counterparts. Here too there are (I argued) certain differences in the aims, in the questions asked, and in the methods used to resolve them or justify the answers, between Greek and pre-Greek inquiries. Yet the nature of the transition – and the nature of the debt – differ from one field to another. If the Greeks were (as they appear to have been) the first to develop the notion of geometrical demonstration, to seek astronomical models to explain the movements of the heavenly bodies, to distinguish explicitly between what they called magic and what they called the 'art' of medicine, they were, of course, not the first to discover many geometrical truths, to undertake sustained observations of the stars, to attempt to record the symptoms of diseases. Here it is too easy arbitrarily to decide on one simple criterion that can be used to mark out 'science' from 'non-science'. Although sometimes the distinctive conceptual breakthrough (the realisation of a problem, the asking of a new kind of question) is the important factor, in other cases one must accept a certain *gradualism* in the emergence of the science. The challenge of the subject I have been discussing is || to do justice to those complexities. We are still in the dark on many problems, and we can expect to know more as time goes on and research continues. But as for some aspects of the question as they appear to one observer today, I have tried to put the issues before you, and I hope that, ancient as the debate is, you will agree to its continuing interest.

13

OBSERVATIONAL ERROR IN LATER GREEK SCIENCE

INTRODUCTION

The basic issue I addressed in the paper I contributed to the Second Symposium Hellenisticum in Paris in 1980, later published in *Science and Speculation* (1982), is the way in which Greek scientists responded to or dealt with observational error. How aware were they of this as a problem, and how did they adjust to it when they recognised it as one? As on so many other important topics in the interpretation of Greek science, generalisation is out of the question since different individual scientists reacted quite differently in different fields of inquiry and at different periods. However, concentrating on what we call the exact sciences – optics, acoustics and especially astronomy – in the Hellenistic period, I showed that a number of Greek scientists were conscious of the issue and had a variety of practical suggestions to cope with it in different circumstances, one of the most notable of these being bracketing, that is securing an upper and a lower bound within which a desired value falls.

In the philosophers' epistemological debates several extreme positions on reason and perception are canvassed, including a variety of ideas concerning the untrustworthiness of perception, some merely preferring reason to perception, others suggesting that reason alone is to be trusted, while others again held that neither reason nor perception provides a sure criterion. But while the practising scientists often express critical attitudes on the same subject of the reliability of sense-perception, it is not surprising that none of those who were seriously engaged in scientific research takes up the extreme position of rejecting it entirely. On the contrary, their discussions of the problem of observational error proceed on the assumption that normally, within certain limits, perception is reliable enough and that the data of observation can be accepted. In several cases illusory effects that were commonplaces to illustrate the fallibility of perception could be, and were, given scientific accounts that *explained* the effect and removed the puzzling features of it.

As I explain (p. 304) my study made no claims to comprehensiveness and was highly selective both in the fields, and in the periods, investigated. But if this was something of a pioneering paper, opening up a new topic for research, subsequent work has suggested further related themes. Two that I may note particularly here are (1) the study of the question of whether or how far the Greeks had a notion of *experimental* error as such, i.e. of observations carried out under experimental conditions, and (2) the philosophical debate concerning problems related to vision, especially illusions, effects due to perspective and the like. I may also mention, in passing, that in my own subsequent work (1987: ch. 5) I have tackled a further aspect of the material I discussed in my 1982 paper, namely the use of *measurement*, both its actual deployment in practice and the awareness of ancient scientists that there is a problem in its use. Studying the problem independently, Grmek (forthcoming) has surveyed the same set of problems and remarked, similarly, on the relative lack of confident deployment of exact measurement.

On the first of the two topics I have identified, G. Hon in an unpublished Ph.D. thesis and several papers (1987, forthcoming) comes to a basically negative conclusion. It is not until the scientific revolution of the seventeenth century that the problem of error in observation under experimental conditions comes to be perceived self-consciously as a problem. I have already noted above (Introduction to chapter 4, p. 71) that experiment is more often used either as a corroborative procedure or in refutation of a rival position – not so much as a neutral heuristic procedure – in Greek antiquity. The over-interpretation of results is a feature of both types of case, especially in the former. Correspondingly there was less focus in Greek science (Hon would say no focus at all) on the problem of experimental error, whether error arising in the theoretical, or in the practical, aspects of the experiment conducted. In any case the experiments carried out in ancient science (as some examples cited below, p. 320–1, show) remain quite simple, with only rudimentary apparatus and the simplest of interventions on the part of the experimenter. The general possibility of failings due to the observer is recognised (see pp. 306–7 especially) and so too is the possibility of error in instruments (pp. 309–11). But otherwise no *extra* points can be adduced to suggest that the sources of error in experimentation were perceived as a separate and additional problem, over and above the general problems encountered in observation as such. While the notion of experimental error is, no doubt, a development from the more general one of observational error, Hon's study provides a useful analysis of the distinctions between the two and of the varieties of experimental error, and I would agree with his general conclusion as to the extreme rarity of any signs of the recognition of the latter *as such* in Greek antiquity.

Secondly, on the question of the philosophical debate concerning vision and perspective, Burnyeat had already, in the year before the Hellenistic conference, delivered his Dawes Hicks lecture, later published in the *Proceedings of the British Academy* for 1979, which contained his masterly survey of the controversy concerning Conflicting Appearances. Since then, he has followed one topic up with a further study (forthcoming) of the archaeological and literary evidence relating to a variety of illusory effects, the actual use of perspective in Greek vase-painting, the evidence concerning scene-painting on the tragic stage, and the use made of related points in epistemological debates from Anaxagoras and Democritus to the Hellenistic philosophers. In 'Conflicting Appearances' he showed how pervasive is the influence of the window model of perception, although he was careful not to claim that it was the *only model* in play in antiquity, let alone that it was the fundamental assumption on which ancient models of *knowledge* were based – the target for the provocative, but exaggerated, interpretation of Rorty (1980). Burnyeat showed in his earlier study how perceptual illusion was exploited by sceptics but accommodated by empiricists in antiquity. Now in his more recent paper he has examined further how perspectival effects – differently interpreted – were common ground to a variety of epistemological positions.

This provides important additional material concerning the philosophical debate, and supplements what I wrote about illusions and their interpretation (pp. 303, 327–8). So far as what I called the practising scientists discussed in my paper go, the striking point to which I drew attention (pp. 327–9) remains. They faced a number of concrete difficulties in securing reliable observational data, and those difficulties are confronted in a severely practical fashion. They show no signs of being tempted to use those difficulties to suggest general difficulties about the practice of observation as such. They exercise their ingenuity in attempting to get round the difficulties they encounter, but the whole of their work presupposes the possibility of basing it on secure enough data. However, on the side of the philosophers, one of the results of Burnyeat's work is to highlight the variety of contrasting epistemological positions all of which happily accommodate and indeed exploit – for different purposes – the common stock of well-known examples of conflicting appearances and perceptual illusions. Moreover it was not just competing epistemologies that all felt confident that they could exploit the data and explain it or explain it away. Each of the two fundamentally opposed physical doctrines in antiquity – atomism and continuum theory – had a different story to tell of the physical processes involved in vision, a different account of light (whether as movement or transport, or as an actuality or tension) and indeed of the geometry of space (see further Brownson, 1981, Lloyd, 1987: 299ff.).

As I observe in my paper (p. 304), a distinction between 'philosophers' and 'scientists' is in general hard to draw in Greco-Roman antiquity. Natural science is a domain that straddles both those disciplines as *we* perceive them. Moreover some of those whom we choose to label primarily as 'scientists' rather than as 'philosophers' had, nevertheless, important interests in epistemology and logic as also in aspects of moral philosophy – as the otherwise different examples of both Ptolemy and Galen amply illustrate. It remains the case, however, that there is a dividing line which can and should be remarked, between those who engaged in detailed empirical work, and those who did not. While the latter, or some of them, raise foundational questions of the type discussed by Burnyeat and others, the former, in general, focused – either primarily or in addition – on the practical issues they encountered at points where specific difficulties occurred in their research.

REFERENCES

Brownson, C. D. (1981) 'Euclid's optics and its compatibility with linear perspective', *Archive for History of Exact Sciences* 24: 165–94

Burnyeat, M. F. (1979) 'Conflicting Appearances', *Proceedings of the British Academy* 65: 69–111

(forthcoming) 'All the world's a stage painting: perspective scenery, optics, and Greek epistemology', *Journal of Hellenic Studies*

Grmek, M. D. (forthcoming)

Hon, G. (1985) 'On the concept of experimental error', Ph.D. thesis, University of London

(1987) 'On Kepler's awareness of the problem of experimental error', *Annals of Science* 44: 545–91

(forthcoming) 'Is there a concept of experimental error in Greek astronomy?', *British Journal for the History of Science*

Lloyd, G. E. R. (1987) *The Revolutions of Wisdom* (Berkeley)

Rorty, R. (1980) *Philosophy and the Mirror of Nature* (Princeton)

OBSERVATIONAL ERROR IN LATER GREEK SCIENCE[1]

The untrustworthiness of perception is one of the oldest themes in Greek philosophy, as the fragments of Heraclitus, Parmenides, Melissus, Empedocles, Anaxagoras and Democritus testify. Already in the Presocratic period the positions adopted and the objections stated differ. For example, Heraclitus said both that 'eyes are more exact witnesses than ears' (Fr. 101a) and that 'eyes and ears are bad witnesses for men if they have souls that do not understand the language' (Fr. 107). Melissus in a famous argument starts from the supposition that 'we see and hear correctly' and ends by contradicting it: 'we did not see correctly' (Fr. 8). Empedocles wrote darkly about the narrow *palamai* spread through the limbs (Fr. 2) though also instructing his hearer to 'consider with every *palamē* in what way each thing is clear' (Fr. 3). According to Anaxagoras, Fr. 21, reported by Sextus, it is 'because of the weakness' (of the senses) 'that we are not able to judge what is true', and Sextus and Galen provide us with our evidence for Democritus' distinction between what is *nomōi* and what *eteēi* (Fr. 9, Fr. 125, cf. Fr. 11).

The philosophical analysis of perception makes considerable advances with Plato and Aristotle, not that they agreed on that analysis, and the arguments about its status continue in Hellenistic philosophy, with both Stoics and Epicureans allotting to *aisthēsis* a basic role in their epistemologies, while the Sceptics attacked it as a criterion of what exists. Thus the ten Aenesideman modes || reported in Sextus all exploit differences in *phantasiai* in different ways in order to recommend suspension of judgement, and many draw on examples relating to sense experience. By Sextus' time a wide variety of examples had become familiar, even commonplace (whether they had originally been used to indicate the radical unreliability of perception or merely the much weaker thesis that perception is sometimes deceptive). They include the tower that appears square close to, but round from a distance (*P.* I 118), the oar that looks bent in water, but straight out of it (*P.* I 119), the body that is light when immersed in water, but heavy in air (*P.* I 125), the marble that looks yellow in a block, but white when planed (*P.* I 130), the distortions of shapes in concave or convex mirrors or when the eyeball is pressed (*P.* I 47–9), the *trompe-l'œil* effects of paintings (*P.* I 92, 120), the sheen of doves' necks (*P.* I 120), the honey that tastes bitter to the jaundiced (*P.* I 101) and the much more puzzling because very largely fictitious[2] cases of white things appearing yellow to the jaundiced (*P.* I 44,

[1] I am most grateful to all those who took part in the discussion of this paper in Paris and to those who have corresponded with me since, and especially for the comments of Jonathan Barnes, Jacques Brunschwig., Ian Mueller, Martha Nussbaum, Heinrich von Staden and Gisela Striker.

[2] The notion that sufferers from jaundice see things yellow persists in nineteenth- and early twentieth-century textbooks on clinical diagnosis, though it loses ground as notes of caution are sounded. The first edition of Finlayson, 1878: 151, remarks: '*Yellow vision* (xanthopsia) is observed in certain cases of jaundice, but it is rare, at least in a highly marked form; it is

and 126) or blood-red to those with eyes suffused with blood (*P.* I 44, 126, cf. 101) – as well as many others.

All of this is well known and needs no elaboration. The problem that this paper addresses relates not to the philosophers' epistemological debates as such, but rather to the question of what ‖ effect, if any, these or similar arguments and objections may have had on those who actually engaged in scientific investigations in the main areas of ancient *phusikē*. To what extent were the philosophers' doubts about the reliability of perception picked up or reflected either in the theoretical or methodological pronouncements, or in the actual practice, of Greek scientists? The field is a vast one and I forthwith enter two major disclaimers. First my investigation is limited temporally: I shall largely ignore the formative period of Greek science, up to Aristotle, and concentrate on the more developed scientific inquiries of the post-Aristotelian period. Secondly, within post-Aristotelian science I shall focus mainly on the exact sciences – where the problems of either the inaccuracy or the inexactness[3] of the observational data might be thought to take their sharpest form. This in turn is my excuse for using what I would be the first to insist is a crude distinction between 'philosophers' and 'scientists'. Many individual Stoic, Epicurean and Sceptic philosophers made a contribution to cosmology or to other areas of ancient natural philosophy. The inquiries I am chiefly concerned with are what Aristotle called the more physical branches of mathematics, especially astronomy, optics and acoustics, where the running was made by specialists, or if not by specialists at least by men who mostly – so far as we know – were not engaged in what was the central preoccupation of Hellenistic philosophy, namely ethics.

occasionally produced by santonine [*sic*] administered internally.' The first edition of French, 1912: 840, has: 'Xanthopsia, or yellow vision, may occur in jaundice or in poisoning by santonin, amyl nitrite, cannabis indica, or picric acid', but in the fourth edition (1928), 926, this becomes: '*Xanthopsia*...has been said to occur in jaundice..., but it is hardly ever met with in practice' (a remark still repeated in the tenth edition, 1973). The twelfth edition of Conybeare and Mann, 1957: 350, has: 'Xanthopsia, or yellow vision, which is very rare, is not dependent on the degree of jaundice, but is probably a toxic effect on the retina', but this is dropped from the thirteenth (1961) and subsequent editions. Many medical dictionaries continue, however, to carry references to xanthopsia in connection with jaundice, for example the twenty-second edition of Stedman (1972), the second edition of Butterworth (1978), and the fourth edition of Blakiston's *Gould Medical Dictionary* (1979), none of which stresses rarity of occurrence. The repetition of this idea is remarkable testimony to the tenacity and conservativeness not just of popular belief but of medical opinion. Mr W. N. Mann, who confirms that he has not encountered a case of xanthopsia in jaundice, has remarked to me (personal communication) that it is striking that the matter has not been tested by a post mortem examination of jaundiced subjects to establish whether the media of the eye (aqueous, vitreous) and/or the lens is discoloured.

3 Greek ἀκρίβεια sometimes connotes exactness or precision, sometimes accuracy. The distinction we draw between precision in the sense of 'the degree of refinement with which an operation is performed or a measurement stated' (as Webster puts it) and accuracy in the sense of 'degree of conformity to some recognised standard value' or 'value accepted as true' would have to be made in Greek by contrasting ἀκρίβεια with ὀρθότης, 'correctness', or ἀλήθεια, 'truth' (cf. e.g. Ptolemy, *Syntaxis* III I, I.i 200.15f.). As Webster also observes, however, exactness, precision and accuracy are often used loosely and interchangeably.

Our first task is to review the evidence for an awareness of the possibility of observational error and to distinguish between the different types of such error that are recognised. We have next to discuss how the difficulties thus identified were met, the different responses or reactions to the problems of the inaccuracy or the inexactness of the observations. My final section will return briefly to the question of the comparison and the contrast between the themes that dominate the philosophers' epistemological debates || on the one hand, and those that represent the chief concern of the practising scientists on the other.

I

We may begin by attempting a rough typology of the various sources of error in observation that Greek scientific writers appear to recognise, and the first and most obvious of these is error arising simply from negligence of one kind or another on the part of the human observers themselves. In such contexts as the law and historical research,[4] the reliability – including the truthfulness – of eyewitness accounts had long been recognised as open to question. Similarly in natural science the writers occasionally flatly deny that what is said to have been observed has indeed been observed. One notable passage in which Aristotle, for instance, does so is in his discussion of the alleged link between the sex of the offspring and the side of the body from which the male seed comes. At *GA* 765a25ff. he reports that some claimed that when one testicle was excised the resulting offspring were all of the same sex, and he then continues: 'but they lie; starting from what is likely, they divine what will happen, and they presuppose that it is so, before they see that it is in fact so'. Similarly Galen in his frequent combative moods often accuses his opponents of lying in their accounts of what they have observed. In *On the Natural Faculties* Asclepiades is said to have done so in claiming that urine does not reach the kidneys, but passes in the form of vapour direct from the region round the vena cava to the bladder,[5] and in *On Anatomical Procedures* Erasistratus is accused of fabricating a report of what happens when a tube is inserted into an artery to test whether the pulse continues distal to the insertion: Galen, who obtained the opposite result to Erasistratus, concludes by remarking || 'so great is the temerity of some who make rash statements about things they have never observed'.[6]

[4] Similarly in geography. Ptolemy, for instance, draws a contrast between the unreliability of travellers' reports on distances and locations and the determination of those facts by astronomical methods, although some of his confidence in the use, for example, of differences in the recorded times of eclipses is misplaced (*Geography* I 4.12.4ff. Müller).

[5] *Nat. Fac.* I 16, *Scr. Min.* III 150.3ff. (II 67.6ff. Kühn), reading κοίλην with Helmreich, rather than κοιλίαν (with Kühn, though contrast 'cavae venae' in Kühn's Latin translation). Cf. a further more general accusation that some of his opponents describe what they have never seen in dissection as if they had seen it accurately, at *De Placitis Hippocratis et Platonis* VIII 1: *CMG* V 4.1.2, 481.31ff., V 650.11ff. K.

[6] *De Anat. Admin.* VII 16 (II 648.2ff. K), cf. also *An in arteriis natura sanguis contineatur* ch. 8 (IV 734.2ff. K). Erasistratus evidently used the test to show that the arteries are dilated because they are filled, not filled because they are dilated, although he believed that what they

In other cases the truthfulness and honesty of the observers are not challenged, but their care and skill are called in question. The need for care and skill is mentioned in general terms by Aristoxenus, for example, when he contrasts the study of music with that of geometry. He notes that while 'the geometrician makes no use of his faculty of sense-perception', for the student of music, on the other hand, 'exactness of sense-perception is a fundamental requirement. For if his sense-perception is deficient, it is impossible for him to deal with those questions that lie outside the sphere of sense-perception altogether.'[7] Here Aristoxenus' point is not, or not only, the obvious one that the student of musical harmonies should not be deaf, but rather, or in addition, that he should not be, as we say, tone deaf. 'It is by hearing that we judge the magnitudes of the intervals', and 'we must therefore accustom ourselves to discriminating particulars exactly.' Whereas the geometrician does not 'in any degree train his sight to discriminate the straight line, the circle or any other figure, such training belonging rather to the practice of the carpenter, the turner or some other such handicraftsman', the student of music, by contrast, must indeed have a trained ear.[8] Observation requires judgement or discrimination, and for this experience is necessary. || Aristoxenus here has some inkling, perhaps, of a point we are all familiar with in scientific education, notably but not exclusively in the context of the use of scientific apparatus such as the microscope or the telescope (let alone more sophisticated instruments), namely that to some degree the student must be *taught* what he *sees*.

Similarly in astronomy the unsatisfactory nature of many of the observations carried out by the earlier Greek astronomers is often mentioned by Ptolemy and was evidently remarked on already by Hipparchus, although it is not always clear on precisely what grounds he considered them to be unreliable. Thus in *Syntaxis* III 1, I i 203.7ff. Ptolemy refers to observations of the summer solstices made by the associates of Meton and Euctemon and after them by those of Aristarchus, and he says that they were carried out 'in

are filled with, in their natural state, is pneuma, not blood. Galen held that the arteries have a natural power of dilating, but that they derive this from the heart. Whereas Erasistratus claimed that the pulse distal to the ligatured tube continues, Galen countered that if the tube is fitted and bound accurately the part of the artery distal to the ligature ceases to pulsate. As Harris, 1973: 378ff. points out, the experiment was repeated many times by later anatomists, notably by Harvey, who remarked on its difficulty and inconclusiveness as a method of testing how the pulse in the arteries is to be explained: in fact the result will depend largely on how the tube is fitted and ligatured.

7 *Harm.* II 33 (translation adapted from Macran). Cf. for example, Didymus' comparison and contrast between music and geometry in Porphyry, *in Harm.* 28.9ff. Düring.

8 *Harm.* ibid. Although Ptolemy disagrees with Aristoxenus on certain fundamental epistemological issues, notably in that he insists – against Aristoxenus – that reason is more trustworthy than hearing as the judge of small intervals (e.g. *Harm.* I 10, 21.25ff., Düring), he shares Aristoxenus' tendency to appeal to what the 'musical man' has to say about harmonies, e.g. *Harm.* III 1, 85.13ff., cf. I 11, 25.5ff., I 15, 37.12. Evidently in acoustics, as in astronomy, it was sometimes recognised that different observers will get different results: see, for example, Porphyry, *in Harm.* 18.12ff., Boethius, *De Inst. Musica* I 9, 195.23ff. (and cf. below n. 12).

a rather rough and ready fashion' (*holoscheresteron*, 203.14, cf. also 205.15ff.), 'as Hipparchus also appears to have thought'. Again in VII 1, I.ii 2.22ff., Ptolemy reports that Hipparchus first 'conjectured rather than affirmed' the precession of the equinoxes 'since he had found very few observations of the fixed stars before him, those being just about only those recorded by Aristyllus and Timocharis and these were not undisputed nor thoroughly worked over' (*oute adistaktois out' epexeirgasmenais*, 3.4f.). Similarly Ptolemy for his own part notes that most of the ancient observations he had to draw on for his planetary theories had been recorded both 'inattentively and at the same time in a rough and ready fashion' (*anepistatōs hama kai holoscherōs*, IX 2, I.ii 209.5ff.).[9]

By themselves such passages suggest merely that some later Greek scientists were conscious of the need for care and accuracy in observation, or at least that they were concerned to present themselves as sticklers for accuracy in observation, and that they found fault with some of their predecessors on that score. But we can go a good deal further than this. The astronomers, especially, specifically refer to and discuss a number of particular difficulties and obstacles to exact observation. We may distinguish broadly between problems that arise from the conditions under which the object is to be observed or from the nature of the object itself, and those that relate to the means or method of observation, for || example in the use of instrumental aids, although this distinction cannot always be firmly drawn.

A prime example of the first kind of problem is atmospheric refraction or, more generally, any type of interference arising from atmospheric conditions. Although Ptolemy discusses atmospheric refraction at some length in his *Optics* (V 23ff.), he does not make systematic corrections for refraction in the *Syntaxis*. But not only *Optics* V 23ff., but also a passage in Cleomedes' *On the Circular Motion of the Heavenly Bodies* illustrate how refraction was sometimes taken into account. In Cleomedes, for instance, it was appealed to, admittedly hesitantly, as one of a variety of possible explanations for certain 'paradoxical' lunar eclipses, when both sun and moon are seen above the horizon at the same time. 'Nevertheless,' Cleomedes writes,[10] 'having regard to the many and infinitely various conditions which naturally arise in the air, it would not be impossible that, when the sun has just set, and is under the horizon, we should receive the impression of its not yet having set.' After mentioning a number of other possibilities he proceeds:

> For if a gold ring is put into a drinking cup or other vessel, then, when the vessel is empty, the object is not visible at a certain suitable distance, since the visual current (*pneuma*) goes right on in a straight line as it touches the brim of the vessel. But when the vessel has been filled with water up to the level of the brim, the ring placed in the vessel is now, at the same distance, visible, since the visual

[9] Cf. IV 9, I.i 327.24ff., where he insists that one should not be ashamed to introduce corrections to old hypotheses, and to one's own, as surer observations become available.

[10] Cleomedes II 6, 222.28ff. Ziegler. My translation is adapted from that in Heath, 1932.

> current no longer passes straight on past the brim as before, but, as it touches, at the brim, the water which fills the vessel up to the brim, it is thereby bent, and so, passing to the bottom of the vessel, meets the right there. Something similar, then, might possibly happen in a moist and thoroughly wet condition of the air, namely that the visual ray should, by being bent, take a direction below the horizon, and there catch the sun just after setting, and so we receive the impression of the sun's being above the horizon.[11]

Moreover even if, in the *Syntaxis*, Ptolemy does not take refraction as such into account, he occasionally there remarks – admittedly rather confusedly – on the possibility of distortions in || the appearance of objects viewed near the horizon. In I 3, I.i 11.20ff., he says that heavenly bodies appear larger when they are near the horizon, and at 13.3ff. he explains this as due not to their being closer to the earth (which they are not), but to the evaporation of the moisture that surrounds the earth (an effect which he claims is similar to the increased apparent size of objects seen in water). Again in IX 2, I.ii 209.16f., he remarks generally that the appearances of planets are difficult to determine because of differences both in atmospheric conditions and in the eye-sight of the observers,[12] and at 210.3ff. he suggests that 'the same angular distances appear greater to the eye near the horizon, and less near the zenith, and so for this reason it is clear that they can be measured sometimes as greater and sometimes as less than the real angular distance'.

The same chapter of the *Syntaxis*, IX 2, mentions two other types of difficulty. Both the stations and the first and last appearances of planets are, Ptolemy says, hard to establish with precision. As for the first and last appearance of a planet, the trouble here is that with the last appearance, for instance, the exact position of the planet disappears with the planet itself (209.13ff.) and he adds that observations of the planets made with reference to a fixed star at a great angular distance are 'hard to calculate and subject to guesswork' (209.20f.). As for the stations, their exact time is difficult to obtain since the planet's local motion remains imperceptible over many days before and after the stationary point (209.9ff.). A precisely similar difficulty arises in determining the solstices, when the sun's position remains little changed over a period of days. In III 1, I.i 203.12ff., he remarks on the greater accuracy of equinox observations, and in II 5, I.i 100.22ff., in discussing the ratios of the sun's shadow at the solstices and equinoxes, he further notes that at the winter solstice the end of the shadow is difficult to determine, although he does not specify how the 'end' is to be defined nor distinguish umbra and penumbra. Moreover in this context he also remarks that the problem about obtaining the length of the shadow at the equinoxes was that the equinox had to be determined independently. ||

[11] Cleomedes II 6, 224.11ff. Lejeune, 1956: 225 n. 9, collects other ancient references to the trick with the ring in the cup.

[12] Cf. VIII 6, I.ii 203.15ff., where Ptolemy again draws attention to the problems of atmospheric conditions and to the discrepancies between different observers attempting to determine, for instance, the heliacal risings and settings of heavenly bodies.

Our second group consists of problems that arise not so much in what was observed as in the means or method by which it was observed, for example in the use of particular sighting aids or other instruments. The use of such aids is certainly not confined to astronomy.[13] In Ptolemy's account of how to measure the amount of refraction between different media (air to water, air to glass and water to glass), for instance, there is a description of the protractor-like disk to be used to obtain the angles of incidence and of refraction.[14] The smallest interval marked on the disk is one degree, and consonantly with this the results are given in degrees or half degrees.[15] Similarly in his *Harmonics*, I 8, 16.32ff., Ptolemy has a number of remarks to make about the difficulties of obtaining exact data concerning harmonies by using clarinets or pipes or by attaching weights to strings: it is only on the *kanōn* that the ratios can be shown reliably, though he has reservations about this too (cf. II 12, 66.6ff.).

It is, however, again in connection with astronomy that Greek scientific instruments were most fully developed. Although the use of simple sighting aids such as the gnomon or upright rod goes back long before the beginnings of Greek astronomy, from the time of Eudoxus, at least, we have good evidence that a number of prominent Greek astronomers paid considerable attention to the development of astronomical instruments.[16] The exact nature of Eudoxus' 'spider', mentioned in Vitruvius (IX 8), is disputed: the controversy has been given a new impetus by the reconstruction recently undertaken by Maula and others on the basis of archaeological finds at Cnidus.[17] Archimedes in an important text in the *Sandreckoner* describes the dioptra he used to obtain the angular diameter of the sun and remarks on a difficulty that was not confined to instrumental observations, namely that the eye itself is not a point, but has a certain magnitude.[18] Passages in || Ptolemy make it clear that Hipparchus described an improved version of the dioptra, the so-called 'four-cubit rod dioptra' (*Syntaxis* V 14, 1.i 417.1ff.), known in some later writers simply as the Hipparchan dioptra,[19] and that Hipparchus was also familiar with the equinoctial (or equatorial) armillary, a ring mounted in the plane of the equator from which the equinoxes could be determined. In *Syntaxis* III 1, 1.i 194.23ff., 196.8ff., two passages are quoted from Hipparchus' lost work *On the Precession of the Tropical and Equinoctial Points* where references are made to observations made on the bronze ring set up in the Square Hall in Alexandria.

[13] Already in the *Philebus*, 55Eff., for example, Plato remarked that some τέχναι are more exact than others, partly because of their use of instruments.

[14] *Optics* V 8, 227.5ff. Lejeune.

[15] Cf. further below, pp. 320–1 and n. 56.

[16] There are brief surveys of ancient astronomical instruments in Dicks, 1953–4: 77–85, and Price, 1957: 582–619.

[17] See Maula, 1975–6: 225–57.

[18] *Sandreckoner* ch. 1, II 224.2ff., cf. further below, pp. 323–4. Cicero (*Rep.* 1.14.21f., *Tusc.* 1.25.63) further reports that Archimedes constructed a mechanical model or orrery to represent the movements of the sun, moon and planets.

[19] See, for example, Proclus, *Hyp.* 120.21 and 126.14. Hero devoted a short treatise to the construction and use of the dioptra.

As for Ptolemy himself, apart from the four-cubit rod dioptra and the equinoctial armillary, four other main instruments are referred to in the *Syntaxis*, the meridional armillary, the plinth or quadrant, the parallactic ruler and the armillary astrolabe.[20] He gives quite detailed instructions concerning the construction of each of the last four as well as for the dioptra.[21] He notes, for instance, in connection with the armillary astrolabe that the concentric rings must be accurately turned and that the convex outer surface of each of the inner rings should exactly fit the concave inner surface of the one above (*Syntaxis* V 1, I.i 351.12ff., 21ff., 352.1ff.). Again in his description of the parallactic ruler he stipulates that the rods should be 'not less than four cubits long' and thick enough to be rigid (V 12, I.i 403.9ff.). Moreover this concern to provide accounts of the astronomical instruments used continues, remarkably, in later writers such as Theon of Alexandria, Pappus and Proclus, who in some cases go beyond the description in the *Syntaxis* and afford us supplementary information on the instruments in question. Thus Pappus remarks that Ptolemy did not specify the dimensions of the rings of the astrolabe and gives a figure of a cubit for the largest, outermost ring,[22] and Proclus devotes several extended passages in his || *Outline* to the construction and use of the main astronomical instruments.[23]

The advantages to be gained from the use of such observational aids were, in some cases, considerable, even though (1) that point should not be exaggerated,[24] and (2) the extent of their actual deployment is controversial.[25] Thus Ptolemy explains, in *Syntaxis* V 1, I.i 353.11ff., how the armillary astrolabe can be used to give the ecliptic coordinates of any heavenly body. The instrument had first to be set with reference to a known point – the sun, if it is the moon that is being investigated, or the moon itself or a bright star, for any other heavenly body – but once that was done, the astrolabe enabled distances both along the ecliptic (i.e. in longitude) and north and south of it (i.e. in latitude) to be read off directly, instead of having to be determined from observations of the object's position in relation to the zenith and the horizon.

Among his particular claims are that he used this instrument (1) to

[20] Although Ptolemy does not mention the plane astrolabe in the *Syntaxis*, it has been thought likely that he refers to it as the 'horoscopic instrument' in the *Planisphaerium* ch. 14, II 249.19ff. (see, for example, Neugebauer, 1949: 240–56, and Drachmann, 1953–4: 183–9.

[21] See *Syntaxis* I 12 (I.i 64.12ff.); I 12 (66.5ff.); V 12 (403.9ff.); and V 1 (351.5ff.), respectively; and on the dioptra, V 14 (417.1ff.).

[22] Pappus, *in Ptol. Synt.* V 4.4ff., 6.6ff., Rome.

[23] Proclus, *Hyp.* ch. 3, 42.5–54.12; ch. 4, 126.13–130.26; ch. 6, 198.15–212.6; and cf. also 72.20ff., 110.3ff., 120.15ff.

[24] Cf. Aaboe and Price, 1964: 1–20, who remark that the characteristic type of measurement depended not on instrumental perfection but on the choice of crucial phenomena, although in insisting on the comparative imprecision of ancient instruments they, for their part, tend to play down the improvements in the data that were obtainable, and obtained, by their use.

[25] See especially the recent exchanges between Newton, 1977 and 1980: 388–99, and Gingerich, 1980: 253–66, and 1981: 40–4.

establish the positions of the stars for his star catalogue in *Syntaxis* VII and VIII,[26] (2) to obtain better data concerning the positions of Mercury (here the problem was that most of the fixed stars are rarely visible at a distance from the sun equal to Mercury's, but this difficulty could be circumvented by taking a fix on more distant stars with the astrolabe, IX 8, I.ii 270.1ff.) and (3) to do so for the moon. In this last case his account of the stages by which his lunar model developed is circumstantial. Previously the only accurate data were those obtained from lunar eclipses. 'The other kinds of observation,' he says in *Syntaxis* IV 1, I.i 265.18ff., 'that depend either on its course with respect to the || fixed stars, or on instruments [he does not specify which], or on solar eclipses, can all be very deceptive because of the moon's parallaxes.' But while his first model for the movement of the moon – in which he followed Hipparchus closely – is based on eclipse data, he returns to the problem in V 2 and remarks on certain discrepancies he had discovered between the predicted and the observed positions of the moon by using the armillary astrolabe described in V 1. 'In general, observing in this way..., we found that the distances of the moon in respect of the sun sometimes agreed with the calculations made according to the hypothesis we have expounded, but sometimes differed and disagreed with them, at times by a little, at times by a great deal' (I.i 354.20ff.). Carrying out what he describes as a 'progressively more complete and more meticulous examination', he found that at conjunctions and at full moons there was little or no discrepancy with what was predicted by the model based on eclipse data. But when the moon was in the first or third quarter, and at the same time midway between the apogee and the perigee on the epicycle, the discrepancies between the predictions and what was observed were appreciable.

Now as already noted, the truthfulness of Ptolemy's claims not just about the use of the astrolabe but about all the observations he said he undertook is currently – and not for the first time[27] – at the centre of controversy. We shall come back to the issue later, but for the moment we may remark that there are important differences between the three particular cases we have referred to. Whatever the grounds for scepticism about the first – Ptolemy's claims concerning the construction of his star catalogue[28] – the Mercury and Moon examples differ from it in that an issue of theory, indeed the simplicity of his whole astronomical model, is at stake. These have in common that they are the two instances where he made radical modifications to his usual

[26] *Syntaxis* VII 4, I.ii 35.11ff., and cf. VII 2, 13.15ff. Ptolemy gives the longitudes and latitudes in degrees and fractions of a degree, using seven simple fractions, $\frac{1}{6}$, $\frac{1}{4}$, $\frac{1}{3}$, $\frac{1}{2}$, $\frac{2}{3}$, $\frac{3}{4}$, $\frac{5}{6}$, i.e. 10′, 15′, 20′, 30′, 40′, 45′ and 50′: thus finer discrimination, below 5′, is not attempted.

[27] Delambre, especially, raised the issue, 1817: e.g. I xxvff., 183 and II 264). The idea that Ptolemy's star catalogue was plagiarised from an earlier astronomer, namely Menelaus, was already suggested by Arabic astronomers: see Björnbo, 1901: 196–212.

[28] It is agreed on all sides that he was here building on earlier work, especially the star-catalogue of Hipparchus. On the thesis that all that Ptolemy has done is to take earlier observations and to adjust them for precession, I entered some caveats in Lloyd, 1979: 183–4, but compare also now Gingerich, 1981.

epicycle–eccentric || model, in both cases introducing an extra circle in addition to the epicycle and the deferent.[29] The very complexities that he thought necessary would appear to be quite gratuitous unless they are a response to what he perceived to be mismatches between the simple model and *some* empirical data (however and by whomsoever these were obtained).[30] This does not, to be sure, prove that his account of his procedures is correct. But it is striking, at the least, that he chose to represent what he claims as better empirical data as the result of the use of his most sophisticated instrument.

But although improvements in the quality and the range of the available data were sometimes attributed, by the Greeks themselves, to the development of astronomical instrumentation, the use of instruments was far from unproblematic and there is good evidence that in some instances, at least, this was clearly recognised both by Hipparchus and by Ptolemy. The discussion of problems connected with the determination of the length of the year in *Syntaxis* III I provides the most striking illustration of this and is worth considering in some detail.

Ptolemy first points out that Hipparchus drew a clear distinction between what we should call the sidereal year (measured by the sun's return to the same fixed star) and the tropical year (measured by the sun's return to the same solstitial or equinoctial point), the latter being less than $365\frac{1}{4}$ days, the former more, the difference between them being due to the phenomenon of the precession of the equinoxes (I.i 191.20ff.). But Ptolemy also notes that Hipparchus suspected that the tropical year might not be constant, though he adds that he was himself sure, on the basis of the successive observations of the solstices and the equinoxes that he had made, that this was not the case (194.3ff.).

> For we find them differing by no important amount from the additional quarter day, but sometimes by just about as much as it is possible to be in error due to the construction and position of the instruments. For we guess from the considerations that Hipparchus adduces that the error || with regard to the inequalities belongs rather to the observations. For after he had first set out, in *On the Precession of the Tropical and Equinoctial Points*, the summer and winter solstices that seemed to him to have been observed accurately and in order, he himself agrees that the discrepancy in them is not so great that the inequality of the yearly period is recognised. For he comments on them thus: 'It is clear, then, from these observations that the differences of the years have been very small. But as regards the solstices I do not despair of my and Archimedes' being in error both in observation and in calculation even up to the fourth part of a day. But the irregularity of the yearly periods can be accurately apprehended

29 For an account of the Mercury and Moon models, see, for example, Pedersen, 1974: 159ff., especially 192ff., and 309ff.

30 Cf. Gingerich, 1980: 261f.: 'Ptolemy must surely have put credence in some specific observations here, or he would not have ended up with such an unnecessarily complicated mechanism for Mercury.' (In the same article, at p. 257, Gingerich produces a table that indicates very clearly the improvements in accuracy Ptolemy obtained in his revised lunar model.)

from observations made on the bronze ring set up in Alexandria in the so-called Square Hall, which – it is agreed – indicates the equinoctial day as that in which its concave surface begins to be lit up on the opposite side.' (I.i 194.10–195.9)

We may conclude from this that Hipparchus was well aware of the difficulty of obtaining precise determinations of the solstices and that he envisaged the possibility of an error of up to six hours arising from one or other or both of two distinct sources, namely (1) in the observations and (2) in calculation.[31]

Ptolemy then cites a number of specific observations of autumn and spring equinoxes made by Hipparchus, from which it emerges that Hipparchus did not simply average his results. The spring equinox data yielded no evidence of a discrepancy with the value of 365¼ days for the tropical year. The autumn equinox data, however, gave values that varied from 365¼ days to 365 days 4 hours. Hipparchus settled, it seems, for a figure of $\frac{1}{300}$th of a day less than 365¼ days for the tropical year, but the procedure he used is not described. Ptolemy follows up the observational difficulties on his own account at 196.21ff. It is possible, he says, for there to be an error of up to a quarter of a day not only in solstice observations, but also in equinoctial ones. There will be an error of that magnitude if the position or calibration of the instruments deviates from the true by a mere 6 minutes of arc.[32] And the error could be greater still where the instruments are not corrected according to the observations themselves, where, for example, they have been fixed on foundations and an unnoticed shift has taken place in their placement. 'And one can see this', he remarks (197.17ff.),

> in the case of the bronze rings in the palaestra in our || city which are supposed to be in the plane of the equator. For so great is the distortion in their position, and especially in that of the bigger and older one, when we make our observations, that sometimes their concave surfaces twice suffer a shift in lighting in the same equinoxes.

Again a similar observation may be ascribed already to Hipparchus, since Ptolemy says that at a particular spring equinox (in 146 B.C.) which occurred in the morning (i.e. sunrise) on a particular date, Hipparchus recorded that the ring in Alexandria was lit up on both sides equally at the fifth hour 'so that the same equinox differently observed differed by about five hours' (196.5ff.).[33]

What Hipparchus took to be stronger evidence for the variation he suspected in the length of the tropical year came from calculations based on eclipse data. But here Ptolemy first complains that this involves already

[31] Observation and calculation are again distinguished as possible sources of error at *Syntaxis* IV 11, I.i 339.13ff., for example.

[32] Price, 1957: 587, notes that an error of 6 minutes corresponds to a shadow movement of about 1½ mm in a 2-cubit instrument.

[33] On how this might be the effect of refraction, for example, see Bruin and Bruin, 1976: 89–111, and Newton, 1977: 85. It is striking that this is referred to as one of the 'exact' observations, *Syntaxis* III 1, I.i 196.5f., indeed 'most exactly' observed, 204.21.

assuming the sun's position as given (198.20ff.) and then protests that the results obtained are far more likely to be due to other factors than the alleged variation in the tropical year.

> For it would seem more possible either that the distances of the moon at the eclipses with respect to the nearest fixed stars had been estimated in a rather rough and ready fashion, or that the calculations either of the moon's parallaxes for the sighting of its apparent positions or of the sun's movement from the equinoxes to the middle of the eclipses had been obtained either not truly or not exactly. (200.9–16)

Ptolemy ends this part of his discussion by stating that he is satisfied that there is no variation in the tropical year, but he emphasises that the actual length of the tropical year is hard to determine. It is slightly less than $365\frac{1}{4}$ days, but the amount less is so small that it remains indistinguishable for many years. The extra amount can only be perceived by taking an extended period of time. Here, as elsewhere in determining periods of return, it is necessary to use observations spaced out over a long period. 'The period of return will be obtained as nearly exactly as possible the longer the time between the observations compared' – for this will have the effect of minimising the error due to the 'weakness' of the observations themselves (202.10ff.). ||

In the detail it provides concerning the inaccuracy of instruments and the errors that might arise in their use, this chapter of the *Syntaxis* is exceptional. Yet the general message it conveys about the unreliability of some of the observational data obtained with the instruments available is one that Ptolemy reiterates often enough in the body of the work. Thus he alludes to the difficulty of obtaining an accurate figure for the variation in the apparent diameter of the moon at perigee and at apogee by direct measurement with the dioptra in *Syntaxis* v 14 (I.i 417.22ff.).[34] In the same chapter (416.20ff.) he also rejects as unsound any attempt to establish the angular diameter of the sun or moon by means of the water-clock, that is by measuring the time taken by the sun or moon to rise or set or pass some given point – a method that is actually used in Cleomedes II 1 (136.26ff.) who mentions a figure of $\frac{1}{750}$ of the orbit, or 28′ 48″, for the angular diameter of the sun thus obtained. Proclus comments (*Hyp.* ch. 4, 124.7ff.) that such a method was, in Ptolemy's view, quite worthless, first because the hole of the clepsydra gets stopped up, secondly because the quantity of water that flows out in a night or day is not

[34] Ptolemy states first that the sun's apparent diameter does not vary appreciably (as Pedersen, 1974: 208, notes, 'this tells us something about the quality of the instrument, since we know that the solar diameter varies between 32′ 36″ and 31′ 31″') and then that the moon's diameter at apogee equals the sun's (Ptolemy appears not to know, or to ignore, the phenomenon of annular eclipses of the sun). He then *calculates* the moon's diameter at perigee from eclipse data. As Goldstein notes (1967: 11), in the *Planetary Hypotheses* 'the apparent diameter given for the Moon indicates that Ptolemy has taken his lunar model as accurately measuring the size as well as the distance of the Moon' – despite the difficulties this involves.

necessarily an exact multiple of the quantity taken at the rising, and thirdly because it is inexact to take the chord as equal to the arc it subtends.[35]

The more general difficulty here – and it was a major one for all Greek astronomy – was that of accurate time-keeping, especially at night, for even though improvements had been made to the water-clock, notably by the introduction of the constant-head water-clock by Ctesibius of Alexandria, the margin of error was still wide. One cautious authority estimates that ancient astronomers could tell the time at night to an accuracy of within ten minutes,[36] which will correspond to between two and three || degrees in the motion of the stars on the celestial equator. In line with this, no actual recorded observation in Ptolemy is more precise than to within one-sixth of an hour.

There is no need to emphasise that while such a level of imprecision in keeping time was a major impediment in astronomy, it must have represented an even greater obstacle to attempts to determine the exact speed of moving terrestrial objects.[37] Although towards the end of antiquity we do have rough and ready tests proposed by Philoponus in order to check the effect of an increase in weight on the time taken for a falling body to traverse a given distance, for example, it should be noticed how his results are set out. Thus in the famous passage in which he objects to certain of the theories he ascribes to Aristotle, *in Ph.* 683.18ff., what Philoponus says is simply that 'if you let fall at the same time from the same height two weights *that differ greatly*, you will see that the ratio of the times of the motions does not correspond to the ratio of the weights, but that the difference is *a very small one*'. Although elsewhere in his discussion he refers to some specific weights and specific times purely for illustrative purposes,[38] no attempt is made to report *precise* results of *actual* tests, and in part the reason for this, no doubt, is the obvious one that to obtain exact results for the times of fall of different weights would have been extremely difficult with the timing devices available.[39]

Finally, as a coda to this brief and highly selective discussion of Greek awareness of difficulties in obtaining precision and accuracy in the observational data, I may mention a rather different case from outside the exact sciences. This concerns the controversy over the value of dissection, where the Empiricists argued against their Dogmatist opponents that dissection is useless, not just on the general grounds that any inquiry into what is hidden and obscure, *ta adēla*, is useless, but for the extra reason that

[35] Cf. Sextus, *M.* v 75ff., and Ptolemy, *Tetrabiblos* III 2.

[36] Dicks, 1953–4: 84; cf. Fotheringham, 1915: 236–8, and 1923: 166f.

[37] Yet as A. Koyré pointed out, e.g. in 1968: 90ff., especially 93, the timing instruments used by Galileo in his discussion of the problem of free fall are not markedly superior to those available in the ancient world.

[38] E.g. *in Ph.* 681.30ff., 682.25ff., 683.13ff.

[39] This is not to deny, however, that other more general factors have also to be taken into account: thus little attempt is made even to specify weights, though there was no technical obstacle to this.

nothing can be learnt concerning the living body from the examination of the dead – nor indeed from the examination of a living body || opened in vivisection. As Celsus reports the argument, it was that

> when the body had been laid open, colour, smoothness, softness, hardness and all similars would not be such as they were when the body was untouched... Nor is anything more foolish, they say, than to suppose that whatever the condition of the part of a man's body in life, it will also be the same when he is already dead.[40]

Here, although there is no question of the problem being the difficulty of obtaining mathematical precision, the awareness of the possibility that the very method that had to be used in undertaking the observation might involve a distortion or change in the object observed is remarkable, even though the evaluation of the possibility was disputed.

II

The next part of our inquiry concerns how Greek scientists attempted to deal with, or how they responded to, the types of inaccuracy or inexactness that they recognised in the data at their command. In some cases the problems could be minimised, if not completely overcome. Doubtful observations could be repeated: the need to base conclusions on as many observations as possible is stated on occasion by Ptolemy.[41] The astronomer who was aware that the faulty construction or positioning of instruments could be a source of error would be wise to check both, even though this was no doubt often omitted: in *Syntaxis* III 1, I.i 197.11ff. (cf. above p. 313), Ptolemy even suggests that equatorial armillary rings should be corrected for each set of observations. Again the problems encountered in using one method might be obviated by checking the results with another. The use of alternative methods to obtain a result is a feature of the discussion of the length of the tropical year in *Syntaxis* III 1 (where he cites both direct observations of solstices and equinoxes and results arrived at by calculation on the basis of eclipse data) and of that of precession in *Syntaxis* VII 2 and 3 (where he uses both declination shifts from which differences in longitude can be calculated and then also values for the longitudes themselves, obtained from observations of the occultations of stars by the moon).[42] ||

In some instances, at least, the effect of observational inaccuracy can be minimised by taking observations separated by a considerable interval. We have seen that in III 1 (I.i 202.12ff., above p. 314) Ptolemy points out that this is, in general, the best way to ensure accuracy in the calculation of periodic returns.[43] In practice, in his discussion of the moon's latitudinal movement

[40] Celsus, *De Medicina*, proem. 41f., Spencer's translation.

[41] E.g. *Syntaxis* III 1, I.i 193.21ff., V 14, 421.14ff., and cf. V 2, 355.5ff.

[42] I.ii 19.8ff. and 25.13ff., cf. further below, pp. 318–19. Cf. also above, pp. 311, on obviating the problem of lunar parallax by using lunar eclipse data, IV 1 I.i 265.15ff.

[43] From *Syntaxis* VII 3, I.ii 18.1ff., it is clear that Hipparchus' initial doubts concerning precession reflected the shortness of time that had elapsed between such reliable earlier

in IV 9 (I.1 328.17ff.), for instance, he even draws on Babylonian data going back to the eighth century B.C. Similarly in his account of each of the planets he aims to correct the figures for their periodic returns by taking observations with a long temporal base. Thus although he starts with a rough figure for the cycle of anomaly (synodic period) of Venus, namely that five such cycles correspond to eight Egyptian years of 365 days, he uses observations separated by nearly 410 Egyptian years to obtain a more exact figure. The first of these is an observation recorded by Timocharis in 272 B.C., the second one of Ptolemy's own in A.D. 138. Dividing the total number of degrees travelled by the total number of days between the two observations Ptolemy arrives at a figure for the mean daily movement in anomaly which he states to six sexagesimal places.[44] This give a synodic period of 583 days 22 hours 24 minutes, or 583.933 days,[45] which compares very closely with the modern value, according to Pedersen, of 583.92 days. We should be under no illusions as to where the *exactness* of the figures in his tables of mean motion comes from: the sexagesimal long division I referred to can be carried out to any number of places you like, and that Ptolemy took it to six places merely reflects the degree of precision he thought he needed for his model.[46] The second key point in this: the accuracy of the two observations themselves does not have to be very great, provided they are separated by a || considerable length of time. Ptolemy gives the *time* of the observations in hours and fractions of an hour, and the longitudinal *position* of the planet in terms of fractions of a degree. But both imprecision and error will have only a negligible effect when spread over a period of several centuries. Thus a combined error in longitudinal position of the planet of one whole degree will only affect the figure for the daily motion in anomaly in the third sexagesimal place.

In his calculations of the two main periodic returns for each of the planets we can see exactly how Ptolemy proceeded and how the effects of observational inexactness and inaccuracy could be, and very largely were, countered. In practice the accuracy of his figures for these returns is very great – to within 0.002 % in every case. There is certainly no need, in this case at least, to suppose with Delambre and Newton, that Ptolemy is engaged in a massive confidence trick, that he is – as Newton put it – the most successful fraud in the history of science.[47]

On the other hand we are often not in such a favourable position to

observations as he had to draw on (those of Timocharis especially) and those he undertook himself. With this device to ensure accuracy in astronomy, one might compare the observation in the Aristotelian *Mechanica*, ch. 1, 848b1ff., that larger balances are more accurate than smaller ones.

[44] As I pointed out in Lloyd, 1979: 194, we obtain a figure of $36^{i}\ 59^{ii}\ 25^{iii}\ 49^{iv}\ 8^{v}\ 51^{vi}$, as against the figure of $36^{i}\ 59^{ii}\ 25^{iii}\ 53^{iv}\ 11^{v}\ 28^{vi}$ given by Ptolemy. Unless Ptolemy has simply made a slip, this suggests that he rounded a value or used a procedure that otherwise differs from our own.

[45] Pedersen, 1974: 426, however, gives 583.98 days.

[46] This, like other such figures, is not the 'abus de calcul' that Tannery called them: cf. Neugebauer, 1975: I 55.

[47] Newton, 1977: 379; Delambre, 1817: I xxvff. and II 250ff.

reconstruct his procedures nor to establish the likely margins of error within which he aimed to work. At a number of points there are lacunae in our evidence concerning both his data and his calculations. His drive to support and confirm his theories (and many of those he took over from Hipparchus) is everywhere apparent – and of course in no way surprising. That, in the process, he discounted some of the evidence available to him is clear. The question is rather the extent and the motivation of this discounting. Some further specific test-cases will help to throw some light on the subject, even if, in many instances, we cannot hope to arrive at clear and definitive answers to our questions.

It is not reassuring that, while he tells us from time to time that he will select the more accurate of his predecessors' observations, these also often happen to be the ones that corroborate this theory. Notoriously, in his discussion of precession in *Syntaxis* VII 2 and 3, he first records a variety of data concerning shifts in declinations, but then uses just those cases that produce the result he wants, the figure of 'very nearly' 1° in 100 years that had some authority from Hipparchus (though it was probably his lower limit for precession) and that had obvious convenience for the calculation of the || effects of precession over extended periods. Yet this is not the *patent* fraud that Newton believes, provided we are right to insist that the *conversion* of declination shifts to longitudinal movements was both more complex and less exact than the application of a simple mathematical formula.[48] Moreover in this case he at least records a fair spread of data, including the data that Delambre and Newton used to suggest he was forging it, and one of the chief weaknesses of their charge of massive fraudulence is that they provide no explanation of why, if Ptolemy was cooking the books, he should have included the evidence from which his deceit could be deduced. The very inclusion of such evidence – of data that do *not* exactly fit his results – was taken by Dreyer, for one, as testimony to Ptolemy's *bona fides*.[49]

But if he is here not plain dishonest, he is, nevertheless, by modern ideals, extraordinarily tolerant of error.[50] Although, as I said, we do not know exactly how he converted declination data into longitudinal movements, we can be sure that if he used the data for all the eighteen stars he cites he would have obtained an average value for precession that is appreciably higher than 1° in 100 years. The average for the set as a whole which is obtained by applying the modern formula for conversion is some 47″ a year.[51] Even for the six stars for which Ptolemy gives a calculation of the longitudinal movement, the average is some 38″ a year. It is true that, having cited his declination data, he proceeds: 'what is required will be even clearer to us from the following observations' (I.ii 25.13f.), and he then gives some

[48] Cf. Lloyd, 1979: 195ff.

[49] Dreyer, 1917–18: 347.

[50] We should, however, emphasise the word 'ideals' and recognise that it was not just in the ancient world that scientists often fall short of these in practice: see further below, n. 59.

[51] See, for example, Pannekoek, 1955: 63f.

longitudinal movements obtained directly from observations of the occultations of certain stars by the moon (which of course unfortunately presuppose his model for the moon). These give values for precession that are, in general, far closer to his figure of 36″ a year:[52] they || range from 3° 45′ in 379 years, i.e. 35″ 37‴ a year, to 10′ in 12 years, i.e. 50″ a year, though that last figure is appreciably higher than the next highest figure (3° 55′ in 391 years, or 36″ 4‴ a year) and is based on a far shorter time span than any other of the comparisons. The average value for this second set of data is 38″ 45‴, if we include the 50″ case, or 35″ 56‴ if we exclude it.

The conclusions we may draw from the occultation data may be expressed in the form of an alternative. *Either* Ptolemy is discounting nearly 3″ per year – rounding down 38″ 45‴ to 36″ – *or* he discarded one apparently aberrant value and then discounted a mere 4‴. In either event he does not specify his procedure: in particular *if* one observation has indeed been discarded as unreliable, he does not indicate this.

Turning back to the declination data, we may remark that Ptolemy does not set out his workings in such a way that we can see precisely what margin of error he allowed himself (as opposed to the error we can establish that he made). But the important points are these: first he was evidently satisfied that the data confirmed his figure of 1° in 100 years well enough, and yet, secondly, the inaccuracy of his result cannot, in this case, be attributed mainly to the observations themselves, for they could have yielded a value for precession much closer to the one arrived at by modern computation for his epoch of 49″ 52‴ a year. The fairly gross inaccuracy, in this instance, must, then, stem largely from a combination of the method of conversion used and the margin of error within which he was working. We are in no position to *apportion* the inaccuracy between these two sources, but there is obviously a distinct possibility that he was, in practice, allowing himself a far wider margin of error than that which appears from his own figures for the occultation data.

In his planetary theory the problem of reconstructing his data is even more severe. In his discussion of the individual planets he cites either the absolute minimum, or very close to the minimum, number of actual observed positions necessary in order to extract the parameters of his model,[53] some 17 particular observations for || Mercury, 11 for Venus and 5 each for Mars, Jupiter and Saturn. The aim is to expound the model and to determine its parameters, but the confrontation between model and data is kept to a minimum. He makes little or no effort to test his model against fresh data, that is data not used in deriving the parameters in the first place. We know

[52] Cf. Mercier's conclusion, that 'the value 36″ per annum would follow from soundly observed occultations if they were reduced in the way indicated by Ptolemy' (1979: 211–17, at 216).

[53] On the potential accuracy of ancient planetary models, with an appropriate selection of parameters, see, for example, Babb, 1977: 426–34. Cf. Gingerich, 1980: 255ff., who has particularly emphasised the superiority of Ptolemy's parameters to his cited observations.

that many of his specific observations are inaccurate,[54] and we can follow him step by step in his interpretation and use of such data as he does record, including his frequent recourse to rounding adjustments of various kinds, both in the purely mathematical features of his calculations (as for example in the conversions of chords to arcs and vice versa and in renorming procedures) and in his rounding of observational data. But while we can be certain that he has been drastically selective in his presentation of that data, he does not indicate the principles on which he made that selection nor even show that he had any such clearly thought out principles at all. Again, the magnitude of the rounding adjustments he allows himself can be as much as 2% of the value concerned.[55] But how much greater latitude he allowed himself in the workings that he does not present can, of course, only be guessed. He is clearly confident (and with some reason) that his theories work well on the whole. No doubt he would be absolutely right not to abandon his model except in the face of seriously discrepant data – though (1) we should distinguish between abandoning the model and revising particular parameters, and (2) we have noted that he *does* revise his model quite drastically in two cases, namely those of the Moon and Mercury. It remains the case, however, that we are left largely in the dark on *just how far* he has discounted discrepant evidence in the data available to him.

However selected and interpreted, the observational data set out in Ptolemy's chapters on the individual planets have this moderately reassuring feature that many of them do not yield results || that *exactly* fit the theory. The situation in his *Optics* is quite different, at least if we may trust the extant Latin version of the Arabic translation of his treatise. There, when he presents what he claims as the results of detailed experiments to determine the amounts of refraction from air to water, from air to glass and from water to glass, these results have clearly already been adjusted to tally with the underlying general theory.[56] To be sure, he signals the approximate nature of the results by the term 'very nearly', *engista*. As already noted, the protractor he used was marked with degree intervals and his results consist of tables giving angles of refraction in degrees and half degrees. Yet although the errors in these values cannot be computed exactly (since we cannot repeat

[54] See, for example, Czwalina, 1959: 1–35; cf. Newton, 1977: 266 and 307, and Gingerich, 1980, especially 260ff.

[55] As, for example, in the roundings he evidently allowed himself in determining the distances of the equant of Venus from the centre of the deferent circle and from the earth, see Neugebauer, 1975: I 154, and other examples given at I 77ff., 91, 127 and 197f. Rounding adjustments are an equally prominent feature of Ptolemy's discussion of planetary distances in the *Planetary Hypotheses*: thus in the calculation for Mercury in I§5, the fraction $\frac{115}{15}$ is first rounded to 8, and that figure is used in a further fraction $\frac{8}{220}$ which is itself then rounded to $\frac{1}{27}$.

[56] All three tables tally exactly with a general law that takes the form $r = ai - bi^2$, where r is the angle of refraction, i the angle of incidence and a and b are constants for the medium concerned (the angle of incidence in Ptolemy's terminology is that from the eye to the perpendicular of the refracting surface). This law is, however, nowhere stated in the *Optics*.

Ptolemy's experiments with precisely the same materials he used), even on the most favourable interpretation they range, in all three sets of results, higher than three-quarters of a degree.[57] Here, then the observations have been interpreted *before* they are recorded. Indeed something similar happened far more frequently, if less noticeably, in the domain of acoustics. In the extensive ancient reports of the results of real or purported experiments investigating the main concords of octave, fifth and fourth, those results are invariably presented in the form of ratios that *exactly* correspond to what acoustic theory demanded – and they do so even when the tests referred to could not conceivably have yielded anything like those results.[58] ||

These last two examples from optics and acoustics show that, in certain circumstances, Greek scientists dealt ruthlessly enough with the discrepancies between their data and their theories: they simply ignored them.[59] Yet that should not lead us to discount entirely all those protestations of carefulness in observation that we reviewed earlier. The contrast between Ptolemy's *Optics* and his *Syntaxis* is as important as the similarities between them. What they have in common is that in both many results, or what are claimed as such, are introduced with the qualifying expression *engista* – very nearly.

[57] The best fit that can be obtained for Ptolemy's values for the refraction between air and water, and between water and glass, in each case involve an error of more than 1° in at least one of the eight values set out in the table: for that between air and glass the error is still over 50′.

[58] This is clearly true of the tests that purported to reveal the principal harmonies from weighing hammers and measuring jars with different quantities of water, where in each case the test as reported does not yield the result claimed: the sources are listed in Lloyd, 1979: 144 n. 95. While both these stories are fictitious, there is this difference between them that the hammers are given, while Pythagoras is represented not as first getting jars to give the harmonies and then measuring the water, but as working back from the result he expected: he poured predetermined quantities of water into the jars and then 'confirmed' that these gave the harmonies. That perception cannot attain to exactness in judging harmonies is repeatedly emphasised in the acoustical writers, for example Ptolemy, *Harm.* I 1, 3.1ff., 16ff., I 2, 5.12f.; Porphyry, *in Harm.* 16.13f., 17.6ff., 18.7ff. From outside the domain of the exact sciences we may note Galen's tenacity in sticking to his anatomical and physiological doctrines and his insistence that only repeated observations will count as counter-evidence to them. Thus at *De Anat. Admin.* I 11 (II 278.14ff. K) he says: 'if ever, when you are dissecting a limb, you see something that contradicts what I have written, recognize that this happens infrequently. Do not prejudge my work until you yourself have seen, as I have, the phenomenon in many examples' (transl. Singer).

[59] Yet the ancient Greeks were not, of course, alone in this. From the 20th century we may cite. Holton's recent study of the dispute between R. A. Millikan and F. Ehrenhaft on the results of oil-drop experiments (1978: ch. 2). Despite Millikan's emphatic, italicised, claim that what he was presenting 'is not a selected group of drops but represents all of the drops experimented on during 60 consecutive days', it is clear from his laboratory notebooks that he selected favourable experiments and discarded unfavourable ones: see the series of Millikan's notes set out by Holton, 1978: 68 and 70–1, for example: 'Very low Something wrong' [November 18, 1911]...'This is almost exactly RIGHT and the best one I ever had' [December 20, 1911]...'Exactly right' [February 3, 1912]. 'Something the matter...' [February 13, 1912]. 'Agreement poor. Will not work out' [February 17, 1912]. 'Publish this Beautiful one...' [February 24, 1912], and on March 15, 1912, '*Error high* will not use'. Other striking examples from astronomy and other fields are mentioned by Gingerich, 1980: 254 and 263f.

But the difference is that, unlike the *Optics*, the *Syntaxis* does not, as a whole, present results that have already been tailored to match the theory precisely. The problem there is not that discrepant observational data are corrected, in a bid to obtain perfect fit with the theories, but rather that they are tolerated – along with a very broad tolerance of other sources of imprecision in the purely mathematical part of the calculations.

We have discussed various types of ancient response to the problems of inaccuracy or inexactness in the observational data. But one further possibility has yet to be mentioned. It was, of course, open to the ancient scientist to meet the problem by bracketing, that is by attempting to obtain upper and lower limits between which the desired value must fall. In fact we find several ancient scientific treatises in which certain results are stated not in terms of exact figures, but in terms of such upper and lower limits.[60] Three of the best known such works are Aristarchus' *On* || *the Sizes and Distances of the Sun and Moon*, Archimedes' *Measurement of the Circle* and his *Sandreckoner*. However, although all three of these treatises share the characteristic I have mentioned, there are important differences in the workings in the three cases.

Archimedes' *Measurement of the Circle*, which arrives at a value for π stated as 'less than $3\frac{1}{7}$ but greater than $3\frac{10}{71}$', is purely geometrical and involves no measurement whatsoever. He first proves that the ratio of the diameter of the circle to the perimeter of a circumscribed 96-sided polygon is greater than $4673\frac{1}{2}:14688$, from which it follows, given that the circumference of the circle is less than the circumscribed polygon, that the ratio of the circumference to the diameter is less than $3\frac{1}{7}$, and he then shows, similarly, that the ratio of the diameter to the inscribed 96-sided polygon is less than $6336:2017\frac{1}{4}$, from which it follows that the ratio of the circumference to the diameter is greater than $3\frac{10}{71}$.

Aristarchus' *On the Sizes and Distances* is again, geometrical throughout the deductions in the body of the treatise, but (unlike the *Measurement of the Circle*) this incorporates as *part of the initial hypotheses* certain values for observable data, namely hypothesis four that 'when the moon appears to us halved its [angular] distance from the sun is then less than a quadrant by one-thirtieth of a quadrant' (i.e. 87°), and the notorious hypothesis six that 'the moon subtends one fifteenth part of a sign of the zodiac' (i.e. 2°). Using these hypotheses, Aristarchus proves geometrically that, for example, 'the distance of the sun from the earth is greater than 18 times, but less than 20 times, the

[60] The notion of approximation to a limit is fundamental to the Greek mathematical method of exhaustion, where, for instance, the area of a curvilinear figure such as a circle may be determined by inscribing successively larger regular polygons. It should, however, be noted that, despite the conventional English name for the method, in the Greek view the area was, precisely, *not* exhausted: the circle was *not* identified with the inscribed polygon. Another context in which approximation techniques were well established is in the extraction of square roots, discussed for example by Hero, *Metrica* I 8, 18.22ff., on which see Heath, 1921: II 323ff., and cf. II 51–2 on Archimedes' approximation for $\sqrt{3}$ in *Circ.* Proposition 3, I 236.12ff.

distance of the moon' and that 'the diameter of the sun has to the diameter of the earth a ratio greater than that which 19 has to 3, but less than that which 43 has to 6'. Here we have astronomical conclusions, yet the limits within which the values arrived at fall are simply the result of the assumptions as set out.[61]

In Archimedes' *Sandreckoner* also we find a mathematical ‖ problem tackled using inequalities. His aim is to show that the number of grains of sand that the universe would hold is less than a given number which is expressible within the notation he develops in the treatise for the expression of very large numbers. Thus he takes an upper or a lower limit for a variety of values which he needs to use, choosing always a limit well beyond what he takes to be likely in order to make his problem more difficult. He assumes, for instance, that there will be not more than 10,000 grains of sand in a poppy seed of diameter not less than $\frac{1}{40}$th of a finger breadth. He also assumes an upper limit for the circumference of the earth that is ten times the value he believes to be approximately correct (not greater than 3,000,000 stades, as opposed to about 300,000 stades), although it turns out that he was not cautious enough in his upper limit for the ratio of the diameter of the sun to that of the moon. Earlier astronomers had all put the diameter of the sun at a value of less than 20 times the diameter of the moon. Archimedes says that 'in order that the truth of my proposition may be established beyond dispute' (II 220.26f.) he will take a figure of not greater than 30 times the diameter of the moon – although this is, of course, still a drastic underestimate.

Now while most of the other limits taken are not directly related to his own observations, the upper and lower limits he obtained for the angular diameter of the sun quite definitely are. In a passage I have mentioned before, he describes how the dioptra is to be used to obtain this angular diameter and he remarks, for instance, on the problem that arises because the eye is not a point but has a certain magnitude. If, however, the eye is assumed to be a point located at the end of the dioptra, this will give an upper limit for the angular diameter of the sun, when the sun itself is completely covered by the disk on the dioptra (226.3ff.). To obtain the lower limit, two conditions must be fulfilled: first the disk on the dioptra must be moved so that it just fails to cover the sun; then allowance has to be made for the magnitude of the eye itself by substituting for it a second disk which is at least as big as the eye[62] and measuring the angles to it rather than to the end-point of the dioptra itself (222.22ff.). The result of his investigation is not a single approximate value for the angular diameter of the sun, but ‖ an upper limit of $\frac{1}{164}$th of a right angle (just under 32′ 55″ 37‴) and a lower one of $\frac{1}{200}$th of a right angle (or 27′).

[61] He does, however, refer to what is perceived when he proves, on the basis of his assumption about the angular diameter of the moon, that the arc of the shadow is not perceptibly different from a great circle (Proposition 4).

[62] How this is to be done is set out at II 224.16ff.

The use of bracketing and of inequalities can, then, be illustrated not just in Greek mathematics but also in certain contexts in astronomy. This is, we might think, precisely the technique that Greek astronomers could and should have adopted wherever they were in doubt about the accuracy of the observational data themselves. Yet the occasions on which they did so are rare. There is some evidence that in his attempt to determine the value of precession Hipparchus aimed to establish a minimum figure, for when Ptolemy quotes from Hipparchus' work *On the Magnitude of the Solar Year* in the *Syntaxis* (VII 2, I.ii 15.19ff.) the result Hipparchus reached is expressed as 'not less than [a shift of] $\frac{1}{100}$th of a degree a year'. Ptolemy himself gives upper and lower limits for the obliquity of the ecliptic in the chapter (I 12) where he attempts a determination of its value, namely between 23° 50′ and 23° 52′ 30″. Yet in his calculations he adopts Eratosthenes' and Hipparchus' result of $\frac{11}{83}$ of two right angles, i.e. 23° 51′ 20″. Elsewhere too – for all the repeated references to the approximate nature of his results – he does not work with upper and lower limits for doubtful values as a general rule. But the – or rather a – reason is not far to seek. If, instead of working with *specific* values for the rate of precession, for the length of the tropical year, for the obliquity of the ecliptic, for the latitude of Alexandria and various other fundamental parameters in his system, Ptolemy had on each occasion tried to work with *upper and lower* limits for all those values, the complexity that this would have introduced into his calculations would have been quite unmanageable.

The point is worth spelling out a little. Take any *one* of these parameters, for instance the value of the tropical year. Instead of settling on a specific figure ($365+\frac{1}{4}-\frac{1}{300}$ days) it would have been preferable to have attempted – as Archimedes does for the angular diameter of the sun in the *Sandreckoner* – to determine the upper and lower limits within which the value fell and to proceed with those figures. The same goes for the other fundamental values I specified. But then consider the problems that would have faced Ptolemy in attempting to determine the parameters of his models for each of the planets. Venus' model, for example, is constructed largely by using positions at which it is at maximum elongation from the sun: but these presuppose the sun's position as given || – not directly observed, but *calculated* according to the tables which *incorporate* Ptolemy's figure for the length of the tropical year. Indeed for each of the planets one of its two main motions is directly linked to the sun's movement. In the case of Venus and Mercury the centre of the epicycle remains on a direct line from the earth to the mean sun. For the three outer planets the line joining the position of the planet on the epicycle to the centre of that epicycle remains parallel to the line joining the earth to the mean sun. Thus in the tables of planetary motion, for Venus and Mercury the table of motion in longitude exactly repeats the table of the sun's mean motion in longitude, and for the other three planets the sum of the movement in longitude and that in anomaly is equal to the mean motion of the sun in longitude. The model of the sun's motion permeates, in fact, the whole analysis of the motion of each of the planets.

Moreover Ptolemy is evidently perfectly well aware of how certain fundamental assumptions underpin the whole of his astronomical theory. Thus his introductory remarks in Book III (I.i 190.15ff.) show that he is absolutely clear both that his account of planetary motions presupposes his solution to the problem of the motion of the sun, and that his account of the moon also does so. Again he points out, as we have noted, concerning Hipparchus' worry about a possible variation in the length of the tropical year, that his calculations from lunar eclipses already assume the sun's position at the eclipse, and so cannot be obtained independently of assumptions about the sun's movement (III I, I.i 198.20ff.).[63]

But if the deductive articulation of his theories in most cases effectively ruled out using upper and lower limits for the main fundamental parameters, we may now return to the more problematic question of the views he may have held on the matter of the basis on which approximations could be tolerated. He is certainly explicit at particular points about particular sources of either inaccuracy or imprecision. We saw that he remarked that errors of up to a quarter of a day are possible in determining solstices and equinoxes (above pp. 312–13). Again in V 10 (I.i 400.10ff.) || he comments that a difference of four minutes of arc or of an eighth of an hour is not surprising in observations of the moon's movement. More generally, at VII 3 (I.ii 18.14ff.) in his discussion of precession he speaks of discrepancies which can be neglected as 'the result of the observations themselves', although he does not specify their magnitude. If *we* go over *his* workings we find many approximations – usually signalled as such – both in his observations and in his calculations, and in one notable chapter (IV 11, I.i 338.5ff.) *he* goes over Hipparchus' workings to show where certain errors have occurred which influenced his figures for the ratio of the moon's epicycle to its deferent. The corrections Ptolemy here introduced range from 9 to 56 minutes in time and from 9 to 36 minutes of arc in the sun's movement. Clearly his expectation of the level of accuracy obtainable in eclipse data is far higher than for solstice and equinox observations, and he explicitly notes that errors of this magnitude are above the 'chance' errors that might be expected in such an investigation (344.8ff., cf. 347.14ff.).

But while this all adds up to excellent evidence of an awareness of the approximate nature of his results and to implicit notions of the limits of tolerable error in particular contexts, not even the more explicit passages can be said to amount to anything like a general theory of error. To begin with,

[63] Thus at 199.9ff. Ptolemy remarks that the sun's positions at the middle of the eclipses are obtained from the spring equinoxes, from the sun's positions the moon's are derived, and from the moon's those of the stars: cf. also 200.9ff. Equally sightings with the astrolabe frequently presuppose the position of the sun or moon.

rather than regularly setting out the whole of a body of data and then arriving at a result by averaging the whole set, for example,[64] he far more often works with selected data, that is data from which some items have already been discarded, but the basis for such discarding is intuitive. Thus he not only tolerates, but frequently positively recommends, the selection of the 'most accurate' data. It is, to be sure, understandable, in his terms, to attempt to exclude observations that might bias or distort the results,[65] and we have found that he sometimes identifies a particular source of inaccuracy or difficulty that casts doubt on results found by a particular || method.[66] Yet elsewhere the basis on which he considers some observations to be more reliable than others is not made explicit and there is an evident possibility of circularity – the observations are judged accurate because they confirm the theories (Hipparchus' or his own) and the theories are accepted on the grounds that the 'best' observations confirmed them.

Again, although he distinguishes broadly between errors in the observations and errors in mathematical calculations, he does not usually discuss where imprecision can be obviated (for example by taking the calculation to further sexagesimal places), and where it cannot (for instance because of the limits of resolution of the observations). Nor does he, in general, draw attention to the points in the workings where imprecision will have far-reaching consequences and the points where it will not, even though he must constantly be exercising his judgement on that issue. Interpolation and extrapolation procedures in the use of tables of arcs and chords and of tables of periods of return are not made explicit, and although this may sometimes be because some procedures could be taken to be well known to practising mathematicians, that can hardly always be the case. Approximations are extremely common, but although in particular cases we can determine their magnitude, we lack any *general* statement of the principles on which they are to be allowed.

We end this section with something of a paradox. Ptolemy is emphatic, in the opening of the *Syntaxis* (I.i 4.7ff., 6.11ff.), that the inquiry he is about to engage on – which he there calls 'mathematics' – is to be contrasted with both theology and physics on the grounds that – unlike them – it is capable of yielding certain and unshakeable knowledge. Yet in practice the entire

[64] In one context, however, the notion of an average value is common enough: it is fundamental to the idea of the *mean* motion of a heavenly body, clearly stated in an elementary text such as Geminus XVIII 19.

[65] Thus it is clear from *Syntaxis* IX 2 I.ii 213.1ff., that in his planetary theory he preferred to work, so far as possible, with observations of the planets taken at contact or in close proximity with the stars or the moon, these being, as he puts it, the 'most undisputed observations'.

[66] Although he sometimes implicitly recognises what *we* should describe as *systematic* errors, he does not explicitly contrast these and random ones. Again he has a term for 'significant' or 'noteworthy' difference, ἀξιόλογος διαφορά (see, for example, I.i 347.14ff., and cf. 194.11, 197.1, 400.12; and compare *Harm.* I 4, 9.23f.), but employs, of course, no procedure that corresponds to a test for significance.

discussion in the body of the work is steeped in inexactness.[67] Yet that is not its weakness: or rather it is not always a mark of its weakness, but on the contrary, at certain junctures at least, associated with one of || its strengths. For in astronomy it is only with reference to inevitably more or less imprecise observational data that the elegant and rigorous geometrical theory can be applied to the explananda – and Ptolemy's *Syntaxis*, after all, is the first extant text to carry this out in detail. The weakness here lies, rather, in the silence with which Ptolemy passes over the general issues connected with the approximation techniques he used and the errors he allowed – though to speak thus is to speak from the point of view of ideals that were not to be expressed, let alone adopted, for many centuries.

III

Finally, we may return briefly to the question of the comparisons and contrasts between points made in the philosophers' epistemological debates and the work of practising scientists. Evidently the scientists are concerned often enough, in certain contexts, with the unreliability of perception. But equally evidently the issues they raise are not those of the types that figure most prominently in the philosophers' debates. None of the examples that I listed at the beginning from Sextus[68] is ever mentioned – so far as I know – in a practical scientific context as a source of radical confusion. On the contrary, several stock examples are cases where some of the scientists were in a position to offer an adequate account of some aspects at least of the more or less unfamiliar phenomenon popularly thought of as puzzling or problematic.

This is true, for example, of puzzles about the weights of objects in different media, where the same object is heavy in air but light in water (as mentioned by Sextus at *P.* I 125). Archimedes' work in hydrostatics removes the paradoxical feature of this. The famous principle enunciated in proposition seven of *On Floating Bodies* book I enables the weight of an object in air to be related to its weight in any fluid. It enables one to predict, for example, what a body fully immersed in water will weigh from its weight in air together with the weight of the corresponding volume of water. It is true that the point in the Sixth mode, reported by Sextus, is that there is a 'mixture', as he puts it, || formed by the combination of the external object and the accompanying conditions under which it is apprehended, and in so far as the moral is that there is no such thing as weight per se, but only weights in given media, the scientist can and must agree with the sceptic. But

[67] Inexactness is not, to be sure, incompatible with a claim that certainty is, in principle, and on particular issues, obtainable. But we may contrast the claims for βεβαιότης in I 1 with the acknowledgement of the lack of βεβαιότης in, for example, IX 2 (e.g. I.ii 208.22) and cf. XIII 2, I.ii 532.12ff.

[68] It is, however, notable that when Sextus comes to attack ἀστρολογία in *M.* V 1ff., he takes as his prime target Chaldaean genethlialogy and explicitly contrasts this with the work of Eudoxus and Hipparchus.

the scientist will draw no radical sceptical conclusions about withholding judgement from this, for he will insist on, and be content with, the point that weights in different media are perfectly investigable.[69]

Similar points apply also to some of the optical examples in Sextus. The oar that looks bent in water (*P.* I 119)[70] and the effects of concave and convex mirrors (*P.* I 48–9) do not lead the student of optics to *epochē*. Rather, it is recognised that optics enables illusory appearances to be explained.[71] Thus the exact amount of the bending of the oar is something that can be measured and predicted. To be sure, the phenomenon did not receive an adequate physical explanation (in terms of the velocity of light in different media) in antiquity. Yet ancient writers on optics were confident that the phenomena of refraction were subject to general laws, even if they did not state the sine law itself. The exact measurement of angles of refraction between two well-defined media was in principle – and sometimes in practice[72] – no *more* difficult than the *exact* measurement of angles of reflection. As for concave and convex mirrors, writers of specialist treatises on catoptrics[73] as well as students of optics in general were in a position to specify the fundamental principles of reflection that applied to every plane or spherical reflecting surface. Ptolemy's *Optics* provides not just a statement of such principles, but simple experimental corroboration of them, both for plane and for spherical convex and concave mirrors.[74]

Such knowledge of optical principles could be used, and was || used, to produce startling or apparently paradoxical effects. These are, indeed, mentioned by Hero in the opening chapter of his *Catoptrics* as one of the aims of his inquiry,[75] and in ch. 18, for instance, he shows how 'to place a mirror so that anyone approaching it sees neither his own image nor that of another but only whatever image one selects'.[76] But the essential point is that, however startling they may seem to the bystander or victim, such effects depended, for their production, on *knowledge* on the part of the individuals who set them up.[77] *They* had to have a firm enough grasp of the principles of optics and know what they were doing. Admittedly the point at issue in Sextus at *P.* I 48–9 is that animals with different shaped eyes may see things differently, and in *P.* I 119 that position may make a difference to how an

[69] Compare also the series of attempts made in antiquity to determine whether air has weight in air, Aristotle, *Cael.* 311b8ff., Simplicius, *in Cael.* 710.14ff. (referring to Ptolemy's investigation) and 710.29ff. (reporting Simplicius' own results).

[70] This was a stock example, appearing in a wide variety of authors: for a list of references see Schöne, 1897: 29 n. 9.

[71] See, for example, Proclus, *in Euc.* 40.9ff.

[72] Contrast, however, the much more problematic case of atmospheric refraction, where, precisely, the media and their boundaries are not well defined.

[73] See, for example, Hero, *Catoptrics*, e.g. ch. 5, 328.9ff., chh. 8ff., 332.8ff. and cf. 'Euclid', *Catoptrics*, ch. 1, 286.21ff., ch. 29, 338.7ff.

[74] See Ptolemy, *Optics* III 67, 120.8ff.; III 97ff., 131.14ff.; IV 1ff., 147.2ff.

[75] Hero, *Catoptrics*, ch. 1, 318.9ff.

[76] Hero, *Catoptrics*, ch. 18, 358.1ff.

[77] Cf., more mundanely, the aims of σκηνογραφία, see, for example, Proclus, *in Euc.* 40.19, and Damianus 28.11ff.

object appears. As in the weight example, the latter is certainly a point that may be agreed, except that the scientist will not go on to draw any radical sceptical conclusions about the suspension of judgement. On the contrary, the firmer his understanding of the laws of reflection and refraction, the less inclined the student of optics will be to draw sceptical morals, the more confident he will be concerning the investigability of the phenomena. Thus in the second book of the *Optics* Ptolemy goes through a long list of illusory phenomena and is able to give satisfactory accounts of many of them: so far from concluding from such cases that sight as a whole is deceptive, he insists on the contrast between the exceptional and the normal case.[78]

The types of problems concerning perception that trouble the scientists relate less to sight or hearing as such and in general, than to particular obstacles to observation that arise in particular circumstances. General points, about the need of the observer to be skilled, and careful, are made, but they are to be understood within the framework of the investigation in question. The astronomer, for instance, as we have seen, may be concerned with the distorting effects of certain atmospheric conditions; he should be aware of possible faults in the construction and positioning of instruments, of errors that may arise in the timing of observations, || in estimating wide angular distances,[79] and so on. Certainly the move to simplify and idealise the problems investigated is common in Greek, as in all, science, and this move often, even normally, involves discarding some of the perceptible phenomena as irrelevant to the inquiry. There are already certain such idealisations in Aristotle, as for example in his being prepared to treat of point sources of light in his discussion of haloes and the rainbow.[80] The study of the lever involves discounting the effects of friction (as we call it),[81] and the principle of the absence of elasticity of fluids is encapsulated in Postulate I of Archimedes' *On Floating Bodies*. The assumption that the earth is as a point in relation to the fixed stars is common in astronomy;[82] for the purposes of his discussion of the longitudinal movements of the planets

[78] See, for example, Ptolemy, *Optics* II 134f., 80.3ff.

[79] Cf. also the problem of estimating very small angles, a difficulty present in Ptolemy's discussion of determining the apparent and true angular diameters of the planets, *Planetary Hypotheses* I §5 and cf. §7.

[80] *Mete.* III, ch. 3, 373a6ff., ch. 5, 375b19ff. See further Owen, 1970: 256ff.

[81] As in Archimedes, *On the Equilibrium of Planes*. The tendency to discount or minimise the effects of friction is also a feature of the discussion of the actions of the simple machines, for example in Hero, *Mechanics* II 21 (wheel and axle), 23 (compound pulley), *Dioptra* 37 (cogged wheels). Cf. also the discussion of the problem of friction in connection with the analysis of forces acting on weights on an inclined plane, Hero, *Mechanics* I 23; cf. Pappus VIII 9, 1054.4ff.

[82] At *Syntaxis* I 6, I.i 20.5ff., Ptolemy argues for this: cf. also Euclid, *Phainomena* Proposition 1, 10.12ff., Cleomedes I 11, 102.23ff. Compare the assumption that the earth is as a point in relation to the *moon's orbit*, in Aristarchus, *On the Sizes and Distances*, Hypothesis 2 – which discounts lunar parallax – and contrast the assumption that the circle in which the earth moves round the sun is as a point in relation to the fixed stars, in Aristarchus' heliocentric theory, as reported in Archimedes, *Sandreckoner*, ch. 1. II 218.13ff.

Ptolemy explicitly leaves out of account their deviations in latitude;[83] and many other examples could be given. But it is one thing to discount some of the perceptible data as irrelevant;[84] it is quite another to discount *them all* as unreliable. To be sure, the latter move *is* made in certain contexts within one strand of a Platonising tradition. For Plato himself, it was thought, astronomy should be reduced to a branch of geometry, acoustics to number-theory. But Aristoxenus is clear that such a reduction is ‖ foreign to acoustics: 'some of those [predecessors] introduced extraneous reasoning, and rejecting perception as inexact fabricated rational principles, . . . a theory utterly extraneous to the subject and quite at variance with the phenomena'.[85] Again although Proclus, many centuries later, began his *Outlines* with a pious reference to Plato's recommendation that the true philosopher should bid the senses good-bye and concern himself with the study of 'slowness itself' and 'speed itself' 'in true number', the whole of the rest of his work deals with the investigation of the *visible* moving objects in the sky.

Idealisations and simplifications there may be, indeed must be. But the key question, whether or not it was made explicit, was, rather, which perceptible phenomena to discard. Those that remained, that provided the explananda of the science in question, had to be as comprehensive and reliable as possible, and considerable efforts were expended, at least in certain quarters, to achieving that end.

The trustworthiness of perception in general was not the main issue in the exact or the natural sciences: the problems related, rather, to particular contexts and to the particular circumstances of an inquiry. The writers we have been studying often show quite a keen sense of where, in their particular subject, the practical problems of securing a reliable data-base lay. They exercise, on occasion, some ingenuity in meeting or getting round the difficulties, and they are, at least sometimes, careful to emphasise the approximate nature of approximate results. The limitations of such methodological discussions as they engage in are, however, apparent. While first-order recognition of particular problems and difficulties is common enough, second-order analysis of the issues connected with error and approximation procedures is rare, that is notably of such questions as the

[83] *Syntaxis* IX 2, I.ii 211.21ff. He comes back to the problem of movement in latitude in *Syntaxis* XIII.

[84] The attempt to isolate the operative variables is a feature of the stories purporting to describe Pythagoras' investigation in acoustics, however fantastic their other elements may be (see above p. 321 and n. 58), and it is also an aspect of the methods used by the Alexandrian engineers, according to Philo, *Bel.* 50, in their attempts to improve the construction of catapults.

[85] Aristoxenus, *Harm.* II 32, cf. also Boethius, *De Inst. Musica* I 10. Porphyry, quoting Ptolemais of Cyrene at *in Harm.* 23.25ff., 25.26ff., suggests that for the Pythagoreans when reason (λόγος) and perception (αἴσθησις) are in conflict, the latter is to be rejected, and in fact the Pythagoreans denied that the interval formed by an octave plus a fourth (i.e. 8:3) is a concord because it did not fit their ideas of the simplicity of the ratios of the numbers to which concords must correspond.

interpolation and extrapolation techniques to be used, and of the methods to be applied to extract results from sets of discrepant data – while there is little or no use at all, of course, of a cluster of concepts associated with probability || in the statistical sense,[86] let alone a theory of error of the form familiar since Gauss. On these and similar questions, not much awareness, let alone sophistication, is shown by practising Greek scientists.[87] In this respect, they could have done with being better epistemologists and philosophers of science. Yet it is not as if they could have learnt much on many of these topics from the usual epistemological discussions in contemporary philosophical writings: for if the points about the problems connected with error and probability were not made in science, they cannot be said to have been part of the philosophical debate either.

[86] The development of this notion has been studied by Hacking, 1975; cf. also Sambursky, 1956: 35–48, Sheynin, 1977: 207–59, and on its application in astronomy in particular, Sheynin, 1973: 97–126. [87] Nor, as we have said, by other scientists for many centuries.

REFERENCES

Aaboe, A., and Price, D. J. de S. (1964) 'Qualitative measurement in antiquity', in *L'Aventure de la science*, 1 (Paris), 1–20

Babb, S. E. (1977) 'Accuracy of planetary theories, particularly for Mars', *Isis* 68: 426–34

Björnbo, A. A. (1901) 'Hat Menelaos aus Alexandria einen Fixsternkatalog verfasst?', *Bibliotheca Mathematica*, Dritte Folge 2: 196–212

Bruin, F., and Bruin, M. (1976) 'The equator ring, equinoxes and atmospheric refraction', *Centaurus* 20: 89–111

Conybeare, J., and Mann, W. N. (1957) *Textbook of Medicine*, 12th edn (Edinburgh)

Czwalina, A. (1959) 'Ptolemaeus: Die Bahnen der Planeten Venus und Merkur', *Centaurus* 6: 1–35

Delambre, J. B. J. (1817) *Histoire de l'astronomie ancienne*, 2 vols. (Paris)

Dicks, D. R. (1953–4) 'Ancient astronomical instruments', *Journal of the British Astronomical Association* 64: 77–85

Drachmann, A. B. (1953–4) 'The plane astrolabe and the anaphoric clock', *Centaurus* 3: 183–9

Dreyer, J. L. E. (1917–18) 'On the origin of Ptolemy's catalogue of stars', *Monthly Notices of the Royal Astronomical Society* 78: 343–9

Finlayson, J. (1878) *Clinical Manual* (London).

Fotheringham, J. K. (1915) 'The probable error of a water-clock', *Classical Review* 29: 236–8

(1923) 'The probable error of a water-clock', *Classical Review* 37: 166–7.

French, H. (1912) *An Index of Differential Diagnosis of Main Symptoms* (Bristol)

Gingerich, O. (1980) 'Was Ptolemy a fraud?', *Quarterly Journal of the Royal Astronomical Society* 21: 253–66

(1981) 'Ptolemy revisited', *Quarterly Journal of the Royal Astronomical Society* 22

Goldstein, B. R. (1967) 'The Arabic version of Ptolemy's *Planetary Hypotheses*', *Transactions of the American Philosophical Society* 57, 4

Hacking, J. (1975) *The Emergence of Probability* (Cambridge)

Harris, C. R. S. (1973) *The Heart and the Vascular System in Ancient Greek Medicine* (Oxford)

Heath, T. L. (1921) *A History of Greek Mathematics*, 2 vols. (Oxford)
(1932) *Greek Astronomy* (London)
Holton, G. (1978) *The Scientific Imagination* (Cambridge)
Koyré, A. (1968) *Metaphysics and Measurement* (London)
Lejeune, A. (1956) *L'Optique de Claude Ptolémée* (Louvain)
Lloyd, G. E. R. (1979) *Magic, Reason and Experience* (Cambridge)
Maula, E. (1975–6) 'The spider in the sphere: Eudoxus' Arachne', *Philosophia* 5–6: 225–57
Mercier, R. (1979) Review of R. R. Newton, *Ancient Planetary Observations and the Validity of Ephemeris Time*, in *British Journal for the History of Science* 12: 211–17
Neugebauer, O. (1949) 'The early history of the astrolabe', *Isis* 40: 240–56
(1975) *A History of Ancient Mathematical Astronomy*, 3 vols. (Berlin and New York)
Newton, R. R. (1977) *The Crime of Claudius Ptolemy* (Baltimore)
(1980) 'Comments on "Was Ptolemy a fraud?" by Owen Gingerich', *Quarterly Journal of the Royal Astronomical Society* 21: 388–99
Owen, G. E. L. (1970) 'Aristotle', in *Dictionary of Scientific Biography*, I, ed. C. C. Gillispie (New York), 250–8
Pannekoek, A. (1955) 'Ptolemy's precession', in *Vistas in Astronomy*, I, ed. A. Beer (London and New York)
Pedersen, O. (1974) *A Survey of the Almagest* (Odense)
Price, D. J. de S. (1957) 'Precision instruments: to 1500', in *A History of Technology*, III, edd. C. Singer *et al.* (Oxford), 582–619
Sambursky, S. (1956) 'On the possible and the probable in ancient Greece', *Osiris* 12: 35–48
Schöne, R. (1897) *Damianos Schrift über Optik* (Berlin)
Sheynin, O. B. (1973) 'Mathematical treatment of astronomical observations (A historical essay)', *Archive for History of Exact Sciences* 11: 97–126
(1977) 'Early history of the theory of probability', *Archive for History of Exact Sciences* 17: 207–59

14

PLATO ON MATHEMATICS AND NATURE, MYTH AND SCIENCE

INTRODUCTION

In 1968 I published a paper on 'Plato as a natural scientist' in the *Journal of Hellenic Studies*. I returned to that topic, broadening it to include others to do with Plato's attitude to and use of mathematics, in a lecture I gave in Tokyo in 1981, afterwards published in *Humanities* for 1983. Since in certain respects this supersedes my earlier discussion I have chosen it for inclusion here.

In both papers my strategic concern can be simply stated. Against those who have represented Plato as either antipathetic to the inquiry into nature, or, if not antipathetic to it, persuaded nevertheless that no such inquiry could yield any worthwhile result, I argued, to the contrary, that Plato was vitally concerned to advocate, and does both advocate and practise, a new style of inquiry into nature, namely a teleological one. His own exercise in cosmology, the *Timaeus*, is not to be dismissed as mere play, let alone as some kind of childish story. On the contrary, it fulfils an important and very serious purpose in Plato's philosophy: it justifies the claim that this world, the likeness of the intelligible model, is (as the last sentence of the *Timaeus* puts it) a 'perceptible god, greatest and best and fairest and most perfect'. One influential line of interpretation of Plato, and one strand in Platonism, represents the perceptible world as no worthwhile object of study, and has Plato turning his back on it, to focus on the intelligible world alone: but that is drastically to oversimplify his position which is, I argue, both subtle and complex. Thus although the perceptible world is said to come to be (in a famous but disputed sentence of the *Timaeus*, 28B) the emphasis could hardly be stronger on the point that it is the construction of a good Craftsman and based on the intelligible model.

Admittedly these topics are still highly controversial. Texts in the *Republic*, especially a famous recommendation, in the passage describing how astronomy should be studied, to 'leave the things in the heavens alone' (530B), have been and continue to be interpreted as support for the view that Plato did indeed, in some sense, 'turn his back on' the perceptible phenomena. I argue briefly against that, in this paper (p. 348), first on the grounds that the context of the passage makes a crucial difference to how we should understand it. It occurs in an account of the education of the

Guardians: Plato is not concerned to discuss astronomical methods as such and in general, but has the limited purpose of identifying the contribution that astronomy can make to training the Guardians in abstract thought. Secondly Plato's actual practice, when it comes to suggesting astronomical models both in mythical guise in the *Republic* (book x) and within the framework of his cosmology in the *Timaeus*, shows that he is far from discounting the phenomena entirely. As I have noted, however, the problem remains disputed: the most recent contribution to the debate, by David Sedley (forthcoming), comes down firmly in favour of taking Plato to be advocating an anything but totally *a priori* astronomy – although that has no doubt not said the last word on the subject.

But if overinterpretation of Plato's alleged rejection of the perceptible world is one view that should be resisted, I also stressed that overenthusiastic representations of Plato's advocacy of the 'mathematisation of physics' are also mistaken – where I have to admit to being somewhat unguardedly enthusiastic myself in the brief chapter I wrote on Plato in my *Early Greek Science* (1970). For the Plato of the *Republic*, mathematics as currently practised undeniably falls into the second, not the topmost, category in his account of the four levels of cognition, namely that of *dianoia*, rather than *noēsis*. Some detailed questions – again mostly controversial ones – as to the precise nature of Plato's criticisms of the mathematicians are discussed in my article. Thus I argue that when he describes them as proceeding as if their starting-points were clear to anyone, that is not to say that Plato thought, or that he thought that they thought, that that is the case: but rather they proceeded (and Plato knew they proceeded) by taking as evident starting-points which they knew to be contested – and what was contested was not just a matter of alternative formulations for the same underlying idea, but some of the underlying ideas themselves.

However, the strategic point is unaffected by these matters of detail. The extent to which Plato explicitly formulates, let alone carries through, any programme that can be called a 'mathematisation of physics' is very limited. He has a geometrical atomism, for sure, and that influences many other areas of his account in the *Timaeus*. But even if we limit ourselves to the sphere of the activity of Reason, that is not always a matter of a mathematically expressible order: and of course once Necessity is brought into play, it seldom or never is.

Too much emphasis on mathematisation is liable to miscue the general thrust of Plato's argument. His overwhelmingly dominant concern is with teleology, with showing how the *good* is instantiated. That the good is sometimes represented by geometrical order is true: but often it is not – at least not directly. But whatever form it takes, we can be certain of its importance. As the ancients themselves for once clearly and unanimously appreciated, the significance of the *Timaeus* lies in its being the first clear and sustained statement of a teleological cosmology.

To see Plato as antipathetic to perceptible phenomena is to risk assimilating him with Parmenides: to see him as clear-sightedly (even, one might say, with second sight) advocating the mathematisation of physics is to assimilate him to Galileo, or to Archimedes at least. My own perception of his seriousness in the enterprise of cosmology, and of the ways in which accounts of perceptible phenomena *can* be justified, will strike many as running the risk of assimilating Plato too closely, after all, to Aristotle (although I draw attention to that danger, and to the differences, in my article, p. 351).

While that topic is (again) controversial, I would now be inclined not to qualify my position, but rather to try to strengthen it with further arguments. I have since argued elsewhere (1987: 138f.) that the *Philebus* provides evidence of two ways in which (even) 'what comes to be' is amenable to inquiry. First, of particular events or objects, an account can be given of what makes them or is otherwise responsible for them (for example a human craftsman or his divine counterpart). Secondly, of kinds of things, objects or events, an account is possible that picks out the element of the determinate (*peras*) in them. That line of argument keeps closely to the text of the *Philebus* itself, both to the account of dialectic given at 16cff. and to the particular examples to which Plato applies the analysis in terms of *peras* and *apeiron*. These include health, music and fine weather (25Eff., cf. 17Bff. on music) where we evidently can become knowledgeable concerning each kind, to wit by grasping the limit, measure or proportion they exhibit. But a further strengthening of the argument might be secured by focusing more directly on a deep-seated but seldom explicitly noticed ambiguity in the reference both of the term *aisthēta* – perceptible things – and of the vocabulary of becoming, *ta gignomena*, *genesis*.

In both cases the expression may refer to tokens (in the terminology of Platonism, to particulars) or to types (or universals). The fundamental distinction between *aisthēta* and *noēta* – between perceptibles and intelligibles – can, then, be read in two quite different ways, depending on whether *aisthēta* refers to tokens or to types.[1] If to tokens, then the contrast between this red particular and redness will do very well as an illustration, the one of an *aisthēton*, the other of a *noēton*. The consequences of that, in turn, for the kinds of account that Plato can allow, are significant: *redness*, as an intelligible object, may, on that score at least, be the object of unqualified understanding. However, if *aisthēta* are taken to pick out types, then the contrast will be between redness and (say) justice. On that reading, redness, as *aisthēton*, falls on the perceptible side of the perceptible/intelligible dichotomy, and on that score would *not* itself be unqualifiedly knowable.

A similar distinction is relevant also to talk of becoming (where some of

[1] This is not an ambiguity confined to Greek, of course, for in equivalent expressions in English, to 'perceptibles', 'perceptible phenomena' or to the 'perceptible world', the reference may be equally unclear.

the complexities of Plato's terminology have recently been explored by Frede, 1988, and by Code, 1988). 'What comes to be' or 'becoming' may range over particular objects as the particulars they are, or over the kinds they exemplify – over this or that healthy body, this or that musical performance (to adapt examples from the *Philebus*) or over health and music themselves.

Now an examination of the texts of Plato himself – and of those who, beginning with Aristotle,[2] have commented on him – does not yield an entirely clear and unequivocal answer to the simple question of which of these *two* distinctions is in play. There are, to be sure, occasions when Plato refers unambiguously to some particular, for example to a particular face (as at *Symposium* 211A6). There are also notable texts in which he postulates an intelligible Form in relation to such an item as fire (*Timaeus* 51Bff., cf. also colours in the *Seventh Letter*, 342D4), and when, as for instance at *Phaedo* 78E2, the many in question are said to share the same name as the Form, that suits the type–token interpretation of the contrast, rather than the type–type one. However, on many occasions his expressions remain ambiguous. Although his point may be no more than that perceptible particulars, as the *particulars* they are, are *not* intelligible, some[3] of his statements do not *rule out* the stronger reading according to which the perceptible *properties themselves* are contrasted with other, intelligible, ones – where the contrast in question would be not one between token and type, but between two kinds of type.

So when remarks are made – including by Plato himself, as at *Philebus* 59A–B – that the objects of the inquiry into nature are always changing, considerable caution is in order. I argued in relation to *Republic* 530B that Plato sometimes allows his polemical stance to run away with him – in that to recommend the abstract study of astronomy it is not *necessary* to denigrate empirical inquiry, and yet Plato makes Socrates do just that. So more generally, the use of intelligible and perceptible as a polar contrast may mask the point that there is an eminently legitimate study directed to the (intelligible) properties that perceptible physical particulars imitate or in which they participate.

Of course Plato still has a number of reservations to enter – and duly does so – concerning the kinds of account that can be given of different aspects of

[2] Aristotle himself draws a clear distinction between perceptible *forms* (*eidē*) and intelligible ones, for example at *De Anima* 424a17ff. However, in some contexts where he discusses earlier philosophers he uses expressions the exact reference of which remains unclear. This is the case where he mentions 'Heraclitean opinions', with which Plato was familiar, according to which all perceptibles are always flowing and there is no knowledge concerning them, *Metaphysics* 987a32ff. (cf. Plato, *Republic* 529B6–C1). However, at *Metaph.* 987b7ff. Aristotle's comment that perceptibles participate in the forms and *share the same name* suits the type–token contrast rather than the contrast between two kinds of type.

[3] This is true particularly where Plato generalises from particular examples to what is the case in a range of 'such-like' cases (using such expressions as *ta toiauta*, as, for instance, at *Timaeus* 28B8, cf. *Phaedo* 83B3).

the physical world. The role of Necessity and the Wandering Cause is one complicating factor. Elsewhere he underlines the difficulty of particular investigations or their conjectural nature – for example of the geometry of the fundamental particles, of astronomy, and of the underlying atomic structures and interactions responsible for perceptible colours and other qualities. Yet these reservations – which are, in some cases at least, as I pointed out, well judged – would have no point if it were the case that *in principle* no account were possible. They provide, then, all the more reason for not underestimating the seriousness and the value of the cosmological enterprise – and this over and above its undeniable teleological significance.

REFERENCES

Code, A. (1988) 'Reply to Michael Frede's "Being and becoming in Plato"', *Oxford Studies in Ancient Philosophy*, Supplementary volume, 53–60

Cornford, F. M. (1937) *Plato's Cosmology* (London)

Cross, R. C., and Woozley, A. D. (1964) *Plato's Republic, A Philosophical Commentary* (London)

Frede, M. (1988) 'Being and becoming in Plato', *Oxford Studies in Ancient Philosophy*, Supplementary volume, 37–52

Lloyd, G. E. R. (1968) 'Plato as a natural scientist', *Journal of Hellenic Studies* 88: 78–92

(1970) *Early Greek Science* (London)

(1987) *The Revolutions of Wisdom* (Berkeley)

Mourelatos, A. P. D. (1980) 'Plato's "real astronomy", *Republic* 527d–531d', in *Science and the Sciences in Plato*, ed. J. P. Anton (New York), 33–73

(1981) 'Astronomy and kinematics in Plato's project of rationalist explanation', *Studies in History and Philosophy of Science* 12: 1–32

Mueller, I. (1980) 'Ascending to problems: astronomy and harmonics in *Republic* VII', in *Science and the Sciences in Plato*, ed. J. P. Anton (New York), 103–21

Robinson, R. (1962) *Plato's Earlier Dialectic*, 2nd edn (Oxford)

Sedley, D. N. (forthcoming) 'Teleology and myth in the *Phaedo*' *Phronesis*

Taylor, A. E. (1928) *A Commentary on Plato's Timaeus* (Oxford)

Vlastos, G. (1980) 'The role of observation in Plato's conception of astronomy', in *Science and the Sciences in Plato*, ed. J. P. Anton (New York), 1–31

(1988) 'Elenchus and mathematics: a turning-point in Plato's philosophical development', *American Journal of Philology* 109: 362–96

PLATO ON MATHEMATICS AND NATURE, MYTH AND SCIENCE*

As my compendious and unwieldy title may suggest to you, this paper consists of a number of I hope not too disjointed observations on some far-reaching topics. Much of what Plato had to say on the issue picked out in my title is well known and I have no quarrel with what I take to be standard, if not orthodox, interpretations. On other points, however, I am doubtful or dissatisfied, and it is in the hope of being able to alleviate some of the difficulties that I have chosen to air them with you today.

First to put three main items down on the agenda. That Plato uses mathematics as a model of knowledge in many contexts is well known. So too is his use of mathematics, in *Republic* VI and VII, to illustrate not the highest mode of cognition, νόησις, but the next highest, διάνοια. My first group of problems relates to the way in which Plato represents what is wrong with διάνοια, or more strictly what is wrong with the way in which the mathematicians use ὑποθέσεις when they practise what Plato calls διάνοια. What light does Plato throw on contemporary mathematics and how does what he says square with what we know otherwise and independently about it?

Then secondly I have no need to remind anyone that Plato calls the account of the physical world that he offers in the *Timaeus* a 'likely story', εἰκὼς μῦθος, and you are well aware of the controversy that there has been over what that means. Taylor's view, that what Plato was offering was merely a provisional account, was criticised by Cornford and has rightly generally been dismissed. Unlike the hypotheses of || modern science, which had better not be in principle incapable of confirmation or refutation, an account of the physical world, in Plato's view, could under no circumstances be converted from a merely probable into a certain one. Yet quite what status the account of the physical world is supposed to have is puzzling and problematic. I attempted, as long ago as 1968, to say something on certain aspects of Plato as a natural scientist, maintaining – as others had before me – that Plato's *seriousness* in the cosmological enterprise in the *Timaeus* is guaranteed (paradoxically perhaps) by what some of us might think of as one of the unsatisfactory features of the account, namely its teleological orientation. It is chiefly because he wants to show how this world, the best possible world, is the work of a wise and benevolent Craftsman that Plato undertook the exercise and investigated in such detail the workings of Reason even when these are confronted with the factor of Necessity. Even so I was perhaps too easily satisfied with the contrast that Plato himself presents, in the *Timaeus*, between Being (or the Forms) on the one hand, and Becoming on the other.

* The lecture delivered on 15 June 1981, as one of the ICC (Institute for the Study of Christianity and Culture) public lecture series entitled "Myth", held at International Christian University, Mitaka, Tokyo.

Now I want with you to press harder on the question of the limitations or constraints on accounts of the latter – on their inadequacies and on how far they can be circumvented.

This in turn will take us towards a third set of problems concerning the relation between Plato's own views and various strands of Platonism, concerning the extent to which one or the other construction of that highly ambiguous slogan 'saving the phenomena' can claim genuine Platonic lineage. That topic too is vast, and what I have to say here is no more than some brief notes to reopen aspects of the discussion.

If our heads may eventually be in the clouds, let us begin nevertheless with our feet firmly on the ground, with a specific text. As you are well aware the procedures of the mathematicians are criticised in *Republic* VI chiefly on the grounds (1) that they use images derived from the lower section of the Line, (2) that they do not proceed from the hypotheses to a starting-point, but to a conclusion and (3) that they do not deign to offer an account of them either to themselves or to the || others; they do not deign to do so 'as they are clear to anyone', ὡς παντὶ φανερῶν. I am not so much concerned with the first point (though there are some interesting reflections to be made on the way in which visible images will be used in different areas of mathematics: if we ask what, in the case of the number-theorist, corresponds to the geometricians' use of diagrams, the answer, for the Greeks, will no doubt be or include the dot representations of odd and even numbers). Rather I am concerned with the latter two, and especially the third. First there is a point about the unclear status of the hypotheses of the mathematicians. Plato's examples are – you will remember – the odd and the even, the figures and the three kinds of angles. The question that a reader of Euclid is inclined to put is this. Does Plato have in mind definitions (compare the definitions of odd and even in Euclid VII, Defs. 6 and 7) or existence assumptions (corresponding to Aristotle's hypotheses – though Aristotle would not allow odd and even that status, since he insists that while arithmetic assumes the definitions of odd and even, it has to prove that they exist) or even, thirdly, as seems possible in the case of the figures, assumptions concerning the possibility of carrying out certain constructions (like the first three of Euclid's postulates)? Others may feel that we can answer that question definitely in favour of one of the alternatives and to the exclusion of the other two. My own view would be that any such answer goes beyond the text and that that text is importantly indeterminate. While the notion of a starting-point as that from which certain conclusions are derived is absolutely clear, the nature of the starting-points the mathematician will use is not – in that different types of such starting-points have not yet been clearly differentiated (as they were to be in Aristotle and Euclid). While we know that books of *Elements* go back to Hippocrates of Chios in the fifth century B.C., and they must have used starting-points of some kind, just how clear the classification of such starting-points was is problematic. To judge from the main surviving fragment of

Hippocrates himself, he was prepared to speak of the 'beginning' (ἀρχή) of a demonstration ‖ in relation to a proposition which could itself be proved.

Whatever we may think on the first point, we can see that what Plato says about the mathematicians using certain starting-points from which other conclusions are derived makes good enough sense – thus far – in terms of contemporary mathematics. When, however, he says that they do not deign to give an account of such hypotheses 'as clear to anyone', the puzzles grow. What has he in mind by 'clear to anyone', ὡς παντὶ φανερῶν? Some interpreters take it that the sense is 'plain to see' – to wit there 'to be seen embodied in the sensible diagrams or models the mathematician uses' (as Cross and Woozley, 1964: 244, put it) or 'plain to see' . . . in the physical sense of being there to see in the geometer's sand' (Robinson, 1962: 156). But will that do? I have my doubts. Certainly it can hardly be the case that what Plato is referring to here is the type of appeal to a visible diagram such as we have in the *Meno* where Socrates takes the slave-boy through a piece of geometrical reasoning and leads him to the realisation that the double square is not the square with a double side with the help of a square drawn in the sand. In the *Republic* 510C Plato is talking of the starting-points of demonstrations, not to references to diagrams in the course of demonstrations. Though it is undoubtedly the case that Greek geometrical proofs depend crucially on constructions, including constructions that incorporate unwarranted assumptions, and that the term γράφειν means both 'construct' and 'prove', it would be quite fanciful to see Plato as wanting to criticise that feature of contemporary mathematics in this passage of the *Republic*. Whatever his point, it is a point concerning an assumption made about the hypotheses themselves, not one that concerns the procedures of argument by which the conclusions are obtained.

The way in which the hypotheses are supposed to be 'evident to anyone' may well include more than a simple appeal to what can be seen in diagrams. But how far is it the case that what Plato has in mind is that the starting-points of mathematics are, as we should say, taken as self-evident? When we refer to the available evidence of approximately ‖ contemporary mathematics, the plot thickens. Of course Euclid starts off with a number of definitions, common opinions and postulates that are presented without questions and without explanations, and one might think that the assumption was that these are self-evident starting-points. Yet one of the striking features of early Greek mathematics is the lack of uniformity – the evident disagreement – on such questions as the definitions of number or point or line, as well as on such famous issues as the inclusion of the parallel postulate as a postulate. When we compare Euclid's definitions with others that we know to have been proposed before him, the divergence is often no mere matter of formulation, no mere stylistic variation, but reflects a substantial disagreement. Euclid defines point (I, Def. 1) as that which has no part. But Aristotle cites two other quite different definitions, a monad having position

(*De An.* 409a6) and the 'extremity of a line' (*Top.* 141b19ff.). Line itself is a breadthless length in Euclid (I, Def. 2) but a 'flux of a point' in a definition given by Proclus but alluded to (it seems) again by Aristotle (*De An.* 409a4). For 'straight line' in turn we have 'a line which lies evenly with the points on itself' (Euclid I, Def. 4) and 'that of which the middle covers the ends' (Plato, *Prm.* 137E). For number too, apart from 'multitude composed of units' (Euclid VII, Def. 2) we have 'finite multitude' or 'limited multitude' (as in Aristotle *Metaph.* 1020a13), as well as quite a variety of later definitions such as Nicomachus' 'aggregate in the realm of quantity composed of units' (13, 8). And so one could go on.

The evidence for early Greek mathematicians shows that disagreements on the definitions of certain key terms were wide-ranging. Can Plato have been ignorant of that fact? It is not impossible, to be sure, that he was, but surely the overwhelming probability is that he was well aware of most of the debates that centred on the definitions of fundamental terms. If we now turn back to the *Republic* passage we are interested in, it is certainly not necessary to suppose that Plato is there assuming that the mathematical hypotheses he is referring to either are or were thought by the mathematicians to be self-evident. Certainly || Plato himself does not think so: the whole point of νόησις is that an account can be given of the hypotheses which were used by διάνοια. But when Plato says that the mathematicians do not deign to give an account of their hypotheses to themselves or to others as 'plain to anyone', that 'as plain to anyone' can be read as their *claim* rather than (or as much as) their *warrant*. As a matter of fact, the nature of 'number' or 'point' or 'line' may be disputed. The mathematician nevertheless proceeds in his argumentation *as if* his starting-points were 'plain to anyone'. They take those starting-points as known – they proceed ταῦτα ὡς εἰδότες – even when alternative views were in the field.

If that reading of the passage is correct, then Plato's complaint against the mathematicians is not merely that they fail to derive their hypotheses from an unhypothetical first principle, or Form of the Good: he has a further possible criticism, that they 'finesse' the disagreements among mathematicians themselves on the question of the nature or definition of certain fundamental concepts. To adopt one view of 'point' for example, rather than any other, is, precisely, *not* to have something that is plain *to anyone* as your starting-point. To proceed *as if* it were is to use a good deal of bluff. It is, however, just that element of bluff that is so prominent in large sections of early Greek mathematics: at least while we have a good deal of evidence of the variety of suggestions of definitions of many basic terms, we are much shorter on information of the justifications for those suggestions, and while that may well reflect, in part, the meagreness of our sources, that is probably not the whole story and in some cases we may suspect that such justifications were not forthcoming.

To recapitulate: it is possible (but I think unlikely) that Plato is unaware of – or chose to ignore – the substantial disagreements that existed among contemporary mathematicians on the matter of the definitions of certain fundamental mathematical terms. When he says that the mathematicians take certain hypotheses as known and give no account of them as 'plain to anyone', this would – on this view – be || because he Plato believes (or assumes for the sake of argument) that the mathematicians *genuinely* think that that is the case: they are confident that the hypotheses are in fact 'plain to anyone'. Plato's own complaint is simply that the hypotheses are not related to the Form of the Good. Alternatively – and this is the view I would favour – Plato *is* aware of the actual disagreements between mathematicians on the subject of certain fundamental hypotheses. When he says that the mathematicians take them as known and give no account of them as 'plain to anyone', it is rather that they act *as if* that were the case. It is, if you like, the mathematicians, not Plato, that ignore the disagreements. They give no account of – they do not justify – the particular hypotheses they adopt (and in point of fact, as we said, we are short of evidence of any attempts on the part of the mathematicians to justify particular views on, for example, the definition of number or line or point). In addition to the particular complaint that Plato makes concerning the failure to get back to an unhypothetical first principle, there is a further point that he could well score against contemporary mathematicians. They may well appreciate that their starting-points should be known and should be uncontroversial; they act as if that were the case, and yet the actual radical disagreements among their colleagues on many questions give them the lie. This text in the *Republic* would, then, be a criticism not so much of a certain naïve confidence on the part of mathematicians, as of their failure to resolve, or even to come to terms with, certain foundational questions.

I turn now from Plato's complaints about the inadequacies of mathematics to his complaints about the inadequacies of any account of the physical world – to the 'probable story' of the *Timaeus*. The emphasis that Plato puts on the status of the account there offered is remarkable. It is true that he sometimes refers to it as an εἰκὼς μῦθος, sometimes as an εἰκὼς λόγος: the latter expression suggests that we need not read the μῦθος in εἰκὼς μῦθος as carrying the associations of fictional account. The point that Timaeus returns to again and again, however, is that his story is not a *certain* one: it is a probable one. It is worth noting || too, that the introductory material in the *Timaeus* also serves to alert the reader to the question of the status of any account. At 20D7 Critias introduces the story of Atlantis as one that is 'very extraordinary, yet true in every respect' λόγου μάλα μὲν ἀτόπου, παντάπασί γε μὴν ἀληθοῦς. At 22A (still in Critias' speech) Solon is said to 'tell the legend' μυθολογεῖν, of Deucalion and Pyrrha, and the Egyptian priest tells him at 23B that his genealogies are little different from 'children's tales' παίδων βραχύ τι διαφέρει μύθων. Again at 26C Critias says that he will 'transport' the citizens and the city that they described yesterday (in the *Republic*) ἐν μύθῳ and bring them here ἐπὶ τἀληθές (and assume that the city is that ancient city and that the citizens you conceived are our actual forefathers). This evokes from Socrates the reply that this is an excellent plan and that it is important that the story is not an invented fable (μὴ πλασθέντα μῦθον) but a true story (ἀληθινὸν λόγον). I am not suggesting that any of these passages is directly relevant to the cosmological account itself. Yet they certainly all serve to draw our attention to the need to be on our guard on the question of the status of any discussion.

But what are the reservations that Plato has about the account that can be offered of the subject matter that Timaeus deals with? The chief reservations, as expressed by Timaeus himself, relate, of course, to the contrast between Being and Becoming. *Timaeus* 27D5ff. introduces the distinction (as a matter, incidentally, of Timaeus' belief or opinion, κατ' ἐμὴν δόξαν) and at 29B5ff. there is the further well-known and important contrast between the status of the accounts that are possible on the one hand of a model and on the other of its likeness. On the first Timaeus demands irrefutable and unchangeable (ἀκινήτοις) or invincible (ἀνικήτοις) accounts 'so far as is possible': such accounts are possible in relation to what is itself stable and discoverable by the aid of reason and there should, as far as possible, be no falling short in this respect. On the second, however, on what is itself a likeness made in the image of the model, there will be accounts that are likely (εἰκότας) and that stand in proportion to it – as Being is to Becoming, || so is truth to belief (πίστιν).

You are, I am sure, well aware of this and other passages making similar points about the probable nature of Timaeus' account of becoming. But the first point that bears repeating is that while accounts of becoming are merely probable, accounts of Being should, in principle at least, be irrefutable. Now that is a very considerable claim. Whenever the cosmologist or natural philosopher has to do with the intelligible model after which the visible cosmos is constructed, there should, in principle, be no falling short of certainty. Whenever we are dealing with the Forms in other words (in Plato's terms) – whenever it is a question of defining a Form or of giving an account of its relationship with other Forms – there should be no question of mere probability. It is true that Timaeus says 'as far as is possible', καθ' ὅσον οἷόν τε, 29B7 – yet where possible, stable and unchanging.

But what about becoming itself? Here it is a question of mere probability. Yet if probable and not certain, nevertheless the 'most likely' account, as he puts it at 44C–D (μάλιστα εἰκός) and again at 67D (μάλιστα εἰκός), the account that is 'inferior to none in probability' as he says at 29C4, again echoed at 48D. Clearly where the visible likeness is concerned, we are dealing with an object that does fall short, in ways that may or may not be specified, of the intelligible model itself. Yet here too the point should not be exaggerated. We are not, clearly, dealing with an *identical* likeness. Yet the Craftsman makes the image *as like the model as he can*. Four points are worth emphasising.

First the model the Craftsman uses is itself eternal and unchanging: the importance of this is spelled out at 28Aff. where the inferiority of any production based on a created model is stressed. Secondly the product of his workmanship is *good*. The theme is a recurrent one and is given a triumphant culmination in the very final sentence of the *Timaeus* where the likeness of the intelligible model is described as 'a perceptible god, greatest and best and fairest and most perfect': μέγιστος καὶ ἄριστος κάλλιστός τε καὶ τελεώτατος. Thirdly what the Craftsman does is to bring *order* into precosmic chaos or disorder, ‖ ἀταξία. Moreover, fourthly, his work is indissoluble – even if the work of the lesser divine Craftsmen does not share that characteristic. At least at 41A–B when the Craftsman addresses the other Gods he describes his own productions as 'indissoluble' 'unless I myself so wish'. But he then goes on: 'while any bond that is fastened can be untied, yet to wish to dissolve what has been well fitted together and is in a good state would be wicked'.

There are, then, certain fundamental considerations that can be adduced to provide reassurance for the natural philosopher. If there is order in the products of the Craftsman, if they are, or in so far as they are, good, and based on an eternal model, then they are clearly investigable and well worth investigating. Yet there is another side to the picture. As is again well known Timaeus draws back from time to time from a particular discussion with remarks that suggest its difficulty. Even if the natural philosopher can hope for an account that is 'inferior to none in probability', the question of just how good and how probable that is is an open one.

Here it is essential to distinguish between different reservations expressed for different reasons at different points in the dialogue. In one of the chief passages in which great stress is laid on the need to be content with a probable account – 29B–C – Timaeus specifies that Socrates should not be surprised if 'on many topics they are unable to give a completely consistent and exact account' 'on many topics – concerning', for example, 'the gods and the generation of the whole' – θεῶν καὶ τῆς τοῦ παντὸς γενέσεως. No doubt when he goes on to observe that 'we should remember that we are mere mortals' and 'not seek more than a probable account', that is meant to apply to some extent to the whole cosmology. Yet we should not fail to remark that the particular example he has given is the account of the gods and of the genesis of the whole. The disclaimer is attached primarily to talk of the divine: we shall indeed be told something a little later on about the stars, and Timaeus introduces a brief paragraph about the traditional gods, Earth, Uranus, Oceanos, Tethys and so on, saying that they ‖ must trust what has been said about them by earlier men, who were, after all, the descendants of the gods and so their statements should not be disbelieved even though they are 'without probable and necessary demonstrations' (40D–E). As for the 'genesis of the whole', this may be taken to refer to that part of the account that deals with how the world came to be, in particular how, for example, fire was constructed – discussed later at 48B (though at 56B he makes the rare claim that they may take it that the pyramid is the 'element and seed' of fire 'according to the correct account as well as to the probable one').

Elsewhere when Timaeus draws back, it is for fear of making his account disproportionately long. This is what happens at 38D–E when he refers to the detailed description of the positions of the planets and the reason for them. Yet there it is not that such an account is, in principle, impossible – just that it is both difficult and long. Timaeus goes on to say that they may perhaps later give these questions the exposition they deserve. Again when shortly later at 40C–D he refers to the paths of the planets, their retrograde and forward movements, their conjunctions and oppositions – and the signs and portents they provide for men – and says that to discuss all of this without having visible models to consult would be vain labour, this too may be taken to represent a practical difficulty, not one that rules out any possible account of the subject-matter in question. The length of the account involved is once again one of the factors mentioned when – at 54A–B – he draws back from an account of why the half-equilateral triangle is the fairest of triangles. Here the possibility of a superior account is mentioned. If someone is able to give a better account of the construction of the elementary bodies, he is a friend not an enemy. The longer account that Timaeus refers to, but does not give, would not necessarily be an end of the matter. 'Should anyone refute us and discover that it is not so, we do not grudge him the prize.' But that is certainly not to deny, but rather to assert, that the problem might be advanced. The very possibility of a refutation and of an improved account depends upon the problem being in principle investigable. ||

The value and importance of parts at least of the exercise are, to be sure, somewhat deflated at 59C–D, when Timaeus speaks of probable accounts of becoming as a 'moderate and intelligent pastime' undertaken 'for the sake of recreation'. The particular aspect of becoming he has in mind concerns the varieties and compounds of the simple bodies. Yet if we recall that in what follows Timaeus not only attempts general classifications of the various kinds of 'water', of 'earth', and of their compounds, but also tries to relate this account to what happens at the level of the fundamental triangles, then a reluctance to claim any more than a certain probability is readily understandable, indeed laudable when we reflect on the excessive dogmatism shown in this general area of inquiry not only by most of Plato's predecessors but also by most of his successors.

It would also seem to be difficulties at the level of the interaction of the primary triangles that are the primary consideration in Plato's mind when at 68B–D Timaeus says that it is foolish to try and state the proportions of the different constituents that go to make up particular colours, and goes on to add that to attempt to investigate the compositions of colours by tests would be to betray an ignorance of the difference between God's nature and man's. When he says that God alone has the knowledge and power to blend the many into one and dissolve the one into many, this blending appears not to be a matter of mixing pigments but one of combining fundamental atomic particles. I say 'appears to be' because one cannot deny that Plato does not distinguish as carefully as he might between the two types of 'blending' and Timaeus' remarks can also be read as suggesting that one cannot even hope to discover which pigments added to which give which compound colours.

I have gone over these mostly very well known passages at some length and in some detail since it is only when we do so that we can see that Plato often has quite specific – and generally readily understandable – motives for the particular reservations about the account that he puts into the mouth of Timaeus. Disclaimers based on the || difficulties of particular parts of the inquiry – as it might be the complexities of astronomy – are often well grounded. The refusal to claim certainty – when so many other Greek theorists did just that – is to be applauded. The picture that emerges is of a Plato who is far from being as *despairing* of natural philosophy as he is sometimes represented. The visible cosmos is an imperfect likeness of the intelligible model: yet it is made as like it as can be. On the original chaotic disorder order has been imposed and is discoverable. The natural philosopher has to deal both with the work of Reason and with the factor of Necessity and we must be even-handed in the emphasis we give to each. Just as we should not ignore that the visible cosmos is not purely and simply the work of Reason, so we should not be misguided enough to think that it is purely and simply the product of Necessity.

The nub of the matter concerns the fundamental ontological theory that provides the framework for the whole cosmology. What belongs to becoming, in so far as it becomes, never is. Using points from Plato's statements elsewhere in connection with the theory of Forms, at least with the version of that theory he adopted in the middle period dialogues, we can say that 'becoming' is not just a matter of change and coming-to-be but also one of the ways in which any particular bears the predicates it bears. The beautiful objects of the *Symposium* (211A) come to be and pass away, but they are not just beautiful at one time, but not at another, but beautiful in some respects, ugly in others, beautiful in one relation but ugly in another, beautiful in one place, ugly in another, beautiful to some people, ugly to others. The equal sticks and stones of the *Phaedo* also appear unequal either to another person, or to another object. The vocabulary of the 'suchlike' in the *Timaeus* itself (49Bff.) has a similar message to convey.

But how far and in what respect does this fundamental ontological gulf between Being and Becoming threaten the inquiry of the natural philosopher? To read some commentators it runs the risk of ruling it out, of completely undermining the inquiry from the start since the phenomena it has to deal with provide evidence that is fatally flawed. || Yet that line of interpretation, at the extreme, collapses Plato into Parmenides, and makes of Plato's world of particulars a world of pure illusion. That we should not so construe it can be argued on a number of counts, most simply perhaps on the grounds that it ignores the distinction Plato himself draws so carefully between εἰκασία, mere conjecture, and πίστις, belief, in the *Republic*. But that is not the only point. So far as the possibility of an inquiry into nature goes, there is not just the actual carrying out of such an investigation in the *Timaeus* to go by. One of the lessons we must surely carry away from that work is that the measure of order in the cosmos is not to be underestimated. The phenomena are ever-changing and unstable. Yet they are modelled on stable patterns.

When Plato insists that it is only of the intelligible world that certain accounts can be given, the natural scientist has, or should have, nothing to quarrel with. If Plato directs attention to the universal and away from the particular, to the essential and away from the contingent or the accidental, here too there is no threat to the natural scientists. They will surely agree that it is the species that the inquiry is directed towards, not the particular individual example – as it might be the specimen he has on his dissecting table. Dissecting tables themselves are not Plato's method, to be sure. And for the Plato of the middle period ontology the imperfection of the specimen follows from its being a particular. Yet if imperfect, not incoherent. Indeed, it may be suggested that it is to give an account of such coherence as the phenomena have that Plato postulated a theory of Forms in the first place. It is in so far as they participate in or imitate the Forms that the particulars have the measure of coherence they possess: but the Forms are the explanation of that coherence, and but for the fact that we can say of particulars that they are – even if only in qualified respects – beautiful or equal, we should not have needed a Form of Beauty or of Equality. Even when the approach to an understanding of the Forms is described in terms of the theory of Recollection, as for example in the *Phaedo*, we may use the point that recollection is stimulated by encounter with || particulars, both by likes and unlikes, as it is put in the *Phaedo* at 74A. Again this would not be possible if the particulars in question were quite incoherent.

There are, then, I submit, many features of Plato's position that allow and even encourage the inquiry into nature, construed as an inquiry into the intelligible ordered world that the changing phenomena presuppose. After all there are many aspects of Plato's position – the focus on Forms, on the essential rather than the accidental, on final causation and the good, on the overall order of the cosmos – in which he agrees with Aristotle. We must, to be sure, resist any temptation to collapse Plato's position into Aristotle's, just as much as we should resist collapsing it into Parmenides'. So far as points of disagreement go, there is first the fundamental issue of transcendence, to be construed in the main in terms of the conditions to be set on the existence of Forms: for Plato the existence of a Form is not dependent on there being any particular exemplifying it, while for Aristotle it is. Again for Aristotle, from a certain point of view, for sure, the individual substance has priority – even though from another point of view he speaks of form as primary substance when in *Metaphysics* Z he raises the question of what makes a substance a substance and answers this in terms of the unity provided by the form it possesses. Above all, for Aristotle there is nothing qualified about a substance being the substance that it is, at least not when we are dealing with what is in actuality. Yet though the ontological differences are profound, the agreement on the answer to the question of what is there to be known remains: even for Aristotle, what is known is not the particular, at least not as the particular it is, but the form it has.

How far, then, we may now ask, does Plato tolerate or encourage *discounting* aspects of the particulars? How far does the philosopher *ignore* the phenomena in order to 'save' them, not that Plato himself speaks in terms of 'saving the phenomena'? Focusing on the universal or on the intelligible model the philosopher will no doubt expect there to be some shortfall in the imperfect particulars. Yet the || evidence of the particulars can hardly be dismissed completely. It is true that Plato appears to say, or has been taken to say, just that in the *Republic*, when in the context of describing the kind of astronomy that will be useful in the education of the Guardians he says that they will 'leave the things in the heavens alone' (530B7). The interpretation of that phrase and of the whole passage continues to be highly controversial. Recent contributions by Vlastos, by Mourelatos and by Mueller to the problem show that the range of views still being canvassed is wide. One interpretation takes the phrase at full force and sees what Plato is advocating as a study that would more correctly be called the geometry of the sphere in motion, than any of study of the stars or astronomy in the normal sense. The or an opposing view takes it that the phenomena provide at least the problems, though these are then dealt with purely geometrically. How far on either of these views – or indeed on any other – the passage is meant to tell us anything relevant to the inquiry into nature is doubtful. Plato's aim is not to enter the debate about the correct method in astronomy as such, but to consider what in this field can be put to use in the educational programme of the Guardians, in their training in abstract thought. In this context the assimilation of what is called astronomy to geometry is understandable, even if the terms in which Plato describes the new study that he advocates for the Guardians are provocative and potentially misleading. If we want to consider what Plato believed about the possibilities and the constraints on the study of the heavenly bodies, then we should turn to the passages in the *Timaeus* we have already cited, which speak of the difficulties of the inquiry and draw back from a detailed exposition, but which make no suggestion either that the inquiry is in principle impossible or that it is to be conducted on a purely *a priori* basis. On the contrary Plato's careful account of the two main revolutions, the Circle of the Same and the Circle of the Other, and his distinction between the apparent and the actual relative speeds of the planets on the Circle of the Other, strongly suggest that the detailed account that he says is possible (but which he draws back from) would pay as || much respect as any other astronomical system would have done to the kind of data about the periods of the planets which formed the starting-point of the work of such astronomers as Eudoxus.

The phenomena to be saved and the conditions of their saving will no doubt vary from one field to another. Yet it is a visible cosmos that the Craftsman produces and orders and that is there to be explained and within limits understood. Becoming is not to be confused with Being, but what comes to be comes to be what it becomes by virtue of participating in or imitating Being. Of Becoming we have and can have only a likely story. It is important to be aware of the different status of different kinds of account dealing with different subject matter. The likely story of Becoming is not *just* like the myths about the traditional gods. We have seen that Plato distances Timaeus' account from *that* type of story, with the express statement that traditional myths concerning the anthropomorphic gods are 'without probable and necessary demonstrations' (40D–E). It is not that the account of Becoming is itself a necessary demonstration: but that it can attain a measure of probability is guaranteed by the fact that it manifests a measure of order and that while not, of course, a replica of the world of being, it is a likeness of it.

I have entered reservations concerning the views of commentators who picture Plato as antipathetic to the study of nature or despairing of it entirely. But the final topic I wish to broach relates to another influential line of interpretation which also carries certain dangers. Plato and Platonism are often seen to stand for one version of an insistence on the mathematisation of physics. Koyré, for example, in his characteristically direct way put it that: 'if you claim for mathematics a superior status, if more than that you attribute to it a real value and a commanding position in physics, you are a Platonist. If on the contrary you see in mathematics an abstract science, which is therefore of a lesser value than those – physics and metaphysics – which deal with real being . . . , you are an Aristotelian.'

The first difficulty is that to speak of mathematics having, for Plato, ‖ a commanding position in physics is to read too much into the specifically methodological texts we have and to present Plato's actual practice in an unduly charitable light. We discussed earlier the view that Plato himself advances concerning mathematics itself in *Republic* VI: there is no question there, to be sure, of mathematics being supreme. It is firmly subordinated to dialectic, just as it continues to be in, for example, the classification of different kinds of knowledge in the *Philebus* (55Dff.). In *Republic* VII we have certain mathematical studies given an important role in the educational programme of the Guardians, again as a propaedeutic to dialectic. Admittedly the passages in the *Republic* tell us only about the relationship between mathematics and dialectic, not that between mathematics and physics: but by the same token they do not help to place mathematics in any commanding role *within* physics. To see what role it does have there we have to turn to the *Timaeus*, and while mathematics is well and truly brought to bear at one key point, in the geometrical atomism of Plato's account of the primary elements, we cannot or should not discount the fact that often elsewhere – in the account of physiological processes or pathological ones, for instance – the role of mathematics is negligible. There are some references to diseases that correspond to certain accidents to the primary elements, but that hardly prevents the account as a whole from being qualitative, vague and impressionistic, rather than exact and quantitative.

So far as the distinctive (and largely original) characteristics of the cosmology offered us in the *Timaeus* go, the fundamental point is not that Plato set out to mathematise physical inquiry, but rather that he insisted on teleology. The geometrical atomism of his theory of the primary elements, like the atomism of Leucippus and Democritus, attempts, to be sure, a reduction of qualitative differences to quantitative differentiae. As a model it may have seemed suggestive: yet in fact few attempted to follow his lead or to build on or develop his theory, and the very arbitrariness of his suggestions must have detracted from their persuasiveness. On the issue of final causes, on the other hand, there can be || no doubt of the importance that he attached to the principle, of the vigour with which he developed it in detailed theories and explanations, or of the subsequent influence that this had, beginning with Aristotle and continuing through a roll call of most of the major names in Greek science.

The challenge presented by the subject we have been discussing is to do justice to Plato's distinctive, but complex and easily misunderstood, position. It is easier to define this negatively – in terms of what Plato wishes the natural philosopher to avoid – than positively, in terms of positive recommendations. First his own use of μῦθος in relation to the cosmology of the *Timaeus* departs from a common use of the term in Greek to indicate a fictitious story, a myth in our sense, even though some of the associations of that usage are still present in the background and Timaeus' μῦθος in so far as it deals with Becoming is certainly no demonstration, ἀπόδειξις, either. The account is clearly set apart from traditional tales about the gods: it is set apart too from that highly traditional, even if at the same time highly original, work, Hesiod's *Theogony*. But Plato distances himself also from the dogmatism of the Presocratic philosophers, from the unrestrained speculation about how the world was in the beginning, about the physical elements and their modes of mixture and combination, from the unqualified assertions on those subjects in such as Empedocles or Anaxagoras. Certainty is still Plato's aim or ideal, but this is to be had only *by* dialectic and *about* Being. If we can and must detect Being – recollecting the Forms and practising both διάνοια and νόησις – we must also be aware that the visible cosmos is subject to change and the objects we perceive have the characteristics they have only in a qualified manner. That they have such characteristics, even if in a qualified manner, saves them from the incoherence that threatens Parmenides' Way of

Seeming, a world of mere illusion. But in so far as we are dealing with what is changing *as* what is changing we face the problems that Plato refers to in the *Timaeus* concerning what is merely 'suchlike', never 'this'.

Plato's position is not that of a Hesiod, not those of Anaxagoras and || Empedocles, nor that of Parmenides: but it is not that of Aristotle either. Becoming can be understood in so far as it is like Being, and it is Being alone that is the stable object of knowledge. But for Aristotle, unlike for Plato, there is no need to qualify the manner in which a particular substance (if actual) is the substance it is. For both Plato and Aristotle science is of the essential and the universal, and it ignores the accidental. What both would say can and must be discounted in the phenomena is the accidental: what remains to be 'saved' is the essential. But the mode of idealisation or simplification that this involves differs in turn from some of those deployed by some of those who engaged in the exact sciences in antiquity. What Plato and Aristotle shared with an Archimedes or a Ptolemy was the discounting of merely observational error – what can be put down to the mistakes of the observers or the inexactness of the methods of observation. But the exact sciences went beyond Plato in the simplification of certain problems (as when an astronomer ignores the parallax that is the effect of our taking observations from the surface of the earth rather than from its centre) and in the idealisation of others (as when an investigation in statics proceeds on the assumption that the lever itself is absolutely rigid, weightless and frictionless, or when one in hydrostatics proceeds on the assumption that the fluid in question is absolutely homogeneous and non-elastic). The move to present a quantitative, mathematical account of certain aspects of the physical world is there in an embryonic form, in the *Timaeus*, in the geometrical atomism of the theory of the fundamental particles. But it *is embryonic*: there is no clear statement of the principle that physics should be mathematised, nor, in fact, does such a principle correspond to any systematic feature of Plato's practice. Just as we must and can clearly differentiate Plato from Hesiod, from Parmenides and from Aristotle, so equally we must and can resist the temptation that Koyré succumbed to, to assimilate Plato with Archimedes, let alone with Galileo.

15

SCIENCE AND MORALITY IN GRECO-ROMAN ANTIQUITY

INTRODUCTION

An inaugural lecture is an occasion bound by certain conventions, where a general public will expect to be told a little about the discipline being inaugurated, its relationship to other studies and its aims and aspirations. My own effort in the genre dates from 1985. Since what I was inaugurating was not tenure of an established chair, but an *ad hominem* professorship in ancient philosophy and science, I had less excuse, but more need, to introduce my audience to some history and to point the way towards the future. To the Classicists in that audience I was keen to underline the erstwhile centrality of *science* in European perceptions of its classical heritage, keen to stress that there was, in a more recent concentration on a literary canon, an imbalance to be corrected, to remind them of what the study of classical antiquity once stood for and should still stand for today. As for looking towards the future, I was able to mention some encouraging signs, in work of the highest quality being done by some younger colleagues, although I neither attempted to elaborate the ambitious programme I have sketched out in my introduction to this collection, nor did I confess to my sense of its great difficulty.

The particular theme I chose to develop to exemplify the practice of the discipline was that of the relationship between science and ethics – or more generally values. There is a certain irony in the changes in our European perception of ancient science on this score. On the other hand, it is clear that in antiquity science maintained close links with philosophy, including moral philosophy, and even when it was not seen just as a branch of philosophy, it was often perceived as contributing to the good life. This was so in two kinds of ways. First the teleologists were clear that science reveals the good at work in the universe in general and in all its parts. But secondly even the anti-teleologists, such as Democritus, valued the inquiry for the sake of the understanding it led to. Indeed those arch anti-teleologists, the Epicureans, went further and thought of it as a necessary means of freeing human beings from superstitious fear.

Yet on the other hand, with the development of science and especially with its increasing specialisation, those links with philosophy, with ethics, with values, came to be seen as mistaken, misleading, a sign of the immaturity of science, and a feature from which it needed to be purged. The ideal that came to be expressed so powerfully and for so long in European thought was of a science that is totally objective, totally value-free, and the intrusion of talk of the good in ancient science was seen as a mark of its failure to emancipate itself from philosophy.

Yet first, even if one accepted such an ideal of a value-free science, it must be recognised that *but for* the ancients' assumptions of its value-ladenness – and of its value as contributing to the good life – there would hardly have been any science then at all. If we ask where the motivations to do science came from, *they* provide most of the answer. There was, after all, no institutional framework within which scientists worked, no profession, no way in which as scientists they could earn a living. It was just as well, then, we may say, that science was seen as an end in itself: for it was evidently not seen, by society in general or even by notable individuals within it, as a means to some other desirable end.

Moreover that ideal itself – of a value-free science – has in recent years been challenged and is now increasingly recognised to be fraught with problems. Quite how far science can indeed claim to be objective and value-neutral is a matter of intense dispute. This is not just a question of the theoretical framework within which scientific inquiry has inevitably to be carried out. The attempt to divorce science from questions of values is particularly dangerous in a situation where scientific institutions are increasingly large and increasingly isolated empires, and where the control of the products of scientific research is increasingly difficult to achieve – whether by society as a whole or by the scientists who do the research. It is obvious that for science not just to pay lip-service to the ideals of moral responsibility, but to fulfil those ideals, is more and more difficult the more competitive science becomes, in independent institutions insulated, in many cases, from public scrutiny and from public accountability. So it becomes easier to appreciate that while most of the history of science is a history of superseded ideas, study of the perception of science itself, its place in society, and the aims and ambitions of its practitioners, may and does hold lessons still for us today.

To rejoin the themes of my introduction to this set of essays, the pluralism of styles of science has to be given due weight. Those styles reflect different assumptions and different claims concerning the aims of the exercise, the proper manner of conducting it, and how it relates to the received values of society or represents a modification of or challenge to them. To study what passes for science in a society is to go to the centre of the values of that society.

Instruction and research in Greek science in this university have sometimes been in the hands of some of its most illustrious members. I am thinking of John Caius, of William Harvey, of Isaac Newton. That was in the heady days when Greek science was still science, not the downgraded subject it then became, not merely through the expansion of science itself, but from the disaffection of Classicists as well, who were content to let it be confined, if not to oblivion, at least to a decent obscurity, to become a backwater of the history of science, itself an unprestigious and accident-prone area of the practice of the historian's craft. That so many Classicists have turned and still turn their backs on this aspect of antiquity is not any the less lamentable in that it seems readily understandable in terms of the early formation, or rather deformation, that most of us receive. In the late twentieth century Classicists include many who have chosen Latin and Greek precisely to *escape* from science at the very early stage of specialisation that our schools' curricula permit: and often a very successful escape it is, to judge from the depth of ignorance of science ancient *and* modern that it often secures.

To be reminded, at school or university, that Archimedes, Galen and Ptolemy are not just disembodied names for a scientist to conjure with, but authors who exist in the shape of substantial extant corpora of texts *in Greek* was the last thing that some students, intent on their Sophocles or their Horace, were going to appreciate. Nor, when they had won their laurels in Tripos and received their D.E.S. awards, were they likely to be overwhelmed by positive recommendations about the research that might be done on – for example – the important problems of text and transmission in Euclid, or on the many works of Galen for which no modern edition exists and which still today, in 1985, have never been translated into English, or indeed || on the Hippocratic gynaecological treatises of which the same is true. They were, of course, far more likely to be steered towards further work on the much loved, but also much trampled, texts of those within the established literary canon of the 'best' Greek and Latin authors – that is, those who are set for translation exercises in the Unseen papers of Part I of the Classical Tripos. That has *never* happened, to my knowledge, to Euclid, to Archimedes, to Galen or to Ptolemy – a preposterous situation, our learned predecessors would have said, and surely it would take a peculiarly blinkered Classicist to fail to recognise that, for their massive and long-lasting impact on subsequent mathematics, biology and astronomy, Euclid, Galen and Ptolemy are among the most influential of all ancient classical authors – with Plato and Aristotle, I would say, *the* most influential.

But I said 'were', because recently there have been signs of some change, here in Cambridge and elsewhere, a readiness to engage on research on the likes of Asclepiades, Soranus, Galen, Philoponus, to mention just four figures on whom dissertations by graduate students of this university are being written or have just been completed.

There were, of course, notable Cambridge exceptions to that otherwise depressingly widespread mid-twentieth-century conspiracy of silence, among Classicists, about Greek science, even if the interests pursued by those exceptions smacked, sometimes, of the idiosyncratic. Cornford, for example, who once expressed the extraordinary opinion that Greek physics went into decline after Aristotle,[1] nevertheless had important points to make both about the relation between early Greek philosophy and science, and on their joint relationship to their background in myth, ritual and religion.[2] There have also been those who have done pioneering work on medicine and on Aristotle's zoology, W. H. S. – affectionately known as Malaria – Jones, and Arthur Peck, both contributors of valuable volumes to the Loeb Classical Library, and John || Raven, himself an expert field botanist, whose J. H. Gray lectures on that subject indicated exciting areas of research that he was, alas, not able to complete. More recently and more centrally there have been Gwil Owen's brilliant studies on, among other subjects, Aristotle's philosophy of science and on his mechanics.

It is not my claim that the study of Greek science must be the centrepiece of our concern for the ancient world. That study presents, however, a number of opportunities at the intersection of current discussions on a number of far from merely parochial subjects. One example is provided by the active debates, in the sociology and philosophy of science, on the nature and causes of scientific revolutions and on the relationship between science and other forms of knowledge. Another relates to the more purely philosophical analyses of problems connected with the incommensurability or otherwise of belief systems, or the radical indeterminacy of translation. A third concerns the anthropological debates on the issues of the Great Divide, the comparison and the contrast between 'hot' and 'cold', 'open' and 'closed' societies, and on the Domestication of the Savage Mind, as well as on the epistemological and methodological problems posed by the understanding of other cultures. Above all there is the question that is raised in especially sharp terms by the chief material that the student of early Greek science has to deal with: namely under what circumstances, under what conditions, to what extent, can a society become radically self-critical, critical, that is, of the fundamental moral and ideological beliefs and institutions that lie at its own very basis and on which its self-perpetuation depends. Not that to speak of the ancient Greeks as having invented science is – as I have insisted elsewhere[3] – to do any more than to offer an exceptionally telegraphic and correspondingly potentially most misleading rubric to cover some highly complex and far from universally commendable phenomena.

[1] Cornford, 1950: 83. [2] Most notably in Cornford, 1912 and Cornford, 1952.
[3] Lloyd, 1979: 226ff.

The topic that I have chosen for a brief discussion this || evening is rather on the periphery of those concerns, but I hope of some general interest: it concerns the relations between science and morality, and more generally between science and values, in ancient Greece. One of the chief forms in which that surfaces as an issue for us today relates, of course, to the question of the social responsibilities of science – and of individual scientists. First, what limits should there be to the types of work done by scientists in such fields as cloning or germ warfare? And secondly how, even if we could agree on the limits, are they to be imposed? The record of the twentieth century to date is none too good, you will agree, either on the matter of the clarity and determination with which scientists, or anyone else, have attempted to think the issues through, or on the creation of institutions, or of any kind of sanctions, national or international, to police such policies as could be said to command widespread support. Nor do the prospects for reversing the trend seem bright. While on the one hand there are reassuring signs of greater awareness of the issues in certain quarters, on the other, as the pace of technological advance quickens, the difficulty of resisting the momentum of the scientific research programmes themselves increases exponentially.

In the infancy of science, problems of this kind were, naturally, sometimes on an altogether different scale. When Philo of Byzantium refers, at one point,[4] to the subventions that certain Alexandrian engineers received from the Ptolemies for armaments research, what is involved is nothing more portentous than some slightly improved versions of the stone-throwing ballista: missile launchers of a different kind from those we, alas, are familiar with. Nor did Archimedes' success in keeping the Roman troops at bay at Syracuse by ingenious mechanical contrivances spark off a sudden fashion to emulate him. Yet even in the early days of science, the morality of particular investigations was sometimes no trivial issue. The Roman medical || encyclopaedist Celsus reports that, among those who joined the ancient debates on how far anatomical knowledge obtained by dissection was useful or necessary to the medical practitioner, some of the so-called Dogmatists argued that the best method was that adopted by the Hellenistic biologists Herophilus and Erasistratus. I quote:

> Herophilus and Erasistratus proceeded in by far the best way: they cut open living men, criminals they obtained out of prison from the kings, and they observed, while their subjects still breathed, parts that nature had previously hidden, their position, colour, shape, size, arrangement, hardness, softness, smoothness, points of contact, and finally the processes and recesses of each and whether any part is inserted into another or receives the part of another into itself.[5]

[4] *Belopoeica* 50.20ff., text and translation in Marsden, 1971: 106ff.

[5] Celsus, *De Medicina*, ed. F. Marx, *Corpus Medicorum Latinorum* I, Proem to book I, 23f., p. 21.15–21. There is a Loeb Classical Library edition by W. G. Spencer (London and Cambridge, Mass., 1935).

The veracity of this report has often been impugned: certainly it would not have been beyond the reach of ancient imaginations to *invent* such a story for polemical purposes, and the absence of confirmation of this account from Galen is sometimes held to tell strongly against it (though in my view it is not difficult to think of reasons that might have led Galen to choose to pass by this episode in earlier medical research in silence[6]). Yet while some later, Christian, polemic on this and other issues relating to pagan science – condemned by many Christians for its insatiable curiosity – *is* suspect, Celsus has no similar axes to grind. Rather, the way he not only reports this Dogmatist view and registers his own moderate outrage,[7] but also tells us how the Dogmatists themselves justified their opinion against moral objections, lends the whole passage some verisimilitude. Besides, whether or not human vivisection was actually carried out by Herophilus and Erasistratus, the report in Celsus certainly shows one thing for sure, namely that the matter of its morality was debated. While most people, according to Celsus, and Celsus himself, condemned such a practice as cruel, the || Dogmatists defended it by appeal to an argument based on the balance of benefit: 'Nor is it, as most people say, cruel that in the execution of criminals, and but a few of them, we should seek remedies for innocent people of all future ages.'[8]

The exceptional nature of this case can be brought out by drawing some contrasts. We already find in Aristotle, for instance, encouraging noises to the effect that scientific research is worthwhile, despite the hard work, inconvenience and unpleasantness involved, unpleasantness, for example, in having to contemplate blood, flesh and the like in animal dissection.[9] But if determination is necessary, it will be well rewarded by the knowledge gained concerning the marvellous workings of nature. Again much later Galen provides both theoretical and practical justifications for his far more extensive programme of animal dissection and vivisection, the theoretical that the scientist discovers how 'nature does nothing in vain' as well as the answers to problematic physiological questions, the practical that the programme yields anatomical knowledge essential for the medical practitioner.[10] The surgeon, after all, had better know where the principal arteries, veins and nerves lie if he is not to run the risk of maiming his patients when he operates on them instead of doing them some good.

But while Galen spends a good deal of time discussing practical problems

[6] Galen was, in general, concerned to present doctors in the best possible ethical light and in his treatise *That the best doctor is also a philosopher* he argues that doctors should display a high moral character, in particular in relation to the financial aspects of the practice of medicine. On the other hand Galen certainly does not refrain from criticising earlier doctors and his own contemporaries for falling short of the ideals that Galen believes were set by Hippocrates himself. [7] See especially *De Medicina*, Proem to book I, 75, p. 29.20–2.

[8] *De Medicina*, Proem to book I, 26, p. 21.29–32.

[9] See especially *De Partibus Animalium* 645a26ff.

[10] See especially *De Anatomicis Administrationibus* II 2–3, Kühn II 283.7–291.18. There is an English translation of the books extant in Greek by Singer, 1956.

encountered in dissection and vivisection, how to deal with haemorrhage, or with incipient rigor in dead subjects, for instance,[11] the morality of killing animals and of causing them suffering for science gives him, it seems, little pause. For many purposes, such as his investigations of the musculature and of the blood-vascular system, he advises using apes, especially those most like humans, though on his own account he dissected and vivisected many other species as well. Thus the intricate operation described in *On Anatomical Procedures* || book 12 involves the exposure of the living goat foetus *in utero* with observation of foetal movements,[12] and he specified goats, dogs and pigs as possible subjects for his famous investigations of the nervous system, in which working systemically up the spinal column he described the effects of sections either right through, or through one side of, the spinal cord.[13] As for his use of apes, his reiterated belief that they are *ridiculous imitations* of humans[14] no doubt contributed to his suppressing or dismissing some awkward questions, though he does on one occasion recommend using a pig or a goat for an operation in which the brain is exposed in the living animal in part to 'avoid seeing the unpleasing expression of the ape when it is being vivisected', though also in part because you need an animal with a 'really loud voice' since this is one of the functions in which – or rather in the interference with which – he is particularly interested.[15] But while Galen occasionally notes the need for an operation to be carried out 'without pity or compassion',[16] he is usually more concerned that the experiments should not be fluffed through hesitation on the part of the experimenter, than with the feelings of the animal. In general, the price paid, in terms of animal suffering, for the knowledge gained is not an important issue for Galen.

Yet it clearly had been, for the Dogmatists reported by Celsus. While for Galen human vivisection is never in question and human dead subjects for post mortem dissection a rarity,[17] Herophilus and Erasistratus – we are told – obtained criminals out of prison from the kings. Those kings are not named, but they must include (and may be confined to) the first two Ptolemies, Soter and Philadelphus,[18] and the question arises of what *their* motivations and interests were. In the closest ancient parallel to this story of humans sacrificed for the cause of science the answer is clear. This is the

[11] See, for example, *De Anat. Admin.* IV 2, K II 427.17ff., and VII 12, 628.5ff, and cf. XIII 6 in Duckworth, 1962 p: 158. [12] *De Anat. Admin.* XII 6, Duckworth, 1962: 120ff.

[13] *De Anat. Admin.* IX 13–14, Duckworth, 1962: 20ff. Parts of Galen's discussion have been preserved in Greek by Oribasius, see French and Lloyd, 1978: 237ff.

[14] See, for example, *De Usu Partium* I 22, Helmreich I 58.18ff., K III 79.18ff., III 8, H I 152.21ff., K III 208.15ff., III 16, H I 194.11ff., K III 264.9ff., XI 2, H II 117.14ff., K III 848.8ff., XIII 11, H II 273.8ff., K IV 126.1ff. There is an English translation of *UP* by May, 1968.

[15] See *De Anat. Admin.* IX 11, Duckworth, 1962: 15.

[16] *De Anat. Admin.* IX 11, Duckworth, 1962: 15.

[17] See, for example, *De Anat. Admin.* I 2, K II 221.2ff., and III 5, 384.16ff.

[18] While there is not doubt that Herophilus' main base was Alexandria, the question of whether the same is also true of Erasistratus is controversial, see Fraser, 1969: 518ff., who argues that he worked chiefly at the Seleucid court, and cf. Lloyd, 1975: 172ff.

evidence which comes chiefly from Galen[19] concerning Mithridates' use of || criminals condemned to death (by Mithridates himself, no doubt) to test the powers of certain drugs and in particular to develop effective antidotes not only to poisonous drugs, but also to the poisonous bites of snakes, scorpions and spiders. Here the interest of the ruler is clear. *His* chief object was to defeat or forestall any attempts to poison him – to defeat them both by discovering antidotes and by establishing safe doses of drugs which he could then take to build up his own immunity. Indeed according to Galen he was so successful that when, after his defeat by the Romans, he tried to take his own life rather than fall into the hands of his enemies, he could find no poison to which he was not immune, and had to die by the sword. So far as the Ptolemies go, it would be a mistake to assume they necessarily had any high ideals about benefiting 'innocent people of all future ages'. At least the *chief* motivation for most of the support they offered to scientists or to anyone else was likely to be to enhance their own prestige. Herophilus and Erasistratus were simply the most *renowned* biologists of the day. We cannot put an exact date to their extensive anatomical discoveries – which include most notably those of the valves of the heart and of the nervous system itself – but their work evidently quickly became sufficiently well known to make an impression well beyond the circles of medical practitioners – on, for example, the likes of the poet-scholars Callimachus and Apollonius of Rhodes.[20] Presumably Herophilus and Erasistratus already had quite a reputation for anatomical skill *before* they ever embarked on human vivisection: and although we have no means of telling who first had the idea – whether the scientists or indeed the rulers – or how much emphasis the balance-of-benefit argument had when it was first proposed, the model of *animal* vivisection undoubtedly already existed and that was no doubt a, if not the, crucial factor in the fateful extension of such a practice to humans. ||

The rejection of such an extension could have been fortified by some appeal to the Aristotelian argument that some acts are such that they should not be done under any circumstances, including under constraint from tyrants (or as we should say dictators). The actual counters recorded by Celsus vary in strength and take three main forms, that human vivisection is futile, that is unnecessary and that it is cruel. Thus some argued, rather weakly, that under vivisection and indeed under dissection the subject is changed and that that invalidates those methods as methods of acquiring knowledge concerning the functioning of the unimpaired living human being. Others maintained that human vivisection, at least, is unnecessary since the information it yields can be obtained from study of the wounded (for that you did not have to serve in the army: Celsus mentions that other well-known training ground for surgeons, the gladiatorial arena). But naturally the strongest, recurrent argument is that from cruelty, and while that by itself

[19] See Galen, K XIV 2.3ff, and cf. Pliny, *HN* 25.5ff., who mentions immunisation but not experiments on criminals.

[20] See most recently Most, 1981: 188ff.

established no firm boundary between animal and human vivisection, the clincher for some of those reported by Celsus is the appeal to the doctor's duty to save human life. For some, what Herophilus and Erasistratus did and later Dogmatists recommended is a crime, *scelus*, and they were cut-throats.[21]

In the background to this debate we should recall that it was common practice, in ancient Greek lawcourts, for slaves to be tortured when giving evidence. As for atrocities committed in the aftermath of victory, antiquity hardly yields to the twentieth or any other century. Human life as such was hardly prized very highly in society in general. Nor can there be any doubt that in general it was the doctors, or most of them, who prized it most highly. The Hippocratic *Oath* is just the best known of a set of often austere works on medical ethics and etiquette dating from the classical or the Hellenistic period. The *Oath* not only forbids the giving of abortive pessaries, || administering poison and so on, but also specifies that the doctor should never act to harm or injure the patient, besides enjoining high standards of morality in relation to such matters sexual intercourse with men or women, free or slave, and insisting on professional confidentiality.[22] True, not every ancient doctor swore to the *Oath* or some equivalent, not even every doctor represented in the extant Hippocratic Corpus: some treatises discuss abortion and the means to procure it in ways that flatly contradict the principles set out in the *Oath*.[23] Nor was the *Oath* any more than a purely private contract, quite unsupported by any specific state or institutional sanction. Yet all that tends to underline, rather than detract from, the efforts that some Greek doctors made to try to set up standards of conduct for medical practice, and it points to the exceptional nature of the gruesome experiments on human subjects attributed to Herophilus and Erasistratus.

So far I have sketched in some of the ancient analogues to problems relating to the morality of particular scientific research. But I now want to broaden the context of the discussion to include the more general issue of the relationship between any scientific activity as such and values, both moral and otherwise, taken in the broadest sense. Two assumptions are, I believe, quite widespread on this topic. The first is that the more that science (or a particular scientific study) is tied to or at least associated with a morality, a political philosophy, an ideology, the worse, the less efficient, the science, as science, is likely to be (and conversely the more a political philosophy or ideology represents itself as based on natural science, the more dangerous it

21 See Celsus, *De Medicina*, Proem to book 1, 40, p. 23.28ff. ('alia possint etiam sine scelere') and 42f., p. 24.11 ('latrocinantis medici') p. 24.13 ('crudeliter iugulet') and p. 24.19 ('non caedem sed sanitatem molientem').

22 The *Oath* is included in J. L. Heiberg's edition of Hippocratic works, *Corpus Medicorum Graecorum* I 1 (Leipzig, 1927), and is translated in Jones, 1923: I, and by J. Chadwick and W. N. Mann in Lloyd, 1978. The controversial issues of who took the *Oath* and what its significance was are discussed, for example, by Edelstein, 1967: 3ff.

23 As, for example, in *De Natura Pueri* ch. 13, Littré VII 490.3ff., on which see Lonie, 1981: 165.

is likely to be). The second is the historical belief or opinion that the separation of science from morality and values was, precisely, a Greek achievement and to a large extent what the invention of science as an independent inquiry was all about. Both opinions have a fair prima-facie plausibility. But both need rather important || qualifications and it is these that I wish to try to bring out here.

Let me begin with the second point, the idea that the Greeks were responsible for a – the first – clear distinction between the proper domain of science (that is, as they would put it, the inquiry into nature) and such studies as moral and political philosophy. Certainly in so far as we can talk – in admittedly shorthand terms – of an invention of science in ancient Greece, that was no merely *intellectualist* development. We have little reliable evidence about the motivations of most of the Presocratic natural philosophers, though it is clear that several of them (Xenophanes, Heraclitus and Empedocles for instance) were concerned to criticise conventional Greek religious beliefs and practices. A disproportionate amount of the information in the so-called doxographic tradition records naturalistic explanations of strange or frightening phenomena such as earthquakes, lightning and thunder, and eclipses, though that may just reflect the interests of our sources. But while in general it would be rash to say how far any given individual *deliberately* set out to demystify nature,[24] the *effect* of the aetiologies they proposed was to provide an alternative framework of explanation rendering appeals to the divine superfluous: a first move in securing nature as the domain of empirical research, even while it was still the domain of some pretty wild speculation.

Moreover we can be sure that some early Greek medical theorising was directed to establishing the *naturalness* of diseases and to refuting assumptions of direct divine intervention there. The form of the attack on such beliefs in such works as *On the Sacred Disease* and *On Airs, Waters, Places* is circumspect. They do not say that the so-called Sacred Disease (that is epilepsy) or the impotence that strikes certain Scythians are not sacred at all: rather they assert that they are no more divine than any other disease. All are divine, but all have natural causes. There is no need || to refer any disease, epilepsy included, to the intervention of gods or demonic agencies and those who do so are cheats and imposters, extracting money from the gullible under false pretences. While parts of the treatment they recommend (such as abstention from certain foods) are not dismissed, their use of ritual purifications, charms and incantations is rejected explicitly as ‘ magic ’.[25]

To get this in perspective, however, it is important to note how thin the ice under the feet of the would-be rationalists was. *On the Sacred Disease* has no

[24] A particular interest in and enthusiasm for ‘aetiologies’ is, however, attributed in our doxographic sources to Democritus: see, for example, Fr. 118 in Diels and Kranz, 1954.

[25] The evidence from *On the Sacred Disease*, especially ch. 1, paras. 1ff (Grensemann), L VI 352.1ff., and ch.18 paras. 1ff. (G), L VI 394.9ff, and from *On Airs, Waters, Places* ch. 22, *CMG* I 1.74.10ff., is set out and discussed in Lloyd, 1979: 15ff.

hesitation rejecting stories about divine intervention. Yet while the writer's description of an epileptic seizure is detailed and careful, his explanations are quite fantastical. 'The brain', he writes,[26]

> may be corrupted both by phlegm and by bile and you can distinguish the two types of disorder thus: those whose madness results from phlegm are quiet and neither shout nor make a disturbance; those whose madness results from bile shout, play tricks and will not keep still . . . Such are the causes of continued madness. But fears and frights also occur from a change in the brain. Such a change happens when it is warmed and that is the effect bile has when, flowing from the rest of the body, it courses to the brain along the blood-vessels...(The converse condition, cooling as the result of phlegm, is responsible for the loss of memory.)'

It is only those with unbounded faith in our man, and already convinced of the correctness of Hippocratic naturalism, who could believe that he knows more about what he is talking about there than the purifiers who diagnosed different types of epilepsy as the work of different gods, Poseidon, Ares and so on. True, *his* framework of explanation is naturalistic, not religious or supernaturalistic. Yet the effects of bile and phlegm to which he appeals, while in principle verifiable, remain at the level of pure speculation. Their effects are invisible entities too, if of a different kind. As for the treatment the Hippocratic writer recommends, it does not || progress beyond the attempt to control hot and cold, wet and dry, by regimen. Indeed by such means, he claims, not just the more striking afflictions, such as epilepsy and madness, but *every* disease can be cured, if you hit upon the right moment (*kairos*) to apply your remedies.

The point can be generalised: the confidence with which many early Greek medical writers proclaim not just that all diseases are natural, but also that they themselves can explain – indeed in many cases also cure – them, is not matched by very adequate theories, or, with the exception of some of the surgical procedures used, by very impressive therapeutic methods. That is not just a point that may occur to *us*. The massive disagreements, already in the Hippocratic period, both in pathology and in therapeutics, the extraordinary proliferation of in many cases wildly speculative theories, the bluff involved in most of the claims made for them, were not lost on many of their own contemporaries. The puzzle is, rather, how Hippocratic naturalism gained any credence at all, except among a few intellectuals already convinced on general grounds that some kind of naturalism must be correct. The solution to that puzzle must depend to some extent on the gap between theory and practice – to the benefit of practice, for as we can see from the less theoretically oriented treatises, in the clinic caution as regards diagnosis, and a defensive commonsense as regards treatment, were often the orders of the day.

Several other Hippocratic texts, as well as the ones I have mentioned,

[26] *Morb. Sacr.* ch. 15, paras. 1ff. (G), L VI 388.12ff. Aspects of Greek 'scientific' explanations of madness and other paranormal phenomena are treated in my 1984 Sather Classical lectures, 'The Revolutions of Wisdom', to be published by the University of California Press.

deploy a contrast between *nomos* (a term that covers custom, convention and law) and *phusis* and it is in connection with that distinction, especially, that we think of the Greeks as carving out the domain of science as the study of nature as such, as a study divorced from any concern with the essentially social issues on the side of *nomos*. Nature, on one view, is objective, constant, investigable, *nomos* is relative to the social group, a matter || where disagreements cannot be resolved by reference to objective criteria. Now indeed that *is* one view, one way in which that contrast is employed, and the relevance this has for the constitution of natural science as an autonomous inquiry is incontestable. However, as many commentators have been at pains to point out,[27] the *phusis–nomos* contrast was interpreted very differently and used to very different ends, even if we limit ourselves to writers in the fifth and fourth centuries B.C. It was anything but the sole intellectual property of those who were intent on securing the independence of science, on demystifying the concept of nature or on establishing its moral neutrality: though it was indeed used by some writers for just that kind of purpose. Others, on the other hand, invoked this antithesis with a quite different, even the reverse, intention. Thus the character Callicles in Plato's *Gorgias* recognises a sharp enough distinction between *nomos* and *phusis*: but for him it is the laws established by the weaker that represent *nomos*.[28] According to the life according to nature, *phusis*, the strong rule the weak. While this is supported by references to what is supposed to hold good of animal behaviour (as well as by appeal to how men behave in war and politics) Callicles draws a quite general conclusion about how we should live: that is if we are powerful enough to get away with it. 'Nature' is here no morally neutral domain of inquiry for the physicist, but the source of a principle of morality that stands in direct contrast to conventional human institutions, a principle deemed to be sanctioned by what is true not just in the animal kingdom, the jungle, but in the universe as a whole.

Interestingly enough, the point that Plato shares with Callicles is that nature is not morally neutral. While Plato is vitriolic in his condemnation not just of what Callicles stands for, but of the whole tradition of what he represents as atheistical science, he continues to insist that cosmic order is a moral order. The trouble with the atheists || criticised in the *Laws*,[29] in Plato's view, is that they *opposed* nature to convention and did not recognise that soul is prior to body and that the whole universe is governed by a divine intelligence. In his very different way, then, Plato is as concerned as any Callicles to deny that the realm of nature is morally indifferent, though the morality be believes to be inherent in nature is not the rule of force, but that of reason and intelligence. Of course Socrates, who in Cicero's famous phrase 'called philosophy down from the sky',[30] is made to express his sense

[27] See especially Heinimann, 1945 and Guthrie, 1969: ch. 4, pp. 55ff.

[28] Plato, *Grg*. 482Cff.

[29] Plato, *Lg*. x 885Cff., 888Eff.

[30] Cicero, *Tusc*. 5.4.10, cf. *Academica* 1.4.15.

of the impasse facing physical inquiry in a well-known text in the *Phaedo* where he speaks of his disappointment with Anaxagoras' failure to apply the principle of reason more extensively in his cosmology.[31] But by the time he came to write the *Timaeus* Plato (at least) clearly saw his way to providing a cosmological account in which the world is the result of the work of a benevolent craftsman-like God imposing order on a pre-existing chaos or disorder. God secures the best possible outcome, within the constraints of necessity, and the result, in the ringing tones of the end of the *Timaeus*, is a world that is 'a perceptible god, made as a likeness of the intelligible, this single universe, greatest and best and fairest and most perfect'.[32]

This brings us back to the first of the two widespread assumptions I spoke of, that the closer the association of science with morality and values, the worse the science as science is likely to be. There is no question of representing Plato as a leading practising scientist: though he was certainly a highly influential philosopher of science, not least for the very insistence on the need for teleological explanations (in science and elsewhere) that I have just mentioned. Not that all the results of teleologically oriented natural science, in those who agreed with Plato's ideal, were bad science. It is not that teleology as such is in principle misguided. On the contrary it could and did prove an enormously fruitful heuristic principle, in antiquity as || later. But the nub of the matter is, of course, how the good – what good – and whose good – is deemed to be manifest in nature: but this is to jump ahead.

The link between, or the reluctance to divorce, science and values may take quite different forms and it is important to distinguish three that are relevant to the ancient world. First scientific inquiries may be undertaken expressly to establish a particular moral or political point of view, where all and only those aspects of science are pursued that can be represented as support for that view. So far as expressed intentions go, Galen perhaps comes closest to allowing the end he sets himself to determine the programme itself when he sets out, in *On the Use of Parts*, to show that all the parts of animals, without exception, are witness to divine providence.[33] But more often the link is weaker: either the results of scientific inquiries are held to have implications for values and the scientists themselves are concerned to spell these out: or, weaker still, the activity of scientific research itself may be deemed to be praiseworthy, to be a part of, even constitutive of, the good life. Both ideas are widespread, from Aristotle and Theophrastus down to Galen and Ptolemy and beyond, not that they should be taken to be representative of the whole of Greek science, though they are typical of one and a dominant strand in it: I shall come back to that at the end.

Aristotle presents a particularly intriguing case since no one could, in general, be more conscientious than he was in drawing distinctions between

[31] Plato, *Phd.* 97Bff.

[32] Plato, *Ti.* 92C.

[33] See, for example, *UP.* I 5, H I 6.18ff., K III 9.4ff.; III.10, H I 177.20ff., K III 242.5ff.; III 16, H I 190.10ff., K III 259.3ff.; V 5, H I 267.12ff., K III 364.17ff.

the subject-matter, aims, methods and degrees of exactness of different inquiries. Among the best known examples where those scruples are in evidence are the contrast between physics and mathematics in *Physics* II and that between ethics and mathematics in the *Nicomachean Ethics*.[34] A realist, but no Platonist, in the philosophy of mathematics, Aristotle puts it that what the geometrician studies – points, lines, surfaces || and so on – are the properties of physical objects (not separate, independently existing entities) though he studies them not *as* physical but *as* mathematical (abstracting from the properties that make the physical objects the physical objects they are). Again he says it is absurd to expect exactness in ethical inquiries – as absurd as to accept merely probable arguments from a mathematician.

But on the relationship between physics and ethics Aristotle's position is complex. In his moral philosophy he recognises, for sure, that specifically moral excellence depends on *proairesis*, moral choice or deliberation. There is no question of animals (in his view there is no question even of children) having moral excellence, since they lack the capacity to make such choices, though they may have, precisely, what he calls natural excellence. Yet when he comes, in the *Politics*, to discuss the political arrangements that are necessary for the practice of moral excellence and for happiness in general, he begins his analysis with a consideration of the kinds of communities or associations that human beings form. His famous dictum that man is by nature a political animal (more strictly a *polis*-, or city-state-, forming animal), is meant, precisely, as the conclusion of a factual analysis. All animals naturally desire to reproduce themselves. In humans, too, male and female naturally form associations for the purposes of reproduction. That legitimates the view that the family or household, the *oikia*, is based on biological needs: but *oikiai* are not self-sufficient, but (naturally) agglomerate to form villages, and the end-result of that process, the complete or perfect (*teleios*) such association is the *polis*. Just as there are natural limits to the size of animals and plants (you do not get giraffes 100 feet tall), so, Aristotle argues, there are natural, proper limits to the size of the *polis*. But more potently he sees the same or a similar principle at work in each of the relationships adult:young, male:female, || master:slave – namely the first member of each pair naturally rules, the second is naturally ruled. Since, in his view, the distinction between the function of ruling and the function of being ruled is a natural one (he takes the relationship between soul and body to illustrate it as well) he holds that slavery is a natural institution, while recognising that many slaves are slaves only by accident and compulsion.[35]

Moreover plants are for the sake of animals, animals for the sake of humans, and when, in his zoology, he encounters prima-facie counter-evidence to his principle that the male is stronger, longer-lived and more aggressive than the female, it does not lead him to modify that principle since

[34] *Ph.* 193b22ff., *EN* 1094b25ff.
[35] Aristotle, *Pol.* 1252a1ff., 24ff., 1253b1ff., 14ff., 1255a4ff.

those exceptions are overridden by another even more important guiding notion, namely that man is the *model* animal. What is true of humans is what *should* be true of all animals: if *they* fail (when for example we find species where females are stronger than males) that is because those species are inferior, defective, even, as Aristotle sometimes puts it, deformed or maimed.[36] He certainly does not ignore the distinction between physics, and moral and political philosophy: on the contrary he points it out. But just as certainly he grounds his political philosophy in principles he holds to apply to nature generally. The concept of 'nature' he works with spans human nature along with animals, plants and the natural elements. The concept of 'good' is not confined to contexts where we can identify individuals or species *whose* good is in question, but is applied to the cosmos as a whole, conceived not merely as orderly but as a hierarchical whole, in which everything from the natural elements, up past plants, animals and humans, to the divine heavenly bodies and the Unmoved Mover himself has its own particular capacities and due place in the series.[37]

For us, brought up, maybe still, on the sacrosanctity of the fact–value dichotomy, the problem of coming to terms || with such a cosmology is acute. Have we not learnt from Hume and others that it is illegitimate to move from an 'is' to an 'ought'? If large parts of ancient science assume you can (as the teleological tradition especially seems to do), does not that suggest a fundamental error? The day before yesterday the answer would probably have been a straight 'yes'. But we would do well, today, to pause. The fact–value contrast itself has come under critical scrutiny from various quarters. One can set out conditions, so it has been argued, where 'ought' statements can be derived from 'is' ones. Factual statements presuppose a conceptual framework and any such framework involves selectivity, a viewpoint, just as equally observation statements presuppose theories. Can there, then, be any discourse that is totally value-neutral or value-free? The idea that natural science is such a discourse – it might be argued, it has been argued – was part of nineteenth-century positivist rhetoric. Science as ineluctably theory-laden is ineluctably evaluative at least in some broad or loose sense of evaluative.

Now arguments of that general type are themselves subject to some exaggeration and abuse. That no observation statements are completely theory-free does not mean that no distinction between observation and theory can be drawn, even if the contrasts will turn out to be matters of degree, a matter of greater or less theory-laden-ness. If the fact–value contrast has occasionally been invoked in a highly simplistic fashion, that too does not mean that it was not, is not, useful and important. Indeed though the fact–value contrast has been criticised and to some extent eroded, in some contexts it is still the case that insufficient, not excessive, attention has been

[36] The evidence is set out and discussed in Lloyd, 1983: 26ff., 40ff.

[37] *Pol.* 1256b15ff., *Metaph.* 1075a11ff.

paid to it. Some recent endeavours to read off conclusions about how human social relations should be organised from biological theories (the selfish gene), from sociobiology (the naked ape), or from physics (the indeterminacy principle), usually illustrate how badly such attempts go astray, if not || in the scientific interpretations used as their basis, at least in the bridging principles – or in both.

But there is a second major difficulty, for us, in Aristotle's cosmology and science and those like them in that talk of *cosmic* good, and exploring this a little way may help to point up some contrasts, and some comparisons, between ancient and modern preoccupations. When in his zoology Aristotle asks the question of the good an organ or a process serves and answers in terms of the contribution it makes to the survival or the flourishing of the species in question, we can follow him well enough. But how to save from incoherence talk of the good from a cosmic perspective (where Heraclitus' dictum that 'to god all things are beautiful and good and just, but men have thought some things are unjust, others just'[38] merely reinforces the problem – for anyone but a god)? Press the question of the meaning of *cosmic* good and a dilemma presents itself. On the one hand, on one line of argument the good is simply a redescription of what is the case, or rather of what is regularly the case, and that way the *vacuity* of calling that *good* threatens (a point on which Stoic philosophy contributed some important arguments). On the other, press the demand for a standpoint from which an evaluation is to be made, and that way leads eventually to a far more complex nexus of problems relating to what we may call the anthropocentric perspective.

The anthropocentricity of much of Aristotle's talk of non-species-specific good is there for all to see, for there in the *Politics*, as I have pointed out, he says that animals are for the sake of humans.[39] Yet while the importance of the assumption of the privileged place of humans in what later came to be called the Scala Naturae is undeniable, that is not all there is to Aristotle's view. Supreme among animals, humans are still inferior to greater beings, the stars and their Unmoved Movers, and Aristotle himself might want to insist that, difficult though the notions of || cosmic good and cosmic order are, they point *away* from an exclusively anthropocentric standpoint.

Some maybe sweeping remarks on some developments of science since antiquity may serve to elaborate these points. We are all Copernicans now: well, almost all. The ancients often assumed, not just that human beings have a privileged place in the animal kingdom on earth, but also that the earth does in the centre of the universe, though neither view went unchallenged.[40] But in cosmology today the opposite assumption is standard, and indeed

[38] Heraclitus, Fr. 102 DK.

[39] *Pol.* 1256b15ff.

[40] Aristarchus' heliocentric theory, reported by Archimedes in his *Arenarius* (*Sandreckoner*) I 4ff., II 218.7ff. Heiberg–Stamatis, was, however, maintained, so far as we know, by only one other ancient astronomer, Seleucus of Seleucia (Plutarch, *Quaest. Plat.* 8.1, 1006c).

invoked under the name of Copernicanism, though applied now not to the position of the earth in the solar system, but rather to that of our galaxy in relation to other galaxies. Now nothing *follows* from that about how you and I should treat one another: nor even about how we should act with regard to our natural environment on planet earth. And you can certainly lead an admirable and full life without any such knowledge. Yet the penetration of Copernican realisations has surely influenced our attitudes deeply if only because it has undermined and demolished earlier cherished assumptions (cherished, I mean, by some). Coming to terms with the (earth-shaking) conclusions that science reached there involved far-reaching adjustments, and not just on the question of the authority of the Church and the interpretation of the Bible. Let me repeat: nothing follows from cosmological Copernicanism for interpersonal behaviour, just as nothing follows from Black Holes (if you will pardon the expression) or from the Big Bang. But realisation of the non-privileged position of earth and greater understanding of the dimensions of the cosmos provide food for thought concerning earlier human delusions.

Anthropocentricity is also the issue in that other question of our relationship to our immediate natural environment. The conservation of nature is not an ancient problem and antidotes to an anthropocentric perspective || may be in short supply for us today. To be sure, conservation can be argued on purely selfish grounds, purely from the point of view of the human species, by appealing, for instance, to such ideas as the recreational value of the wilderness. But again others, bearing in mind, perhaps, the destruction that has been committed in the name of human interests, would say that is not to go far enough. The fact that the notion of a respect for nature and that of its beauty, whether or not there are conscious beings there to appreciate it, are problematic, disputed, hard to apply and no doubt often misused does not mean that their invocation is inappropriate. Aristotle is in no doubt that, strictly, you cannot keep a contract or fail to do so with an animal: yet anthropocentrist as he was he asserted that there is something of the fine, the *kalon*, in every species of animal – nor did he mean *just when* the scientist studies them.[41]

The turn the argument has taken reminds us that when, in the ancient world, science challenged certain conventional religious beliefs, it sometimes did so by appropriating to itself the discourse of the divine. That ancient science was so often cast – or cast itself – in the role of being able to bring back, from the frontiers of knowledge, tablets of stone for the human predicament, carries with it warnings, no doubt, for science today. But there is of course a balance to be struck. On the one hand, in the search for tablets (the demand for them) they have often been believed to lie on those frontiers, and that way lies one kind of danger. On the other, the information passed

[41] *PA* 645a7ff., 21ff.

back from those frontiers, some of it at least, cannot fail to be relevant to our attitudes to and understanding of that (our) predicament, for even if we cannot expect to read off conclusions about how we ought to behave straightforwardly from such information, just as surely such information will often need to be taken into account, if we are to have any hope of making intelligent, not to say wise, decisions. For || that, to be sure, we shall need more than science can provide, and some earlier pretensions of science to provide it have now been shown by science itself to be just that. But if the chief lesson to be learnt from the demise of ancient anthropocentric delusions is a negative one, it may be no less important for that. Indeed the more that modern science puts into our hands technical means of control that far surpass any ancient dream, the greater is the danger of a resuscitation of a modern version of those delusions, founded on misguided reflection on the capacity of the species we belong to to produce those technical means of control. Fifth-century Greece already discovered that values, once subjected to scrutiny, forfeit the authority they derive from their unquestioned acceptance. The bid to fill the credibility gap thus created, from within the resources of the study of nature itself, was often, we can see, opportunistic – not that, in our own chill world, we are at all close to being able to make confident suggestions, in theory let alone in practice, for the filling.

Let me now, by way of conclusion, come back to some of the more purely historical aspects of my subject, adding some points and qualifying others in some final summary observations. Under five heads. First I said, but let me now elaborate, that there is no uniformity in ancient attitudes to the relationship between science, the study of nature, and morality. And the fact that widely differing views were adopted is of some importance. Apart from such as Aristotle, Galen, Ptolemy, there were others, such as Archimedes and Euclid, who, so far as we know, were quite unconcerned to place their research in a wider perspective: and this is true of the admittedly scantier evidence available to us for such other denizens of Greek science as Apollonius and Hipparchus. While for many, *phusis*, nature, was a normative, as much as a descriptive, concept, some early investigators sought to secure the autonomy of the study of nature as an objective inquiry independent of the claims of || *nomos*, and some later ones too were loud in proclaiming that that study was the way to free mankind from superstition. What counted as 'superstition' was, to some extent, up for grabs: for the Epicureans not just the belief in wilful gods, but also much of physics as generally practised was 'myth':[42] but it was not just the case that 'superstition' was the label you used for other people's beliefs when you disapproved of them, even though it was often used in just that way. It was not just the case that what the new scientists substituted for old superstition

[42] Arguing for the principle of plural explanation in relation to what is obscure, Epicurus puts it in the *Letter to Pythocles*, D.L. x 87, that to attempt to establish a single cause is to fall into myth.

was just new make-believe, though again some of what some passed off as objective knowledge was little more than wishful thinking – a point true not just of *ancient* science. But the main point is that the pluralism of Greek thought manifests itself on this topic, as on so many others, a pluralism that no doubt reflects the pluralism of the kind of society that produced it. It is not that you could get away with anything (Socrates' fate shows that), but you *could* get away with a very great deal, in societies that were small-scale, face-to-face, self-governing, and where political power and responsibility were often widely devolved.

Secondly we find many ancient expressions of the idea that scientific or philosophical inquiry is part of the good life. The ancients spoke not so much of the creativity of such activity, as of its contributing to understanding and to wisdom. Again they more often focused on the worthwhileness of science as an end in itself, than on the benefits to be gained from its application to practical contexts – though an important exception to this is the sense that many doctors had that their medical research could and did directly benefit the sick. While knowledge as a value in itself was the principal motivation of many scientists, there are forceful statements of the practical importance of work done in anatomy, physiology, pharmacology, dietetics: we saw that even the arch-teleologist Galen stressed the || vital importance, to the surgeon, of the knowledge to be gained from dissection.

To be sure, thirdly, what the elite activity of pure science presupposed in terms of inegalitarian, hierarchical and authoritarian political and social institutions was not lost on them and is not lost on us: and the splendours of the life of pure theory find, hardly surprisingly, their most eloquent spokesmen among those who were the beneficiaries of those inequalities.

Moreover fourthly, there are clear instances where the end-results of the scientific inquiries that were undertaken were represented as supporting or legitimating the type of hierarchical principle that was invoked in justification of the social order that those inquiries depended upon. Even if ideology did not dictate the programme, its conduct was sometimes under strain from the side of those presuppositions.[43]

Yet fifthly and finally, even though a first reflection on the issue of the connections between science and morality in the ancient world is one of the pitfalls that went with those connections remaining too close – pitfalls both from the side of the distorting effects on the science, and from that of the narrowness of the morality sometimes grounded in that science – a second point to ponder is the unwisdom of the notion that it is better for *no* link to remain, for rather, clearly, the *connection* is of the utmost concern. This is unlikely to be forgotten, for sure, in the context of the ever-increasing problems of the morality of particular scientific investigations. But more generally, it may not be inopportune, from the perspective of what is

[43] Aspects of this problem are discussed in Lloyd, 1983 in relation to test cases in the life sciences in particular in Greco-Roman antiquity.

supposed to be par excellence a discipline contributing to humane education, to insist on the relevance to such of science. This is not with the objective that some of the first explorers in the field had, to teach us about the privileged place of humans in the scheme of things. But now rather || the reverse: it is precisely to help us unlearn – as some of us, scientists and non-scientists alike, may still need to unlearn – our anthropocentricity, while, indeed, preserving our humanity, and while (let us hope) not careering towards the destruction of the human race.[44]

[44] It is a pleasure to record my special thanks to Professor Myles Burnyeat and to Dr Malcolm Schofield for their constructive criticisms of the ideas adumbrated in this lecture. What I owe more generally to the stimulus they and all my other friends and colleagues provide to the study of ancient philosophy and science in this university can never adequately be expressed.

REFERENCES

Cornford, F. M. (1912) *From Religion to Philosophy* (London)

(1950) 'Greek natural philosophy and modern science', in *The Unwritten Philosophy*, ed. W. K. C. Guthrie (Cambridge)

(1952) *Principium Sapientiae* (Cambridge)

Diels, H., and Kranz, W. (1954) *Die Fragmente der Vorsokratiker*, 7th edn (Berlin)

Duckworth, W. L. H. (1962) *Galen, On Anatomical Procedures: The Later Books*, edd. M. C. Lyons and B. Towers (Cambridge)

Edelstein, L. (1967) 'The Hippocratic Oath', in *Ancient Medicine*, edd. O. and C. T. Temkin (Baltimore)

Fraser, P. M. (1969) 'The career of Erasistratus of Ceos', *Rendiconti del Istituto Lombardo*, Classe di Lettere e Scienze Morali e Storiche 103: 518–37

French, R. K., and Lloyd, G. E. R. (1978) 'Greek fragments of the lost books of Galen's Anatomical Procedures', *Sudhoffs Archiv* 62: 235–49

Guthrie, W. K. C. (1969) *A History of Greek Philosophy*, III, *The Fifth-Century Enlightenment* (Cambridge)

Heinimann, F. (1945) *Nomos und Physis* (Basel)

Jones, W. H. S., ed. (1923) *Hippocrates*, Loeb edn (Cambridge, MA)

Lloyd, G. E. R. (1975) 'A note on Erasistratus of Ceos', *Journal of Hellenic Studies* 95: 172–5

ed. (1978) *Hippocratic Writings* (Harmondsworth)

(1979) *Magic, Reason and Experience* (Cambridge)

(1983) *Science, Folklore and Ideology* (Cambridge)

(1987) *The Revolutions of Wisdom* (Berkeley)

Lonie, I. M. (1981) *The Hippocratic Treatises 'On Generation' 'On the Nature of the Child' 'Diseases IV'*, Ars Medica Abt. II Bd 7 (Berlin)

Marsden, E. W. (1971) *Greek and Roman Artillery: Technical Treatises* (Oxford)

May, M. T. (1968) *Galen, On the Usefulness of the Parts of the Body*, 2 vols. (Ithaca, NY)

Most, G. W. (1981) 'Callimachus and Herophilus', *Hermes* 109: 188–96

Singer, C. (1956) *Galen, On Anatomical Procedures* (Oxford)

16

ARISTOTLE'S ZOOLOGY AND HIS METAPHYSICS: THE STATUS QUAESTIONIS. A CRITICAL REVIEW OF SOME RECENT THEORIES

INTRODUCTION TO CHAPTERS 16–18

The last three papers in this collection consist of as yet unpublished studies that need no special introduction other than a note concerning their provenance. 'Aristotle's zoology and his metaphysics: the status quaestionis' is the revised text of a paper that I gave to a conference at Oléron in June–July 1987 devoted to Aristotle's zoology, the proceedings of which are to be edited by Pierre Pellegrin. As my paper explains, it attempts an overview of some of the many recent studies concerned with what can be learned about Aristotle's metaphysics from the theory and practice of his zoological investigations.

'Galen on Hellenistics and Hippocrateans' is the second of two papers that I have written for the series of international conferences on Galen inaugurated at Cambridge in 1979 (the first was entitled 'Scholarship, authority and argument in Galen's *Quod Animi Mores*' and was published in *Le Opere psicologiche di Galeno*, edd. P. Manuli and M. Vegetti, in 1988). This study develops some themes adumbrated in its predecessor and considers the problem of the reasons and motives that weighed with Galen in choosing Hippocrates as the major authority on whom to base his own medical theory and practice and in developing his own interpretation of what Hippocrates himself could be represented as maintaining. The paper was written for the Galen conference in Berlin in August 1989 which I was unfortunately unable to attend: the proceedings are to be edited by J. Kollesch.

Finally 'The invention of nature' is the text of my contribution to the 1989 series of Spencer Lectures at Oxford, whose general theme was nature. My aim there was to present to a general audience a picture of the controversiality of the notion as it was developed in ancient Greece. I argue that that factor provides the essential background against which we should understand both the original development of the concept and its continued deployment in rival natural and indeed moral philosophies.

ARISTOTLE'S ZOOLOGY AND HIS METAPHYSICS: THE STATUS QUAESTIONIS. A CRITICAL REVIEW OF SOME RECENT THEORIES

After many decades of comparative neglect, the zoological treatises of Aristotle have been the subject of a considerable resurgence of interest in the last dozen years.[1] It is now no longer a matter of a handful of specialists studying the finer details of Aristotle's descriptions of the reproduction of octopuses. A wide variety of scholars have come to see that the zoological works present rich materials to test theories and interpretations of Aristotle's thought on many fundamental issues, in metaphysics, in philosophy of science and in psychology especially. But if the scholars in question are united by the ambition to use the zoology to support readings of Aristotle's views on topics from causation to the philosophy of mind, they are anything but agreed on how the zoology itself should be interpreted or on what lessons are to be drawn from it for the interpretation of Aristotle's thought more generally. That no simple orthodoxy has emerged as the result of that resurgence of interest in the zoology is neither surprising nor in itself cause for concern. After all a fair divergence of interpretation in the field can be a sign of lively ongoing debate. Yet that hardly characterises the current situation in some areas of the study of zoology, which border, rather, on a state of interpretative anarchy. My aim in this paper is first and foremost to spell out some of the implications – for the interpretation of Aristotle's thought in general – of some of the theses that have been based on a study of the zoology or that have been advocated by appealing to ideas and theories claimed to be in evidence in his work in that area.

As I shall devote most of what I have to say to a critical review of some of the 'findings' claimed in recent work in the zoology, it is only right and proper for me to preface my remarks with some recognition of the positive aspects of that resurgence of interest. First that very resurgence itself should be applauded (even if one may feel that the results so far obtained are disappointing: compare developmental studies when they first became the rage). At least one may say that it is now going to be very much more difficult than before for anyone to get away with strategic generalisations about Aristotle's philosophising that do *not* pay *some* attention to his work on the study of animals.

Then secondly, among the points emerging from recent work that command widespread (if not universal) agreement are the following: first, following pioneering work by David Balme, Pierre Pellegrin has shown how the use of the terms *genos*, *eidos* and *analogia* is context- or level-relative.[2]

[1] Recent books include Kullmann, 1974; Preus, 1975; Pellegrin, 1982 (transl. 1986); Gotthelf, 1985b; Gotthelf and Lennox, 1987; Furth, 1988.

[2] See Balme's reference to Pellegrin at Balme, 1987b: 72 n. 2 and 79 n. 8, and Lennox at Lennox, 1987a: 100. At Pellegrin, 1985: 105 there is the further claim that 'the word *ousia*, like *genos* and *eidos*, designates realities of a variable level of generality': but in this area, on the question of substance, Pellegrin's views are more questionable, as I shall argue below.

While in certain prominent, programmatic passages in the *PA* and elsewhere Aristotle stratifies *analogia, genos, eidos as if* he were interested in fixing their taxonomic levels, his use elsewhere and in general runs counter to any such strategic interest. That in practice *genos* and *eidos* each designate classes of very varying extension is, now, abundantly clear. Nor, secondly, can there be any serious doubt over the absence of any Linnaean-style taxonomy from Aristotle's zoology – though, on the question of whether Aristotle had any interest in *eventually* supplying a comprehensive classification of animals, recidivists like myself still resist drawing the conclusion that that *further* question must *also* receive an emphatic negative answer. But for my present purposes it is enough to record unanimity on the minimum fact that a *comprehensive systematic* classification of animals proceeding *from* the highest groups *via* their principal divisions to end with the *infimae species* all clearly identified is nowhere to be found.[3] Third, Jim Lennox has won much support for his view that an interest in securing the widest class to which a property belongs provides *one* important link between the principles set out in the *Posterior Analytics* and the practice in the zoology: though again that is far from saying, of course, that there is general agreement on other aspects of the question of the applicability of the former to the latter, let alone on the extent of their actual application. Quite the contrary: I shall be returning to that.

However, while on certain points concrete (if sometimes negative) results have been obtained, on others the impression that recent work creates is one of continuing radical divergence on fundamental issues – of interpretative anarchy, as I put it. Due allowance should be made, to be sure, for the tentativeness with which some interpretations have been proposed. It is a feature of much of the new work in zoology that the scholars in question draw attention to the need for further work. It seems to be *de rigueur* in this field not just to revise opinions maintained some time ago, but to do so with regard to positions published no more than a couple of years back, even, at the limit, of positions in work as yet unpublished but forthcoming. David Balme himself, without a doubt the doyen of English-speaking scholars who have attempted to take Aristotle's zoology seriously, has modified his earlier published views on the authenticity of parts of *HA*, on its relationship with the rest of the zoology, on teleology, and on classification.[4] Flexibility,

[3] Even in 1961 and 1968 when I optimistically suggested that developments can be traced in Aristotle's procedures in classifying animals, I spoke only of the broad classification into greatest kinds being generally clear with some minor reservations (Lloyd 1961: 73) and in Lloyd, 1968: 86 I explicitly denied that a definitive, systematic classification of animals is to be found in the zoological works.

[4] Thus on questions of authenticity at Balme, 1987a: 16, and on teleology at Balme, 1987c: 285 n. 33. Compare also the different formulations used in different versions of his influential 1961 article. In the original version he wrote (Balme, 1961: 212): 'it is difficult to imagine that the Stagirite had abandoned or lost interest in the classification of animals, to which he attaches such importance and such careful rules in the *Organon* and *De Part. Anim.* I'. When the paper was reprinted in 1975, he put it (p. 192) thus: 'This [the collection of differences] would have

tentativeness, anti-dogmatism are all laudable qualities: but when as so often in this area at the present time, we are faced with a bewildering variety of hypotheses, the urgent need is to spell out and explore their implications: the chief task then becomes one of evaluation. It is with that end in view that I wish to scrutinise critically some of the interpretative suggestions currently in the field. If the tone of my comments appears particularly critical, I would plead that the highest compliment that can be paid to an interpretation is to submit it to the severest testing.

Let me begin with one of the results proposed by Pierre Pellegrin from his careful, pioneering and immensely influential studies. Already in his *La Classification des animaux chez Aristote* he spoke of one of the central themes of the zoology in terms of what he dubbed 'moriology'. In two recent papers[5] he notes that many of his colleagues remain opposed to these views[6] but he reiterates the fundamentals of his position and maybe goes even further on some points. Thus in the collective volume, *Philosophical Issues in Aristotle's Biology*, edited by Gotthelf and Lennox, he writes: 'I am convinced that the *moria* constitute the cardinal level of Aristotelian biology.'[7] It is to *moria* (alone) that the correct division of a *genos* into *eidē* can be applied. 'But it is only when the conceptual schema *genos–eidos* is applied to *moria* that it must have recourse to all the "logical information" which it contains and that the division of the *genos* can be made according to contrary *eidē*.' 'One might say that the division of the parts according to the conceptual schema *genos–eidos* is "more" a definitional division in the Aristotelian sense of the word than is the division of animal classes.' Nevertheless 'if it is to *moria* that the conceptual schema *genos–eidos* is applied most *completely*, it is to animal classes that it is applied the most *explicitly*'. But if there is a tension between these two viewpoints, something like a 'reconciliation' between the two fields of application is to be found – Pellegrin claims – in the famous passage in *Politics* IV, where (in his view) 'this schema is applied sometimes to animal classes, sometimes to *moria*, with the latter level being determinant since it is the conjunction of the *moria* which makes possible animal diversity'.[8]

Moreover in his contribution to the Balme Festschrift Pellegrin tackles questions to do with the notion of substance. There the thesis of the paper is, as its title suggests, that in a certain sense (which he specifies) Aristotle's zoology is a 'zoology without species', but in the process Pellegrin argues not just that 'for the biologist . . . [the] strategic level is that of the *moria*',[9] but further that 'in Aristotelian biology the *ousiai*, in the primary and strong

yielded the explanatory classification of animals demanded by his rules of division, in which the genus is no arbitrary class of common characters but a statement of the potentialities which its species actualise.' But in the 1987 reprint (Balme, 1987b) all talk of an eventual classification of animals has disappeared. The statement that 'The *HA* is a collection and preliminary analysis of the *differences* between animals' (Balme, 1987b: 88, original emphasis, see also 80, and cf. Balme, 1975: 192) is *not* followed by any reference to a possible explanatory classification.

[5] Pellegrin, 1985: 104ff., and 1987: 336.

[6] Cf. e.g. Lennox's review of Pellegrin, 1982, and contrast Furth, 1987: 52 n. 66, who applauds the suggestion that divisions focus on parts.

[7] Pellegrin, 1987: 336f.

[8] Quotations from Pellegrin, 1987: 336–8.

[9] Pellegrin, 1985: 106.

sense, are the *moria*'.[10] Again the *Politics* passage is discussed and the explanation of Aristotle's evident interest there in the definition of animal species is that this relates to the nature of the *political* objects to be explained, namely political constitutions. These last, Pellegrin says, are comparable 'only to a whole living organism and not to a "part"'.[11] But Pellegrin further discusses texts from the *Metaphysics*, notably first one from Z.16 which says that the parts of living things are potentialities (*dunameis*).[12] While he begins by noting that this 'might seem to hold directly against [the] moriological interpretation', he argues that correctly understood it does not. It does not assert (so he writes) that 'because the "parts" are "potentialities" they are not *ousiai*', but rather (merely) that the concrete individual is primary *ousia*[13] because it is separable, which the parts obviously are not. Similarly in the paper in the Gotthelf–Lennox volume Pellegrin concedes that separability is a characteristic of *ousia* and yet Aristotle continues to qualify as *ousiai* certain items that do not meet the separability requirement.[14] But then in the Balme Festschrift article a further passage, from *Metaphysics* Z.2, is added (1028b8), on which Pellegrin comments: 'Not only did some contemporary philosophers think it natural that the *moria* should be *ousiai* but Aristotle, in *defending this thesis* [my italics], joined that part of the Presocratic tradition which held that the true reality of things is in their components.'[15]

There are complexities, subtleties and I fear I must confess for me also some obscurities in Pellegrin's position on this nexus of issues: but as I understand the notion, at least, the implications of the moriological interpretation for Aristotelian metaphysics are enormously wide-ranging. But is the interpretation well-grounded? First I have a number of perhaps minor queries on the question of definition, before I come to a fundamental objection on the score of substance.

First on questions to do with definition: Pellegrin notes that in Aristotle, as in Plato, division is a definitional method and he acknowledges that the dichotomists whom Aristotle spent so much time refuting had as *their* aim the definition of species.[16] It might be thought surprising, then, that Aristotle does not explicitly take issue with them for *mistaking the proper objects of definition* (if, that is, Pellegrin is right, that *they* are the *moria*). Yet in all the extensive criticisms Aristotle offers of the method of the dichotomists, of the differentiae they appealed to, and of the results they got, there is no text that does just that. On the contrary he seems to suppose that their definienda are the definienda that he too should be concerned with, even though the way they set about getting definitions is radically mistaken.

Pellegrin has some supplementary arguments on the point and stresses as

[10] Pellegrin, 1985: 106. [11] Pellegrin, 1985: 101ff.

[12] Pellegrin, 1985: 105 on *Metaphysics* 1040b5–8.

[13] Pellegrin, 1985: 105: the expression 'primary *ousia*' in connection with the concrete individual in *Metaphysics* Z is unguarded: at least at p. 114 n. 7 Pellegrin shows that he recognises that 'first *ousia*' does not have the same meaning in the *Categories* as in *Metaphysics* Z. [14] Pellegrin, 1987: 337. [15] Pellegrin, 1985: 107.

[16] Pellegrin, 1987: 323 and 1985: 104.

the chief objection to the idea that Aristotle was attempting definitions of animal species that 'he never gives us even a single example' of such a definition.[17] Yet that does not of course rule out the possibility that that was one of his *aims*, and indeed one of his chief quarrels with the dichotomists was, as he puts it at *PA* 644a10f., that they are unable to grasp any of the particular *animals* (*zōōn*, cf. also *PA* 642b32, 643a16ff., b10ff.). I shall come back to the problem of the gap between *aims* and *results* in the zoology in general terms later.

Secondly Pellegrin distinguishes between the concern to give a definition of such an item as *man* and the concern to define 'the human way of having feet' (the more correct way, he argues, to specify Aristotle's aim[18]). But then the definiendum, on this account, is clearly not foot (in general) nor even human foot (because one of the characteristics invoked is that humans are *two*-footed), but rather – to rephrase Pellegrin's point – the mode of locomotion of humans. But that is one of the faculties of the human soul, and even on the orthodox view of definition would certainly be one item in the eventual full definition of *human*. Indeed that concern (with the mode of locomotion of humans) might be thought to belong more appropriately to a programme of defining *humans*, than to one aimed at definitions of parts such as *feet*. At this point some of Pellegrin's talk of the definitions of parts seems rather to obscure a distinction between a definition of a part (such as foot) *per genus et differentiam* where the *genus* is e.g. foot itself and the *differentia* the kind of foot, and a definition of a part set in the context of definition of the whole organism of which it is the part. On the latter reading it could be argued that the human way of having feet is essentially to be related to what it is to be a human, not to what it is to have feet.

But that cluster of puzzles is of minor importance compared with the difficulties in the interpretation offered of substance. The main problem here concerns not the zoology but the *Metaphysics*, specifically the relationship between the varying parts of Aristotle's discussion in *Metaphysics* Z. Z.2 is a summary of the usual views, as *dokei* at 1028b8 (and cf. 16) shows. That chapter cannot be taken to set out Aristotle's *own* views (despite Pellegrin) for two reasons: first having mentioned the view that the parts of animals and plants are substances (among other views) Aristotle immediately proceeds to insist that the question of whether they *are* indeed substances must be investigated, *skepteon*, 1028b15 (cf. also 31). Z.2 sets out an *agenda* and does not *defend* any thesis.

Secondly the sequence of argument in Z as a whole tells against Pellegrin's interpretation. Z.16 clearly picks up the suggestion of Z.2 (the *dokousōn* of 1040b5 even echoes the *dokei* of 1028b8) and gives Aristotle's own views on the matter, and when he pronounces that most of what are thought to be substances are potentialities (including specifically the parts of animals,

[17] Pellegrin, 1985: 99: contrast the claims made by Gotthelf (1985a: 27ff.) and by Lennox (1987a: 90ff.), that at least partial definitions of animal kinds are common enough.

[18] Pellegrin, 1985: 102, on further thoughts on *PA* 644a1–11.

1040b6) that does not allow that they may still be substances (as Pellegrin wishes to suppose) but must be taken as an argument *against* that view. By dealing with Z.16 first, and then Z.2, Pellegrin gives the impression that Z.2 can be taken as offering Aristotle's own views. But that is surely mistaken. In Z.16 the parts of animals fail to be substances on three grounds, all made explicit in the text. First there is the separability requirement mentioned at 1040b6ff.: though Pellegrin protests that separability is not an overriding criterion,[19] that does not mitigate the point that in *Metaphysics* Z at least it *is* invoked as fundamental (cf. e.g. Z.3, 1029a27ff.). Secondly the parts of animals fail the test of unity. The passage Pellegrin quotes from 1040b5–8[20] continues as follows: 'for none of them [viz. the parts of animals and the physical elements, earth, fire, air] is a unity, but they are like a heap, before they are concocted and some one thing comes to be from them'. Then Aristotle immediately goes on to say that while one might suppose that the parts of living creatures (and 'what is close to soul') are both, as being both in actuality and in potentiality, yet nevertheless they are still all potentially, when they are one and continuous *phusei*. When we are told that they are potentialities, this is indeed to tell against their being substances.

Thirdly and surely conclusively the end of Z.16 provides yet a further argument for the same conclusion. No substance, we are told (1041a3ff., picking up Z.13, 1039a3ff.) consists of substances. Evidently the individual animals themselves, Socrates or that dog or this horse, are paradigmatic substances, maybe even, if we add in the argument from Z.17, 1041b28ff., the only substances. But if *they* are substances, then on the argument that no substance consists of substances, their parts are not.

Nor would it be easy, I think, to rescue Pellegrin's position on the primary objects of definition at least as an interpretation of *Metaphysics* Z. The argument of Z.4, as is well known, is that the primary objects of definition are substances,[21] and if those arguments are added to those of Z.2 and Z.16, the upshot would clearly be that the primary definienda are the animals, not their parts. When in chh. 10–12 Aristotle warns against doing away with the matter, and specifies that – given that the animal is something perceptible – it is not possible to define it without movement and so not without the parts

[19] Cf. above at n. 14.

[20] Pellegrin, 1985: 105. The whole passage, 1040b5–16 runs:

φανερὸν δὲ ὅτι καὶ τῶν δοκουσῶν εἶναι οὐσιῶν αἱ πλεῖσται δυνάμεις εἰσί, τά τε μόρια τῶν ζῴων (οὐθὲν γὰρ κεχωρισμένον αὐτῶν ἐστίν· ὅταν δὲ χωρισθῇ, καὶ τότε ὄντα ὡς ὕλη πάντα) καὶ γῆ καὶ πῦρ καὶ ἀήρ· οὐδὲν γὰρ αὐτῶν ἕν ἐστιν, ἀλλ' οἷον σωρός πρὶν ἢ πεφθῇ καὶ γένηταί τι ἐξ αὐτῶν ἕν. μάλιστα δ' ἄν τις τὰ τῶν ἐμψύχων ὑπολάβοι μόρια καὶ τὰ τῆς ψυχῆς πάρεγγυς ἄμφω γίγνεσθαι, ὄντα καὶ ἐντελεχείᾳ καὶ δυνάμει, τῷ ἀρχὰς ἔχειν κινήσεως ἀπό τινος ἐν ταῖς καμπαῖς· διὸ ἔνια ζῷα διαιρούμενα ζῇ. ἀλλ' ὅμως δυνάμει πάντ' ἔσται, ὅταν ᾖ ἓν καὶ συνεχὲς φύσει, ἀλλὰ μὴ βίᾳ ἢ συμφύσει· τὸ γὰρ τοιοῦτον πήρωσις.

[21] E.g. *Metaphysics* 1030a11ff. At 1030a17ff., however, Aristotle says that definition and essence belong secondarily also to the other non-substantial categories.

being in a certain state (1036b28ff.),[22] that emphatically does *not* say that the *parts* are the objects of definition. The definienda he (still) has in mind are, e.g., man and animal, as the examples make clear,[23] even while he insists that their definitions must incorporate reference to their parts. Which parts are parts of the *sunolon* and which of the *form* or *essence* are tricky questions which lead Aristotle into a complex discussion of several varieties of part/whole relationships.[24] But that discussion (and the whole of Z) presupposes that both the definiendum and the definition must, in a strong sense, be unities. The locus of Aristotle's interest in *Metaphysics* Z where both definition and substance are concerned remains throughout the *animal* considered as the unity it is, not such parts as the finger of 1034b29f., the hand of 1036b31, the flesh and bones of e.g. 1035a33, or even the heart of 1035b26.

That set of clear lessons from *Metaphysics* Z does not, of course, rule out the possibility that Pellegrin's views on the cardinal level of the *moria* are correct as an interpretation of the *zoology*. Yet the contrast between metaphysics and zoology would then be very striking indeed: as I said, the implications of the moriology for the metaphysics are very wide-ranging. But just how that contrast could be accounted for is highly problematic. The differences between a whole-orientated *Metaphysics* and the moriological orientation Pellegrin finds in the zoology are no mere minor shifts in emphasis, and it would seem that the only way to reconcile the two would be via some developmental hypothesis.[25] Yet neither of the two main possibilities is at all an attractive candidate. Thus it could be argued that *Metaphysics* Z implies a rejection on Aristotle's part of the part-oriented zoological studies whose results are set out in the zoological treatises. Alternatively – and no less drastically – the zoology might be seen as implying a rejection of the lessons of *Metaphysics* Z on the question of the status of animal parts, on the doctrine of substance and on the primary objects of definition. The revisions in either case would, as I say, be *drastic*. Thus, on the first option, if the *Metaphysics* represents Aristotle's (new) realisation that the parts of animals do not count as substances and are not strictly definable, at least not the primary objects of definition, then the whole effort of the zoology (as Pellegrin presents it) is founded on a misapprehension. Alternatively (on the second option) if the zoology represents a (new) discovery on Aristotle's part that the determinant factors in zoology are the parts, then the discussion of substance oriented to wholes in the *Metaphysics* stands in need of serious revision to take that into account.

[22] I come back to this below.

[23] E.g. *Metaphysics* 1036b3ff., 10ff., 28ff.

[24] Especially in *Metaphysics* Z. 10 and 11.

[25] Pellegrin considers the possibility of a developmental hypothesis in connection with the *Politics* IV text, though he concludes by rejecting any such solution: 'faced by the difficulties of these chronological speculations, I would prefer to say that there is in Aristotle a coexistence without interpenetration of two methods of definition which differ at least in terms of their object' (Pellegrin, 1985: 104).

I do not say that such developmental hypotheses could not be suggested. But that some fairly massive effort at reconciliation would be needed between metaphysics and zoology, if Pellegrin's view of the latter is to be accepted, is, in my opinion, clear. It is not enough, in any event, merely to postulate a change of heart on Aristotle's part – although that was the way in which some developmental arguments used to be promulgated. What we have to see is *why* Aristotle should have held each of the conflicting views successively: we need to understand the motivations of the change, if indeed he did change his views. The moriological interpretation of the zoology in its strong form has, then, that high, perhaps unacceptably high, price to pay. It would seem preferable, rather to retrench: to reconsider the factors that led to its proposal, to accept, rather, at most a weaker version of the thesis, according to which the interest in the parts in the zoology is *not* to be seen as cardinal nor as representing Aristotle's *ultimate* strategic concerns, nor as superseding the ultimate focus of interest in *wholes*. On the modified view, the interest in parts would be a means to an end, not the end itself: though even on this modified view there are still, of course, interesting repercussions from Pellegrin's researches on the question, since they might well be taken to indicate the difficulty Aristotle faced in practice, in the zoology, in carrying through the programme of definition, that is to say the programme of the investigation of form that was so clearly one of his primary philosophical motivations. I do not know how far, if at all, Pierre Pellegrin himself would agree with that suggestion. But I shall adduce further arguments at the end which might be used to support a similar conclusion from reflection on Aristotle's practice in other areas of his zoology.

I turn now to a second, perhaps even more influential and far-reaching suggestion that has been proposed on the basis of a reading of the zoology, namely the set of arguments that Balme advanced in connection with his denial that Aristotle's biology was essentialist. The particular features of his line of interpretation that I wish to consider are the following: first of all there is the distinction between (*a*) species taken as a generalisation over individuals, (*b*) essence (which picks out those features for which a teleological account can be given) and (*c*) the (individual) animal form (which on Balme's view included such material accidents as sex and colour).[26] Secondly, following his conception of (*c*), Balme argues that matter can be, indeed must be, included in the definitions of animals. As he puts it[27] 'a definition of Socrates includes a complete account of all his matter at a given moment'. That implies not merely that matter should be included in definitions, according to Balme, but also the possibility of definition of an individual (Socrates), indeed of an individual in process. Balme argues that *Metaphysics* H.6 has it that 'at the moment of actualization matter and form are one thing', and he proceeds:[28]

[26] See especially Balme, 1987d:295ff. [27] Balme, 1987d: 295. [28] Balme, 1987d: 310.

considered as if frozen at a moment, a man is not two items, body and soul or matter and form, but one: a complex but graspable form. On the other hand, considered as he is in nature (which H.6 assumes to be the right way to consider him), a man is a process, not a static subject–predicate state. The analysis of a man, therefore – or of a snub nose – should be either a causal account of the process or a complete description of every detail as at a given moment. Either will include matter and movement.

Let me begin with the first distinction, between species, essence and animal form, and certainly one may agree that there are sufficient explicit texts in Aristotle to legitimate the distinction between the species taken universally and its individual members. One of the clearest passages is Z.10, 1035b27ff.: 'man and horse and the things said thus in relation to individuals, but universally, are not substances, but a *sunolon* made up of this *logos* and this matter as universal'. Certainly, too, one may go some way towards agreeing with the connection Balme suggests between essence and teleological explanation. Clearly in the case of animal kinds (which is what Balme is speaking about in the first instance) a teleological explanation of what it is to be that animal will be possible, and required. However, the extension of the notion of *to ti ēn einai* to non-substance categories in *Metaphysics* Z, ch. 4 may cause one to hesitate before going all the way with Balme here. As I have already remarked, that chapter says that one can talk of essences in a secondary or derived sense, *hepomenōs* (1030a22) of qualities, quantities and so on. Given that the applicability of essence in this secondary sense to the non-substance categories seems quite unrestricted, the coincidence of essence and teleological explanation appears highly problematic. White is one of Aristotle's examples in that chapter. Even if we may concede that where all the members of a species have eyes of a particular colour, that may be part of that animal's essence and capable of final causal explanation,[29] it is coloured eyes in this kind of animal that have a final cause, not this or that colour as such. Whether colours as such regularly have teleological explanations seems doubtful, and the same is no doubt true of many other non-substance items, which nevertheless will have secondary or derivative essences.

But it is of course in relation to item (*c*), animal form, taken to include 'all the material details and accidents',[30] that Balme has put forward some of his most striking, surprising and radical suggestions. One motivation for his view comes from reflection on the account of reproduction in *GA*, and the argument (without I hope too much distortion) goes like this.[31] In *GA* Aristotle clearly states that the male parent contributes form alone. But in *GA* IV.3 especially we have a fairly detailed account of how the offspring comes to resemble the father (and how too the mother, or the grandparents, or indeed no one at all, in which case the offspring is just an animal, not a

[29] This is to develop the concession implied by the *plēn* cause at *GA* 778a33.

[30] Balme, 1987d: 309.

[31] Balme, 1987d: 294f.

human being or whatever). But if the offspring comes to resemble the father in being male (say) or in skin or hair or eye colour, then these characteristics must belong to the father's form. Thus Balme concludes:[32] 'the definition of essence can never be the complete formal description, for it must always exclude such material accidents as sex and colour which *are* included in the form contributed by the sire'.

Now one may note, to begin with, a puzzling feature of this argument, which is that it starts from the firm distinction between form and matter and the insistence that the father's contribution to the offspring is form *and not* matter. But by the time that we get to the conclusion it appears that the complete formal description is taken actually to *include* material accidents, such as sex and colour. (On the female side of the equation Balme explicitly notes that she does not contribute *just* matter, but also some formal characteristics: indeed all differences are for Balme formal differences[33] and so any contribution from the female parent that helps to differentiate the offspring will be set on the formal side of the form/matter dichotomy.) On the view that all differences are formal differences, the characteristics that the offspring owes to the male parent belong, indeed, to form: but then should not be deemed to be matter – and so the idea that the form includes matter (even in the shape of 'material accidents') falls to the ground. But of course it may be that the weak point in the argument as thus set out lies not in the conclusion, so much as in that assumption that all differences *are* formal ones.[34] While one can see that in a sense to differentiate is to pick out some determinate character, and given that matter is in itself indeterminate, differentiation must be through form, there is another sense in which it is perfectly possible and indeed desirable to speak of differences in the *matter* of two individuals of the same kind. Aristotle still needs to distinguish the way in which a bronze triangle differs from a wooden one *from* the way in which a bronze triangle differs from a bronze statue.

But whether or not Balme would feel inclined to save his argument by modifying the modes of applicability of the principle that all differences are formal differences, the chief problem remains the interpretation of Aristotle's position, in *GA* IV.3, on the resemblances of offspring to their male and female parents. Though the analysis offered in that chapter is clear on some points, it is desperately indeterminate on others. To begin with some of the former: evidently the levels at which the male parent acts in its generative function are clearly distinguished. Coriscus is not just an animal, and a man, but is said to act as such and such a male, and indeed that means as Coriscus, the individual he is.[35] Aristotle's account of how it is that certain offspring resemble or do not resemble each of their parents proceeds by appealing to these differences in level together with a further distinction between the process he calls *existasthai* (which results in an opposite) and what he calls

[32] Balme, 1987d: 294f.
[33] This is explicitly stated at Balme, 1987d: 294.
[34] Cf. Hamlyn's comments in 1985: 56ff.
[35] E.g. *GA* 767b24ff., 768a1f.

luesthai (where change is to what 'stands near', e.g. to a characteristic of a grandparent or of a more remote ancestor).[36] This enables Aristotle to account for the cases (*a*1) of a male offspring that takes after the father, (*a*2) of a female offspring that takes after the mother, (*b*1) a male taking after the mother, (*b*2) a female taking after the father, (*c*1) a male that takes after a grandfather or more remote ancestor, (*c*2) a female that takes after the maternal grandmother, and so on, not to mention cases where some parts of the offspring resemble one parent, while others do the other.[37]

Moreover *qua* generator Coriscus acts first and foremost as Coriscus (as the individual father) – more, that is, as the particular man he is than as man, and more as man than as animal.[38] Aristotle leaves us in no doubt of the priority of *to idion* and *to kath'hekaston* to *to katholou*, and though, as is well known, what counts as *to kath'hekaston* depends always on the context, the repeated references to the named individuals Socrates and Coriscus show that it is indeed individuals, not species, that Aristotle here privileges.

But if so much is reasonably clear, elsewhere *GA* IV.3 leaves many questions unanswered. This applies particularly to the all-important issue of the nature of the resemblances between offspring and parent that the account is supposed to cover. So far as the generator goes, certain accidental features are explicitly discounted: we are not talking about Socrates as literate (*grammatikos*) or as someone's next-door neighbour.[39] But while resemblance in being male or female is clear enough, otherwise the talk of offspring 'being like' father, mother or grandparent is left quite unspecific. Given this indeterminacy, the way ahead in interpretation must be acknowledged to be risky. But if we use what Aristotle says elsewhere in *GA* I on the topics (1) of the resemblances between offspring and parents and (2) of the account to be given of certain characteristics by which individuals of the same species are distinguished (as opposed to characteristics that belong to the species as a whole), some conjectures seem possible. It is in *GA* I.17 and 18, of course, that Aristotle has a good deal to say about the first topic (and the danger in using that as evidence in relation to *GA* IV.3 is obvious: *GA* I.17 and 18 are a polemical examination and refutation of pangenesis, a doctrine that used resemblances between offspring and parents among other arguments to suggest that the seed must be drawn from the whole of the body). Two sets of remarks that Aristotle makes in this avowedly polemical discussion are, however, particularly relevant to how we interpret his own position. Having set out the pangenesists' *tekmēria* in *GA* I.17 (including (1) the alleged fact that mutilated parents produced mutilated offspring, and (2) the general resemblance between children and parents not just in inherent, *sumphuta*, i.e. congenital characteristics, but also in acquired ones, *epiktēta*, such as scars[40]), Aristotle's opening gambit in I.18 is to object that children resemble

[36] *GA* 768a14ff., b15ff.
[37] *GA* 768a21–b15.
[38] *GA* 767b25ff., 30ff., 768a1ff., 5ff., 24ff., b13ff.
[39] *GA* 767b28f.
[40] *GA* 721b11ff., 14ff., 20ff., 29ff.

their parents in certain respects where (even his opponents will have to agree) *nothing* is drawn from the part in question: he specifies *voice*, *nails*, *hair*, *movements*.[41] There are too some characteristics that the parent does not yet possess when the child is generated, such as grey hair or a beard. Again the children resemble their remote ancestors 'from whom nothing comes' (viz. *they* do not make a direct contribution to the seed of the parents themselves). More strikingly still, at 722a18ff. he argues (still within this polemical context of course) that the resemblances hold rather (*mallon*) in respect of the anhomoiomerous parts (such as face, hands and legs), rather, that is, than in the homoiomerous ones (flesh, bone, sinew) – a remark that does not rule out resemblances in the latter as well.

That gives us at least a preliminary checklist of the items that Aristotle's own account should, in theory or in principle, be able to accommodate. Recognising that there are resemblances between parents and offspring in respect of hair, for instance (that is not in respect of their having hair, but in respect of their having hair of a particular sort, curly or straight, or of a certain colour), and again in voice (again not in respect of having a voice, but in respect of having a voice of a particular sort, deep, high-pitched, big or small for instance), and again in respect of hands and legs, and even flesh and bone, Aristotle *ought* to be able to give *some* account of these 'facts', obviously not a pangenesist account that would have it that the explanation lies in the principle that the seed is drawn from the whole of the body, but an alternative to that account and presumably superior to it.

But of course an account of a number of the items in our checklist is actually offered by Aristotle in *GA* v, not so much in the context of a discussion of parent–offspring resemblances, but rather in his general account of what he calls the *pathēmata* he there identifies, where he leads off with the examples of eye-colour, of voice-pitch and differences in colour, hair and feathers.[42] *GA* v distinguishes clearly between characteristics that regularly belong to all (normal) members of a kind and those that vary between individuals of the same kind: and evidently it is the latter that are his concern when he discusses resemblances of offspring to parents – for he is not there interested, obviously, in what all offspring have in common with all the parents in the species in question, as it might be having a heart, having legs, having eyes, but rather in the resemblances in having legs or eyes of some particular sort. But *GA* v specifically discusses the type of account that can be given of the *pathēmata* it mentions. We are told that they are not for the sake of something, but they come to be 'by necessity' – and although the interpretation of the necessity involved here and elsewhere is certainly controversial, notably the cash-value of the distinction drawn between two types of necessity at 778b16ff. (of having an eye, and of having a particular

[41] *GA* 722a5ff.

[42] *GA* 778a17ff. Eye colour is discussed in *GA* v.1, voice in *GA* v.7, differences in colour, hair and feathers in *GA* v.3, 4 and 6.

sort of eye), that should not deter us unduly, since the statement at 778a35 makes it plain enough that the necessity there opposed to 'that for the sake of which' is such that the causes of the items in question should be referred back, as he says, 'to the matter and the moving cause'.

It is worth recalling that at the outset[43] *GA* announces that it is particularly concerned with the moving cause. The first chapter of *GA* I divides the four causes there identified into two pairs, where that for the sake of which (the end) and the *logos tēs ousias* (which are said almost to amount to one and the same, 715a5f.) are together opposed to (3) matter and (4) the *archē kinēseōs*. As we should expect, then, it is the interplay of (3) and (4) that provides the basis of his account of reproduction, with (3) being identified as the contribution of the female (for the male supplies no matter) and (4) being the chief male contribution. But while there is no wavering on Aristotle's part on the principle that the male parent supplies nothing material to the offspring, just how it acts as *archē kinēseōs* is less transparent than one might suppose. It is tempting to assume that the efficient cause always just is the form in action, in its dynamic function, that is it always just transfers or imposes form. But we should be careful: the relationships between the form of the object produced (itself a *sunolon* of form and matter) and the form of that which produced it (where again we may be dealing with an element in a *sunolon*, a composite object, though sometimes it is just the form that acts) can be varied and complex. First we may note those texts in *GA* I.1, II.1 and V.1 where the efficient cause is linked with the material cause and this pair is contrasted with the final cause and the *logos tēs ousias*.[44] But Balme might accommodate these texts by insisting that what that last expression, *logos tēs ousias*, picks out is the essence, not the animal form.

However, secondly and more importantly, if we consider the range of modalities of efficient causes in Aristotle a number of possibilities suggest themselves. In some cases a proximate moving cause acts by transmitting its own form (shape) directly to the matter: a signet ring leaves its impression in wax.[45] But in other accounts of the action of moving causes the situation is more complicated. Take some of the analogies Aristotle in fact repeatedly uses to illustrate features of sexual reproduction, such as those that appeal to the action of human craftsmen,[46] the carpenter making the bed, the builder the house, and the series of comparisons with cooking, concocting and curdling. In the former, what makes the bed (in the sense of the proximate moving cause) is the carpenter's tools, and (unlike the signet-ring case) they

[43] *GA* 715a3ff.

[44] *GA* I.1, 715a3ff., is cited in the previous note. *GA* V.1, 778a35, is cited in my text, above p. 385. In *GA* II.1, 731b21ff., proximate mover and matter are together opposed to that for the sake of which.

[45] Cf. *GA* 729b17f., where, however, Aristotle's purpose is to illustrate general features of the form–matter doctrine, and the point at issue in the theory of reproduction is limited to the doctrine that the male supplies no matter.

[46] See e.g. *GA* 723b29ff., 729b16f., 730b5ff., 11ff., 734b36ff.

do not themselves *have* the shape of the bed. Of course the tools are moved by the carpenter and he has the form of a bed in mind (as Aristotle often puts it, it is the house without matter, viz. in the builder's mind, that creates the house with matter).[47] But *that* form is to be equated with the essence. At least I recall no passage where Aristotle specifies that the craftsman's thoughts about what he is making include the material accidents that Balme says are included in form.

The cooking, concocting, curdling analogies differ from building and carpentry – and differ from one another, notably that in the curdling case the fig-juice, we are told,[48] forms no part of the end-product, whereas in cooking the effect is the result not of a body, but of heating. Yet in these cases too the proximate efficient causes do not themselves *have* the form eventually exemplified in the end-product. The heat that cooks the eggs, sugar etc. into a soufflé is not itself a soufflé, nor even soufflé-like. That image is particularly appropriate since it provides a particularly clear illustration of the way in which the varieties of the end-product depend on the *proportion* or *balance* of the heat applied to the materials to be cooked – a point that Aristotle repeatedly stresses in relation to the illustrand, the need for *summetria* between the male efficient cause and the material supplied by the female.[49]

Now none of these other cases of efficient causes *exactly* fits the case of sexual reproduction: none of the analogies is perfect. Nevertheless we may ask how far they can take us towards resolving the issue of the role of the male parent. From one point of view, given that the male parent produces or can produce a look-alike, his blue eyes being reproduced in the blue eyes of his offspring, it might seem that the signet-ring model might be invoked. But it clearly will not do, given that the father acts via the semen (described as the tools used)[50] and – unlike the signet-ring case – the *semen* does not of course look like Socrates: it is not blue-eyed, it does not even have eyes; it is not snub-nosed, for it has no nose. It does its work thanks to the *movements* that it initiates: and throughout the account of resemblances in *GA* IV.3 Aristotle pays due attention to the fact that the outcome is the result of an *inter*action between what initiates the movement and the matter involved. When the matter is totally worked up, the result is a male resembling the father (evidently the semen initiates movements that in the normal or ideal case lead to the new *sunolon* being as like the old as possible – as is stated at *GA* 766b15 and 767b15). But deviations of various kinds are possible and to be expected, when either the semen is weaker, or the material stronger, than is ideally desirable.[51]

[47] See e.g. *Metaphysics* Z 1032b12: at 1032b1f. (cf. 1035b32) Aristotle makes clear that by *eidos* here he means essence. [48] See *GA* 737a13ff.

[49] See especially *GA* 767a13ff., 768b25ff., 772a17ff.; cf. also 723a29ff., 727b11ff., 729a16ff., 739b3 (of the womb), 743a28f., 777b27ff. [50] E.g. *GA* 730b19ff., cf. 766a3ff.

[51] The possibility of failures of perfect match is also allowed for by Aristotle's talk of potentiality and actuality. The embryo as it develops proceeds through a series of stages of the successive actualisation of higher and higher potentialities, and given that this continues

Balme's argument was that the father supplies only form and so *that* must include all the items, such as sex and colour, which are or may be reproduced in the offspring. But an alternative account of resemblances in such items as colour, at least, seems possible and maybe preferable. Where such factors as eye-colour, hair-colour, pitch of voice and so on are concerned, the clear lesson of *GA* v is that these all depend on an *inter*action of two factors, the moving cause and the matter (in some instances in *GA* v Aristotle invokes other material conditions such as diet and climate, for example in the explanation of straight and curly hair).[52] And if it is by *inter*action that we should explain eye-colour, the same will also apply, presumably, to *similarity* in eye-colour between parent and offspring. Even when the offspring has blue eyes like the father, those blue eyes depend (as the father's did) on a particular outcome of the interaction of matter and moving cause. The moving cause cannot operate on its own, evidently, even though when it does act on the matter, it may act as far as possible to reproduce its own pattern of movement, and for it to fail to do so is, precisely, a failing, either in its capacity to move or in that of the matter to be moved. The capacity of the semen is better described, that is, as a capacity to produce movement than (just) as a matter of possessing a form that it transmits. It *is* responsible for transmitting essence, the *logos tēs ousias*, where a teleological account is possible: there is no dispute there. But where having an eye of a particular colour is concerned (as opposed to having an eye) that outcome, according to *GA* v, seems to depend crucially on the complication in the equation introduced by the *inter*action of movement and matter. Accidents, that way, are to be explained by that interaction, not included in the account to be given of form, or rather not explained, we should say, by whatever is to be included under the heading of form.

The issue is and is likely to remain controversial (cf. the different account recently offered by Cooper, 1988 and cf. Code, 1987). The talk of resemblances of offspring to parents in *GA* IV.3 is quite general and as I said indeterminate. There are problems in using *GA* I.17 and 18 as evidence of cases of resemblances Aristotle should be able to accommodate, but if we do and appeal to *GA* v for its account of some of them, the upshot is a different possible story, in those cases, to the one that led Balme to include material accidents in animal form. So far as references to the priority of Coriscus acting as Coriscus goes, those need not lead to any clear division between animal form on the one hand, species and essence on the other. Aristotle would clearly have many reasons to deny that what generates is a *disembodied* form and many reasons to deny that it is a disembodied essence that does so

to be the case for some time *after* the semen has initiated the first movement, this allows Aristotle to identify a series of (increasingly significant) potentialities, each of which may fail to be actualised, in the stages of development through which an embryo passes. If the first stage depends *directly* on the action of the semen, later stages do so only indirectly.

52 Climate is mentioned as a factor at *GA* 782b34f. (curly hair), cf. 783a15f., and 788a17f. (pitch of voice). The food eaten is a factor in colour at 786a34ff. Cf. also 767a28ff., 30ff.

or again some universal (the species as such). Whatever we say on the complex and controversial questions of individual form,[53] Aristotle never ceased to believe that the concrete *sunolon*, Socrates or Coriscus, is substance, as many texts in *Metaphysics* Z and H testify[54] even when those texts occur in the context of discussions where the term 'first' substance is reserved for form or essence.[55] Certainly in generation it is the individual that does the work: but if I am right to stress the role of moving causes in Aristotle's account, then the individuality in question, what makes it the individual moving cause it is, could as well be a matter of it being the individual *sunolon* it is as one of its being an individuated form – one individuated in any of the ways that have been suggested by Frede and others in part to meet the well known difficulties of the refutation of universal as substance in *Metaphysics* Z.13. Otherwise put, that talk of Coriscus acting as Coriscus in *GA* IV.3 seems indecisive on that other problem of the individuation of form.

However, if those issues remain open to argument, on further points the consequences Balme drew from his analysis pose problems that seem insurmountable. I refer to some of his remarks on the subject of *definition*, some of which I have already quoted, Citing passages in *Metaphysics* Z Balme argued[56] that the species Man as a universal generalised over individual men-in-flesh is not the substance whose definition is sought. 'The only two contenders for valid definition', Balme proceeds, 'are Socrates' essence (soul) and Socrates in the flesh.' A string of further passages in *Metaphysics* Z are listed in the footnote, but he goes on that while the *Metaphysics* Z discussion leaves the issue open (between those two alternatives, that is), *Metaphysics* H resolves it. There 'at the moment of actualization matter is identical with the form realized in it, so that the composite is a definable unity'. 'It follows that a definition of Socrates includes a complete account of all his matter at a given moment.' The account to be favoured is one of man as a process, and so includes both matter and movement.[57]

Now some of the problems in all of this are referred to by Balme himself a little later in Appendix 2. 'This solution raises the question whether Aristotle now envisaged definition only at the level of the individual particular: to be valid, must the definition of "man" be a definition of Socrates at a moment?'[58] If so, Balme goes on, 'it is a change of view from the *Topics*, where the definiendum is always a class, not a particular', and he further notes that the view would need accommodating with the view that Socrates and Callias are 'the same thing in form' in *Metaphysics* Z. But the

[53] See most recently Frede, 1985 and Frede and Patzig, 1988.

[54] E.g. *Metaphysics* Z 1033b16ff., 1035a1, 1039b20ff.; H 1042a26ff.

[55] As for example at *Metaphysics* 1032b2, 1037a28.

[56] *Metaphysics* 1033b25, 1035b28, 1037a6 and Z.13 are cited by Balme at 1987d: 295 n. 24.

[57] Balme, 1987d: 295, where n. 25 cites *Metaphysics* Z 1039b20–31; cf. 1035a33, b14–31, 1036a1–9, 1037a24–33.

[58] See Appendix 2 to Balme, 1987d: 306ff., at p. 311.

problems are far worse than those remarks acknowledge, and they do not just concern squaring the 'solution' with the *Topics* and the end of Z.8. Let me outline briefly the four most serious difficulties, which stem as much from problems in the reading of the *Metaphysics* as they do from those of the zoology.

(1) That talk of the primacy of considering man as a process runs directly counter to the repeated insistence, both in the *Metaphysics* and in the zoology, that Aristotle is concerned with the *ousia* rather than with *genesis*, and with the latter only for the sake of the former. *PA* 640a18 is one of a whole series of texts that make the point unequivocally, and *GA* 778b6 is another that does so in the heart of *GA* v.1. It might be thought that Balme could easily accommodate this objection by rephrasing his point in terms of actualisation, not process; yet that would involve a quite different reading of the sense in which *movement* can be included in the definition: I shall come back to that.

(2) In the particular text in H.6 on which so much is made to rest, which Balme takes to show that 'at the moment of actualization matter is identical with the form realised in it', what Aristotle actually says is rather more guarded: it is that the proximate matter and the form are one and the same, the one in potentiality, the other in actuality.[59] That that continuation is important and provides the right reading becomes clear three lines later, when he puts it that what is in potentiality and what is in actuality are one in a way (*pōs*). It is only with what has no matter, that they are *unqualifiedly* one.[60] This permits no erosion of the distinction between potentiality and actuality, no erosion of that between proximate matter and form. Even if we are considering the axe doing some cutting (viz. actualizing its potentiality for cutting) there is no question of our not being able to distinguish (in thought) between the matter of the axe, of the mere potentiality for cutting, and the form, or its actuality. So far from providing a unique solution to the problem of the unity of form and matter, H.6 says no more (and no less) than many other passages that discuss form and matter, or (in the case of living creatures) soul and body, as the two aspects into which the given *sunolon* can be analysed.[61]

(3) Thirdly and more damagingly, there is the question of definitions of individuals. The difficulties that Balme mentions are much less serious than others that might be thought to arise from some of the texts he refers to. Not just in the *Topics* but in the *Metaphysics* itself, indeed in the chapters of Z Balme cites, Aristotle insists that definition is of the universal, *and* that no definition of the individual is possible. As texts that make the first point one may cite 1035b34 in Z.10, 1036a28f. in Z.11: as texts that make the second

[59] Whether *to men* is to be read at H.6, 1045b19, is disputed, but Ross's note gives cases where *ho men* or *to men* suffer ellipse before *ho de, to de* in Aristotle, even though Ross goes on to add that the ellipse would be unusually harsh here.

[60] *Metaphysics* 1045b23.

[61] See especially *Metaphysics* Z.11, 1037a7ff.; Z.15, 1039b20ff.

1036a2ff. in Z.10, and 1039b27ff. in Z.15, which says: 'For this reason, of the perceptible individual substances there is neither definition nor demonstration.' And why? 'Because they have matter whose nature is such as to be able both to be and not to be.' And later in the same chapter (1040a5ff.) he remarks that it is always possible to refute anyone who tries to define a particular:[62] for it is not possible to define them. As for the texts in *Metaphysics* Z that Balme referred to in support of the claim that the only two contenders for valid definition are Socrates' essence and Socrates in the flesh, those passages[63] do absolutely nothing to legitimate the assumption that an individual (however described) is a possible object of definition: all they do is make the well-known distinction (which can always be made in the case of any perceptible *sunolon*) between the *sunolon* as the *sunolon* it is (viz. a composite of matter and form) and the form that gives the *sunolon* its distinctive character (or essence). (The denial of the universal's claims to be substance, expressed already in Z.10, 1035b27ff., before it is argued for in detail in Z.13, is a denial that e.g. horse taken universally is substance, viz. this form and this matter so taken – universally. But whatever we make of that doctrine, neither there nor anywhere else in Z, nor anywhere else in the Aristotelian Corpus I should say, is there any statement defending the definability of individuals as such, or reneging on the clear doctrine ruling out such definitions in Z.10, 11 and 15).[64]

(4) Finally the attempt to allow matter into definition runs foul of similar objections. Z.11 states categorically that of the *sunolon* consisting of matter and form there is no *logos*,[65] where *logos* presumably has a strong sense, definition, since that some *logos* in the weaker sense of account is possible is clear from Z.7, 1033a4f., for instance. Z.11 gives the argument: 'it' (the

[62] Some of those who attempted to define particulars were Platonists who had in mind Platonic Forms: so Aristotle believes he has arguments not only against defining his own individual *sunola* but also against defining Platonic Forms conceived as belonging to the class Aristotle labels as *ta kath' hekasta* (*Metaphysics* 1040a8ff.).

[63] The first text Balme cites, 1039b20–31, *includes* at b28ff. a clear statement to the effect that there is no definition and no demonstration of perceptible individuals. The second, 1035a33, is immediately preceded by a text that states that the matter is no part of the form (*eidos*) (1035a19ff.). The third, 1035b14–31, ends with a clear statement that Socrates already contains matter, and the fourth, 1036a1–9, similarly refers to the perceptible or intelligible matter of individuals and states explicitly (1036a5f.) that there is no definition in such cases. The last, 1037a24–33, explains both the sense in which there is, and that in which there is not, a *logos* of the *sunolon*, specifying that there is *not* a *logos* of the *sunolon* as it is taken to include the matter, since matter is indeterminate. The very fact that the *grounds* that Aristotle consistently invokes to *rule out* definition of individuals is that the individual contains matter (perceptible or intelligible) will be grounds for rejecting any view that the animal form, construed as Balme construes it to *include* all the material accidents, can be a possible subject of definition.

[64] The problem that is posed by the conjunction of the two doctrines, (1) that definition is primarily of substance, and (2) the universal is not substance, does not get resolved by Aristotle by abandoning the view that definition is not of individuals, which seems firmly in place still in *Metaphysics* Z.15. How those several views are to be reconciled is, however, of course, one of the most controversial topics in the interpretation of *Metaphysics* Z.

[65] *Metaphysics* 1037a25ff.

sunolon) 'is with matter: for that is indeterminate, *aoriston gar*'.[66] (Whereas the *logos* is according to the primary substance, e.g. of soul in the case of man.) The passage carries all the more weight since it comes in a recapitulation of the lessons to be learnt from Z.10 and 11 together. 1037a25ff. picks up the argument in 1036a2ff. which specifies that of the *sunolon* particular (this circle, whether perceptible or intelligible) there is no *horismos*: but they are always said and recognised by virtue of the universal *logos*: while matter is unknowable in itself.[67]

The concessions to the argument that not everything should be reduced to number, and that matter should not be done away with (1036b21ff.) evidently do *not* in Aristotle's view in the recapitulation at the end of that chapter, legitimate any view that matter can now straightforwardly be included in definition. True we are told that a living creature cannot be defined 'without *kinēsis*' and so not 'without the parts being in a particular state'[68]: but overinterpretation of this must be avoided. If we bear in mind the way in which the faculties of soul *are* defined in the *De Anima*, it seems likely that we are invited to specify such items as reproduction and nutrition, perception, locomotion (*kinēsis*), imagination and reason. No doubt in specifying the locomotive faculty we shall need to refer to the animal being biped, quadruped, footless or whatever. But while this encourages us to specify the modalities of locomotion, it is doubtful how far it represents any departure from Aristotle's customary view, that definition is of the *soul*, though we no doubt have to bear in mind that with the exception of *nous* all the faculties of soul are first actualities of parts of the body. Yet clearly including 'biped' in the definition of man is still a long way from countenancing the inclusion of – as Balme puts it – 'all his matter at a given moment'. That thesis, with its startling suggesting that we apparently need to include in our account of 'Socrates in the flesh' all his warts and bunions not to mention the contents of his stomach, goes well beyond anything for which support can be found in Z – or indeed in the zoological works. No doubt both in Z and in the zoology, especially *PA* 1.2–4, the model of definition Aristotle works with is appreciably more complex than the simple combination of genus plus ultimate differentia that many of the standard Academic examples presuppose. No doubt in practice he realised that a fair range of differentiae will have to be included in any zoological definition. Yet the guiding principle is still, surely, differentiae of the soul, of the vital activities that is, and there is no need and no justification for extending the definition to include all the matter.

Thus far I have examined some cases where if the results of recent studies are accepted, the implications for Aristotle's metaphysics would be momentous: and the gist of my argument has been that the case for ascribing

[66] *Metaphysics* 1037a27ff.

[67] *Metaphysics* 1036a7ff.

[68] *Metaphysics* Z.11, 1036b28ff., cf. 'not without the *ergon*', 'not without perception' at Z.10, 1035b16ff.

the drastic changes in viewpoint imagined is not proven. It is not, however, that – against the trend of some of my own earlier essays – I now wish to advocate or defend some kind of diehard unitarian thesis where Aristotle's zoology and metaphysics are concerned. Rather it has always been the case and always will be that we have to have good reason for attributing major (or even minor) shifts in theory to Aristotle, and where such seem inescapable we should further attempt to specify the grounds that suggested the need for change. So far as differences in perspective between the zoology and the metaphysics go, it seems necessary to be more cautious than some recent speculations. Yet even within the range of topics I have discussed, some differences in emphasis, if not shifts in doctrine, seem detectable. Certainly in his account of the generation of animals the *pairing* of efficient and material causes and the contrast between them as a pair and the final cause and *logos tēs ousias* represent not, it is true, any *revision* of the doctrine of the four causes (for all four continue to be identified and distinguished) but at least a particular emphasis that can perhaps be contrasted with the canonical line-up where matter is often opposed to the other three.[69] There is no need whatsoever to see Aristotle as having changed his mind (in one direction from physics to zoology, or in the other from zoology to physics): but we have here, perhaps, one example (and no doubt others might be suggested) where the practice of a particular inquiry involves Aristotle in putting a *distinctive* emphasis on certain particularities.[70]

On the question of the proper objects of definition, on causation, on substance, the implications of the zoology are not, in my view, as far-reaching as some recent claims have it. But in one other respect I believe they may be far-reaching enough. Let me introduce very briefly one further topic, following up points that I have argued for recently elsewhere.[71] The Organon sets out certain rather stringent requirements on predication, for the sake of demonstration and for syllogistic reasoning generally, notably on the univocity of terms. For demonstrations in particular, as is well known, the primary premises must in addition be true, immediate, better known than, prior to and explanatory of the conclusions. Clearly if the univocity requirement, at least, is not met, valid inference will not be possible. But when it comes actually to doing some physics, especially though not exclusively zoology, that requirement is under considerable strain. Aristotle devotes some extended discussion in *PA*[72] to the ways in which such fundamental terms as hot, cold, dry and wet are 'said in many ways'. Yet while he there distinguishes, for example, between accidental and essential heat, between potential and actual, and gives various signs by which heat can be judged, for instance by various effects, this hardly amounts to a definitive

[69] As at *Ph.* 198a24ff. for instance.

[70] Thus the requirements of the analysis of the subject-matter of the *Meteorologica* have consequential effects on the causal schemata actually deployed in that treatise.

[71] Lloyd, 1987: ch. 4.

[72] See especially *PA* 648a21–649b8, 649b9ff.

resolution of the difficulties: no more does the account offered in the *De Generatione et Corruptione*.[73] Yet given both the role of these opposites as the primary qualitative differentiae in his element theory, and more especially the recurrent appeal to vital heat in particular throughout his physiological doctrines, one might think it to be absolutely crucial that Aristotle has absolutely clear criteria to appeal to, and moreover criteria that are independent of the differentiae he uses these opposites to explain.

A similar and related case is presented by such a term as *pepsis*, 'concoction'. Here we have an attempt to distinguish different types of *pepsis* in *Mete.* IV, where he identifies ripening, boiling and roasting/baking and claims that there are natural counterparts to the last two artificial processes, though these have not been given distinct names.[74] Yet while some problems in the range of application of the terms are recognised, including some cases where metaphor is involved,[75] Aristotle still allows himself extraordinary freedom, using *pepsis* not just of the processes of digestion, but of the production of semen and its action on the menses, the development of the embryo, the hatching of eggs, the formation of blood, fat, suet, milk and residues such as urine.[76] Are we dealing with the *same* process in each case? Why does concoction of nourishment lead in one case to semen, in another to fat, in yet another to marrow?[77] Again if digestion is like ripening and like cooking, the problem arises of why we cannot just eat unripe and uncooked food and let the stomach do *all* the necessary concoction. There had better be some justification available to Aristotle for the application of the same term to such widely disparate phenomena: we had better be able to say we are dealing with clearly defined species of the same general process, or with processes that can be said to be the same 'by analogy'. The instances are indeed all linked in that they are effects of heat, but heating is not *just* what *pepsis* is, not even if we specified 'vital heat': we still need to differentiate it from other cases of heating and indeed to differentiate *its* various types – other than merely by their effects: for *so* to differentiate them will not be explanatory but merely circular.

The *APo.* gives as an illustration of an explanation the syllogism that accounts for deciduousness in terms of the coagulation of fluid – Aristotle eventually specifies sap[78] – and presumably coagulation, fluid, sap had all

[73] *GC* II.2, 329b7ff., with a characterisation of the four primary opposites in terms of their ability to combine other things and of their capacity to be delimited by their own boundary. On the difficulties of seeing those characterisations as providing the clear definitions needed for the deployment of hot, cold, wet and dry in the zoology see Lloyd, 1987: ch. 4.

[74] *Mete.* 379b10ff., 380a11ff.

[75] *Mete.* 380b13ff., 28ff., in relation to the 'boiling' of gold or of wood.

[76] For some representative texts, see *PA* 652a9f., *GA* 719a32ff., b2, 727a34ff., 744b1ff., 753a18ff., 756b28f., 775a17ff., 776a20f., b33ff., 780b6ff., *Mete.* 380a1ff.

[77] See, for example, *GA* 727a34ff., cf. *PA* 651a20ff., b20ff., 28ff.

[78] *APo.* 98a35ff., b5ff., 33ff., 99a23ff.: contrast 'fluid' at 98b37, with *opos* at 99a27. The addition of *ē ti allo toiouton* at 99a27 suggests that the account in terms of coagulation of sap is meant merely as an illustration of the *type* of explanation that might be invoked.

better be terms that meet the univocity requirement. I do not say that there is any evidence of Aristotle ever modifying that model: but certainly the zoology provides plenty of evidence of the problems encountered in his *practice* of natural science.[79] It is not just that actual explanations set out in syllogistic form are difficult to find: the whole discourse of the practising natural scientist resists, one might say, being recast in the mould of the ideal formal language that the Organon desiderates.[80] Problems will arise not just with terms like fluid or wet, *hugron*, but also for example with coagulation, where Aristotle thinks this can result from heat as well as from cold.[81] But though the *APo.* evidently hopes that the results of research can eventually be expressed in the ideal terms of demonstrative syllogisms, the actual practice of Aristotle's zoology is the richer and maybe the more fruitful for being some way away from that ideal.

So I return finally and in conclusion to the question of the applicability of the *APo.* to the zoology – to its applicability, not to its actual application, since so far as such issues as the actual presentation of explanations in syllogistic form go there is general agreement on *their* rarity (though there may remain disagreements on how easy it would be to recast the explanations actually given in standard form). There are well known passages in the zoology in which Aristotle speaks of *apodeixis* as the aim of the biology.[82] Certainly no one would expect him *not* to be interested in explanations of the *dioti*. Yet for the *APo.* model to be applicable *in detail*, not only must there be the possibility of recasting the conclusions in syllogistic form, but these demonstrations *should* proceed from indemonstrable primary premises. Now Gotthelf has recently considered the question of the first principles in play in the *PA* especially and has concluded that Aristotle's discussion follows a 'broadly axiomatic' structure.[83] But so 'broad' – I should say – as to be almost unrecognisable. The *APo.* sets out clear distinctions, of course, between three kinds of primary indemonstrables, (1) axioms, (2) 'hypotheses', (3) definitions. But how far can these be imagined as applicable to

[79] See further Lloyd, 1987: ch. 4.

[80] Following Kosman, Gotthelf, 1987a: 195 distinguishes between the *APo.* as a demand for a formal account of proper science, and *APo.* as a demand that proper science be formal. But even on the first view, as Gotthelf concedes, proper science should be formalisable, and even if we limit ourselves to *that* demand, there is still a gap between that claim and the practice of, e.g. *PA*. There is not only no apparent attempt to formalise the results: but no signs of concern with their formalisability, a concern, for instance, with the need eventually to secure the appropriate indemonstrables, or even a concern to limit the discussion to terms that can meet the strict univocity requirement. The failure of many key terms to meet that requirement represents an insuperable obstacle to the *APo.*-style formalisation of the results – the proposed explanations – in which they figure, and the tolerance of such terms suggests a lack of any preoccupation with such an endeavour.

[81] See *PA* 649a30ff., *Mete.* 388b10ff. Among the effects of *pēxis* we find mentioned curdling of milk (*GA* 729a11ff.): cf. also *Mete.* 382b30ff.

[82] E.g. *HA* 491a13f., cf. the more controversial *PA* 640a6ff. and *GA* 742b23ff., 28f.

[83] Gotthelf, 1987a: see for example 179, cf. 194. I intend to devote a separate study to this question.

zoology? The two general principles, the law of non-contradiction, and that of excluded middle, must be counted to be fundamental to all intelligible discourse, to be sure. But nothing *follows* from them in zoology, at least. There are, however, other axioms limited to specific fields, such as the mathematical axiom that if equals are taken from equals, equals remain. There are two questions here: *are* there such axioms in zoology? And indeed could there be? One of Gotthelf's suggestions about the 'quasi-axiomatic' principles at work in the zoology is that they include the principle that nature does nothing in vain. That is, it may be agreed, some kind of regulative principle that has to be assumed for fruitful work to be done in the inquiry into animals. But so far from being able to assume it as an *axiom*, Aristotle spends a good deal of time and energy justifying and recommending it against those who, he knew, denied it. The situation is, then, quite different from the tactics he uses in giving an elenctic demonstration of the principle of non-contradiction in *Metaphysics* Γ. Nor can the principle that nature does nothing in vain be compared with the equality axiom – for which, indeed, no parallel seems to be suggestible from the zoology. There would seem to be no possible axioms of that type in natural science – nor, again, does Aristotle appear to use, or even contemplate using, hypotheses in the sense defined in *APo.*

The only likely candidate for indemonstrable starting-points in the zoology is, then, definitions. But we come back to the point that *in fact* Aristotle often shows some signs of hesitation in offering definitional accounts, and often acknowledges that the terms that are in play in his own discussion are 'said in many ways'. It is ironic, to my mind, that Gotthelf opts for hot, cold, wet and dry as examples of *APo.*-style first principles,[84] at least if I am right that the *GC* account just will not do as a resolution to the difficulties identified in *PA* II.2 and 3.

APo.-style indemonstrables are not, we surely have to conclude, in evidence in the zoology, but that is not to say that Aristotle may not have continued to hope that the results of his work in that area might be got into good *APo.*-style demonstrative order. Demonstrations, at least *apodeixeis*, are – in *some* sense – the aim. But if we just had Aristotle's actual practice in zoology to go by, we would surely attribute to him a notion of demonstration, in this area, that is a good deal less formal and rigid than that we find in *APo.* Although in *APo.* he clearly expected his schema to be applicable in the study of both animals and plants, when it actually comes to the study of the former, at least, the questions of just how far he remained wedded to that schema, of just how far he realised the difficulties in its implementation, are open ones. From the practice of the zoology it cannot be shown that he consciously revised the schema. Yet given that in certain respects at least Aristotle shows no great inclination to cast his results in the form the schema dictates, we have two possible lines of interpretation. On the

[84] Gotthelf, 1987a: 185ff.

one hand there will be those who will prefer to believe that the *APo.* remains the unaltered *ideal*: that has been one of the motivations of recent work on the zoology, and it has brought to light some positive features of Aristotle's discussion that had hitherto been neglected (as I noted in connection with Lennox on the concern for the widest class to which a property belongs). On the other hand there will be those who may suspect that in some respects, at least, the actual investigation of animals may have led Aristotle to reconsider some aspects of that *APo.* schema.

If that alternative view can certainly not be *proved*, it may still be *recommended* with lines of argument that draw on two sets of considerations. First there is the evident price that Aristotle would have had to pay, had he set out to secure, in zoology, indemonstrables of the types he demands in *APo.* and that can most readily be exemplified from mathematics. Was it really relevant to seek the equivalent of the equality axiom? Might not Aristotle have realised that the differences between mathematics and physics extended further than his use of biological and botanical illustrations in *APo.* appeared to allow? Secondly I am struck by one feature of that modern scholarly endeavour to explore the possible translation of the zoological investigations into canonical *APo.* form, namely the artificiality that that introduces into the discussion. Of course the syllogisms claimed to be recuperable from the materials in the zoology are not claimed, by those scholars who do the recuperating, to be great science:[85] no more are the proposed definitions, *per genus et differentiam*, taken to be candidates for the title of zoological indemonstrables. Yet the suspicion remains that Aristotle, once fully launched on the enterprise of the investigation of animals – an enterprise undeniably stimulated by high-level metaphysical notions of form, finality, substance, actuality and the like – may not have even aimed at recasting the results of that investigation, eventually, to conform to all of the ideals of the model of syllogistic demonstration set out in *APo.*

[85] See, for example, the syllogism proposed by Gotthelf, 1987a: 178 n. 33 with the conclusion that viviparousness without polydactylity and with no non-horn means of defence belongs to all horn-possessors, and cf. Bolton's discussion of definition (Bolton 1987: especially 152ff., 163ff.).

REFERENCES

Balme, D. M. (1961) 'Aristotle's use of differentiae in zoology', in *Aristote et les problèmes de méthode*, ed. S. Mansion (Louvain), 195–212

(1975) 'Aristotle's use of differentiae in zoology', revised version of Balme, 1961, in *Articles on Aristotle*, I, edd. J. Barnes, M. Schofield and R. Sorabji (London), 183–93

(1987a) 'The place of biology in Aristotle's philosophy' in Gotthelf and Lennox, 1987: 9–20

(1987b) 'Aristotle's use of division and differentiae', revised and expanded version of Balme, 1961 in Gotthelf and Lennox, 1987: 69–89

(1987c) 'Teleology and necessity' in Gotthelf and Lennox, 1987: 275–85

(1987d) 'Aristotle's biology was not essentialist', revised and expanded version of article originally published (1980) in *Archiv für Geschichte der Philosophie* 62: 1–12, in Gotthelf and Lennox, 1987: 291–312

Bolton, R. (1987) 'Definition and scientific method in Aristotle's *Posterior Analytics* and *Generation of Animals*', in Gotthelf and Lennox, 1987: 120–66

Code, A. (1987) 'Soul as efficient cause in Aristotle's embryology', *Philosophical Topics* 2: 51–9

Cooper, J. M. (1988) 'Metaphysics in Aristotle's embryology', *Proceedings of the Cambridge Philological Society* 34: 14–41

Frede, M. (1985) 'Substance in Aristotle's *Metaphysics*' in Gotthelf, 1985b: 17–26

Frede, M., and Patzig, G. (1988) *Aristoteles 'Metaphysik* Z', 2 vols. (Munich)

Furth, M. (1987) 'Aristotle's biological universe: an overview', in Gotthelf and Lennox, 1987: 21–52

(1988) *Substance, Form and Psyche* (Cambridge)

Gotthelf, A. (1985a) 'Notes towards a study of substance and essence in Aristotle's *Parts of Animals* II–IV', in Gotthelf, 1985b: 27–54

ed. (1985b) *Aristotle on Nature and Living Things* (Pittsburgh)

(1987a) 'First principles in Aristotle's *Parts of Animals*' in Gotthelf and Lennox, 1987: 167–98

(1987b) 'Aristotle's conception of final causality', in Gotthelf and Lennox, 1987: 204–42

Gotthelf, A., and Lennox, J. G., edd. (1987) *Philosophical Issues in Aristotle's Biology* (Cambridge)

Hamlyn, D. W. (1985) 'Aristotle on form' in Gotthelf, 1985b: 55–65

Kullmann, W. (1974) *Wissenschaft und Methode* (Berlin)

Lennox, J. G. (1987a) 'Divide and explain: the *Posterior Analytics* in practice', in Gotthelf and Lennox, 1987: 90–119

(1987b), 'Kinds, forms of kinds, and the more and the less in Aristotle's biology' in Gotthelf and Lennox, 1987: 339–59

Lloyd, G. E. R. (1961) 'The development of Aristotle's theory of the classification of animals', *Phronesis* 6: 59–81

(1968) *Aristotle: the Growth and Structure of His Thought* (Cambridge)

(1987) *The Revolutions of Wisdom* (Berkeley)

Pellegrin, P. (1982) *La Classification des animaux chez Aristote*, (transl. by A. Preus as *Aristotle's Classification of Animals*, University of California Press, 1986) (Paris)

(1985) 'Aristotle: a zoology without species', in Gotthelf, 1985b: 95–115

(1987) 'Logical difference and biological difference: the unity of Aristotle's thought', in Gotthelf and Lennox, 1987: 313–38

Preus, A. (1975) *Science and Philosophy in Aristotle's Biological Works* (Hildesheim)

17

GALEN ON HELLENISTICS AND HIPPOCRATEANS: CONTEMPORARY BATTLES AND PAST AUTHORITIES

Galen's Hippocratism is so familiar to us that it is easy to take it too much for granted.[1] In this paper I wish to explore various aspects of Galen's attitudes to, and use of, his predecessors, via a number of simple, even maybe naïve, questions about the alternatives that were open to him. We know what position Galen came to maintain – a complex one when we take four principal strands into account. (1) There are many points on which he professes agreement with Plato and to a lesser extent with Aristotle. (2) He has laudatory as well as critical judgements to express on the work of some others of his medical predecessors (notably Herophilus and Erasistratus). Moreover (3) he is increasingly aware, as time goes on,[2] of aspects of what we call the Hippocratic question, particularly problems to do with authenticity. (4) He allows himself to correct Hippocrates on a few occasions and he positively claims to go beyond him on a number of topics, such as pulse lore.[3]

Yet none of that detracts from the importance of the almost totally unbounded admiration he always expressed, throughout his life, for Hippocrates, his 'guide in all that is good'.[4] But if all of that is well known, we do not want to slip into the assumption that there was anything automatic about the preferences that Galen came to express. My aim in this paper is to explore some of the underlying reasons for those preferences. My first task is to restore the sense of the possibility of alternatives and to review those that were, in principle, open to him. My second is to tackle the question of the possible underlying reasons – by which I mean those that go beyond Galen's expressed views on the subject, obviously a difficult and speculative area where we shall inevitably be engaged in conjecture. Following up some of the lines of argument I proposed in my study of *QAM*[5] I hope to throw

[1] Aspects of the topic have recently been explored by Diller, 1974; Harig and Kollesch, 1975; Smith, 1979; Vegetti, 1986; and cf. also De Lacy, 1972 and Manuli, 1983.

[2] See especially Smith's extended discussion of developments in Galen's attitudes towards Hippocrates: Smith, 1979: 61ff.

[3] See, for example, *CMG* v 8.1, 134.1ff. For other claims to have made advances in anatomy see, for example, *UP* II, ch. 3, Helmreich I 70.10ff. (Kühn III 96.8ff.), and in therapeutics see, for example, K x 420.9ff, 425.6ff, 672.1ff.

[4] *Prognosis* ch.1, *CMG* v 8.1, 70.16f., cf. *PHP* VII ch. 8, *CMG* v 4.1.2, 478.3ff.

[5] Lloyd, 1989.

further light on Galen's scholarship and on his use of past authorities to fight his own, contemporary, battles.

It has been a recurrent fault, among historians of later Greek science, to exaggerate the extent to which it was in thrall to the past and correspondingly to underestimate its own originality. True, when so much work came to take the form of commentaries on previous writers, it is easy to gain the impression that the ambitions of the commentators were limited to the mere preservation and faithful interpretation of ancient texts. But we have to be careful. There was always more to faithful interpretation than mere repetition, and sometimes there was sophisticated, original thought stimulated by contemporary debate – as could be amply illustrated still in the sixth century A.D. from the polemic between Simplicius and Philoponus even while both purport to be explaining Aristotelian texts.

Of course two of the giants of the second century A.D. take their stand by tradition, for what Hippocrates was for Galen, Hipparchus was – up to a point – for Ptolemy. But only up to a point. First, in Ptolemy's case, too, to take Hipparchus' work as the basis of his own was the outcome of a definite decision, even though, in that case, we know far less about other astronomical theorists from the period between Hipparchus and Ptolemy himself as Ptolemy chose rather to ignore, than to polemicise with, them.[6] Secondly, even if in astronomy we can say that Ptolemy followed and developed Hipparchus' work, in both optics and harmonics he is far more difficult to represent as a straightforward adherent of any particular tradition. Indeed in neither of those cases was there just one single dominant tradition, but rather competing approaches divided on fundamental questions to do with the aims, methods and even subject-matter of the inquiry concerned.[7] There is no question in those cases, then, of any ancient investigator burying his own individuality totally in an all-encompassing tradition even if he had wanted to.

So far as medicine goes, in Galen's day there were three live questions the answers to which were anything but a foregone conclusion. First *whether* to follow tradition: more precisely whether legitimacy was to be sought (for a doctrine, a method, a practice) via the authority of the past. Second (if the answer to the first question was 'yes') *which* figure or figures from the past were the ones to invoke to confer such legitimacy. Third (once the answer to the second question was settled) *how* that figure or figures were to be interpreted.

The evidence that attitudes towards the past in general as well as to Hippocrates in particular varied widely in medicine in the second century A.D. comes from a variety of sources. Galen himself, of course, frequently tells us about contemporaries of his who – he says – completely neglect the

[6] For much of our information on Greek astronomy and astrology in the period intervening between Hipparchus and Ptolemy we have to turn to Indian sources, see Pingree, 1963, 1981, and especially 1978: 533, 559ff.

[7] Some of these divergences are discussed briefly in Lloyd, 1987: 296ff., 299ff.

great traditions of the past. A fundamental point that must be mentioned straight away is that Galen repeatedly makes the accusation, both against contemporaries and against some of his predecessors, that *they* were motivated, in their attitudes towards the past, by overweening ambition, *philotimia*, contentiousness, *philonikia/philoneikia*, and arrogance, *hubris*: they wanted to outdo the great names from the past in their bids to claim superiority for themselves, some going so far as to establish new sects.[8]

Galen is certainly not an impartial witness concerning his rivals' motivations, but for the general point – the variety of possible attitudes towards past authorities – we do not need to rely just on him. We have, first, near-contemporary evidence from the Methodist Soranus by which to check and qualify what Galen tells us on their views on this question. Three points are fundamental. First the Methodists in general evidently did not look back further than Themison for the beginnings of their own approach: they certainly did not seek authority for that in the remote antiquity of Greek medicine. Secondly and more importantly, Soranus shows no uncritical reverence for Themison, Thessalus or indeed any Methodist: on the contrary, he frequently criticises 'our people' in the *Gynaecia*[9], and a similarly critical attitude towards fellow-Methodists is to be found in Caelius Aurelianus' *Chronic* and *Acute Diseases*, whether that simply reflects what Caelius found in Soranus or also Caelius' own views.[10] Thirdly and quite

[8] Although *philotimia*, *philoneikia/philonikia* and cognate terms do not invariably carry pejorative undertones, they are used by Galen very commonly in treatises of many different types to accuse his predecessors or contemporaries of contentious rivalry. This is a complaint directed not only against medical theorists but also against philosophers (for example against the Stoics repeatedly in *PHP*, *CMG* V 4.1.2, 288.12ff., 294.11, 17ff., cf. 102.12ff., but also more generally, K I 420.11ff., VIII 642.10ff., *CMG* V 4.1.1, 62.22ff., cf. V 8.1, 96.25ff.). Among the medical theorists who are often so accused are Praxagoras (e.g. *CMG* V 4.1.2, 82.2), Erasistratus and the Erasistrateans (e.g. *Scr. Min.* III 182.1ff., 198.8ff., *CMG* V 4.1.2, 510.5ff., K XI 166.16ff., 167.8ff., 168.9ff., 228.3ff.), the Empiricists (e.g. *CMG* V 4.2, 202.23ff., K VIII 780.16ff., 785.5f., XIII 366.2ff., 563.6ff., 607.17ff., cf. also K X 137.9ff., 140.4, 145.6), Asclepiades (e.g. K I 499.11ff., X 20.1ff., XI 163.6ff.), Thessalus and the Methodists (e.g. *CMG* V 9.1, 145.19ff., V 10.3, 33.19ff.), Martialius (*Scr. Min.* II 94.26ff.), Julian (*CMG* V 10.3, 33.16ff., 34.7ff.), and many of the 'younger' doctors, *hoi neōteroi* (e.g. K VII 373.12ff., VIII 484.10ff., 642.10ff., 955.12, X 20.2ff.). Sometimes this contentiousness is said to be directed specifically against Hippocrates (e.g. K XI 166.15ff., 167.8ff., 168.9ff., 340.8ff), or the physicians from Cos (e.g. *CMG* V 4.1.2, 510.5ff.), or 'the ancients', though it is sometimes a matter of a general rivalry between sects (e.g. *Scr. Min.* III 15.20ff., 125.15ff.) or between individuals (e.g. *CMG* V 4.2, 211.6, V 10.2.1, 87.15, K VII 605.3ff., VIII 640.1ff.). Galen is careful to claim that Hippocrates himself was free from contentiousness (*CMG* V 4.1.1, 84.30ff.) though he occasionally admits to writing in a *philotimoteron* manner himself when stung by a contentious opponent (e.g. *Scr. Min.* II 94.22ff., 95.12) and it is clear that he was himself subjected to counter-accusations of *philoneikia* by his rivals (e.g. *CMG* V 4.1.2, 194.16ff., K VIII 655.17). The passion with which Galen attacks those who in a spirit of contentious rivalry with the ancients set up new sects or propose new doctrines of their own emerges especially clearly at *Nat. Fac.* II, ch. 9, *Scr. Min.* III 203.6–204.6 and at *De Bonis Malisque Sucis*, *CMG* V 4.2, 391.11–392.3.

[9] Thus some at least of 'our people' are criticised by Soranus at *Gynaecia* I, ch. 27, *CMG* IV 17.25ff., and Mnaseas and Dionysius in particular are at I, ch. 29, *CMG* IV 19.10ff. and 19.16ff.

[10] See, for example, Caelius Aurelianus, *Morb. Acut.* II, ch. 24, III, chh. 47, 172–4, 189f., *Morb. Chron.* II, chh. 16f., III, chh. 137f.

specifically, it is well known that so far as Hippocrates and the followers of Hippocrates go, on the great majority of occasions when Soranus mentions their ideas or practices it is to criticise them and to expose their mistakes.[11] A century or so earlier, Celsus, too, we may add, shows that criticism of Hippocrates was perfectly possible in his day – as indeed surely it had *always* been.[12]

No doubt the Methodists represent one extreme end of the spectrum of possible attitudes towards authority and tradition, but that spectrum encompassed a wide range. On Galen's account, many past and contemporary doctors represented themselves as followers of one or other great figure from earlier medicine, though some, the Empiricists especially, chose not to do so, but rather to name themselves after the method they adopted. However, even among the former group the variety of individuals chosen as figure-heads is considerable. They included not just self-styled Hippocrateans (more on them shortly), Herophileans and Erasistrateans, but also, for example, Praxagoreans and Asclepiadeans.

There is no need to suppose that the members of those groups *slavishly* followed the precepts of the person by whose name they called themselves or were called by others. On the contrary, certain developments *within* the Herophilean and again within the Erasistratean sects are clearly discernible, even though Galen tends to represent those developments as forlorn attempts to save consistency, the last shreds of plausibility, or both.[13] Again 'sect' may be too strong an expression, in some cases, for what may have been very loosely defined groups with quite tenuous loyalties. But the basic point remains: the use of such labels would be unintelligible if there were *no* sense in which the individuals so labelled looked back to, or picked up ideas from, Herophilus, Erasistratus, Asclepiades and so on themselves, however much the followers might then elaborate, modify and revise those same ideas. Although the spirit in which what were perceived as the great figures of the past were invoked varied from one sect, group or individual to another, there were plenty of such figures to choose from.

Most importantly, so far as Hippocrates himself goes, Galen was far from having the field to himself. First there are those self-styled Hippocrateans, including, notably, Sabinus from a generation or so before Galen himself.[14]

[11] See Soranus, *Gyn.* I, ch. 45, *CMG* IV 31.26ff., III, ch. 29, 112.14ff., IV, ch. 13, 144.2ff., IV, chh. 14f., 144.21ff., 145.14ff.

[12] See, for example, Celsus, *De Medicina* III, ch. 4.12, *Corpus Medicorum Latinorum* I 107.1ff., VI, ch. 6.1e, 260.3ff. Earlier still criticisms of 'Hippocrates' made by Diocles and by Ctesias are reported by Galen, see *CMG* V 10.1, 112.31ff., K XVII B 530.9ff., XVIII A 731.5ff.

[13] On developments among the Herophileans, see now von Staden, 1989. On the divergences that Galen claims to detect among the Erasistrateans (e.g. *Scr. Min.* III 169.6ff., 172.8ff.) see especially Lonie, 1964. On the development of the notion of a sect, *hairesis*, in Hellenistic medicine and philosophy in general, see von Staden, 1982.

[14] Galen refers generally to self-styled Hippocrateans on several occasions (for example *CMG* V 9.1, 75.21ff., V 10.1, 17.11ff., V 10.2.1, 154.15ff., V 10.2.2, 20.13ff., 242.17ff., 243.22f., K I 478.10ff., VII 764.9ff.), and it is clear that these included, among others, Sabinus and his pupil Metrodorus (*CMG* V 4.1.1, 78.23f., V 10.2.1, 154.17ff.). At *CMG* V 10.2.1, 17.22ff., Sabinus and Metrodorus or their followers are said to have passed as more accurate interpreters than

Galen repeatedly accuses them of misinterpreting Hippocrates, for example from their ignorance of anatomy, or again or *blindly* following Hippocrates – for Galen himself is careful to claim that *he* follows Hippocrates not because he is Hippocrates, but because what he says is true.[15] Secondly and in addition, it is clear not just that many of the Empiricists engaged in careful study of Hippocratic texts,[16] but also that some of them claimed Hippocrates as an Empiricist.[17] Certainly Galen often bewails the neglect from which Hippocrates was suffering in his day, and there is evidence enough to confirm that there were plenty of theorists (and not just Methodists) who were in no sense Hippocrateans. But it is not as if Galen were the *sole* reviver and champion of Hippocratism. He certainly could not be thought to have chosen Hippocrates as his ideal simply because no one else had, nor simply because there was somehow more room for manoeuvre in choosing a figure from the *more* remote past. There was indeed more room for manoeuvre in the interpretation of Hippocrates (we shall come back to that), But *Galen's* interpretation did not have the field to itself but had to prevail against rivals, including rivals who claimed, like Galen, to be faithful followers, not critics, of Hippocrates.

the earlier Hippocrateans and at *Scr. Min.* II 87.19f. Galen also recognises some merit in them. However, Galen still has plenty of criticisms, some of them hard-hitting ones, to make of Sabinus' interpretations in particular, as at *CMG* V 9.1, 15.18ff., 87.18ff., V 10.1, 329.11ff., V 10.2.2, 174.7ff. The picture that emerges from Galen's comments, both on his teachers (including Satyrus and Pelops) and on his fellow-pupils, is one of sustained discussion of Hippocratic texts from an early stage in Galen's career. On the one hand those who disagreed with Hippocrates are criticised, especially Lycus, named as a 'bastard' of the Hippocratic sect at *CMG* V 10.2.1, 17.7f. and the subject of the detailed refutation in the *Adversus Lycum*. On the other hand even those who claimed to be faithful followers of Hippocrates are often said to have misinterpreted his theories, out of an ignorance of anatomy, or of his texts, or both (for example *CMG* V 9.1, 75.21ff., V 10.1, 329.20ff., V 10.2.2, 242.17ff.). Thus Galen is particularly careful to distance himself from the views of his teacher Pelops, who argued that the brain is the source of the blood-vessels as well as of the nerves. It is clear that Pelops put forward this opinion in his *Hippocratic Introductions* (see *CMG* V 4.1.2, 392.10ff) and one might conjecture that he did so on the authority, partly, of the anatomy in *On the Nature of Man* ch. 11: at *CMG* V 4.1.2, 378.32ff., 36ff., Galen turns immediately from expressing his disagreement with Pelops' anatomical views to a restatement of his, Galen's firm opinion that *Nat. Hom.* ch. 11 does not contain the authentic teaching of Hippocrates. While *Scr. Min.* II 86.23–87.23 throws light on the extent of discussion of Hippocratic texts by Galen's teachers and fellow-pupils, the distinct impression we are sometimes left with is that Galen alone interprets Hippocrates correctly, just as Galen alone has the correct medical doctrines. From among his own contemporaries and close predecessors it is not just the likes of Lycus and Julian who are criticised for their interpretations of Hippocrates, but also Sabinus, Quintus, Numesianus, Stratonicus, Aephicianus, and even Satyrus and Pelops as well as many otherwise unidentified 'younger' doctors.

15 See especially *Scr. Min.* II 64.10ff., *CMG* V 4.1.2, 198.25f., 380.5ff., V 10.1, 375.22ff. At *Scr. Min.* II 95.6ff. Galen says that he calls those who named themselves after any authority, Hippocrates, Praxagoras or anyone, slaves.

16 At *CMG* V 9.2, 73.11ff., Zeuxis is said to have been the first Empiricist to have commented on *all* the works of Hippocrates: cf. also *CMG* V 10.2.1, 16.23ff., 154.13ff., V 10.2.2, 20.17ff. Study of earlier views corresponds to the Empiricist recommendation of *historia* (*Subf. Emp.* ch. 7).

17 See especially *CMG* V 10.2.2, 174.20ff., K XVIII A 524.15ff. It is clear, for example, from *CMG* V 10.2.2, 243.22ff., that Galen is particularly exercised by the possible threat of contamination from Empiricist readings of Hippocrates.

So our agenda of questions includes first why Galen should have shown such respect for traditional authority, second why he should have chosen the particular authorities he did, and third how he could vindicate the particular interpretations of those authorities, Hippocrates especially, that he promulgated.

Now if we consider those questions from the point of view of what Galen himself wishes us to believe, the answers run something like this. Tradition had been seriously neglected and much of value had thereby been lost or temporarily mislaid from the medical art, thanks partly to the laziness and ignorance of practitioners, partly to their excessive eagerness to advance their own claims to originality. Secondly, so far as Galen's chief authority, Hippocrates, goes, he deserves to be revered, indeed to be called 'divine', because of the superiority of his medical art, a superiority that can be claimed on several distinct accounts – thereby to answer the third along with the second of my three questions. First there is his scientific method (praised by Plato in the *Phaedrus* and to be found, of course, according to Galen, in *On the Nature of Man* especially, which could then become the foundation for the reconstruction of the authentic Hippocrates).[18] Secondly there is Hippocrates' expressed moral principles and evident high moral practice, the model he provided of the unselfinterested, dedicated medical man. Third his medical practice was based on correct physiology, pathology and even psychology. Fourth there is the superiority of his medical practice itself, its prognostic and therapeutic techniques, as amply demonstrated, Galen would claim, in treatise after treatise.

Galen's own picture of his reasons for following Hippocrates, as thus sketched out, must be our starting-point, but it has its weak points and it leaves some explaining to be done. The questions we should raise concern not just those aspects of the picture that may now strike *us* as ill-founded or over-optimistic, but also and more particularly those aspects that would (or at least might) have struck Galen's own contemporaries as such – where, for example, the consistency of Galen's account is problematic. The evidence in Galen himself can, I believe, be pressed to answer those questions and to supplement that picture.

First there are some well-known fudges on the topic of Hippocratic anatomy. If there was not much by way of detailed guidance on anatomical points in the Hippocratic writings, that was not – Galen sometimes argued – because Hippocrates' knowledge in that field was inadequate, but rather

[18] It should be noted that, even if one accepted that the method Plato ascribed to Hippocrates in the *Phaedrus* tallied with that in *Nat. Hom.* chh. 1–8, that would, strictly speaking, still not prove conclusively that Hippocrates wrote those chapters, among other reasons because others might have adopted the same method either independently or in imitation of Hippocrates. If the conjecture offered above, n. 14, is correct, namely that Galen's teacher Pelops argued in part on the basis of *Nat. Hom.* ch. 11 for what Galen considered the unacceptable view of the brain as the source of the blood-vessels, then Galen may be presumed to have been concerned with the interpretation of that treatise from very early on in his career. However, when precisely he saw the importance of the evidence in Plato as support for *his own* interpretation of *Nat. Hom.* chh. 1–8 cannot now be determined.

largely because in his day it was not necessary to go into those questions in any detail.[19] But if we look closer at that apology two problems arise. First there are some straightforward mistakes (as Galen himself perceived them) on anatomical questions in some texts in the Corpus. But when he encounters an account of the blood-vessels in *Nat. Hom.* ch. 11 that is badly flawed (not least because it treats the brain as the source), his line is to deny its authenticity. Indeed he denies that that account is the work of either Hippocrates or Polybus – despite the evidence in Aristotle, *HA* III, ch. 3 where the account in question or something very close to it is expressly ascribed to Polybus.[20] One can see why Galen needs to deny that Polybus was responsible, since elsewhere he uses him as indirect evidence for what his father-in-law Hippocrates himself maintained. However, with that denial the problem does not entirely vanish. Even if *Nat. Hom.* ch. 11 is not authentic, it is an *early* interpolation, since it was known to and discussed by earlier commentators.[21] However, this evidence of *mistaken* anatomical views in a work that is of early date, even if not composed by Hippocrates or Polybus themselves, does not mesh entirely happily with the other, general, argument in Galen that in ancient times it was not necessary to go into anatomical questions in any detail.

Secondly Galen is honest enough to give the credit for much important anatomical work to Diocles, Praxagoras and especially to Herophilus and Erasistratus. Those last two, as is well known, are credited with the first detailed descriptions of the nerves, though Galen still considers Herophilus' work sketchy and he contrasts Erasistratus' earlier accounts with the more accurate work done in his later years, when he had the leisure to do research.[22] However, Galen can – in all honesty – only give that credit where it was due by allowing the implication that Hippocrates' own knowledge, at least on these points, was imperfect – though Galen is in general careful to leave that just *as* an implication.

Of course if anatomy had been all there were to being a doctor, then we might have said, and Galen might even have agreed, that he would have done better to align himself with Herophilus and Erasistratus. But that would not do, for a whole series of reasons. I shall be coming back to these again later,

[19] See for example *De Anat. Admin.* II, ch. 1, K II 280.2ff., and cf. Harig and Kollesch, 1975: 260ff.

[20] See, for example, *CMG* V 4.1.2, 378.36ff., 380.18ff., 492.22ff. It is at *HA* 512b12ff. that Aristotle ascribes a very similar set of views to Polybus. For Galen's knowledge of *HA*, see, for example, *QAM* ch. 7, *Scr. Min.* II 55.13ff., 56.6ff.

[21] Galen's view is that the material after *Nat. Hom.* chh. 1–8 and before *Salubr.* was inserted by someone who wanted to pad out the book and make it bigger, a common practice, as he believes, 'at the time of the Attalid and Ptolemaic kings' (*CMG* V 9.1, 57.12ff., cf. 55.6ff.). Although we cannot give precise dates for when Galen thought the interpolated material was written or inserted into the text of *Nat. Hom.–Salubr.*, he appears to believe that it was known from early on in the Hellenistic period to Alexandrian Hippocratic scholarship.

[22] See especially *CMG* V 4.1.2, 440. 20ff., 442.9ff., 476.36ff. on Erasistratus. *Med. Exp.* ch. 13 (where an Empiricist speaks) is particularly fulsome in its praise of Herophilus, described as having surpassed the great majority of the ancients both in the width of his knowledge and in intellect, and as having advanced the art of medicine in many ways.

but the principal among them are these. First Galen would have insisted that both Herophilus and more especially Erasistratus were seriously mistaken in their physiological doctrines. This was not just a matter of Erasistratus' notorious theory that the arteries contain air and his treating the heart as the source of the veins as well as of the arteries, but also concerned his inaccurate views on digestion and his unfounded doctrine of the basic *triplokia* of vein, artery, nerve.[23] Secondly, even if it could be claimed that Herophilus and Erasistratus were expert in dissection, their reputation as medical practitioners could not compare (Galen believed) with Hippocrates. In their case Galen could not cite (or at least he did not cite) substantial evidence to suggest a brilliant and successful clinical practice. Indeed he concentrates, in the case of Erasistratus at least, rather on the *failures* of his performance in that regard.[24]

Evidently what Galen sought was a figure for whom it could be claimed *both* that he was an outstanding doctor *and* that he was *no mere* doctor. Let me take each of those points in turn. On the face of it the Hippocratic writings might seem to provide plenty of promising material to support the thesis of Hippocrates as a brilliantly successful physician. However, several basic reservations need to be borne in mind. First there is – *we* should say, at least – a radical indeterminacy in the retrospective evaluation of the efficacy of the therapies favoured in the Hippocratic writings, and indeed when cures are claimed or recovery recorded there are always elements of doubt as to the cause. That point, however, it must be conceded, is not one that troubles Galen.

However, secondly, there is a good deal of evidence in those writings, including in those that Galen took to be authentic works of Hippocrates himself, that might suggest that the remedies available were largely *in*effective, at least for the more severe acute diseases. There are plenty of texts in the surgical treatises and the *Epidemics* especially where the ineffectiveness of remedies is explicitly remarked, as well as plenty of cases recorded where the outcome was death, not recovery. However, the very recording of failures and of mistakes in treatment[25] could be turned to advantage, as redounding to the credit of their author, a Hippocrates thereby revealed as worthy – not of blame for his mistakes – but of praise for his honesty. This is indeed what happens in Celsus – though we may remark the contrast in Galen's treatment of the failures recorded by Erasistratus.[26]

Moreover, thirdly, we have Galen's own word for it that some prominent doctors who were near contemporaries of Hippocrates (Diocles, and even earlier Ctesias of Cnidos) criticised him for some of his treatments.

[23] Particularly strenuous attacks on Erasistratus' views are mounted in *Nat. Fac.* and in the treatises on venesection and on respiration (see Brain, 1986; Furley and Wilkie, 1984). On the ambiguities of Erasistratus' theory that the heart is *archē* of the veins as well as of the arteries, see Lonie, 1964.

[24] See especially K XI 200.1ff., 206.5ff., 209.14ff.

[25] As in a famous text in the Hippocratic work *On Joints* ch. 47, Littré IV 210.9–212.5, discussed with other cases in Lloyd, 1987: 124ff.

[26] See Celsus, *Med.* VIII 4.3, *CML* I 378.3ff.

How, then, could Galen be so confident about Hippocrates' clinical expertise? Two points suggest themselves in reply, though since they go beyond what Galen himself draws attention to in so many words, there is an inevitable element of conjecture in making use of them. One may presume, first, that the fact that both Plato and Aristotle[27] testified to the fame of Hippocrates counted for a good deal. Doctors should, of course, count for more than philosophers as judges of other doctors and Galen has plenty of reservations about some philosophers (more on that later). But the fact that two of the most prestigious endorsed Hippocrates' reputation as a physician must have weighed with Galen (not that he *ever* reveals any *doubt* on the score of the greatness of Hippocrates' medical art). Moreover, secondly, Galen had reason enough, we may agree, to believe that a wealth of valuable clinical experience is contained in the particular records and general observations in the Hippocratic Corpus, even if those records do not describe an uninterrupted sequence of successful cures. Then once he had satisfied himself that the evidence of Plato's *Phaedrus* established the authenticity of *Nat. Hom.* chh. 1–8, the next step was all too deceptively simple. Galen was not the first, nor was he the last, even if he was the most influential commentator to associate whatever seemed most praiseworthy in the Corpus with the author of *Nat. Hom.* chh. 1–8 identified as the man whom Plato and Aristotle already knew as a famous doctor.

However, it was clearly not just for his medical art that Galen idealised Hippocrates, and this takes us to a second strand of argument. For Galen, 'the best doctor' is, of course, 'also a philosopher', a point he argues on a number of grounds, for example the need to base medicine on scientific method, and indeed on moral philosophy. Moreover in addition to the grounds that Galen explicitly sets out for this thesis, we may see it as fulfilling a further role. The evidence of Vitruvius, for instance, shows that others besides doctors sometimes sought a higher standing for their *technē* (in his case architecture) by assimilating it to philosophy and we can hardly doubt that this is a factor in Galen's case as well, even though the importance we attach to it is a matter of judgement.

As the embodiment of the thesis that the best doctor is also a philosopher, Hippocrates, as Galen represents him, must have seemed far and away the most attractive of the ancients to associate himself with. Of course it was not enough just to have philosophical theories. Galen is vividly aware of the disputes among philosophers and he is highly critical not just of atomists and anti-teleologists, but also often of Stoics and of Sceptics.[28] Nor even with his favoured philosophers does he endorse everything they proposed, certainly not in the case of Aristotle, but not even in the case of Plato either. The point was, rather, that Hippocrates had the *right* theories, specifically the correct

[27] See Aristotle, *Politics* 1326a14ff.

[28] On Galen's deep-seated concern with the threat posed by Scepticism, see now Hankinson, forthcoming.

scientific methodology, the right theory of the physical elements, the right psychology, the right moral philosophy – as well as himself embodying those moral principles in practice.

As a matter of principle – it is important to note – Galen saw the need to justify, and often did attempt to justify, those claims for correctness *independently*. There is no question of his asserting that Hippocrates was right *because Plato said so* – let along that Hippocrates was right because *Hippocrates* said so.[29] The justification of the claims (which are also claims, of course, for the correctness of the positions that Galen himself adopts) does not proceed *simply* by appeal to *authority*. But as secondary confirmation that endorsement from authority counted for a good deal. Why Hippocrates' philosophical positions (rather than those of Herophilus, say) were the ones to admire was because they were right – *and also* because they were endorsed by and/or coincided with those of Plato. Hippocrates' scientific method was directly approved by Plato. Better still, both his physics and his psychology could, with a bit of fudging, be said to agree with Plato's, whose theories in those areas could, therefore, be said to have been *anticipated by* Hippocrates. This concern with Hippocrates' priority claims is important since it tallies with Galen's *negative* concern to expose his own contemporaries' claims to innovate as the *unfounded* claims he takes them to be.

But in the case of the physics and the psychology there was, as I put it, a bit of fudging to do, and this needs careful analysis – for the extent of the fudging may be taken as an indicator of the strength of Galen's prior motivation to get to his conclusion. Let us take element theory first, and for the sake of argument concede the first step, that *Nat. Hom.* chh. 1–8 contains Hippocrates' considered views. The strength of the general claims that Galen makes in *PHP* and in *El. sec. Hipp.* varies. Sometimes it is put that Hippocrates and Plato agreed: sometimes Galen adds that theirs was the best account, indeed the true one; sometimes he puts it that they were the earliest to propose this element theory – and sometimes he is more explicit, that Hippocrates was the very first to do so.[30]

First, then, there is the thesis of the agreement between Hippocrates and Plato on element theory, and the remarkable feature of this is that although this is one of the principal themes and theses of *PHP*, Galen recognises plenty of divergences between them. He recognises, for instance, that Plato has a distinctive theory analysing the four simple bodies into their elementary triangles,[31] and he has some defensive arguments on the point that Plato does not actually call the simple bodies elements – but then no more does

[29] As in the texts already noted above, n. 15.

[30] Compare, in *PHP*, *CMG* v 4.1.2, 424.7ff. (where the question is whether Hippocrates and Plato agreed) with 334.20ff. (where the question is whether their doctrines are true). That Plato followed Hippocrates in his theory of the four simple bodies is asserted at *PHP*, *CMG* v 4.1.2, 492.31ff.: that Hippocrates was the very first to have discovered the elements and to have defined their qualities is said at *El. sec. Hipp.* K I 456.16ff., 487.7ff., and cf. also *Nat Fac.* II ch. 4, *Scr. Min.* III 165.12ff. and *MM* K x 16.1ff.

[31] *CMG* v 4.1.2, 496.4ff.

Hippocrates.[32] Moreover when he comes to outline Hippocrates' theory of the four humours as the chief constituents of the human body, he is quite clear that that goes far beyond what can be found in the *Timaeus*. Plato is represented as holding that the four humours are the causes of most diseases, just as Hippocrates did.[33] But quite apart from other discrepancies both in pathology[34] and in physiology [35] Plato made a number of mistakes, for example on the nature of the blood and even on the basic point that the humours exist naturally in the body.[36]

This says a great deal for Galen's careful exegesis and his scruples: on a number of points he is prepared to qualify, and he does qualify, his overall thesis of the general agreements between Hippocrates and Plato. But those qualifications – we may say – *still do not go far enough*. Justification for attributing a theory of four simple bodies to the author of *Nat. Hom.* depends crucially on *combining* the destructive arguments rejecting monistic doctrines based on one or other of air, fire, water or earth in chapter I with the constructive theories identifying the four primary opposites and the four constituent humours in later chapters. But we should be clear that those later chapters do not in fact set out a theory of the four *simple bodies*: they do not mention earth, water, air and fire at all. To ascribe that theory to their author is an inference and involves indeed not so much a Platonic as an Aristotelian reading of that text. To that it may be said that Galen's point is sometimes expressed in the form that Hippocrates was the first to define the *qualities* of the simple bodies:[37] yet that is not the only claim Galen makes and he often goes further and suggests that Hippocrates was the first to propose the four simple bodies as elements.[38] Galen would have us believe that Hippocrates and Plato were the first to suggest what we should think of, rather, as the Aristotelian synthesis in which the four simple bodies are defined in terms of four primary opposites:[39] yet while talk of the four fundamental opposites suits the text of *Nat. Hom.* and talk of other physical objects being constituted by earth, water, air and fire suits the text of the *Timaeus* it is only

[32] *CMG* V 4.1.2, 494.26ff., cf. 498.9ff.

[33] *CMG* V 4.1.2, 508.9ff.

[34] For example at *CMG* V 4.1.2, 520.3ff., Galen says that Plato neglected to consider the problem of the correlations between the age of patients and the complaints they suffered from and that he was in error in his statements about periodic fevers.

[35] Plato's doctrine of respiration, based on the idea of circular thrust, is said to be badly mistaken at *CMG* V 4.1.2, 530.12ff., 532.3ff. (though he was correct in agreeing with Hippocrates that inhalation is for the sake of cooling the innate heat, 532.27ff.).

[36] At *CMG* V 4.1.2, 506.14ff., Plato is said to be mistaken in including blood, along with bone, flesh and so on, as a secondary formation: in *Nat. Hom.* chh. 1–8 Hippocrates is taken to have shown that blood is a humour and one of the four primary constituents of the body. At *CMG* V 4.1.2, 510.8ff., 512.4ff., Hippocrates is contrasted favourably with Plato as he demonstrated that the four humours exist naturally, while Plato did not even attempt to do so.

[37] As at *El. sec. Hipp.* K I 456.16ff. and in *MM* K X 16.1ff., texts cited above, n. 30.

[38] Indeed he does so in the same text, *El. sec. Hipp.* K I 456.16ff., cited in n. 37 in which he goes on to claim that Hippocrates was the first to define their qualities.

[39] However, in Aristotle's theory each of the simple bodies is associated not just with one of the primary qualities, but with a pair of them, *GC* 330b3ff., but cf. 331a3ff. giving priority to one of each pair in each case.

by assimilating items from both texts that Galen can arrive at his interpretation of what, according to him, *both* Hippocrates *and* Plato maintained.[40]

Moreover on the question of psychological theory the claim that Hippocrates and Plato were in basic agreement faced appreciably more formidable obstacles. In *PHP* Galen tacitly acknowledges that the names of the three parts of the soul in Plato, *logistikon*, *thumoeides*, *epithumētikon*, are Plato's own. In arguing for the harmonisation of Plato and Hippocrates Galen concentrates, rather, on the question of where those three parts are localised, and he remarks that it was somehow more appropriate for a physician to present his teaching in terms of bodily organs, and for a philosopher to do so in terms of powers or faculties of the soul.[41] It is the *Timaeus*, of course, that Galen uses to substantiate the claim that Plato maintained the view that corresponds to Galen's own, namely that the *archai* of the three principal faculties of the soul are brain, heart and liver, the sources of the nerves, arteries and veins respectively. That interpretation has *broad* Platonic justification, even though we should resist the notion that Plato would have seen the brain, the seat of the *logistikon*, as the origin of the *nerves*, and even though in the case of the *epithumētikon* Galen adopts a rather more precise interpretation than is strictly warranted of the text in the *Timaeus* (77B3f.) that refers to the region between the diaphragm and the navel.[42]

Yet it is finding Platonic tripartition in Hippocrates that presents the biggest problem. Galen has, to be sure, a text in *On Nutriment* ch. 31 which states that the heart is the *rhizōsis* of the *artēriai*, the liver that of the *phlebes*, and that might seem to secure two of the three localisations. Meanwhile a variety of texts[43] could be used to suggest not, it is true, that the brain is the source of the nerves, but at least that it is the seat of intelligence, and so of the *logistikon*. However there is something distinctly opportunistic about Galen's use of *On Nutriment*. One might not expect him to be unduly troubled about what may strike *us* as evidence of a comparatively late date,[44] at least

[40] Moreover the further question of whether Hippocrates can be represented as the *very first* to have proposed the four-element theory that Galen ascribes to him involves the additional difficulty of the interpretation of other early philosophers and medical writers. Galen is aware that Empedocles has a theory of four roots (for he quotes his theory of perception, for instance, at *CMG* V 4.1.2, 462.4ff.) but he holds that Empedocles was mistaken in maintaining that the elements are subject to no mutual interaction, *El. sec. Hipp.* K I 484.1ff. Other problems, such as the possibility that Philistion also maintained a four-element theory (Anon. Lond. XX 25ff.) or that Petron had a theory of four primary opposites (Anon. Lond. XX 1ff.) or again that the author of the Hippocratic treatise *On Fleshes* proposed a theory of four elements that diverges in certain respects from that which Galen finds in *Nat. Hom.* (see L VIII 584.9ff.) are not mentioned in this connection either in *PHP* or in *El. sec. Hipp.*

[41] *CMG* V 4.1.2, 418.30ff., cf. Vegetti, 1986: 234.

[42] However, at *CMG* V 4.1.2, 370.1ff., Galen quotes *Timaeus* 77B perfectly accurately: cf. also 418.10ff.

[43] For example *On the Sacred Disease*, especially ch. 14, L VI 386.15ff. Galen cites this treatise, for example, at *CMG* V 9.2, 206.13ff.

[44] See, for example, Diller, 1936–7; Deichgräber, 1973; and cf. Joly, 1975.

not in general terms. But it is striking that when Galen repeatedly points out that Hippocrates used *phlebes* not just for veins but also for what he, Galen, calls arteries – and he knows further that *artēria* is the regular name for the trachea – he should nevertheless coolly cite *Alim.* ch. 31 as evidence that Hippocrates held that the heart is the source of the *arteries*. Galen might have stopped to ponder why Hippocrates should there – exceptionally, if not uniquely[45] – have used the term *artēriai*, not the usual *phlebes*, thereby introducing a term for a distinction normally ignored by the generic use of *phlebes*.[46]

Nor is that the end of the problem. To get to the conclusion that Hippocrates located what Plato called the spirited part in the heart Galen cites as perhaps his chief evidence a text from *Epidemics* II 5.16 which runs (in part) 'the man in whose elbow the *phleps* throbs is frenzied and quick to anger, *ozuthumos*'. Galen then argues (1) that the throbbing (*sphugmos*) here refers to the violent pulsing of the artery (for as he has often pointed out elsewhere the ancients called the arteries *phlebes*),[47] and (2) that therefore the source of anger is here located, by Hippocrates, in the arteries, which themselves stem (as he has argued) from the heart. Ergo Hippocrates thought the heart was the seat of the spirited part – it being assumed, in *PHP*, that *Epidemics* II can be used as evidence for Hippocrates' views (indeed it is crucial for Galen's reconstruction of Hippocrates' views on the blood-vascular system in particular)[48] even though in his commentaries on the *Epidemics* Galen more cautiously concluded that the author of *Epid.* II was not Hippocrates, but Thessalus – who, however, based it on Hippocrates' notes.[49]

Whatever one might think of the hazards of identifying Plato's tripartite psychology with *anything* to be found anywhere in the Hippocratic Corpus, there are palpable weaknesses in Galen's arguments as he himself presents them. As I tried to show in my discussion of the way in which Galen handles his authorities in *QAM* – where he cites not just Hippocrates and Plato but also Aristotle in support of the *vague* thesis that the faculties of the soul 'follow' the *kraseis* of the body –[50] so too in his general assimilation of the psychology of Hippocrates and Plato there are shortcomings in Galen's

[45] *Artēriē* is, however, also used in the other text that Galen cites, *Epid.* II 4.1, L V 120.13ff., viz. at 122.9, 13ff., 124.3ff., quoted by Galen at *CMG* V 4.1.2, 420.2ff., and Galen evidently took it there to have the sense 'artery' (not, as usual in the Hippocratic writings, 'trachea' or 'bronchi'). One problem there (as we shall see, n. 49) is that in his Commentary on *Epidemics* II Galen concluded that that book is the work of Thessalus.

[46] Moreover in *Alim.* ch. 31, *CMG* I 1, 82.13f., the *phlebes* and *artēriai* are said to be the source of the blood and the pneuma. While the text does not specify *which* of these two is carried by *which* type of vessel, and Galen might hold the statement is compatible with his own view that the *phlebes* contain blood and the arteries blood and pneuma, that statement in *Alim.* is *also* compatible with Erasistratus' doctrine – which Galen strenuously rejects – that the veins carry blood, but the arteries (just) air. However, Galen does not mention this difficulty.

[47] *CMG* V 4.1.2, 416.16ff.

[48] The key text is *Epid.* II 4.1, L V 120.13ff., mentioned above n. 45.

[49] See *in Epid.* II, *CMG* V 10.1, 213.23ff., 310.23ff., cf. V 10.2.2, 76.1ff.

[50] See Lloyd, 1989: 33ff. especially.

arguments that a close reading of the very evidence that Galen himself chooses to put before the reader would bring to light – even before any reader went further afield and consulted evidence that Galen himself ignores. In *QAM* his strategic goal appears to be, or to include, justification for the special claims about what a doctor can hope to achieve beyond merely an improvement in physical well-being.[51] *PHP* can be thought of as helping to secure another part of Galen's general programme, his theses concerning the prestige and standing of the model doctor and his view of the best doctor as philosopher. For that programme it was important for Galen to be able to represent Hippocrates as having a theory of the faculties of the soul, indeed as having basically the same theory as Plato's, indeed (more boldly) as having put that forward *before* Plato, even (more boldly still) as being the very first to propose such a psychology. It is true that Galen recognises a minor query on that last score. He quotes Posidonius to the effect that, so far as the distinction between the rational soul and the affections, *pathē*, go, that had already been put forward by Pythagoras.[52] But to that Galen comments that Posidonius had to infer that from the writings of some of Pythagoras' pupils, since no book of Pythagoras himself survived, and secondly that he, Galen, was not undertaking a historical account of early opinions, but merely an examination of the views of Hippocrates and Plato.[53] But it should be noted that Galen had *just* said that the *best* view (i.e. in psychology) was the one that Hippocrates and Plato were the first of all (*hapantōn prōtoi*) to expound.[54]

Let me now turn back to the three questions that I said were open questions in Galen's day and so for Galen himself at the very beginning of his career, and see where Galen's own account of the answers may need supplementing. Tradition is to be respected since there is much in ancient medical practice that is of great value – a point that should, and can, be established independently of the authority of tradition itself. However, to this should perhaps be added the further point that I mentioned at the outset. Galen is vociferous in his criticisms of the arrogance of those who turned their backs on tradition and who claimed to have new and better theories and practices themselves. The overall charge that he often repeats is, as we saw, that of *philoneikia*.[55] Yet Galen himself, obviously, was not the least ambitious of men: nor even, I dare say, the least arrogant. He is perfectly frank, on many occasions, about his anatomical discoveries, about his brilliant diagnoses and cures and much else besides. But we may notice how, if some of his opponents had tried to accuse him of precisely what *he* accused *them* of, namely of being excessively ambitious to innovate and claim

[51] See *QAM* ch. 9, *Scr. Min.* II 67.2ff., where the claim is made that the doctor, by making recommendations about diet and regimen generally, will be able to contribute to a person's moral excellence and intellectual capacity, cf. Lloyd, 1989: 39ff.

[52] At *CMG* V 4.1.2, 290.3ff., Galen apparently endorses Posidonius' view, but later in *PHP* V Galen is decidedly more guarded: see n. 53.

[53] *CMG* V 4.1.2, 334.30ff., 33ff., cf. Vegetti, 1986: 230.

[54] *CMG* V 4.1.2, 334.29, cf. also 168.8f.

[55] See above, n. 8.

superiority for the new ideas and practices thus introduced, Galen could use his own adherence to Hippocratism in reply. He himself, he could counter, was doing no more than elaborating the views and theories of the great names of the past, of great philosophers and of great doctors, and especially of Hippocrates, his 'guide in all that is good'. It would be unfair to suggest that Galen *merely* used Hippocrates as a *cover*. But the work of elaboration, systematisation and creative reinterpretation that goes into his account of what Hippocrates stood for should not be underestimated. There is a generosity, to be sure, in finding so much that he could agree with in Hippocrates, and in seeing himself as following his lead. But we should not fail to remark that there was something in that generosity also for Galen, for it provided him with an argument in his polemic with his contemporaries: for he could accuse them of *philoneikia* but defend himself on that same score on the grounds that he was the faithful follower of the ancients.

Some particularly good examples of this come in the *Prognosis*. There he goes through a number of cases of what were hailed (he tells us) as miracle cures or marvellous feats of prediction. But, he says with a disarming modesty, there was nothing *thaumaston* about most of them, for he merely followed what Hippocrates had set down in the *Epidemics*.[56] However, he leaves us in no doubt that the problems presented by the cases he described had defeated all his rivals and that *they* were convinced that what he had done was amazing. But it is particularly striking, surely, that Galen should claim that he was doing no more than follow Hippocrates' teaching on crisis in the *Epidemics*, *as if* the views expressed on that topic in those works were (*a*) consistent and (*b*) self-explanatory.[57] However, Epigenes is brought in to testify that Galen had said that 'everything that I have written about all the predictions you have seen me make was demonstrated by Hippocrates'.[58]

To turn, now, to the second of my three main questions, the reasons for Galen opting for Hippocrates as the chief authority to follow. Obviously he was the most promising and attractive ancient physician to cast in this role since he could be represented as meeting all the criteria that Galen demanded. These included not just Hippocrates' fame as a successful practitioner. The crucial extra factor was that Hippocrates could be used as a perfect demonstration of *how*, in methodology, in natural philosophy, even in moral philosophy, the best doctor is also a philosopher. Many able physicians might go some way to meet the first criterion, but most failed miserably on the other scores: and the other criteria were certainly essential to the picture of the model physician that Galen wanted – one who could justify the strongest claims for the *prestige* of the medical art.

Conversely some of the more successful and renowned theorists and researchers might be passable physicists or natural philosophers, but fall

[56] See, for example, *CMG* v 8.1, 126.1ff., 12ff.: cf., however, the claim made at 126.16ff.

[57] On divergences on the subject of critical days in the Hippocratic writings, including between *Prognostic* and various texts in *Epid.* I and III, see Lloyd, 1975: 184f.

[58] *CMG* v 8.1, 134.1ff.

down on other counts. The case of Herophilus is particularly interesting, and his achievements can now be much more clearly appreciated thanks to Heinrich von Staden's magnum opus. Certainly he had a methodology, based in part on the famous dictum that the phenomena are to be treated as primary even if they are not – although the interpretation of that is still disputed.[59] He had, too, an element theory, a humour theory, a physiology, and he was a master anatomist, responsible for a whole series of discoveries of first-rate importance not just for anatomy but also for clinical practice.[60] Yet however great Galen's admiration for his work in that last area especially, he shows no inclination to call himself a Herophilean, and not just because he would have had to redefine that term in order to distinguish himself from others who called themselves such (for after all he had to do that also with Hippocrates).

Piecing together the possible reasons for Galen's coolness towards Herophilus is – we said – bound in places to be speculative. Some have even suggested that Galen would not have associated himself with a man who had the reputation of having conducted human vivisections, but since Galen makes no mention of that whatsoever, that must be thought *entirely* speculative. Whatever may be thought about the evidence that was available to Galen on Herophilus' clinical practice, Galen's remarks suggest that he rated this as no more than moderate,[61] and Herophilus certainly suffered from one unavoidable disadvantage, in that he had no endorsement from Plato. It is also possible that the very detail of Herophilus' work in anatomy was an obstacle, paradoxically, in the following way. However much of that work Galen could and did take over, it was an area where appreciable progress continued to be made, not least by Galen himself.[62] Claims for superiority in clinical practice are on the whole easier to make because they are *less* easily or less straightforwardly verifiable than similar claims in the domain of anatomy, where 'Hippocrates' was, in general, tactfully silent. Where Hippocrates, by contrast, scored, with Galen, was for his reputation as practitioner as well a theorist. While Plato spoke directly of the fame of Hippocrates as doctor, Platonic admiration could also be claimed for other areas of Hippocrates' work as well. Given those Hippocratic anticipations of some of the major theses of Plato's natural philosophy, his element theory, his psychology, his teleology, Plato's endorsement could be represented as extending to those other fields as well. From Galen's point of view it was neat that a philosopher could thus be used to testify that Hippocrates was a better example of the doctor as philosopher, as well as an outstanding doctor.

Yet for Hippocrates to play the role of the ideal that Galen wanted, that is as the best *advertisement* for the medical art that Galen could desire, the

[59] See, for example, Anon. Lond. XXI 22f., and cf. von Staden, 1989: 117ff.

[60] See von Staden, 1989: 138ff., 242ff.

[61] See von Staden, 1989: 408ff.

[62] However, the other main area in which Galen makes claims to have innovated, namely pulse lore (see above n. 3) was one where verification was problematic.

Corpus, we said, had to be subjected to a massive effort of interpretation and reinterpretation – the topic of the third and final of my initial questions. Alternative views of Hippocrates had certainly been proposed before Galen – in addition to those versions of Hippocratism we hear about from Galen himself.[63] Galen has a whole battery of different types of arguments to defeat one or other alternative view of Hippocrates. Sometimes he is concerned merely with points of detail, with the detailed *mis*interpretation (as he sees it) of therapeutic or diagnostic recommendations.[64] But where a strategic view of Hippocrates is at issue – for example when he was claimed as an Empiricist – Galen has a more difficult battle on his hands. Different commentators might at that point attach different weights to the various internal, and external, arguments that Galen deploys. But we should surely all agree that to defeat rival interpretations it was, once again, of crucial importance to Galen that he could (he thought) invoke the authority of *Plato* in support of his own reconstruction. Thereby that reconstruction could be said to be based not just on internal evidence and not just on some commonly accepted opinions about Hippocrates. It had as one of its chief foundations the external evidence provided by the account of Hippocrates' method in the *Phaedrus*. That alone would be enough, in Galen's view, to show that Hippocrates was no sceptic and no Empiricist.

Problems to do with authenticity, which might have seemed a major deterrent telling heavily against the usefulness of 'Hippocrates' for Galen's purposes, could, at least sometimes, be turned to positive advantage. The texts that Galen could not longer accept or that contained theories that he knew to be plain false could be written off as interpolations in authentic work or be taken as evidence *of in*authenticity.[65]

However, as that last remark suggests, Galen's reconstruction, like so many others, involves picking and choosing from among a wide range of disparate material. The major problem in his interpretation, too, is that of *consistency*. Within the group of treatises Galen draws on, the *inconsistencies* on points of doctrine strike *us* as glaring. This is true even if we confine ourselves to the favoured works, the 'most authentic ones', the surgical treatises, *Epidemics* I and III, *Prognosis*, *Aphorisms*, *On Regime in Acute Diseases*, *On Airs, Waters, Places*, *On the Nature of Man* chh. 1–8.[66] Even if we limit ourselves to that group, there are many blatant incompatibilities in the physical, physiological, anatomical, pathological and therapeutic theories, for example in humoral theories, in theories of the constituents of

[63] Thus we have direct evidence concerning the interpretations put forward by Apollonius of Citium (*CMG* XI 1.1) as also by Celsus.

[64] The early editors, Artemidorus Capiton and Dioscorides, and their schools, are criticised, for example, at *CMG* V 9.1, 15.11ff., V 10.1, 197.10ff., 275.12ff., K XVIII B 631.7ff., XIX 63.13ff., cf. also K I 438.11ff., 476.2ff., 478.10ff., VII 764.9ff., and *CMG* V 10.1, 401.7ff. (the last an extended criticism of a pupil of Metrodorus).

[65] As happens with the account of the blood-vascular system in *Nat. Hom.* ch. 11, see above, p. 404.

[66] See, for example, *CMG* V 10.2.1, 60.13ff.

the human body, in doctrines concerning critical days, even in recommendations concerning dietetics and so on.[67] If we spread our net wider, as Galen does, to take in the likes of such treatises as *On Breaths* and *On Nutriment*, the problems increase exponentially.

Now *if* Galen had seriously confronted this question, he might have attempted at least something of a first-stage defence with the argument he sometimes deploys, to the effect that too much precision in terminology is boorish.[68] If there are four cardinal humours in *Nat. Hom.*, but an apparently different humour theory – a different group of four, or a theory based more simply just on bile and phlegm[69] – in other treatises, Hippocrates should not be expected to present the whole of his considered theory, nor necessarily in precisely the same terminology, every time any part of it is mentioned. General consistency might be saved with regard to some apparently conflicting suggestions about diet in a similar fashion. However, these are problems which as a whole, we must say, do not occupy much of Galen's attention: they do not, it seems, present themselves to him in the way they might to us. Nevertheless that is not an end to the matter, since if we confine ourselves to the problems that Galen *does* discuss, the examples I took from *PHP* of his discussion of Hippocrates on the blood-vascular system indicate that even with the evidence that Galen selects for his own purposes, some problems of consistency arise.

A cynic might remark that one of the advantages of using Hippocrates as an ideal was that that allowed a good deal of room for manoeuvre in the interpretation of what he stood for. Galen certainly had nobler motives for focusing on Hippocrates, and yet to exploit that room for manoeuvre to the extent that Galen does certainly leads him into slipshod, verging at times on the downright unscrupulous, scholarship. The picture that Galen chose to present was one that suited his ambitions for the medical art and it has, it must be said, much that is worthy of admiration. No doubt it would be quite wrong to suggest that Galen first formed those ambitions and then looked round for a sufficiently 'flexible' authority in the past on whom to foist them retrospectively. On the other hand the converse extreme position has also to be rejected, namely that Galen's ideal of medicine is simply the distillation of his admiration for Hippocrates, an admiration conceived *prior to* those ambitions themselves. Obviously the two went hand in hand, the arrival at his picture of Hippocrates and the making concrete of his ambitions. At the same time so forceful is the rhetoric of Galen's presentation that we do well to remind ourselves not just of that very effort of interpretation that has gone

[67] The chief such discrepancies are discussed briefly in Lloyd, 1975.

[68] See, for example, *UP* IV, ch. 9, H I 213.9ff. (K III 290.16ff.), *De Anat. Admin.* VI, ch. 13, K II 581.1ff., *De Anat. Admin.* X, ch. 9, XII, ch. 2 and XV, ch. 1 (Duckworth, 1962: 65, 115, 224), K VIII 52.2ff., 494.10ff., 498.13ff.

[69] For a theory based on bile and phlegm, see, for example, *Aff.* ch. 1, L VI 208.7ff., *Morb.* I, ch. 2, L VI 142.13ff.: for a theory based on four principal humours identified as blood, phlegm, bile and water, see *Genit.* ch. 3, L VII 474.7ff., and *Morb.* IV, chh. 32 and 38, L VII 542.6ff., 556.7ff.

into the construction of the picture, but also of the particular personal motives Galen had for that interpretation. If Hippocrates had not existed, Galen would have had to invent him. But then, in a sense, he did.

REFERENCES

Brain, P. (1986) *Galen on Bloodletting* (Cambridge)

Deichgräber, K. (1973) *Pseudhippokrates Über die Nahrung*, Akademie der Wissenschaften und der Literatur, Mainz, Abhandlungen der geistes- und sozialwissenschaftlichen Klasse, Jahrgang 1973, 3 (Wiesbaden)

De Lacy, P. H. (1972) 'Galen's Platonism', *American Journal of Philology* 93: 27–39

Diller, H. (1936–7) 'Eine stoisch-pneumatische Schrift im Corpus Hippocraticum', *Sudhoffs Archiv für Geschichte der Medizin und der Naturwissenschaften*, 29: 178–95

(1974) 'Empirie und Logos: Galen's Stellung zu Hippokrates und Platon', in *Studia Platonica: Festschrift H. Gundert*, edd. K. Döring and W. Kullmann (Amsterdam), 227–38

Duckworth, W. L. H. (1962) *Galen On Anatomical Procedures: The Later Books*, transl. W. L. H. Duckworth, edd. M. C. Lyons and B. Towers (Cambridge)

Furley, D. J. and Wilkie, J. S. (1984) *Galen On Respiration and the Arteries* (Princeton)

Hankinson, R. J. (forthcoming) 'Galen's account of scientific knowledge', in *Proceedings of Madrid Galen conference*, March 1988, ed. J. A. Lopez Ferez (Madrid)

Harig, G. and Kollesch, J. (1975) 'Galen und Hippokrates', in *La Collection hippocratique et son rôle dans l'histoire de la médecine*, edd. L. Bourgey and J. Jouanna (Leiden), 257–74

Joly, R. (1975) 'Remarques sur le "De Alimento" pseudo-hippocratique', in *Le Monde grec*, edd. J. Bingen, G. Cambier and G. Nachtergael (Bruxelles), 271–6

Lloyd, G. E. R. (1975) 'The Hippocratic Question', *Classical Quarterly* 25: 171–92

(1987) *The Revolutions of Wisdom* (Berkeley)

(1989) 'Scholarship, authority and argument in Galen's *Quod Animi Mores*', in *Le Opere psicologiche di Galeno*, edd. P. Manuli and M. Vegetti (Napoli), 11–42

Lonie, I. M. (1964) 'Erasistratus, the Erasistrateans, and Aristotle', *Bulletin of the History of Medicine* 38: 426–43

Manuli, P. (1983) 'Lo stile del commento', in *Formes de pensée dans la collection hippocratique* edd. F. Lasserre and P. Mudry (Genève), 471–80

(1986) 'Traducibilità e molteplicità dei linguaggi nel *De placitis* di Galeno', in *Storiografia e Dossografia nella filosofia antica*, ed. G. Cambiano (Torino), 245–65

Pingree, D. (1963) 'Astronomy and astrology in India and Iran', *Isis* 54: 229–46

(1978) 'History of mathematical astronomy in India', in *Dictionary of Scientific Biography*, XV, ed. C. C. Gillespie (New York), 533–633

(1981) *Jyotiḥśāstra* (A History of Indian literature 6.4) (Wiesbaden)

Smith, W. D. (1979) *The Hippocratic Tradition* (Ithaca, New York)

Staden, H. von (1982) 'Hairesis and heresy: the case of the *haireseis iatrikai*', in *Jewish and Christian Self-Definition*, III, edd. B. F. Meyer and E. P. Saunders (London), 76–100, 199–206

(1989) *Herophilus: The Art of Medicine in Early Alxandria* (Cambridge)

Vegetti, M. (1986) 'Tradizione e verità: Forme della storiografia filosofico-scientifica nel *De placitis* di Galeno', in *Storiografia e Dossografia nella filosofia antica*, ed. G. Cambiano (Torino), 227–44

18

THE INVENTION OF NATURE

Nothing, one might think, could be more natural or more straightforward than the Greeks' conception of nature. After all, does not our own concept of the contrast between the natural and the supernatural stand in direct descent from the ideas of the Greeks? Do we not, thereby, owe to the Greek conception of nature one of the fundamental principles upon which science is based – the science we think of, so naturally, as *natural* science? Does not the concept of nature encapsulate the condition of the possibility of science, that of the intelligibility of the cosmos?

If we pursue such a line of thought, we might – naturally – be led to expect that most of what there is to be said about the Greek conception of nature would consist of an extended testimonial to our indebtedness, a pious rehearsal of what we like to call our legacy. Surely there is not much *new* to be said on that topic – to which I must say immediately that I am very conscious that a vast amount has indeed already been said on it.

But maybe not everything, and maybe not what needs saying on the subject today. For despite the undeniable fact that we are indeed indebted to our Greek past, the line of thinking that I have just sketched out is seriously flawed. Two elementary points will serve as a first indication of this. First it is not as if there ever were *the* Greek concept of nature, by which I mean just the one. To talk of such is to bracket the enormous differences between one philosophical position and another, and between philosophy and what passed as common opinions, as also the divergences between one period and another. It is to talk as if we could blithely generalise over Homer and Proclus, or even over Plato and Aristotle: and that is before we begin to pay attention to the chorus of voices of those who – then as now – invoked the natural to contrast it with the deviant, to justify their own particular attitudes, beliefs and behaviour, including, not least, their prejudices on gender difference and on sexual practices, where what passes for natural to insiders appears to outsiders as all too obviously culturally determined. What a writer such as Artemidorus tells us about what some Greeks thought *natural* sexual intercourse is enough to jolt one out of any unreflecting assumption that the Greeks were very much like us – though that is not the subject I shall concentrate on today.

Secondly, if we approach the Greek material not through our term 'nature', but through their term φύσις and their term for its study, namely φυσική, it soon becomes evident just how strained it is to assimilate what they did under that rubric with what we now think of as physics. If we turn to the treatise called the *Physics* of Aristotle in the expectation of finding anything *we* would recognise as physics, or even anything we would immediately recognise as the ancestor of our physics, we shall be disappointed. Instead of dealing with fundamental particles, or even with matter and energy, Aristotle devotes much of his time to problems to do with causation, time, infinity, continuity. *They* seem to *us* to belong not to physics but to metaphysics and philosophy of science – and to understand how that came about poses quite a challenge, though again that is not one that I can take up today.

So my principal task is to try to recover some of the original, and at points quite alien, complexities of the subject of Greek view*s* (in the plural) about nature. Let me begin, nevertheless, with what may seem some of the more familiar aspects. Let us begin with some of that natural science, though we shall have to move – for the second part of our discussion – from science to politics, and then, in a third, from politics back to some fundamental questions in metaphysics and philosophy of science. 'Scientific, political, speculative', it will be recalled, was how Spencer categorised one of his collections of essays. That suits me very well today, for certainly a study of Greek views of nature must span all three. My aim throughout will be not just to report some ancient Greek thoughts, but to focus more particularly on the contexts of their thinking. We must consider not just what they said, but why they said it (in so far as that can be recovered). Whom were they trying to persuade, and what grounds had they to hope to be successful in their persuasion: what were their explicit arguments and how far did they rely on implicit assumptions?

So I turn first to some of that seemingly familiar natural science, and the first point that needs stressing – to *de*familiarise ourselves with this material – is that there was nothing intrinsic in the Greek conception of the *naturalness* of natural phenomena. On the contrary, that idea had to be *invented*, and the most important factor of which we can be sure concerning the circumstances of its invention is the *context of polemic* that surrounded it. Let me elaborate those two points briefly at this stage.

That the idea required invention can be seen most easily by reflecting on its absence from the earliest Greek writings that we have. True, the term φύσις occurs in a famous passage in the *Odyssey* (10.302ff.) where Hermes shows Odysseus a plant, though whether the primary sense here is 'nature'/'character' or more simply 'growth' is disputed. But to have the idea of the nature of some particular object is not to have the general conception of a *domain of nature* encompassing all natural phenomena. Besides, the plant in question in the *Odyssey* is a *magic* one, μῶλυ. Of course no one should expect Homer or Hesiod to discourse on natural science. But it is not just that they do not have occasion to deliver lectures on physics: that would be merely a matter of what they *omit* to say. It is rather what they actually *do* say that is indicative. They are, after all, very free in referring to what *we* might take to be cases of the suspension of the normal regularities of nature. This is high literature, to be sure, and Circe's turning Odysseus' companions into pigs has a symbolic appropriateness that transcends the difficulties that the literal-minded may feel when they ask the question of how precisely she did it: what kind of alchemy was this? Again Hesiod's *Theogony* populates the world with a wild array of hundred-armed creatures, fifty-headed dogs, Chimaeras, Hydras and the like, which belong to no zoological menagerie but to the no doubt equally vivid representations of the world of the imagination.

We should certainly not imagine that Homer and Hesiod and the audiences for whom they composed were somehow unaware of the regularities of what we call natural phenomena. It did not take Aristotle to point out that a human begets a human. It is just inconceivable that Hesiod's contemporaries (or anyone else) were somehow in two minds about the need to sow seed if they wanted corn, even though many no doubt believed that the success of the crop depended also on Zeus, and even though it was only sensible – Hesiod thought – to follow the advice he offered not just on when to plough or to shear the sheep, but also about how to avoid the anger of the gods. In that sense some notion that corresponds to nature is assumed – I dare say – universally. But there is all the difference in the world between an implicit assumption and the *explicit* concept.

Nor, once explicit concepts begin to be elaborated in this field, is there any inevitability that the phenomena will come to be grouped in such a way as to make the concept of *nature* central. It so happens that there are certain similarities between our own ideas of nature and some ancient Greek notions of φύσις: and that is no mere coincidence, of course, but reflects more or less determinate historical influences. However, a glance at the very different but also very sophisticated concepts developed by the ancient Chinese, for example – where *we* will tend to interpret them as referring to what *we* call nature – will serve to make the fundamental point. While Joseph Needham in his pioneering explorations of Chinese science in *Science and Civilisation in China* has much to say on their ideas concerning nature, no less than six primary concepts as well as several further subsidiary ones are in play in the texts on which he is commenting – where the more literal renderings of the key terms would be more like Heaven or Sky (tian), pattern (li), things (wu), the way (dao), as well as human nature or disposition (xing) and spontaneity (zi ran, literally 'self so', the term which with the prefix da, 'great', comes eventually to form the word used in modern Chinese for nature as in natural science).

So we have two contrasts to bear in mind, not just one: the first that between making certain assumptions concerning certain regularities and having an explicit concept or concepts, and the second within the concepts used in mapping those regularities. The people who were chiefly responsible for explicitly developing some of the characteristically Greek ideas about φύσις as a domain of nature were the natural philosophers as they were called (φυσικοί) and the early medical writers. The philosophers usually take pride of place in the discussion of this development, and certainly the earliest of them, Thales in the early sixth century B.C., Anaximander and Anaximenes somewhat later, antedate the earliest medical texts we have. But while we have plenty of secondary evidence in the so-called doxographers that suggests that the early natural philosophers went in for naturalistic explanations of natural phenomena in a big way, there are well known difficulties in evaluating this material. We do not even know how far this emphasis reflects the interests of the natural philosophers themselves, or how far it merely represents those of the doxographers – and the need *they* experienced to have *some* theory they could attribute to each early thinker on the various items that were later treated as standard examples of problematic phenomena requiring explanation. As it is, we are presented with a bewildering list of theories, fifteen or so different explanations of lightning and thunder, eleven of earthquakes, twelve of comets and shooting stars, but we are generally *not* given the grounds for them nor the contexts in which they were proposed.

That is true also of one of the few early cases where we can be fairly sure that what we have is the words of the philosopher himself, not a reformulation of them. This is the excerpt from one of Xenophanes' poems we are given by a scholiast to Homer, to the effect that 'she whom men call Iris also is a cloud, purple and red and yellow to behold'. Now that does not seem a particularly inspired suggestion, even if we make allowances for Xenophanes as a very earlier debutant natural scientist: it is not even as if a rainbow obviously resembles a cloud. But it may be that the thrust of Xenophanes' point (and of other such ideas attributed to other early philosophers) is not so much what is said as what is implicitly denied. Iris – the message is – is no messenger of the Gods, no omen for the future: even though we should beware of assuming that every time some Greek before Xenophanes saw a rainbow they automatically thought of it as a portent.

Yet if that *may have* been the thrust of Xenophanes' point, that is just conjecture on our part. Yet there is no need to guess when it comes to the medical writers' similar ideas and explanations, for there we are dealing with whole original texts and they provide us with all the evidence we need to evaluate not just the basis for the explanations proposed, but also the contexts and the motivations for their proposal. We can give some answers to the questions I said we should bear in mind, of whom they were trying to persuade, and why, and what the grounds were on which they hoped to be persuasive. One *principal* context in which nature comes to be invoked in the medical writers is in relation to the claim that *all* diseases are natural. Against those who maintained or assumed either that particular types of disease are sacred, or that particular incidences of diseases are signs of the gods' displeasure (as when Apollo sends the plague on the Achaeans in the first book of the *Iliad*), some of the Hippocratic writers flatly denied that gods or demons had anything to do with diseases or with their cures.

The best-known example is the treatise called *On the Sacred Disease* which is entirely devoted to the claim that that disease, epilepsy, is natural. There are many interesting details to this writer's arguments that I have discussed at length elsewhere, but I shall concentrate here on the strategy of his attack. It is nonsense, he suggests, to claim that epilepsy is caused by the gods, for every kind of disease has its own nature, φύσις, and its own cause, πρόφασις. Epilepsy is no exception and the writer offers his own naturalistic account of what causes epileptic fits: I shall come back to that. Actually it is positively impious to think of the gods causing diseases. Moreover it is not just that this is nonsense – a mistaken inference, he suggests, from the startling character of epileptic attacks. There is more to it than that. The people who go around claiming that it *is* a sacred disease, that they can diagnose which deity is responsible for which variety, and that they can administer the appropriate ritual purification for each, are charlatans and quacks who are in it for the money and who exploit the gullibility of the public.

The obvious but important point about this evidence is that we are dealing with no merely intellectual debate, no mere abstract, theoretical discussion about the nature of nature. On the contrary, this text gives us one side of a bitter controversy between rival traditions of medicine. This is not just a matter of Hippocratic rationalists on the one hand, purifiers on the other. The situation is far more complex than that. To start with, the Hippocratic authors may all invoke natural causes, but they otherwise disagree among themselves fundamentally not just on questions of pathology and treatment, but also on the issue of the status and methodology of the art of medicine itself. On the traditionalist side of the debate there was not just one strand of religious medicine, but more, and less, established kinds, ranging from the medicine practised in the shrines of Asclepius, all the way to the itinerant sellers of charms and incantations who are the main, and softer, target of *On the Sacred Disease*.

The fundamental point is that *no* ancient healer could justify his or her right to practise with an appeal to legally recognised qualifications. There were no teaching hospitals; there were no hospitals. There was nothing remotely equivalent to the hallowed initials, M.D., F.R.C.P. In classical antiquity, in Greece, there were not even any legal sanctions that could be invoked against medical practitioners of any kind (though the situation changed in this regard in the Roman empire). But this means that every style of healing competed on equal terms with every other (and temple medicine, we know, was as popular as any). It is all very well our Hippocratic author remarking that the purifiers were in it for the money: he was himself. We know, then, whom this and other Hippocratic authors were trying to persuade: they include potential clients and potential pupils as much as anyone who might be interested in joining a theoretical – philosophical or scientific – debate.

We can, too, evaluate the grounds and justification for his counter-claims to the ones the purifiers made. His explanation of the sacred disease is that it is caused by the blocking of the veins in the brain, which he says happens especially to the phlegmatic – the bilious are less affected. That last point gives him an additional argument that it was nothing to do with gods, for they would not discriminate thus between phlegmatic and bilious constitutions. But this explanation of epilepsy is, of course, quite fanciful. Worse: so too are the anatomical theories with which he backs it up, his equally imaginary account of the blood-vessels in the body – I shall spare you the details. Worse still, he appears to claim, against the purifiers, that he has the right technique to effect a cure – of epilepsy as of most other diseases. This turns out to be a matter of controlling the temperature and humidity of the body by regimen (food and exercise), and this too, so far as epilepsy is concerned, must be considered pie in the sky.

Nature was, no doubt, invoked by medical writers and natural philosophers on some occasions when something like a plausible explanatory theory was available. Eclipses would be a case in point. But, as my example shows, on many others it was a mere act of faith – we might even say bluff – to claim to be able to understand, let alone to control, the phenomena in question.

My argument thus far is that some of those who insisted on the category of the natural used it to demarcate and justify their style of inquiry, their methodology, in contrast to those of rivals whom they were hoping to put out of business. We cannot be sure that Xenophanes had it in for diviners (though he certainly criticised on several grounds a number of prestigious professions which were rival claimants to excellence). But some Hippocratic authors used nature to rule out any possibility of any *super*natural interference in diseases. The concept of the natural had its attractions for them precisely because it enabled a wedge to be driven between *their* medical practice and that of the competition. Their rivals, the Hippocratics would claim, make an elementary category mistake. All diseases are natural phenomena, each has its nature, its own causes, its own natural explanation. However, the grounds those same Hippocratic writers themselves had to justify their own positive claims to have understood those causes were often tenuous or non-existent.

Again if one may interject a Chinese comparison and contrast to point up features of the Greek experience, there were Chinese too who were as critical as any Greeks of certain traditional Chinese beliefs and practices that they considered to be groundless or based on superstitious fears. But they did not attempt to defeat whole classes of opponents by invoking a category of the natural that ruled out what is contrary to nature. Rather they dealt with error, folly, superstition, as they encountered them – by exposing their consequences, for example – without recourse to some general categorial principle concerning the natures of things which was supposed to secure a firm distinction between the investigable and the superstitious – except that the Greeks' expressed confidence that everything had its nature and its causes generally lived uneasily with a fundamentally shaky grasp of what these actually were.

But to those criticisms of mine of the Hippocratics a counter might be offered that might go like this. Maybe the Hippocratic theorists could not explain all or even many diseases, and could not cure them either, and maybe most of the Presocratic natural philosophers were all at sea in their explanations of rainbows and comets and earthquakes. That point might be conceded. But, the counter might be, at least their explanations were of the *right type*. Eventually more and better explanations would be given: but they would share the essential characteristic of the earliest hesitant attempts, namely that they appealed purely to natural factors. So if the expression of what *could* be explained *then was* an act of faith (even with an element of bluff thrown in), it was a *legitimate* act of faith – in the *promise* of delivery of the new style of wisdom, even if that new style had not *actually* delivered much at the time the original faith was expressed.

That counter has some force, but its main weakness is obvious. It was not as if the justification could reasonably take the form that the act of faith was legitimate because the way ahead – for science – was clear, in the sense that the path to follow was. It could not take that form for the simple reason that – except perhaps in the broadest possible terms – the path that science *should* follow was anything but agreed. Even those who shared a view of the importance and desirability of the goal of understanding nature were locked in bitter dispute over what would constitute such understanding – and accordingly also over how to set about securing it. I shall have more to say on this at the end.

More immediately, the invocation of the category of the natural in such a manner as we have seen in the early philosophers and medical writers depends, for its plausibility, on having a reasonably clear answer to the question of what that category included. At first sight the answer may seem simple: the answer must be everything, where 'everything' ranges over all material objects, their properties and characteristics. But three problems immediately present themselves, of varying degrees of difficulty, the first to do with exceptions to the rule, the second to do with human nature, and the third with the contrast between nature and culture (or as the Greeks said, φύσις and νόμος) – where the last two will take us into the second main section of our inquiry, into politics.

As for exceptions to the rule – my first difficulty – the point for the moment is straightforward and we can be brief. As Aristotle insisted, what is natural comprises what is true always or for the most part. An explanation, to be an explanation, must bring the particular explanandum in question under a general law and Aristotle will see proper explanations as making reference to the formal cause, the essence, the nature of the object or event investigated. But if that does splendidly for the regularities of nature – when a human being begets a human being – what about breaches to those regularities, monsters, sports? They had, of course, quite often been grist to the mill of those who saw the hands of the divine or demonic at work in the world – so the natural philosophers had better have *some* account that they could offer on this type of question. Aristotle's first-stage answer is to insist on a distinction. 'According to nature', κατὰ φύσιν, in one sense picks out the regularities, the law-like – where the contrast is with what is contrary to nature, παρὰ φύσιν, in the sense of an exception to the rule. But the exceptions are still not *super*natural – not παρὰ φύσιν in that other sense – for they arise, for example, from the chance intersection of two or more causal chains each of which is a perfectly good example of some regularity. Chance just is the name for such an intersection and there is no more to it than that. Nature evinces regularities and that is what entitles us to speak of the essential characteristics of things as their natures: but those regularities are not exceptionless, even if the exceptions themselves do not *stand outside* the domain of nature (for nothing does that). There will be more to say about other aspects of this problem later, but as a first-stage answer it may suffice for now.

But that problem is nothing like so severe as those that arise in connection with the issue of *human* nature. It was, perhaps, one of the strengths of the pagan Greek view of humans that there was no question of human beings *not* being part of nature. Humans are living creatures, ζῷα, and clearly belong to the same genus as all other animals. Where other cultures and religions may so stress the *gap* between humans and animals that 'animals' do not include 'humans', the pre-Christian Greeks generally assumed co-membership in a common genus.

One asymmetry was, however, quite widespread. The animal series was often used as a template to apprehend and describe the differences between human characters. This was not a formally elaborated part of any natural philosopher's theory, but rather a common and deeply ingrained way of thinking and talking about the world. One of the ways animals were 'good to think with' was as providing a set of models for human characters – the fox for cunning, the lion for courage, the boar for steadfastness, the deer for timidity and so on. But one feature of this way of thinking and talking that stands out is that, on the animal side, it is distinct species and genera that provide the markers, while on the human side, what is thus marked is character types *within* the *one* (human) species. That tends to stress and enlarge the differences, to suggest more permanent character traits in humans than would otherwise be assumed – as if Ajax were *always* like a wild boar. That is partly *why* the animal series is so used (and was so used not just by the ancient Greeks, of course), but we should be clear that that use is not neutral, nor entirely innocent, in its implications for our understanding of human behaviour. No doubt to make sense of one another's behaviour we need to assume some more or less stable character traits. Yet with some uses of animal comparisons it is not just stability, but fixity or even unmodifiability that is assumed: for the leopard cannot change his spots.

Nor was it just human character traits that were sometimes thus type-cast. Another context in which the Greeks favour a strong differentiation within humans is that of their physical constitutions. Indeed this notion interacts with the differentiation of human characters in the context of theories of the humours. The phlegmatic, the bilious, the sanguine, the melancholic man or woman were assumed to possess not just stable character dispositions, but also (as it were) different biochemistries. To be sure, that is mainly a development of the post-classical period. But differentiation between the physical constitutions of different groups already figures in the fifth century B.C., in such classic discussions as that of the different natures, φύσιες, of the Egyptians, Libyans, Scythians, Greeks and others in the Hippocratic treatise *On Airs, Waters, Places*. As that writer puts it (ch. 13) there are human natures that are like wooded, well-watered mountains, others like light, dry land, others like marshy meadows, others like a bare, parched earth. This writer happens to believe that everything grows to a greater size and beauty in Asia (ch. 12), even though the Greeks have superior characters. But the potentially ominous racialist implications of the type of thesis he advances are obvious, even though, let me repeat, whatever their sense of their own superiority to Barbarians and to slaves, and their readiness to deploy a rich vocabulary of abuse for those – including other Greeks – unlike themselves, the ancient Greeks generally were clear that inferior humans too are still members of the same, human species.

The writer of that Hippocratic treatise holds that while human physique is largely determined by ecology, human character depends in part on another factor. What, I asked earlier, was to be included under φύσις, nature? I first answered that everything was, all material objects – and that was the answer the natural philosophers needed in order to squeeze out the category of the *super*natural. But of course in the sphere of human behaviour φύσις was regularly opposed to its standard antonym, νόμος, covering customs and conventions as well as laws. It is this factor that *On Airs, Waters, Places* appeals to in order to explain how it is that members of the same γένος or race, brought up in the same ecological conditions, may nevertheless behave quite differently. This happens, he says, when they *live under different political systems*. As clear evidence for this (a μέγα τεκμήριον) he cites the fact that where the inhabitants of Asia are *not* ruled by tyrants, they are the most warlike of peoples (ch. 16), even though bravery is not, by nature, part of their character (cf. ch. 24).

Yet as is well known, just how the antithesis between nature and convention was to be taken was itself enormously controversial in antiquity, a topic on which many a modern book and article has been written. From one point of view the contrast was crucial as the chief means of securing what (on *that* view) the domain of science is to include. For one type of aspiring natural scientist 'nature' encompasses what holds of natural phenomena, including of humans as the animals they are, while 'custom' stands for society-specific modes of behaviour. Broadly, φύσις falls to science, νόμος to sociology or political philosophy. Yet that was far from being the only point of view expressed, either on where the dividing line between the two came, or on the moral and political connotations and implications of the two terms.

For some, νόμος was *mere* custom and convention, the rules and regulations that a person with the power to do so will ignore – or manipulate to their own advantage. Social codes in all their variety, Callicles says in Plato's *Gorgias* (492C), are a nonsense, φλυαρία: they are set up by the weak (483B–C) but according to nature it is *just* for the stronger to have more than the weak. Thrasymachus in the *Republic* (338E) takes a different line on the origins of laws, when he puts it that each interest group, once it gets into power, fixes them to suit their own advantage. But while there are different developments and formulations of the point in yet other texts in Plato (in his account of the atheists in *Laws* X, for instance), in Thucydides (the Melian debate, 5.85ff.), and in the sophist Antiphon, a common theme found in many variations is that the only universally valid principle is that might is right.

But against that group of positions there were those who adopted a more positive evaluation of νόμος in the sense of law, as the guarantor of justice and, precisely, what marks humans out from other animals. Justice and shame, the sophist Protagoras is made to say in Plato (*Prt.* 322C), are given to all humans, and it is they that provide the basis for civilised social life. And there are others again who resist too sharp a contrast between the two terms, not least Plato himself, who sees the same demiurgic intelligence at work in nature as should be present also in the ideal human *law*-giver.

No agreement obtained, therefore, either on whether *both* nature and law are charged with moral significance, or on that significance, if they are. While for some, we said, nature is *not* the domain of moral or evaluative judgements, for many others it was, even though how they cashed that out varied all the way from the view that might is right to the notion that there are, in some sense, unwritten laws of nature – moral laws, that is. The whole controversy is, of course, often associated with the challenge to traditional moral values for which those favourite bogeymen of Plato, the sophists, are often held to be primarily responsible. But whatever the degree of their involvement, let alone responsibility, it would clearly be wrong to assume that this was *just* a sophistic controversy, as the continuation of some themes in Aristotle amply shows. It is time now to explore his contribution to the issues in some detail.

Aristotle takes as firm a line as any on the investigability of nature – the topic we began with. We have seen that he *dis*allows the *super*natural with an insistence on the distinction between it and what is merely an exception to a general rule: the former is not, the latter is, countenanced. He gives us, too, a definition of nature as what has an inner source of movement and rest, and he sets out with great lucidity the task of the natural philosopher in giving causal explanations of four types, formal, final, efficient, material. The way in which the concept of nature is deployed in the heart of his political philosophy is, then, all the more striking. For there, as is so well known, humans are defined as by *nature* political animals, more strictly as animals that live in city-states. Moreover in a further notorious section of *Politics* book I, slavery is defended as a *natural* institution. Again even certain types of economic exchange – those that do not involve wealth-getting for its own sake – are said to be natural. It is not that Aristotle ignores the differences between moral and political philosophy on the one hand, physics and natural philosophy on the other. On the contrary, he points them out repeatedly. Thus the sphere of *moral* excellence is quite distinct from that of merely natural excellence, for moral excellence depends on (moral) choice, προαίρεσις, which only adult humans possess, not the other animals and not even children. Yet there are these in no sense merely figurative appeals to nature in his political philosophy.

Coming to terms with this at first sight quite alien feature of his thought is no easy task; but there are arguments to evaluate as well as deep-seated assumptions, not to say prejudices, with which to grapple. That humans are political animals (to use that conventional translation) is arrived at not as a result of some piece of Academic scholastic definition-mongering of the type that gave us the shattering insight that man is a rational two-legged animal. Rather it is the conclusion of a piece of analytic reasoning. The argument takes an evolutionary form, though Aristotle is not committed to all the evolutionary aspects of the hypothesis. All animals naturally desire to reproduce. Like other animals, male and female humans naturally form associations for reproductive purposes: so that the basic mode of association, the household (οἰκία) is (as we might put it) founded on biological needs. But the household is not self-sufficient: to fulfil more than their daily, ephemeral, needs several households agglomerate first into villages, then into more complete or perfect associations, a process that culminates in the πόλις, the city-state, which, we are told, *came to be* for the sake of life, but *is* for the sake of the good life. So the πόλις is by nature, φύσει, given that the first associations are: for *it* is *their* end, τέλος, and nature is an end. Whatever we may think about where the argument ends, some modern commentators would agree at least to its beginning, to the proposition that humans are social animals with a minimum size for a viable human community.

His argument concerning slavery shares some of the same features. He is well aware of an alternative view, the idea that it is merely by convention, νόμῳ that slaves are slaves, and that naturally, φύσει, there is no distinction between slave and free. Evidently when the naturalness of what he *claims* to be natural had been flatly denied, he has that much more of an obligation to *show* its naturalness, and he concedes to the opposition straight away that some do become enslaved unjustly and are slaves merely by convention or law. However, that does not lead him to make any concessions at all as to the general principle, that the distinction between master and slave *is* natural, a principle he supports, first, by citing a battery of proportional analogies. Master is to slave as soul is to body, or as old is to young, or as male to female. Yet (as so often) the argument is not merely one by analogy, for all those paired relationships exemplify the generic distinction to be found (he says) in every composite whole constituted of parts, namely that between what rules and what is ruled.

Here too then the determination of what is natural involves a biological and a sociobiological dimension, but the way the sociobiological data at Aristotle's command are put to work is remarkable. He can, to be sure, claim that the distinction between soul and body is to be found in all living creatures, for 'soul' just picks out what makes the living creature the *living* thing it is. But as for his representation of the relationship between males and females, Aristotle the zoologist knows very well that there are plenty of species of animals where the females are stronger, bigger, more dominant, and longer-lived than the males, and some too (such as the bear and panther) where they are more courageous. If we add up the exceptions that Aristotle allows to the rule that males are longer-lived than females, they amount to a considerable list, one that includes most of the ovipara and larvipara. Yet that does not stop him from reiterating that naturally, φύσει, males are longer-lived than females.

There is a recurrent move, here, in both arguments, that relates to a fundamental tension in Aristotle's conception of nature. On the one hand the natural is equated with what is true always or for the most part. On the other, what is natural is the goal, the end, the ideal. Thus it is *better*, Aristotle claims, for right to be differentiated from left, and again male from female, and again master from slave. But the first of each of those pairs is the τέλος or end, the second *for the sake of* that end. From the point of view of what just is the case, females are as *regular* as males, of course. But from the point of view of their function or capacity, they are, he says, like natural deformities, natural (no doubt) because regular, but deformities because Aristotle is convinced that they are to be defined by an *in*capacity, the incapacity to concoct the blood into semen (viz. in the way males do). From the point of view of regularities he might just as well have defined males by *their* incapacity to produce menses and to give birth: but Aristotle would not dream of doing so.

The nature of the species is, then, captured by the mature – male – specimen. But nature is a goal not just in an intraspecific perspective, but also in certain interspecific ones (though this is more controversial). Throughout Aristotle's zoology the human species is the yardstick by which other animals are measured. Anomalies such as species where the females are longer-lived do not shake his belief – cannot shake his belief – that *naturally* (now in the sense of the ideal) the male is longer-lived – for that is true, he believes (and it was true in his day), of humans. Similarly it is better for right (the side from which movement begins) to be differentiated from left: but when he encounters animals with no strong differentiation between the two sides, that is a mark of their inferiority. Again he defines upper as the direction from which food is taken in – and accepts the consequence that plants, fed from their roots, are upside down. In humans alone, indeed, the upper parts are directed towards the upper part of the universe. In humans *alone*, he is prepared to say (*De Partibus Animalium* 656a10ff.), the *natural* parts are *according* to nature. What is normal or natural in the animal kingdom is evidently no matter, here, of counting heads or species, but arrived at by reflection on the principles instantiated in the animals assumed to be *superior*, or more particularly in the species assumed to be supreme, namely humans.

The application of similar ideas in the *Politics* is particularly blatant. Humans are the *only* species of animals in which the distinction between master and slave is found. They are the only πόλις-forming animals, too, though other species are gregarious and are described as political, πολιτικά, in the loose or general sense of *social* animals. But these unique features of human beings do not cause Aristotle to hesitate to attach the characteristic 'natural' to them – rather than treating them as belonging to the νόμος, law, convention, culture, side of the dichotomy. The uniqueness of the features in question does not deter him because what is natural is here equated with the ideal. The truly natural specimen is the animal in its prime. The truly natural species, the species that is most in accord with nature as what is capable of fulfilling the most potentialities for the good life, is the human species.

There is, or course, much more to Aristotle's political arguments than I can indicate here, including much of his analysis for which no claim as to the naturalness of human social institutions is entered. But I hope to have said enough to bring out one fundamental feature of his use of the concept of nature, and not just in politics, namely that while it may often appear merely descriptive (where it corresponds to what is just usually the case) it is also and just as frequently profoundly normative. We should be clear that there is nothing covert about this. It is not that Aristotle slips unwittingly into some crass confusion. On the contrary: it is an explicit and avowed part of Aristotle's whole programme of inquiry in *every* area of thought that explanations should be teleological in character and include references to the good, where this is appropriate. It is true that he explicitly *denies*, in his zoology, that *everything* (without exception) has a final cause, that is that all the parts of animals serve some end. Some parts are as they are *not* because they serve some good directly, but merely because they are the by-products of other processes (though *they* do). He specifies the gall-bladder as an example, the end-product of the processes of digestion, and if they certainly serve an obvious good – the survival of the creature no less – not all their residues do. However, the natural philosopher can, and Aristotle insists should, consider the goods that objects and events serve, and where these are present, they form part of the *explanations* of the objects and events in question. There can be no question of giving a satisfactory account of the blood-vessels, say, if just their structure and constitution are considered. Their function, the good they serve (which Aristotle thinks of in terms of nourishing the body) has to be included also, a principle he applies not just in zoology but throughout his natural science and beyond – notably within his political philosophy as we have seen.

So this takes me now to the third and final subject area I identified at the outset, the metaphysical and philosophical assumptions that underlie the various competing and conflicting Greek conceptions of nature. It was Aristotle's view, and one he shared with Plato, that the natures of things include their goals, the good they fulfil or actualise. On this view, the natural philosopher, we said, must consider and include, indeed *especially* include, teleological explanations. But that was not the only view put forward in classical antiquity. Much to the chagrin of Plato and of Aristotle, there were those who pursued the goal of understanding the world on the basis of the directly opposed, anti-teleological, assumption – namely that the *only* explanations that are to count as explanations are those that relate to the physical (we often say mechanical) interactions of things. The atomists' programme was represented by Plato as atheistical (and by Aristotle sometimes as appealing to mere chance). But on *their own* terms, *they* sought to investigate the necessary causal connections of things.

Nor was this the only fundamental disagreement that separated opposing schools of thought, whether among theorists who agreed at least on the possibility of understanding, or between them and others who denied that very possibility. There were, for instance, radical sceptics for whom it is futile to attempt to comprehend nature. These sceptics were careful not to say that it is *impossible* to comprehend nature, for to *assert* that would be to be as dogmatic as their opponents. Rather *no* assertions as to how nature is, nor about the underlying realities or hidden causes of things, can be made. These radical sceptics content themselves with saying how things appear. The honey appears sweet: but as to its being sweet or not, on that judgement should be suspended.

But even among those who rejected scepticism and maintained the possibility and the value of the investigation of nature, there were disputes that stretch beyond the major quarrel between teleologists and anti-teleologists that I have already referred to. This is yet another vast topic to which I cannot attempt to do justice here. But just two aspects may be noted briefly.

First, on an issue that sees Plato and Aristotle on different sides, there was a question of the admissibility of change and coming-to-be in what is investigable. In Plato's Theory of Forms the range of what is fully knowable does not extend beyond that of unchanging being. Particulars that come to be and are subject to change are then assigned to the realm of opinion as contrasted with that of knowledge. Now Aristotle shares Plato's reservations about the possibility of attaining knowledge of the particular *as the particular it is*: he agrees that understanding is of the universal. But he is clearer as to the investigability of changing objects and more positive on the status of particulars. The regularities that the natural philosopher reveals are the regularities instantiated by physical objects, not (as in some formulations in Plato) merely imitated by them. For Aristotle, as I have already remarked, nature is indeed defined as a *principle* of change. While you and I, natural objects that we are, indeed change, that does not diminish our claim to substancehood: indeed, of course, in the terminology of the *Categories* we are primary substances.

The second debate involves a larger cast of characters but again sees Plato and Aristotle on different sides – on the question of the relations between physics (the study of nature) and mathematics. For a claim to full understanding to be sustained does it or does it not have to have a mathematical form or be expressible mathematically? For Plato, certainly, mathematics is superior to the study of becoming, though itself inferior to dialectic – and we should not exaggerate the extent to which Plato was clear about a programme of mathematising physics. But for many practitioners in the exact sciences it was precisely through the mathematisation of the phenomena that the underlying regularities were to be revealed. That was the great strength of what we correctly call the mathematical astronomy of antiquity, and of Archimedes' statics and hydrostatics, as also of such other exact, mathematical sciences as optics and harmonics. Yet for Aristotle the priorities between physics and mathematics are clear. Not for him the view that it is only what is mathematisable that can be fully understood, and if the rest of physics could not be, so much the worse for physics. His position is that the truths that mathematics reveals are truths *about* the physical realities. Mathematics deploys a powerful technique of abstraction, to be sure, but its subject-matter is no separate realm of mathematical entities but, precisely, the mathematical properties of *physical* objects.

I issued warnings about generalising about the Greek view of nature and I have put a bewildering variety of ideas before you. But it is time now to take stock. I began by referring to a naïve view that might suppose that the Greek concept of nature is natural. By now you will have some idea of how controversial it was – I mean among the Greeks themselves. My argument has been that the theorists we have been studying did not (so much) discover nature – like Columbus hitting America. Rather they created, they invented, their own distinctive and divergent ideas, often in direct and explicit confrontation with their rivals. The concept was forged in controversy, notably as the underpinning to the claims made by new styles of wisdom in their attempts to outbid more traditional kinds. The paradox was that (as some have said of mythology) the idea of nature was supposed to stand simply for what is there, for what can be taken for granted. Yet what that comprised was repeatedly contested, not just so far as the natural world in general went, but also as far as human nature is concerned. For some the domain of natural science was sharply contrasted with that of human culture, and nature was opposed to art as well as to convention. But for others nature was itself permeated with values, and a resource for moral philosophy, while for yet others it was rather a covert source of moralising where the category of the natural was used to legitimate a point of view specific to the interests of some particular group.

So if we stand back and ask what the Greeks stood for, the answer must be complex and almost every generalisation has to be qualified. One recurrent notion was that of humans as part of nature, humans as members of the animal kingdom, though special members no doubt. Another, of prime importance in one of the leading controversies, was the idea of the investigability of the causal relations of natural phenomena, although that was contested (by the sceptics), and even those who did not contest it disagreed about the character of the understanding that could be attained and the way to set about attaining it. In their enthusiasm for their own investigations, many ancients – as we have seen – promised a good deal more than they could deliver. If eventually there were to be some remarkable deliveries, we should not imagine that the ancients themselves had a clear and uncluttered vision of the way ahead, let alone were unanimous in their views. On the contrary, that was as disputed as many of the solutions to particular problems were. We have almost as many theories of nature as of...earthquakes. However, the value of those disputes is not diminished, but may if anything be increased, by the very range of disagreement – since that secured the exploration of the widest possible range of answers to the questions of the proper subject-matter of the study of nature, and the outer limits of its intelligibility. On that view, one of the most notable products of classical antiquity lies not so much in the actual natural scientific theories proposed, as in the competing theories of nature and of natural science themselves. It would be an exaggeration to say that the sole Greek contribution to science lies in the philosophy of science, but it can be argued that that was one of their more durable contributions.

But the paradoxicality of the situation deserves underlining. Nature was what was presupposed to be there to investigate: its supposed objective reality was what guaranteed the viability of the investigation. Yet what that vaunted objective reality consisted in was contested in every conceivable respect. If nature was invoked as a rallying cry for the new natural science, the investigators, in Greek antiquity, were not exactly *rallied*, and while today no one can doubt the strength of the forces that stand for natural science, it is not that our own more mundane ideas of what is natural have been completely sanitised in the process.

Two last points to conclude. In the early days the bid to give naturalistic explanations of natural phenomena went, one might say, not just with a demystifying of the universe, but with a certain trivialising of it. Poet that he himself was, how could Xenophanes reduce Iris to a cloud? Yet if the advance of what passed for science meant in some cases the exclusion of poetry, we should be careful not to exaggerate the point. There is poetry and there is poetry: there is elevated thought in verse and elevated thought in prose. I would not claim that such verse as most ancient scientists wrote is great poetry. Ptolemy's epigram (referring to his feeling when he does astronomy that his feet no longer touch the earth and it is as if he were feasting with the gods) ranks perhaps not much higher than doggerel. Yet there is no mistaking the thrill the scientists sometimes felt and expressed at the exploration of nature and the discovery of its workings. Aristotle has to defend the study of anatomy against the prejudices of the day. But he does well to quote Heraclitus in that defence: there are gods even here. The point is that one of the chief motivations of science (as again Aristotle remarks in the opening of the *Metaphysics*) was curiosity, the desire to learn, the excitement of discovery, even on occasion a certain wonder at the objects of that investigation.

My second point is the converse of that one. The motivations of the ancient scientist had indeed mainly to be personal and private, and they were often moral, even moralistic, or religious. There was no way in which society was going to support science, there were not even many (though there were some) rich patrons who would do so for the prestige attached. So science existed with a minimum institutional framework, certainly without the complex institutions of education and research we are familiar with, all of which testify to the standing of science in our own culture. But with that standing goes, of course, a certain aggressiveness, in the modern bid to convert knowledge to what are represented as useful purposes, an aggression also sometimes with regard to the means used to get the knowledge, where questionable means are justified on the off-chance that some useful ends *might* be served.

Many ancient Greek views of nature were simplistic, and on many occasions they were used to bolster dubious conclusions as to the place of human beings in the scheme of things. But the Greeks were not driven to study nature in order to control and appropriate it. To be sure, that may be as much because the possibilities of the exploitation of such knowledge as they had were limited, as for any other reason: for what can you do with a system of astronomical models *but* contemplate them? And Aristotle certainly spoke of plants and other animals being, in some sense, for the sake of humans. Yet that does not mean that *we* have any reasons to be complacent, in our attempts to strike a balance between the notion that nature is just there to be exploited and the reservations that might be held to follow from the recognition of ourselves as part of that nature. Ineluctably modern as we are, we are still in no position to use the criticism and analysis of ancient opinions as any grounds for self-congratulation about our own capacity to reach a steady view on the problems which those opinions addressed, on the possibility of science, on the stability of human character, on the boundaries of nature and culture, and on the proper relationship between ourselves and our environment. Indeed for reaching a steady view on those problems it may even be wise to make the most of those ancient opinions and controversies as resources for our own self-criticism and analysis. Certainly one may take a first, salutary, step towards unmasking the powerful claims to inevitability that often accompany the appeal to nature by following up those ancient controversies and the other indications that point to the circumstances of what I have called its invention.

INDEX OF PASSAGES CITED

GENERAL INDEX